Oracle Database Programming Using Java and Web Services

Oracle Database Related Book Titles:

Oracle Database Programming Using Java and Web Services

Kuassi Mensah

ELSEVIER
DIGITAL
PRESS

AMSTERDAM • BOSTON • HEIDELBERG • LONDON
NEW YORK • OXFORD • PARIS • SAN DIEGO
SAN FRANCISCO • SINGAPORE • SYDNEY • TOKYO

Elsevier Digital Press
30 Corporate Drive, Suite 400, Burlington, MA 01803, USA
Linacre House, Jordan Hill, Oxford OX2 8DP, UK

∞ Recognizing the importance of preserving what has been written, Elsevier prints its books on acid-free paper whenever possible.

Library of Congress Cataloging-in-Publication Data
Application Submitted.

ISBN 13:   978 1-55558-329-3
ISBN 10:   1-55558-329-6

British Library Cataloguing-in-Publication Data
A catalogue record for this book is available from the British Library.

For information on all Elsevier Digital Press publications
visit our Web site at www.books.elsevier.com

06 07 08 09 10 9 8 7 6 5 4 3 2 1

Printed in the United States of America

To the memory of my mother and my father.

To my loving wife, Gabrielle, and my wonderful sons, Gareth and Kenneth.

Contents

2   OracleJVM: Under the Hood   23

Foreword

I spend the bulk of my time working with Oracle database software and, more to the point, with people who use this software. Over the last 18 years, I've worked on many projects—successful ones as well as complete failures—and if I were to encapsulate my experiences into a few broad statements, they would be

- An application built around the database—dependent on the database—will succeed or fail based on how it uses the database. Additionally, in my experience, all applications are built around databases. I cannot think of a single useful application that does not store data persistently somewhere.

- Applications come, applications go. The *data*, however, lives forever. In the long term, the goal is not about building applications; it really is about using the data underneath these applications.

- A development team needs at its heart a core of database-savvy developers who are responsible for ensuring the database logic is sound and the system is built to perform from day one. Tuning after the fact (tuning after deployment) typically means you did not give serious thought to these concerns during development.

These may seem like surprisingly obvious statements, but I have found that too many people approach the database as if it were a *black box*—something that they don't need to know about. Maybe they have a SQL generator that they figure will save them from the hardship of having to learn the SQL language. Maybe they figure they will just use the database like a flat file and do keyed reads. Whatever they figure, I can tell you that thinking along these lines is most certainly misguided: you simply cannot get away with not understanding the database and how best to work with it.

That is where this book comes in – it provides a balanced view of how a Java programmer can approach the Oracle database and use it successfully. Where and when database features such as stored procedures make sense – and how they fit in. The author explains how things work – which leads to an understanding of when to use a particular feature; and as importantly when *not* to use a particular feature.

That is what I like best about this book – it explains how things work. It does not just prescribe methods of doing something, it explains in detail the inner workings. With this knowledge you yourself will be able to make the judgment call as to whether a particular feature of Oracle is something you should or should not be using in your application. Additionally - the exposure to these features, many of which you might not otherwise be exposed to – is important as well. If you don't know something exists – you will never use it.

If you are a Java programmer looking to exploit Oracle, or a database developer looking to exploit Java – this is the book for you.

Thomas Kyte

Vice President (Public Sector)

Oracle Corporation

Preface

"This—is now my way: where is yours?"

Thus I answered those who asked me "the way."

For the way—does not exist!

Zarathustra, in Thus Spoke Zarathustra —Friedrich Nietzsche

I've been working with the Oracle database, at Oracle, for more than 15 years now but for the last six years, I have been serving as group product manager within the Java and Web services products group, part of Oracle's server technologies development organization. Like Janus, the Roman god, I have to face two opposite directions: (1) the development organization, to represent customer interest (e.g., requirements, application design choices) and (2) customers, to represent the development organization (e.g., features, implementation design choices). Working closer to both worlds (i.e., customers and developers) gave me a very broad and sound knowledge of the products, how customers are using them, and ultimately what customers want. This book is my attempt to share this experience with a larger audience and provide a practical overview of Java and Web services technologies (APIs, products, and utilities) that are embedded within or gravitate around the Oracle database.

When I submitted the draft of this book to my publisher, I proposed the following title: *360-Degree Programming the Oracle Database with Java and Web Services*. The final title lost the "360-degree" reference, but this is the spirit of the writing. The audiences of this book are (1) database developers—a community that includes DBAs, stored procedures developers, JDBC applications developers, persistence frameworks developers (i.e., OR Mapping, JDO), and data architects[1]; (2) Java developers who want to get the most out of their RDBMS; and (3) Web services assemblers (as you will see, you don't develop Web services, you assemble or turn an existing component into a Web service). The book describes simple techniques accessible to non-Java audiences such as DBAs as well as advanced techniques for experts and power developers. The Java community has already developed tons of Java libraries and code samples; therefore, you don't need to reinvent them or be a Java expert or Web services guru to wrap existing libraries, applications with SQL, or bridge Web services and SQL. You won't need to dig into the mysteries of Java programming or SOAP programming.

The techniques are powerful, as with minimal effort, you will instantaneously add new capabilities and fully exploit all the potential of your Oracle database and RDBMS in general. The techniques are cost effective, as these will help you save development time and, more important, costs.

After practicing the samples in this book, DBAs and database developers in general will add Java and Web services to their skills set and contemplate their next move with confidence; Java/J2EE applications developers and Web services assemblers will broaden their scope and build applications that straddle both the middle tier and the database tier; and finally infrastructure developers (e.g., J2EE containers and OR mapping frameworks designers) will get advanced tips and insights for building more efficient persistence and datasource layers.

The ability to run Java in the database is not a new concept; it has been available in the Oracle database since the release of 8.1.5, and also in other RDBMS such as DB2 and Sybase. However, J2EE in the middle tier has eclipsed Java in the database, partly because some vendors, such as Oracle, have earlier trumpeted J2EE support in the database and then, realizing that the J2EE programming models (EJB, Servlet, JSP) do not fit well within the RDBMS, smartly changed their strategy.[2] This abandonment of J2EE in the database leads the public to think that the baby has been thrown out with the bath water (i.e., dropped entirely Java support in the database). Fortunately, Java in the database is well alive and being adopted by a growing number of database developers as an open language for stored procedures, as validated by the following survey.

Evans Data Corporation conducted a survey in Winter 2004 on database development and found that 46% of database developers like Java in the database because it offers the choice of a standard procedural language for database packages. Another 43% of database developers are attracted to Java

---

1.   Data Architect or Data Tier Architect is an emerging high-profile database-centric job.
2.   Oracle dropped J2EE from the database starting with Oracle 9i Release 2, in favor of a more competitive and lightweight J2EE stack in the Oracle Application Server.

because of the large pool of programmers now available. Skills can be easily redeployed from project to project. Another benefit is the reusability of the applications, as cited by 41% of respondents. Forty-one percent also cite the flexibility by which Java code can be run on any tier of the IT infrastructure.

I will show you that beyond tactical use for stored procedures, Java in the database allows you to bridge and glue database capabilities with J2EE, Web services, and ERP. With Java, you can turn your database into an agile and extensible data logic server.

If you Google "Java persistence," you will get more than 700,000 hits. Java persistence accounts for a significant part of the Java/J2EE applications development effort. Simply put, there is no enterprise Java application that does not involve persistence, and usually using an RDBMS. There are many choices of APIs and design patterns, including JDBC, SQLJ, Data Access Object (DAO), Java Data Object (JDO), EJB CMP, POJO, OR mapping, POJI (even MOJO[3]), and so on. There also are tons of products, frameworks, and utilities. I will distinguish between explicit persistence mechanisms (i.e., SQL-intrusive or "do-it-yourself") and transparent persistence mechanisms (i.e., non-SQL-intrusive or "do-it-for-me"). Transparent persistence refers to mapping, storing, and retrieving the states of complex Java objects and object graphs to relational tables without the explicit use of SQL-intrusive API such as JDBC or SQLJ. Transparent persistence mechanisms ultimately generate JDBC/SQLJ and are used by those who do not want to deal directly with JDBC or SQLJ. It is mandated by Container-Managed Persistence EJB, POJO, and JDO design models and implemented by OR mapping frameworks such as Toplink, Hibernate, and so on. A discussion of this topic is beyond the scope of this book.

Explicit persistence refers to storing and retrieving the states of Java objects, mapping SQL types to and from Java types in procedure parameters and function returns, and using JDBC, SQLJ, and related utilities such as Oracle's JPublisher. It is used by stand-alone J2SE applications, J2EE components that handle persistence directly (i.e., Bean-Managed Persistence EJB), and under the covers (i.e., through code generation) by the transparent persistence design models or frameworks mentioned previously. I will show you how to take advantage of new and advanced Oracle JDBC features, how SQLJ simplifies JDBC programming, and how JPublisher simplifies overall database programming.

Beyond persistence, Java SQL data access must also face a set of new requirements in terms of managing database connections in clustered data-

3. Plain Old Java Object, Plain Old Java Interface, Mapped Old Java Objects

bases and enterprise grid computing[4] environments such as load-balancing of connection requests and high availability. These requirements can be addressed either programmatically at the application level—you don't want to do that!—or at the application server level (i.e., J2EE containers, Java frameworks)—this is currently the norm—or at an even lower level (i.e., the JDBC drivers). I will describe how the new connection services in Oracle Database 10g JDBC address these requirements.

RDBMS vendors are also adding Web services support to their databases. A couple of years ago, I humbly coined the term "database Web services"[5] to designate the new trend of accessing and manipulating a database through Web services protocols. The Evans Data Corporation survey (mentioned earlier) also found that "more than two out of three respondents, 68%, say they are in the process on exposing or invoking their database operations (including SQL query, DML and stored procedures) through standard Web services mechanisms." What are Web services and what can you expect from their integration with the database? I will provide an overview of the core technologies that are part of Web services and describe in detail the emerging concept of database-related Web services with practical examples. I will provide concrete examples of turning your database into a Web service provider and consumer, and also how you can turn your database into a first-class citizen of a service-oriented architecture (SOA).

Programming the Oracle Database using Java and Web services is not a panacea, but as you will see, it furnishes pragmatic solutions to real life database-related problems.

I am convinced that you will have fun playing with the code samples; the soft copies are available on the publisher's web site http://www.elsevier.com and linked from my blog http://db360.blogspot.com, where I share thoughts on database programming, beyond this book.

Kuassi Mensah

San Francisco, California

April 2006

---

4.   Grid computing within the enterprises, as opposed to academic/research grids
5.   www.oracle.com/technology/tech/webservices/htdocs/dbwebservices/Database_Web_Services.pdf

Introduction

The time for action is now. It's never too late to do something.

—Antoine de Saint Exupery

The traditional division of labor between the RDBMS—manages SQL, XML, text, and binary data—and the application server—runs applications (i.e., business logic and presentation logic)—is obsolete. First, relational databases now host frameworks and run packages that furnish data services; they also communicate with the external world through standard mechanisms such as JDBC, RMI, HTTP, and IIOP. Second, the traditional application servers have been subsumed by the more comprehensive and integrated application platform suites,[1] which comprise the core J2EE containers (or equivalent) and a broad set of frameworks, including HTTP listeners, Web services, enterprise integration, portals, Web caches, business intelligence, report, wireless, and so on. Ultimately, the RDBMS, the application platform suite, higher-level ERP (e.g., Oracle E-Business Suite, SAP), and collaboration frameworks (e.g., Oracle Collaboration Suites) will all interoperate through standard protocols or middleware such as the emerging enterprise service bus.[2] At a humble and immediate scale, this book will address server-side database programming (i.e., programming models that run within the database) as well as client-side database programming (i.e., programming models that run in the middle tier or client tier, against the database).

This book is organized into six parts. Part I will look at Java in the database: the requirements, the programming model, and the various pragmatic applications. Part II (JDBC), Part III (SQLJ) , and Part IV (JPublisher) will

---

1. Term coined by the Gartner Group to designate the integration of all middleware components as a single product.
2. Savant term for Web services standards-based middleware that provide secure and reliable messages routing, data transformation, and connectors.

address the requirements and APIs for Java SQL data access, as well as advanced techniques for connecting Java/J2EE applications to clustered databases. Part V will focus on database Web services, the requirements, the techniques, and concrete examples. Finally, Part VI will put everything together and illustrate how far developers can go using Java in the database, using JDBC, J2EE, Web services, and SQL together. An introduction to Oracle, Java, and Web services is beyond the scope of this book; a minimal knowledge of Java, JDBC, SQL, Oracle RDBMS, and PL/SQL is required.

Server-Side Database Programming (Stored Procedures)

Stored procedures are traditionally used to encapsulate a batch of CRUD[3] operations, but in this book, we will look at advanced and more powerful usage. Imagine database-resident frameworks (i.e., code running in the database)—homegrown (see "Putting Everything Together") or packaged database frameworks such as Oracle iMedia (see Chapter 17)—exposing their entry points as stored procedures (i.e., the tip of the iceberg), and you will get an idea of the power of this programming model.

Database Programming Using Java in the Database

Java is a complete, portable, object-oriented, safe, flexible, and versatile language, but why consider it when it comes to database programming? Well, this is the whole purpose of Part 1 of this book, but let's say in a nutshell that the integration of a Java engine (J2SE) with a database engine, closer to the data, gives you the best of both worlds and opens the door to powerful, versatile/flexible, and sophisticated data-driven applications that are not possible with non-Java-enabled RDBMS. The greatest benefit Java brings to the database is the ability to implement data-driven functionalities or services, by just reusing the *huge* set of Java libraries, with minor changes, directly in the database, resulting in an extraordinary productivity and cost savings. These libraries solve concrete problems such as custom enterprise integration, advanced image processing, Excel-like expressions to SQL transformers, and a set of outbound capabilities including JDBC callout to remote databases, HTTP callout to Web components (i.e., Servlet and JSP), callout to RMI servers, RMI/IIOP callout to EJB and CORBA objects, and SOAP/HTTP callout to external Web services. Several RDBMS support Java for writing stored procedures; however, the level of integration of Java with the RDBMS engine varies from one vendor to another.

---

3.   Acronym for Create, Read, Update, and Delete

In this book, I will focus on Oracle's implementation, which is by far the most integrated, as discussed in Chapter 2. I will discuss the rationale for running Java in the database as opposed to Java outside the database. This book covers Oracle 9i R2, up to Oracle Database 10g Release 2.[4] At platform level, Java in the database complements Java/J2EE in the middle tier; applications can be partitioned or migrated across tiers.

DBAs are adamant when it comes to data security or data integrity breaches that might originate in code running in "their" database but foreign to them and outside their control. This book is your opportunity to regain control or confidence in Java in your database, or at least be knowledgeable enough to discuss it with the Java geeks. You will see that Java code cannot surreptitiously be downloaded from the Internet and run in your database without your explicit consent; in other words, Java runs even safer in the database. With the emergence of self-managed databases that require less DBA time, you will be expected to manage more databases to support an increasing number of applications, but also be involved in the support of data-driven applications and the deployment of Java and Web-enabled products.[5] The techniques described in this book will help you extend your skill set in these areas, thereby strengthening your position. If you love PL/SQL, you will see that Java in the database complements and opens new frontiers to PL/SQL.

In Chapter 2, I will take you inside the Java runtime in the database (i.e., OracleJVM). I will explain its architecture, memory management, byte-code interpreter, and native compiler, but more important, I will provide performance tips. In Chapter 3, I will explain the necessary steps for developing and deploying Java applications in the database. In Chapter 4, I will describe advanced database applications as well as practical code samples in terms of data conversions and callout to external Web components, EJB components, ERP frameworks, external databases, and external Web services. These are building blocks for more complete applications such as the TECSIS custom integration framework and Corporate Online (see "Putting Everything Together"). Scripting languages are becoming more and more popular for RAD and Web publishing; in Chapter 5, I will show you how you can run non-Java scripts written in TCL, PYTHON, SCHEME, and GROOVY in the Oracle database, using the OracleJVM.

---

4.   It won't cover the pre-Oracle 9i R2 attempt to run J2EE in the database.

5.   Web Services, BI fuel DBA job market http://searchdatabase.techtarget.com/originalContent/ 0,289142,sid13_gci970019,00.html

Database Programming Using JDBC, SQLJ, and JPublisher

When it comes to database programming, Java in the database is just one side of the coin. The other side of the coin is made of JDBC and SQLJ. These APIs are used both within Java in the database and also with J2EE/J2SE in the middle tier, and J2SE (Applets) in the client tier to access and invoke database operations and applications. In Part II, III, and IV of the book I will investigate JDBC, SQLJ, and Oracle JPublisher.

The Good Old JDBC

Used by millions of Java applications to persist Java states in RDBMS either explicitly, or under the covers, JDBC has evolved from a mere call-level interface API modeled from ODBC to a complete data access middleware and a key player in enterprise applications development and deployment. Beyond the standard API, vendors such as Oracle have taken JDBC one step further by adding scalability, high availability, debugging, diagnostic ability, tracing, and logging capabilities in clustered databases and grid environments.

JDBC and Grid Computing

Servers consolidation, resource virtualization, and provisioning—in other words, enterprise grid computing—aims at consolidating IT resources (infrastructure and applications) and optimizing their usage, thereby cutting costs substantially. Enterprise grid computing put new requirements on RDBMS, such as reliably deploying over a farm of servers to allow thousands of concurrent users to efficiently access peta-bytes of data. Consequently, deploying Java and J2EE applications against a Grid-enabled database poses a set of new challenges to JDBC. I will describe new connection services in Oracle JDBC drivers, including the advanced connection caching, fail-over, and load-balancing mechanisms in RAC and GRID environments.

In Chapter 6, I will introduce the JDBC technology and Oracle's implementation. In Chapter 7, I will describe the essential JDBC structures, and then we'll look at type mapping in Chapter 8; finally in Chapter 9, we'll look at JDBC best practices and performance tips.

SQLJ: Bundling SQL and Java Together

For those who find JDBC programming cumbersome, the ANSI ISO SQLJ Part 0,[6] which specifies the integration of SQL statements in Java programs, came to the rescue. SQLJ is to JDBC what JavaServer Pages are for Java Servlets; it simplifies JDBC programming. However, SQLJ is not part of the Enterprise Java platform (i.e., J2EE), hence its adoption is mostly among database developers. In Chapters 10, 11, and 12, I will cover the SQLJ technology and Oracle's implementation.

JPublisher: The Java Developer's Swiss Army Knife for Accessing the Oracle Database

If you are handling Java persistence programmatically, neither JDBC nor SQLJ allows you to easily map complex database types such as object types, object type references, and user-defined SQL types. Oracle JPublisher is a pure Java utility that simplifies SQL data access as well as publishing database entities to Java and Web services. In Chapter 13, I will show you how to avoid the pains of JDBC programming (if any) using JPublisher.

Database Programming with Web Services

Web services refer to core technologies (SOAP, WSDL, UDDI) that allow client applications to access remote applications as services (currently, mostly through HTTP). At the database level, this translates into the ability to invoke database operations through Web services mechanisms (i.e., SOAP, WSDL) without using vendor-specific protocols and through the Internet. Database Web services extend the client base of the database (i.e., inbound/inward reach) to heterogeneous environments and unconnected applications. Similarly, the ability to access remote data as dynamic data (i.e., data produced on demand), using Web services mechanisms and federating such data with resident data, extends the outreach of the database. In Part V of this book, I will describe Oracle's implementation of database Web service[7]s and how it leverages all technologies available in the Oracle database, including SQL, PL/SQL, Streams AQ, XDB, Java-in-the-Database, JDBC, SOAP, and HTTP. Beyond bare Web services, the industry is geared toward the service-oriented architecture (SOA), to help consolidate enterprise resources and expose these through standard Internet and Web services mechanisms, thereby optimizing their utilization and reducing costs. Chapter 14 will cover Web services and SOA for DBAs, data architects, and others. In Chapter 15, we will look at how you can turn your Oracle database into a Web services provider and first-class member of your

6.   SQLJ Part 1 is about Java stored procedures.
7.   www.sys-con.com/webservices/articleprint.cfm?id=515

SOA. In Chapter 16, we will examine how you can invoke external Web services from within the database.

Putting Everything Together: The "All-You-Can-Eat Buffet"

In this final part of the book (Chapter 17), I will describe real-life customer case studies, which implement many of the technologies described so far. The TECSIS/Tenaris and CorporateOnline case studies are the best illustrations of combining Java, Web services, and database capabilities. These case studies will inspire and give software architects, designers, application developers, database developers, DBAs, and data architects a complete, 360-degree perspective of programming the Oracle database. Like all-you-can-eat buffets, you can get more from your investment in the Oracle database without necessarily paying for more software (or just a very little more).

Acknowledgments

First of all, I would like to thank my wife and my sons for letting me steal evenings and week-ends, from them for almost two years, not sure I will ever make up for this time.

My special thanks to my friends Herve Lejeune and Soulaiman Htite for their moral support throughout the whole process and for putting up with my eternal excuse, the book, for not getting together.

I would like to thank numerous friends and colleagues, notably Barbara Krag, Penny Avril, Angela Long, Eric Belden, Shandra Cheevers, Jyotsna Laxminarayanan, Vladimir Barriere, Bojana Simova, Matthieu Devin, and Agnes Devin who have morally helped by persistently asking "How's the book?" you cannot imagine how supportive this simple question can be.

Without the backing of publishers there won't be so many books out there as you may not have the opportunity to publish and it will be more tempting to just give up when you are stuck in front of your computer, with no inspiration (i.e., the blank page syndrome). I would like to thank, a million time, Sheila Cepero for liaising me with Theron R.Shreve, my publisher – a gentle man, who trusted me based on the draft outline of the book.

But the gist, the technical content in this book would not have been possible without the active contribution, and/or technical support, and/or advice, of numerous developers and engineers inside and outside Oracle. In particular, I'd like to express my gratitude to, in disorder: Robert H. Lee, Allison Lee-Waingold, Malik Kalfane, David Unietis, Mark. Jungerman, Dmitry Nizhegorodov, Ernest Tucker, Peter Benson, Srivatsan Govindarajan, Yimin Huang, Paul Lo, Douglas Surber, Edward Shirk, Jean de Lavarene, Rajkumar Irudayaraj, Tong Zhou, Ashok Shivarudraiah, Soulaiman Htite, Steve Ding, Ekkehard Rohwedder, Eric Rajkovic, Omar Alonzo, Quan Wang, Mehul Bastawala, Lakshminaray Chidambaran, Harlan Sexton, Gregory Colvin, Xuhua Li, Susan Mavris, Andrew Lamb, Amit Bande,

Ali Shehadeh, Mark Scardina, Michael Alshouse, Venkatasubramaniam Iyer, Troy Anthony, Marcello Ochoa, Francisco Juarez, Esteban Capoccetti, Thor Heinrichs-Wolpert, and many others that I am sure I have missed (in advance, my sincere apologies).

The content would not be accurate or intelligible without technical reviewers who have the hard task of "parsing" raw materials from the author. I am very grateful to Avi Abrami, Oracle ACE and very popular on the Oracle OTN forums for his deep review of Part I; my special gratitude to the discrete but efficient Quan Wang for reviewing the entire book as well as contributing to its content.

I am blessed and honored that Tom Kyte, in spite of his busy agenda and numerous engagements, accepted to go over the entire book while it was in hard to read state (i.e., not proof read), and eventually wrote the foreword. Tom is one of the most passionate and knowledgeable person about the Oracle database and its components that I know.

Finally, to turn my Word documents into this book that you are holding in your hands, it took the dedication of an entire production team. I would like to express my gratitude to the Elsevier editorial and production teams for working hard to compensate my retard in delivery the manuscript (my day job is a good excuse, though!): Alan Rose, Tim Donar, the administrative staff, the marketing staff and the anonymous behind-the-scene workers.

Part I: Java in the Database

At the beginning, there was SQL, a high-level query language for relational databases. Then the need to extend SQL with procedural logic gave birth to the concept of stored procedures and their corresponding languages, such as Oracle's PL/SQL. Stored procedures allow developing data logic that run in the database, decoupled from business and computational logic, which runs in the middle tier. However, the proprietary nature of stored procedure languages, leads to some concerns (or perceptions) of vendor lock-in and skills shortage. Java is a response to these concerns. The ANSI SQLJ Part I specification[1] defines "*SQL Routines and Types Using Java.*" Although there are differences in their specific implementations, most RDBMSs, including Oracle, DB2, Sybase, and open source RDBMSs such as PostgreSQL and to some extent MySQL, support Java as a language for stored procedures and user-defined functions.

Chapter 1 discusses the rationale for stored procedures, the programming model, and languages. Chapter 2 tells you everything you ever wanted to know about the OracleJVM, its architecture, memory management, threading, class-sharing techniques, the native Java compiler (NCOMP), and security management and contrasts it with the JDK VM. Chapter 3 delves into the details of developing, deploying, and invoking Java applications in the database, including an extensive section on PL/SQL wrappers (also known as Call Spec) for publishing Java (i.e., make it known) to SQL, and mapping SQL datatypes to/from Java/JDBC datatypes. Chapter 4 describes atypical Java applications, which implement new database functionality using standard Java libraries. Finally, just for fun, in Chapter 5, you will run basic JACL, Jython, Scheme, and Groovy scripts in the data-

---

1. See Oracle JDBC, Oracle SQLJ, and JPublisher in Part II; then Database Web Services in Part III; and Putting Everything Together in Part IV.

base, as proof of the concept of supporting non-Java languages in the database.[2] There is a growing adoption of Java in the database, among DBAs and database developers, and after reading this book, you will probably become an aficionado, if that is not already the case!

2.   I must say that this proof of concept does not correspond to any Oracle product plan.

Stored Procedures as Database Programming Model

1

Although stored procedures have been around for more than a decade now, there still is a recurrent, almost ideological, debate on this programming model. Although it takes position in favor of stored procedures, the intent of this book is not to fuel this discussion but to elaborate on the benefits, assuming that there are situations where stored procedures are the right design choices. In this chapter, I will discuss the rationales for stored procedures, the obstacles to their adoption, languages used for writing stored procedures, and proprietary procedural languages such as PL/SQL versus open standards languages such as Java.

1.1   Rationale for Stored Procedures

As database developers and database administrators (DBAs) already know, stored procedures allow the exploitation of capabilities of relational database management systems (RDBMSs) to their fullest extent. The motivations to use stored procedures range from simplifying database programming to advanced data access to performance to centrally managed data logic and to optimizing network traffic.

1.1.1   Simplifying Database Programming

Procedural programming (also known as modular programming), as the name indicates, is based on the concepts of modules (also known as packages) and procedures (also known as functions, routines, subroutines, or methods). Each module consists of one or more procedures. The resulting code is simple and easier to read, debug, and maintain. Stored procedures are a mix of procedural code and SQL. The runtime of stored procedures is usually tightly integrated with the RDBMS but could also be loosely coupled, as an external runtime. Procedural languages include vendors' extensions to SQL, such as PL/SQL, as well as BASIC/Visual BASIC, COBOL, Pascal, C/C++, C#, Perl, and Java.

1.1.2 Centrally Managed Data Logic

By centralizing data logic, you can share it across all database projects, thereby avoiding code duplication and allowing flexible application development.

Avoids Code Duplication

Stored procedures are written once, centralized, and not dispersed across applications. When the procedure is updated, all consumer applications will automatically pick up the new version at the next invocation.

Fosters Data Logic Sharing

Irrespective of their implementation language (e.g., proprietary, Java, 3GL), stored procedures are declared and known to the database catalog through their SQL signature. In the Oracle case, this is achieved via a PL/SQL wrapper known as Call Spec. Through this PL/SQL wrapper, SQL, PL/SQL, Java in the database, thin clients (Web), rich clients (desktop), stand-alone Java, and middle-tier components[1] access the same, centrally managed data logic. For example, a stored procedure can be used to send a notification email when a new order is placed or to invalidate the middle-tier cache to notify data change (see "Poor Man's Cache Invalidation" example in Chapter 4).

Implementation Transparency

Interfaces allow effective modularization/encapsulation and shield consumers from implementation details, allowing multiple implementations. By decoupling the call interface (i.e., Call Spec in Oracle's vocabulary) from its actual implementation, the stored procedure may change over time from being written in PL/SQL to Java or the opposite, transparently to the requesters.

1.1.3 Performance: Run JDBC Applications Faster in the Database

Performance is one of the main motivations for using stored procedures. A few years ago, Oracle used PL/SQL stored procedures to optimize the performance of a benchmark version of the infamous J2EE Blueprints

---

1.   Mastering Enterprise JavaBeans,2nd edition, by Ed Roman, Scott W. Ambler, and Tyler Jewell (New York: John Wiley & Sons, 2002).

"PetStore"[2] application. This optimization prompted a heated debate in the Java/J2EE community. On the heels of this debate, Microsoft implemented and published the results of a .NET variant of the same benchmark, using—guess what?—stored procedures! The main criticism[3] was the lack of portability of PL/SQL or Transact SQL stored procedures across RDBMSs. Well, this is precisely the raison d'être of Java stored procedures.

The conclusion to derive from these experiences, as database programmers already know, is that stored procedures are the right design choice for efficient database programming. Stored procedures inherently incur minimal data movement, compared with a set of individual SQL statements that ship data outside the database. By processing data within the database (sorting, filtering) and returning just the results, stored procedures reduce network traffic and data movement. To cut to the chase, let's compare the performance of a Java application used as a stand-alone Java database connectivity (JDBC) application deployed on a Java development kit (JDK) virtual machine (VM) versus the same code deployed as a Java stored procedure running in the database (this is, by the way, an illustration of the claim that you can reuse existing Java/JDBC applications, with minor changes, in the database). The following example will already give you an overview of the few steps involved in creating, compiling, publishing, and executing Java in the database.

Setup

Configuration:

A Pentium 4 M 1.80-GHz laptop, with 1 GB of RAM using Windows XP Professional Version 2002, Oracle Database 10*g* Release 1, and the associated JDBC drivers.

Create a table with a Varchar2, BLOB, and CLOB columns, using the following script (in a SQL*Plus session):

```
SQL> connect scott/tiger;
SQL> drop table basic_lob_table;
SQL> create table basic_lob_table (x varchar2 (30), b blob, c clob);
```

2.   http://www.oracle.com/technology/tech/java/oc4j/pdf/9ias_net_bench.pdf
3.   http://java.sun.com/blueprints/qanda/faq.html#stored_procedures

The Java Aplication

Listing 1.1   *TrimLob.java*

```
============================
/*
 * This sample shows basic BLOB/CLOB operations
 * It drops, creates, and populates table basic_lob_table
 * with columns of blob, clob data types in the database
 * Then fetches the rows and trim both LOB and CLOB
 */

// You need to import the java.sql package to use JDBC
import java.sql.*;

/*
 * You need to import the oracle.sql package to use
 * oracle.sql.BLOB
 */
import oracle.sql.*;

public class TrimLob
{
  public static void main (String args []) throws SQLException {
  Connection conn;
 /*
  * Where is your code running: in the database or outside?
  */
  if (System.getProperty("oracle.jserver.version") != null)
  {
  /*
   * You are in the database, already connected, use the default
   * connection
   */
  conn = DriverManager.getConnection("jdbc:default:connection:");
  }
  else
  {
  /*
   * You are not in the database, you need to connect to
   * the database
   */
```

```
DriverManager.registerDriver(new oracle.jdbc.OracleDriver());
conn =
      DriverManager.getConnection("jdbc:oracle:thin:", "scott",
      "tiger");
}
long t0,t1;
 /*
  * Turn auto commit off
  * (Required when using SELECT FOR UPDATE)
  */
 conn.setAutoCommit (false);
 t0=System.currentTimeMillis();
 // Create a Statement
 Statement stmt = conn.createStatement ();
 // Make sure the table is empty
 stmt.execute("delete from basic_lob_table");// sure we could use
truncate
 stmt.execute("commit");

 // Populate the table
 stmt.execute ("insert into basic_lob_table values ('first', " +
              "'0101010101010101010101010101', " +
              "'one.two.three.four.five.six.seven')");
 stmt.execute ("insert into basic_lob_table values ('second', " +
              "'0202020202020202020202020202020202', " +
              "'two.three.four.five.six.seven.eight.nine.ten')");

  /*
   * Retreive LOBs and update contents (trim); this can be done by
doing
   * "select ... for update".
   */
  ResultSet rset = stmt.executeQuery
              ("select * from basic_lob_table for update");

  while (rset.next ())
  {
    // Get the lobs
    BLOB blob = (BLOB) rset.getObject (2);
    CLOB clob = (CLOB) rset.getObject (3);

    // Show the original lengths of LOBs
```

```
System.out.println ("Show the original lob length");
System.out.println ("blob.length()="+blob.length());
System.out.println ("clob.length()="+clob.length());

// Truncate the lobs
System.out.println ("Truncate LOBs to legnth = 6");
blob.truncate (6);
clob.truncate (6);

// Show the lob length after truncate()
System.out.println ("Show the lob length after truncate()");
System.out.println ("blob.length()="+blob.length());
System.out.println ("clob.length()="+clob.length());
}

// Close the ResultSet and Commit changes
rset.close ();
stmt.execute("commit");

// Close the Statement
stmt.close ();

t1=System.currentTimeMillis();
System.out.println ("====> Duration: "+(int)(t1-t0)+
"Milliseconds");
// Close the connection
conn.close ();
}
}
```

Running the Java Application as a Stand-alone JDBC Application

Stand-alone JDBC applications run on JDK VM, against the database. For my test, the database, the JDBC driver, and application, all run on the same machine. The following steps compile the Java class and execute it:

```
javac TrimLob.java
java -classpath %CLASSPATH% TrimLob
```

Running the Java Application as a Java Stored Procedure

```
TrimLobSp.sql (contains Java source and SQL commands)
```

```
=============

connect scott/tiger;
create or replace java source named TrimLob as

rem
rem -> Insert here the above Trimlob.java here
rem

/

show errors;

alter java source TrimLob compile;

show errors;

create or replace procedure TrimLobSp as
  language java name 'TrimLob.main(java.lang.String[])';
/

show errors;
set serveroutput on
call dbms_java.set_output(50000);

call TrimLobSp();
```

Table 1.1 contrasts the performance of 10 invocations of the same Java code as stand-alone JDBC, and as Java stored procedure, on the same laptop, using exactly the same configuration (i.e., Oracle Database 10*g* Release 1 and its embedded OracleJVM).

Although we cannot draw a universal conclusion, because of the elimination of network roundtrips and because it runs within the same address space as SQL, this JDBC application runs four to five times faster in the database than outside it. This example proves that, when appropriate, you can move Java/JDBC applications to the database and run them faster.

Table 1.1   *Performance Contrasts*

Run#	Stand-alone JDBC	Java Stored Procedure
1st	570 ms	121 ms
2nd	241 ms	61 ms
3rd	240 ms	60 ms
4th	250 ms	50 ms
5th	230 ms	50 ms
6th	281 ms	50 ms
7th	280 ms	50 ms
8th	241 ms	50 ms
9th	250 ms	50 ms
10th	251 ms	50 ms

1.1.4   Encapsulation

Encapsulation is an object-oriented design principle that lets you structure an application into modules that hide data structures from outside view and also protect it from unauthorized access. Stored procedures allow building specialized modules, which can be tuned by domain specialists and DBAs, shielding consumers from the arcane data structure and SQL programming. Encapsulation also hides differences between RDBMSs by presenting the same call interface over different enterprise information systems (see "TECSIS System Use" case in Part VI).

1.1.5   Security: Advanced Data Access Control

Database-related applications that have explicit knowledge of database schema login and password may compromise the security of your system and may break upon schema change. You can enforce security as part of your design by using JDBC data sources that remove and defer the actual database and login information to deployment time, and, in addition, implement security policies in stored procedures (validate login information on each procedure call) and only allow users/apps to call these stored procedures. You can control database access use through customized, advanced, sophisticated data access logic that does CRUD (i.e., Create, Retrieve, Update, Delete) operations on tables while denying users direct access to these tables. Database triggers are traditionally used to enforce referential integrity and constraints, thereby making sure that only valid data enters the database; stored procedures that implement more complex constraints and additional operational security restrictions (e.g., forbid salary table update during weekends!) can be implemented as triggers, on top of the built-in security mechanisms offered by the RDBMS engine.

1.1.6 Resource Optimization

All database clients accessing the same database schema run the same in-memory copy of the procedure, thereby reducing overall memory allocation. Also, as demoed previously, depending on the level of integration, stored procedures can run within the same address space as the SQL engine, incurring minimal call overhead and optimizing memory utilization. In Chapter 2, I will describe in detail the internal mechanisms of the Java VM in the Oracle database.

1.1.7 Low-Cost Deployment

Independent software vendors (ISVs) and integrators already know that the ability to bundle their products on top of the database considerably simplifies installation, platform support, and product distribution. Java integration with the database eliminates the need for an external JDK/JRE and the headache of platform compatibility; furthermore, it works the same way on every platform on which the database runs.

1.1.8 Fully Utilize Database Capabilities

Part VI of this book describes how Oracle *interMedia*, TECSIS Systems, Oracle Text, British Columbia Corporate Online, and DBPrism CMS case studies use the database to its full extent.

1.2 Obstacles to the Adoption of Stored Procedures

The following concerns are usually invoked as showstoppers for adopting stored procedures: portability across database vendors, scalability, maintainability, and debugability. As discussed in the following text, some of these concerns are valid, but others are misperceptions.

1.2.1 Lack of Portability across RDBMS Vendors

In corporate IT environments that use more than one RDBMS, DBAs and database developers have to learn different procedural languages, such as PL/SQL, T-SQL, SQL/PL, and so on. Large IT organizations can afford to dedicate specific resources to each RDBMS for handling tasks ranging from managing databases to writing stored procedures. However, most organizations are looking for the flexibility of redeploying their staff of DBAs and developers according to their business priorities. Using Java across tiers and an RDBMS enables the portability of skills. Also, in the unlikely situation where an organization decides to move to a different RDBMS, it will have to migrate not only the schema and data but also the set of stored procedures developed over the years. Using Java leaves the door open for such a move because the Java sources and classes can be migrated smoothly, with minimal changes, losses, and cost.

1.2.2 Scalability

In typical application deployments, the clients (i.e., Web client, rich client, desktop) run against middle-tier nodes, which in turn funnel threads corresponding to clients against a pool of fewer database connections, typically an order of magnitude less than the number of concurrent clients/threads. Still, database scalability is crucial to middle-tier scalability. The session-based architecture of the Oracle database makes it scale linearly on symmetric multiprocessing (SMP) using a single RDBMS instance and quasi-linearly on clusters and grid nodes using multiple RDBM instances (i.e., Real Application Clusters [RAC]). To conclude, PL/SQL and Java stored procedures scale very well as far as the platform permits. In other words, the scalability of stored procedures is a by-product of the architecture of the target RDBMS and not a limitation of the stored procedure programming model per se.

1.2.3 Maintenance and Resilience to Schema Change

Upon schema change (i.e., when changes to table/column names, locations, or references occur), the stored procedures need to be updated to adapt to the new schema however, all of the applications built on top of those stored procedures remain unchanged and still return the exact result sets from the new database design. Shielding your applications (i.e., business logic) from the inevitable schema change by encapsulating the database schema within centralized stored procedures and validation logic is a small price to pay compared with the benefits of maintenance. Stored procedures act as interfaces between the data schema and the business logic layer, shielding each layer from changes occurring in the others. Encapsulation significantly reduces the ripple effect.

1.2.4 Hard to Debug

Most RDBMSs support stored procedures development and debugging through an integrated development environment (IDE) using either proprietary mechanisms such as the former Oracle's java.debugAgent, which has now fallen into obsolescence, or standard mechanisms such as the Java Debug Wire Protocol (JDWP). Oracle JDeveloper integrates JDWP and allows simultaneous debugging of PL/SQL and Java stored procedures in the same session. Third-party IDE, which support JDWP, would also allow debugging PL/SQL and/or Java directly in the database. Alternatively, and this is what most Java developers currently do, you debug your Java code first outside the database (as a JDBC application), and then deploy it in the database. The bottom line is that debugging stored procedures is a bit less straightforward than debugging middle-tier applications or presentation logic using your favorite development tool; hence, there is this legitimate concern.

1.2.5 Weak Support for Complex Types

This concern is rather a question of perception. As shown in Chapter 3, stored procedures can pass complex database types, such as user-defined types (ADT), SQL object types, nested tables, VARRAY, and multilevel collections between the client program and the database. The standard SQL-Data interface allows custom mapping of user-defined types (ADT) in JDBC applications and stored procedures; furthermore, the Oracle JDBC extensions allow exchanging Oracle Object types between SQL (RDBMS) and JDBC applications (i.e., Java stored procedures).

1.3 Languages for Stored Procedures

This section discusses the pros and cons of using proprietary languages, Java, and the emerging category of .NET languages in the database.

1.3.1 Proprietary Languages

The following discussion applies to most proprietary languages for stored procedures;[4] however, I focus on the Oracle PL/SQL, which is widely used and regarded as one of the best vendor-supplied languages for stored procedures.

Seamless Integration with SQL

Proprietary languages for stored procedures such as Oracle's PL/SQL are an extension to SQL and as such are well integrated into SQL with little or no data type conversion and optimized for faster SQL data access. PL/SQL is well suited for wrapping intensive SQL operations with moderately complex procedural logic.

IDE Support

Those languages benefit from a strong vendor-supplied development environment and also third-party IDE. As an example, the Oracle JDeveloper, as well as third-party IDE, provides a nice environment for writing, debugging, and maintaining PL/SQL programs.

Portability

Cross-platform portability of proprietary language such as PL/SQL is inherited from the portability of the RDBMS. As an example, compiled PL/SQL packages can be moved to different platforms where the Oracle database runs—from Solaris to Linux or Windows or vice versa—without recompilation. Cross-vendor portability (e.g., run one vendor's language in another vendor's database) is technically possible (see section 1.3.3) but not yet a sure thing.

1.3.2 Java for Stored Procedures

Complete Programming Language

The Java language is by design an object-oriented programming language that supports many programming models, including simple models such as JavaBean, POJO, JDBC applications, Java stored procedures, and more complex J2EE programming models such as Servlets, JavaServer Pages, and Enterprise Java Beans.

Secure Language

The Java language has built-in security mechanisms, such as the lack of pointer arithmetic, which prevents it from computing offending memory offset; the Garbage Collector, which reduces the risk of memory corruption

---

4.   Not including languages supported by Microsoft's Common Language Runtime, such as Visual BASIC and C#.

by cleaning up dead objects and reclaiming unused memory; the type safety, described next; the byte-code verifier described later in this chapter; and Java 2 security for accessing system resources or remote systems (described in Chapter 2).

Type Safety

Java's strong typing[5] and static typing (i.e., compile time type checking) make the language less vulnerable to viruses and buffer overflow security holes. The creators of Java carefully designed the language and byte code formats to facilitate static type checking. The byte code verifier effectively checks static types at compile time, giving Java developers the opportunity to fix any type errors before deployment, resulting in a type safe program that runs efficiently.

Robustness

Java requires catching exceptions that can be thrown by methods in any class, thereby making Java stored procedures more robust. The automatic memory Garbage Collector also enforces robustness because it reduces the likelihood of memory corruption.

Productivity: Rapid Design Features

The Java language comes with a set of built-in rapid application design (RAD) features, such as the following:

- Built-in automatic bounds checking on arrays
- Built-in network access classes (java.net, java.rmi)
- Automatic Garbage Collector, which eliminates whole classes of memory management issues
- Standard data types and application programming interfaces (APIs) contain many useful and ready-to-use classes (or easy-to-implement interfaces)

Using Java as a Procedural Language

Like most RDBMSs, the Oracle database promotes a simplified programming model that can be summarized as "no threading within applications code." Although OracleJVM lets you deploy a threaded Java code, its

---

5.   Strong typing refers to the requirement that the type of each field and variable and the return type of each method be explicitly declared.

scheduler is nonpreemptive; in other words, the active thread will run until it is no longer runable. The running Java application in a session is practically the only code running in the embedded Java VM. Java stored procedures also share the same simplicity with J2EE programming models: no threading within components code; the container itself is threaded, but the components (i.e., EJB, Servlet, JSP) are nonthreaded. Furthermore, Java experts discourage threading and recommend having only a very few for application robustness and portability [Bloch01]. This simplified programming model also simplifies memory management by removing the need to place memory allocation locks during garbage collection (GC).

Standard Specifications for Java Stored Procedures

The following American National Standards Institute (ANSI) specifications define SQLJ, Java stored procedures, and SQLJ Object types:

- *SQLJ Part 0.* "Database Language SQL—Part 10: Object Language Bindings (SQL/OLB)," ANSI X3.135.10-1998. Specifications for embedding SQL statements in Java methods. Similar to the traditional SQL facilities for embedded SQL in COBOL and C and other languages. The Java classes containing embedded SQL statements are precompiled to pure Java classes with JDBC calls. Also known as *SQL.*

- *SQLJ Part 1.* "SQL Routines Using the Java Programming Language," ANSI NCITS N331.1. Specifications for installing Java classes in a SQL system and for invoking Java static methods as SQL stored procedures and functions. Also known as *Java stored procedures.*

- *SQLJ Part 2.* "SQL Types Using the Java Programming Language," ANSI NCITS N331.2. Also known as *SQLJ Object Types.*

POJO-like Programming Model

What are POJOs? If you Google "Java POJO," you'll get the following definition.

> *POJO = "Plain Old Java Object." Term coined by Martin Fowler, Rebecca Parsons, and Josh MacKenzie to denote a normal Java object that is not a JavaBean, an EntityBean, a SessionBean, etc., and does not*

serve any other special role or implement any special interfaces of any of the Java frameworks (EJB, JDBC, . . .).

Any Java object can run within an EJB container, but many people don't know that or forget it. Fowler et al. invented the acronym POJO so that such objects would have a "fancy name," thereby convincing people that they were worthy of use.

POJOs are useful for creating a Domain Model. In contrast, the various types of beans and other special Java objects often have constraints that make it difficult to use them directly to model a domain.

Stored procedures use explicit SQL statements through JDBC and aren't, therefore, pure POJOs; however, they have in common the simplicity of their programming models. Unlike when using Enterprise JavaBeans (EJBs), you don't need to be a rocket scientist to get a Java stored procedure right. As a matter of fact, the next EJB specification (EJB 3.0) is looking at simplifying the EJB model by integrating the POJO programming model.

Stored Procedures and O/R Mapping

O/R mapping generally refers to transparent mapping of Java objects to a relational database, which is achieved through several mechanisms (or programming models), including EJB CMP, POJO, and Java Data Object (JDO).[6] Stored procedures may be used by O/R mapping frameworks to perform a custom mapping of a specific object but are by no means a substitute. Stored procedures belong to explicit persistence mechanisms (i.e., SQL intrusive), whereas O/R mapping frameworks address transparent persistence (i.e., non-SQL intrusive).

Cross-Database Portability

Most RDBMSs (except SQL Server) support Java, either through a loosely coupled external JDK-based runtime or through a tight integration of the Java runtime with the database kernel (i.e., OracleJVM). Database developers who choose Java in the database motivate this choice, among other things, by its cross-vendor portability. Although Java stored procedures implementations differ from one vendor to another, Java is by far the most portable language for stored procedures. This book offers in-depth coverage of Oracle's implementation.

---

6.   http://java.sun.com/products/jdo/.

Huge Class Library and Tools: Reduced Development Time and Costs

As we all know, the ability to reuse existing libraries results in quicker and lower-cost applications development. The availability of a rich and very large set of standard libraries as well as third-party class libraries is one of the biggest benefits that Java brings to database developers. The smart and lazy developers will extend their databases with new capabilities (see Chapter 4) in no time, writing only a few lines of code and scripts to adapt and glue Java with the database.

Skills Reuse

Because Java is one of the most dominant and widespread programming languages, it is likely that Java programmers already exist within your organization; furthermore, most new hires graduating from college have Java programming skills. The ability to use the same language across the middle tier (business/application logic) and the database tier (data logic) bolsters skills reuse, which in turn simplifies resource allocation, thereby reducing project costs.

Java Database Connectivity and SQL Data Access

The OracleJVM embeds a special JDBC driver and a SQLJ runtime for direct SQL data access. This enables redeploying J2SE/JDBC/SQLJ applications in the database (see section 1.1.3).

Starting with Java

An introduction to Java is beyond the scope of this book; however, here are some pointers to start with Java:

- Online Java Tutorial: http://java.sun.com/docs/books/tutorial

- The comp.lang.java FAQ List: http://www.ibiblio.org/javafaq/javafaq.html

- The *Java Developer Almanac*, by Patrick Chan and Lan-Ahn Dang (Reading, MA: Addison Wesley)

1.3.3   .NET Languages

SQL Server 2005 introduces the Common Language Runtime (CLR) on top of the .NET framework, for running stored procedures written in C#, VB.NET, J#, and other languages. CLR can be viewed as a generic virtual machine, which supports multiple languages in the database. The most interesting aspect of CLR is its support by the latest releases of DB2 and

Oracle; as a result, and similarly to Java, CLR would in theory allow the portability of code not only across the Microsoft middle tier and database tier,[7] but also across RDBMSs.[8] Java may no longer be the only portable language for stored procedures across RDBMSs but remains by far the most portable,[9] the most widely used, and the one that offers the largest reusable set of code and class libraries. Because the version of CLR might vary across vendors, it is not yet clear what will be the uptake of C#, J#, VB.NET beyond SQL Server 2005.

1.4 PL/SQL or Java

This is the $72,526 techno-political question being asked all the time: "*When should we use PL/SQL and when should we use Java for stored procedures?*" The short but correct answer is, "*It depends!*" It indeed depends on your goals; your requirements, such as the profile of the code being executed in the database (i.e., data access intensive versus computation intensive); the available skills within your organization; and whether you might, in the future, need to migrate the code in question from the database to the middle tier or vice versa. According to a survey conducted by Evans Data Corporation among database developers (across all RDBMSs), 22 percent declare using PL/SQL (which must be the majority of Oracle database customers) while 41 percent to 46 percent declare using Java, across all RDBMSs that support it. These figures are not exclusive; the person who declared using Java also uses PL/SQL when dealing with the Oracle Database. As you have already figured out, there is no straight answer; however, here are my own rules of thumb for choosing between Java and PL/SQL, but each DBA, database developer, and data architect has his or her own rules or motivations for choosing one approach versus another:

- Prefer PL/SQL when (i) *your data logic (i.e., data processing or data validation logic) is SQL intensive,* or (ii) *you already have the skills.* Modeled after the ADA programming language, PL/SQL is an advanced procedural language. Its seamless integration with SQL and the Oracle database allows faster SQL data access with little or no type conversion. There is a large community with Oracle-supplied packages[10] and third-party libraries.

---

7. Enabled by the integration of .NET with the SQL Server 2005 RDBMS.
8. IBM DB2 Release 8.2 and Oracle Database 10g Release 2 support CLR 1.x.
9. DB2, Oracle, Sybase, PortGresSQL, and MySQL.
10. http://www.oracle.com/technology/tech/pl_sql/index.html.

- Prefer Java in the database when (i) *your data logic has moderate SQL data access requirements (as opposed to SQL intensive) and moderate computational requirements (as opposed to compute intensive),* or (ii) *you already have the skills (Java skills are more pervasive, most college graduates know Java),* or (iii) *you need to accomplish things you cannot do in PL/SQL, such as interaction with ERP systems, RMI servers, Java/J2EE, and Web services,* or (iv) *you want to leave the door open for partitioning your application between the middle tier and the database tier.* There is a large Java community with tons of class libraries (standard and third party) that you can reuse. When your data logic becomes too complex, you just migrate it to the middle tier.

- Furthermore, you should consider Java/J2EE in the middle tier (stand-alone JDBC, JavaBeans, POJOs, EJBs, Servlets/Java Server-Pages, and so on) when (i) *your business logic is complex or compute intensive with little to moderate direct SQL access,* or (ii) *you are implementing a middle-tier-driven presentation logic,* or (iii) *you require transparent Java persistence (i.e., POJOS, CMP EJB) as opposed to SQL intrusive persistence,* or (iv) *you require container-managed infrastructure services (transaction, security),* or (v) *many other reasons not specified here.* If your business logic becomes SQL data access bound, you may migrate it into the database tier. JavaBeans, POJOs, and J2EE design models may orthogonally use stored procedures (PL/SQL and/or Java) directly through JDBC or indirectly through O/R mapping frameworks.

If performance is the key requirement, since Java in the database is sandwiched between PL/SQL (SQL intensive) and Java/J2EE in the middle tier (compute intensive), when is it competitive? As illustrated in section 1.1.3, when your code combines Java and SQL, Java in the database wins, since it incurs less roundtrips (minimal network overhead) and less data traffic.

[A poster on Slashdot.org] *"While I agree that I would tend to abstract all SQL to some PL/SQL call that 'DBAs who get it' have control over, there are LOTS of things that Java can do that are VERY handy, when viewed at in the application architecture point of view and not just in a SQL context."*

1.4.1 **PL/SQL and Java!**

The pragmatic database developers use both Java and PL/SQL, because these complement each other very well to glue together the rich set of database features. Now that we have set the stage, in the next chapters, I'll walk you through the entrails of the Java runtime in the Oracle database, how to reuse standard libraries, how to deploy your own Java classes, and examples of real-life cases.

2

OracleJVM: Under the Hood

In Chapter 3 we will delve into the details of developing, deploying, and invoking Java applications in the database. Before that, this chapter takes you inside Java in the Oracle database. You may ask, "What for? Why dive into the internals of the OracleJVM?" Java developers do not usually care about the internals of the Java Virtual Machine they are using. First, understanding the implementation of the OracleJVM and contrasting its architecture, its memory management, its thread management, the class-sharing techniques, the native Java compiler, and the security management with the JDK VM is, in my opinion, a prerequisite for using it efficiently, at least for those who build infrastructures and frameworks. Second, when you want to better know your car, you look under the hood; similarly, database developers and DBAs will be in a better position to take full advantage of Oracle-JVM by reading this chapter.

2.1   Design Goals and Architecture

The initial design goals of the OracleJVM were tight integration with the RDBMS (à la PL/SQL), J2SE compatibility, scalability (memory footprint), portability across the platforms where the RDBMS ships, robustness, and performance of Java with SQL. The attempt to support J2EE in the database (pre-9.2 releases) was an afterthought, which did not work very well. Scalability, the ability to support a large number of simultaneous users while keeping memory requirements under control, was another key requirement that has been addressed by sharing system classes, class state, and strings as much as possible. Support for large Java programs has been addressed by designing efficient memory management. Robustness, or resilience, was another requirement that was addressed through the integration with the RDBMS session model.

2.1.1   Tight Integration with the RDBMS

The tight integration with the RDBMS consists of allowing Java to execute in the same address space as SQL and PL/SQL, while making no compromise on security and data integrity. This goal was accomplished by espousing the session model of the Oracle database. Each database process hosting a Java-enabled session literally has its own private Java VM along with SQL and PL/SQL engines; there is, therefore, no need for a separate process for running Java.

2.1.2   J2SE Compatibility

J2SE compatibility is a key requirement from a Java developer's perspective. The OracleJVM keeps up with J2SE specifications through database releases. In other words, you cannot upgrade the Java VM in the database independently of the database release. As examples, the Oracle 9*i* Release 2 is J2SE 1.3 compatible, while the Oracle Database 10*g* Release 1 and 2 are J2SE 1.4 compatible. OracleJVM support for J2SE allows the extension of the database capabilities by the use of standard Java libraries. As an example, the Java Secure Socket Extension (JSSE) allows Java programs to communicate with other systems, using SSL. This feature is optional in J2SE 1.3 and therefore not offered by default in the Oracle 9*i* Release 2, but you can extend the database by loading the standard JSSE libraries in OracleJVM. What is the usefulness of JSSE for Java in the database? It can communicate securely with external systems, using HTTPS callouts. See, in Chapter 4, step-by-step instructions for secure communication with external systems, using HTTPS callout.

OracleJVM Is J2SE 1.3 Compatible in Oracle9i Release 2

There are few implementation differences with the JDK VM, because of the server-side (or embedded) nature of the OracleJVM runtime:

- It does not materialize GUI objects. (This is now standardized in J2SE 1.4 by headless AWT.)

- Another implementation difference is that OracleJVM does not support delete-on-close mode for zip and jar.

An additional feature in Oracle 9*i* Release 2, beyond the standard J2SE features, includes the support for Java Debug Wire Protocol (JDWP), a standard protocol (part of the Java Platform Debugger Architecture) that allows debuggers to communicate with Java virtual machines.

OracleJVM Is J2SE 1.4.x in Oracle Database 10g (Release 1 and 2).

This includes mostly support for standard JDK 1.4 features such as:

- Support for Logging (JSR-041)
- Complete Security (JAAS, JCE)
- Support for Preferences API (JSR-010), a replacement for Properties
- Assertions (JSR-041)
- Exception chaining
- Support for Headless AWT allows the manipulation of graphic objects without materializing the UI, and therefore without throwing an exception
- Regular expression java.util.regex
- JDBC 3.0 support in the server-side JDBC

2.1.3   How Is Java Stored in the Database?

The JDK VM stores, loads, and runs Java sources/classes from the file system; the OracleJVM stores each Java class (and derived classes), its source, the potential/optional Java resources (used for properties and miscellaneous needs), and the metadata in a managed, stand-alone database object called "*libunit*" (short for library unit). Let's see the storage structures involved.

Where Is the Java Source Stored?

Unlike PL/SQL sources, which are stored in human-readable format as `VARCHAR` columns of system tables, Java sources are stored in nonhuman-readable format as Opaque types,[1] using `UTF8` character set, in internal system tables. Upon the reception of the instruction to create a new managed Java source—from SQL*Plus interactive session ("`CREATE JAVA SOURCE...`"), from client-side `loadjava` utility, or from server-side `dbms_java.loadjava()`[2] or IDEs[3]—the SQL DDL creates a library unit ("*libunit*") in the internal system table. It is also possible to create managed

---

1.   A data type whose details are not visible (i.e., hidden).
2.   See Oracle documentation for more details on DBMS_JAVA supplied package.
3.   IDEs such as JDeveloper use loadjava under the covers.

Java sources from existing Java sources in external system files using the `BFILE` mechanism (described later) or regular database structures such as `VARCHAR`, `BLOB`, `CLOB`, or any other mechanism that can transmit large sequences of characters separated by newlines (i.e., source code).

What Are Java Resources and How Are These Used?

Java resources allow storing, of **properties** files but also **.xml, .jar, .zip** files in the database, as well as any arbitrary file type used by Java classes and applications running in the database. They are used mainly during the resolution of Java classes. They are not compiled by the OracleJVM. They are loaded as is in the database using the `loadjava` utility or the SQL command `CREATE JAVA RESOURCE NAMED` "<name> ... . The resources objects are looked up by the Java VM (within the scope of the resolver spec of the calling class), using *ClassLoader.getResource()* or *ClassLoader.findResource()* methods, which return a URL of the actual resource. The Native Java compiler (described later) stores platform-specific executables (i.e., DLL) in the database as Java resource. Here is a basic example of a config.properties file:

Listing 2.1   *Propty.sql*

```
=======================

create or replace and resolve java source named propty as
import java.sql.*;
import java.util.*;
import java.io.*;

public class propty
{

 public static void getppty(String fname)
                             throws java.io.IOException
 {
   InputStream is = null;

   // Get input stream from the properties file
    is = ClassLoader.getSystemResourceAsStream(fname);
   Properties p = new Properties();
     p.load(is);
     is.close();

    // Print poperties values
```

```
       System.out.println ("foo in config file: " +
                                      p.getProperty("foo"));
       System.out.println ("bar in config file: " +
                                      p.getProperty("bar"));
       System.out.println ("url in config file: " +
                                      p.getProperty("url"));
       System.out.println ("sid in config file: " +
                                      p.getProperty("sid"));
   }
}
/
show errors;
create or replace procedure getproperties
  as language java name
  'propty.getppty(java.lang.String)';
/
show errors;

rem At this stage, you need to grant scott the permission to read the
the properties file for loading
rem
rem SQL> connect sys as sysdba
rem Enter password: *****
rem Connected.
rem SQL> call dbms_java.grant_permission
rem                 ( 'SCOTT','java.io.FilePermission',
rem   2  'C:\temp\config.properties', 'read' );
rem
rem Call completed.
rem
rem SQL>connect scott/tiger
rem
call dbms_java.loadjava('-v -f C:\temp\config.properties');
```

Notice the literal name of the resource object that is created (with the "ROOT/" prefix):

```
SQL>select object_name from user_objects where object_type = 'JAVA
RESOURCE';
```

```
OBJECT_NAME
-----------------------------------------------------
ROOT/tmp/config.properties

set serveroutput on
Call dbms_java.set_output(50000);
call getproperties('ROOT/tmp/config.properties');
```

Alternatively, you may archive the resource file in a JAR file as follows:

```
C:\Book>jar  -cf resource.jar config.properties
C:\Book>jar -tf resource.jar
META-INF/
META-INF/MANIFEST.MF
config.properties
```

Notice that `dbms_java.loadjava` will explode the JAR file; the config.properties file can now be referenced without the "ROOT/" prefix:

```
SQL*Plus scott/tiger

SQL>call dbms_java.loadjava('-v -f /tmp/resources.jar');

SQL>select object_name from user_objects where object_type = 'JAVA
RESOURCE';
OBJECT_NAME
---------------------------------------
META-INF/MANIFEST.MF
config.properties

SQL>call getproperties('config.properties');
```

Where Is the Java Bytecode Stored?

In the current implementation, a Java class must be physically stored in the database before it can be executed. You can compile the Java source on the client-side and then upload the resulting class, but you can load the source file and compile directly within the database. During the in-database compilation phase (i.e., using "ALTER JAVA COMPILE..." or "create or `replace and resolve java source.."`), the Java source is "loaded" into the compiler's memory by reading the previously stored text out of the internal system table. This is to ensure that the original Java source has not been altered out of the control of the DDL since it has been loaded—such alteration could break the dependencies maintained within the OracleJVM. The compiler produces a set of bytecodes. During the compilation phase, the references to other objects are "resolved" by a "resolver," using the "resolver specification," which is similar to the notion of CLASSPATH in JDK VMs (see section 2.1.6). However, a resolver specification is used only once to resolve referenced names to other classes. Once the resolution has been done, the name bindings persist indefinitely. On the other hand, the CLASSPATH may be different at each invocation, which may bind different classes to the referenced names.

Optionally, but recommended, the bytecodes can be compiled into machine code (static native compilation), to accelerate the execution speed; in this case, the native compiler library information (or metadata)—including the name of the DLL that contains the machine code, the name of the function stored in the DLL that loads the class, and flags—is associated with the class.

In summary, a "*stand-alone Java object*" or "*managed Java object*" contains the source text (if loaded in the database), the bytecode of the class, the "resolver specification,"[4] OracleJVM-specific metadata, and, optionally, the native compiler (NCOMP) metadata. It is stored as a "*library unit.*" Similar to PL/SQL objects, the metadata of "Java objects" does not currently reference external objects. During runtime, the bytecode of the Java classes is loaded into shared memory (see section 2.2).

How Are Java Archives Handled?

Java/J2EE applications are usually packaged as JARs (Java ARchives), WARs (Web ARchives), and EARs (Enterprise ARchives). The OracleJVM does not currently handle JARs as a unit of deployment; as a result, signed JARs[5] are not currently supported. However, it allows uploading JAR and ZIP files into the database. Once loaded, the JAR and ZIP files are unbundled into individual classes before compilation and resolution. By default, JAR files are treated as resource files (only looked up during runtime) and are not processed recursively. However, the "–recursivejars" option of loadjava forces the recursive processing of JAR files.

---

4.   Once resolved, the referenced names are bound to (and depend on) particular database objects (i.e., other classes).
5.   Signed JARs tracks the origin/signature (digest attribute, magic number) of each member in the Manifest file, along with other security files.

2.1.4 Class Sharing

In section 2.1.3, I have described how Java is stored in the database. In order to support thousands of simultaneous sessions and users, the Oracle-JVM must reduce the average memory footprint per session. This goal is achieved through class sharing, both for system and user classes.

Sharing JVM Runtime Classes and Metadata

The following classes and metadata, from largest sized to smallest sized, are shared between all clients in the same database instance: the bytecodes of interpreted methods, the in-memory representation of the constant pool,[6] the virtual method tables (i.e., a list of pointers to actual methods that support polymorphic[7] methods), the list of implemented methods and fields, the "hot-loaded" states, and various implementation-specific metadata. Figure 2.1 pictures the sharing of system classes.

Sharing User Application Classes

Each active Java class comprises a shared part and a nonshared part, described here as follows:

- The read-only and hence shareable part includes the bytecodes and the method tables. Sharing the read-only part of Java classes results in smaller average memory footprint and scalability.

- The unshared part contains the static class variables; this private part is carved out of the Sessionspace (a session memory area described later).

The invocation of Java methods causes the read-only part to be brought into the Shared Global Area (SGA) by the class loader—if not yet present, since there is only one copy per instance—and the creation of the private part. Keeping private copies of Java classes in every schema would be a waste of resources and would quickly become a maintenance nightmare. Figure 2.1 depicts the sharing of user classes. The best practice to derive from this is that applications libraries should be designed to be shareable across multiple database schemas.

---

6.   The constant pool is an area in the Java class that keeps a reference of strings and other metadata, similar to the symbol table in conventional languages.
7.   Object-oriented concept where a virtual method has multiple implementations (behaviors).

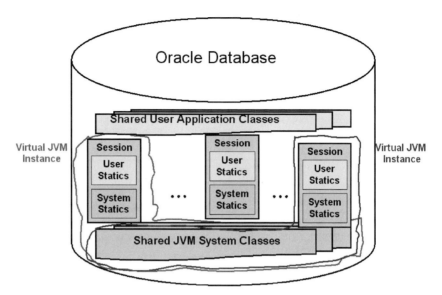

Figure 2.1
Session-Based
Virtual JVM

Applications class sharing occurs automatically as soon as two or more schemas share the same classes and jars. At any given time, there is only one in-memory (SGA) representation of each Java class per database instance.

Sharing "Interned Strings"

To further reduce the per-session footprint, OracleJVM also uses a memory space in SGA to hold string literals that are common to several Java classes and arrange these in a way that allows quick search and retrieval.

Sharing "Constant States" (Class Hot Loading)

Another memory optimization technique, known as "class hot loading," consists of sharing constant states across all sessions, based on the observation that many system classes have static variables that are initialized to the same value across all sessions and then never changed (i.e., constant values). This technique is implemented by saving in system tables the static states of selected system classes, during the installation of Java (part of or post database installation), and then restoring the saved states into shared memory when loading the classes in question.

Sharing Read-Only System Objects

By design (e.g., scalability, data integrity), the Oracle database sessions are isolated and watertight, whereas the Oracle JVM manages to share selected system objects. This sharing is achieved by persisting selected read-only objects into the database and then loading these into shared memory. Sharing read-only system objects significantly reduces the per-session memory. This technique is used internally only by the OracleJVM and Oracle products that use Java in the database but is not productized and therefore not exposed or available for user objects.[8]

2.1.5 Interapplication Isolation (JSR 121)

As explained earlier, the session architecture of the Oracle database does not allow sharing user data across sessions. This lack of data sharing across sessions is often pointed out as a limitation of Oracle's implementation of Java in the database. In the JDK VM world, sharing across threads works fine within a single Java VM boundary; however, this perceived advantage goes away in a multiple Java VM environment, which is now the norm for large-scale deployment. There is a growing need (i.e., scalability, security) for interapplication isolation. The JSR 121,[9] which specifies the Application Isolation API, is a materialization of such a requirement. OracleJVM already offers interapplication isolation by design without the need for a specific API (a by-product of session isolation) but will support JSR 121 when it is finalized.

2.1.6 Contrasting OracleJVM with the JDK VM

Although OracleJVM maintains J2SE compatibility, it currently differs from the JDK VM in terms of architecture, scalability, robustness behavior, threading, invocation mechanisms, isolation, and security.

Session-Based Architecture and Scalability

Session isolation is the foundation for scalability and data integrity in the Oracle database; an application should not be able to see/read uncommitted data or update another application's data. The OracleJVM is integrated into this architecture while keeping system resources (needed by each session) minimal to maximize the number of concurrently executing Java sessions on a given database instance. Conceptually, as illustrated in Figure 2.1, there is a dedicated, private Java VM per session. In reality, all sessions share the same JVM system classes—only statics and private states are kept in individual session space, resulting in unbound scalability as far as the capacity of the system permits. Row-level locking and multilevel read con-

---

8. This is discussed here in the context of memory footprint reduction techniques.
9. http://www.jcp.org/en/jsr/detail?id=121.

sistency ensure that one application would not be able to prevent another application from performing its database operations. Session isolation, row-level locking, and multilevel read consistency result in high concurrency or scalability.

As a poster on Slashdot.org stated: "We were doing some benchmarking and found that our app 'died' at about 3,000 sessions (as defined by us) in the tweaked/tuned native JDK JVM, whereas the OracleJVM handled almost 150,000 before croaking."

Robustness

Because each session has its own "virtual Java VM," a process failure impacts only the virtual JVM of the session being serviced by the failed process; as a result, it does not crash as a whole (unless the entire system crashes), and it has the same robustness as the Oracle database.

Threading

JDK-based Java VMs are multithreaded (i.e., use threads for scalability to serve multiple users or requests concurrently). OracleJVM, on the other hand, is based on the database session model, which is a single-client non-preemptive model. Although Java in the Oracle database allows running threaded programs, such as SQL and PL/SQL, it is single threaded at the execution level. To be clearer, multiple clients or threads cannot be multiplexed to run simultaneously within the same process. Therefore, unless the currently running Java thread completes or blocks on socket operation or voluntarily pauses (i.e., calls   `java.lang.Thread.yield()`), another thread will not be capable of running. This model is independent of the server process type (i.e., dedicated or shared server); even in shared server mode, clients are scheduled and run serially. This model increases thread safety and robustness by reducing the need for object locking (i.e., synchronization) and therefore reduces the likelihood of deadlocks; it also simplifies memory management and Garbage Collection.

Java Output

Currently, and unlike JDK VMs, the outputs of OracleJVM go to the trace files (.trc) associated with the session (process). However, you can redirect the standard output to the console (i.e., the SQL output) using the `DBMS_JAVA.SET_OUTPUT()` method. But, the output is only printed when the stored procedure exits, and this setting works only for one call (i.e., the SQL call that immediately follows the invocation of `DBMS_JAVA.SET_OUTPUT()`). The minumum and default value is 2,000 characters and the maximum is 1,000,000 (1 million) characters. Notice the "SET SERVEROUTPUT ON" command, which enables displaying the outputs of stored procedures (Java or PL/SQL blocks) in SQL*Plus.

```
Usage:
SQL> SET SERVEROUTPUT ON
SQL> call dbms_java.set_output (5000);
```

See examples in Listing 2.1.

Invocation Mechanisms, Locating Classes, and Transitive Closure

The top-level invocation of Java is primarily done via a PL/SQL wrapper called Call Spec. As of Oracle Database 10*g*, you can also use a JPublisher-generated client-stub, which shields you from defining a Call Spec at the expense of the overhead of serializing/deserializing parameters and return values (see "Developing and Deploying Java in the Database" in Chapter 4 for more details). The notion of CLASSPATH is replaced by the corresponding notion of "Resolver Spec," which is short for "Resolver Specification" (see section 2.3 later in this chapter for more details). To be executed, the Java classes must reside in database schemas, and all references to other classes and objects must be "resolved" within the database (i.e., cannot reference external classes).

Preferences

Starting from JDK1.4, the preferences API (in package "java.util.prefs") allows Java applications to persist small amounts of states. Designed as a replacement for java.util.Properties, the Preferences API provides persistent storage and retrieval of *key-value* pairs, mostly to store user and system configuration values as well as GUI/Window positions. The system preferences are available to all users, whereas user-specific preferences are private to that user. In Oracle Database 10*g*, OracleJVM is J2SE 1.4 compatible and therefore implements java.util.prefs.Preferences. The JDK implementation uses platform-dependent mechanisms to persistently store the name/value pairs, such as registries on Windows and xml file on UNIX. The OracleJVM implementation uses a platform-independent storage (i.e., an internal database table); the name is restricted to VARCHAR2(2000); and the value is stored as a BLOB. In addition to supporting the standard API for setting and retrieving the stored values, the OracleJVM implementation also offers a PL/SQL interface dbms_java.set_preference() for setting preferences. However, there currently is no symmetric function to retrieve the value (i.e., *dbms_java.get_preferences()*) .

The PL/SQL interface, which is implemented by the Java method, is as follows:

```
    procedure set_preference(user varchar2, type varchar2,
        abspath varchar2, key varchar2, value varchar2);
user: <login schema> or 'SYS'
type: User preference('U') or System preference ('S')
abspath: absolute path
key: for looking up the value
value: the value associated with the key


Usage: Setting preferences using dbms_java.set_preferences()


SQL> call dbms_java.set_preference('SCOTT','U',
        '/my/package/class/method','CONSTANT','20');
```

The Java method:

```
java.util.prefs.OraclePreferences.DbmsSetPreference(
        java.lang.String, java.lang.String, java.lang.String,
        java.lang.String, java.lang.String);
```

See java.util.prefs.Preferences[10] for more details on the API itself.

Consistent Behavior across Platforms

As part of the Oracle database code, the OracleJVM is built once and then ported to the various platforms where the database code runs; as a result, its behavior is consistently the same across all of the platforms where the Oracle database is available; most of you are familiar with the headaches incurred by the difference in behavior of JDK VM across platforms. As already mentioned, there is no need to install or upload an external JDK or JRE to run Java in the database; however, you need to make sure that the Java option is selected during the database installation.

---

10. http://java.sun.com/j2se/1.4.2/docs/api/java/util/prefs/Preferences.html.

Java 2 Security

OracleJVM also differs from the JDK VM in terms of Java 2 Security implementation and permission administration, which are covered in detail in section 2.3 in this chapter.

2.1.7   Resource Control

The Oracle database limits system resource consumption through DBA-defined profiles (i.e., `CREATE PROFILE p, ALTER USER u PROFILE p`). In addition, the Database Resource Manager allows you to group users and applications into *resource consumer groups* and allocate a percentage of CPU resources to each consumer group through a *resource plan*. The Database Resource Manager is not addressed in this book, but the OracleJVM enforces a database resource profile. Defining and enforcing resource limitations on a schema involves the following steps:

1.   Enable resource limitation at the database system level using either of the following two ways:

     ■   Statically, in the database initialization file, using the

         ```
         RESOURCE_LIMIT parameter
         RESOURCE_LIMIT  = true | false
         ```

     ■   Dynamically, using the "`ALTER SYSTEM`" command (requires `ALTER SYSTEM` privilege)

         ```
         ALTER SYSTEM RESOURCE_LIMIT  = true | false
         ```

2.   Define a resource profile: a set of limits on database and system resources (requires `CREATE PROFILE` privilege).

     ```
     Example
       CREATE PROFILE greedy LIMIT
          SESSIONS_PER_USER          UNLIMITED
          CPU_PER_SESSION            UNLIMITED
          CPU_PER_CALL               4000
          CONNECT_TIME               50
          LOGICAL_READS_PER_SESSION  DEFAULT
          LOGICAL_READS_PER_CALL     2000
          PRIVATE_SGA                30K
          COMPOSITE_LIMIT            5000000;
     ```

3.   Assign the defined profile to a user (schema).

     ```
     ALTER USER Java_nerd1 PROFILE greedy;
     ```

See the Oracle Database 10*g* SQL Reference for more details on defining resource limitations.

2.1.8 SQL Data Access from Java in the Database

One of the motivations for embedding Java in the database is to take advantage of the close proximity to the SQL engine for efficient data access and manipulation. OracleJVM furnishes a type-2 server-side JDBC driver, as well as a SQLJ runtime, which runs in the same address space as the SQL engine. The Oracle JDBC drivers are covered in detail in Part II; in this section, I will briefly address the server-side JDBC driver, which is used when calling SQL directly from Java code running in the database. This JDBC driver is instantiated and preregistered at Java initialization in the session. Java initialization happens during the first invocation of Java since the creation of the session. Because you are already connected to the database by the time you invoke Java, the connection object you get by invoking *getConnection()* is a mere handler to the default connection. The following three methods look syntactically different but all return the same kind of connection (i.e., a lightweight server-side default connection handler):

- Connection conn =
  DriverManager.getConnection("jdbc:default:connection:");
- Connection conn =
  DriverManager.getConnection ("jdbc:oracle:kprb:");
- OracleDriver t2server = new OracleDriver();
  Connection conn = t2server.defaultConnection();

These syntaxes are required because the OracleJVM does not yet allow associating a JDBC data-source name with the actual connect string through the JNDI namespace. The consequence of this limitation is that you need to code the connection section in such a way that you can determine where your code is running and then use the right connection string.

```
/*
 * Where is your code running: inside or outside the database?
 */
Connection conn;
if (System.getProperty("oracle.jserver.version") != null)
{
  /*
   * You are in the database, use the default connection
   */
  conn = DriverManager.getConnection("jdbc:default:connection:");
```

```
}
else
{
  /*
   * You are not in the database, use standard JDBC connection
   */

  DriverManager.registerDriver(new oracle.jdbc.OracleDriver());
  conn =
      DriverManager.getConnection("jdbc:oracle:thin:", "scott", "tiger");
}
```

Alternatively, you may use properties files to adapt and pass-in the JDBC URL.

All SQL operations in OracleJVM are part of the current transaction; however, because auto-commit is disabled (not supported is the right statement), you must explicitly COMMIT or ROLLBACK all of your changes. JDBC best practices recommend closing all statements and result sets when they are no longer needed. However, the close() method closes the connection object instance but not the physical database connection; you cannot close this one as long as the session lives.

For accessing remote Oracle databases from within Java in the database, a type-4 "*Server-side JDBC-thin*" is provided. Existing JDBC applications that access a remote Oracle database should work as is, but the cancel() and setQueryTimeout() methods are not supported. Also, in order to open a socket from within the server-side JDBC-thin, the database session must be granted java.net.SocketPermission as follows:

```
SQL> create role CALLOUT;
SQL> call dbms_java.grant_permission('CALLOUT',
'java.net.SocketPermission',
'*', 'connect' );
SQL> grant callout to scott;
```

See section 2.3, for more details on permissions, and "JDBC Call-out to Non-Oracle Databases" in Chapter 4 for an example of accessing a remote non-Oracle database from within the Oracle database.

Both server-side drivers (type-2 and type-4) and their classes are automatically installed as part of the database install (when the Java option is selected) or during manual OracleJVM reinstall. In Part II, all Oracle JDBC driver types are compared, including their features' differences.

2.1.9   DBMS_JAVA: The All-Purpose Tool for Administering OracleJVM

DMBS_JAVA is a comprehensive package of PL/SQL wrappers (see the "PL/SQL Packaged Call Spec" section in Chapter 4) that exposes a set of Java methods for administering the OracleJVM from SQL (and, therefore, JDBC). You will see a lot of references to DBMS_JAVA throughout the book, so that is why I am introducing this topic at this early stage. DBMS_JAVA contains documented interfaces for DBAs and Java developers but also undocumented interfaces that are used internally. Each interface is in the form of a **DBMS_JAVA.<Java_method()>** procedure of function and each has a corresponding Java method that implements the procedure or function in question. However, the implementation classes and the Java methods may change from one release to another. Therefore, it is highly recommended to use only the PL/SQL interface (or wrapper); your applications will not brake throughout successive database releases. The corresponding DBMS_JAVA interfaces will be highlighted under the appropiriate sections (e.g., security, compiler setting).

Let's look at one example of DBMS_JAVA usage through the longname/ shortname interfaces.

Longnames and Shortnames

The maximum length of a SQL identifier or a database schema object name is 31 characters, and all characters must be legal and convertible to the target database character set. The full name of Java classes and methods usually exceeds this limit and may contain illegal characters such as dots. To work around this issue, the Oracle database uses abbreviated names (i.e., shortname) internally, but maintains a correspondence between this shortname and the full name (i.e., longname), as well as the methods used to transform shortname into longname and vice versa. *A longname is only generated when the actual name is regarded as invalid* (i.e., it has passed the maximum size or contains illegal characters). The longname and shortname functions have been designed to help you query shortname and longname of your Java classes, sources, and resources.

longname: Returns the longname of a class when given the shortname, if it exists.

```
FUNCTION longname (shortname VARCHAR2) RETURN VARCHAR2 as
language java name
```

```
'oracle.aurora.rdbms.DbmsJava.longNameForSQL(java.lang.String
) return java.lang.String';
```

shortname: Returns the shortname of a class when given the longname.

```
FUNCTION shortname (longname VARCHAR2) RETURN VARCHAR2 as
language java name
'oracle.aurora.rdbms.DbmsJava.shortName(java.lang.String)
return java.lang.String';
```

.

Example: Let's create a Java source and class where the package name contains illegal characters (e.g., dots are illegal, from a database object name perspective) and see its conversion.

```
SQL>CREATE OR REPLACE AND RESOLVE JAVA SOURCE NAMED LongNameSample AS
package longnamepkg.subpackage.foo;

  class LongNameSample {
    public static void main (String argv[]) {
      System.out.println ("Hello LngNameSample");
    }
  }
/

Java created.

SQL> show errors;
No errors.
SQL>

SQL> col DBMS_JAVA.LONGNAME(OBJECT_NAME) format a45

SQL> col DBMS_JAVA.LONGNAME(OBJECT_NAME) format a45
SQL> select dbms_java.longname(object_name), object_type, status from
     user_objects
  2     where object_type not in ('TABLE', 'VIEW', 'INDEX') and
  3           dbms_java.longname(object_name) like '%LongNameSample'
  4  order by dbms_java.longname(object_name)
  5  /
```

```
DBMS_JAVA.LONGNAME(OBJECT_NAME)                OBJECT_TYPE
STATUS
--------------------------------------------- -----------------------
longnamepkg/subpackage/foo/LongNameSample      JAVA CLASS
VALID


SQL> col DBMS_JAVA.SHORTNAME(OBJECT_NAME) format a40
SQL> l
  1  select dbms_java.shortname(object_name), object_type, status
  2  from user_objects
  3  where object_type not in ('TABLE', 'VIEW', 'INDEX')
  4  and dbms_java.shortname(object_name) like '%LongNameSample'
  5* order by dbms_java.shortname(object_name)
SQL> /


DBMS_JAVA.SHORTNAME(OBJECT_NAME)              OBJECT_TYPE          STATUS
-------------------------------------------- -------------------- -------
/3277131c_LongNameSample                      JAVA CLASS           VALID
```

2.2   Java Memory Management

The goal of the OracleJVM memory manager is to map Java memory management semantics (automatic memory management) to the Oracle database memory management framework. I will first introduce the memory structures of the Oracle database—including SGA, CGA, PGA, and UGA (see section 2.2.1), and then describe the OracleJVM memory structures, memory allocation, and Garbage Collection techniques. Once again, this information might appear unnecessary for Java developers, but remember this is Java in the database, and you have to have the big picture by factoring in the overall RDBMS memory management. You will learn how to retrieve and alter the default values of memory areas. Another reason why you want to know more about memory management for Java in the database is when the DBA sets a maximum size target for the instance's shared memory, a.k.a SGA (i.e., setting `PGA_AGGREGATE_TARGET parameter`), it influences the behavior of the Garbage Collector in Java-enabled sessions. In this case, when the overall RDBMS memory allocation approaches `PGA_AGGREGATE_TARGET`, the OracleJVM will make sure to use less memory at the expense of the execution speed.

2.2.1   Key Memory Structures of the Oracle Database

In order to understand the memory management of OracleJVM, you need a basic knowledge of the memory structures of the Oracle database. Those familiar with the Oracle database structures can skip this section and go to section 2.2.2. The installation, configuration, and administration of the database is beyond the scope of this book; however, for those interested in these topics, I recommend the *Oracle Database 2 Day DBA documentation*[11]—a concise, task-oriented book that will get you up to speed with the Oracle database in two days!

A Database Instance: An Oracle database instance comprises one (and only one) SGA and a set of database processes. A database is usually accessed and managed by a single instance. However, an Oracle database can also be concurrently accessed and managed by multiple instances—Oracle's Real Application Clusters (RAC) technology[12]—for scalability and high-availability requirements. RAC is also the cornerstone of Oracle database deployment in Enterprise Grid environments (which will be addressed in Part II of this book). Figure 2.2 depicts the key memory structures of an Oracle database instance.

The Shared Global Area (SGA): This is a shared memory area that contains data and control information, which is visible and accessible to the server processes that are part of the database instance. The data buffer cache, the redo buffer, and the various pools are part of the SGA and therefore visible and accessible to all Oracle server processes. The SGA has the same lifetime as the database instance.

The Process Global Area (PGA): This is a memory area that contains data and control information, which is private, visible and accessible only to a server process (dedicated or shared). The PGA has the same lifetime as the server process.

The User Global Area (UGA): This is a memory region associated with a user session. With dedicated server processes, the session is tied to the process; therefore, the UGA is allocated out of the PGA. With shared servers, the session is not attached to any process; therefore, its UGA is allocated out of the SGA.

11.   http://www.oracle.com/pls/db10g/
db10g.to_pdf?pathname=server.101%2Fb10742.pdf&remark=portal+%28Getting+Started%29.
12.   See the Oracle Database RAC documentation for more details.

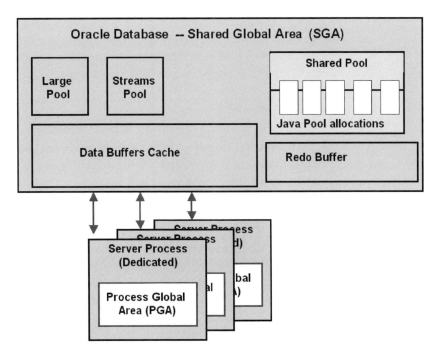

Figure 2.2
*Oracle Database
Key Memory
Structures*

CGA (Call Global Area): This is a memory area allocated out of the PGA (dedicated or shared servers) for the duration of a SQL call; its contents are visible and accessible only to this call. It is freed at the end of the call.

In the OracleJVM memory manager lexicon, "*object*" refers to a program state, and "*object memory*" or "*objmem*" refers to a memory space used to hold live objects as well as garbage objects. Live objects are objects that a program will likely access at some point in the future, as opposed to garbage objects, which are regarded as dead objects. Before examining the various object memories, their allocation, and clean-up policies, let's first define a baseline in terms of memory allocation and clean-up vocabulary and techniques used by the OracleJVM.

2.2.2 Java Memory Allocation Techniques

OracleJVM uses mainly the "frontier consing" and "buddy allocation" memory allocation techniques for the various object memories.

Frontier consing

Frontier consing (or "cons operation") is a very fast allocation strategy, which consists of incrementing a pointer that maintains a frontier boundary between allocated and unused memory space in the heap.

Buddy allocation

Buddy allocation is a strategy that rounds up memory allocation requests to predetermined sizes (e.g., next multiple of 16, next power of 2). For example, an allocation request for 10-Kb will result in a 16-Kb space allocation, a request for 28-Kb will result in a 32-Kb allocation and so on.

2.2.3 Garbage Collection Techniques

Garbage Collection designates a set of techniques used by Java VM for automatic memory reclamation; those familiar with these techniques can skip this section. Garbage Collection generally consists of three steps: (1) mark, (2) collect, and (3) clean-up. The mark step finds the objects that need to be retained. The collect step removes unused objects. The clean-up step returns the reclaimed memory to the pool of free memory (i.e., return to a usable state). The OracleJVM memory manager uses a set of GC techniques for its various memory structures (listed in Table 2.1), including the generational GC, mark-sweep GC, and copy GC.

Generational GC

Generational GC is a technique that segregates memory areas by their age (i.e., generations). Allocations happen in the most recent area. When an area is full, a collector is used to "move" the live objects to the next older area (hence, the term *generational*). Different collection algorithms may be used across generations. As a result, most objects are reclaimed upon the first GC, resulting in many inexpensive GCs instead of fewer large ones.

Mark-sweep GC

A mark-sweep GC consists of two phases: (1) the mark phase (garbage detection) and the (2) sweep phase (Garbage Collection). The sweep phase places the "garbaged" memory on the freelists. The allocation is serviced out of the freelists. Lazy sweeping is a variation technique that marks objects normally, but, in the sweep phase, leaves it up to the allocation phase to determine whether the marked objects are live (no need to reclaim) or not (can be reclaimed), rather than sweeping the object memory at that time.

Copy GC

Copy GC consists of recursively copying objects, referenced by root objects, into an empty region of the object memory. It combines marking and compacting into one operation. This technique is very efficient when most of the objects need to be reclaimed—which is the case most of the time.

Reference-counting GC

In reference-counting GC, each object stores a count of the number of references to it. This count is incremented every time a reference to that object is stored and decremented every time a reference to that object is overwritten. The object is reclaimed when the count reaches zero.

Self-tuning GC

Starting with Oracle 9*i* Release 2, the Garbage Collector automatically and dynamically adjusts the threshold at which the GC is triggered; for most applications, you don't have to play with GC thresholds, using `OracleRuntime.getSessionGCThreshold()` and `OracleRuntime.setSessionGCThreshold()`. In Oracle Database 10*g* Release 2, the GC supports `PGA_AGGREGATE_TARGET` and a smoother memory growth.

Supporting `PGA_AGGREGATE_TARGET`: The DBA or database developers with DBA privileges can set the `PGA_AGGREGATE_TARGET`[13] parameter, which will instruct the GC to trade memory for speed and vice versa. The values differ as follows:

- *Low values optimize memory at the expense of execution speed.* In other words, if the only active Java thread at the end of the top-level call is the main thread (i.e., there are no user threads),[14] then perform a full GC of *oldspace* to free up memory, irrespective of the type of server (dedicated or shared). This results in optimizing the PGA space usage, much like the end-of-call migration, which happens systematically in pre-10*g* and only in shared server mode in 10*g*.

- *High values optimize the execution speed at the expense of memory.* In other words, state migration is not performed at the end of the call, when in dedicated mode.

---

13.   See the Oracle Database Performance Tuning Guide for a more detailed discussion.
14.   Pre-10g Database releases, OracleJVM kills any remaining live threads at the end of the call.

Smoother Memory Growth: In Oracle database 10*g* Release 2, the clean-up and growth of the memory space used for holding long-lived or large objects (i.e., Oldspace) is smoother. In previous releases, the growth of Oldspace was too aggressive, resulting in that a user who allocates a lot of objects and then drops these ends up with a large unused memory space. In 10*g* Release 2, Oldspace grows only if the growth is inversely proportional to the amount of space freed. In other words, Oldspace cannot grow more than 100 percent of its current size.

2.2.4 Java Memory Areas

In OracleJVM, the states of Java objects are preserved in special data structures called "object memories." There are several object memory types, including Newspace, Oldspace, Runspace, Stackspace, and Unscanned Stackspace. Each object memory type is used for a specific need. Why would you care? Well, although the default sizes of the various memory areas, described as follows, suffice for most applications, some Java applications or frameworks running in the database might have extreme memory requirements; in this case, you want to know the default allocations and behavior of the Garbage Collector. Table 2.1 summarizes what each object memory type is used for and how these are allocated and cleaned (i.e., garbage collected).

Sessionspace

Sessionspace, also called "session memory," is an object memory residing in the User Global Area (UGA), which is associated with each session (each session has its own Sessionspace) and lives as long as the session lives. Sessionspace is used to preserve state of system objects, user objects, and metadata used by the Java runtime. In shared server mode, the UGA resides in the SGA (hence, the Sessionspace), and the states of the objects that are live at the end of the previous call are recursively copied from the Call Global Area (see Newspace and Oldspace in the following text) to the Sessionspace; this process is called "end-of-call migration" or "session migration." In dedicated server mode, the Sessionspace resides in the PGA (as opposed to the SGA); starting with release 10*g*, the end-of-call migration is no longer performed when in dedicated mode. You can programmatically get the size of the Sessionspace using `OracleRuntime.getSessionSize()` (see memtest.sql code sample).

Oldspace

Oldspace is an object memory used for holding long-lived or large objects (i.e., larger than 1-K Bytes) for the duration of a call. It is cleaned up using Marksweep GC (described earlier) for large objects; it uses a variation of "lazy sweeping" for small objects.

Runspace

Runspace is an object memory residing in CGA or PGA and is used to hold system objects (e.g., classloader objects) allocated for the duration of a call. It is managed (allocation and clean-up) in the same way as Oldspace. You can use the `OracleRuntime.getMaxRunspaceSize()` method to see the current value in your system (see the following memtest code sample in Listing 2.2).

Stackspace

Stackspace is an object memory residing in CGA or PGA and is used to allocate system objects and objects used by the Java interpreter (no user objects). Memory allocation in stackspace is achieved using the "Frontier Consing" technique. You can use `OracleRuntime.getJavaStackSize()`, `OracleRuntime.setJavaStackSize()`, `OracleRuntime.getThread-StackSize()`, and `OracleRuntime.setThreadStackSize()` to get and set the size of the Stackspace (see the following memtest code sample in Listing 2.2).

Newspace

Newspace is the default memory for allocating almost all Java objects, except large objects, which are allocated in Oldspace. Memory allocation in newspace is achieved using "Frontier Consing," and Garbage Collection is done using the "Copy GC" technique. You can use `OracleRuntime.getNewspaceSize()` and `OracleRuntime.setNewspaceSize()` to programmatically get and set the size of Newspace (see Listing 2.2).

Listing 2.2   *Memtest.sql*

```
===========================
create or replace and resolve java source named memtest  as
import oracle.aurora.vm.OracleRuntime;
public class memtest
{
/*
```

```
 * The following code sample is provided for for illustration purposes
only.
 * The default values should work for most applications.
 * Before altering these values for your production system, please
 * go under tuning and testing exercises beforehand
 */
public static void Tests ()
{
    System.out.println("getSessionSize(): "
                   + OracleRuntime.getSessionSize());

    System.out.println("Old NewspaceSize(): "
                               + OracleRuntime.getNewspaceSize());
    OracleRuntime.setNewspaceSize(2 *
OracleRuntime.getNewspaceSize());
    System.out.println("New NewspaceSize(): "
                   + OracleRuntime.getNewspaceSize());

    System.out.println("Old MaxRunspaceSize(): "
                               + OracleRuntime.getMaxRunspaceSize());
    OracleRuntime.setMaxRunspaceSize(2 *
OracleRuntime.getMaxRunspaceSize());
    System.out.println("New MaxRunspaceSize(): "
                   + OracleRuntime.getMaxRunspaceSize());

    System.out.println("getJavaPoolSize(): "
                               + OracleRuntime.getJavaPoolSize());
    System.out.println("getSessionSoftLimit(): "
                               + OracleRuntime.getSessionSoftLimit());
    System.out.println("Old SessionGCThreshold(): "
                           + OracleRuntime.getSessionGCThreshold());
    OracleRuntime.setSessionGCThreshold(2 *
                           OracleRuntime.getSessionGCThreshold());
    System.out.println("New SessionGCThreshold(): "
                           + OracleRuntime.getSessionGCThreshold());
    System.out.println("Old NewspaceSize: " +
OracleRuntime.getNewspaceSize());
    OracleRuntime.setNewspaceSize(2 *
OracleRuntime.getNewspaceSize());
    System.out.println("New NewspaceSize: " +
OracleRuntime.getNewspaceSize());
    System.out.println("Old MaxMemsize: " +
OracleRuntime.getMaxMemorySize());
```

```
    OracleRuntime.setMaxMemorySize(2 *
OracleRuntime.getMaxMemorySize());
    System.out.println("New MaxMemsize: " +
OracleRuntime.getMaxMemorySize());
    System.out.println("Old JavaStackSize(): "
                              + OracleRuntime.getJavaStackSize());
    OracleRuntime.setJavaStackSize(2 *
OracleRuntime.getJavaStackSize());
    System.out.println("New JavaStackSize(): "
                              + OracleRuntime.getJavaStackSize());
    System.out.println("Old ThreadStackSize(): "
                              + OracleRuntime.getThreadStackSize());
    OracleRuntime.setThreadStackSize(2 *
OracleRuntime.getThreadStackSize());
    System.out.println("New ThreadStackSize(): "
                              + OracleRuntime.getThreadStackSize());
  }
}
/
show errors;


create or replace procedure memtests
  as language java name
  'memtest.Tests()';
/
show errors;


set serveroutput on
Call dbms_java.set_output(50000);
call memtests();
```

Swapping and Pinning Libunits

Under heavy load, the OracleJVM also uses a disk storage (tablespace) to age out libunits (i.e., swapped out and reconstructed in memory when needed), unless the libunits in question are "pinned" in memory.

2.2.5   Shared Servers versus Dedicated Processes

The Java VM runtime was initially designed for the shared server mode and reused as is in dedicated mode. In mode, because there is no guarantee that subsequent calls (within the session) will be executing in the same server process, an end-of-call migration is performed in order to preserve pro-

Table 2.1   *Summary of OracleJVM Memory Structure*

Name	Contents	Location	Property	Allocation	GC Type
New-space	Small & New Objects	PGC (CGA*)	Contiguous, fixed-size	Frontier Consing	Copy GC
Old-space	Large & Old Objects	PGC (CGA*)	Contiguous, fixed-size	Buddy	Mark-Sweep
Stack-space	Java Stack Stratch Objects	PGC (CGA*)	Segmented, may grow	Frontier Consing	No GC
Session-space	Java Objects (Session Lifetime)	PGC (UGA* Javapool)	Unpaged, may grow (Paged*)	Buddy/ (Frontier Consing*)	Mark-Sweep (Copy GC*)
Run-space	System Objects	PGC (CGA*)	Contiguous, fixed-size	Buddy	Mark-Sweep

*Shared Server mode.

gram/objects state across calls in the Sessionspace. Starting with Oracle database 10*g* Release 1, the memory management has been optimized for dedicated servers; in this case, the session always runs in the same process, and an end-of-call migration is not necessary for preserving states across calls. As a result, threads remain quiescent, and file handles persist (remain open) across calls. Applications that needed to keep file handles open across calls will now work properly. Use the (SERVER = SHARED) or (SERVER = DEDICATED) connection descriptor in the tnsnames.ora file to specify the server type. See the Oracle Database Administration Guide for more details on configuring shared server or dedicated servers.

Session in Dedicated Process

Figure 2.3 summarizes the location of the main object memories in a dedicated server environment. The user memory (UGA) is allocated out of the dedicated process memory (PGA) and not out of the Javapool in SGA.

Session in Shared Server Process

Figure 2.4 summarizes the location of object memories in a shared server environment. The user memory (UGA) is allocated out of the Javapool in

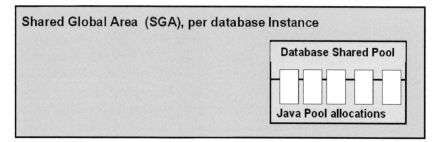

Figure 2.3
*Dedicated Server –
Java Memory Areas*

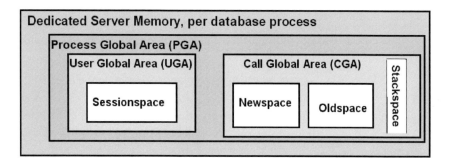

Figure 2.4
*Shared Server –
Java Memory Areas*

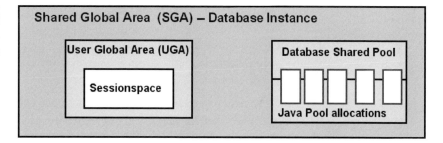

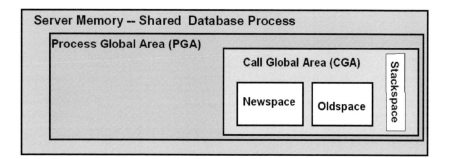

global database instance memory (SGA). End-of-call migration is enforced in this case.

2.2.6　The Javapool

The size of the Javapool in SGA is defined by the `JAVA_POOL_SIZE` parameter. `JAVA_POOL_SIZE` specifies (in bytes) the size of the instance-wide Javapool, from which the Java class loader allocates space for bytecodes and other read-only class metadata when a class, not actually in SGA, needs to be loaded. This memory also contains the Java states that are migrated from the Session space at the end of call. You can see its value using the `SHOW PARAMETER` command under SQL*Plus using `SYSTEM` or `SYS` schemas, or programmatically from any session, using `OracleRuntime.get-JavaPoolSize()` (see Listing 2.2). Starting with Oracle database 10*g*, `JAVA_POOL_SIZE` can be dynamically adjusted through the `ALTER SYSTEM` command.

`JAVA_SOFT_SESSIONSPACE_LIMIT` specifies (in bytes) a ***soft limit*** on Java memory usage in a session. When a user's session exceeds this size, Oracle generates a warning that goes into the trace files. You can also use `OracleRuntime.getSessionSoftLimit()` to programmatically get the value of the soft session space limit.

`JAVA_MAX_SESSIONSPACE_SIZE` specifies (in bytes) the maximum amount of session space made available to a Java program executing in the server. When a user session attempts to exceed this limit, the session is killed, with an out-of-memory message. You can programmatically get its value, using `OracleRuntime.getSessionSize()`. See the previous memtest code sample.

Also, two new views, `V$JAVA_POOL_ADVICE` and `V$JAVA_LIBRARY_CACHE_MEMORY`, have been added to help enforce the Self-Tuning SGA.

`V$JAVA_POOL_ADVICE` displays information about estimated parse time in the Javapool for different pool sizes.

Column	Datatype	Description
JAVA_POOL_SIZE_FOR_ESTIMATE	NUMBER	Javapool size for the estimate (in megabytes)
JAVA_POOL_SIZE_FACTOR	NUMBER	Size factor with respect to the current Javapool size
ESTD_LC_SIZE	NUMBER	Estimated memory in use by the library cache (in megabytes)
ESTD_LC_MEMORY_OBJECTS	NUMBER	Estimated number of library cache memory objects in the Javapool of the specified size

Column	Datatype	Description
ESTD_LC_TIME_SAVED	NUMBER	Estimated elapsed parse time saved (in seconds), owing to library cache memory objects being found in a Javapool of the specified size. This is the time that would have been spent in reloading the required objects in the Javapool if they had aged out because of insufficient amount of available free memory.
ESTD_LC_TIME_SAVED_FACTOR	NUMBER	Estimated parse time saved factor with respect to the current Javapool size
ESTD_LC_LOAD_TIME	NUMBER	Estimated elapsed time (in seconds) for parsing in a Javapool of the specified size
ESTD_LC_LOAD_TIME_FACTOR	NUMBER	Estimated load time factor with respect to the current Javapool size
ESTD_LC_MEMORY_OBJECT_HITS	NUMBER	Estimated number of times a library cache memory object was found in a Javapool of the specified size

V$JAVA_LIBRARY_CACHE_MEMORY displays statistics about memory allocated to library cache memory objects in different namespaces for Java objects. A library cache object consists of one or more memory objects.

Column	Datatype	Description
LC_NAMESPACE	VARCHAR2(15)	Library cache namespace
LC_INUSE_MEMORY_OBJECTS	NUMBER	Number of library cache memory objects currently in use in the Javapool
LC_INUSE_MEMORY_SIZE	NUMBER	Total size of library cache in-use memory objects (in megabytes)
LC_FREEABLE_MEMORY_OBJECTS	NUMBER	Number of freeable library cache memory objects in the Javapool
LC_FREEABLE_MEMORY_SIZE	NUMBER	Size of library cache freeable memory objects (in megabytes)

2.2.7   Top-Level Calls and Recursive Calls

The top-level call to Java in the database is generally through a SQL call; in other words, entering the OracleJVM is achieved by invoking public static methods through PL/SQL wrappers. Starting with Oracle Database 10*g*

Release 1, a client-side stub generated by JPublisher and referred to in the Oracle Database Java Developers documentation[15] as "Native Java Interface" offers another alternative for calling into Java in the database, with an additional overhead associated with serializing and deserializing the parameters and return values. A detailed example of the various invocation mechanisms is given in Chapter 3.

Once you enter Java in the database, you can recursively invoke other Java classes within the same top-level call, provided the classes in questions are visible to you (see section 2.3) and you have been granted execute rights on these. When Java is recursively invoked,[16] the same session and the same JVM are used. Therefore, the inner Java code (i.e., the recursively called java class) has access to the same Java states as the originating call; in other words, the Java state(s) manipulated in the recursive procedure is visible to the outer calls.

2.2.8 State Preservation across Calls and End-of-Call Migration

Java in the database operates repeatedly on the same object instances, but the OracleJVM was initially designed for shared database server environments (i.e., the database sessions are not attached to a particular server process). At the end of a call, and in order to preserve Java states that originate (i.e., are reachable) from the static variables of the active classes in the session, all of the significant information necessary for subsequent calls is saved in sessionspace (described earlier); this state migration is known as "end-of-call migration." End-of-call migration happens systematically in pre-10g releases of the Oracle database irrespective of the server type (i.e., dedicated or shared). Starting with Release 10g of the Oracle database, in dedicated server mode, end-of-call migration is no longer performed, because the session is bound to the same process during its entire lifetime. By saving the time spent after each call performing state migration and restoration, the absence of end-of-call migration results in better overall execution performance, at the expense of an overall increase in memory consumption (a result of keeping all states). Listing 2.3 illustrates state preservation across calls.

15.   Look also for Publishing Server-side Java in the Oracle JPublisher documentation.
16.   Consider procedures A (Java), B (Pl/SQL), and C (Java); recursive call occurs when A calls B, which in turn calls C.

Listing 2.3   *StateXCall.sql (contains both Java source and SQL scripts)*

```
create or replace java source named StateXCall as

import oracle.*;
import oracle.aurora.vm.OracleRuntime;
public class StateXCall
{
  public static String state1 = "initial state";
  public static int     state2;

 // state2 is initialized each time the class is loaded
  static {
    state2 = 0;
  }

  public static void pass1() {
    state1 = "got this state in pass1";
    state2 = 111;
    System.out.println("Pass 1" + "\n state1: " + state1 + "\n state2: " +

                        String.valueOf(state2));
    OracleRuntime.exitCall(0); // graceful end-of-call, preserves states
  }

  public static void pass2() {

    System.out.println("Pass 2" + "\n state1: " + state1 + "\n state2: " +

                        String.valueOf(state2));


    if (state2 != 0 || !state1.equals("initial state"))
       System.out.println("SESSION STATE PRESERVED!");
     else
       System.out.println("SESSION STATE LOST!");
     state1 = "got this state in pass2";
     state2 = 222;
     OracleRuntime.exitSession(0); //terminates the VM
  }

  public static void pass3() {
```

```
        System.out.println("Pass 3" + "\n state1: " + state1 + "\n state2: " +

                            String.valueOf(state2));
   if (state2 != 0 || !state1.equals("initial state"))
      System.out.println("SESSION STATE PRESERVED!");
    else
      System.out.println("SESSION STATE LOST!");

   OracleRuntime.exitSession(1);


  }
}
/
show errors;

alter java source StateXCall compile;
show errors;

create or replace procedure pass1
    is language java
    name 'StateXCall.pass1 ()';
/
show errors

create or replace procedure pass2
    is language java
    name 'StateXCall.pass2 ()';
/
show errors

create or replace procedure pass3
    is language java
    name 'StateXCall.pass3 ()';
/
show errors
exit;
```

And here is the output of the invocation of pass1, pass2, and pass3:

```
set serveroutput on
call dbms_java.set_output(50000);
```

```
call pass1();
Pass 1
state1: got this state in pass1
state2: 111

Call completed.
SQL> call dbms_java.set_output(50000);

Call completed.

SQL>
SQL> call pass2();
Pass 2
state1: got this state in pass1
state2: 111
SESSION STATE PRESERVED!
call pass2()
     *
ERROR at line 1:
ORA-29515: exit called from Java code with status 0


SQL> call dbms_java.set_output(50000);

Call completed.

SQL>
SQL> call pass3();
Pass 3
state1: initial state
state2: 0
SESSION STATE LOST!
call pass3()
     *
ERROR at line 1:
ORA-29515: exit called from Java code with status 1
SQL>
```

Be aware that when a Java class being used is recompiled, all sessions using this class in question will receive an "ORA-29549 Java Session State Cleared" message the next time they invoke methods belonging to the class in question. Although this is normal during the development process (develop/test/debug cycles), this is annoying in production environments. DBAs just need to pay attention before redeploying new versions of Java classes on a live system.

Most Java database applications work well with the default/automatic end-of-call migration or avoid it using dedicated servers. However, you may want to programmatically control the end-of-call migration and trade the memory overhead—incurred by keeping statics in Sessionspace across calls—for faster execution by releasing objects at the end of the call and recreating these on demand (lazy initialization), using the `oracle.aurora.memoryManager.EndOfCallRegistry` and `oracle.aurora.memoryManager.Callback` interfaces, documented in Oracle's *Java Developer's Guide*.

2.2.9   End-of-Call, VM Termination, and Session Termination

As you have probably noticed in the state preservation code samples, we used both `OracleRuntime.exitCall()` and `OracleRuntime.exitSession();` what are their differences and how about the standard `System.exit()`? Let's look into this in greater detail:

1.   `System.exit()` terminates the Java VM (i.e., all threads) in the RDBMS session with no state preservation. As illustrated by the state across calls sample, it does not and should not terminate the RDBMS session nor cause the client to disconnect (i.e., the SQL*Plus session continues).

2.   `OracleRuntime.exitSession()` terminates the Java VM as well as the RDBMS session, causing the client to disconnect.

3.   The behavior of `OracleRuntime.exitCall()` requires a little more explanation, because it varies depending on the `OracleRuntime.threadTerminationPolicy()`. This method returns a Boolean, which, if true, means that any active threads should be terminated (rather than left quiescent) at the end of a database call.

      ■ In 9*i* R2, all threads (i.e., daemon and nondaemon) are terminated abruptly, irrespective of the server type (i.e., shared and dedicated).

      ■ In 10*g*, shared server mode, `threadTerminationPolicy()` is always true, and all active threads are terminated abruptly.

- In 10*g*, dedicated server, the value may be changed by the user by calling `OracleRuntime.setThreadTerminationPolicy()`.

  - If the value is false (the default), all threads are left quiescent but receive a ThreadDeath exception for graceful termination.
  - If the value is true, all threads are terminated abruptly.

4. In addition, the `OracleRuntime.callExitPolicy()` controls when a call exits, if none of the `OracleRuntime.exitSession()`, `OracleRuntime.exitCall()` or `System.exit()` methods were ever called. `OracleRuntime.callExitPolicy()` may be set (by using `OracleRuntime.setCallExitPolicy()`) to one of the following:

- `OracleRuntime.EXIT_CALL_WHEN_ALL_NON_DAEMON_THREADS_TERMINATE`

  This is the default value; the call ends when only daemon threads are left running.[17]

  - If `threadTerminationPolicy()` true, always in shared server mode, the daemon threads are killed. In 9*i* R2, the Java VM behaved as if the `callExitPolicy()` were set to `OracleRuntime.EXIT_CALL_WHEN_ALL_NON_DAEMON_THREADS_TERMINATE` and `threadTerminationPolicy()` = true.
  - If `threadTerminationPolicy()` false, the daemon threads are left quiescent until the next call (default for dedicated servers).

- `OracleRuntime.EXIT_CALL_WHEN_ALL_THREADS_TERMINATE`

  The call ends only when all threads have returned (or ended upon uncaught exception), irrespective of the value of `threadTerminationPolicy()`.

- `OracleRuntime.EXIT_CALL_WHEN_MAIN_THREAD_TERMINATES`

  When the main thread returns (or an uncaught exception occurs):

---

17.   Normal Java VM behavior, when all nondaemon threads terminate, the VM exists (i.e., the call ends).

- If `threadTerminationPolicy()` is true, always in shared server mode, all remaining threads (i.e., daemon and non-daemon) are killed.
- If `threadTerminationPolicy()` is false, all remaining threads (i.e., daemon and nondaemon) are left quiescent until the next call.

In summary:

- In all database releases—namely, 9*i* R2, 10*g* R1, and 10*g* R2—`System.exit()` and `OracleRuntime.exitSesssion()` end the Java VM abruptly; all threads are terminated without running the finally blocks.[18]

- In all releases, `OracleRuntime.exitCall()` attempts to end each thread "gracefully" by throwing a `ThreadDeath` exception on each thread, which results in the execution of finally blocks.

- Otherwise, if none of these applies, in other words, no invocation of `System.exit()`, `OracleRuntime.exitSesssion()`, or `OracleRuntime.exitCall()`—which is the case for most Java programs—then `OracleRuntime.callExitPolicy()` controls how the call is terminated.

2.3   Security in OracleJVM

Security requirements are even more stringent when it comes to the database. Java code running in an Oracle database benefits from a rich database security environment, including user authentication, database-schema security, login-user security, and effective-user security. The OracleJVM itself provides additional features such as class-resolution security and Java 2 security.

2.3.1   User Authentication

An Oracle database user—which is typically a client application or a JDBC connection—needs to be identified, authenticated, and authorized before it can create a session. Oracle Net and Oracle JDBC drivers support several user-authentication mechanisms. These methods include traditional user-name/password authentication, as well as strong authentication mecha-

---

18.   Block of statements prefixed by finally { } for cleaning up the state of the method before passing control.

nisms such as Kerberos, CyberSafe, RADIUS, token cards, smart cards, biometrics, public-key infrastructure (PKI), certificate-based authentication, proxy authentication and authorization, and Single Sign-On (SSO). Once the database client is authenticated, a new database session is associated with it. For more details on Oracle database authentication, see the Oracle Net documentation.

2.3.2   Database-Schema Security

JDK JVM lets you execute Java classes downloaded from the Web. With OracleJVM, Java classes reside in the database and are governed by the same security features that protect other database objects. Specifically, Java classes, sources, and resources are organized, stored, searched, and executed within database schemas. Before you can execute a Java class with OracleJVM, you need to load it into a specific database schema and then validate it (i.e., resolve it). To load a Java class, you can use the loadjava command-line utility or an integrated development environment (IDE) such as Oracle JDeveloper. You must have *CREATE PROCEDURE* privilege in order to load classes into your own schema and *CREATE ANY PROCEDURE* privilege to load classes into a schema owned by another user. These protections provide a reliable Java execution environment, which is less likely to be attacked by malicious code.

Java classes are owned by the schema, which loads them (i.e., the defining schema). You can provide different levels of security for Java classes by grouping them into separate schemas. For example, suppose you define class A and class B in different schemas. In order for class A to refer to class B, the defining schema of class A must be granted execute rights on class B. To accomplish this, you can use the grant option in the loadjava utility. By creating new schemas for particular classes and controlling execute rights to those classes, you can design fine-grained security for your Java applications. In the following example, Betty and Bob are granted the right to execute class alpha in the schema TEST:

```
loadjava -thin -schema test -u SCOTT/
TIGER@localhost:5521:orcl
    -grant BETTY,BOB alpha.class
```

2.3.3 Resolver Specification and Class-Resolution Security

The OracleJVM class-resolution architecture provides flexible and fine-grained control over class visibility and security. It uses a resolver specification (also known as resolver spec) to search for and locate Java classes within database schemas. A *resolver spec* usually contains multiple schemas. It is similar in concept to the CLASSPATH in the JDK world. In contrast with JDK, resolver specs are defined on a class-by-class basis. There is no general CLASSPATH, however; there's a default *resolver spec* per schema, instead.

The following examples show different ways of defining the scope of a resolver spec.

1. The default resolver spec contains the defining schema (i.e., SCOTT) and the PUBLIC schema (i.e., all classes exposed through the PUBLIC synonym).

    The default resolver spec for the SCOTT schema is '{(* SCOTT) (* PUBLIC)}'.

2. The following command loads a Java class using the default resolver spec; as a result, loadjava will search the definer's schema and PUBLIC:

    ```
    loadjava —resolve Foo.java
    ```

3. In the following example, a Java class is loaded using a resolver spec that will search the SCOTT, OTHER, and PUBLIC schemas:

    ```
    loadjava -resolve -resolver "((* SCOTT)(* OTHER)(*
    PUBLIC))" ...
    ```

    Before resolving a class, it must be visible and the requester must have execution permission on it. All references to other classes must have been resolved before a class can be executed. Furthermore, OracleJVM requires that the resolution be done at deployment time, unless it is told to defer such resolution until runtime. For example, the following resolver spec skips the references not found within SCOTT or PUBLIC schemas:

```
loadjava -resolve -resolver "((* SCOTT)(* PUBLIC))" -
genmissing
```

genmissing is an option of loadjava that lets you deal with nonexistent classes. It instructs *loadjava* to create and load placeholders for classes that are not defined but referenced. By skipping the missing classes, *genmissing* allows the Java code to run, but the methods in the missing classes cannot be invoked.

Note: A Java resource can have a "resolver spec" but is only looked up and used during the resolution of the class, which refers to it; in other words, loadjava does not resolve Java resources. The following PL/SQL interface and the Java method return the resolver spec of a specific object.

```
function resolver (name VARCHAR2, owner VARCHAR2, type VARCHAR2)
   RETURN VARCHAR2;

oracle.aurora.rdbms.DbmsJava.resolver(java.lang.String,
                                      oracle.sql.CHAR,
                                      java.lang.String)
   return oracle.sql.CHAR;
```

Example: returning the resolver spec for a given object:

```
SQL> select dbms_java.resolver('TrimLob', 'SCOTT', 'CLASS') from
dual;

   DBMS_JAVA.RESOLVER('TRIMLOB','SCOTT','CLASS')
   ----------------------------------------
   ((* SCOTT)(* PUBLIC))
```

This output indicates that all the references to external objects in Trimlob class should be resolved by looking up the SCOTT and PUBLIC schemas (PUBLIC schema is a pseudoschema that refers to all objects that have a public synonym).

2.3.4 **Login-User and Effective-User Security**

When a user logs in to the database, a new session is created with a login-user identity or schema identity. All database operations—including SQL statements, PL/SQL packages, and PL/SQL wrappers for Java stored procedures—are executed under the login-user identity. A session can execute Java classes defined in other schemas, provided the login user's schema has been granted execute permission on the other classes. However, you can dynamically override the effective identity under which a Java class runs. By default, the effective identity is the login-user identity. You can alter the identity at the Java class level or the PL/SQL stored-procedure level by using the database's effective-user mechanism, similar to the UNIX setuid facility.

You can set the effective identity by assigning invoker's rights or definer's rights to a class; these are defined as follows:

- *Invoker's rights.* By default, a Java class is associated with invoker's rights; the class is not bound to its defining schema. The current user of any session executing the class is the same as the session's login user. The privileges are checked at runtime, and external references are resolved in the schema of the current user. With invoker's rights, you can centralize and share code across multiple schemas and applications while keeping data stored in each schema private and isolated.

- *Definer's rights.* By assigning definer's rights to a class, you bind the class to its defining schema. The effective user of any session executing the class is changed temporarily to the identity of the class's defining schema, and all unqualified references are looked for in the defining schema. Java classes loaded with definer's rights can be executed without requiring the invoking session to be connected as the schema to which the code belongs.

You can specify effective-user rights on the PL/SQL wrapper (by using Call Spec, which exposes public static Java methods to the SQL world) or on the Java class itself (by using the loadjava utility). These rights are in effect only when a Java class or PL/SQL package is invoked through server-side JDBC. In the following examples, the effective-user rights are defined on the PL/SQL wrapper and on the Java class:

- Specifying invoker's rights (current user) through the PL/SQL interface:

  ```
  CREATE [OR REPLACE] PROCEDURE
  [schema_name.]procedure_name

  [(parameter_list)]

  [AUTHID CURRENT_USER] AS ...
  ```

- Specifying invoker's rights (current user) on the Java class with load-java:

  ```
  loadjava {-user | -u} <user>/<password>[@<database>]
  [options]

  <file>.java | <file>.class | <file>.jar |

   <file>.zip |<file>.sqlj | <resourcefile> ...[-
  nodefiner]
  ```

- Specifying definer's rights through the PL/SQL interface:

  ```
  CREATE [OR REPLACE] PROCEDURE
  [schema_name.]procedure_name

  [(parameter_list)]

  AUTHID DEFINER ...
  ```

- Specifying definer's rights on the Java class with loadjava:

  ```
  loadjava {-user | -u} <user>/<password>

  [@<database>] [options]

  <file>.java | <file>.class | <file>.jar |

   <file>.zip |<file>.sqlj | <resourcefile> ...-definer
  ```

For more details on effective-user rights, see Oracle's *PL/SQL User's Guide and Reference*.

2.3.5 Java 2 Security

The goal of Java 2 security is to provide an easily configurable security policy, fine-grained access control (i.e., permissions), and an easily extensible access-control structure. In this section, I will briefly describe the key Java 2 security concepts, including permissions, security policy, and the security manager, and then describe how they are implemented and supported in the OracleJVM.

Permissions

Permissions are represented by (encapsulated in) Java objects, which represent the authorization or access to system resources. Each permission object controls one or several targets and zero, one, or several actions it authorizes on those targets. As an example, files and directories are the targets of **java.io.FilePermission,** which controls their access and authorizes **read, write, delete,** and **execute** actions (or access) on those files and directories.

Here is a sample of built-in fine-grained security permissions, with their targets and actions. (See the Java Security Architecture documentation for the complete list of Java security permissions.)[19]

- **java.util.PropertyPermission** Controls read/write access to JVM properties such as `java.home`, `os.name`.

- **java.lang.RuntimePermission** Controls use of some system/runtime functions like `exitVM()`, `getClassLoader()`, `setSecurityManager()`, `setIO()`, and so on.

- **java.io.FilePermission** Controls access to files and directories; the actions on files and directories are **read, write, delete,** and **execute**.

- **java.net.SocketPermission** Controls use of network sockets; the actions on sockets are **accept, connect, listen,** and **resolve**.

- **java.net.NetPermission** Controls use of multicast network connections, no action.

- **java.lang.reflect.ReflectPermission** Controls use of reflection for class introspection; it has one target and no action.

- **java.security.SecurityPermission** Controls access to security methods such as `getPolicy()`, `setPolicy()`, ... and so on but has no action.

---

19.   http://java.sun.com/j2se/1.4.2/docs/guide/security/spec/security-spec.doc3.html#20107.

- **java.security.AllPermission** Allows access to all permissions, just as if you were running Java without a SecurityManager

The Java Security Manager

The SecurityManager (`java.lang.SecurityManager`) is a runtime object that controls permissions. Once activated, Java classes/methods request permission to allow or disallow certain operations proactively (before performing the operation). Each operation type has its specific check*XXX*() method. For example, the `Connect()` method invokes the security manager's check-Connect() method to approve the socket connection operation:

```
SecurityManager security = System.getSecurityManager();
if (security != null) {
    security.checkConnect(status);
}
. . .
// catch SecurityException
```

If the security manager approves the connect operation, the checkConnect() returns normally; otherwise, the checkConnect() method throws a SecurityException.

Figure 2.5 illustrates how it works.

Figure 2.5
Java Security
Manager

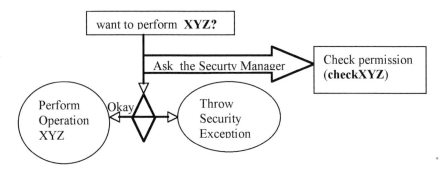

The following operations or activities are regulated by the Java security manager (i.e., have "checkXXX" methods):

- **Network operations** (i.e., opening, waiting, or accepting a socket connection from a host and a port number) require *SocketPermission* and *RuntimePermission*.

- **Thread operations** (i.e., modify a thread) require *RuntimePermission*.

- **File System operations** (i.e., read, write, delete a file) require *FilePermission* and *RuntimePermission*.

- **Operating System operations** (i.e., create a new process) require *FilePermission, RuntimePermission,* and *AWTPermission*.

- **JVM operations** (i.e., create a new class loader, exit the current application) require *FilePermission, PropertyPermission,* and *AWTPermission*.

- **Packages and Classes operations** (i.e., add a new class to a package, unload a class from a package) require *FilePermission* and *RuntimePermission*.

- **Security operations** (i.e., access or modify system properties) require *SecurityPermission*.

See the `java.lang.SecurityManager` method permissions checks for more details.[20]

2.3.6 Java 2 Security in OracleJVM

OracleJVM fully complies with Java 2 security; it supports all default Java 2 permissions as well as Oracle-defined permissions but differs from JDK VM implementation on the following points: permission determination, security policy management, and security manager.

Security Policy

A security policy is a set of permissions that represents what a code source[21] is and is not allowed to do.

In the JDK VM:

- The security policies are represented by entries in one or several policy file(s), which can be updated with proper permissions, using a text editor or specific tool. The system policy file is by default located at:

  $JAVA_HOME/lib/security/java.policy (Unix platforms)

  $JAVA_HOME\lib\security\java.policy (Windows platforms)

---

20. http://java.sun.com/j2se/1.4.2/docs/guide/security/permissions.html#SecMgrChecks.
21. A code source is an object that captures the location (URL) from which a code originates (loaded from) and also the certificate(s), if any, that was used to sign the code in question.

In OracleJVM:

- Although there is a `java.security` file under `$ORACLE_HOME/javavm/lib/security`, the security policy is not read from the file system. Security policy objects are defined as rows in the PolicyTable, which is a secure/internal database table. This table can be updated (i.e., update policies, insert user-defined policies) through the `DBMS_JAVA` package, but you must be granted `PolicyTablePermission` on the specific permission type (i.e., `PolicyTablePermission` on FilePermission) before doing so. By default, only the `JAVA_ADMIN` role is granted `PolicyTablePermission` to update the PolicyTable.

Querying the PolicyTable

The policy table is an internal system table that is not queryable as a traditional table; however, two views have been provided for viewing its contents: `USER_JAVA_POLICY` gives each schema access to its permissions rows, and `DBA_JAVA_POLICY` for viewing all permissions requires DBA privilege.

Example:

```
SQL*Plus scott/tiger
SQL> describe user_java_policy;
 Name                                      Null?    Type
 ----------------------------------------- -------- ------------------

 KIND                                               VARCHAR2(8)
 GRANTEE_NAME                              NOT NULL VARCHAR2(30)
 TYPE_SCHEMA                               NOT NULL VARCHAR2(30)
 TYPE_NAME                                          VARCHAR2(4000)
 NAME                                               VARCHAR2(4000)
 ACTION                                             VARCHAR2(4000)
 ENABLED                                            VARCHAR2(8)
 SEQ                                                NUMBER
```

Notice the SEQ column, which serves as the row key!

```
SQL> column grantee_name format a15
SQL> col grantee_name format a10
SQL> col type_schema format a10
SQL> col name format a35
SQL> col type_name format a35
```

```
SQL> col action format a10
SQL> select kind, grantee_name, name, action, enabled from
user_java_policy
SQL> /


KIND      GRANTEE_NA NAME                             ACTION     ENABLED
--------  ---------- -------------------------------- ---------- --------
GRANT     PUBLIC     createSecurityManager                       ENABLED
GRANT     PUBLIC     exitVM                                      ENABLED
RESTRICT  PUBLIC     loadLibrary.*                               ENABLED
GRANT     PUBLIC     modifyThread                                ENABLED
GRANT     PUBLIC     modifyThreadGroup                           ENABLED
GRANT     PUBLIC     preferences                                 ENABLED
GRANT     PUBLIC     *                                read       ENABLED
GRANT     PUBLIC     user.language                    write      ENABLED
RESTRICT  PUBLIC     0:java.lang.RuntimePermission#              ENABLED
                     loadLibrary.*


KIND      GRANTEE_NA NAME                             ACTION     ENABLED
--------  ---------- -------------------------------- ---------- --------
GRANT     PUBLIC     DUMMY                                       DISABLED
GRANT     PUBLIC     LoadClassInPackage.*                        ENABLED
RESTRICT  PUBLIC     LoadClassInPackage.java.*                   ENABLED
RESTRICT  PUBLIC     LoadClassInPackage.oracle.auro              ENABLED
                     ra.*

RESTRICT  PUBLIC     LoadClassInPackage.oracle.jdbc              ENABLED
                     .*


14 rows selected.



SQL> select name, type_name from user_java_policy;


NAME                             TYPE_NAME
-----  ------------------------- ------------------------------------
createSecurityManager            java.lang.RuntimePermission
exitVM                           java.lang.RuntimePermission
loadLibrary.*                    java.lang.RuntimePermission
modifyThread                     java.lang.RuntimePermission
modifyThreadGroup                java.lang.RuntimePermission
```

```
preferences                        java.lang.RuntimePermission
*                                  java.util.PropertyPermission
user.language                      java.util.PropertyPermission
0:java.lang.RuntimePermission#     oracle.aurora.rdbms.security.Policy
loadLibrary.*                      TablePermission


NAME                               TYPE_NAME
-------------------------------    ------------------------------------
DUMMY                              oracle.aurora.security.JServerPermi
                                   ssion


LoadClassInPackage.*               oracle.aurora.security.JServerPermi
                                   ssion


LoadClassInPackage.java.*          oracle.aurora.security.JServerPermi
                                   ssion


LoadClassInPackage.oracle.auro     oracle.aurora.security.JServerPermi
ra.*                               ssion


NAME                               TYPE_NAME
-------------------------------    ------------------------------------


LoadClassInPackage.oracle.jdbc     oracle.aurora.security.JServerPermi
.*                                 ssion


14 rows selected.
```

- Security permissions are assigned to the defining schema; therefore, all classes within the same schema are regarded as belonging to the same "protection domain."[22]

- You can grant, restrict, and revoke permissions (granting, restricting, and revoking permissions is explained later).

- End users with proper privileges can define and store their own permissions. However, a custom permission (i.e., not a default/built-in permission) can only be granted by the schema that created such permission in the PolicyTable. The granting schema must have been

---

22. A protection domain is a dynamic object (created by class loaders) that associates a set of permissions to given code source; in other words, it defines which permissions are granted to each running Java class.

granted the PolicyTablePermission or the `JAVA_ADMIN` role before being in position to grant defined permission to other schemas.

The Security Manager

In the JDK environment:

- The Security Manager is not initialized or enforced by default. You can use the default Security Manager or write and launch your own security manager.

In OracleJVM:

- Security Manager is always initialized/enforced at database startup. It is recommended to use the default database security manager, but you may extend it (see the Oracle Database Java Developer's Guide for more details).

Determining and Granting Permissions

In JDK VM:

- The permissions are determined by code location: `CLASSPATH`, `URL`, and keycode (a set of private keys and associated certificates). All classes within the `CLASSPATH` are trusted. The `CodeSource` is used to identify the code/class:

```
grant { permission java.io.FilePermission "/tmo/
myfile", "read";};
```

Permissions can also be granted programmatically; the following instruction in a Java program creates a permission object for reading the file named "myfile" in the /tmp directory:

```
p = new java.io.FilePermission("/tmp/myfile", "read");
```

- In the standard Java 2 security environment, permissions are only granted, by contrast in the OracleJVM implementation, as described later; permissions can also be revoked or restricted.

In OracleJVM:

- Each Java 2 permission is represented by a permission object, stored in the PolicyTable and identifiable by a row key. The permissions are determined by the defining schema (i.e., the schema in which they are loaded). In OracleJVM, the notion of CLASSPATH is replaced by the notion of Resolver Spec. Classes in the database are trusted on a class-by-class basis (even classes within the reach of the Resolver Spec are not blindly trusted). The permissions are granted using either the `dbms_java.grant_permission()` method or the underlying Java method `PolicyTableManager.grant()` programmatically.

```
dbms_java.grant_permission(grantee, permission_type, permission_name,

permission_action, key);
```

grantee: is the name of a schema.
permission_type: is the fully qualified name of a class that
        extends java.lang.security.Permission. If the class does
        not have a public synonymn then the name should be
        prefixed by <schema>:.
        For example 'myschema:scott.MyPermission'.
permission_name: is the name of the permission
permission_action: is the action of the permission
key: is set to the key of the created row or to -1 if an error occurs.

This command attempts to create an active row in the policy table that will grant the permission specified to the grantee. If a row granting the exact permission does not already exist, then a new row is inserted. If a row granting the exact permission already exists, then the new row is not inserted and the table remains unchanged. If a row granting the exact permission exists but is disabled, then the permission is reenabled.

Alternatively, you can directly invoke the PolicyTableManager grant method from a Java program as follows:

```
oracle.aurora.rdbms.security.PolicyTableManager.grant(grantee
,
   permission_type, permission_name, permission_action, key);
```

```
Signature:
oracle.aurora.rdbms.security.PolicyTableManager.grant(
        java.lang.String, java.lang.String, java.lang.String,
        java.lang.String, long[]);
```

Examples:

1.   The following command creates a permission entry in the Poli-
     cyTable for reading the file named "myfile" in the /tmp directory:

```
SQL>call
DBMS_JAVA.GRANT_PERMISSION('scott','java.io.FilePermiss
ion',
```
                              `'/tmp/myfile','read');`

The SCOTT schema may execute this command, provided it
has been granted the PolicyTablePermission.

2.   In order to open a socket from within the server-side JDBC
     Thin,   the   database   session   must   be   granted
     java.net.SocketPermission; in the following example, we
     first grant the permission to a role and then grant the role to the
     schema; this technique is useful when you want to predefine a
     set of permissions as a role and then assign such a role as a
     coarse-grained permission to one or several schemas.

```
SQL> create role CALLOUT;
SQL> call dbms_java.grant_permission('CALLOUT',
'java.net.SocketPermission',
'*', 'connect' );
SQL> grant callout to scott;
```

Let's grant the SCOTT schema, the permission to read an existing file,
C:\temp\myfile:

```
SQL>connect system/xxxx as sysdba

SQL> call
dbms_java.grant_permission('SCOTT','java.io.FilePermission',
  2 'C:\temp\myfile', 'read, write');

Call completed.

SQL>connect scott/tiger
Connected.

SQL> select kind, grantee_name, name, action, enabled from user_java_policy;
```

```
KIND       GRANTEE_NA NAME                            ACTION     ENABLED
--------   ---------- ------------------------------- ---------- --------
GRANT      PUBLIC     createSecurityManager                      ENABLED
GRANT      PUBLIC     exitVM                                     ENABLED
RESTRICT   PUBLIC     loadLibrary.*                              ENABLED
GRANT      PUBLIC     modifyThread                               ENABLED
GRANT      PUBLIC     modifyThreadGroup                          ENABLED
GRANT      PUBLIC     preferences                                ENABLED
GRANT      PUBLIC     *                               read       ENABLED
GRANT      PUBLIC     user.language                   write      ENABLED
RESTRICT   PUBLIC     0:java.lang.RuntimePermission#             ENABLED
                      loadLibrary.*


KIND       GRANTEE_NA NAME                            ACTION     ENABLED
--------   ---------- ------------------------------- ---------- --------
GRANT      PUBLIC     DUMMY                                      DISABLED
GRANT      PUBLIC     LoadClassInPackage.*                       ENABLED
RESTRICT   PUBLIC     LoadClassInPackage.java.*                  ENABLED
RESTRICT   PUBLIC     LoadClassInPackage.oracle.auro             ENABLED
                      ra.*

RESTRICT   PUBLIC     LoadClassInPackage.oracle.jdbc             ENABLED
                      .*

GRANT      SCOTT      C:\temp\myfile                  read,writ  ENABLED

15 rows selected.
```

See more examples of permissions granting in Chapter 4, "Pragmatic Applications Using Java in the Database," "Advanced Applications Using Java in the Database," as well as "Running Non-Java Languages in Oracle-JVM" in Chapter 5.

Restricting Permission

Permission restriction is usually applied to an existing generic/ broad permission grant (such as allowing all users the permission to load Java classes in their own schema), by placing a restriction to it such as: (1) restricting the permission to a specific schema, (2) restricting a specific permission on a specific target, or (3) restricting the permission on a specific action.

The PL/SQL interface(s) is:

```
procedure restrict_permission(
        grantee varchar2, permission_type varchar2,
        permission_name varchar2, permission_action varchar2);

procedure restrict_permission(
        grantee varchar2, permission_type varchar2,
        permission_name varchar2, permission_action varchar2,
        key OUT number);
```

The corresponding Java method(s) is:

```
oracle.aurora.rdbms.security.PolicyTableManager.restrict(
        java.lang.String, java.lang.String, java.lang.String,
        java.lang.String);

oracle.aurora.rdbms.security.PolicyTableManager.restrict(
        java.lang.String, java.lang.String, java.lang.String,
        java.lang.String, long[]);
```

As an example, in the previous section (grant_permission) we granted both read and write on C:\temp\myfile to SCOTT. We may change our mind and place a restriction on write action; therefore, SCOTT can only read the file in question.

```
SQL> connect system/manager as sysdba;
Connected.
SQL> call dbms_java.restrict_permission('SCOTT','java.io.FilePermission',
    2 'C:\temp\myfile', 'write');

Call completed.

SQL> connect scott/tiger;
Connected.
SQL> select kind, grantee_name, name, action, enabled from user_java_policy;
```

KIND	GRANTEE_NA	NAME	ACTION	ENABLED
GRANT	PUBLIC	createSecurityManager		ENABLED
GRANT	PUBLIC	exitVM		ENABLED
RESTRICT	PUBLIC	loadLibrary.*		ENABLED
GRANT	PUBLIC	modifyThread		ENABLED
GRANT	PUBLIC	modifyThreadGroup		ENABLED
GRANT	PUBLIC	preferences		ENABLED
GRANT	PUBLIC	*	read	ENABLED
GRANT	PUBLIC	user.language	write	ENABLED
RESTRICT	PUBLIC	0:java.lang.RuntimePermission#loadLibrary.*		ENABLED

KIND	GRANTEE_NA	NAME	ACTION	ENABLED
GRANT	PUBLIC	DUMMY		DISABLED
GRANT	PUBLIC	LoadClassInPackage.*		ENABLED
RESTRICT	PUBLIC	LoadClassInPackage.java.*		ENABLED
RESTRICT	PUBLIC	LoadClassInPackage.oracle.aurora.*		ENABLED
RESTRICT	PUBLIC	LoadClassInPackage.oracle.jdbc.*		ENABLED
GRANT	SCOTT	C:\temp\myfile	read, write	ENABLED
RESTRICT	**SCOTT**	**C:\temp\myfile**	**write**	**ENABLED**

```
16 rows selected.

SQL>
```

Having initially granted all users (i.e., PUBLIC) the right to load any class in their own schemas, the following commands place restrictions on the `JServerPermission` permission, preventing all users from loading system classes in their own schema:

```
call dbms_java.restrict_permission('PUBLIC',
'SYS:oracle.aurora.security.JServerPermission', 'LoadClassInPackage.java.*',
null);
call dbms_java.restrict_permission('PUBLIC',
'SYS:oracle.aurora.security.JServerPermission',
'LoadClassInPackage.oracle.aurora.*', null);
```

```
call dbms_java.restrict_permission('PUBLIC',
'SYS:oracle.aurora.security.JServerPermission',
'LoadClassInPackage.oracle.jdbc.*', null);
```

As a result, the ability for any schema to load classes/packages in their own schemas won't apply for system classes.

Revoking Permission

Unlike RESTRICT_PERMISSION, which adds restrictions to a broader permission grant, REVOKE_PERMISSION revokes entirely the permission in question. In the previous example, instead of placing a write restriction on SCOTT on C:\temp\myfile, we could have revoked the initial permission from SCOTT and granted it a new one.

PL/SQL interface(s):

```
procedure revoke_permission( grantee varchar2, permission_type
varchar2,
  permission_name varchar2, permission_action varchar2)
```

The corresponding Java method is:

```
oracle.aurora.rdbms.security.PolicyTableManager.revoke(
    java.lang.String, java.lang.String, java.lang.String,
    java.lang.String)';
```

Disabling Permissions

The command dbms_java.disable_permission(key number) disables the existing permission row, identified by the specified key (SEQ#). The corresponding Java method(s) is:

```
oracle.aurora.rdbms.security.PolicyTableManager.disable(long);
```

Deleting Permissions

Deletes the existing permission row identified by the specified key (SEQ#). The permission must have been previously disabled (see previous section), in order for the delete to work; otherwise, if the permission is still active, then this procedure does nothing.

PL/SQL interface(s):

```
dbms_java.delete_permission(key number);
```

Java method interface(s)

```
oracle.aurora.rdbms.security.PolicyTableManager.delete(long);
```

System Classes Security

User Java class needs to share the J2SE system classes. The system classes are loaded once in the `SYS` schema and are made accessible from any other schema through `PUBLIC` synonyms (a database mechanism that provides public visibility to common objects or resources). As described in rectrict_permission, OracleJVM prevents all users from replacing system classes (e.g., `java.*`, `oracle.aurora.*`, and `oracle.jdbc.*`), loading new classes into system packages, or loading system classes into their own schema. However, in order to load system classes into your own schema, a user schema may be explictly granted `JserverPermission` on the classes or package in question. As an example, the following command grants SCOTT the permission to load its own version of the `oracle.aurora.tools.*` package into its schema `call`:

```
dbms_java.grant_permission('SCOTT','SYS:oracle.aurora.sec
urity.JServerPermission',
'LoadClassInPackage.oracle.aurora.tools.*, null);
```

2.3.7 OracleJVM Security Best Practices

Do not grant unnecessary permissions. Use the principle of "Least Privileges"; in other words, only grant explicit or specific permission to a particular code for accessing a particular resource. Such attitude gives you a fine-grained security control, in the spirit of Java 2 security.

An example of a bad practice would be to grant the SCOTT schema "read" access to all files, like this:

```
call dbms_java.grant_permission('SCOTT',
'SYS:java.io.FilePermission',
'<<ALL FILES>>','read');
```

On the other hand, a good practice would be to grant permission only to the explicit document root file path, as we did earlier.

```
call dbms_java.grant_permission('SCOTT',
'SYS:java.io.FilePermission',
'(<actual directory path>)','read');
```

Discourage the use of granting a coarse-grained group of permissions such as JAVASYSPRIV and JAVAUSERPRIV roles that are still provided for backward compatibility with Oracle 8*i* so as not to break programs that used to work in previous RDBMS releases.

In general, be conservative about granting permissions related to Classloader and java.lang. For example, granting *RuntimePermission* to *createClassLoader* has the same effect as granting all permissions.

2.3.8 JNI Calls

Java Native Interface (JNI) is a standardized interface to call procedures written in other languages to access platform facilities such as AWT fonts, file locks, and registries from Java. There are safety considerations when calling native methods; JavaSoft/SUN recommends that, only experienced programmers should attempt to write native methods or use the Invocation API! In order to reduce the need for JNI, the latest J2SE specifications have added most platform-specific facilities such as `java.util.prefs` to deal with registries. Because OracleJVM does not have control over the behavior of foreign code, and in order to guarantee data integrity, it does not allow end users the use of JNI calls. See the "Calling-out SAP from within a Stored Procedure" case study in Chapter 4 for a discussion of working around the JNI restriction. However, OracleJVM uses JNI calls internally for its own needs (by expert programmers only!), such as the C-based bytecode verifier, the headless AWT fonts, and miscellaneous interactions with the RDBMS kernel.

2.4   Java VM Life Cycle

2.4.1   OracleJVM Install, Uninstall, and Reinstall

One frequent question people ask is, "Can I upgrade the Java VM in the database?" As you have seen throughout this chapter, the OracleJVM is intimately integrated with the RDBMS release and cannot be upgraded independently; however, similar to most Oracle database components, its packaging allows independent install or reinstall. OracleJVM is automatically installed as part of the Oracle database software installation, but you can choose to disable this option, knowing that some database components such as interMedia, UltraSearch, Data Mining, Oracle Spatial, the XML Developers Kit (XDK), the XML SQL Utility (XSU), the XML Query, and so on require a Java-enabled database in order to function properly. In case you need to uninstall or manually reinstall the OracleJVM, see Metalink note 209870.1, "How to Reload the JVM in 9.2.0.X," and note 276554.1 "How to Reload the JVM in 10.1.0.X." In Oracle Database 10*g*. The native compiler libraries (NCOMP) and the compiled system classes reside on the companion CD and have to be installed in a second step.

2.4.2 Java VM Initialization and Termination

Java VM or Java Application Initialization

You may have noticed that sometimes the first invocation of Java in the database session is slower than subsequent calls. It is likely that the first call is paying either the cost of Java VM initialization in the session and/or the cost of the initialization of the application. But this is not a high price remember that only the private/unshared part of the runtime and the applications reside in Sessionspace; everything else is in Javapool in the SGA so as to be shared by all sessions.

Java VM Termination

See the "End-of-Call, VM Termination, and Session Termination" discussion in section 2.2.9.

2.5 Java Execution in the Database

In general, there are many ways to execute Java bytecode, including strict interpretation, threaded interpretation, JIT compilation, native compilation, and so on. Discussing Java bytecode execution techniques is beyond the scope of this book.

The OracleJVM currently furnishes a threaded interpretation and static native compilation (NCOMP) of Java; both techniques are described in the following sections. The portability of the interpreter and the compiler is a key requirement for the Oracle database.

There are three modes for running Java in the database: (1) interpreted system classes and interpreted user classes, (2) compiled system classes and interpreted user classes, and (3) compiled system classes and compiled user classes. For (1), you only need to install Java during the database installation. For (2) and (3), you need to install the NCOMP libraries (covered later) from the companion CD, in a second step.

Note: To check whether NCOMP is installed (from the companion CD), use the following query, which gives ORA-29558 when it has not been installed.

```
select dbms_java.full_ncomp_enabled from dual;
```

2.5.1   The OracleJVM Interpreter

I will briefly describe what a threaded interpreter is, and then, more important for application developers, indicate best practices for optimizing the performance of interpreted Java code.

Threaded Interpreter

A traditional Java interpreter can be regarded as a large *switch-and-loop* statement over an array of bytecodes:

```
char *current_vm_instruction;
while(1) {
  char vm_instruction = *current_vm_instruction;
  switch (vm_instruction) {
  case OPCODE_0:
    /* C code for VM instruction */ ... ;
    current_vm_instruction += OPCODE_0_LENGTH;
    break;
  ...
  ...
  case OPCODE_255:
    /* C code for VM instruction */ ... ;
    current_vm_instruction += OPCODE_255_LENGTH;
    break;
  }
}
```

It fetches an array of bytecodes at the current_vm_instruction, and for each bytecode entry, switches to corresponding vm_instruction *"opcode"* for its execution and then starts the loop over for the next byte-code. The cost of dispatching interpreted bytecode is expensive and may often surpass the execution cost. For simple bytecodes, this overhead can be extremely costly. *Direct-threaded* interpreters reduce this overhead by replacing the *loop-and-switch* code—which a traditional interpreter will place after every case to execute the next bytecode—with a direct *jump (goto)* to an address offset corresponding to the bytecode implementation (see following example).

```
char **current_vm_instruction;

OPCODE_0:
  /* C code for VM instruction */ ... ;
  current_vm_instruction += OPCODE_0_LENGTH;
  goto *current_vm_instruction;
...

...
OPCODE_255:
  /* C code for VM instruction */ ... ;
  current_vm_instruction += OPCODE_255_LENGTH;
  goto *current_vm_instruction;
```

Performance Optimization

Performance optimization starts in general with profiling to reveal the hot spots or bottlenecks; then you tune the specific codes by implementing the appropriate best practices, and validate your changes with another profiling and iterate the process until you achieve satisfaction. The following standard programming best practices—not specific to Java—will help you get a decent performance out of the Java interpreter:

1. *Avoid excessive interface and virtual method calls.* Virtual method dispatch incurs a runtime lookup cost. Interface method dispatch incurs an even greater runtime lookup cost. As a result, calling interface methods or virtual methods are slower than calling methods on a regular Java class. Use private, static, or final methods whenever possible, because these method calls are directly bound to the Java class, incurring less overhead.

    - Use the following optimization techniques, described in detail in *Practical Java Programming Language Guide*:[23]

      - Empty method removal
      - Dead code removal
      - Strength reduction: replacing expensive operations with more effective ones such as compound assignment operators
      - Constant folding: precalculating constant expressions

23. Practical Java Programming Language Guide, by Peter Haggar (New York: Addison-Wesley, 2000).

- Common subexpression elimination: replace duplicate expressions by a temporary variable
- Loop unrolling: replace the loop construct by the sequence of the operations to be performed
- Algebraic simplification: use algebra rules to simplify expressions
- Loop invariant code motion: avoid redundant object accessors in tight loops (see following example).

Instead of:

```
int[] a = ...;
 for(int i = 0; i < a.length; i++) {
     a[i] = o._x;
 }
```

Use this one:

```
int[] a = ...;
int x = o._x;
int max = a.length;
for(int i = 0; i < max; i++) {
  a[i] = x;
}
```

2.   Browse online Java performance-tuning Web sites such as JavaPerformanceTuning.com.[24]

However, the best Java performance is achieved by the means of natively compiled code (i.e., dynamic compilation [JIT] or static compilation); OracleJVM Native Compiler is described in the following section.

2.6   The Native Java Compiler (NCOMP)

2.6.1   What Is NCOMP?

Java developers are more familiar with Just-In-Time (JIT) compilation in JDK VM environments. JIT compilation consists of dynamically compiling the Java bytecode into platform-specific executables on the fly. It is a runtime process that happens transparently under the covers, which is great from a usability perspective but has a recurrent recompilation cost

---

24.   http://www.JavaPerformanceTuning.com.

(this is minor, though). NCOMP, which is short for Native Compilation of Java (also known as JAccelerator), aims at the same goal—that is, speed up Java execution by compiling the Java bytecode into platform-specific binary executables. However, NCOMP uses a static compilation approach, which must be performed ahead of the deployment time. It is an explicit, additional operation (you have to invoke it), which, from a usability perspective, is not great but which, on the plus side, avoids the repeating cost of on-the-fly compilation. The JIT versus NCOMP discussion is beyond the scope of this book, because the Oracle database does not currently offer a JIT compiler.

2.6.2   Requirements and Design Choices

The ultimate goal of NCOMP is to convert Java bytecode into platform-dependent binary, in the most efficient and portable manner. To reach this goal, it had to meet the following requirements: portability, scalability, security, and interoperability between interpreted bytecode and native code. The first design choice was to take advantage of the portability of C code across all platforms where a C compiler is available. The second design choice was to take advantage of the optimization techniques offered by C compilers.

Portability

The main piece of the native compiler is a Java-to-C translator. Unlike traditional "platform-specific assembly-based" native compilers, NCOMP must be portable across multiple platforms and support the different hardware platforms with which the Oracle database ships. To meet this requirement, the NCOMP team leveraged the Oracle standards C Pre-Processor (CPP) macros, a highly portable subset of ANSI C, used for writing the Oracle database software. This design choice allows performance optimizations such as caching and simplified maintenance.

Scalability

The native code must offer the same scalability, throughput, and support for large loads as the database. To meet these requirements, the designers chose to store native code as shared libraries (called DLLs)—using Java resources—that can be dynamically loaded and shared concurrently by a large number of user sessions.

Security/Integrity

The native code must be safe for execution directly into the server's address space, avoiding context-switching overhead while preserving the security aspects of the Java runtime. Security requirements were met by preserving all necessary runtime checks, thus making native code as safe as interpreted Java bytecodes.

Java Bytecode to C Translation

Java bytecodes residing in the database have been resolved and verified during the loading phase (loadjava) and can therefore be trusted and expected to execute correctly. The translator takes the trusted bytecodes as inputs and converts them into a subset of ANSI C, applying data flow analysis and optimization techniques, as described by the following internal steps (transparent to the end user), which you might want to skip, unless you share my curiosity.

1. Each operation on Java stack is replaced with an equivalent but much faster operation using local temporary C variables.

2. Wherever possible, Java VM calling conventions are replaced by faster C calling conventions. The natively compiled Java code executes directly on the C stack and does not use the Java VM stack.

3. Performance-critical properties of Java classes such as instance layouts and virtual method table layouts are computed at compile time, and the corresponding C code is generated.

4. The translator performs a range of interprocedural optimizations by analyzing large groups of classes at compile time, thereby reducing the overhead of method dispatch in Java code.

5. The translator emits data structures that enable caching of the results of runtime method dispatch, further improving the speed of runtime execution.

In summary, the NCOMP-generated code can be regarded as a regular Java class, which preserves the semantics of Java such as class invalidation and reloading. The OracleJVM class loader can invalidate both interpreted or NCOMPed classes and their dependents by marking every affected NCOMPed class as non-ncomped and a candidate for reload.

Interoperability between Interpreted Bytecode and Native Code

A Java application may result in a mix of bytecodes (interpreted) and natively compiled binaries. Therefore, the natively compiled code must be fully interoperable with the Java VM. The native compiler has been designed to generate C code that allows natively compiled routines to call (and be called from) interpreted Java bytecode. The interaction between the OracleJVM runtime, the interpreted bytecode, and the native code is pictured in Figure 2.6.

Figure 2.6
The OracleJVM Execution Mechanisms

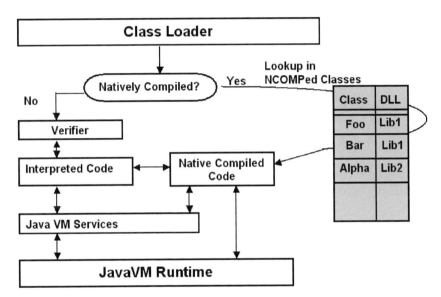

The interaction can be summarized as follows (see Figure 2.7):

1. *At the OracleJVM runtime level:* The NCOMP translator generates CPP macros that behave just like the system native code written by hand by OracleJVM developers. This ensures tight integration at the runtime level. In addition, the generated code expands inline into platform-specific raw C code, resulting in greater configurability and flexibility.

2. *At the OracleJVM services level:* The OracleJVM preserves dynamic aspects of code execution through a special execution context passed as an argument to all routines that require dynamic services. The native compiler produces C code that follows the same calling convention. In addition, the generated C code contains calls to high-level VM APIs, such as exception

handling primitives, predefined and cached standard objects, and so on.

3.   *At the OracleJVM interpreter level:* The OracleJVM supports a mixed execution model, which allows mixing interpreted byte-code and natively compiled code.

2.6.3   **The NCOMP Process**

NCOMP comprises three commands/steps: `'NCOMP'`, `'STATUSNC'`, and `'DEPLOYNC'`. Figure 2.8 depicts the compilation and linkage phase.

1.   the normal/traditional deployment phase of Java in the database (loadjava, interpreted mode execution)

2.   The translation, compiling, and linking phase

    a.   Translation of the Java bytecode (application JAR) into C source files and headers

    b.   Compilation of the generated C files resulting in plat-form-specific object files

    c.   Linkage of the object files, resulting in platform-specific binaries library (DLL)

3.   The deployment phase

    a.   Loadjava uploads every resource by default. When load-java loads an NCOMP deployment JAR, it treats it as a Java resource. These are "special resources"; a hook in loadjava dumps these DLLs in the `$ORACLE_HOME/javavm/deploy` directory on the database server for the duration of the deployment.

    b.   Loadjava invokes the installers serially. When a Java pack-age is successfully validated, the corresponding DLL file is enabled by the corresponding installer and copied from `$ORACLE_HOME/javavm/deploy` to `$ORACLE_HOME/javavm/admin`.

Compilation and Linkage

Figure 2.8 depicts the NCOMP process.

2.6.4   **The NCOMP Command**

From the end-user's perspective, the NCOMP command does three things:

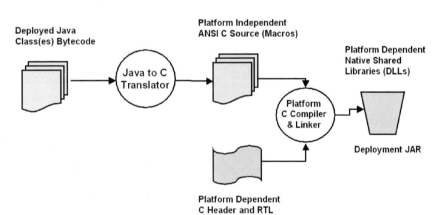

Figure 2.7
The NCOMP Steps

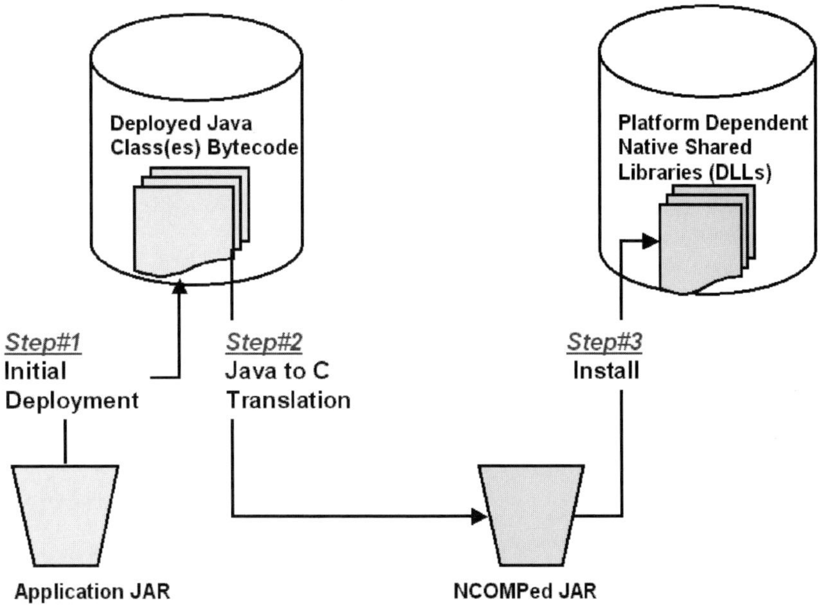

Figure 2.8
The Compilation and Linkage Phase

1.   Gathers class info, generates a script that will drive the NCOMP-ing process, and produces the list of NEED_NCOMPNG or ALREADY_NCOMPED methods

2.   Pauses for the Java-to-C translation: C compilation and linkage of each package involved into platform-specific DLLs

3.   Deployment/installation of the resulting DLL (unless -noDeploy) is specified

```
ncomp [ options ] <class_designation_file>
```

```
-user | -u <username>/<password>[@<database_url>]
[-load]
[-projectDir | -d <project_directory>]
[-force]
[-lightweightDeployment]
[-noDeploy]
[-outputJarFile | -o <jar_filename>]
[-thin]
[-oci | -oci8]
[-update]
[-verbose]
```

Argument	Description and Values
`<file>.jar`	The full path name and file name of a JAR file that contains the classes that are to be natively compiled. If you are executing in the directory where the JAR file exists and you do not specify the `-projectDir` option, you may give only the name of the JAR file.
`<file>.zip`	The full path name and file name of a ZIP file that contains the classes that are to be natively compiled. If you are executing in the directory where the ZIP file exists and you do not specify the `-projectDir` option, you may give only the name of the ZIP file.
`<file>.classes`	The full path name and file name of a CLASSES file, which contains the list of CLASSES to be natively compiled. If you are executing in the directory where the classes file exists and you do not specify the `-projectDir` option, you may give only the name of the CLASSES file.
`-user	-u <username>/ <password>[@<database>]`	Specifies a user, password, and database connect string; the files will be loaded into this database instance. The argument has the form *<username>/<password>[@<database>]*. If you specify the database URL on this option, you must specify it with OCI syntax. To provide a JDBC Thin database URL, use the -thin option.
`-force`	The native compilation is performed on all classes, excluding previously compiled classes.
`-lightweightDeployment`	Provides an option for deploying shared libraries and native compilation information separately. This is useful if you need to preserve resources when deploying.
`-load`	Executes `loadjava` on the specified class designation file. You can not use this option in combination with a *<file>*.`classes` file.

Argument	Description and Values
`-outputJarFile <jar_filename>`	All natively compiled classes output into a deployment JAR file. This option specifies the name of the deployment JAR file and its destination directory. If omitted, the `ncomp` tool names the output deployment JAR file the same name as the input *<file>* with "`_depl.jar`" appended as the suffix. If directory is not supplied, it stores the output JAR file into the project directory (denoted by -`projectDir`).
`-noDeploy`	Specifies that the native compilation results only in the output deployment JAR file, which is not deployed to the server. The resulting deployment JAR can be deployed to any server using the deploync tool.
`-thin`	The database URL that is provided on the -`user` option uses a JDBC Thin URL address for the database URL syntax.
`-oci` | `-oci8`	The database URL that is provided on the -user option uses an OCI URL address for the database URL syntax. However, if neither -`oci` nor -`thin` is specified, then the default assumes that you used an OCI database URL.
`-projectDir` | `-d` `<absolute_path>`	Specifies the full path for the project directory. If not specified, Accelerator uses the directory from which `ncomp` is invoked as the project directory. This directory must exist; the tool will not create this directory for you. If it does not exist, the current directory is used.
`-update`	If you add more classes to a *<class_designation_file>* that has already been natively compiled, this flag informs Accelerator to update the deployment JAR file with the new classes. Thus, Accelerator compiles the new classes and adds them to the appropriate shared libraries. The deployment JAR file is updated.

Forced NCOMPing

The normal usage is to natively compile already loaded (then trusted) Java classes or packages. NCOMP requires that each library (JAR, ZIP) contains only a single package. It recompiles only packages that contain classes that have changed since the last time these were loaded in the database. However, you can "force" the recompilation of any package using the –force option.

```
ncomp -user SCOTT/TIGER Project1.jar, Project2.zip,
Class1.class
ncomp -user SCOTT/TIGER –force Project1.jar, Project2.zip,
Class1.class
```

Note: OracleJVM does not support mixing Java classes and Java sources within the same library.

NCOMPing nonloaded java classes

NCOMP only uses loaded and trusted classes; however, you may ask for the compilation of a class or library that has not yet been loaded using the "load" option.

```
ncomp -user SCOTT/TIGER@<dbhost>:<port>:<sid> -<driver_type>
-load  <library>
ncomp -user SCOTT/TIGER@host1:5521:orcl -thin —load
Project1.jar
```

2.6.5   The STATUSNC Command

Class-level Check

The OracleJVM offers the STATUSNC command as a standard method for checking whether your JAR files, ZIP files, or CLASSES files are NCOMPed or not.

```
statusnc [ options ] <file>.jar | <file>.zip |
<file>.classes.

-user <user>/<password>[@database]
[-output | -o <filename>]
[-projectDir | -d <directory>]
[-thin]
[-oci | -oci8]
```

The possible values of the status are:

- *ALREADY_NCOMPED* The class is natively compiled.

- *NEED_NCOMPING* A class within the shared library probably reloaded after the native compilation process. Needs to natively recompile the entire shared library.

   - **INVALID** The native compiler tried to validate an invalid class but failed. The class will be excluded from the natively compiled shared library.

   The results of STATUSNC are stored in the JACCELERATOR$STATUS table.

Method-level Check

Sometimes, not all methods within a class are NCOMPed. To find out whether a specific method within a class has been natively compiled or not, you can leverage new points in the OracleJVM runtime (as of 10g Release 2) to programmatically determine the status of a method with reference to native compilation.

1. From SYSTEM or SYS account grant SCOTT the following permission:

    ```
    call
    dbms_java.grant_permission('SCOTT','SYS.java.lang.Runti
    mePermission','accessDeclaredMembers', '');
    ```

2. Once granted SYS.java.lang.RuntimePermission you can query the status of loaded methods, using the program shown in Listing 2.4:

Listing 2.4   *Method-Level Check*

```
CREATE OR REPLACE AND RESOLVE JAVA SOURCE NAMED Method_nc AS
import java.lang.reflect.*;
import oracle.aurora.vm.OracleRuntime;

public class Method_nc {
  public static void foo(String s) throws Exception {
  Class c = Class.forName(s);
    printMethods(c);
  }

  public static String methodStatusString(int status) {
    switch(status) {
    case OracleRuntime.INTERPRETED_METHOD:
      return "interpreted";
    case OracleRuntime.SYSTEM_NATIVE_METHOD:
      return "system-native";
```

```
        case OracleRuntime.JNI_METHOD:
      return "JNI-native";
    case OracleRuntime.NCOMP_METHOD:
      return "NCOMP'd";
    default: return "Unknown";
      }
    }

  public static void printMethods(Class c) throws Exception {
    System.out.println("Methods report for class "+c);
    Constructor[] ctors = c.getConstructors();
    for(int i = 0; i < ctors.length; i++) {
      int status = OracleRuntime.methodRuntimeType(ctors[i]);
      System.out.println("\t"+ctors[i]+" is a
"+methodStatusString(status)+" method");
    }
    Method[] meths = c.getDeclaredMethods();
    for(int i = 0; i < meths.length; i++) {
      int status = OracleRuntime.methodRuntimeType(meths[i]);
      System.out.println("\t"+meths[i]+" is a
"+methodStatusString(status)+" method");
    }
  }
}
/
show errors;
/
CREATE OR REPLACE PROCEDURE MethodNC (C VARCHAR2) AS LANGUAGE JAVA
NAME
'Method_nc.foo(java.lang.String)';
/
show errors;
/
```

Generates the following output:

```
SQL> call dbms_java.set_output(50000);

Call completed.

SQL> call MethodNC('Method_nc');
```

```
Methods report for class class Method_nc
        public Method_nc() is a interpreted method
        public static void Method_nc.foo(java.lang.String) throws
java.lang.Exception
is a interpreted method
        public static java.lang.String
Method_nc.methodStatusString(int) is a
interpreted method
        public static void Method_nc.printMethods(java.lang.Class)
throws
java.lang.Exception is a interpreted method


Call completed.

SQL>
```

Create the list of classes to be natively compiled into the file: my.classes:

```
my.classes
==========
import Method_nc;
```

Invoke the native compiler with my.classes as input:

```
C:\> ncomp -u scott/tiger my.classes
#
# this list is produced by query
#   select status, class_name  from jaccelerator$status;
#
NEED_NCOMPING Method_nc
# Deployment History, produced by query:
# select timestamp, status, dll_name  from jaccelerator$dlls order by
dll_name
2005-06-09 09:41:18 installed /
libjox10_104648c91ac_scott_UnnamedPackage.so
```

Let's run the method-level status check again to find out if the class has been NCOMPed:

```
SQL> set serveroutput on
```

```
SQL> call dbms_java.set_output(50000);

Call completed.

SQL> call MethodNC('Method_nc');
Methods report for class class Method_nc
    public Method_nc() is a NCOMP'd method
    public static void Method_nc.foo(java.lang.String) throws

        java.lang.Exception is a NCOMP'd method
    public static java.lang.String
        Method_nc.methodStatusString(int) is a NCOMP'd method
    public static void Method_nc.printMethods(java.lang.Class)
throws
        java.lang.Exception is a NCOMP'd method
Call completed.
SQL>
```

2.6.6 Dumping Java Classes with NCOMP

NCOMP takes as input already compiled and resolved classes. The following command will dump the Java class FooBar:

```
echo "include FooBar; " > my.classes
ncomp -u sys/install -noDeploy -force my.classes
ls -l classes/foo/Bar.class
```

2.6.7 NCOMP Configuration and Planning

Configuring C Compiler Optimizations

C compiler optimizations are controlled through platform-specific options. These settings are specified in the `$ORACLE_HOME/javavm/jahome/Settings_os.properties` file.

On Linux (on Solaris these are slightly different but quite similar to Linux):

```
CC = gcc
c.compile.opt.level = -O3

LINK_COMMAND = ld -shared -h $(@:f) -o $@ $<
```

On Windows:

```
CC = $(visual.c.home)/bin/cl
c.compile.flags.platform = -Ox -Oy-

LINK_COMMAND = $(visual.c.home)/bin/LINK  /DLL /OUT:$@ \
/LIBPATH:"$(visual.c.home)/lib" /DEF:$(*:b).def $< \
$(oracle.home)/lib/orajox10.lib /NODEFAULTLIB msvcrt.lib
kernel32.lib
```

The flag `c.compile.opt.level` controls the level of optimization. In general, a higher level of optimization produces faster code at the expense of a longer NCOMPing process.

Platform Dependencies

Platform dependencies information comes from three sources:

1.   The javavm/jahome/jtc.h file, which contains platform-specific CPP definitions

2.   The JDK Java system properties

3.   The OracleJVM system properties and other platform-specific variables and system methods

NCOMP gathers most platform-specific information from a file produced by the Oracle database porting teams (i.e., the `javavm/jahome/Settings_os.properties` file), which contains the C compiler optimization specifics, file extensions, flags, and so on. This file can be modified to reflect a specific path to the C compiler or the location of C temporary storage or specify a new level of C compiler optimization (e.g., O3 performs level 3 optimization).

On Linux:

```
file.extension.obj = o
library.prefix = lib
file.extension.dll = so

LINK_COMMAND = ld -shared -h $(@:f) -o $@ $<

CC = gcc
```

```
c.compile.opt.level = -O3

c.compile.flags.platform = $(c.compile.opt.level) \
-fPIC -DLINUX -D_GNU_SOURCE -DSLTS_ENABLE -DSLMXMX_ENABLE
-D_REENTRANT -DNS_THREADS    -D_SVID_GETTOD

makefile.maker = $(one.c.unit.per.dll.makefile.maker)
```

On Windows:

```
file.extension.exe = exe
file.extension.obj = obj
library.prefix = "ora"
file.extension.dll = dll

visual.c.home = c:/devstudio/vc
oracle.home = $(ORACLE_HOME)
LINK_COMMAND = $(visual.c.home)/bin/LINK  /DLL /OUT:$@ \
/LIBPATH:"$(visual.c.home)/lib" /DEF:$(*:b).def $< \
$(oracle.home)/lib/orajox10.lib /NODEFAULTLIB msvcrt.lib
kernel32.lib

CFLAGS =   $<  -Fo$@ $(c.compile.include) \
$(c.compile.flags.platform) $(c.compile.flags.aurora)

CC = $(visual.c.home)/bin/cl
COMPILE.c = $(CC) $(CFLAGS) $(CPPFLAGS) -c
c.compile.flags.platform = -Ox -Oy-

makefile.maker = $(one.c.unit.per.dll.makefile.maker)
```

NCOMP: Time Planning

The system classes are provided fully NCOMPed; their deployement in the database happens during database creation. For the end users or application classes, the NCOMPing process consists of, as described previously, three steps/phases: (1) the C-to-Java translation, (2) the compilation and linkage of the generated C code, and (3) the deployment/uploading of the platform-specific binary libraries (also called DLLs) in the database. Here is an estimate of resource requirements for each phase based on the proof of concept "Run Groovy Scripts in the Database" (see Chapter 5):

1.   The translation of 500 Java classes (i.e., 80 MB of uncompressed bytecodes) generates approximately 24 million lines of C code and takes from one to three hours depending on the CPU power of the platform.

2.   The compilation and linkage phases depend on the speed of the C compiler and its optimizer; it may take from three to five times the duration of the translation phase; in other words, from 3 hours up to 15 hours!

3.   The duration of the deployment phase depends on the speed of JDBC LOBs access. It takes, on average, a few seconds to deploy a class. Based on the same application, the deployment of NCOMPed 500 classes—a 10-MB deployment JAR—takes less than three minutes on modern Intel boxes under Linux. The deployment process requires the pinning in memory of the classes and access to the database storage. Tuning the speed of deploying large NCOMPed JARS involves the typical database tuning process (i.e., table storage, rollback segment, and Javapool).[25]

NCOMP: Disk Space Planning

How much disk space does NCOMP need? To answer that question, let's look at everything NCOMP produces and their disk space considerations:

1.   Using the same Groovy example as above: unloading 500 Java classes requires 8 MB zipped or 17MB uncompressed.

2.   NCOMP generates temporary C source code: for 500 Java classes, 1400 C files (and headers) generated, approximately 1.3 million lines, occupying 39 MB disk space; the object file occupies 19 MB.

An NCOMP deployment Jar contains:

1.   The installer: Java code that contains tables used to validate and enable the DLLs.

2.   The DLLs: platform-specific binaries that are managed as a Java resource file. The typical bytecode/DLL ratio ranges from 1:2 to 1:5 (on average), up to 1:10, depending on the size of the individual classes and their "density."[26] With JDK 1.4, classes are less

---

25.   See Oracle High-Performance Tuning for 9i and 10g, by Gavin Powell (Boston: Elsevier Science, Digital Press, 2003).
26.   The ratio between the size of the bytecodes and the list of strings, methods, and fields names (also known as constant pool).

dense, resulting in a ratio of bytecode size over DLL size closer to 1:1. However, for heavyweight C-style applications with very large methods and few classes, it will be closer to 1:10. As an example, the Groovy bytecode/DLL ratio is 8 MB/10 MB.

2.6.8 NCOMP Performance Tips, Improper Use, and Troubleshooting

The ultimate question you were dying to ask is: "What is the performance improvement of NCOMP?" As usual, there is no absolute figure; it all depends on what exactly you are NCOMPing. NCOMP speeds up only Java code, not the embedded SQL, NCOMP may give you up to an order of magnitude speed up (i.e., 10 times) compared with interpreted execution. But remember, in Chapter 1 we saw that the combination of Java and SQL runs faster in the database, even interpreted. This section gives you some tips to get the best performance out of NCOMP.

Performance-Tuning Tips for Java in the Database

1. General considerations:

   a. Private, final, static, and constructor methods turn into direct function calls within the DLL, so there is almost no overhead. When static methods are called within the same package (and hence the same DLL), the overall performance is even better, because you save the overhead of indirectly calling into another DLL.

   b. Interface methods[27] are slower, so avoid them if possible.

2. Not all methods in an NCOMPed class are natively compiled:

   a. Some are not translated from Java to C because they are too complicated or because of other mitigating circumstances.

   b. Methods that are not NCOMPed are skipped based on some rules. Among them are:

      ▪ Methods whose compiled bytecode is larger than 16K are not NCOMPed.
      ▪ Static initializer blocks[28] are not NCOMPed either.

3. Try-catch-finally blocks:

---

27. Method signature for all classes implementing the interface.
28. Static initializer blocks are used to initialize static variables the first time the class is loaded.

a. The Java compiler generates complex exception-handling code out of try-catch-finally; avoid using this in performance-critical code.

b. If you absolutely need try-catch-finally semantics, put the critical code in another method (ideally a private, static, or final method so it will be a fast C function call) and call that method from the try-catch-finally block.

c. Do not use try-catch as a control primitive. For portability reasons, the NCOMP translator converts try-catch blocks into code relying on the nonlocal GOTO of ANSI C: `setjmp/longjmp`. These facilities are indeed portable but may incur an overhead compared with machine code GOTOs. Hence, following these recommendations helps avoid the performance penalty of `setjmp/longjmp`:

   ■ Don't use the try block as conditionals and "catch" as a branching construct as follows:

```
try {
        ((CCC)obj).fooBar(); // the main case
      } catch (NullPointerException npe) {
        // obj was null, do something specific to that
case
      } catch (ClassCastException cce) {
        //it was a different type, do something else
yet..
      }
```
Instead, use explicit checks:
```
      if (obj == null) {
        // obj is null, do something to that case
      } else if (obj instanceof CCC) {
        ((CCC)obj).fooBAr(); // the main case
      } else {
        // obj is of a different type, do something else
yet..
      }
```

   ■ Do not use exceptions to terminate loops!
Instead of this:
```
      try {
```

```
myArray = ....
for (int i;;i++)
    dosomething(myArray[i]);
} catch (ArrayIndexOutOfBoundsException e) {
// exit loop
}
```

do this:

```
myArray = ....
int myArrayLen = myArray.length;
for (int i;i < myArrayLen ;i++)
    dosomething(myArray[i]);
```

4. Avoid redundant array accessors and object accessors in tight loops.

    Example:

    Instead of:

    ```
    int[] a = ...;
    for(int i = 0; i < a.length; i++) { // redundant array
    accessors
        a[i] = o._x; // redundant object accessor
    }
    ```

    Use:

    ```
    int[] a = ...;
    int x = o._x;
    int max = a.length;
    for(int i = 0; i < max; i++) {
      a[i] = x;
    }
    ```

    This code snippet saves `(max-1)*times` the array check and `length` attribute retrieval.

5. Array access is more expensive than primitive operators because array must be validated (i.e., not null and array bounds) before an access happens. In some cases, the NCOMP translator eliminates null checks, but not always, and the bounds checks are not eliminated. Similarly, instance accessors need null pointer checks and also are expensive if repeatedly performed in loops. Hence, the programmer can maximize performance by making sure object and array accessors are not needlessly repeated in performance-critical loops.

6. The same is true for other expensive operations such as 'instanceof' and casts. Example:

```
DON'T:
for (int i = 0;
obj instanceof CCC && ((CCC)obj).getSomeArrray != null
        && i < ((CCC)obj).getSomeArrray.length;
    i++) ...

DO:
if (obj instanceof CCC) {
    CCC myobj = (CCC)obj;
        SomeArray myarray = myobj.getSomeArrray;
        if (myarray != null) {
          int max = myarray.length;
          for (int i = 0; i < max; i++) ...
        }
    }
}
```

The performance gain will be significant, and code maintenance will also be improved.

7. Crossing the NCOMP/non-NCOMP boundary is relatively expensive (especially calling interpreted methods from the NCOMPed code).

8. Avoid using finalizers. Finalizers are inadvisable from a memory point of view: objects with finalizers (especially ones that release large amounts of memory) typically need to be held onto across session call boundaries (end-of-call migration), which could be expensive in shared servers mode.

9. If you use the permissions framework (e.g., doPriviledged), there is a significant one-time startup cost.

2.7   Conclusion

Having explored the internals of the OracleJVM through this chapter, you are now in a position to understand its specifics and take the best of it. In the next chapter, I will walk you through the process of developing, compiling, and executing Java in the database.

3

Developing and Running Java in the Database

In the previous chapter, we explored the Java runtime in the database. You are now well armed to tackle your initial goal, which is developing and running Java in the database. I'll walk you through (1) the most-used techniques for putting Java sources and/or classes in the database; (2) how to expose/map Java procedures, functions, their parameters, and return values to SQL; and (3) the various mechanisms for invoking Java in the database; then, you can get busy!

3.1 Developing Java in the Database

This section explains the various techniques for creating or loading Java in the database, how to remove Java from the database, setting or querying environment variables or system properties, and the Java compiler within the database.

3.1.1 Turning JDBC Applications into Java Stored Procedures

As already mentioned, one of the key benefits of Java is the availability of a *huge* set of libraries that can be reused as is or with minor changes, resulting in a substantial productivity gain. In general, any J2SE Java program may be reused within OracleJVM; however, you want to run Java in the database because you are doing data-related manipulations that are more efficient in the database than from the middle tier or client tier. Which changes are required for running a standard JDBC application in the database? We'll answer that question in the following section.

JDBC Connections

Because you are already connected to a database session when you run Java in the database, the JDBC connection, also known as the *default connection*, is in reality just a handle to the session. OracleJVM does not yet support data-source lookup in JNDI; instead, you have to use the following syntaxes:

```
Connection conn =
DriverManager.getConnection("jdbc:default:connection:");
```

or:

```
Connection conn =
DriverManager.getConnection ("jdbc:oracle:kprb:");
```

or:

```
OracleDriver t2server = new OracleDriver();
Connection conn = t2server.defaultConnection();
```

Turning Instance Methods into Public Static Methods

Only public static methods can be exposed to the external world using either a PL/SQL wrapper or a client-side stub. However, you can simply wrap the instance method with a public static wrapper as follows:

```
public static void <instance_method_wrapper>() {
    new <myclass>().<instance_method>();
}
```

Invoking the wrapper will create a new instance and the class and invoke the method in question; that's it. Now that you know how to turn JDBC applications into Java stored procedures that run faster in the database, how do you get these into the database? The following section answers this question.

3.1.2   Creating or Loading Java in the Database

There are several ways to create or upload Java into OracleJVM-managed structures. Java sources, classes, and resources can be created interactively during a SQL*Plus session, uploaded from files residing on your development client machine, uploaded from files residing on the server machine (same machine as the database instance), or created from database storage structures such as CLOB/BLO/BFILE.

First of all, the session must have the following database privileges to load classes: CREATE PROCEDURE, CREATE TABLE, CREATE ANY PROCEDURE, CREATE ANY TABLE and JServerPermission. As explained in the security section in Chapter 2, at database creation all schemas have been granted JServerPermission permission through the following command: dbms_java.grant_permission('PUBLIC', 'SYS:oracle.aurora.security.JServerPermission', 'LoadClassInPackage.*', null);.

Let's look at the most commonly used techniques for creating Java in the database.

Method 1: Create Java Sources in the Database, Interactively

This is the quickest way of creating Java in the database. The SQL syntax for creating a Java source, class, or resource in the database is:

```
CREATE [ OR REPLACE ]
  [ AND { RESOLVE | COMPILE } ]
  [ NOFORCE ]
  JAVA { { SOURCE | RESOURCE }
        NAMED [ schema. ]primary_name
      | CLASS [ SCHEMA schema ]
      }
  [ invoker_rights_clause ]
  [ RESOLVER
    ((match_string [,] { schema_name | - })
      [ (match_string [,] { schema_name | - }) ]...
    )
  ]

  AS source_text
  } ;
```

Using SQL*Plus, enter the text of your Java source directly, as shown in Listing 3.1:

Listing 3.1   *Workers.java*

```
========================
create or replace java source named Workers as
/*
  * Adapted from existing JDBC demo
  * this code sample retrieves a worker
  * from a database, then updates its position and salary.
  */

import java.sql.*;
import oracle.jdbc.driver.*;

public class Workers
{

  public static void main (String args []) throws SQLException
  {

        String name = null;
String pos = null;
int sal;
int id;
long t0,t1;
Connection conn = null;
Statement stmt = null;
PreparedStatement pstmt = null;

if ( args.length < 1 ) {
 System.err.println("Usage: Java Workers <wid> <new position>
                                       <new salary>");
 System.exit(1);
 }

// Get parameters value
id = Integer.parseInt(args[0]);
pos = args[1];
sal = Integer.parseInt(args[2]);

  /*
 * Where is your code running: in the database or outside?
 */
```

```
      if (System.getProperty("oracle.jserver.version") != null)
{
/*
 * You are in the database, already connected, use the default
 * connection
 */
conn = DriverManager.getConnection("jdbc:default:connection:");
System.out.println ("Running in OracleJVM,in the database!");
}
else
{
/*
 * You are not in the database, you need to connect to
 * the database
 */

DriverManager.registerDriver(new oracle.jdbc.OracleDriver());
conn = DriverManager.getConnection("jdbc:oracle:thin:",
                "scott", "tiger");
      System.out.println ("Running in JDK VM, outside the
database!");
        // Disable autocommit  - Not suppoted in OracleJVM
          conn.setAutoCommit(false);
      }


      // Start timing
         t0=System.currentTimeMillis();

   /*
    * find the name of the workers given his id number
    */

      // create statement
         stmt = conn.createStatement();

      // find the name of the worker
         ResultSet rset = stmt.executeQuery(
               "SELECT WNAME FROM workers WHERE wid = " + id);

      // retrieve and print the result (we are only expecting 1 row
         while (rset.next())
```

```
            {
              name = rset.getString(1);
            }

    // return the name of the worker who has the given worker number
            System.out.println ("Worker Name: "+ name);

      /*
        * update the position and salary of the retrieved worker
        */

    // prepare the update statement
              pstmt = conn.prepareStatement("UPDATE WORKERS SET WPOSITION
= ?, " +
                  " WSALARY = ? WHERE WNAME = ?");

    // set up bind values and execute the update
              pstmt.setString(1, pos);
              pstmt.setInt(2, sal);
              pstmt.setString(3, name);
              pstmt.execute();

    // double-check (retrieve) the updated position and salary
              rset = stmt.executeQuery(
              "SELECT WPOSITION, WSALARY FROM WORKERS WHERE WNAME = '" +
                              name + "'");
              while (rset.next())
              {
                pos = rset.getString ("wposition");
                sal = rset.getInt ("wsalary");
              }
            System.out.println ("Worker: Id = " + id + ", Name = " + name +
                      ", Position = " + pos + ", Salary = " + sal);

    // Close the ResultSet
              rset.close();

    // Close the Statement
              stmt.close();

    // Stop timing
              t1=System.currentTimeMillis();
```

```
        System.out.println ("====> Duration: "+(int)(t1-t0)+ "
Milliseconds");

    // Close the connection
        conn.close();
    }
 }


/


Java created
```

Provided you have been granted ALTER ANY PROCEDURE privilege and
EXECUTE object privilege on the Java sources/classes in question, you can
use either of the following commands (these are synonymous) to compile
the loaded Java source in the database (the embedded compiler is covered
later):

```
SQL> alter java source Workers resolve;
SQL> alter java source Workers compile;
```

When everything goes well, you get:

```
Java created
```

Otherwise, you get:

```
Warning: Java altered with compilation errors.
```

In this case, you can check the errors using the following command:

```
SQL> select text from user_errors;
```

The following syntax combines the creation of the Java source follow-up
with the compilation within a single command:

```
SQL>create or replace and resolve java source named Workers as
//
// -> Insert the above code, here

/
SQL>show errors;
```

However, command-line tools such as SQL*Plus offer limited editing capabilities; therefore, this method is only convenient for small or short programs.

Method 2: Uploading Client-Side Java Files into the Database

Oracle furnishes client-side command-line utilities, loadjava and drop-java, for loading or removing Java sources (.java), Java classes (.class), Java resources (.properties), and JAR and ZIP files into/from the database. This is the most-used technique, because it allows you to upload already debugged/validated Java sources and Java classes from your development environment into OracleJVM structures; furthermore, this method allows you not only to upload an individual Java source, class, or resource but also JAR and ZIP files—which are convenient and fast ways of loading an entire application or framework into the database.

The loadjava Utility

Syntax for invoking the "loadjava" (command-line) utility:

```
loadjava {-user | -u} <user>/<password>[@<database>] [options]
<file>.java | <file>.class | <file>.jar | <file>.zip |
<file>.sqlj | <resourcefile> ...
  [-action][-andresolve][-casesensitivepub][-cleargrants] [-noaction]
  [-debug]
  [-d | -definer]
  [-dirprefix <prefix>]
  [-e | -encoding <encoding_scheme>]
  [-fileout <file>]
  [-f | -force]
  [-genmissing] [-genmissingjar <jar_file>]
  [-g | -grant <user> [, <user>]...] [-nogrant]
  [-help]
  [-jarasresource]
    [-nocasesensitivepub]
  [-nocleargrants]
  [-nodefiner]
    [-norecursivejars] [-recursivejars]
  [-noschema] [-S | -schema <schema>]
  [-noserverside]
  [-nosynonym] [-s | -synonym]
  [-nousage]
  [-noverify]
```

```
[-o | -oci | oci8]
[-optionfile <file>]
[-optiontable <table_name>]
[-publish <package>]
[-r | -resolve] [-R | -resolver "resolver_spec"] [-resolveonly]
[-stdout]
[-stoponerror]
[-tableschema <schema>]
[-t | -thin]
[-time]
[-unresolvedok]
[-v | -verbose]
```

Loadjava offers way too many options, and not all of these are needed or used; Table 3.1 describes the most important options. See the Oracle Database Java Developer Guide for a comprehensive list of all options.

Table 3.1   *Loadjava Options*

Argument	Description
-definer	By default, class schema objects run with the privileges of their invoker. This option confers the privileges of the definers instead. Chapter 2 explains definer's rights and invoker's rights.
-force	Forces files to be loaded, even if they match digest table entries.
-genmissing	genmissing is an option of loadjava that lets you deal with non-existent classes. It instructs loadjava to create and load place-holder definitions of classes that are referenced but not defined. By resolving the references to the missing classes, the genmissing option allows the Java code to run, but because the missing classes have placeholder definitions, their methods cannot be invoked.
-help	Prints the usage message on how to use the loadjava tool and its options.
-noverify	Used along with –resolver, this option causes the classes to be loaded without bytecode verification. The following privilege is required: oracle.aurora.security.JServerPermission ("Verifier").
-optionfile <file>	Look up the loadjava options in <file>, instead. All of the command-line options (except -thin, -oci, -user, -password) can be specified in the file in question.

Table 3.1   *Loadjava Options (continued)*

Argument	Description
-recursivejars	By default (see [-jarasresource], loadjava treats JAR files within the loaded JARs as resources and does not process these recursively. If this option is specified, loadjava will process contained JARs as if they were top-level JARs (read their entries and load classes, sources, and resources.)
-resolve	Compiles (if necessary) and resolves external references in classes after all classes on the command line have been loaded. If you do not specify -resolve, loadjava loads files but does not compile or resolve them. However, they will be resolved at the first invocation.
-synonym	Creates a PUBLIC synonym for loaded classes, making them accessible to all schemas. You must have the CREATE PUBLIC SYNONYM privilege to exeute this option.

Method 3: Uploading Server-Side Java Files into the Database

When already running in the database, DBMS_JAVA.loadjava() allows loading Java sources, classes, or resources residing on the same machine as the database, using the same options as the client tool. When operating from the server side, because you are already in the database, there is no need to provide connection credentials (username/password) or specify the driver type to be used. Running the following SQL script in the database will load an existing Java source file, /tmp/foo.java, into the scott/tiger schema.

```
connect scott/tiger
set echo on
set serveroutput on
call dbms_java.set_output(1000000);
Rem
Rem  Call server-side loadjava. For the loation of file to upload,
Rem  Use either absolute or relative pathname to $ORACLE_HOME
Rem
call dbms_java.loadjava('-v —r —f /tmp/foo.java');
```

Method 4: Using JDeveloper and Third-party IDE

The Oracle JDeveloper and third-party IDE allow you to develop and debug Java applications on the JDK, and then upload the resulting classes (and sources) to the database, using method 2, under the covers!

Method 5: Creating Java Objects from an Existing CLOB/BLOB/BFILE

As explained in Chapter 2, OracleJVM operates only on managed objects, which are stand-alone objects with no external references. As a result, even if you have existing Java sources, Java classes, and Java resources already stored in regular database structures such as CLOB or BLOB columns, or an external file system (on the same system as the database), you still need to create the corresponding managed objects using the following syntax:

```
CREATE [ OR REPLACE ]
  [ AND { RESOLVE | COMPILE } ]
  [ NOFORCE ]
  JAVA { { SOURCE | RESOURCE }
          NAMED [ schema. ]primary_name
        | CLASS [ SCHEMA schema ]
        }
  [ invoker_rights_clause ]
  [ RESOLVER
    ((match_string [,] { schema_name | - })
      [ (match_string [,] { schema_name | - }) ]...
    )
  ]
  {USING { BFILE (directory_object_name ,
                  server_file_name)
          | { CLOB | BLOB | BFILE }
            subquery
          | 'key_for_BLOB'
          };
```

Example:

Assume you have an existing Foo.java file in the /java/test directory. A BFILE (covered in detail in Part II) is an Oracle database mechanism rather than a data type, which allows manipulating the content of external files. The BFILE definition associates an alias (stored in table column) with the actual external file. You can create a managed Java source in the database from the external Java file, using the following steps:

1.   The schema must have been granted "CREATE ANY DIRECTORY" privilege, by another schema (i.e., SYSTEM).

```
SQL> grant create any directory to scott;

Grant succeeded.
```

2.   Create the alias name ("bfile_dir") for the existing external directory.

```
SQL> connect scott/tiger
Connected.
SQL> create or replace directory bfile_dir as '/java/
test';

Directory created.
```

3.   Create a new Java source using the content of the existing external Java source file.

```
SQL> create or replace java source named "Bar.java"
using bfile (bfile_dir, 'Foo.java')
  2  /

Java created.

SQL>
```

Similarly, you may create a new Java class or Java resource from existing external files.

```
SQL>CREATE JAVA CLASS USING BFILE (bfile_dir,
'Bar.class');

SQL>CREATE JAVA RESOURCE NAMED "config.properties"
USING
       BFILE (bfile_dir, 'properties.dat');
```

Method 6: Creating Java Objects from XML (XDB folder)

XDB is Oracle's native support for XML in the database.[1] XDB supports direct HTTP, WebDAV, and FTP access (the database listener has been enhanced to listen for FTP requests on port 2100 and HTTP requests on port 8080). The following example assumes you have an existing Java source or Java class in an XDB folder; otherwise, you can use either one of the following (1), (2), or (3) techniques to populate the XDB folder with a valid Java source text. See the XDB documentation[2] for more details:

1. Drag and drop Java source from your desktop or client machine to the WebDAV-mapped XDB folder.

2. Use FTP to push Java source from your desktop or client machine to the WebDAV-mapped XDB folder.

3. Use the PL/SQL-supplied package dbms_xdb.createResource() as described hereafter. Use SQL*Plus to create a Java source in the XDB folder using dbms_xdb.createResource() (replace the Java skeleton with a valid Java source).

```
SQL>
declare
source CLOB := 'public class Class1 {
 public Class1()  {  }
 public static void main(String[] args)
{System.out.println("Hello");   }
}';
res boolean;
begin
  if dbms_xdb.existsResource('/public/test.java') then
    dbms_xdb.deleteResource('/public/test.java');
  end if;
  res := dbms_xdb.createResource('/public/test.java',source);
end;
/
SQL> commit;
```

Assuming you have enabled the listener to listen to HTTP requests, point your browser to http://localhost:8080; you should see the newly created Java source within the XDB /public folder.

---

1. See http://www.oracle.com/technology/tech/xml/xmldb/index.html for more details.
2. http://www.oracle.com/technology/tech/xml/xmldb/Current/TWP_XMLDB_Content_Mgmt.pdf.

From an existing Java source stored in XDB[3] folders, here is how you can create managed Java source in OracleJVM from it:

1.   Browse the XDB repository (Note: this mechanism is only available with 10*g* R2); point your browser to http://local-host:8080 to browse the `/public` folder to list existing Java sources.

2.   Create a Java source in OracleJVM from an XDB folder.

```
SQL> create or replace and resolve java source named
"Class1"
          2  using clob
          3  (
          4    select xdburiType('/public/
test.java').getClob() from dual
          5  );
          6  /
          SQL>Select object_name from user_objects;
```

You should see the newly created Java source. At this stage you may compile it, create a PL/SQL wrapper, and execute it.

Dumping the Java Class Bytecode

You can use the following PL/SQL interface to dump the bytecode of the Java class(es) managed by the OracleJVM into a class file(s):

```
procedure dumpclass(arg1 varchar2, arg2 varchar2,  arg3
varchar2);
arg1: the longname of the class to be dumped
 arg2: the defining schema
 arg3: where to dump


Usage:
SQL>call dumpclass('foo', 'SCOTT', '/tmp/foo.class');
```

Alternatively, Java code running in the database may directly invoke the underlying Java method, which implements the PL/SQL interface.

```
oracle.aurora.server.tools.dumpclass.ServerDump.dumpClassToFile(
java.lang.String, java.lang.String, java.lang.String);
```

---

3.   Oracle's native support for XML support in the database.

See section 2.6.6 for another method for dumping classes.

Checking the Status of Java Classes in Your Schema

Once you've created your Java classes in the database, run the following self-explanatory SQL queries to check their status:

```
SQL>select count(*) from user_objects where object_type='JAVA CLASS';

SQL>select object_name from user_objects
            where object_type = 'JAVA CLASS'

SQL>select count(*) from user_objects
            where object_type = 'JAVA CLASS' and status = 'VALID';

SQL>select object_name from user_objects
            where object_type = 'JAVA CLASS' and status != 'VALID';
```

3.1.3   Removing Java Sources, Classes, and Resources from the Database

Dropjava is a client-side utility for dropping Java sources, classes, and resources from the database. From within the database, use dbms_java.loadjava(). Loadjava is invoked directly from the OS prompt as follows:

```
dropjava [options] {<file>.java | <file>.class | file.sqlj |
<file>.jar | <file.zip> | <resourcefile>} ...
```

Dropjava syntax

```
dropjava [options] {<file>.java | <file>.class | file.sqlj |
<file>.jar | <file.zip> | <resourcefile>} ...
  -u | -user <user>/<password>[@<database>]
  [-jarasresource]
  [-noserverside]
  [-o | -oci | -oci8]
  [-optionfile <file>]
  [-optiontable <table_name>]
  [-S | -schema <schema>]
  [ -stdout ]
```

```
[-s | -synonym]
[-t | -thin]
[-time]
[-v | -verbose]
```

From SQL and PL/SQL, and Java in the database, use:

```
SQL>call dbms_java.dropjava (foo.java);
```

From Java in the database, use:

```
oracle.aurora.server.tools.loadjava.DropJavaMain.serverMain(
    java.lang.String);
```

See the Oracle Database Java Developer's Guide for more details, especially the required precautions when using dropjava.

Alternatively, from SQL, you may use the DDL command:

```
DROP JAVA SOURCE|CLASS|RESOURCE <java object name>;
```

```
SQL> drop java class "Method_nc";
```

You must have EXECUTE permission on the object in question and DROP ANY PROCEDURE if the Java object does not belong to your schema. However, DROP JAVA may throw ORA- 29537 if the Java class or Java resource has dependencies on a Java source(s) within the database.

3.1.4 Setting/Querying Environment Variable and System Properties

OracleJVM currently allows setting few compiler options.

Setting Options for the Java Compiler in the Database

OracleJVM allows you to specify: Encoding, Online, and Debug options on Java sources, as follows:

Encoding: Similar to javac –encoding, this option specifies the file encoding of the Java source, such as 8859_x, SJIS, and so on. The Java source is converted from the file encoding to Unicode.

Online: A Boolean value that turns on (true) or off (false), the SQL semantic check (i.e., correctness) of SQLJ programs in the database. The default value is true.

Debug: A Boolean value, similar to javac –g, which turns the debug mode on (true) or off (false); the default value is false. When the debug mode is on, Java classes are compiled with debugging information.

From SQL, PL/SQL, and JDBC, use the DBMS_JAVA PL/SQL interfaces with the following signature:

```
FUNCTION get_compiler_option(what VARCHAR2, optionName
VARCHAR2)
  RETURN varchar2;

  PROCEDURE set_compiler_option(what VARCHAR2, optionName
VARCHAR2,
 value VARCHAR2);

  PROCEDURE reset_compiler_option(what VARCHAR2, optionName
VARCHAR2);
```

Examples:

First, let's initialize Java in the session using the following basic SQL query (assuming Java has never been invoked since the creation of the session):

```
SQL> select dbms_java.longname('foo') from dual;

DBMS_JAVA.LONGNAME('FOO')
--------------------------
foo
```

Then, let's get the default values for Encoding, Online, and Debug, using dbms_java.get_compiler_option(name VARCHAR2, option VARCHAR2).

An empty NAME string causes the same options to be applied to all Java sources in the schema.

```
SQL> select dbms_java.get_compiler_option('', 'encoding') from dual;

DBMS_JAVA.GET_COMPILER_OPTION('','ENCODING')
--------------------------------------------
8859_1
```

The default value is the value of the system property file.encoding, which can be queried using System.getProperty("file encoding").

```
SQL> select dbms_java.get_compiler_option('', 'online') from dual;

DBMS_JAVA.GET_COMPILER_OPTION('','ONLINE')
------------------------------------------
true
```

The default values can be reset for all schema objects (using a null name string) or for a specific Java source object (inputting the object name).

```
SQL> SQL> execute dbms_java.reset_compiler_option('', 'online');

PL/SQL procedure successfully completed.

SQL> select dbms_java.get_compiler_option('', 'online') from dual;

DBMS_JAVA.GET_COMPILER_OPTION('','ONLINE')
------------------------------------------
true

SQL> select dbms_java.get_compiler_option('', 'debug') from dual;

DBMS_JAVA.GET_COMPILER_OPTION('','DEBUG')
-----------------------------------------
false
```

Java in the database may directly use the Java methods, which implement the PL/SQL interfaces.

oracle.aurora.jdkcompiler.CompilerOptions.get(java.lang.String,
java.lang.String) return java.lang.String ;

oracle.aurora.jdkcompiler.CompilerOptions.set(java.lang.String,
java.lang.String, java.lang.String);

oracle.aurora.jdkcompiler.CompilerOptions.reset(java.lang.String,
java.lang.String);

Specifying Compiler Options Using Loadjava: The encoding option can also be specified/changed through loadjava.

```
loadjava  [-e | -encoding <encoding_scheme>]
```

Specifying Compiler Options Using the JAVA$OPTION *table:* A compiler option table (JAVA$OPTION) is also created in each schema, upon the first invocation of:

```
dbms_java.set_compiler_option('<name>','<option>','<value>');

SQL> execute dbms_java.set_compiler_option('', 'online', 'false');

PL/SQL procedure successfully completed.

SQL> select dbms_java.get_compiler_option('', 'online') from dual;

DBMS_JAVA.GET_COMPILER_OPTION('','ONLINE')
-----------------------------------------
```
false

```
SQL> desc java$options;
 Name                                     Null?    Type
 ---------------------------------------- -------- ---------------------------
 WHAT                                              VARCHAR2(128)
 OPT                                               VARCHAR2(20)
 VALUE                                             VARCHAR2(128)
SQL>
SQL> col what format a40
SQL> col opt format a15
```

```
SQL> col value format a15
SQL> select * from java$options

WHAT                                     OPT           VALUE
---------------------------------------- ------------- -----------------
                                         online        false
```

Each row of the JAVA$OPTION table contains the name of a Java source to which a setting applies. Different options can be set for different Java sources in the same schema, using multiple entries/rows in the JAVA$OPTION table. However, the command-line setting (loadjava) has precedence over the JAVA$OPTION table setting.

Turning the Bytecode Verifier ON/OFF

The bytecode verifier is part of the Java language security mechanisms. It ensures that bytecodes have a valid storage format, valid instruction set, and meet other security checks. The following PL/SQL interface and Java method allow you to turn the bytecode verifier on ('0') or off ('1').

The schema must have been granted JServerPermission("Verifier") permission (see Chapter 2).

The PL/SQL interface:

```
procedure set_verifier(flag number);
```

The Java method:

```
oracle.aurora.rdbms.Compiler.sessionOptionController(int);
```

3.1.5   The Java Compiler within the Database

The OracleJVM also embeds a Java compiler, which is almost identical to Sun's standard JDK compiler. It allows explicit compilation at development time and implicit/automatic compilation at runtime.

Invoking the OracleJVM Compiler

In the previous section, we covered the setting of the compiler options. There are several ways to invoke the compiler in the OracleJVM:

1.   Using the "resolve" (command-line) option of the "loadjava" utility:

```
loadjava —resolve ... <name>
```

2. Using the DBMS_JAVA (PL/SQL) package to upload, compile, and
    resolve external references:

    ```
    dbms_java.loadjava('<blank separated
    options>','<resolver options>');
    ```

3. Using the CREATE JAVA SOURCE (DDL) statement to explicitly
    request the compilation of a Java source that is entered interac-
    tively (by the user):

    ```
    SQL> create or replace and compile java source named
    <name> AS <Java source>

      SQL> create or replace and resolve java source named
    <name> AS <Java source>
    ```

4. Using the ALTER JAVA SOURCE (DDL) statement to force the
    compilation:

    ```
    SQL> alter java source <name> compile;
    ```

Automatic Compilation and Java Classes Dependencies Management

Let's compare Java class dependency resolution with the PL/SQL dependency
resolution (between packages).

A PL/SQL package has two parts: a specification part and a body part.
Let's assume we have two PL/SQL packages, A and B, A depending on B.

- At the SPEC level, if the spec of B is changed, then A is invalidated,
  because A depended on the old version of B's spec. Therefore, if you
  try to run A, its spec must either be explicitly rewritten before it
  could run again or implicitly recompiled first, then run; if the recompilation fails, it won't run.

- At the package BODY level, if B is changed, A will not be invalidated;
  there is no dependency at the package body level.

Unlike PL/SQL, Java programs do not have a specification part and a
body part. The dependency mechanism is set in such a way that when a

class changes in a way that might make another class "un"-runnable without re-resolution, then the other class is marked invalid.

Assume we have two Java classes: `A.class` and `B.class`. Class A is said to be dependent on B if B is mentioned in any way in `A.class` file, or if B is a superclass of A.

- If class A depends on class B and B is changed, then A will be invalidated. Similarly to PL/SQL, an attempt to run class A will result in implicit revalidation (i.e., compilation and resolution) of A and recursively of B if it hasn't previously been re-resolved. If the revalidation is successful, it will run.

In summary:

- Both PL/SQL and Java have the same invalidation model. When an object is changed, its dependents are marked as invalid, thus leaving them in a state where a subsequent attempt to run them will cause revalidation.

- Both PL/SQL and Java have the same automatic recompilation model. If an object is invalid when invoked, an automatic (implicit) attempt to revalidate is done. If successful, the object is then run; otherwise, an error message is thrown.

- But PL/SQL and Java differ in the definition of "dependency" (i.e., the relationship among objects).

3.2   Turning Java in the Database into Stored Procedures

Once you've developed, loaded, compiled, and NCOMPed your Java applications in the database, the next step consists of "publishing" them to the SQL world. In other words, make the Java procedures and functions, their parameters/arguments, and return types known to the database dictionary as stored procedures and functions, callable from SQL, PL/SQL, and Java/J2EE in the middle tier (through JDBC) and any language that supports stored procedures/functions. Publishing is accomplished by means of user-defined or JPublisher-generated[4] PL/SQL wrappers, known in Oracle literature as Call Spec (short for Call Specification). Once published through the Call Spec, the mapping between the Java methods, the Java types, and

---

4.   See the JPublisher utility, covered in Part IV of this book.

SQL or PL/SQL types happens automatically, at runtime. The most challenging part in writing Call Spec is mapping SQL types or PL/SQL types to Java types and vice versa. This section describes the various Call Spec types; in the next section, we'll dive deeper into type mapping.

3.2.1 Call Spec Types

This section briefly describes the various types of call specifications, including top-level Call Spec, PL/SQL-packaged Call Spec, and object type Call Spec. Then, section 3.3 provides an extensive list of call specification examples.

Top-Level Call Spec

Top-level Call Specs publish Java static public methods as entry points to OracleJVM. These can be viewed as interfaces implemented by the Java methods. They are created either interactively, using command-line tools such as SQL*Plus, or offline (in SQL scripts files).

Syntax:

```
CREATE [OR REPLACE]

{ PROCEDURE procedure_name [(param[, param]...)]

| FUNCTION function_name [(param[, param]...)] RETURN
sql_type}

[AUTHID {DEFINER | CURRENT_USER}]

[PARALLEL_ENABLE]

[DETERMINISTIC]

{IS | AS} LANGUAGE JAVA

NAME 'method_fullname (java_type_fullname[,
java_type_fullname]...)
  [return java_type_fullname]';
```

- *procedure_name* uniquely identifies the Java method; it may have the same name as the Java method name; however, procedure_name must be different when publishing the Java method name. The full Java method names use dot notation; long names can be broken across lines at dot boundaries:

```
this.is.a.long.java.class.
        full.name()
```

- *param* represents the following syntax: parameter_name [IN | OUT | IN OUT] sql_type. There is a one-to-one correspondence between the Java method signature and the Call Spec parameters, which are mapped by position.

- the *AUTHID* clause determines whether a stored procedure executes with the privileges of its definer or invoker (the default).

- Note: The unqualified references to schema objects are resolved in the schema of the definer or invoker.

- The *PARALLEL_ENABLE* option declares that a stored function can be used safely in the slave sessions of parallel DML evaluations. See the Oracle Database SQL reference documentation for more details.

- The hint *DETERMINISTIC* helps the optimizer avoid redundant function calls. See the Oracle Database SQL reference documentation for more details.

Example of a Top-level Call Spec (from a *SQL*Plus* session):

```
create or replace procedure TrimLobSp as
 language java name 'TrimLob.main(java.lang.String[])';
/
show errors;
set serveroutput on
call dbms_java.set_output(50000);

call TrimLobSp();
```

PL/SQL Packaged Call Specs

PL/SQL Packaged Call Specs allow the grouping of multiple Call Spec methods belonging to the same Java class or belonging to the same functional package—or just for convenience—into a PL/SQL package. Unlike

Top-level Call Specs, in a PL/SQL Packaged Call Spec, the *procedure_name* **cannot** have the same name as the *java method name*. The package specification contains only the signature of the methods to be published.

Syntax:

```
CREATE [OR REPLACE] PACKAGE package_name

  [AUTHID {CURRENT_USER | DEFINER}] {IS | AS}

  [type_definition [type_definition] ...]

  [cursor_spec [cursor_spec] ...]

  [item_declaration [item_declaration] ...]

  [{subprogram_spec | call_spec} [{subprogram_spec | call_spec}]...]

END [package_name];
```

The package body contains the full Call Spec of the Java methods to be published.

```
[CREATE [OR REPLACE] PACKAGE BODY package_name {IS | AS}

  [type_definition [type_definition] ...]

  [cursor_body [cursor_body] ...]

  [item_declaration [item_declaration] ...]

  [{subprogram_spec | call_spec} [{subprogram_spec | call_spec}]...]

[BEGIN

  sequence_of_statements]
END [package_name];]
```

Example: The following user-defined PL/SQL Packaged PL/SQL Call Spec is from the "JDBC Callout to Non-Oracle Databases," covered in Chapter 4.

The Package Specification:

```
create or replace package JDBC_PKG is

    -- Public function and procedure declarations
    PROCEDURE setConnection (Driver IN VARCHAR2, Url IN VARCHAR2, User
IN VARCHAR2, dbPassword IN VARCHAR2, dbSchema IN VARCHAR2);

    PROCEDURE open;
    PROCEDURE execSQL (sqlString IN VARCHAR2, isQuery IN Boolean);
    FUNCTION afetch RETURN boolean;
    FUNCTION getColumnValue ( col IN number ) RETURN VARCHAR2;
    FUNCTION getColumnCount RETURN NUMBER;
    PROCEDURE commit;
    PROCEDURE rollback;
    PROCEDURE close;

end JDBC_PKG;
```

The Package Body:

```
create or replace package body JDBC_PKG is

    -- Function and procedure implementations
    PROCEDURE setConnection
    (Driver IN VARCHAR2, Url IN VARCHAR2, User IN VARCHAR2, dbPassword
IN VARCHAR2, dbSchema IN VARCHAR2)
        AS LANGUAGE JAVA
        NAME
'jdbcConnection.setConnection(java.lang.String,java.lang.String,java.
lang.String,java.lang.String,java.lang.String)';

    PROCEDURE open as
    LANGUAGE JAVA NAME 'jdbcConnection.open()';

    PROCEDURE execSQL
    (sqlString IN VARCHAR2, isQuery IN Boolean )
    AS LANGUAGE JAVA
    NAME 'jdbcConnection.execSQL(java.lang.String,boolean)';

    FUNCTION afetch RETURN boolean
    AS LANGUAGE JAVA
    NAME 'jdbcConnection.fetch() return java.lang.String';

    FUNCTION getColumnValue ( col IN number ) RETURN VARCHAR2
    AS LANGUAGE JAVA
```

```
    NAME 'jdbcConnection.getColumnValue(int) return
java.lang.String';

    FUNCTION getColumnCount RETURN NUMBER
    AS LANGUAGE JAVA
    NAME 'jdbcConnection.getColumnCount() return int';

    PROCEDURE commit AS
    LANGUAGE JAVA NAME 'jdbcConnection.commit()';

    PROCEDURE rollback AS
    LANGUAGE JAVA NAME 'jdbcConnection.rollback()';

    PROCEDURE close AS
    LANGUAGE JAVA NAME 'jdbcConnection.close()';
end JDBC_PKG;
```

The DBMS_JAVA package used abundantly throughout this book is an example of an Oracle-supplied PL/SQL Packaged Call Spec.

Object Type Call Spec

Top-level Call Spec and PL/SQL Packaged Call Spec can only publish public static Java methods. The data structures of user-defined object types are known as *attributes*. The member functions (or procedures) that define the behavior are known as *methods*. These can be written in Java (see section 3.3). Object Type Call Spec can publish member methods of object types that are either public static methods using the STATIC keyword or nonstatic methods (instance methods) using the MEMBER keyword. Nonstatic methods can accept or reference SELF, a built-in parameter that refers to the active instance of the object type. For SQLJ Object types (see section 3.3), the Java class must implement the standard java.sql.SQLData interface,[5] more specifically, the getSQLTypeName(), readSQL(), and writeSQL() methods.

Object Type Specification:

```
CREATE [OR REPLACE] TYPE type_name
    [AUTHID {CURRENT_USER | DEFINER}] {IS | AS} OBJECT (

    attribute_name datatype[, attribute_name datatype]...
```

---

5.   SQLData and JPublisher support for Object Types will be addressed in Part IV.

```
[{MAP | ORDER} MEMBER {function_spec | call_spec},]

[{MEMBER | STATIC} {subprogram_spec | call_spec}

[, {MEMBER | STATIC} {subprogram_spec | call_spec}]...]

);
```

Object Body Specification:

```
[CREATE [OR REPLACE] TYPE BODY type_name {IS | AS}

  { {MAP | ORDER} MEMBER function_body;

    | {MEMBER | STATIC} {subprogram_body | call_spec};}

  [{MEMBER | STATIC} {subprogram_body | call_spec};]...

END;]
```

```
Basicobjtyp.sql
===============

/*
 *  Basic Object type (scalar data types)
 *
 */

create or replace and resolve java source named BasicObjTyp as


import java.sql.*;
import java.io.*;
import oracle.sql.*;
import oracle.jdbc.*;

public class BasicObjTyp
{
  public static String fString (String s) { return s; }
  public static int fint (int n) { return n; }
  public static DATE fDATE (DATE d) { return d; }
```

```
      public static RAW fRAW (RAW r) { return r; }
}
/


set serveroutput on

create or replace type myobjtyp as object (
  num_attr number,
  chr_attr varchar2(20),
  dat_attr date,
  raw_attr raw(20),

  static function intfunc (x number) return number,
  static function strfunc (x varchar2) return varchar2,
  static function datfunc (x date) return date,
  static function rawfunc (x raw) return raw
);
/


create or replace type body myobjtyp as

  static function intfunc (x number) return number
        as language java name 'BasicObjTyp.fint(int)
        return int';

  static function strfunc (x varchar2) return varchar2
        as language java
        name 'BasicObjTyp.fString(java.lang.String)
        return java.lang.String';

  static function datfunc (x date) return date
        as language java
        name 'BasicObjTyp.fDATE(oracle.sql.DATE)
        return oracle.sql.DATE';

  static function rawfunc (x raw) return raw
        as language java
        name 'BasicObjTyp.fRAW(oracle.sql.RAW)
        return oracle.sql.RAW';
end;
/
```

```
rem
rem  Test Object type Call Spec
rem

declare
n number;
c varchar2(20);
d date;
r raw(20);
obj myobjtyp;

begin
  n := 469;
  c := 'Basic Object Type';
  d := '12-JUN-2005';
  r := '0102030405';

  obj := myobjtyp(n, c, d, r);

  dbms_output.put_line('*** Print Object Attributs ***');
  dbms_output.put_line(obj.num_attr);
  dbms_output.put_line(obj.chr_attr);
  dbms_output.put_line(obj.dat_attr);
  dbms_output.put_line(obj.raw_attr);
  dbms_output.put_line('** Invoke Object Methods *** ');
  dbms_output.put_line(myobjtyp.intfunc(n));
  dbms_output.put_line(myobjtyp.strfunc(c));
  dbms_output.put_line(myobjtyp.rawfunc(r));
  dbms_output.put_line(myobjtyp.datfunc(d));
  dbms_output.put_line('**** ');
end;
/


*** Print Object Attributs ***
469
Basic Object Type
12-JUN-05
0102030405
```

```
*** Invoke Object Methods  ***
469
Basic Object Type
0102030405
12-JUN-05
****
PL/SQL procedure successfully completed.

SQL>
```

3.3   Mapping SQL and PL/SQL Types to/from Java Types

Defining a Call Spec that matches the Java signature can be challenging and is the root cause of the most frequent error message when invoking Java in the database (see section 3.4.5). It is important to understand type mapping, but you can avoid the pain, the hassle, and the mistakes by just using JPublisher to do it for you, as we will see in Part II, III, and IV (covering JDBC, SQLJ, and JPublisher). This section provides an extensive but still not exhaustive list of mapping the different SQL and PL/SQL types to Java (and vice versa). Let's start by looking at the mapping matrix.

3.3.1   Mapping Matrix

Tables 3.2 and 3.3 provide the mapping of SQL and PL/SQL types to Java/JDBC types supported by the Oracle Database, including Java in the database, JDBC, SQLJ, and JPublisher. These tables will serve as a reference in the following examples.

1.   `oracle.sql.NCHAR`, `oracle.sql.NCLOB`, and `oracle.sql.NString` are not part of JDBC but are distributed with the JPublisher runtime (see Part IV) to represent the NCHAR form of `oracle.sql.CHAR`, `oracle.sql.CLOB` and `java.lang.String`.

2.   See JPublisher "Type Map" in Part IV of this book.

3.   SQL URL types, also known as "data links," are mapped to `java.net.URL`.

4.   Mapping of PL/SQL `BOOLEAN` to SQL `NUMBER` and Java boolean is defined in the default JPublisher type map.

Table 3.2   *Mapping SQL and PL/SQL Types to Java and JDBC Types*

SQL Types, and PL/SQL Types	Oracle JDBC Mapping*	Standard Java Mapping
`CHAR, CHARACTER, LONG, STRING, VARCHAR, VARCHAR2`	`oracle.sql.CHAR`	`java.lang.String, java.sql.Date, java.sql.Time, java.sql.Timestamp, java.lang.Byte, java.lang.Short, java.lang.Integer, java.lang.Long, java.sql.Float, java.lang.Double, java.math.BigDecimal, byte, short, int, long, float, double`
`NUMBER`	`oracle.sql.NUMBER`	`java.lang.Byte, java.lang.Short, java.lang.Integer, java.lang.Long, java.sql.Float, java.lang.Double, java.math.BigDecimal, byte, short, int, long, float, double`
`DATE`	`oracle.sql.DATE`	`java.sql.Date, java.sql.Time, java.sql.Timestamp, java.lang.String`
`NCHAR, NVARCHAR2`	`oracle.sql.NCHAR (note 1)`	`n/a`
`RAW, LONG RAW`	`oracle.sql.RAW`	`byte[]`
`BINARY_INTEGER, NATURAL, NATURALN, PLS_INTEGER, POSITIVE, POSITIVEN, SIGNTYPE, INT, INTEGER`	`oracle.sql.NUMBER`	`int, java.lang.Integer`
`DEC, DECIMAL, NUMBER, NUMERIC`	`oracle.sql.NUMBER`	`java.math.BigDecimal`

Table 3.2   *Mapping SQL and PL/SQL Types to Java and JDBC Types (continued)*

SQL Types, and PL/SQL Types	Oracle JDBC Mapping[*]	Standard Java Mapping
DOUBLE PRECISION, FLOAT	oracle.sql.NUMBER	Double, java.lang.Double
SMALLINT	oracle.sql.NUMBER	short, Int
REAL	oracle.sql.NUMBER	Float, Float
TIMESTAMP TIMESTAMP WITH TZ TIMESTAMP WITH LOCAL TZ	oracle.sql.DATE, oracle.sql.TIMESTAMP oracle.sql.TIMESTAMPTZ oracle.sql.TIMESTAMPLTZ	java.sql.Date, java.sql.Time, java.sql.Timestamp, byte[]
INTERVAL YEAR TO MONTH INTERVAL DAY TO SECOND	String (note 2)	String (note 2)
URITYPE DBURITYPE XDBURITYPE HTTPURITYPE	java.net.URL (note 3)	java.net.URL (note 3)
ROWID	oracle.sql.ROWID, oracle.sql.CHAR	java.sql.String
BOOLEAN	boolean (note 4)	boolean (note 4)
CLOB LOCATOR	oracle.sql.CLOB	java.sql.Clob
BLOB LOCATOR	oracle.sql.BLOB	java.sql.Blob
BFILE	oracle.sql.BFILE	n/a
NCLOB	oracle.sql.NCLOB (note 1)	n/a
User-defined objects types	oracle.sql.STRUCT, oracle.sql.ORAData	java.sql.Struct, java.sql.SqlData
User-defined collection	oracle.sql.ARRAY, oracle.sql.ORAData	java.sql.Array
OPAQUE types	oracle.sql.OPAQUE	Generated or predefined class (note 5)
RECORD types	Through mapping to SQL object type (note 5)	Through mapping to SQL object type (note 5)

Table 3.2   *Mapping SQL and PL/SQL Types to Java and JDBC Types (continued)*

SQL Types, and PL/SQL Types	Oracle JDBC Mapping[*]	Standard Java Mapping
Nested table, VARRAY	oracle.sql.ARRAY, oracle.sql.ORAData	java.sql.Array
Reference to SQL object type	oracle.sql.REF, oracle.sql.SQLRef, oracle.sql.ORAData	java.sql.Ref
REF CURSOR	oracle.jdbc.OracleResultSet	java.sql.ResultSet
Indexed-by tables	Through mapping to SQL collection (note 6)	Through mapping to SQL collection (note 6)
Scalar Indexed-by tables (numeric or character)	Through mapping to java array (note 7)	Through mapping to java array (note 7)
User-defined subtypes	Same as base type	Same as base type

[*]   The **oracle.sql.*** datatypes lets you store and retrieve data without loosing information/precision.

5.   Java classes implementing the `oracle.sql.ORAData` interface.

6.   See JPublisher "Type Mapping Support for PL/SQL RECORD and Indexed by Table Types" in Part IV.

7.   See JPublisher "Type Mapping Support for Scalar Indexed by Tables" in Part IV.

Table 3.3   *Mapping Java Types to Oracle Types*

	Java Types	Oracle Types (SQL and PL/SQL)
Primitive (Built-in) Types		
	boolean, byte, short, int, long, float, double	NUMBER
	java.lang.String	CHAR, VARCHAR2,LONG
	byte[]	RAW, LONGRAW
	java.sql.Date, java.sql.Time, java.sql.Timestamp	DATE

Table 3.3 *Mapping Java Types to Oracle Types (continued)*

	Java Types	Oracle Types (SQL and PL/SQL)
	`java.math.BigDecimal`	NUMBER
Reference Types (Wrapper Classes)		

	`java.lang.Boolean,`
	`java.lang.Byte,`
	`java.lang.short,`
	`java.lang.Integer,`
	`java.lang.Long,`
	`java.lang.Float,`
	`java.lang.Double`
		NUMBER

JDBC 2.0 Mapping		
	`java.sql.Clob`	CLOB
	`java.sql.Blob`	BLOB
	`java.sql.Struct`	STRUCT
	`java.sql.Ref`	REF
	`java.sql.Array`	ARRAY
Oracle Extensions		
	`oracle.sql.NUMBER`	NUMBER
	`oracle.sql.CHAR`	CHAR
	`oracle.sql.RAW`	RAW
	`oracle.sql.DATE`	DATE
	`oracle.sql.ROWID`	ROWID
	`oracle.sql.BLOB`	BLOB
	`oracle.sql.CLOB`	CLOB
	`oracle.sql.BFILE`	BFILE
	`oracle.sql.STRUCT`	STRUCT
	`oracle.sql.REF`	REF
	`oracle.sql.ARRAY`	ARRAY

3.3.2   Code Segments for Mapping

In this section, you will find code segments that will help you map both simple and complex SQL and PL/SQL types to the corresponding Java types, including Strings, Numbers, Int, Date, Float, BLOB LOCATOR, CLOB LOCATOR, Opaque types, VARRAY (Scalar, ADT), NESTED TABLE (Scalar, ADT), and so on. The purpose of these code segments is to show the mapping between SQL and Java—which can be challenging—not to show the functionality of the data types in question.

Setup

Listing 3.2 will create a table, TypesTab, with the various column types that we will use later to map Java states to SQL columns.

Listing 3.2   *TypesTab.sql*

```
===========================
connect scott/tiger
set echo on

drop table TypesTab;

create table TypesTab(
    num number,
    bfloat binary_float,
    bdouble binary_double,
    vchar2 varchar2(24),
    xchar char(24),
    xraw raw(24),
    xdat date);

insert into TypesTab values (
    111,
    10000000.000001,
    1000000000000.000000002,
    'this is a varchar2',
    'this is a char',
    hextoraw (lpad ('b', 24, 'b')),
    '19-Apr-2005');
commit;
```

```
SQL> select * from TypesTab;

       NUM      BFLOAT    BDOUBLE VCHAR2
---------- ---------- ---------- ------------------------
XCHAR                      XRAW
------------------------ -------------------------------------------
----
XDAT
---------
       111    1.0E+007   1.0E+012 this is a varchar2
this is a char            BBBBBBBBBBBBBBBBBBBBBBBB
19-APR-05
SQL>
```

Mapping java.sql.Date to/from SQL DATE

This code sample maps a SQL DATE column to java.sql.Date and vice versa. The same technique can be utilized to map java.sql.Time, java.sql.Timestamp, and java.lang.String to DATE (see Table 3.2). Mapping oracle.sql.DATE to SQL DATE is shown in Listing 3.3. This example uses JDBC PreparedStatement and executeQuery, which will be described in the Part II.

Listing 3.3 *javasqlDate.sql*

```
==========================

create or replace java source named javasqlDate as
/*
 * Mapping java.sql.Date  to/from SQL DATE
 */

import java.sql.*;
import java.io.*;
import oracle.sql.*;
import oracle.jdbc.*;

public class javasqlDate
{

/*
 * Update SQL DATE column with java.sql.Date
 */
```

```
public static void xputDat (Date x) throws SQLException
{
  Connection conn =
   DriverManager.getConnection("jdbc:default:connection:");

   PreparedStatement ps =
      conn.prepareStatement("UPDATE TypesTab SET xdat = ?");
   ps.setDate (1, x);
   ps.execute();
   ps.close();
}


/*
 * Rerieve SQL DATE column as java.sql.Date
 */

public static String xgetDat() throws SQLException
{
 Connection conn =
  DriverManager.getConnection("jdbc:default:connection:");
  Statement stmt = conn.createStatement();
  Date dat = null;
  ResultSet rs = stmt.executeQuery("SELECT xdat FROM TypesTab");
  while (rs.next())
  {
    dat = rs.getDate(1);
  }
  stmt.close();
  return dat.toString();
 }
}
/
show errors;
alter java source javasqlDate compile;
show errors;

create or replace procedure putjavaDate (x DATE)
  as language java
  name 'javasqlDate.xputDat (java.sql.Date)';
/
```

```
show errors;

create or replace function getjavaDate return VARCHAR2
  as language java
  name 'javasqlDate.xgetDat() return java.lang.String';
/
show errors;

call putjavaDate(sysdate);
set serveroutput on
select getjavaDate from dual;
```

Mapping oracle.sql.DATE to/from SQL DATE

Listing 3.4 is similar to Listing 3.3, except that it maps the SQL DATE column to oracle.sql.DATE instead of java.sql.Date.

Listing 3.4   *orasqlDATE.sql*

```
===============================

create or replace java source named orasqlDATE as
/*
 * Mapping oracle.sql.DATE  to/from SQL DATE
 */
import java.sql.*;
import java.io.*;
import oracle.sql.*;
import oracle.jdbc.*;

public class orasqlDATE
{

/*
 * Update SQL DATE with oracle.sql.DATE
 */
 public static void xputDat (DATE x) throws SQLException
 {
    Connection conn =
    DriverManager.getConnection("jdbc:default:connection:");
    OraclePreparedStatement ops = (OraclePreparedStatement)
       conn.prepareStatement("UPDATE TypesTab SET xdat = ?");
    ops.setDATE (1, x);
```

```
      ops.execute();
      ops.close();
  }

 /*
  * Retrieve SQL DATE column as oracle.sq.DATE
  */
  public static DATE xgetDat() throws SQLException
  {
    Connection conn =
        DriverManager.getConnection("jdbc:default:connection:");
    OracleStatement ostmt = (OracleStatement) conn.createStatement();
    DATE dat = new DATE();
    OracleResultSet ors =
        (OracleResultSet) ostmt.executeQuery("SELECT xdat FROM
TypesTab");
    while (ors.next())
    {
      dat = ors.getDATE(1);
    }
    ostmt.close();
    return dat;
  }
}
/
show errors;
alter java source orasqlDATE compile;
show errors;

create or replace procedure putoraDATE (x DATE)
  as language java
  name 'orasqlDATE.xputDat (oracle.sql.DATE)';
/
show errors;

create or replace function getoraDATE return DATE
  as language java
  name 'orasqlDATE.xgetDat() return oracle.sql.DATE';
/
show errors;

call putoraDATE(sysdate);
```

```
set serveroutput on
select getoraDATE() from dual;
```

Mapping java.lang.Integer to/from SQL NUMBER

Listing 3.5 maps an int and/or java.lang.Integer to SQL NUMBER and vice versa. The same technique can be utilized to map java.lang.Byte, java.lang.Short, java.lang.Integer, java.lang.Long, java.sql.Float, java.lang.Double, java.math.BigDecimal, byte, short, long, float, and double (see Table 3.2). Mapping oracle.sql.NUMBER to SQL NUMBER is shown in Listing 3.5.

Listing 3.5   *javalangInt.sql*

```
================================
create or replace java source named javalangInt as

/*
 * Mapping int, java.lang.Integer to/from SQL NUMBER
 */
import java.sql.*;
import java.io.*;
import java.lang.Integer;
import oracle.sql.*;
import oracle.jdbc.*;

public class javalangInt
{

  /*
   * Update SQL NUMBER column with java.lang.Integer
   */

  public static void xputInt (Integer x) throws SQLException
  {
    Connection conn =
    DriverManager.getConnection("jdbc:default:connection:");
    PreparedStatement ps =
       conn.prepareStatement("UPDATE TypesTab SET num = ?");
    int n = x.intValue();
    ps.setInt (1, n);
    ps.execute();
    ps.close();
```

```
    }

    /*
     * Retrieve SQL NUMBER column as int
     */

  public static int xgetInt() throws SQLException
  {
    Connection conn =
    DriverManager.getConnection("jdbc:default:connection:");
    Statement stmt = conn.createStatement();
    int n = 0;
    ResultSet rs = stmt.executeQuery("SELECT num FROM TypesTab");
    while (rs.next())
    {
      n = rs.getInt(1);
    }
    stmt.close();
    return n;
  }
}
/
show errors;
alter java source javalangInt compile;
show errors;

create or replace procedure putjavaInt (n NUMBER)
  as language java
  name 'javalangInt.xputInt (java.lang.Integer)';
/
show errors;

create or replace function getjavaInt return NUMBER
  as language java
  name 'javalangInt.xgetInt() return int';
/
show errors;

call putjavaInt(888);
set serveroutput on
select getjavaInt from dual;
```

Mapping oracle.sql.NUMBER to SQL NUMBER

Listing 3.6 is similar to Listing 3.5, except that it maps SQL NUMBER to oracle.sql.NUMBER instead of java.lang.Integer.

Listing 3.6   *orasqlNUMB.sql*
================================

```
create or replace java source named orasqlNUMB as
/*
 * Mapping oracle.sql.NUMBER  to/from SQL NUMBER
 */
import java.sql.*;
import java.io.*;
import oracle.sql.*;
import oracle.jdbc.*;

public class orasqlNUMB
{

/*
 * Map oracle.sql.NUMBER to SQL NUMBER
 */
  public static void xputNum (NUMBER n) throws SQLException
  {
    Connection conn =
    DriverManager.getConnection("jdbc:default:connection:");


    OraclePreparedStatement ops = (OraclePreparedStatement)
       conn.prepareStatement("UPDATE TypesTab SET num = ?");
    ops.setNUMBER (1, n);
    ops.execute();
    ops.close();
  }


  /*
   * Map SQL NUMBER column to oracle.sq.NUMBER
   */
  public static NUMBER xgetNum() throws SQLException
  {
```

```
        Connection conn =
        DriverManager.getConnection("jdbc:default:connection:");
        OracleStatement ostmt = (OracleStatement) conn.createStatement();
        NUMBER onb = new NUMBER();
        OracleResultSet ors =
            (OracleResultSet) ostmt.executeQuery("SELECT num FROM
TypesTab");
        while (ors.next())
        {
          onb = ors.getNUMBER(1);
        }
        ostmt.close();
        return onb;
    }
}
/
show errors;
alter java source orasqlNUMB compile;
show errors;

create or replace procedure putoraNUMB (n NUMBER)
  as language java
  name 'orasqlNUMB.xputNum (oracle.sql.NUMBER)';
/
show errors;

create or replace function getoraNUMB return NUMBER
  as language java
  name 'orasqlNUMB.xgetNum() return oracle.sql.NUMBER';
/
show errors;

call putoraNUMB(999);
set serveroutput on
select getoraNUMB from dual;
```

Mapping oracle.sql.CHAR to/from SQL CHAR

Listing 3.7 maps a CHAR column to oracle.sql.CHAR and vice versa. The same technique can be used to map CHARACTER, LONG, STRING, and VARCHAR2 to the corresponding standard Java mapping (see Table 3.2).

Listing 3.7   *orasqlCHAR.sql*

```
================================

create or replace java source named orasqlCHAR as
/*
 * Mapping oracle.sql.CHAR to/from SQL CHAR
 */
import java.sql.*;
import java.io.*;
import oracle.sql.*;
import oracle.jdbc.*;

public class orasqlCHAR
{

 /*
  * Update SQL CHAR column with oracle.sql.CHAR
  */

  public static void xputChar (CHAR c) throws SQLException
  {
    Connection conn =
    DriverManager.getConnection("jdbc:default:connection:");


    OraclePreparedStatement ops = (OraclePreparedStatement)
       conn.prepareStatement("UPDATE TypesTab SET xchar = ?");
    ops.setCHAR (1, c);
    ops.execute();
    ops.close();
  }


  /*
   * Retrieve SQL CHAR column as oracle.sq.CHAR
   */

  public static CHAR xgetChar() throws SQLException
  {
    Connection conn =
```

```
      DriverManager.getConnection("jdbc:default:connection:");
      OracleStatement ostmt = (OracleStatement) conn.createStatement();
      String ochar = null;
      OracleResultSet ors =
          (OracleResultSet) ostmt.executeQuery("SELECT xchar FROM
TypesTab");
      while (ors.next())
      {
        ochar = ors.getString(1);
      }
      ostmt.close();
      return new CHAR(ochar, null);
  }
}
/
show errors;
alter java source orasqlCHAR compile;
show errors;

create or replace procedure putoraCHAR (c CHAR)
  as language java
  name 'orasqlCHAR.xputChar (oracle.sql.CHAR)';
/
show errors;

create or replace function getoraCHAR return CHAR
  as language java
  name 'orasqlCHAR.xgetChar() return oracle.sql.CHAR';
/
show errors;

call putoraCHAR('Foooooooooooo');
set serveroutput on
select getoraCHAR from dual;
```

Mapping oracle.sql.RAW to/from SQL RAW

Listing 3.8 maps a RAW column to `oracle.sql.RAW`, and the same technique can be used to map LONG RAW to a java byte array (see Table 3.2).

Listing 3.8   *orasqlRAW.sql*

```
==============================

create or replace java source named orasqlRAW as
/*
 * Mapping oracle.sql.RAW  to/from SQL RAW
 */
import java.sql.*;
import java.io.*;
import oracle.sql.*;
import oracle.jdbc.*;

public class orasqlRAW
{

 /*
  * Update a SQL RAW column to oracle.sql.RAW
  */

 public static void xputRAW (RAW r) throws SQLException
 {
   Connection conn =
   DriverManager.getConnection("jdbc:default:connection:");

   OraclePreparedStatement ops = (OraclePreparedStatement)
      conn.prepareStatement("UPDATE TypesTab SET xraw = ?");
   ops.setRAW (1, r);
   ops.execute();
   ops.close();
 }


  /*
   * Retrieve a SQL RAW column as oracle.sq.RAW
   */

 public static RAW xgetRAW() throws SQLException
 {
   Connection conn =
   DriverManager.getConnection("jdbc:default:connection:");
```

```
    OracleStatement ostmt = (OracleStatement) conn.createStatement();
    RAW oraw = new RAW();
    OracleResultSet ors =
        (OracleResultSet) ostmt.executeQuery("SELECT xraw FROM
TypesTab");
    while (ors.next())
    {
      oraw = ors.getRAW(1);
    }
    ostmt.close();
    return oraw;
  }
}
/
show errors;
alter java source orasqlRAW compile;
show errors;

create or replace procedure putoraRAW (c RAW)
  as language java
  name 'orasqlRAW.xputRAW (oracle.sql.RAW)';
/
show errors;

create or replace function getoraRAW return RAW
  as language java
  name 'orasqlRAW.xgetRAW() return oracle.sql.RAW';
/
show errors;

call putoraRAW('Foooooooooooo');
set serveroutput on
select getoraRAW from dual;
```

Setup for CLOB, BLOB, and BFILE Mapping

This script creates and populates a table of BLOB, CLOB, and BFILE columns used in the next three examples. Per the Oracle Database Glossary,[6] these are defined as follows:

- *Binary FILE (BFILE)* is a LOB data type that represents a binary file residing in the file system, outside of the database datafiles and tablespace (also referred to as an **external LOB**).

- *Binary Large Object (BLOB)* is a LOB data type that contains binary data and is used to hold unstructured data (also referred to as **persistent LOBs** because it resides in the database).

- *Character Large Object (CLOB)* is a LOB data type that contains character data in the database character set. A CLOB may be indexed and searched by the interMedia Text search engine.

Steps

1. Copy and paste a random pdf file as `Figure1.pdf`, `Figure2.pdf`, and `Figure3.pdf`, under `C:\temp` or equivalent directory (i.e., `/tmp`).

2. Connect under a DBA account (i.e., system or sys-as-sysdba) and grant the SCOTT schema the right to create an alias directory in the database as follows:

```
SQL> grant create any directory to scott;
SQL> exit
```

Run the following script as SCOTT. Notice the use of `EMPTY_BLOB` and `EMPTY_CLOB` SQL function for returning an empty LOB locator to initialize the LOB variable or column before populating the LOB in question.

```
XobTypesTab.sql
===============
connect scott/tiger
rem
rem Create a file system directory alias in the database
rem

create or replace directory bfiledir as 'C:\TEMP';

drop table Xobtab;

create table XobTab (id number, blob_col blob, clob_col clob,
bfile_col bfile);

insert into XobTab values (1, empty_blob(), empty_clob(),
```

```
          bfilename('BFILEDIR', 'Figure1.pdf'));

insert into XobTab values (2, hextoraw(lpad('b', 1500, 'b')),
    lpad('c', 3500, 'c'), bfilename('BFILEDIR', 'Figure2.pdf'));

insert into XobTab values (3, hextoraw(lpad('b', 2000, 'b')),
    lpad('c', 4000, 'c'), bfilename('BFILEDIR', 'Figure3.pdf'));

commit;
```

Mapping CLOB Locator to/from java.sql.Clob

In reality, all LOB data types store a locator, which points to the actual storage inside or outside of the database. Listing 3.9 maps a CLOB locator column to java.sq.Clob.

1. Inserts a new CLOB into the database using JDBC PreparedStatement.

2. Appends text to the inserted CLOB using JDBC CallableStatement and PL/SQL DBMS_LOB_WRITEAPPEND procedure.

3. Returns the locator of the updated/modified CLOB and the augmented NUMBER. The PL/SQL procedure Clobwrap wraps the method Clobproc and takes a NUMBER and a CLOB as IN/OUT parameters. The same technique can be used to map CLOB to oracle.sql.CLOB. The JDBC techniques for inserting and retrieving LOB will be covered in Part II.

Listing 3.9   *ClobMap.sql*

```
========================
create or replace and resolve java source named ClobClass   as
/*
 *ClobClass.java
 */

import java.sql.*;
import oracle.sql.*;
import oracle.jdbc.*;

public class ClobClass
```

```
{
  /*
   * Insert a Clob into XobTab and returns the modified Clob
   * IN and OUT parameters are passed as arrays (of NUMBER, Blob)
   */

  public static void Clobproc (NUMBER id[], Clob cl[]) throws
SQLException
  {
    Connection conn = DriverManager.getConnection
("jdbc:oracle:kprb:");
    Statement stmt = conn.createStatement();

    OraclePreparedStatement ps = (OraclePreparedStatement)
       conn.prepareStatement ("INSERT INTO XobTab (ID, Clob_col)
VALUES(?, ?)");

    ps.setNUMBER (1, id[0]);
    ps.setClob (2, cl[0]);
    ps.execute ();
    ps.close();

    String buf = "This is an Outbound CLOB";
    long amount = buf.length();

    OracleCallableStatement cs =
      (OracleCallableStatement)
        conn.prepareCall ("begin dbms_lob.writeappend (?, ?, ?);
end;");

    cs.setClob (1, cl[0]);
    cs.setLong (2, amount);
    cs.setString (3, buf);
    cs.registerOutParameter (1, OracleTypes.CLOB);
    cs.execute ();

    cl[0] = cs.getClob (1);
    id[0] = new NUMBER(id[0].intValue() + 1000);
    cs.close();
  }
}
/
```

```
show errors;

create or replace procedure Clobwrap (x IN OUT number, y IN OUT Clob)
  as language java
  name 'ClobClass.Clobproc(oracle.sql.NUMBER[], java.sql.Clob[])';
/

show errors;
set serveroutput on
declare
x Clob;
a number;
begin
  select id+200, Clob_col into a, x from Xobtab where id = 1 for
update;

  dbms_output.put_line('IN ID NUMBER = ' || a);
  dbms_output.put_line('IN CLOB length = ' || dbms_lob.getlength(x));

  Clobwrap(a, x);

  dbms_output.put_line('OUT ID NUMBER = ' || a);
  dbms_output.put_line('OUT CLOB length = ' ||
dbms_lob.getlength(x));
end;
/
```

Mapping java.sql.Blob to/from SQL BLOB

Listing 3.10 maps a BLOB locator column to java.sq.Blob.

1.   Inserts a new BLOB into the database using JDBC Prepared-Statement.

2.   Appends text to the inserted BLOB using JDBC CallableStatement and PL/SQL DBMS_LOB.WRITEAPPEND procedure.

3.   Returns the locator of the updated/modified BLOB and the augmented NUMBER. The PL/SQL procedure Blobwrap wraps the method Blobproc and takes a NUMBER and a BLOB as IN/OUT parameters. The same technique can be used to map BLOB to oracle.sql.BLOB.

Listing 3.10 *BlobMap.sql*

```
========================

create or replace and resolve java source named BlobClass  as
/*
 *BlobClass.java
 */

import java.sql.*;
import oracle.sql.*;
import oracle.jdbc.*;

public class BlobClass
{
  /*
   * Insert a BLOB into XobTab and returns the modified BLOB
   * Notice IN and OUT parameters are passed as array of NUMBER
andarray of Blob
   */


  public static void Blobproc (NUMBER id[], Blob bl[]) throws
SQLException
  {
    Connection conn = DriverManager.getConnection
("jdbc:oracle:kprb:");
    Statement stmt = conn.createStatement();

    OraclePreparedStatement ps = (OraclePreparedStatement)
      conn.prepareStatement ("INSERT INTO XobTab (ID, blob_col)
VALUES(?, ?)");

    ps.setNUMBER (1, id[0]);
    ps.setBlob (2, bl[0]);
    ps.execute ();
    ps.close();

    byte[] buf = { 00, 01, 02, 03, 04, 05, 00, 01, 02, 03, 04, 05,
                   00, 01, 02, 03, 04, 05, 00, 01, 02, 03, 04, 05,
                   00, 01, 02, 03, 04, 05, 00, 01, 02, 03, 04, 05 };
    long amount = buf.length;
```

```
    OracleCallableStatement cs =
      (OracleCallableStatement)
        conn.prepareCall ("begin dbms_lob.writeappend (?, ?, ?);
end;");

    cs.setBlob (1, bl[0]);
    cs.setLong (2, amount);
    cs.setRAW (3, new RAW(buf));
    cs.registerOutParameter (1, OracleTypes.BLOB);
    cs.execute ();

    bl[0] = cs.getBlob (1);
    id[0] = new NUMBER(id[0].intValue() + 1000);
    cs.close();
  }
}
/
show errors;

create or replace procedure blobwrap (x IN OUT number, y IN OUT blob)
  as language java
  name 'BlobClass.Blobproc(oracle.sql.NUMBER[], java.sql.Blob[])';
/

show errors;
set serveroutput on
declare
x blob;
a number;
begin
  select id+100, blob_col into a, x from Xobtab where id = 1 for
update;

  dbms_output.put_line('IN ID NUMBER = ' || a);
  dbms_output.put_line('IN BLOB length = ' || dbms_lob.getlength(x));

  Blobwrap(a, x);

  dbms_output.put_line('OUT ID NUMBER = ' || a);
  dbms_output.put_line('OUT BLOB length = ' ||
dbms_lob.getlength(x));
end;
/
```

Mapping oracle.sql.BFILE to/from SQL BFILE

Listing 3.11 illustrates mapping the BFILE data type to JDBC type
oracle.sql.BFILE. The PL/SQL procedure Bfilewrap wraps the method
Bfileproc and takes a NUMBER and a BFILE as IN/OUT parameters and
a BFILE as an IN parameter. This method uses the PL/SQL
DBMS_LOB.FILEOPEN, which opens the bfile in read-only mode (remember
we are manipulating PDF files). It also uses JDBC PreparedStatement and
CallableStatement, which are described in Part II.

Listing 3.11   *BfileMap.sql*

```
===========================
create or replace and resolve java source named BfileClass   as
/*
 *BfileClass.java
 */

import java.sql.*;
import oracle.sql.*;
import oracle.jdbc.*;

public class BfileClass
{
  /*
   * Insert a Bfile into XobTab and returns the modified Bfile
   * Notice IN and OUT parameters are passed as array of NUMBER
   * and array of Blob
   */

  public static void Bfileproc (NUMBER id[], BFILE bf[], BFILE bf2)
     throws SQLException
  {
    Connection conn = DriverManager.getConnection
("jdbc:oracle:kprb:");
    Statement stmt = conn.createStatement();

    OraclePreparedStatement ps = (OraclePreparedStatement)
       conn.prepareStatement ("INSERT INTO XobTab (ID, Bfile_col)
VALUES(?, ?)");

    ps.setNUMBER (1, id[0]);
```

```
    ps.setBFILE (2, bf[0]);
    ps.execute ();
    ps.close();

    OracleCallableStatement cs =
      (OracleCallableStatement)
        conn.prepareCall ("begin dbms_lob.fileopen (?, 0); end;");

    cs.setBFILE (1, bf2);
    cs.registerOutParameter (1, OracleTypes.BFILE);
    cs.execute ();

    bf[0] = cs.getBFILE (1);
    id[0] = new NUMBER(id[0].intValue() + 1000);
    cs.close();
  }
}
/
show errors;

Rem
Rem Call Spec for the Bfileproc method, mapping Bfile to
Rem oracle.sql.BFILE
Rem
create or replace procedure Bfilewrap (x IN OUT number, y IN OUT
Bfile, z bfile)  as language java
  name 'BfileClass.Bfileproc(oracle.sql.NUMBER[], oracle.sql.BFILE[],
oracle.sql.BFILE)';
/


show errors;
set serveroutput on

declare
x bfile;
y bfile;
a number;
begin
  select id+300, bfile_col into a, x from XobTab where id = 1;
  select bfile_col into y from XobTab where id = 3;
```

```
  dbms_output.put_line('IN ID NUMBER = ' || a);
  dbms_output.put_line('IN BFILE length = ' ||
dbms_lob.getlength(x));

  Bfilewrap(a, x, y);

  dbms_output.put_line('OUT ID NUMBER = ' || a);
  dbms_output.put_line('OUT BFILE length = ' ||
dbms_lob.getlength(x));
end;
/
```

Mapping User-Defined Object Types to oracle.sql.STRUCT

This script (`XADTTab.sql`) creates a user-defined object type, ADTTYP2, and then creates a table, ADTTAB2, of ADT TYP2 objects, which will be used to map ADTTYP2 objects to `oracle.sql.STRUCT`.

```
XADTTab.sql
===========
create type ADTTYP2 as object (n1 number, n2 varchar2(30), n3 date)
/
create table ADTTAB2 (id number, adtcol ADTTYP2)
/

insert into ADTTAB2 values (1, ADTTYP2(101, 'Row One', '01-JAN-
2001'));
insert into ADTTAB2 values (2, ADTTYP2(102, 'Row Two', '02-JAN-
2002'));
insert into ADTTAB2 values (3, null);
insert into ADTTAB2 values (4, ADTTYP2(104, 'Row Four', '04-JAN-
2004'));
insert into ADTTAB2 values (5, ADTTYP2(105, 'Row Five', '05-JAN-
2005'));
commit;
```

The following code sample, `ADTTab.sql`, creates and compiles `ADTTabClass` directly into the database. The class has two methods: `ADTTabProc()` and `ADTTabFunc()`; the corresponding Call Specs have the same name as the Java methods.

- The method ADTTabClass.ADTTabProc takes an array of NUM-BER as IN/OUT parameter, an array of STRUCT as IN/OUT parameter, a STRUCT as IN parameter, and inserts an oracle.sql.STRUCT into the ADTTyp2 type table.

■ The function ADTTabClass.ADTTabFunc takes an array of NUMBER as IN/OUT parameter, an array of STRUCT as IN/OUT parameter, a STRUCT as IN parameter, and retrieves and returns an instance of ADTTyp2 as oracle.sql.STRUCT.

```
ADTTab.sql
==========
create or replace and resolve java source named ADTTabClass   as
/*
 *Mapping ADT Table to oracle.sql.STRUCT
 */

import java.sql.*;
import oracle.sql.*;
import oracle.jdbc.*;

public class ADTTabClass
{

 /*
  * inserts an oracle.sql.STRUCT object into an ADT Type table
  */

  public static void ADTTabProc (NUMBER id[], STRUCT adt[], STRUCT
adt2)
     throws SQLException
  {
    Connection conn = DriverManager.getConnection
("jdbc:oracle:kprb:");
    Statement stmt = conn.createStatement();

    OraclePreparedStatement ps = (OraclePreparedStatement)
       conn.prepareStatement ("INSERT INTO ADTTAB2 (ID, ADTCOL)
VALUES(?, ?)");

    ps.setNUMBER (1, id[0]);
    ps.setSTRUCT (2, adt[0]);
    ps.execute ();
    ps.close();
```

```
      id[0] = new NUMBER(id[0].intValue() + 1000);
      adt[0] = adt2;
  }


 /*
  * retrieves an ADT as oracle.sql.STRUCT
  */


   public static STRUCT ADTTabFunc (NUMBER id[], STRUCT adt[], STRUCT
adt2) throws SQLException
   {
     Connection conn = DriverManager.getConnection
("jdbc:oracle:kprb:");
     Statement stmt = conn.createStatement();

     OraclePreparedStatement ps = (OraclePreparedStatement)
        conn.prepareStatement ("SELECT ADTCOL FROM ADTTAB2 WHERE ID =
?");

     ps.setNUMBER (1, id[0]);
     OracleResultSet rs = (OracleResultSet) ps.executeQuery();

     STRUCT st = null;

     while (rs.next())
     {
       st = (STRUCT) rs.getObject(1);
     }
     ps.close();

     id[0] = new NUMBER(id[0].intValue() + 1000);
     adt[0] = adt2;

     return st;
   }
}
/

show errors;

create or replace procedure ADTTabProc (x IN OUT number, y IN OUT
ADTTYP2, z IN ADTTYP2)
```

```
    as language java
    name 'ADTTabClass.ADTTabProc(oracle.sql.NUMBER[],
oracle.sql.STRUCT[],
        oracle.sql.STRUCT)';
/
show errors;
create or replace function ADTTabFunc (x IN OUT number, y IN OUT
ADTTYP2, z IN ADTTYP2)
    return ADTTYP2 as language java
    name 'ADTTabClass.ADTTabFunc(oracle.sql.NUMBER[],
oracle.sql.STRUCT[],
        oracle.sql.STRUCT) return oracle.sql.STRUCT';
/
show errors;
set serveroutput on
declare
a number;
x ADTTYP2;
y ADTTYP2;
z ADTTYP2;

begin
    dbms_output.put_line('Calling ADT Type  Procedure ');
    a := 11;
    x := ADTTYP2(11, 'JAVA record in', '11-MAY-2001');
    y := ADTTYP2(81, 'JAVA record OUT', '18-MAY-2001');
    dbms_output.put_line('IN number = ' || a);
    dbms_output.put_line('n1 = ' || x.n1 || ', n2 = ' || x.n2 || ', n3 =
' || x.n3);
    ADTTabProc(a, x, y);
    dbms_output.put_line('OUT number = ' || a);
    dbms_output.put_line('n1 = ' || x.n1 || ', n2 = ' || x.n2 || ', n3 =
' || x.n3);

    dbms_output.put_line('Calling ADT Table Function');
    a := 1;
    x := ADTTYP2(11, 'JAVA record in', '11-MAY-2001');
    y := ADTTYP2(81, 'JAVA record OUT', '18-MAY-2001');
    dbms_output.put_line('IN number = ' || a);
    dbms_output.put_line('n1 = ' || x.n1 || ', n2 = ' || x.n2 || ', n3 =
' || x.n3);
    z := ADTTabFunc(a, x, y);
```

```
   dbms_output.put_line('OUT number = ' || a);
   dbms_output.put_line('n1 = ' || x.n1 || ', n2 = ' || x.n2 || ', n3 =
' || x.n3);
end;
/
```

Mapping REF of ADT Table Types

REF types are built-in data types that represent references to objects of a specified type. To create a REF, you select the object from the table and apply the REF operator (see example). Similarly, to access the object referenced by a REF, you dereference the REF, which can be done using the Oracle-supplied DEREF operataor (see example). This script (XREFADTTab.sql) creates a user-defined object type ADTtyp, and then creates a table ADTtab of ADTtyp objects, and then a table of REF ADTtyp. We will use this table for mapping the REF of ADTtyp to oracle.sql.REF.

```
XREFADTTab.sql
==============


create type ADTtyp as OBJECT (a1 number, a2 varchar2(20), a3 date)
/
create table ADTtab of ADTtyp
/

create table REFtab (id number, refcol REF ADTtyp)
/


insert into ADTtab values (ADTtyp(1, 'One', '01-JAN-2001'));
insert into ADTtab values (ADTtyp(2, 'Two', '02-JAN-2002'));
insert into ADTtab values (ADTtyp(3, 'Three', '03-JAN-2003'));
insert into ADTtab values (ADTtyp(4, 'Four', '04-JAN-2004'));
insert into ADTtab values (ADTtyp(5, 'Five', '05-JAN-2005'));

insert into REFtab select 1, REF(R2) from ADTtab R2 where R2.a1 = 1;
insert into REFtab select 2, REF(R2) from ADTtab R2 where R2.a1 = 2;
insert into REFtab values (3, NULL);
insert into REFtab select 4, REF(R2) from ADTtab R2 where R2.a1 = 4;
insert into REFtab select 5, REF(R2) from ADTtab R2 where R2.a1 = 5;
commit;
```

The following code sample, `REFADTTab.sql`, creates and compiles
`REFADTTabClass` directly into the database. The class has two methods:
`REFADTTabProc()` and `REFADTTabFunc();` the corresponding Call Specs
have the same name as the Java methods.

- The method `REFADTTabClass.REFADTTabProc` takes an array of
  NUMBER as IN/OUT parameter, an array of `REF` as IN/OUT parameter, a `REF` as IN parameter, and inserts an `oracle.sql.REF` into
  the `REFtab` table.

- The function `REFADTTabClass.REFADTTabFunc` takes an array of
  NUMBER as IN/OUT parameter, an array of `REF` as IN/OUT parame-
  ter, a `REF` as IN parameter, and retrieves and returns an instance of
  REF `ADTTyp` as `oracle.sql.REF`.

```
REFADTTab.sql
============
create or replace and resolve java source named REFADTTabClass   as
/*
 *Mapping REF of ADTtype to oracle.sql.REF
 */

import java.sql.*;
import oracle.sql.*;
import oracle.jdbc.*;

public class REFADTTabClass
{

  /*
   * inserts oracle.sql.REF object as REF of ADTtyp
   */
  public static void REFADTTabProc (NUMBER id[], REF rf[], REF rf2)
    throws SQLException
  {
    Connection conn = DriverManager.getConnection
("jdbc:oracle:kprb:");
    Statement stmt = conn.createStatement();

    OraclePreparedStatement ps = (OraclePreparedStatement)
```

```
        conn.prepareStatement ("INSERT INTO REFTAB (ID, REFCOL)
VALUES(?, ?)");

   ps.setNUMBER (1, id[0]);
   ps.setREF (2, rf[0]);
   ps.execute ();
   ps.close();

   id[0] = new NUMBER(id[0].intValue() + 1000);
   rf[0] = rf2;
 }

/*
 * retrieves an return a REF of ADTtyp as oracle.sqlREF
 */
 public static REF REFADTTabfunc (NUMBER id[], REF rf[], REF rf2)
   throws SQLException
 {
   Connection conn = DriverManager.getConnection
("jdbc:oracle:kprb:");
   Statement stmt = conn.createStatement();

   OraclePreparedStatement ps = (OraclePreparedStatement)
      conn.prepareStatement ("SELECT REFCOL FROM REFTAB WHERE ID =
?");

   ps.setNUMBER (1, id[0]);
   OracleResultSet rs = (OracleResultSet) ps.executeQuery();

   REF r = null;

   while (rs.next())
   {
     r = (REF) rs.getObject(1);
   }
   ps.close();

   id[0] = new NUMBER(id[0].intValue() + 1000);
   rf[0] = rf2;

   return r;
 }
```

```
}
/
show errors;

create or replace procedure REFADTTabProc(x IN OUT number, y IN OUT
REF ADTTYP, z IN REF ADTTYP) as language java
  name 'REFADTTabClass.REFADTTabProc(oracle.sql.NUMBER[],
oracle.sql.REF[], oracle.sql.REF)';
/

create or replace function REFADTTabfunc(x IN OUT number, y IN OUT REF
ADTTYP, z IN REF ADTTYP) return REF ADTTYP as language java
  name 'REFADTTabClass.REFADTTabfunc(oracle.sql.NUMBER[],
oracle.sql.REF[], oracle.sql.REF) return oracle.sql.REF';
/
show errors;
set serveroutput on
declare
a number;
x REF ADTTYP;
y REF ADTTYP;
z REF ADTTYP;
t1 ADTTYP;
begin
  a := 11;
  select refcol into x from reftab where id = 1;
  select refcol into y from reftab where id = 2;
  dbms_output.put_line('Input number = ' || a);
  select deref(x) into t1 from dual;
  dbms_output.put_line('Input: a1= ' || t1.a1 || ', a2= ' || t1.a2 ||
', a3= ' || t1.a3);
  dbms_output.put_line('Calling REF of ADT Table  Procedure ');
  REFADTTabProc(a, x, y);
  select deref(x) into t1 from dual;
  dbms_output.put_line('Ouput number = ' || a);
  dbms_output.put_line('Ouput: a1= ' || t1.a1 || ', a2= ' || t1.a2 ||
', a3= ' || t1.a3);

  a := 5;
  dbms_output.put_line('Calling REF of ADT Table Function ');
  z := REFADTTabfunc(a, x, y);
  select deref(x) into t1 from dual;
```

```
    dbms_output.put_line('Output number = ' || a);
    dbms_output.put_line('Output: a1= ' || t1.a1 || ', a2= ' || t1.a2 ||
 ', a3= ' || t1.a3);
    select deref(z) into t1 from dual;
    dbms_output.put_line('Output Z = ');
    dbms_output.put_line('Output: a1= ' || t1.a1 || ', a2= ' || t1.a2 ||
 ', a3= ' || t1.a3);

end;
 /
```

Mapping REF Cursors to java.sql.ResultSet

Cursors are database areas where the results of a query are stored. REF cursor (or cursor variable) allows sharing query result sets on the server side (i.e., between PL/SQL and Java in the database) and also passing the query results from the server side to the client side (i.e., as a return object). The following code sample illustrates mapping the REF cursor to java.sql.ResultSet. It uses the EMP table in the SCOTT schema. Setting setCreateStatementAsRefCursor() to true turns any statements created from this connection into a REF CURSOR; this is required for returning Resultset from Java in the database. The same technique can be used for mapping REF CURSOR to oracle.jdbc.OracleResultSet.

```
Resultset.sql
=============
create or replace and resolve java source named refcur as
import java.sql.*;
import java.io.*;
import oracle.jdbc.*;
/*
 *  Mapping REF CURSOR to java.sql.Resultset
 */
public class refcur
{
  /*
   * Procedure returning a REF CURSOR via OUT parameter
   */
  public static void refcurproc (ResultSet rs[])
    throws SQLException
  {
    Connection conn = null;
```

```
    conn = DriverManager.getConnection("jdbc:oracle:kprb:");
    ((OracleConnection)conn).setCreateStatementAsRefCursor(true);
    Statement stmt = conn.createStatement();
    ((OracleStatement)stmt).setRowPrefetch(1);
    ResultSet rset = stmt.executeQuery("select * from EMP order by
empno");
    rs[0] = rset;
    // fetch one row
    if (rset.next())
    {
      System.out.println("Ename = " + rset.getString(2));
    }
   }


  /*
   * Function returning a REF CURSOR
   */
  public static ResultSet refcurfunc ()
    throws SQLException
  {
    Connection conn = null;
    conn = DriverManager.getConnection("jdbc:oracle:kprb:");
    ((OracleConnection)conn).setCreateStatementAsRefCursor(true);
    Statement stmt = conn.createStatement();
    ((OracleStatement)stmt).setRowPrefetch(1);
    ResultSet rset = stmt.executeQuery("select * from EMP order by
empno");
    // fetch one row
    if (rset.next())
    {
      System.out.println("Ename = " + rset.getString(2));
    }
    return rset;
   }
}
/
show errors;


create or replace package refcur_pkg as
type EmpCurTyp IS REF CURSOR;
  function rcfunc return EmpCurTyp;
```

```
   procedure rcproc (rc OUT EmpCurTyp);
end refcur_pkg;
/
show errors;

create or replace package body refcur_pkg as

procedure rcproc(rc OUT EmpCurTyp)
 as language java
 name 'refcur.refcurproc(java.sql.ResultSet[])';

function rcfunc return EmpCurTyp
 as language java
 name 'refcur.refcurfunc() returns java.sql.ResultSet';

end refcur_pkg;
/
show errors;

set serveroutput on
call dbms_java.set_output(50000);

declare
   type EmpCurTyp IS REF CURSOR;
   rc EmpCurTyp;
   employee emp%ROWTYPE;
begin
   dbms_output.put_line(' ** Calling REF CURSOR PROCEDURE' );
   refcur_pkg.rcproc(rc);
   ---
   --- Alternatively the refcurfunc could be called as follows
   --- rc = refcur_pkg.refcurfunc();
   ---
   LOOP
       fetch rc into employee;
       exit when rc%notfound;
        dbms_output.put_line(' Name = ' || employee.ENAME ||
               ' Department = ' || employee.DEPTNO);
   end loop;
close rc;
end;
```

```
/
show errors;
```

Mapping VARRAY of Scalar SQL Types

Along with Nested Tables (covered later), VARRAY, or Variable-Length Array, are parts of user-defined SQL collection types. They define a type, which represents an ordered set of elements of the same type. VARRAY columns are stored inline within the same tablespace; however, when they are too large (i.e., over 4 K), the Oracle database stores these as a BLOB. The following script defines a VARRAY of number type, a VARRAY of varchar2 type, and a VARRAY of date type. It then creates and populates a table using the defined VARRAY types as columns.

```
XVARRAY.sql
===========
drop table VarrayTab;
rem
rem VARRAY of Number type
rem
create or replace type NVARRAY as VARRAY(10) of number
/
rem
rem VARRAY of VARCHAR2 type
rem
create or replace type VC2VARRAY as VARRAY(10) of varchar2(30)
/
rem
rem VARRAY of date type
rem
create or replace type DATVARRAY as VARRAY(10) of date
/
rem
rem Table of VARRAYs
rem (number varray, varchar2 varray, date varray)
rem
create table VarrayTab (id int, nva nvarray,
    vc2va vc2varray,  datva datvarray);

insert into VarrayTab values (1,
    NVARRAY(1, 2, 3, 4, 5, 6, 7, 8, 9, 10),
    VC2VARRAY('One', 'Two', 'Three', 'Four', 'Five', 'Six',
```

```
                      'Seven','Eight', 'Nine', 'Ten'),
       DATVARRAY('01-JAN-2005', '02-JAN-2005', '03-JAN-2005', '04-JAN-
    2005',
                 '05-JAN-2005', '06-JAN-2005', '07-JAN-2005', '08-JAN-
    2005',
                 '09-JAN-2005', '10-JAN-2005')
       );

insert into VarrayTab values (2, null, null, null);

insert into VarrayTab values (3,
       NVARRAY(31, 32, 33, 34, 35, 36, 37, 38, 39, 40),
       VC2VARRAY('Thirty One', 'Thirty Two', 'Thirty Three',
                 'Thirty Four', 'Thirty Five', 'Thirty Six',
                 'Thirty Seven', 'Thirty Eight'),
       DATVARRAY('01-MAR-2005', '02-MAR-2005', '03-MAR-2005', '04-MAR-
    2005',
                 '05-MAR-2005', '06-MAR-2005', '07-MAR-2005', '08-MAR-
    2005',
                 '09-MAR-2005', '10-MAR-2005')
       );
commit;
```

The following code sample, `NumVarray.sql`, creates and compiles `NVArrayClass` directly into the database. The class has two methods: `nvaproc()` and `nvafunc()`; the corresponding Call Specs have the same name as the Java methods.

- The method nvaproc inserts a `java.sql.Array` row into VarrayTab table as NVARRAY; it takes an array of NUMBER as IN/OUT parameter, an array of NVARRAY as IN/OUT parameter, and an NVARRAY as IN parameter.

- The method nvafunc retrieves and returns a NVARRAY as a `java.sql.Array`; it takes an array of NUMBER as IN/OUT parameter, an array of NVARRAY as IN/OUT parameter, and an NVARRAY as IN parameter.

```
NumVarray.sql
=============
create or replace and resolve java source named NVarrayClass  as
```

```
/*
 *Mapping NUMBER VARRAY to/from java.sql.Array
 */

import java.sql.*;
import oracle.sql.*;
import oracle.jdbc.*;

public class NVarrayClass
{
 public static void nvaproc (NUMBER id[], Array va[], Array va2)
    throws SQLException
  {
    Connection conn = DriverManager.getConnection
("jdbc:oracle:kprb:");
    Statement stmt = conn.createStatement();

    OraclePreparedStatement ps = (OraclePreparedStatement)
        conn.prepareStatement ("INSERT INTO VarrayTab (ID, NVA)
VALUES(?, ?)");

    ps.setNUMBER (1, id[0]);
    ps.setARRAY (2, (ARRAY)va[0]);
    ps.execute ();
    ps.close();
    id[0] = new NUMBER(id[0].intValue() + 1000);
    va[0] = va2;
  }

 public static Array nvafunc(NUMBER id[], Array va[], Array va2)
    throws SQLException
  {

    Connection conn = DriverManager.getConnection
("jdbc:oracle:kprb:");
    Statement stmt = conn.createStatement();

    OraclePreparedStatement ps = (OraclePreparedStatement)
        conn.prepareStatement ("SELECT NVA FROM VarrayTab WHERE ID = ?
");
    ps.setNUMBER (1, id[0]);
    OracleResultSet rs = (OracleResultSet) ps.executeQuery();
```

```
   Array a = null;
   while (rs.next())
   {
     a = (Array) rs.getObject(1);
   }
   ps.close();

   id[0] = new NUMBER(id[0].intValue() + 1000);
   va[0] = va2;
   return a;
  }
}
/
show errors;

create or replace procedure nvaproc (x IN OUT number, y IN OUT
NVARRAY,
  z IN NVARRAY)
  as language java
  name 'NVarrayClass.nvaproc(oracle.sql.NUMBER[], java.sql.Array[],
      java.sql.Array)';
/
show errors;

create or replace function nvafunc (x IN OUT number, y IN OUT NVARRAY,

  z IN NVARRAY) return NVARRAY
  as language java
  name 'NVarrayClass.nvafunc(oracle.sql.NUMBER[], java.sql.Array[],
      java.sql.Array) return java.sql.Array';
/

show errors;

set serveroutput on
declare
a number;
x NVARRAY;
y NVARRAY;
z NVARRAY;
begin
```

```
dbms_output.put_line('Calling Number VARRAY Procedure ');
a := 11;
x := NVARRAY(101, 102, 103, 104, 105, 106);
y := NVARRAY(201, 202, 203, 204, 205, 206);

dbms_output.put_line('IN number = ' || a);
for i IN 1 .. x.COUNT loop
  dbms_output.put(x(i) || ' ');
end loop;
dbms_output.put_line(' ');


nvaproc(a, x, y);

dbms_output.put_line('OUT ID = ' || a);
 dbms_output.put_line('OUT X = ');
for i IN 1 .. x.COUNT loop
  dbms_output.put(x(i) || ' ');
end loop;
dbms_output.put_line(' ');


dbms_output.put_line('Calling Number VARRAY Function ');
a := 1;
x := NVARRAY(101, 102, 103, 104, 105, 106);
y := NVARRAY(201, 202, 203, 204, 205, 206);

dbms_output.put_line(' ');


z := nvafunc(a, x, y);

dbms_output.put_line('OUT ID = ' || a);
dbms_output.put_line('OUT X = ');
for i IN 1 .. x.COUNT loop
  dbms_output.put(x(i) || ' ');
end loop;
dbms_output.put_line(' ');

dbms_output.put_line('OUT Z = ');
for i IN 1 .. z.COUNT loop
  dbms_output.put(z(i) || ' ');
end loop;
dbms_output.put_line(' ');
```

```
end;
/
```

The following code sample, `VC2Varray.sql`, creates and compiles `VC2VArrayClass` directly into the database. The class has two methods: `vc2vaproc()` and `vc2vafunc()`; the corresponding Call Specs have the same name as the Java methods.

- The method `vc2vaproc` inserts a `java.sql.Array` row into Varray-Tab table as `VC2VARRAY`; it takes an array of NUMBER as IN/OUT parameter, an array of `VC2VARRAY` as IN/OUT parameter, and a `VC2VARRAY` as IN parameter.

- The method `vc2vafunc` retrieves and returns a `VC2VARRAY` as a `java.sql.Array`; it takes an array of NUMBER as IN/OUT parameter, an array of `VC2VARRAY` as IN/OUT parameter, and a `VC2VARRAY` as IN parameter.

```
VC2Varray.sql
=============
create or replace and resolve java source named VC2VarrayClass   as
/*
 *VARCHAR2 VARRAY
 */

import java.sql.*;
import oracle.sql.*;
import oracle.jdbc.*;

public class VC2VarrayClass
{
 public static void vc2vaproc (NUMBER id[], Array va[], Array va2)
    throws SQLException
  {
    Connection conn = DriverManager.getConnection
("jdbc:oracle:kprb:");
    Statement stmt = conn.createStatement();

    OraclePreparedStatement ps = (OraclePreparedStatement)
       conn.prepareStatement ("INSERT INTO VarrayTab (ID, VC2VA)
VALUES(?, ?)");
```

```
      ps.setNUMBER (1, id[0]);
      ps.setARRAY (2, (ARRAY)va[0]);
      ps.execute ();
      ps.close();
      id[0] = new NUMBER(id[0].intValue() + 1000);
      va[0] = va2;
    }

  public static Array vc2vafunc(NUMBER id[], Array va[], Array va2)
      throws SQLException
    {

      Connection conn = DriverManager.getConnection
("jdbc:oracle:kprb:");
      Statement stmt = conn.createStatement();

      OraclePreparedStatement ps = (OraclePreparedStatement)
        conn.prepareStatement ("SELECT VC2VA FROM VarrayTab WHERE ID =
? ");
      ps.setNUMBER (1, id[0]);
      OracleResultSet rs = (OracleResultSet) ps.executeQuery();
      Array a = null;
      while (rs.next())
      {
        a = (Array) rs.getObject(1);
      }
      ps.close();
      id[0] = new NUMBER(id[0].intValue() + 1000);
      va[0] = va2;
      return a;
    }
}
/
show errors;

create or replace procedure vc2vaproc (x IN OUT number, y IN OUT
VC2Varray,
  z IN VC2Varray)
  as language java
  name 'VC2VarrayClass.vc2vaproc(oracle.sql.NUMBER[],
java.sql.Array[],
        java.sql.Array)';
```

```
/
show errors;

create or replace function vc2vafunc (x IN OUT number, y IN OUT
VC2Varray,
  z IN VC2Varray) return VC2Varray
  as language java
  name 'VC2VarrayClass.vc2vafunc(oracle.sql.NUMBER[],
java.sql.Array[],
        java.sql.Array) return java.sql.Array';
/

show errors;

set serveroutput on
declare
a number;
x VC2Varray;
y VC2Varray;
z VC2Varray;
begin

  dbms_output.put_line('Calling VARCHAR2 VARRAY Procedure ');
  a := 12;
  x := VC2VARRAY('ONE', 'TWO', 'THREE', 'FOUR', 'FIVE', 'SIX');
  y := VC2VARRAY('one', 'two', 'three', 'four', 'five', 'six');

  dbms_output.put_line('Input number = ' || a);
  dbms_output.put_line('Input VC2ARRAY = ');
  for i IN 1 .. x.COUNT loop
    dbms_output.put(x(i) || ' ');
  end loop;
  dbms_output.put_line(' ');

  vc2vaproc(a, x, y);

  dbms_output.put_line('Ouput number = ' || a);
  dbms_output.put_line('Ouput VC2ARRAY = ');
  for i IN 1 .. x.COUNT loop
    dbms_output.put(x(i) || ' ');
  end loop;
  dbms_output.put_line(' ');
```

```
dbms_output.put_line(' ');
dbms_output.put_line('Calling VARCHAR2 VARRAY Function ');
a := 1;
x := VC2VARRAY('ONE', 'TWO', 'THREE', 'FOUR', 'FIVE', 'SIX');
y := VC2VARRAY('one', 'two', 'three', 'four', 'five', 'six');

dbms_output.put_line(' ');

z := vc2vafunc(a, x, y);

dbms_output.put_line('Output number = ' || a);
dbms_output.put_line('Ouptput x = ');
for i IN 1 .. x.COUNT loop
  dbms_output.put(x(i) || ' ');
end loop;
dbms_output.put_line(' ');

dbms_output.put_line('Output Z = ');
for i IN 1 .. z.COUNT loop
  dbms_output.put(z(i) || ' ');
end loop;
dbms_output.put_line(' ');

end;
/
```

The following code sample, `DATVarray.sql`, creates and compiles `DATVArrayClass` directly into the database. The class has two methods: `DATvaproc()` and `DATvafunc()`; the corresponding Call Specs have the same name as the Java methods.

- The method **DATvaproc** inserts a `java.sql.Array` row into VarrayTab table as `DATVARRAY`; it takes an array of `NUMBER` as IN/OUT parameter, an array of `DATVARRAY` as IN/OUT parameter, and a `DATVARRAY` as IN parameter.

- The method `DATvafunc` retrieves and returns a `DATVARRAY` as a `java.sql.Array`; it takes an array of `NUMBER` as IN/OUT parameter, an array of `DATVARRAY` as IN/OUT parameter, and a `DATVARRAY` as IN parameter.

```
DATVarray.sql
=============
create or replace and resolve java source named DATVarrayClass   as
/*
 *DATVarrayClass.java
 */

import java.sql.*;
import oracle.sql.*;
import oracle.jdbc.*;

public class DATVarrayClass
{
 public static void DATvaproc (NUMBER id[], Array va[], Array va2)
    throws SQLException
  {
    Connection conn = DriverManager.getConnection
("jdbc:oracle:kprb:");
    Statement stmt = conn.createStatement();

    OraclePreparedStatement ps = (OraclePreparedStatement)
      conn.prepareStatement ("INSERT INTO VarrayTab (ID, DATVA)
VALUES(?, ?)");

    ps.setNUMBER (1, id[0]);
    ps.setARRAY (2, (ARRAY)va[0]);
    ps.execute ();
    ps.close();
    conn.commit();

    id[0] = new NUMBER(id[0].intValue() + 1000);
    va[0] = va2;
  }

 public static Array DATvafunc(NUMBER id[], Array va[], Array va2)
    throws SQLException
  {

    Connection conn = DriverManager.getConnection
("jdbc:oracle:kprb:");
    Statement stmt = conn.createStatement();
```

```
        OraclePreparedStatement ps = (OraclePreparedStatement)
           conn.prepareStatement ("SELECT DATVA FROM VarrayTab WHERE ID =
? ");
        ps.setNUMBER (1, id[0]);
        OracleResultSet rs = (OracleResultSet) ps.executeQuery();
        Array a = null;
        while (rs.next())
        {
          a = (Array) rs.getObject(1);
        }
        ps.close();
        id[0] = new NUMBER(id[0].intValue() + 1000);
        va[0] = va2;
        return a;
     }
}
/
show errors;


create or replace procedure DATvaproc (x IN OUT number, y IN OUT
DATVarray,
   z IN DATVarray)
   as language java
   name 'DATVarrayClass.DATvaproc(oracle.sql.NUMBER[],
java.sql.Array[],
        java.sql.Array)';
/
show errors;


create or replace function DATvafunc (x IN OUT number, y IN OUT
DATVarray,
   z IN DATVarray) return DATVarray
   as language java
   name 'DATVarrayClass.DATvafunc(oracle.sql.NUMBER[],
java.sql.Array[],
        java.sql.Array) return java.sql.Array';
/

show errors;

set serveroutput on
```

```
declare
a number;
x DATVarray;
y DATVarray;
z DATVarray;
begin

  dbms_output.put_line('Calling DATE VARRAY Procedure ');
  a := 13;
  x := DATVARRAY('01-JAN-2005', '02-JAN-2005', '03-JAN-2005', '04-
JAN-2005');
  y := DATVARRAY('01-MAR-2005', '02-MAR-2005', '03-MAR-2005', '04-
MAR-2005');


  dbms_output.put_line('Iinput number = ' || a);
  dbms_output.put_line('Input DATARRAY = ');
  for i IN 1 .. x.COUNT loop
    dbms_output.put(x(i) || ' ');
  end loop;
  dbms_output.put_line(' ');

  DATvaproc(a, x, y);

  dbms_output.put_line('Ouput number = ' || a);
  dbms_output.put_line('Ouput DATARRAY = ');
  for i IN 1 .. x.COUNT loop
    dbms_output.put(x(i) || ' ');
  end loop;
  dbms_output.put_line(' ');

  dbms_output.put_line(' ');
  dbms_output.put_line('Calling DATE VARRAY Function ');
  a := 1;
  x := DATVARRAY('01-JAN-2005', '02-JAN-2005', '03-JAN-2005', '04-
JAN-2005');
  y := DATVARRAY('01-MAR-2005', '02-MAR-2005', '03-MAR-2005', '04-
MAR-2005');

  dbms_output.put_line(' ');

  z := DATvafunc(a, x, y);
```

```
  dbms_output.put_line('Output number = ' || a);
  dbms_output.put_line('Ouptput x = ');
  for i IN 1 .. x.COUNT loop
    dbms_output.put(x(i) || ' ');
  end loop;
  dbms_output.put_line(' ');

  dbms_output.put_line('Output Z = ');
  for i IN 1 .. z.COUNT loop
    dbms_output.put(z(i) || ' ');
  end loop;
  dbms_output.put_line(' ');

end;
/
```

Mapping Nested Tables of Scalar SQL Types

Like VARRAY, Nested Tables, or tables within a table, are parts of the user-defined SQL collection types. They define a type, which represents an unordered set of elements of the same type. The nested table columns of a table are stored out of line from the rows of the parent table, using the "*store as*" clause. Unlike VARRAY, which has fixed boundaries, Nested Tables offer more flexibility because their size can dynamically grow or shrink at the cost of inefficient storage. The following script defines a Nested Table of number type, a Nested Table of varchar2 type, and a Nested Table of date type. It then creates and populates a table using the defined Nested Table types as columns.

```
XNTABLE.sql
===========
rem
rem Nested Table of Number type
rem
create or replace type NTab_Num as TABLE of number
/
rem
rem Nested Table of VARCHAR2 type
rem
create or replace type NTab_Vc2 as TABLE of varchar2(30)
/
```

```
rem
rem Nested Table of date type
rem
create or replace type NTab_Dat as TABLE of date
/

drop table NSTableTab;

rem
rem Table of Nested Tables
rem (nested table of number, nested table of vachar2, neted table of
date)
rem
create table NSTableTab (id int, numnt NTab_Num, vc2nt NTab_Vc2, datnt
NTab_Dat)
    nested table numnt store as NSTabNum,
    nested table vc2nt store as NSTabVc2,
    nested table datnt store as NSTabDat;

insert into NSTableTab values (1,
    NTab_Num(1, 2, 3, 4, 5, 6, 7, 8, 9, 10),
    NTab_Vc2('One', 'Two', 'Three', 'Four', 'Five', 'Six', 'Seven',
            'Eight', 'Nine', 'Ten'),
    NTab_Dat('01-JAN-2003', '02-JAN-2003', '03-JAN-2003', '04-JAN-
2003',
            '05-JAN-2003', '06-JAN-2003', '07-JAN-2003', '08-JAN-2003',
            '09-JAN-2003', '10-JAN-2003')
    );

insert into NSTableTab values (2, null, null, null);

insert into NSTableTab values (3,
    NTab_Num(1, 2, 3, 4, 5, 6, 7, 8, 9, 10, 11, 12, 13, 14, 15),
    NTab_Vc2('Sixty One', 'Sixty Two', 'Sixty Three', 'Sixty Four',
            'Sixty Five', 'Sixty Six', 'Sixty Seven'),
    NTab_Dat('01-MAR-2005', '02-MAR-2005', '03-MAR-2005', '04-MAR-
2005',
            '05-MAR-2005', '06-MAR-2005', '07-MAR-2005', '08-MAR-2005',
            '09-MAR-2005', '10-MAR-2005', '11-MAR-2005', '12-MAR-2005')
    );
commit;
```

The following code sample, `NumNSTable.sql` creates and compiles `NumNTabClass` directly into the database. The class has two methods: `NumNTabProc()` and `NumNTabFunc()`; the corresponding Call Specs have the same name as the Java methods.

- The method `NumNTabProc` inserts a `java.sql.Array` row into `NSTableTab` as `NTab_Num`; it takes an array of `NUMBER` as IN/OUT parameter, an array of `NTab_Num` as IN/OUT parameter, and an `NTab_Num` as IN parameter.

- The method `NumNTabFunc` retrieves and returns an `NTab_Num` as a `java.sql.Array`; it takes an array of `NUMBER` as IN/OUT parameter, an array of `NTab_Num` as IN/OUT parameter, and an `NTab_Num` as IN parameter.

```
NumNSTable.sql
==============
create or replace and resolve java source named NumNTabClass   as
/*
 *NUMBER NESTED TABLE
 */

import java.sql.*;
import oracle.sql.*;
import oracle.jdbc.*;

public class NumNTabClass
{

 public static void NumNTabProc(NUMBER id[], Array nt[], Array nt2)
    throws SQLException
  {
    Connection conn = DriverManager.getConnection
("jdbc:oracle:kprb:");
    Statement stmt = conn.createStatement();

    OraclePreparedStatement ps = (OraclePreparedStatement)
      conn.prepareStatement ("INSERT INTO NSTableTab (ID, NUMNT)
VALUES(?, ?)");

    ps.setNUMBER (1, id[0]);
```

```
    ps.setARRAY (2, (ARRAY) nt[0]);
    ps.execute ();
    ps.close();

    id[0] = new NUMBER(id[0].intValue() + 1000);
    nt[0] = nt2;
  }

 public static Array NumNTabFunc (NUMBER id[], Array nt[],
    Array nt2) throws SQLException
  {
    Connection conn = DriverManager.getConnection
("jdbc:oracle:kprb:");
    Statement stmt = conn.createStatement();

    OraclePreparedStatement ps = (OraclePreparedStatement)
      conn.prepareStatement ("SELECT NUMNT FROM NSTableTab WHERE ID =
?");

    ps.setNUMBER (1, id[0]);
    OracleResultSet rs = (OracleResultSet) ps.executeQuery();

    Array a = null;

    while (rs.next())
    {
      a = (Array) rs.getObject(1);
    }
    ps.close();

    id[0] = new NUMBER(id[0].intValue() + 1000);
    nt[0] = nt2;

    return a;
  }
}
/
show errors;

create or replace procedure NumNTabProc (x IN OUT number, y IN OUT
NTab_Num, z IN NTab_Num) as language java
```

```
      name 'NumNTabClass.NumNTabProc(oracle.sql.NUMBER[],
java.sql.Array[],
        java.sql.Array)';
/
show errors;

create or replace function NumNTabFunc (x IN OUT number, y IN OUT
NTab_Num, z IN NTab_Num) return NTab_Num as language java
   name 'NumNTabClass.NumNTabFunc(oracle.sql.NUMBER[],
java.sql.Array[],
        java.sql.Array) return java.sql.Array';
/
show errors;

set serveroutput on
declare
a number;
x NTab_Num;
y NTab_Num;
z NTab_Num;
begin

  dbms_output.put_line('Calling NUMBER Nested Table Procedure ');
  a := 11;
  x := NTab_Num(11, 101, 102, 103, 104, 105, 106);
  y := NTab_Num(21, 201, 202, 203, 204, 205, 206);
  dbms_output.put_line('Input number = ' || a);
  dbms_output.put_line('Input NTab_Num x = ');
  for i IN 1 .. x.COUNT loop
    dbms_output.put(x(i) || ' ');
  end loop;
  dbms_output.put_line(' ');

  NumNTabProc(a, x, y);

  dbms_output.put_line('Output number = ' || a);
  dbms_output.put_line('Output NTab_Num x = ');
  for i IN 1 .. x.COUNT loop
    dbms_output.put(x(i) || ' ');
  end loop;
  dbms_output.put_line(' ');
```

```
dbms_output.put_line('Calling NUMBER Nested Table Function ');
a := 1;
x := NTab_Num(101, 102, 103, 104, 105, 106);
y := NTab_Num(201, 202, 203, 204, 205, 206);
dbms_output.put_line('Input number = ' || a);
dbms_output.put_line('Input NTab_Num x = ');
for i IN 1 .. x.COUNT loop
  dbms_output.put(x(i) || ' ');
end loop;
dbms_output.put_line(' ');

z := NumNTabFunc(a, x, y);

dbms_output.put_line('Ouput number = ' || a);
dbms_output.put_line('Output NTab_Num x = ');
for i IN 1 .. x.COUNT loop
  dbms_output.put(x(i) || ' ');
end loop;

dbms_output.put_line(' ');
dbms_output.put_line('Output NTab_Num z = ');
  for i IN 1 .. z.COUNT loop
  dbms_output.put(z(i) || ' ');
end loop;
dbms_output.put_line(' ');

end;
/
```

The following code sample VC2NSTable.sql creates and compiles NumNTabClass directly into the database. The class has two methods: VC2NTabProc() and VC2NTabFunc(); the corresponding Call Specs have the same name as the Java methods.

- The method VC2NTabProc inserts a java.sql.Array row into NSTableTab as NTab_Vc2; it takes an array of NUMBER as IN/OUT parameter, an array of NTab_Vc2 as IN/OUT parameter, and an NTab_Vc2 as IN parameter.

- The method VC2NTabFunc retrieves and returns an NTab_Vc2 as a java.sql.Array; it takes an array of NUMBER as IN/OUT parameter, an array of `NTab_Vc2` as IN/OUT parameter, and an `NTab_Vc2` as IN parameter.

```
VC2NSTable.sql
==============
create or replace and resolve java source named VC2NTabClass   as
/*
 *VARCHAR2 NESTED TABLE
 */

import java.sql.*;
import oracle.sql.*;
import oracle.jdbc.*;

public class VC2NTabClass
{

 public static void VC2NTabProc(NUMBER id[], Array nt[], Array nt2)
    throws SQLException
  {
    Connection conn = DriverManager.getConnection
("jdbc:oracle:kprb:");
    Statement stmt = conn.createStatement();

    OraclePreparedStatement ps = (OraclePreparedStatement)
       conn.prepareStatement ("INSERT INTO NSTableTab (ID, VC2NT)
VALUES(?, ?)");

    ps.setNUMBER (1, id[0]);
    ps.setARRAY (2, (ARRAY) nt[0]);
    ps.execute ();
    ps.close();

    id[0] = new NUMBER(id[0].intValue() + 1000);
    nt[0] = nt2;
  }

 public static Array VC2NTabFunc (NUMBER id[], Array nt[],
    Array nt2) throws SQLException
  {
```

```
      Connection conn = DriverManager.getConnection
("jdbc:oracle:kprb:");
      Statement stmt = conn.createStatement();

      OraclePreparedStatement ps = (OraclePreparedStatement)
        conn.prepareStatement ("SELECT VC2NT FROM NSTableTab WHERE ID =
?");

      ps.setNUMBER (1, id[0]);
      OracleResultSet rs = (OracleResultSet) ps.executeQuery();

      Array a = null;

      while (rs.next())
      {
        a = (Array) rs.getObject(1);
      }
      ps.close();

      id[0] = new NUMBER(id[0].intValue() + 1000);
      nt[0] = nt2;

      return a;
    }
}
/
show errors;

create or replace procedure VC2NTabProc (x IN OUT number, y IN OUT
NTab_Vc2, z IN NTab_Vc2) as language java
   name 'VC2NTabClass.VC2NTabProc(oracle.sql.NUMBER[],
java.sql.Array[],
        java.sql.Array)';
/
show errors;

create or replace function VC2NTabFunc (x IN OUT number, y IN OUT
NTab_Vc2, z IN NTab_Vc2) return NTab_Vc2 as language java
   name 'VC2NTabClass.VC2NTabFunc(oracle.sql.NUMBER[],
java.sql.Array[],
        java.sql.Array) return java.sql.Array';
/
```

```
show errors;

set serveroutput on
declare
a number;
x NTab_Vc2;
y NTab_Vc2;
z NTab_Vc2;
begin

  dbms_output.put_line('Calling VARCHAR2 Nested Table Procedure ');
  a := 12;
  x := NTab_Vc2('ONE', 'TWO', 'THREE', 'FOUR', 'FIVE', 'SIX');
  y := NTab_Vc2('one', 'two', 'three', 'four', 'five', 'six');
  dbms_output.put_line('Input number = ' || a);
  dbms_output.put_line('Input NTab_Vc2 x = ');
  for i IN 1 .. x.COUNT loop
    dbms_output.put(x(i) || ' ');
  end loop;
  dbms_output.put_line(' ');

  VC2NTabProc(a, x, y);

  dbms_output.put_line('Output number = ' || a);
  dbms_output.put_line('Output NTab_Vc2 x = ');
  for i IN 1 .. x.COUNT loop
    dbms_output.put(x(i) || ' ');
  end loop;
  dbms_output.put_line(' ');

  dbms_output.put_line('Calling VARCHAR2 Nested Table Function ');
  a := 1;
  x := NTab_Vc2('ONE', 'TWO', 'THREE', 'FOUR', 'FIVE', 'SIX');
  y := NTab_Vc2('one', 'two', 'three', 'four', 'five', 'six');

  dbms_output.put_line('Input number = ' || a);
  dbms_output.put_line('Input NTab_Vc2 x = ');
  for i IN 1 .. x.COUNT loop
    dbms_output.put(x(i) || ' ');
  end loop;
  dbms_output.put_line(' ');
```

```
z := VC2NTabFunc(a, x, y);

dbms_output.put_line('Ouput number = ' || a);
dbms_output.put_line('Output NTab_Vc2 x = ');
for i IN 1 .. x.COUNT loop
  dbms_output.put(x(i) || ' ');
end loop;

dbms_output.put_line(' ');
dbms_output.put_line('Output NTab_Vc2 z = ');
  for i IN 1 .. z.COUNT loop
  dbms_output.put(z(i) || ' ');
end loop;
dbms_output.put_line(' ');

end;
/
```

The following code sample `DATNSTable.sql` creates and compiles `DAT-NTabClass` directly into the database. The class has two methods: `DATNT-abProc()` and `DATNTabFunc();` the corresponding Call Specs have the same name as the Java methods.

- The method `DATNTabProc` inserts a `java.sql.Array` row into `NSTableTab` as `NTab_Dat`; it takes an array of `NUMBER` as IN/OUT parameter, an array of `NTab_Dat` as IN/OUT parameter, and an `NTab_Dat` as IN parameter.

- The method `DATNTabFunc` retrieves and returns an `NTab_Dat` as a `java.sql.Array`; it takes an array of `NUMBER` as IN/OUT parameter, an array of `NTab_Dat` as IN/OUT parameter, and an `NTab_Dat` as IN parameter.

```
DATNSTable.sql
==============
create or replace and resolve java source named DATNTabClass  as
/*
 *DATE NESTED TABLE
```

```
    */

import java.sql.*;
import oracle.sql.*;
import oracle.jdbc.*;

public class DATNTabClass
{

 public static void DATNTabProc(NUMBER id[], Array nt[], Array nt2)
    throws SQLException
  {
    Connection conn = DriverManager.getConnection
("jdbc:oracle:kprb:");
    Statement stmt = conn.createStatement();

    OraclePreparedStatement ps = (OraclePreparedStatement)
        conn.prepareStatement ("INSERT INTO NSTableTab (ID, DATNT)
VALUES(?, ?)");

    ps.setNUMBER (1, id[0]);
    ps.setARRAY (2, (ARRAY) nt[0]);
    ps.execute ();
    ps.close();

    id[0] = new NUMBER(id[0].intValue() + 1000);
    nt[0] = nt2;
  }

 public static Array DATNTabFunc (NUMBER id[], Array nt[],
    Array nt2) throws SQLException
  {
    Connection conn = DriverManager.getConnection
("jdbc:oracle:kprb:");
    Statement stmt = conn.createStatement();

    OraclePreparedStatement ps = (OraclePreparedStatement)
        conn.prepareStatement ("SELECT DATNT FROM NSTableTab WHERE ID =
?");

    ps.setNUMBER (1, id[0]);
    OracleResultSet rs = (OracleResultSet) ps.executeQuery();
```

```
     Array a = null;

     while (rs.next())
     {
       a = (Array) rs.getObject(1);
     }
     ps.close();

     id[0] = new NUMBER(id[0].intValue() + 1000);
     nt[0] = nt2;

     return a;
   }
}
/
show errors;

create or replace procedure DATNTabProc (x IN OUT number, y IN OUT
NTab_DAT,
   z IN NTab_DAT) as language java
   name 'DATNTabClass.DATNTabProc(oracle.sql.NUMBER[],
java.sql.Array[],
        java.sql.Array)';
/
show errors;

create or replace function DATNTabFunc (x IN OUT number, y IN OUT
NTab_DAT,
   z IN NTab_DAT) return NTab_DAT as language java
   name 'DATNTabClass.DATNTabFunc(oracle.sql.NUMBER[],
java.sql.Array[],
        java.sql.Array) return java.sql.Array';
/
show errors;

set serveroutput on
declare
a number;
x NTab_DAT;
y NTab_DAT;
z NTab_DAT;
```

```
begin

  dbms_output.put_line('Calling DATE Nested Table Procedure ');
  a := 13;
  x := NTab_DAT('01-JAN-2005', '02-JAN-2005', '03-JAN-2005', '04-JAN-
2005');
  y := NTab_DAT('01-MAR-2005', '02-MAR-2005', '03-MAR-2005', '04-MAR-
2005');

  dbms_output.put_line('Input number = ' || a);
  dbms_output.put_line('Input NTab_DAT x = ');
  for i IN 1 .. x.COUNT loop
    dbms_output.put(x(i) || ' ');
  end loop;
  dbms_output.put_line(' ');


  DATNTabProc(a, x, y);

  dbms_output.put_line('Output number = ' || a);
  dbms_output.put_line('Output NTab_DAT x = ');
  for i IN 1 .. x.COUNT loop
    dbms_output.put(x(i) || ' ');
  end loop;
  dbms_output.put_line(' ');


  dbms_output.put_line('Calling DATE Nested Table Function ');
  a := 1;
  x := NTab_DAT('01-JAN-2005', '02-JAN-2005', '03-JAN-2005', '04-JAN-
2005');
  y := NTab_DAT('01-MAR-2005', '02-MAR-2005', '03-MAR-2005', '04-MAR-
2005');

  dbms_output.put_line('Input number = ' || a);
  dbms_output.put_line('Input NTab_DAT x = ');
  for i IN 1 .. x.COUNT loop
    dbms_output.put(x(i) || ' ');
  end loop;
  dbms_output.put_line(' ');


  z := DATNTabFunc(a, x, y);

  dbms_output.put_line('Ouput number = ' || a);
```

```
dbms_output.put_line('Output NTab_DAT x = ');
for i IN 1 .. x.COUNT loop
  dbms_output.put(x(i) || ' ');
end loop;

dbms_output.put_line(' ');
dbms_output.put_line('Output NTab_DAT z = ');
  for i IN 1 .. z.COUNT loop
  dbms_output.put(z(i) || ' ');
end loop;
dbms_output.put_line(' ');

end;
/
```

Mapping SQLJ Object Types

The Oracle JPublisher utility (covered in Part IV), allows mapping or "publishing" database entities such as used-defined SQL types, SQL object types, and PL/SQL types and packages to Java. Conversely, SQLJ object types, specified by ANSI SQLJ Part II allow creating user-defined SQL types, using Java classes that implement the SQLData interface (covered in Part II), as templates. Once published to SQL, the defined SQLJ object types can be used as column types or as subtypes of a coarse-grained object type, as illustrated in the following example. Furthermore, the static fields of the instances of the Java class can be accessed or changed using SQL functions, which invoke their Java implementation under the covers. You can consider SQLJ object types as a pragmatic mechanism for persisting and retrieving Java objects to/from RDBMS tables; however, these are not a substitute for an O/R mapping framework such as Toplink, which offers a complete and transparent mapping of Java objects (POJO) and their relationship (i.e., graph of objects) to RDBMS tables. The Oracle SQL syntax (i.e., the DDL) has been extended with EXTERNAL NAME and USING clauses to accommodate SQLJ object types.

The steps involved in creating a SQLJ object type are as follows:

1.   Assume an existing or a new Java class, which implements java.sql.SQLData interface (oracle.sql.ORAData interface[7] is covered in Part II). In summary, the Java class must:

---

7.   Java classes that implement the java.io.Serializable interface are not currently supported.

- Implement a `getSQLTypeName()` method.

- Implement a `readSQL()` method to retrieve the state of the Java object, using SQLInput stream.

- Implement a `writeSQL()` method to store the state of the Java object, using SQLOutput stream.

The attributes, the setters (mutators), and the getters of the Java class can be mapped to SQL through the `EXTERNAL NAME` clause; more specifically, public class methods (i.e., `public static`) are exposed as `STATIC FUNCTION`, and public instance methods (i.e., `public`) are exposed as `MEMBER FUNCTION`.

2.   Load the Java class into the database—if not already present.

3.   Use the SQL `CREATE TYPE` command to create the SQLJ object type that represents the Java type.

```
CREATE TYPE <SQLJ object> AS OBJECT EXTERNAL NAME
'<Class name>'
            LANGUAGE JAVA USING SQLData ...;
```

All attributes of the SQLJ object type must map to a Java field using the `EXTERNAL NAME` clause; however, not all Java fields are exposed to SQL. Furthermore, the Java methods may not be exposed at all.

4.   Example of SQLJ object type(s).

In this example, we will define a simple SQLJ object type (`AddressObj`), and then a complex SQLJ object type (`PersonObj`), which uses the `AddressObj` type; then create and populate a `PersonObj` table and perform the mapping between the user-defined type and `java.sql.Array`. Finally, the `SQLJ_Object` Java program inserts and retrieves an instance of `PersonObj` type.

This code sample comprises four files: `AddressObj.sql`, `PersonObj.sql`, `PersonObtTab.sql`, and `SQLJ_Object.sql` (which contains both the Java code and the test code).

The following example defines:

a.   New SQL object type `address_t` using the `AddressObj` Java class

```
AddressObj.sql
===============
```

```java
create or replace and resolve java source named
AddressObj   as
/*
 *Template for the adress_t SQLJ Object Type
 */
import java.sql.*;
import java.io.*;
import java.util.Date;
import oracle.sql.*;


public class AddressObj implements SQLData {

  String sql_type ="address_t";
  public String street1;
  public String street2;
  public String city;
  public int zip;

// Constructors

  public AddressObj() {}
  public AddressObj(String sql_type, String street1,
String street2, String
  city, int zip)
  {
    this.sql_type = sql_type;
    this.street1= street1;
    this.street2= street2;
    this.city= city;
    this.zip= zip;
  }

 // Methods implementing the SQLData interface

  public String getSQLTypeName() throws SQLException
  {
    return sql_type;
  }

  public void readSQL(SQLInput stream, String typeName)
    throws SQLException
```

```
    {
       sql_type = typeName;

       SQLInput istream = (SQLInput) stream;

       street1 = istream.readString();
       street2 = istream.readString();
       city = istream.readString();
       zip = istream.readInt();
    }

    public void writeSQL(SQLOutput stream)
       throws SQLException
    {
       SQLOutput ostream = (SQLOutput) stream;
       ostream.writeString (street1);
       ostream.writeString (street2);
       ostream.writeString(city);
       ostream.writeInt(zip);
    }
  }
  /
  show errors;
```

b.   New SQL object type person_t using the PersonObj Java class

```
PersonObj.sql
=============

create or replace and resolve java source named
PersonObj   as
/*
 *Template for the person_t SQLJ Object
 *     the previously created address_t Object type is
used to map
 *     an attribute of PersonObj type
 */
import java.sql.*;
import java.io.*;
import java.util.Date;
import oracle.sql.*;
```

```java
public class PersonObj implements SQLData {

  String sql_type = "person_t";
  public String name;
  public int age;
  public AddressObj addrObj;

// Constructors
  public PersonObj () {}
  public PersonObj(String sql_type, String name, int
age, AddressObj addrObj)
    {
      this.sql_type = sql_type;
      this.name = name;
      this.age = age;
      this.addrObj = addrObj;
    }

// Methods implementing the SQLData interface
  public String getSQLTypeName() throws SQLException
    {
      return sql_type;
    }

  public void readSQL(SQLInput stream, String typeName)
    throws SQLException
    {
      sql_type = typeName;

      SQLInput istream = (SQLInput) stream;

      name = istream.readString();
      age = istream.readInt();
      addrObj = (AddressObj) istream.readObject();
    }

  public void writeSQL(SQLOutput stream)
    throws SQLException
    {
      SQLOutput ostream = (SQLOutput) stream;
```

```
        ostream.writeString (name);
        ostream.writeInt (age);
        ostream.writeObject(addrObj);


    }
}
/
show errors;
```

c.   Java class for exchanging (insert and retrieve) Java objects with SQL objects

```
SQLJ_object.sql
===============
create or replace and resolve java source named
SQLJ_Objetc   as
/*
 *Inserting and Retrieving a UDT to/from the
PersonObjTab
 *(using person_t and address_t types)
 */

import java.sql.*;
import java.io.*;
import java.util.*;
import oracle.sql.*;
import oracle.jdbc.*;
import java.math.*;

public class SQLJ_Object
{
/*
 * Retrieving an instance of Person object type
 */
  public static PersonObj getPersonObj(int id)
          throws SQLException
  {
    OracleConnection oconn =

(OracleConnection)DriverManager.getConnection("jdbc:ora
cle:kprb:");
```

```
        java.util.Dictionary map =
            (java.util.Dictionary) (oconn.getTypeMap());
        Statement stmt = oconn.createStatement();
        try
        {
          map.put("person_t", Class.forName("PersonObj"));
          map.put("address_t",
  Class.forName("AddressObj"));
          oconn.setTypeMap((Map)map);
          oconn.commit();
        }
        catch(Exception e)
        {
         throw new SQLException(e.getMessage());
        }
        PersonObj pobj = null;
        PreparedStatement ps =
          oconn.prepareStatement("SELECT adtcol1 from
  PersonObjTab where id = ?");
         ps.setInt(1,id);
         OracleResultSet ors =(OracleResultSet)
  ps.executeQuery();
        java.util.Hashtable ht = new java.util.Hashtable();
        try
        {
          ht.put("person_t",Class.forName("PersonObj"));
          ht.put("address_t",Class.forName("AddressObj"));
        }
        catch(Exception e)
        {
          throw new SQLException(e.getMessage());
        }
        while(ors.next())
        {
          oconn.commit();
          pobj =(PersonObj)ors.getObject(1,(Map)ht);
        }
        ps.close();
        oconn.close();
        stmt.close();
        return pobj;
    }
```

```java
/*
 * Inserting an instance of Person object type
 */
 public static void insPersonObj(int id, PersonObj
personin,
    PersonObj [] personout) throws SQLException
 {
   Connection conn =
DriverManager.getConnection("jdbc:oracle:kprb:");
   OracleConnection orconn = (OracleConnection)conn;

   PreparedStatement ps = conn.prepareStatement
      ("insert into PersonObjTab values(?,?)");
   java.util.Dictionary map =
      (java.util.Dictionary)(orconn.getTypeMap());
   try
   {
     map.put("person_t",Class.forName("PersonObj"));
     map.put("Address_t",Class.forName("AddressObj"));
     orconn.setTypeMap((Map)map);
   }
   catch(Exception e)
   {
      throw new SQLException(e.getMessage());
   }
   ps.setInt(1,id);
   ps.setObject(2,personin);
   ps.executeUpdate();
   ps.close();
   PreparedStatement ps1 = conn.prepareStatement
       ("select adtcol1 from PersonObjTab where id = ?
");
   ps1.setInt(1,id);
   OracleResultSet ors1 = (OracleResultSet)
ps1.executeQuery();
   while(ors1.next())
   {
     personout[0] = (PersonObj) ors1.getObject(1);
   }
   ors1.close();
   conn.close();
```

```
    }
    }
    /
    show errors;
```

d.   Defining the SQL Object types and creating the corresponding
      table

```
CREATE OR REPLACE TYPE address_t AS OBJECT EXTERNAL
NAME 'AddressObj'
  LANGUAGE JAVA USING SQLDATA
( street1  varchar2(25)  external name 'street1',
  street2  varchar2(25)  external name 'street2',
  city     varchar2(25)  external name 'city',
  zip      number        external name 'zip'
);
/
show errors;


CREATE OR REPLACE TYPE person_t AS OBJECT EXTERNAL NAME
'PersonObj'
  LANGUAGE JAVA USING SQLDATA
( name varchar2(25) external name 'name',
  age  number  external name 'age',
  addrObj address_t external name 'addrObj'
);
/

show errors;

drop table PersonObjTab;
create table PersonObjTab (id number,adtcol1 person_t);

insert into PersonObjTab
values(10,person_t('Jack',25,Address_t(' 10
Embarcadero',' Ferry Plazza',
'San Francisco',93126)));

insert into PersonObjTab
values(11,person_t('Bob',26,Address_t('12 Jr
MLK','Alley3','Chicago',1090)));
```

```
insert into PersonObjTab
values(12,person_t('Doug',27,Address_t('10
Alley1','Alley2','Denvers',1091)));

commit;
```

e.   Defining the `Call Spec` for publishing the Java methods to SQL

```
create or replace function getPersonObj (id IN number)
return person_t
as language java
name 'SQLJ_Object.getPersonObj(int) returns PersonObj';
/
show errors;

create or replace procedure insPersonObj(id IN number,
personin IN person_t,
personout IN OUT person_t) as language java
name 'SQLJ_Object.insPersonObj(int, PersonObj,
PersonObj [])';
/
show errors;
```

f.   Running the example from a SQL*Plus command

```
declare
m3      person_t;
m4      person_t;
par     number := 25;
cnt     number := 0;

begin
m3 := person_t('Jane',31,address_t('Oracle Parkway','of
101','Redwood Shores',94065));

dbms_output.put_line('*** Calling insPersonObj
Procedure *** ');
select count(*) into cnt from PersonObjtab;
dbms_output.put_line(' Number of Records is ' || cnt);
```

```
insPersonObj(par,m3,m4);

dbms_output.put_line(' After calling the procedure ');
select count(*) into cnt from PersonObjTab;
dbms_output.put_line('Number of Records is ' || cnt);

dbms_output.put_line(' *name is '|| m4.name ||'*age is
'||m4.age ||
' *street1 is '|| m4.addrObj.street1 ||' *street2 is '
||
m4.addrObj.street2 ||' *city is '||m4.addrObj.city || '
*zip is ' || m4.addrObj.zip);

dbms_output.put_line('*** Calling getPersonObj
Function*** ');

m4 := getPersonObj (11);

dbms_output.put_line(' *name is '|| m4.name ||'*age is
'||m4.age ||
' *street1 is '|| m4.addrObj.street1 ||' *street2 is '
||
m4.addrObj.street2 || ' *city is '||m4.addrObj.city ||
' *zip is '|| m4.addrObj.zip);

end;
/
```

Voilà! This extensive but not exhaustive coverage of Call Spec should have armed you to tackle the most common publishing requirements. Having loaded, compiled, NCOMPed, and published Java in the database, the next step is how to invoke it.

3.4   Invoking Java in the Database

Currently, there are three methods for invoking Java in the database: (1) the OJVMJAVA command-line approach, (2) the PL/SQL wrapper approach, and (3) the client-side stub approach. Let's examine each of these.

3.4.1   Setup

We need a database table and a Java program.

Setting Up the Database Table

Let's reuse the Workers table. The following SQL script will prepare a table to be used by our code sample:

```
rem
rem Workers.sql
rem
connect scott/tiger

rem
rem Set up the Workers table
rem

drop table workers;
create table workers (wid int, wname varchar2(20),
      wposition varchar2(25), wsalary int);

insert into workers values (103, 'Adams Tagnon', 'Janitor',
10000);
insert into workers values (201, 'John Doe', 'Secretary',
20000);
insert into workers values (323, 'Racine Johnson', 'Junior
Staff Member', 30000);
insert into workers values (418, 'Abraham Wilson', 'Senior
Staff Member', 40000);
insert into workers values (521, 'Jesus Nucci', 'Engineer',
50000);
insert into workers values (621, 'Jean Francois', 'Engineer',
60000);
commit;
```

At this stage, the "*workers*" table has been created and populated (feel free to add/change).

Reusing a JDBC Code in the Database

We'll reuse the same JDBC program we used at the beginning of this chapter.

Listing 3.1   *Workers.java*

```
==============================
```

```
create or replace and resolve java source named Workers as
```

```
/*
 * The following code retrieves from the Worker table, a worker
 * based on his id then updates position and salary.
 * Adapated from existing JDBC demo
 */

import java.sql.*;
import oracle.jdbc.*;

public class Workers
{

   public static void main (String args []) throws SQLException {

        String name = null;
        String pos = null;
        int sal;
        int id;
        long t0,t1;
        Connection conn = null;
        Statement stmt = null;
        PreparedStatement pstmt = null;

        if ( args.length < 1 ) {
          System.err.println("Usage: Java Workers <wid> <new position>
                                                   <new salary>");
          System.exit(1);
         }

        // Get parameters value
        id = Integer.parseInt(args[0]);
        pos = args[1];
        sal = Integer.parseInt(args[2]);

          /*
         * Where is your code running: in the database or outside?
         */
         if (System.getProperty("oracle.jserver.version") != null)
      {
      /*
        * You are in the database, already connected, use the default
```

```
 * connection
 */
conn = DriverManager.getConnection("jdbc:default:connection:");
System.out.println ("Running in OracleJVM, in the database!");
    // Disable autocommit  - Not suppoted in OracleJVM
    conn.setAutoCommit(false);
}
else
{
/*
 * You are not in the database, you need to connect to
 * the database
 */

DriverManager.registerDriver(new oracle.jdbc.OracleDriver());
conn = DriverManager.getConnection("jdbc:oracle:thin:",
                "scott", "tiger");
    System.out.println ("Running in JDK VM, outside the
database!");
        }


    /*
     * Auto commit is off by default in OracleJVM (not supported)
     */
    conn.setAutoCommit (false);

    // Start timing
        t0=System.currentTimeMillis();

    /*
     * find the name of the workers given his id number
     */

    // create statement
        stmt = conn.createStatement();

    // find the name of the worker
        ResultSet rset = stmt.executeQuery(
            "SELECT WNAME FROM workers WHERE wid = " + id);

    // retrieve and print the result (we are only expecting 1 row
```

```
        while (rset.next())
        {
         name = rset.getString(1);
        }

    // return the name of the worker who has the given worker number
        System.out.println ("Worker Name: "+ name);

    /*
     * update the position and salary of the retrieved worker
     */

    // prepare the update statement
        pstmt = conn.prepareStatement("UPDATE WORKERS SET WPOSITION
= ?, " +
            " WSALARY = ? WHERE WNAME = ?");

    // set up bind values and execute the update
        pstmt.setString(1, pos);
        pstmt.setInt(2, sal);
        pstmt.setString(3, name);
        pstmt.execute();

    // double-check (retrieve) the updated position and salary
        rset = stmt.executeQuery(
        "SELECT WPOSITION, WSALARY FROM WORKERS WHERE WNAME = '" +
                        name + "'");
        while (rset.next())
        {
         pos = rset.getString ("wposition");
         sal = rset.getInt ("wsalary");
        }
      System.out.println ("Worker: Id = " + id + ", Name = " + name +
                ", Position = " + pos + ", Salary = " + sal);

    // Close the ResultSet
        rset.close();

    // Close the Statement
        stmt.close();

    // Stop timing
```

```
      t1=System.currentTimeMillis();
      System.out.println ("====> Duration: "+(int)(t1-t0)+ "
Milliseconds");

   // Close the connection
      conn.close();
   }
 }
/
```

```
show errors;
```

At this stage, assuming there are no errors, the Workers.class has been created in the schema and is ready to be used. Let's see the various ways of invoking Java in the database.

3.4.2 Invoking Java in the Database Using OJVMJAVA

Description

OracleJVM furnishes an interactive command-line utility called OJVM-JAVA, which can run Java classes in the database (i.e., classes with a `public static main()` method) from the client machine. In reality, OJVMJAVA is made of a client (let's call it ojvmjava-client) and a server (let's call it ojvmjava-server).

Here is how it works:

1.   The ojvmjava-client uses the provided JDBC connection to create a database session, and then starts the ojvmjava-server.

2.   Then the ojvmjava-client passes a byte array (LONG RAW) across the wire to the ojvmjava-server.

3.   The ojvmjava-server looks up the user class (i.e., the first argument) and passes the remaining arguments as a string to its main method. The user class must have at least one method.

4.   When the method completes, the results are sent back to the client across the wire using a byte array (LONG RAW).

The end user starts ojvmjava, and then issues valid commands.

Here is the syntax:

```
ojvmjava {-user <user>[/<password>@database] [options]
```

The valid options are:

```
[@<filename>]
[-batch]
[-c | -command <command> <args>]
[-debug]
[-d | -database <conn_string>]
[-fileout <filename>]
[-o | -oci | -oci8]
[-oschema <schema>]
[-t | -thin]
[-version | -v]
```

where command can be: echo, exit, help, java, version, whoami.

See the Oracle Database Java Developer's Guide for more details; for the purpose of this chapter, we'll only consider the java command.

Example:

Invoking the Workers program in the database, using OJVMJAVA:

```
C:\test>ojvmjava -thin -user scott/tiger
--OJVMJAVA--
--type "help" at the command line for help message

$ java Workers 621 "Senior VP" 650000
Running in OracleJVM,  in the database!
Worker Name: Jean Francois
Worker: Id = 621, Name = Jean Francois, Position = Senior VP, Salary =
650000
====> Duration: 10 Milliseconds


$ java Workers 201 "Senior VP" 650000
Running in OracleJVM,  in the database!
Worker Name: John Doe
Worker: Id = 201, Name = John Doe, Position = Senior VP, Salary =
650000
====> Duration: 10 Milliseconds


$ exit
```

3.4.3   Invoking Java in the Database through the PL/SQL Wrapper

Calling Java in the database using a user-defined or JPublisher-generated PL/SQL wrapper (also known as *Call Spec*) is the traditional and most-used approach, for the following reasons:

- It hides the implementation language of the stored procedures—could be Java, PL/SQL, or any other supported language.
- It can be invoked by SQL, PL/SQL, client-side JDBC, server-side JDBC, and middle-tier Java/J2EE.

Invoking Java through the PL/SQL wrapper involves two steps:

1. Publishing the Java method to SQL (this step is also known as defining the Call Spec and has been covered extensively in the previous section.

2. Calling the PL/SQL wrapper.

Example:

Step 1: Publishing the PL/SQL wrapper (from a SQL*Plus session)

The Call Spec is registered in the system dictionary, which maintains the correspondence with the actual Java method. The parameters and the arguments of the published Java methods and the PL/SQL wrapper must correspond one to one; however, this rule does not apply to the main() method, which only has an array of String as parameter (String[ ]). Because Array of String can only be mapped to CHAR or VARCHAR2 types, both worker id and worker salary, which hold int values, are mapped to VARCHAR2.

```
SQL>create or replace procedure WorkerSP (wid IN varchar2,
wpos IN
    varchar2, wsal IN varchar2) as
    language java name 'Workers.main(java.lang.String[])';
/
Procedure created.
```

```
SQL> show errors;
No errors.
```

Step 2: invoking the Java method through the PL/SQL wrapper (from a SQl*Plus session)

```
C:\My_data>sqlplus scott/tiger

SQL*Plus: Release 10.1.0.2.0 - Production on Wed Feb 2
17:10:08 2005

Copyright (c) 1982, 2004, Oracle.  All rights reserved.

Connected to:
Oracle Database 10g Release 10.1.0.2.0 - Production

SQL> set serveroutput on
SQL> call dbms_java.set_output(50000);

Call completed.

SQL> call WorkerSp('621', 'Senior VP', '650000');
Running in OracleJVM, in the database!
Worker Name: Jean Francois
Worker: Id = 621, Name = Jean Francois, Position = Senior VP,
Salary = 650000
====> Duration: 12 Milliseconds

Call completed.
SQL>  call WorkerSp('201', 'Senior VP', '650000');
Running in OracleJVM, in the database!
Worker Name: John Doe
Worker: Id = 201, Name = John Doe, Position = Senior VP,
Salary = 650000
====> Duration: 10 Milliseconds

Call completed.

SQL>
```

3.4.4   Invoking Java in the Database through Client-side Stub

What Is the Problem with Call Specs?

Call Specs publish methods on Java classes in the database, allowing these methods to be invoked from different languages, including Java/JDBC, non-Java languages, and SQL and PL/SQL. However, Call Specs suffer from the following limitations:

- JDBC is the least common denominator across all RDBMS vendors, and, as such, it does not support all Oracle-specific complex types. Invoking stored procedures that use complex native database types, such as user-defined SQL types, user-defined SQL collection types, object types, VARRAYS, nested tables types, PL/SQL RECORD types, and PL/SQL INDEXED-BY tables, is challenging, unless you use JPublisher (see Part IV).

- For each procedure or function, a wrapper has to be manually published with a SQL signature, which only supports SQL types that have direct mapping.

- Exceptions in Java in the database are not properly returned to the caller.

The Solution

Starting with Oracle Database 10*g* Release 1, a new mechanism allows calling methods on Java classes in the database, without the provision of a user-defined Call Spec, and by the same token, and probably more important, avoids the limitations of Call Spec. The solution consists of letting Java/J2EE invoke methods locally on the client-side stub,[8] resulting in transparent transfer of Java objects between Java in the middle tier and Java in the database and better exceptions returning. However, only serializable parameters and return types are supported; methods that take nonserializable types as parameter or return type will not be published; also, only invoker's rights are supported.

If you need to support JDBC types, arrays of supported types, Java-Beans, and serializable Java types, Oracle Database 10*g* Release 2 furnishes a new -dbjava option of JPublisher. It generates a server-side Java wrapper for instance methods, which converts Java types into types that can be

---

8.   Old-timers will recall the CORBA client-side stub.

exposed to the PL/SQL call specification and then the PL/SQL wrapper in question. See the Oracle Database JPublisher User's Guide 10*g* Release 2 (10.2) for more details.

How Does Java Invocation through the Client Stub Work?

The process consists of two steps:

1. *Generating the client stub.* In Oracle Database 10*g* Release 1, JPublisher provides the –java option for generating the stub; however, it supports only primitive and serializable Java types.

```
jpub -u scott/tiger -java=<Class>:<StubImpl>#<Stub>
```

When using 10*g* JPublisher against pre-10*g* databases, the sqljutl.jar must be preinstalled in the SYS schema.

2. *Creating an instance of the stub.* The client application or middle-tier Java/J2EE creates a new instance of the stub.

```
<Class>Stub <handler> = new <Class>StubImpl(conn);
```

This step is in fact two substeps:

   a. A new database session is created using the connection object passed to the stub in step 1. An instance of the Java class in the server is created, and its handle is returned to the stub.

   b. The client application invokes methods on the stub; the stub in turn calls the corresponding methods of the server-side Java class, using the provided JDBC connection (it uses JDBC but does not have the limitations mentioned previously).

```
<handler>.method ((new String[]{<parameter list>});
```

```
<handler>.main(new String[]{arg[0], arg[1], ...,
arg[n]});
```

Example:

Let's see a complete step-by-step example using the Workers class previously loaded in the database.

Step 1: Generate the client stub

The Oracle Database 10*g* JPublisher utility[9] generates a client-side stub class with the following characteristics:

1. Two constructors: one that uses a JDBC connection and another that uses the SQLJ default connection context instance.

2. Public static methods correspond to the public static methods of the server class

3. An extra method, `newinstance()` in the stub class, is used to create a new instance of the server class and its handle is returned; the server-side class must have an empty public constructor.

4. Public methods corresponding to public methods of the server class, but with an extra "handle" parameter, which refers to the instance of the class in question.

5. Only serializable Java types (as parameters and arguments) are supported.

Given a Java class X, the following command:

```
jpub -u scott/tiger -java=X:XStubImpl#XStub
```

JPublisher generates the stub interface (`WorkersStub.java`) and its implementation (`WorkersStubImpl.java`):

```
C:\My_Data\jpub -u scott/tiger -
java=Workers:WorkersStubImpl#WorkersStub
WorkersStub.java
WorkersStubImpl.java
```

WorkersStub.java(generated code)

```
public interface WorkersStub
{
    public void main(java.lang.String[] p0)
        throws java.sql.SQLException;
```

---

9.   This topic is fully described in Part IV of this book..

```
}
```

WorkersStubImpl.java (generated code)

```
public class WorkersStubImpl implements WorkersStub
{
    public WorkersStubImpl(java.sql.Connection conn) throws
java.sql.SQLException
    { m_ctx = new sqlj.runtime.ref.DefaultContext(conn); }

    public WorkersStubImpl(sqlj.runtime.ref.DefaultContext
ctx)
    { m_ctx = ctx; }

    public WorkersStubImpl() throws java.sql.SQLException
    {}

    public void
_setConnectionContext(sqlj.runtime.ref.DefaultContext ctx)
    { m_ctx = ctx; }

    protected sqlj.runtime.ref.DefaultContext _context()
    { return m_ctx; }

    public void _close(boolean closeJdbcConnection) throws
java.sql.SQLException
    { m_ctx.close(closeJdbcConnection); }
    private sqlj.runtime.ref.DefaultContext m_ctx;

    public void main(java.lang.String[] p0)
        throws java.sql.SQLException
    {

        Object __jRt_0 = null;
        __jRt_0 =
oracle.jpub.reflect.Client.invoke(_context(),"Workers","main"
,
                            "[Ljava/lang/String;",new
Object[]{p0,});
        if (__jRt_0 instanceof java.sql.SQLException) throw
((java.sql.SQLException)__jRt_0);
    }
```

```
}
```

Step 2: Define the client application

WorkersClient.java

```
import java.sql.*;
import oracle.jdbc.*;

public class WorkersClient
{
 public static void main(String[] arg) throws Exception{
   long t0,t1;
   DriverManager.registerDriver(new OracleDriver());
   Connection conn =
DriverManager.getConnection("jdbc:oracle:thin:","scott","tige
r");
   System.out.println ("==> Calling Workers from CLient
Stub");

   WorkersStub wk = new WorkersStubImpl(conn);

   /*
    * We should use a session where JavaVM is already
initialized
    * This first method call initializes Java in the database
session
    * Workers.java does not commit its changes so this is a no-
op
    */
     wk.main(new String[]{arg[0], arg[1], arg[2]});

  // Start client-side timing
     t0=System.currentTimeMillis();
 // Invoke server-side Workers.main method
     wk.main(new String[]{arg[0], arg[1], arg[2]});
  // Stop client-side timing
     t1=System.currentTimeMillis();
     System.out.println ("==> Client-Side Duration:
"+(int)(t1-t0)+ " Milliseconds");

  }
```

```
}
```

Step 3: Compile the client application

```
C:\My_Data\Jpub>javac WorkersClient.java
```

Step 4: Invoke Java in the database through the client stub

```
C:\My_Data\Jpub>java WorkersClient 621 "Senior VP" 650000
==> Calling Workers from CLient Stub
==> Client-Side Duration: 30 Milliseconds
```

```
C:\My_Data\PM\Book\Jpub>java WorkersClient 201 "Senior
Director" 250000
==> Calling Workers from CLient Stub
==> Client-Side Duration: 20 Milliseconds
```

```
C:\My_Data\PM\Book\Jpub>
```

Depending on the number of parameters and return values, there might be a significant overhead incurred by marshaling/unmarshaling (i.e., serialization/deserialization). The client stub approach makes sense when the server-side processing and the flexibility of supported types outweigh the cost of serialization/deserialization; reducing the number of parameters will greatly reduce the overhead.

3.4.5   Errors and Exceptions Handling

Java programs can retrieve SQL error code and the text of the message of SQL exceptions through the `getErrorCode()` and `getMessage()` methods of the `java.sql.SQLException` class. However, when Java in the database is invoked through the PL/SQL wrapper, Java exceptions such as `NullPointerException`, `IllegalArgumentException`, `DivisionByZero`, and so on are not properly returned to the caller; instead, the following error message is returned:

ORA-29532 Java call terminated by uncaught Java exception

When invoking Java in the database through the client-side stub instead (10.1.0.3 upward), exceptions objects are properly returned to the caller.

Example:

1.   Create a basic Java class in the database that throws a user-defined exception.

```
SQL> CREATE OR REPLACE AND RESOLVE JAVA SOURCE NAMED
ExceptionTest AS
      public class ExceptionTest {
      public static void exception1() throws Exception {

            throw new Exception("Test User-defined
Exception");
          }
      };
/   2   3   4   5   6   7

Java created.

SQL> show errors;
No errors.
SQL> exit
```

2.   Create a PL/SQL wrapper for `ExceptionTest.exception1()` and invoke it.

```
SQL> CREATE OR REPLACE PROCEDURE exceptiontest AS
      LANGUAGE JAVA NAME 'ExceptionTest.exception1()';
/   2   3

Procedure created.

SQL> set serveroutput on
SQL> call dbms_java.set_output(50000);

SQL> call exceptiontest();
java.lang.Exception: Test User-defined Exception
        at ExceptionTest.exception1(EXCEPTIONTEST:3)
call exceptiontest()
    *
```

```
ERROR at line 1:
ORA-29532: Java call terminated by uncaught Java
exception:
java.lang.Exception: Test User-defined Exception

SQL>
```

3.   Generate the client stub, using the –dbjava option of JPublisher
       (.java and .sqlj stub implementation sources as well as a PL/
       SQL wrapper are also generated).

```
$ jpub -u scott/tiger -
java=ExceptionTest:XtestStubImpl#XtestStub
./XtestStub.java
./XtestStubImpl.java

XtestStub.java ((generated code with hand-made
comments)
==============
public interface XtestStub
{
 /*
  * The extra method newInstance(), creates a new
instance of
  *  ExceptionTest in the server and returns its handle.
  */
   public long newInstance();

   public void exception1()
      throws java.lang.Exception;
}

XtestStubImpl.java (generated code)
==================
public class XtestStubImpl implements XtestStub
{
   public XtestStubImpl(java.sql.Connection conn)
throws java.sql.SQLException
   { m_ctx = new sqlj.runtime.ref.DefaultContext(conn);
}
   public XtestStubImpl(sqlj.runtime.ref.DefaultContext
ctx)
```

```
    { m_ctx = ctx; }
    public XtestStubImpl() throws java.sql.SQLException
{}
    public void
_setConnectionContext(sqlj.runtime.ref.DefaultContext
ctx)
    { m_ctx = ctx; }
    protected sqlj.runtime.ref.DefaultContext _context()
    { return m_ctx; }

    public void _close(boolean closeJdbcConnection)
throws java.sql.SQLException
    { m_ctx.close(closeJdbcConnection); }
    private sqlj.runtime.ref.DefaultContext m_ctx;

    // newInstance methods
    public long newInstance()

    {
     Object __jRt_0 = null;
     try {
          __jRt_0 =
oracle.jpub.reflect.Client.invoke(_context(),null,
"ExceptionTest","ExceptionTest","",new Object[]{});
       }
     catch (Throwable e) {e.printStackTrace();}
     return ((java.lang.Long)__jRt_0).longValue();
    }

    public void exception1() throws java.lang.Exception
    {
      Object __jRt_0 = null;
      try {
           __jRt_0 =
oracle.jpub.reflect.Client.invoke(_context(),null,
"ExceptionTest","exception1","",new Object[]{});
       }
      catch (java.lang.Exception e) {throw e;}
      catch (Throwable e) {e.printStackTrace();}
    }
}
```

4.   Define and compile the client code (could be any middle-tier Java/J2EE).

```
XtestClient.java
================
import java.sql.*;
import oracle.jdbc.*;

public class XtestClient
{
 public static void main(String[] arg) throws
Exception{
   DriverManager.registerDriver(new OracleDriver());
   Connection conn =

DriverManager.getConnection("jdbc:oracle:thin:@127.0.0.
1:5521:lab","scott","tiger");
  /*
   * get a handle to the client-side stub
   */
  XtestStub xt = new XtestStubImpl(conn);
  /*
   * Invoke the main method of the client-stub
   */
  xt.exception1();
 }
}
```

5.   Invoke the client code, which in turn will invoke Java methods in the database and will return the exception properly, as you would expect.

```
$ java XtestClient
Exception in thread "main" java.lang.Exception: User-
defined Exception
        at ExceptionTest.exception1(EXCEPTIONTEST:3)
        at
sun.reflect.NativeMethodAccessorImpl.invoke0(NativeMeth
odAccessorImpl.java)
        at
sun.reflect.NativeMethodAccessorImpl.invoke(NativeMetho
dAccessorImpl.java)
```

```
            at
sun.reflect.DelegatingMethodAccessorImpl.invoke(Delegat
ingMethodAccessorImpl.java)
         at java.lang.reflect.Method.invoke(Method.java)
         at
oracle.jpub.reflect.Server.invoke(Server.java)
         at
oracle.jpub.reflect.Server.invoke(Server.java)
```

ORA-29531 no method %s in class %s

Because PL/SQL doesn't check the signature of Java methods at wrapper definition time, but rather at runtime, this error is usually caused by data type mismatch between the Call Spec and the Java signature; here is an example:

```
SQL> create or replace and resolve java source named test as
public class X {static public void foo (java.sql.Date d){}}
  2  /

Java created.

SQL>  create or replace procedure foo(x date) as language java
name 'X.foo(dummy)';
  2  /

Procedure created.

SQL> call foo(sysdate);
call foo(sysdate)
     *
ERROR at line 1:
ORA-29531: no method foo in class X

SQL>
```

The reasoning is that the class can be defined at a later time, hence avoiding a hard dependency from the call spec to the Java underlying class. Therefore, the following PL/SQL wrapper is successfully created on a non-existent Java class:

```
SQL> create or replace procedure fake as language java name
  2  'Dummy.Method()';
  3  /

Procedure created.

SQL> call fake();
call fake()
      *
ERROR at line 1:
ORA-29540: class Dummy does not exist
```

ORA-29549 Java Session State Cleared

This error message was covered in Chapter 2. When a Java class being used is recompiled, the in-memory copy is invalidated, and any session using this class receives this message the next time it invokes the class in question and will lose any associated state. Rerun the command that gives this error message to use the newer recompiled version of the class.

3.5   Managing Java in the Database

3.5.1   Java Audit

In the 9*i* R2 and 10*g* R1 database releases, SQL audit can be used to audit the PL/SQL wrappers of Java classes that are published and known to SQL; however, it cannot audit changes to the underlying Java source, class, or resource. Starting with release 10*g* R2, Java audit allows you to trace any modification of Java sources, Java classes, or Java resources using "audit." The SQL syntax has been extended to support Java audit.

Example:

```
SQL> audit create java source by scott;
SQL> audit execute on java class sys.myJavaClass by scott;
```

Tables 3.4 and 3.5 summarize Java audit.

The audit options for a session are initialized at session creation. Hence, if you connect as sys and change the audit option after a user session has

Table 3.4 *Java Audit Option*

Java Audit Option	SQL/DDL to Be Audited
CREATE JAVA SOURCE	CREATE JAVA SOURCE CREATE OR REPLACE JAVA SOURCE
ALTER JAVA RESOURCE	ALTER JAVA RESOURCE
DROP JAVA SOURCE	DROP JAVA SOURCE
CREATE JAVA CLASS	CREATE JAVA CLASS CREATE OR REPLACE JAVA CLASS
ALTER JAVA CLASS	ALTER JAVA CLASS
DROP JAVA CLASS	DROP JAVA CLASS
CREATE JAVA RESOURCE	CREATE JAVA RESOURCE CREATE OR REPLACE JAVA RESOURCE
ALTER JAVA RESOURCE	ALTER JAVA RESOURCE
DROP JAVA RESOURCE	DROP JAVA RESOURCE

Table 3.5 *Audit Option versus Target Objects*

Audit Option versus Target Objects	Java Source	Java Resource	Java Class
ALTER	X		X
EXECUTE			X
AUDIT	X	X	X
GRANT	X	X	X

been started, the change will not be effective until you restart the session. See the Oracle Database Java Developer's Guide for required privileges and more details on Java audit.

3.5.2 Oracle Enterprise Manager (Database Control) Support for Java in the Database

The Oracle Enterprise Manager tool allows managing Java sources and classes through a GUI (Oracle 9*i* R2) or Web interface (10*g*). Through these interfaces, you can perform the following actions: Edit, View, Delete, Create, Create Like, Compile, Status, Creation date, Last Modified date, Create Synonym, Grant privileges, Load Java, and Drop Java. The ability to show dependencies is very handy. In addition, the visual error handling gives you an indication of errors and details on the right-hand pane.

This chapter walked you through the various steps for developing, deploying, and running Java in the database. Now that you know how to use Java in the database, let's see what you can do with it. The next chapter describes interesting usage of Java in the database.

4

Pragmatic Applications Using Java in the Database

JDBC-style applications (i.e., a mix of Java and SQL) are the typical Java applications for the database, commonly known as Java stored procedures. As illustrated in Chapter 1, JDBC applications will likely run faster in the database because there is only one roundtrip and the proximity with the SQL layer (same memory space). This chapter walks you through a few examples of atypical Java applications in the database that implement new database functionality simply by using standard Java libraries. The examples include secure credit card processing using JSSE, calling out a non-Oracle database using a pure Java foreign JDBC driver, Calling Out to SAP Systems using SAP JCO, Using Java in the database and J2EE in the Middle tier Together (calling out to EJB, calling out to Web components using HTTP, JMS over Oracle streams/AQ), and an Excel-like expressions evaluator. These applications are either self-sufficient solutions for tactical needs or building blocks for more complete, complex, or strategic frameworks running in the database.

4.1   CNXO: Secure Credit Card Processing with Oracle and JSSE

This application[1] is furnished courtesy of Francisco J. Juarez-Rivas of Appropriate Solutions, Inc. The CNXO (CN!*Express* for Oracle) product adds credit card processing abilities to a basic Oracle installation (either Workgroup or Enterprise). The processing is performed through an Internet gateway (such as Authorize Net or Paymentech's Orbital Gateway). This application showcases the ability to perform secure Web transactions from within an Oracle 9*i* database using HTTPS protocol (secure HTTP).

---

1.   Previously published in Java in the Database @ Work: Customer Case Studies http://www.oracle.com/technology/tech/java/jsp/pdf/JavaDB_Use_Case.pdf.

Architecture Overview and Design

As Figure 4.1 illustrates, this application is made of a PL/SQL interface, a Java interface, and the processor. All end-user interfaces are written in PL/SQL to allow backward compatibility with existing applications, interfaces, and schemas; all interaction with the processors is written in Java, using the Java Secure Socket Extension (JSSE) libraries by Sun Microsystems.

The end user calls a PL/SQL procedure with XML or Delimited Text input describing the transaction. Next, the PL/SQL interface parses the incoming data and makes any necessary transformations. It then checks permissions, invokes the appropriate packages, and sends validated data to a Java stored procedure. Finally, it gets results back from the Java stored procedure, formats the data according to end-user specifications, performs logging, and delivers the report.

The Java stored procedure retrieves the processor, its URL, and the type of the transaction from the incoming data. It then opens a secure HTTP connection (HTTPS) to the processor, which handles the transaction. Finally, it passes the results back to the PL/SQL interface.

A basic credit card transaction call flows in the following way:

1. The registered user calls a PL/SQL procedure with XML or delimited text data input.

2. The PL/SQL package validates the data, stores some information on the system, and calls a Java stored procedure.

3. The Java stored procedure checks with the JAVA_POLICY_TABLE to ensure that the target URL is registered.

4. The Java stored procedure opens a secure HTTPS connection using JSSE. This connection can also be made through a proxy if desired.

5. The Java stored procedure negotiates the transaction with the processor and sends the results back to the calling PL/SQL package.

6. The PL/SQL package logs the result of the transaction and formats the data to the same format that the procedure received (XML or Delimited Text).

7. The procedure sends the result back to the schema, application, or Web site that made the call.

The user remains isolated from all the HTTPS, Java, and SQL code and does not need to perform any type of programming to set up or run this system.

Implementation Challenges

Because security is a key requirement for CNXO, all Web interactions must be performed through HTTPS protocol implemented by Sun Microsystems', JSSE libraries. Because JSSE is pure Java, it can be loaded to the OracleJVM using the LOADJAVA utility. We decided to use it as a way to implement HTTPS calls from Java procedures; however, JSSE is an optional package in pre-1.4 releases of J2SE and therefore is not supported by Oracle Database 9*i* Release 2. Oracle Database 10*g* is J2SE 1.4 compatible and supports natively JSSE. The ability to invoke Java in the database through a PL/SQL wrapper provides a seamless integration with the SQL engine, thereby eliminating the need for an external mechanism to make secure connections to the Web server from within the database.

All HTTPS interactions must be performed with registered URLs in the Oracle JAVA_POLICY_TABLE.[2] URLs must be added to the policy table before being used. CNXO performs checks to ensure that a given URL is already registered before accessing it.

CNXO does not store sensitive data. Instead, when a client provides a credit card number, it is stored in one-way hash MD5 encryption format by an activity log. To find transaction information, the client must provide a credit card number, which is encrypted by CNXO into MD5 hash format. CNXO uses the encrypted format to look up the transaction information in the activity log.

CNXO is currently being integrated with the Hospitality Suite and CareTrakker product lines from Computrition, Inc. With CNXO, Computrition can now provide an integrated credit card processing solution for its existing food service management products.

JSSE-enabling Oracle 9i Release 2

JSSE is mandated in J2SE 1.4; therefore, steps 1 through 7 are not needed with an Oracle Database 10*g*; these are required only if you are implementing this example with an Oracle 9*i* Database Release 2.

---

2.   See Chapter 2.

Figure 4.1
CNXO Overview

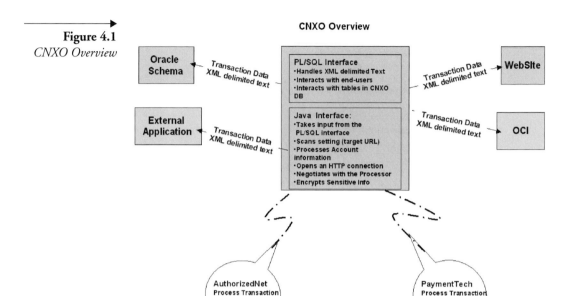

1. Download JSSE version 1.0.3 from the Sun Microsystems Web site: `http://java.sun.com/products/jsse/index-103.html`. Save and unzip the file on your local disk. Locate the three JSSE JAR files: `jnet.jar`, `jcert.jar`, and `jsse.jar` under your local directory. For example:

    ```
    D:\jsse1.0.3_01\lib
    ```

    Copy the certificates to the database security folder.

    Copy the file `jsse1.0.3_01/samples/samplecacerts` to:

    ```
    $ORACLE_HOME/javavm/lib/security/cacerts
    ```

2. Copy the JSSE JAR files: `jnet.jar`, `jcert.jar`, and `jsse.jar` to the `$ORACLE_HOME/javavm` directory.

3. Because Oracle 9*i* does not allow overloading of an existing system class, you must load the JSSE classes into a non-SYS schema. Connect as SYS, and create the schema you want to use for JSSE, using the following command:

```
SQL> GRANT connect, resource, unlimited tablespace,
create public synonym, drop public synonym, javasyspriv
TO JSSE IDENTIFIED BY <password>
```

4.   From SQL*Plus, load the JSSE JAR files to the JSSE schema
      using DBMS_JAVA.LOADJAVA, assuming that your JAR files are in
      the $ORACLE_HOME/javavm directory:

```
SQL> CONNECT jsse/jsse
SQL> SET serveroutput on
SQL> CALL dbms_java.set_output(100000);
SQL> CALL dbms_java.loadjava(' -r -v -definer -g public
$ORACLE_HOME/javavm/jcert.jar $ORACLE_HOME/javavm/
jnet.jar $ORACLE_HOME/javavm/jsse.jar');
```

5.   Create a PUBLIC synonym for the HTTPS handler and the SSL
      Provider:

```
SQL> CREATE PUBLIC SYNONYM "com/sun/net/ssl/internal/
www/protocol/https/Handler" for "com/sun/net/ssl/
internal/www/protocol/https/Handler";
```

```
SQL> CREATE PUBLIC SYNONYM "com/sun/net/ssl/internal/
ssl/Provider" for "com/sun/net/ssl/internal/ssl/
Provider";
```

6.   Set the following permissions for communicating with external
      sites. If you are behind a firewall, you will need extra permissions
      for the proxy machine. You must grant those permissions to every
      schema that is going to use the JSSE. Log in to Oracle as SYS and
      issue the following commands, in the order given:

```
SQL> CALL dbms_java.grant_permission( 'SYS',
'SYS:java.security.SecurityPermission',
'insertProvider.SunJSSE', '' );
```

```
SQL> CALL dbms_java.grant_permission( 'SYS',
'SYS:java.security.SecurityPermission',
'putProviderProperty.SunJSSE', '' );
```

```
SQL> CALL dbms_java.grant_permission( 'SYS',
'SYS:java.security.SecurityPermission',
```

```
'getProperty.ssl.ServerSocketFactory.provider', '' );

SQL> CALL dbms_java.grant_permission( 'SYS',
  'SYS:java.security.SecurityPermission',
'getProperty.cert.provider.x509v1', '' );

SQL> CALL dbms_java.grant_permission( 'SYS',
'SYS:java.util.PropertyPermission',
'java.protocol.handler.pkgs', 'write' );
SQL> CALL dbms_java.grant_permission( 'SYS',
  'SYS:java.util.PropertyPermission',
  'https.proxyHost', 'write' );

SQL> CALL dbms_java.grant_permission( 'SYS',
  'SYS:java.util.PropertyPermission',
  'https.proxyPort', 'write' );

SQL> CALL dbms_java.grant_permission( 'SYS',
'SYS:java.security.SecurityPermission',
'getProperty.ssl.SocketFactory.provider', '');

SQL> CALL dbms_java.grant_permission( 'SYS',
'SYS:java.security.SecurityPermission',
'getProperty.sun.ssl.keymanager.type', '' );

SQL> CALL dbms_java.grant_permission( 'SYS',
  'SYS:java.security.SecurityPermission',
  'getProperty.sun.ssl.trustmanager.type', '' );
```

7.   In order for a specific schema to use the HTTPS protocol, you
     must grant the schema in question the following permissions:

```
SQL> CALL dbms_java.grant_permission( 'SCOTT',
  'SYS:java.security.SecurityPermission',
  'insertProvider.SunJSSE', '' );

SQL> CALL dbms_java.grant_permission( 'SCOTT',
  'SYS:java.util.PropertyPermission',
  'java.protocol.handler.pkgs', 'write' );

SQL> CALL dbms_java.grant_permission( 'SCOTT',
```

```
              'SYS:java.util.PropertyPermission',
              'https.proxyHost', 'write' );

     SQL> CALL dbms_java.grant_permission( 'SCOTT',
              'SYS:java.util.PropertyPermission',
              'https.proxyPort', 'write' );

     SQL> CALL dbms_java.grant_permission( 'SCOTT',
              'SYS:java.security.SecurityPermission',
              'setProperty.cert.provider.x509v1', '' );
```

Compile the URLReader.java source code as follows, which is a JSSE sample program for accessing a secure HTTP Web server, and then load it to the JVM using the LOADJAVA utility, as follows (this step is all you need to do using an Oracle Database 10*g*):

```
loadjava —f —u scott/tiger —resolver "((* SCOTT) (* JSSE)(*
PUBLIC)"
     —r —v URLReader.class
```

URLReader as Java Stored Procedure

The following code snippet issues HTTPS call-out from within the Oracle-JVM to connect to the Verisign secure Web site. Uncomment instructions for proxy setting if you are connecting through a proxy server.

Step 1: URLReader.java

```
// JSSE sample program for accessing a secure http web server.

import java.net.*;
import java.io.*;
import java.security.*;

public class URLReader {
    public static void main(String[] args) throws Exception {
      URLReader r = new URLReader();
      r.URLReader();
    }
```

```
public static void HTTPSCallout() throws IOException
{
  Security.addProvider(new com.sun.net.ssl.internal.ssl.Provider());
System.setProperty("java.protocol.handler.pkgs",

"oracle.aurora.rdbms.url|com.sun.net.ssl.internal.www.protocol");
/*
 *
 * If you are running inside a firewall, please also set the following
 * Java system properties to the appropriate value and uncomment:
 *
 *  System.setProperty("https.proxyHost","< secure proxy server >");
 *  System.setProperty("https.proxyPort","< secure proxy port >");
 *
 *
 */


    URL verisign = new URL("https://www.verisign.com/");
BufferedReader in =
new BufferedReader(new InputStreamReader(verisign.openStream()));
String inputLine;
while ((inputLine = in.readLine()) != null)
   System.out.println(inputLine);
   in.close();
}
}
```

Step 2: Create a PL/SQL Wrapper

```
// PL/SQL Wrapper Code for this Sample

create or replace procedure testssl as language java
 name 'URLReader.HTTPSCallout()';
/
Step 3: Call the PL/SQL Wrapper
SQL> Set Serveroutput ON
SQL> Call dbms_java.set_output(1000000);
SQL> Call testssl();
```

CNXO Conclusion

Using Java stored procedures from within the OracleJVM provides reliable, robust, and secure credit card processing. The implementation uses the Sun Microsystems JSSE package to provide HTTPS interaction with the credit card processing system. Because Java is standardized on the various platforms, it becomes the best choice when dealing with different systems. The implementation uses the Sun Microsystems JSSE package to provide HTTPS interaction with the credit card processing system. For all these reasons, and in addition to its sophisticated built-in JVM, Oracle became the database of choice—it provided flexibility to load any JAR files to its JVM. The ability to wrap those Java objects with PL/SQL provides integration between Java, SQL, XML, and PL/SQL worlds, resulting in greater database flexibility and expandability. A future step will be to expose the transaction processing engine through a Web service—suitably sheltered behind an HTTPS proxy. Send questions and comments to:

fjuarez@AppropriateSolutions.com

4.2   Using J2EE and Java in the Database Together

Traditionally, J2EE components invoke Java in the database as stored procedures through JDBC using the PL/SQL wrapper. Starting with Oracle Database 10*g* Release 1, J2EE components can also use the JPublisher-generated client stub, described in Chapter 3. This section describes additional ways to make Java in the database and J2EE work together, including the implementation of auto-generating primary keys for BMP EJB or finder methods for CMP EJB.

4.2.1   Auto-generating Primary Keys for BMP Entity Beans

A BMP entity bean instance[3] can be uniquely identified by the auto-generated primary key associated with the newly inserted data as return value for *ejbCreate()*. Retrieving this value within *ejbCreate()* can be performed in one database operation by using a stored procedure that will insert the corresponding data and then retrieve or compute the primary key. Alternatively, you can insert the data using a simple INSERT statement and then retrieve the value of the pseudo column (*ROWID*) of the newly inserted row using JDBC 3.0 Retrieval of Auto-Generated Key;[4] but the stored procedure approach is more portable across JDBC drivers and databases. The following code snippet is excerpted from *EJB Design Patterns* (OUT parameters registration has been omitted):

---

3.   Described in Mastering Enterprise JavaBeans, by Ed Roman (New York: John & Sons, Wiley, 2004).
4.   The Oracle Database 10g Release 2 supports JDBC 3.0 retrieval of auto-generated keys.

- Define the `insertAccount()` Java method as part of the GenPK Java class:

```
create or replace and resolve java source named GenPK as
    import java.sql.*;
import java.io.*;
import oracle.sql.*;
import oracle.jdbc.*;

public class GenPK
{

    public static insertAccount(String account)
    throws SQLException
    {
/*
 * pseudo-code
 *
 * insert data
 * compute unique key by
 * either passing out a sequence number
 * or using the JDBC 3.0 Retrieval of auto-
 * generated keys then return the primary key
 */
    }
}
/
show errors;
```

- Create the Call Spec corresponding to the Java method:

```
CREATE OR REPLACE PROCEDURE insertAccount{owner IN
varchar, bal IN number, newid OUT number)
AS LANGUAGE JAVA NAME
'GenPK.insertAccount(java.lang.String [])';
/
```

- Use the Java stored procedure in the BMP `ejbCreate()` method:

```
public AccountPK ejbCreate(String ownerName, int
balance) throws CreateException
{
 try
 {
 CallableStatement call = conn.prepareCall{
 "{call insertAccount(?, ?, ?)}";
 }

 return new AccountPK(accountID);
}
```

Mapping CMP Beans Finders Using Java Stored Procedures

You can use Java-based stored procedures in conjunction with O/R mapping frameworks such as Toplink to implement custom finder methods such as findByStoredProcPK (or whatever you want to call it)—in contrast to findByPrimaryKey, which is generated by the EJB container. As an example, Toplink allows you to define the EJB finders as *SQL finders* and then implement the finder as a Java stored procedure wrapped by a PL/SQL wrapper. See the Oracle Toplink documentation for further details.

4.2.2 Calling-out EJB from OracleJVM

Enterprise JavaBeans typify J2EE programming models by allowing you to declaratively enable, disable, and change the behavior of infrastructure services such as transaction and security management. These are generally complex or pure computational logic that implement a business function such as tax calculation (i.e., Session Beans) or business entities such as a purchase order (Entity Beans).

Rationales for EJB Call-Out

Why call an EJB from within the database? The motivation will become obvious through the following example. Assume a batch job iterates through a queue or table of pending customers' requests (e.g., car rental quotes, loan quotes, tax calculations). For each request, the batch job invokes a stateless EJB implementing a rate engine. The stateless EJB takes input parameters from the queue or the table and produces rate proposals. EJB call-out, as pictured in Figure 4.2, represents the cooperation between the database and the middle tier to accomplish a business service. Several business services can be efficiently implemented by partitioning the job between the database and the middle tier.

Figure 4.2
*Direct EJB Call-
out*

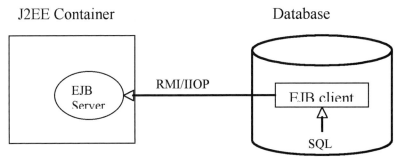

Listing 4.1 describes the steps involved in turning a standard EJB client into a Java stored procedure that invokes an external stateless Session Bean. A stateful Session Bean will be more appropriate if the application requires multiple interactions between the same database session and the same EJB instance. However, multiple interactions between the same session and the same EJB won't work in Oracle 9.2, a result of the end-of-call migration that closes all user threads and file descriptors, no matter which server mode you use (shared server or dedicated); see Chapter 2 for more details.

In 10*g* R1 and up, in dedicated server mode only, threads and file descriptors are preserved across calls, which makes possible multiple inter-actions such as stateful Session Beans invocation. Another consideration when dealing with EJB is transaction demarcation. Enterprise Java Beans are, by nature, transactional; however, the EJB specification does not mandate client-side transaction demarcation, and therefore such capability is not offered by most J2EE containers. As a result, you cannot validate (i.e., commit) or undo (i.e., rollback) the changes performed by the EJB from a remote client, which in our case is a Java stored procedure.

There are additional considerations, such as the ability to propagate the transaction context between the RDBMS and the EJB container; such ability is not available as of this writing. EJB call-out works well in release 10.1.0.5 and up; for previous releases (including 9.2 and initial 10.1.0.x releases, x < 5), an indirect approach[5] consists of calling out[6] a Servlet or JavaServer Page first, which is collocated with the EJB (within the same container and/or JVM), and in turn calls it.

Calling out a Stateless Bean in OC4J from Java DB using RMI/IIOP

Step 1: Download, Install, and Start up OC4J

---

5.   http://www.oracle.com/technology/sample_code/tech/java/jsp/samples/ejbcallout/Readme.html.
6.   HTTP call-out—see section 4.2.3.

a.   Download a recent edition of OC4J stand-alone (for development and test purposes only).

```
http://www.oracle.com/technology/software/products/ias/
index.html
```

a.   Install OC4J stand-alone by extracting the ZIP file in a directory of your choice (e.g., C:\OC4J) and follow the Basic Installation instructions in the Readme file.

a.   By default, OC4J uses RMI over ORMI (an Oracle/Orion proprietary but optimized protocol as opposed to standard IIOP); *GeneratedIIOP* startup option enables RMI/IIOP instead. Start OC4J as follows (from <install dir>/j2ee/home, referred to as $J2EE_HOME):

```
java -DGenerateIIOP=true -jar oc4j.jar
```

Step 2: Deploying the Demo EJB to OC4J

The `ejb_demos.zip`[7] contains several EJB demos for OC4J; this proof of concept will use the basic Helloworld stateless Session Bean.

Listing 4.1   *From ejb_demos.zip*

```
====================================
// HelloBean.java

package hello;

import javax.ejb.*;

public class HelloBean implements SessionBean
{

  public SessionContext ctx;

  public HelloBean()
  {
    // constructor
  }

  public void ejbCreate()
    throws CreateException
```

---

7.   http://www.oracle.com/technology/tech/java/oc4j/demos/904/EJB/ejb_demos.zip.

```
{
  // when bean is created
}

public void ejbActivate()
{
  // when bean is activated
}

public void ejbPassivate()
{
  // when bean is deactivated
}

public void ejbRemove()
{
  // when bean is removed
}

public void setSessionContext(SessionContext ctx)
{
  this.ctx = ctx;
}

public void unsetSessionContext()
{
  this.ctx = null;
}


public String sayHello(String myName) throws EJBException
{
  return ("Hello " + myName);
}

}
```

The following instructions make minor changes to jndi.properties and the EJB client (to mostly deal with lookup services for EJB being called from within OracleJVM):

a.   Unzip ejb_demos.zip into $J2EE_HOME.

```
cd $J2EE_HOME; unzip ejb_demo.zip
cd ejb/helloworld/etc/
```

b.   In order to use the org.omb.CORBA lookup services, edit the
jndi.properties file to become as follows:

java.naming.factory.initial=com.sun.jndi.cosnaming.CNCtxFactory
java.naming.provider.url=corbaname::localhost:5555#helloworld
java.naming.security.principal=admin
java.naming.security.credentials=welcome

c.   Edit the EJB client HelloClient.java file and rebuild.

cd ../src/ejb/client

```
// HelloClient.java

package hello;

import javax.ejb.*;
import javax.naming.*;
import javax.rmi.PortableRemoteObject;
import java.io.*;
import java.util.*;
import java.rmi.RemoteException;

/*
 * A simple client for accessing an EJB.
 */

public class HelloClient
{
  public static void main(String[] args)
  {
    System.out.println("client started...");
    try {

      // Initial context properties are set in the
      // jndi.properties file

      Context context = new InitialContext();
```

```
              // This for use with
com.evermind.server.rmi.RMIInitialContextFactory
          // Object homeObject = context.lookup("HelloBean");


              // This is for use with
          // com.evermind.server.ApplicationClientInitialContextFactory
             Object homeObject = context.lookup("java:comp/env/
Helloworld");


              // Narrow the reference to HelloHome.
                HelloHome home =
             (HelloHome) PortableRemoteObject.narrow(homeObject,
HelloHome.class);


              // Create remote object and narrow the reference to Hello.
                Hello remote =
             (Hello) PortableRemoteObject.narrow(home.create(),
Hello.class);


                System.out.println(remote.sayHello("James Earl"));


             } catch(NamingException e) {
             System.err.println("NamingException: " + e.getMessage());
          } catch(RemoteException e) {
          System.err.println("RemoteException: " + e.getMessage());
       } catch(CreateException e) {
                System.err.println("FinderException: " + e.getMessage());
           }
         }
      }
```

- Remove any exit(1) instruction from the EJB client so the database session is not terminated when the application ends.

- The following changes are needed to use the org.omb.CORBA lookup services:

    - Uncomment the lookup statement at line 29 to become:
      ```
            Object homeObject = context.lookup("HelloBean");
      ```

    - Comment out the following lookup statement at line 31 to become:

```
//Object homeObject = context.lookup("java:comp/env/
Helloworld");
```

d.   Go to the top and build the application.

```
cd ../../..
ant
```

The application should build with no errors; otherwise, refer to the Oracle Application Server Containers for J2EE (OC4J) User's Guide; all you need is a stand-alone packaging.

e.   Deploy the application as follows:

```
java -jar $J2EE_HOME/admin.jar ormi://localhost admin welcome
    -deploy -file dist/helloworld.ear -deployment_name
    helloworld - iiopClientJar dist/stub_helloworld.jar
```

Several notifications will appear.

f.   Test the whole thing in the middle tier.

```
$JAVA_HOME/bin/java -classpath
  $J2EE_HOME/oc4j.jar:dist/helloworld-client.jar:dist/helloworld-
  ejb.jar:dist/ stub_helloworld.jar hello.HelloClient
    client started...
    Hello James Earl
```

Step 3: Turning EJB Client into a Java Stored Procedure

Note: The _Tie.class files would not resolve in OracleJVM and should not be loaded; however, if loaded, harmless error messages will appear.

From the ORACLE_HOME of the database server, perform the following:

a.   Set J2EE_HOME to point to OC4J home.

```
setenv J2EE_HOME <install dir>/j2ee/home
```

b.   Load the following JARS in the database:

```
loadjava -u scott/tiger@localhost:port:instance_name -r -v
  $J2EE_HOME/ejb/helloworld/dist/stub_helloworld.jar
  $J2EE_HOME/lib/ejb.jar
  $J2EE_HOME/ejb/helloworld/dist/helloworld-ejb.jar
  $J2EE_HOME/ejb/helloworld/dist/helloworld-client.jar
```


Note: `helloworld-client.jar` must be the last JAR in the list.

Lots of output that can be ignored will be generated, including the following harmless error messages:

```
class _HelloHome_StatelessSessionHomeWrapper3_Tie: resolution
class _Hello_StatelessSessionBeanWrapper2_Tie: resolution
exiting  : Failures occurred during processing
```

    c.   Create and run the following script as SYS to grant SCOTT the permissions required to access system resources (replace <$ORACLE_HOME> with the actual ORACLE HOME directory):

```
set echo on

grant ejbclient to scott;

call dbms_java.grant_permission( 'SCOTT',
'SYS:java.io.FilePermission',
'<$ORACLE_HOME>/javavm/lib/orb.properties', 'read' );

call dbms_java.grant_permission( 'SCOTT',
'SYS:java.io.FilePermission',
'/orb.properties', 'read' );

call dbms_java.grant_permission( 'SCOTT',
'SYS:java.net.SocketPermission',
'localhost:1024-', 'listen,resolve' );

call dbms_java.grant_permission( 'SCOTT',
'SYS:java.util.PropertyPermission', 'java.naming.factory.initial',
'write' );

call dbms_java.grant_permission(
'SCOTT','SYS:java.lang.RuntimePermission',
'shutdownHooks','' );

call dbms_java.grant_permission(
'SCOTT','SYS:java.util.logging.LoggingPermission', 'control', '' );
```

```
call dbms_java.grant_permission( 'SCOTT',
'SYS:java.util.PropertyPermission', 'java.naming.provider.url',
'write' );

exit;
```

Step 4: Call out the EJB from within the Database

a.   Using OJVMJAVA command-line utility:

```
ojvmjava -u scott/tiger -c "java hello.HelloClient"
client started...
Hello James Earl
```

b.   Through a PL/SQL wrapper:

```
SQL> create or replace procedure hello_client as
language java name
'hello.HelloClient.main(java.lang.String[])';
  2  /

Procedure created.

SQL> connect scott/tiger
SQL> set serveroutput on
SQL> call dbms_java.set_output(1000);

Call completed.


SQL> call hello_client();
client started...
Hello James Earl

Call completed.

SQL>
```

4.2.3 HTTP Call-Out: The Poor Man's Cache Invalidation

The OracleJVM embeds a pure Java HTTP client stack, which allows Java applications running in the database to invoke Web components (Servlet, JSP) running in the middle tier using HTTP and/or HTTPS, as described in the previous CNXO and JSSE examples. Another pragmatic usage of

HTTP call-out is a trigger-based notification of Web components that I call the "poor man's cache invalidation," as opposed to a complete/industrial solution based on Oracle database Change Notification feature. As illustrated by Figure 4.3, assume we have a Web application, which caches and publishes infrequently updated data such as product catalog or price list. The table could be modified by different applications accessing the database. A trigger associated with the table storing the Web content (i.e., catalog) ensures the freshness and accuracy of the published data. Upon changes to the table, an associated database trigger is fired to invalidate the middle-tier cache and force it to be repopulated with fresh data. The database trigger sees all changes to the table, regardless of the origin (e.g., Web applications, PL/SQL, SQL*Plus, C/C++).

Figure 4.3
HTTP Call-Out
(Cache
Invalidation)

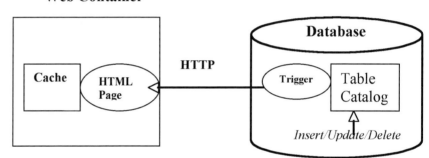

A complete application,[8] posted on the Oracle Technology Network, uses the Java Object Cache mechanism for caching data in the middle tier, but you may use a different caching mechanism. Listing 4.2 shows the required steps (the Java Object Caching is not shown; see the OTN example).

Listing 4.2   *HttpCallout.sql*

```
=================================

connect scott/tiger

create or replace and resolve java source named HttpCallout as
/*
 * HttpCallout — basic code to callout a static HTML pages
 */
import java.sql.*;
```

---
8.   http://www.oracle.com/technology/sample_code/tech/java/jsp/samples/jwcache/Readme.html.

```
import java.io.IOException;
import java.io.InputStream;
import java.util.StringTokenizer;

import HTTPClient.HTTPConnection;
import HTTPClient.HTTPResponse;
import HTTPClient.AuthorizationInfo;

public class HttpCallout {

    public static void getURL(String hostname, String portnum, String
url)
        throws InterruptedException {

        try {

            // process arguments
            String protocol = "http";
            String host = hostname;
            int port = Integer.parseInt(portnum);
            String page = url;

            // Uncomment for Debugging
            // System.setProperty("HTTPClient.log.mask", "3");

            // Establish HTTPConnection
            HTTPConnection con = new HTTPConnection(protocol, host, port);
            con.setTimeout(20000);
            con.setAllowUserInteraction(false);

            // Place a Get request
            HTTPResponse rsp = con.Get(page);

            /*
             * Alternatively, send a Post Request
             *
             * NVPair form_data[] = new NVPair[<n>];
             * form_data[0] = new NVPair("<name>", "<value>");
             * form_data[1] = new NVPair("<name>", "<value>");
             * ...
             * HTTPResponse   rsp = con.Post("<URL.jsp", form_data);
             *
             */
```

```
        // Process the response
        byte[] data = rsp.getData();
        if ( data == null ) {
          System.out.println("no data");
        } else {
          System.out.println("data length " + data.length);
          System.out.println(new String(data));
        }
      }
    catch ( Throwable ex ) {
      ex.printStackTrace();
    }
  }
}
/

show errors;


create or replace procedure callout_sp (host VARCHAR2,
    port VARCHAR2, url VARCHAR2) AS LANGUAGE JAVA
NAME 'HttpCallout.getURL(java.lang.String, java.lang.String,
java.lang.String)';
/
show errors;

create or replace trigger callout_tri
after delete or insert or update on scott.catalog
  begin
    scott.callout_sp('<host>', '<port>',  '<URL of JSP>');
  end;
/
show errors;
```

From a DBA account, grant SCOTT the permission to create a socket, as follows:

```
call dbms_java.grant_permission( 'SCOTT',
'SYS:java.net.SocketPermission', '<host>:<port>', 'resolve,connect');
/
```

At this stage, the invocation of `callout_trig` () with the appropriate parameters will cause the HTML page located at the URL (i.e., a Java ServerPage) to invalidate the middle-tier cache and force a refresh with data from the database.

4.2.4   JMS over Streams/AQ in the Database

What Is Oracle Database Streams/AQ?

The Oracle Advanced Queuing system (known as Oracle Database Streams AQ) is a messaging system tightly integrated with the database; it provides robust, secure, scalable, transactional/recoverable, and auditable functions. The integration of AQ with the RDBMS avoids the use of "two-phase commit" for committing transactions involving queue operations and regular table operations.. Streams AQ furnishes point-to-point as well as publish/subscribe messaging, message propagation to the external world, dynamic message prioritization, on-the-fly message transformation, and single-consumer as well as multiconsumer queues. The other benefit of Streams/AQ integration with the database is that the payload of the message can carry any/most of the data types managed by the RDBMS (e.g., Text, XML). See the Oracle Streams Advanced Queue User's Guide for more details. Because it is integrated with the database, Advanced Queuing messages can be concurrently accessed from SQL, PL/SQL, Java in the Database, as well C/C++ and Java/J2EE in the middle tier. Advanced Queuing furnishes extra features that cannot be mapped to the standard JMS API, such as multiple named recipients. Consequently, Oracle provides proprietary extensions to JMS for Java developers who are willing to take advantage of these features.

JMS in OracleJVM

The Java Message Service API defines a portable interface to message providers. With minimal change, JMS applications can run against different messaging systems that implement the JMS interface. It specifies two message delivery models: (1) point-to-point (or Queue domain for transactional messaging) and (2) publish/subscribe (or Topic domain for broadcasting). J2SE applications, as well as J2EE components, such as Message-Driven Beans, Servlets, and JSPs, can use the JMS APIs. Oracle JMS (OJMS) is Oracle's JMS provider implementation on top of Oracle Streams/Advanced Queuing. It is mainly used from within the Oracle Application Server J2EE containers (OC4J); however, you can run JMS applications in OracleJVM to emit (sender queue) and consume (receiver queue) AQ messages. Listing 4.3 details the necessary steps:

Listing 4.3 *JMS_DB.sql*

```
============================
-- Add the following parameters to the init.ora file:
-- compatible = 9.2.0 # or higher
-- aq_tm_processes = 1
-- job_queue_processes = 2
--
-- connect system/<password> to Create "jmsuser" and grant
-- required privileges
--


SET SERVEROUTPUT on

CREATE USER jmsuser IDENTIFIED BY jmsuser;

GRANT CONNECT, RESOURCE, AQ_ADMINISTRATOR_ROLE, AQ_USER_ROLE
        TO jmsuser;
GRANT EXECUTE ON DBMS_AQADM TO jmsuser;
GRANT EXECUTE ON DBMS_AQ TO jmsuser;

execute dbms_java.grant_permission('JMSUSER',
'java.net.SocketPermission', 'localhost:1024-', 'accept, listen,
resolve');

execute dbms_java.grant_permission( 'JMSUSER',
'SYS:java.lang.RuntimePermission', ' getClassLoader', '' );

execute dbms_java.grant_permission( 'JMSUSER',
'SYS:java.lang.RuntimePermission' , 'setContextClassLoader', '' );


--
-- Connect as the JMSUSER created above
-- Create the JMS_DB Java class
-- Create a Send and Receive Queues
--

connect jmsuser/jmsuser

create or replace and resolve java source named JMS_DB as
/*
```

```
   * JMS in the Database over AQ
   */

  import oracle.jms.*;
  import oracle.jdbc.*;
  import javax.jms.*;
  import java.sql.*;

  public class JMS_DB
  {

    public static void main(String[] args)
    throws Exception
    {
      GetPutMsg(args[0]);
    }

   // send and receive a message
    public static void GetPutMsg(String msgBody)
    {
      java.sql.Connection conn = null;

      QueueConnection send_conn = null;
      QueueSession send_session = null;
      QueueSender sender = null;
      Queue send_queue = null;
      TextMessage send_msg = null;

      QueueConnection rec_conn = null;
      QueueSession rec_session = null;
      QueueReceiver receiver = null;
      Queue rec_queue = null;
      TextMessage rec_msg = null;

      try
      {
       /*
         * get connection (session handle)
         */
        conn = DriverManager.getConnection("jdbc:default:connection:");
       /*
```

```
 * setup receiver
 */
rec_conn =
 AQjmsQueueConnectionFactory.createQueueConnection(conn);
rec_conn.start();
rec_session =
 rec_conn.createQueueSession(true,Session.CLIENT_ACKNOWLEDGE);
rec_queue =
 ((AQjmsSession) rec_session).getQueue("jmsuser", "JMSDBQ");
receiver = rec_session.createReceiver(rec_queue);
System.out.println("receiver created");

/*
 * setup sender
 */
send_conn =
 AQjmsQueueConnectionFactory.createQueueConnection(conn);
send_conn.start();
send_session =
 send_conn.createQueueSession(true,
       Session.CLIENT_ACKNOWLEDGE);
send_queue =
 ((AQjmsSession) send_session).getQueue("jmsuser", "JMSDBQ");
sender = rec_session.createSender(send_queue);
System.out.println("sender created");

/*
 * create a message
 */
send_msg = send_session.createTextMessage(msgBody);
System.out.println("message created");

/*
 * send/produce the message and commit the operation
 */
sender.send(send_msg);
send_session.commit();
System.out.println("message sent");

/*
 * receive/consume  message
```

```
          */
          rec_msg = (TextMessage) receiver.receive();
          rec_session.commit();
          System.out.println("message received");

        /*
         * display the payload (text) of the received message
         */
         String body = rec_msg.getText();
         System.out.println("message was '"+body+"'");

        /*
         * release resources
         */
         send_session.close();
         send_conn.close();
         rec_session.close();
         rec_conn.close();
      }
      catch (java.sql.SQLException sql_ex)
      {
        System.out.println("Exception: " + sql_ex);
        sql_ex.printStackTrace();
      }
      catch (JMSException aq_ex)
      {
        System.out.println("Exception: " + aq_ex);
        aq_ex.printStackTrace();

        if(aq_ex.getLinkedException() != null)
        {
          aq_ex.getLinkedException().printStackTrace();
        }
      }
    }
  }
/
show errors;


--
-- create the JMS Queue "JMSDBQ",
```

```
-- create the queue table
--
execute dbms_aqadm.create_queue_table(queue_table => 'JMSDBQ',
queue_payload_type => 'SYS.AQ$_JMS_TEXT_MESSAGE', comment => 'JMS DB
Queue', multiple_consumers => false, compatible => '9.2.0');

execute dbms_aqadm.create_queue( queue_name  => 'JMSDBQ', queue_table
=> 'JMSDBQ' );
execute dbms_aqadm.start_queue(queue_name => 'JMSDBQ');


--
-- create the Packaged PL/SQL Call Spec
--

create or replace package jmsDb_pkg authid current_user as
  procedure jmsdb(t1 VARCHAR2);
end jmsDb_pkg;
/
show errors;

create or replace package body jmsDb_pkg as
  procedure jmsdb(t1 VARCHAR2) is language java
  name 'JMS_DB.main (java.lang.String[])';
end jmsDb_pkg;
/
show errors;


--
-- Execute
--
set serveroutput on
call dbms_java.set_output(50000);
call jmsDb_pkg.jmsdb('Oracle Streams Advanced Queue Demo');
call dbms_java.set_output(50000);
call jmsDb_pkg.jmsdb('Message from Oracle Streams Avanced Queue');

SQL> set serveroutput on
SQL> call dbms_java.set_output(50000);

Call completed.
```

```
SQL> call jmsDb_pkg.jmsdb('Oracle Streams Advanced Queue Demo');
receiver created
sender created
message created
message sent
message received
message was 'Oracle Streams Advanced Queue Demo'

Call completed.

SQL> call dbms_java.set_output(50000);

Call completed.

SQL> call jmsDb_pkg.jmsdb('Message from Oracle Streams Avanced
Queue');
receiver created
sender created
message created
message sent
message received
message was 'Message from Oracle Streams Avanced Queue'

Call completed.

SQL>
--
-- Clean up
--

execute dbms_aqadm.drop_Queue_table(queue_table => 'JMSDBQ', force =>
true);
drop package jmsDb_pkg;


--
-- connect system/<password>;
--
drop user jmsuser cascade;
exit;
```

In Part VI, I will describe a real-life application that uses JMS in the database to trigger Message-Driven EJB (MDB) in the middle tier (J2EE).

4.3   JDBC Call-Out to Non-Oracle Databases

4.3.1   Description and Rationales

As pictured in Figure 4.4, JDBC call-out consists of calling out a remote database using JDBC from within OracleJVM. This section will show you how Java, SQL, and PL/SQL running in the database can query, insert, update, or delete records stored in a remote non-Oracle database.

Corporate data is sometimes distributed within multiple databases, not necessarily managed by the same RDBMS. The need to access secondary or legacy databases from within a primary Oracle database is driven by data integration and data warehousing requirements. There are several third-party data integration or gateway products, but these products are expensive and might require additional skills or training. JDBC call-out is a simpler, faster-to-implement, and cheaper solution. This technique has been successfully used as a building block by TECSIS for implementing the custom integration framework described in Part VI.

Figure 4.4
Calling out Non-Oracle Database

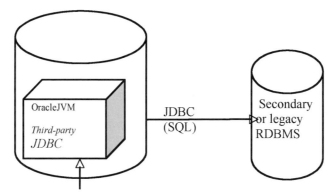

4.3.2   How Does It Work?

Most RDBMSs furnish a pure Java JDBC driver that can be loaded into the OracleJVM. Once the driver is loaded and the call-out Java program is working, we can expose the solution to the entire database user population as Java stored procedures, through PL/SQL wrappers.

The following instructions will guide you through your first experience of JDBC call-out. This example will show you how to remotely access SQL Server from within an Oracle database. The example assumes that you have both SQL Server and Oracle database up and running within the same local area network.

Step 1: Downloading and Uploading the Corresponding JDBC Drivers

First of all, you need to license a pure Java JDBC driver that supports the target database. The publicly accessible link listed is for demo purposes only; you need to check with the vendor (Microsoft, in this case) before using such a solution in a production environment.

a. Download the driver from `http://www.microsoft.com/sql/downloads/default.asp`.

b. Click "SQL Server 2000 Driver for JDBC Service Pack 3 (SP3)."

c. Download and unzip the JDBC drivers.

> You'll get the following three JAR files:
>
> `msutil.jar`
> `msbase.jar`
> `mssqlserver.jar`

d. Load these three files into the Oracle VM using the Oracle load-java utility, as follows:

> ```
> loadjava -v -user user/password@SID msutil.jar
> msbase.jar mssqlserver.jar
> ```

Step 2: Creating a Generic Java Program

The next step is to implement a Java class that contains all of the required methods to interact with the remote database, including `setConnection()`, `open()`, `execSQL()`, `fetch()`, `getColumnValue()`, `getColumnCount()`, `commit()`, `rollback()`, and `close()`.

> `setConnection(Driver, Url, User, Password, Schema)`: Holds parameter values for setting up the connection.
>
> `open()`: Loads the corresponding JDBC driver by creating a new Java object instance of the driver class and finally opens the connection to the external SQL Server.
>
> `execSQL(sql, isAquery)`: Executes a given SQL statement against the remote SQLServer database, upon opening the connection. This method can execute a SQL DML statement (i.e.,

Update/Delete/Insert) that does not return any data or a SQL Query statement (i.e., SELECT) that returns a result set. The value of the Boolean parameter *isAquery* determines whether the statement is a query (isAquery value is "true") or DML (isAquery value is "false").

`fetch()`: Self-explanatory (fetch through the results set)

`getColumnValue(index)`: Access a specific column within a record.

getColumnCount():

```
commit()
rollback()
close()
```

See Listing 4.4.

Listing 4.4   *jdbcConnection.java*

```
====================================

import java.sql.*;
public class jdbcConnection {
    // jdbc database connection parameters.
    private static String jdbcDriver;
    private static String jdbcUrl;
    private static String dbUser;
    private static String dbPwd;
    private static String dbDefaultSchema;
    // Control variables
    private static Connection jdbcConn;
    private static ResultSet dbResultSet;
    private static boolean moreRecords = false;

    public static void setConnection(String Driver, String Url, String
User,String Password, String Schema) {
        jdbcDriver = Driver;
        jdbcUrl = Url;
        dbUser = User;
        dbPwd = Password;
        dbDefaultSchema = Schema;
```

```
        }

        public static void open() throws ClassNotFoundException,
                    IllegalAccessException, InstantiationException,
    SQLException  {
            // Loads the database driver, opens a connection and selects
    the schema
            Class.forName(jdbcDriver).newInstance();
            jdbcConn = DriverManager.getConnection(jdbcUrl, dbUser,
    dbPwd);
        jdbcConn.setAutoCommit(false);
            jdbcConn.setCatalog(dbDefaultSchema);
        }

        public static void execSQL(String sql, boolean isAQuery ) throws
            ClassNotFoundException, IllegalAccessException,
    InstantiationException,
            SQLException {
            if (jdbcConn == null) open();

            // Execute the sql
      if (isAQuery) {
    dbResultSet
    jdbcConn.createStatement().executeQuery(sql);
     fetch();
        }
        else
        jdbcConn.createStatement().execute(sql);

        }

        public static boolean fetch () throws SQLException
        {
          moreRecords = dbResultSet.next();
              return moreRecords;
        }

        public static String getColumnValue (int column) throws
    SQLException
        {
          return dbResultSet.getObject(column).toString();
        }
```

```
public static int getColumnCount() throws SQLException
{
   return dbResultSet.getMetaData().getColumnCount();
}

public static void commit() throws SQLException
{
   jdbcConn.commit();
}
public static void rollback() throws SQLException
{
   jdbcConn.rollback();
}

public static void close() throws SQLException {

    if (dbResultSet != null) {
        dbResultSet.close();
        dbResultSet = null;
    }
if (jdbcConn != null) {
        jdbcConn.close();
        jdbcConn = null;
    }
moreRecords = false;

    }
}
```

a.   *Compiling the Java source*:

Save the previous code as `jdbcConnection.java` and invoke the client-side javac compiler as follows:

```
javac jdbcConnection.java
```

Alternatively, you may load the Java source directly into the database and compile within the database.

b.   *Loading the new class into the Oracle Database:*

```
loadjava -v -user user/password@SID
jdbcConnection.class
```

c.   *Publishing the API to database-side SQL, PL/SQL, and client-side JDBC:*

Create a PL/SQL wrapper package by executing the following block within your Oracle Database (see Chapter 3 for more details on user-defined Call Specs).

The Package Specification:

```
create or replace package JDBC_PKG is

   -- Public function and procedure declarations
   PROCEDURE setConnection (Driver IN VARCHAR2, Url IN
VARCHAR2, User IN VARCHAR2, dbPassword IN VARCHAR2, dbSchema
IN VARCHAR2);

   PROCEDURE open;
   PROCEDURE execSQL (sqlString IN VARCHAR2, isQuery IN
Boolean);
   FUNCTION afetch RETURN boolean;
   FUNCTION getColumnValue ( col IN number ) RETURN VARCHAR2;
   FUNCTION getColumnCount RETURN NUMBER;
   PROCEDURE commit;

   PROCEDURE rollback;
   PROCEDURE close;

end JDBC_PKG;
```

The Package Body:

```
create or replace package body JDBC_PKG is

   -- Function and procedure implementations
   PROCEDURE setConnection
   (Driver IN VARCHAR2, Url IN VARCHAR2, User IN VARCHAR2,
dbPassword IN VARCHAR2, dbSchema IN VARCHAR2)
      AS LANGUAGE JAVA
      NAME
'jdbcConnection.setConnection(java.lang.String,java.lang.Stri
ng,java.lang.String,java.lang.String,java.lang.String)';

   PROCEDURE open as
   LANGUAGE JAVA NAME 'jdbcConnection.open()';

   PROCEDURE execSQL
   (sqlString IN VARCHAR2, isQuery IN Boolean )
   AS LANGUAGE JAVA
   NAME 'jdbcConnection.execSQL(java.lang.String,boolean)';
```

```
FUNCTION afetch RETURN boolean
AS LANGUAGE JAVA
NAME 'jdbcConnection.fetch() return java.lang.String';

FUNCTION getColumnValue ( col IN number ) RETURN VARCHAR2
AS LANGUAGE JAVA
NAME 'jdbcConnection.getColumnValue(int) return
java.lang.String';

FUNCTION getColumnCount RETURN NUMBER
AS LANGUAGE JAVA
NAME 'jdbcConnection.getColumnCount() return int';

PROCEDURE commit AS
LANGUAGE JAVA NAME 'jdbcConnection.commit()';

PROCEDURE rollback AS
LANGUAGE JAVA NAME 'jdbcConnection.rollback()';

PROCEDURE close AS
LANGUAGE JAVA NAME 'jdbcConnection.close()';
end JDBC_PKG;
```

Step 3: Creating a Generic JDBC Call-out Application

Because this example opens a socket to the external world, you need to grant `java.net.SocketPermission` to the package's defining schema, as follows. Assuming your session is listening on `yourSQLServerIP:1433`, then the following instruction should be executed:

```
Exec
dbms_java.grant_permission('<TheSchemaWhoOwnsThePackage
>', 'java.net.SocketPermission','
yourSQLServerIP:1433','connect, resolve');
```

You need some privileges before granting socket permission; this is one reason why you don't want to alienate your Oracle DBA!

a.   This first example connects to the remote database and retrieves U.K. customers' IDs; notice that isAquery is set to "true."

```
declare
ret boolean;
```

```
qCol number;
begin

jdbc_pkg.setConnection('com.microsoft.jdbc.sqlserver.SQLServe
rDriver','jdbc:microsoft:sqlserver://
yourSQLServerIP:1433','user','pwd','Northwind');
 jdbc_pkg.open;
 jdbc_pkg.execSQL('SELECT CustomerId, CompanyName FROM
CUSTOMERS WHERE Country = ''UK'' ',true);
 qCol := jdbc_pkg.getColumnCount;
 dbms_output.put_line('COLUMNS: ' || qCol );
 loop
    for i in 1..qCol loop
      dbms_output.put_line(jdbc_pkg.getColumnValue(i));
    end loop;
   exit when not jdbc_pkg.aFetch;
 end loop;

 jdbc_pkg.close;

end;
```

b.   In the second example, nothing fancy, we set the employee First-
      Name to "Paula" and ID to 1. Notice that isAquery is set to
      "false."

```
begin
Jdbc_pkg.setConnection('com.Microsoft.jdbc.sqlserver.SQLServe
rDriver','jdbc:Microsoft:sqlserver://<your SQL Server
IP>:1433', '<user>','<pwd>', 'Northwind');
   jdbc_pkg.open;
   jdbc_pkg.execSQL('update Employee set FirstName = 'Paula''
WHERE employeeId =
   1', false);
   jdbc_pkg.commit;
   jdbc_pkg.close;
end;
```

This example shows how you can easily and quickly integrate a remote
database as part of your data sources. Any RDBMS accessible through a
type-4 pure JDBC driver can be reached using this simple technique. Fur-

thermore, the PL/SQL interface makes the remote database transparent to Java, SQL, PL/SQL, and any code running in the database.

4.4   SAP Java Connector: Accessing the SAP System from the Oracle Database

The following case study is provided courtesy of Esteban Capoccetti of TECSIS System. TECSIS System is one of the world's largest tubular systems providers based in Argentina. SAP Java Connector (SAP JCO)[9] allows two-way remote procedure or function calls between a Java application (i.e., a Java stored procedure) and a SAP system. You need to be a SAP customer or partner (with a valid SAPnet [OSS] userid) to download SAP JCO (http://service.sap.com/connectors).

Because SAP JCO is not pure Java and uses JNI calls, which are restricted in the OracleJVM, it is deployed as an external stand-alone RMI server, as illustrated in Figure 4.5. The system is made of three parts: (1) a Java-enabled Oracle database hosting the SAP/BAPI RMI client, (2) the stand-alone RMI server, and (3) a SAP/BAPI system.

Figure 4.5
Calling out SAP System from within the Database

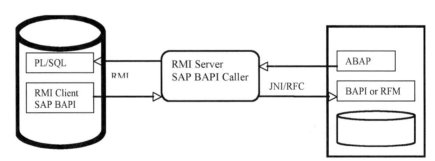

An Oracle database session can invoke operations in a remote SAP/BAPI system by the means of a Java RMI client running within Oracle-JVM. The Java RMI client can be made available to all schemas in the database as a stored procedure. Calling the stored procedure results in an RMI call-out to the SAP JCO, which, in turn, invokes functions/procedures in the SAP/BAPI, and the response is returned to the calling session.

A SAP/BAPI application invokes operations in the Oracle database by calling the SAP Java connector, which, in turn, calls stored procedures (not

---

9.   See an overview of SAP connectors and the SAP JCO FAQ at http://www.sapgenie.com/sapgenie/docs/
        SAP%20Connectors.doc and http://www.sapgenie.com/faq/jco.htm#q10.

necessarily Java based) in the Oracle database; the response from the stored procedure is returned to the calling application.

The RMI Server (SapBapiCaller.Java, SapBapiCallerRmiServer.Java) This server is responsible for connecting and calling a SAP/BAPI function. It is a simple and generic class (SapBapiCaller) that allows you to call any SAP/BAPI function accessible within your organization; it only exposes one single method: *BAPIexecute().*

```
public String BAPIexecute(String bapi_name, String sapUser,
        String sapPwd, String client, String language,
        String sapServer, String sysNumber, String aRequestXml)
```

The key idea is to use XML messages as unique request and response vehicles. The class imports the `com.sap.mw.jco.*` package shipped in the SAP JCO connector distributed by SAP. For a flexible design, we also defined an interface, SapBapiCallerInterface.java, that the SapBapiCaller class implements.

```
SapBapiCallerInterface.Java
===========================

public interface SapBapiCallerInterface extends java.rmi.Remote
 {
  public String BAPIexecute(String bapi_name, String sapUser,
        String sapPwd, String client, String language,
        String sapServer, String sysNumber, String aRequestXml)
        throws java.rmi.RemoteException;
 }


SapBapiCaller.Java
==================

import com.sap.mw.jco.*;

public class SapBapiCaller
   extends java.rmi.server.UnicastRemoteObject
   implements SapBapiCallerInterface
 {
```

```java
JCO.Client mConnection;
// The repository we will be using
JCO.Repository mRepository;

public SapBapiCaller()
      throws java.rmi.RemoteException
{
    super();
}

public String BAPIexecute(String bapi_name, String sapUser,
      String sapPwd, String client, String language,
      String sapServer, String sysNumber, String aRequestXml)
      throws java.rmi.RemoteException
{
 String aux_ret_xml = null;

 synchronized(this) {
 try {
    // Create a client connection to a dedicated R/3 system
    mConnection =
  JCO.createClient(client,sapUser,sapPwd,language,
                                     sapServer,sysNumber);
    // Open the connection
    mConnection.connect();
    // Create a new repository
    // The repository caches the function and structure definitions
    // to be used for all calls to the system mConnection
    mRepository = new JCO.Repository("Repository", mConnection);

    // Get a function template from the repository
    IFunctionTemplate ft = mRepository.getFunctionTemplate(bapi_name);

    // if the function definition was found in backend system
     if ( ft != null)
     {
      // Create a function from the template
      JCO.Function function = ft.getFunction();

      // Creates a request object from the template and returns it
      JCO.Request req = ft.getRequest();
```

```
  // Fill in BAPI input parameters from an XML
  req.fromXML(aRequestXml);

  // Executes the SAP Bapis
  JCO.Response resp = mConnection.execute(req);

  // Returns the whole response in XML format
  aux_ret_xml = resp.toXML();

  // fromXML() and toXML() sentences allow you to pass
  // and receive xml to and from the jco connector avoiding
  // the complexities of dealing with different kinds of SAP BAPI
  // parameters and tables.
  // These 2 methods are key part of this Service.


  }
  // Any error will be traped and returned as an xml instance
  // and prefixed with <ERROR> tag
  else
    aux_ret_xml = "<ERROR>BAPI " + bapi_name +
                   " NOT FOUND WITHIN SAP " + sapServer +
                   ":" + sysNumber + ":" + client + ":" + sapUser
                   + ":" + language + "</ERROR>";
  }
  catch (Exception ex) { aux_ret_xml = "<ERROR>" +
            ex.toString() + "</ERROR>"; }
  }
  // Closes the connection
  mConnection.disconnect();

    return aux_ret_xml;
  }
}
```

In order to simplify the RMI server startup, we have created a helper class, *SapBapiCallerRmiServer.java,* that registers the service for listening to RMI requests on the port passed as a parameter:

```
java.rmi.registry.Registry regobj =
java.rmi.registry.LocateRegistry. createRegistry(rmiPort)
```

```
SapBapiCallerRmiServer.Java
===========================


import java.rmi.Naming;
import java.rmi.registry.Registry;
import java.rmi.registry.LocateRegistry;

public class SapBapiCallerRmiServer {

    public SapBapiCallerRmiServer(String rmiServer, int rmiPort) {
        try {
            // creates a registry running on the local host on the given
            // port number. This method removes the need to also run
            // "rmiregistry" as stand-alone process prior to starting
            // this class as a stand-   alone process
            Registry regobj = LocateRegistry.createRegistry(rmiPort);

            // Instantiate the implementation of the interface that will
             // persist as long as this server runs
            SapBapiCallerInterface c = new SapBapiCaller();

            // Give this process the name that rmi clients use with
             // Naming.lookup()
            Naming.rebind("rmi://" + rmiServer + ":" + rmiPort +
                        "/SapBapiCallerRmiServer", c);

            System.out.println(c.getClass().getName() +
                                " ready to receive requests...");
        }
        catch (Exception e) {
            System.out.println("Trouble: " + e);
        }
    }
    public static void main(String args[]) {
        // Starts the rmi Server on the given port number ( args[0] )
        //   from a java command
        new SapBapiCallerRmiServer("localhost",
                        java.lang.Integer.parseInt(args[0]));
    }
}
```

The SAP RMI Client:

```
SapBapiCallerClient.Java
========================


import java.rmi.Naming;
import java.rmi.RemoteException;
import java.net.MalformedURLException;
import java.rmi.NotBoundException;
import oracle.sql.CLOB;


public class SapBapiCallerClient  {

   public static void main(String[] args) {
      try {
         SapBapiCallerInterface  c = (SapBapiCallerInterface)
         Naming.lookup("rmi://" + args[0] +
                                "/SapBapiCallerRmiServer");
         System.out.println( c.BAPIexecute(args[1], args[2],
            args[3], args[4], args[5], args[6], args[7], args[8]) );
      }
      catch (MalformedURLException murle) {..}
      catch (RemoteException re) {..}
      catch (NotBoundException nbe) {..}


   }
   public static void execute (String rmiUrl,String BapiName,
         oracle.sql.CLOB xml_request, oracle.sql.CLOB xml_response[],
         String sapUser,String sapPwd,String client,String language,
         String sapServer, String sysNumber )
   throws java.rmi.RemoteException,java.rmi.NotBoundException,
                java.net.MalformedURLException,java.sql.SQLException
   {
    String send_buffer = new String();
    long xml_longitud = 0;
    int v_chunk = 0;
      // rmi client as c
      SapBapiCallerInterface  c = (SapBapiCallerInterface)
      Naming.lookup(rmiUrl);

      // Copies an oracle.sql.CLOB into a String
      xml_longitud = xml_request.length();
```

```
v_chunk = xml_request.getChunkSize();
for (long v_from=1;v_from <= xml_longitud;v_from +=v_chunk)
      send_buffer += xml_request.getSubString(v_from,v_chunk);
// Calls the rmi Server, puts the response xml into xml_reponse
//  output parameter


 xml_response[0].putString(1,c.BAPIexecute(BapiName,sapUser,
     sapPwd,client,language,sapServer,sysNumber,send_buffer));



 }
}
```

Install and Configuration:

The following steps are required to install and configure the system:

1.   *Compiling the RMI Server*

Compile the RMI Server-related classes, as follows:

```
javac -classpath . SapBapiCallerInterface.java
javac -classpath sapjco.jar;. SapBapiCaller.java
note: sapjco.jar is the sapJCO Connector api.
javac -classpath . SapBapiCallerRmiServer.java
```

2.   *Generating RMI Stubs and Skeletons*

```
rmic SapBapiCaller
```

Note: `SapBapiCaller_Stub.class` and `SapBapiCaller_Skel.class` will be automatically generated.

Compiling the RMI client:

```
javac -classpath .;classes12.zip
SapBapiCallerClient.java
```

At this point, you should have the following class files:

```
SapBapiCaller.class
SapBapiCaller_Skel.class
SapBapiCaller_Stub.class
SapBapiCallerClient.class
SapBapiCallerInterface.class
```

```
SapBapiCallerRmiServer.class
```

If so, try starting the RMI server as follows:

```
java -classpath .;sapjco.jar SapBapiCallerRmiServer
1099
```

Now, from another session or from a remote computer, make an RMI call to our already running RMI server:

```
java -classpath . SapBapiCallerClient localhost:1099
BAPI_NAME
user password yourClient en your.sapapp.server
yourSystemNumber "<INPUT></INPUT>"
```

Your first XML response packet will probably look like the following:

```
<ERROR>com.sap.mw.jco.JCO$Exception: (102) RFC_ERROR_COMMUNICATION:
 Connect to SAP gateway failed
 Connect_PM  GWHOST=your.sapapp.server, GWSERV=sapgw00,
 ASHOST=your.sapapp.server, SYSNR=00

LOCATION     CPIC (TCP/IP) on local host
ERROR        hostname 'your.sapapp.server' unknown

TIME         Fri Jul 02 03:08:31 2004
RELEASE      620
COMPONENT    NI (network interface)
VERSION      36
RC           -2
MODULE       ninti.c
LINE         385
DETAIL       NiPHostToAddr
SYSTEM CALL gethostbyname
COUNTER      1
</ERROR>
```

Already a very good start! You just have to contact your internal SAP support group to check and fix your SAP connection information. Once you fix your SAP connection, your RMI Server is up and working as expected!

3.   *Uploading the RMI Client in the Database*

We have to load the following three classes into the database:

```
SapBapiCallerClient.class
SapBapiCallerInterface.class
SapBapiCaller_Stub.class
```

Create a JAR file containing these classes:

```
jar cvf SapBapiOracle.jar SapBapiCallerClient.class
SapBapiCallerInterface.class SapBapiCaller_Stub.class
```

Once the SapBapiOracle.jar has been created, we upload it into the database using the loadjava utility:

```
loadjava -verbose -user user/password@sid -resolve
SapBapiOracle.jar
```

The following lines have to be shown after completing the loading:

```
creating : class SapBapiCallerClient
loading  : class SapBapiCallerClient
creating : class SapBapiCallerInterface
loading  : class SapBapiCallerInterface
creating : class SapBapiCaller_Stub
loading  : class SapBapiCaller_Stub
resolving: class SapBapiCallerClient
skipping : class SapBapiCallerInterface
resolving: class SapBapiCaller_Stub
```

4.   *Dealing with Security*

The correct permissions must be granted to the schema that owns the wrapper. In this case, the Java permissions "connect" and "resolve" will be granted to the Java class `java.net.SocketPermission` in order to connect to the RMI server.

Assuming your RMI server *my.rmi.server* listens on port 1099, the following command should be executed:

```
exec
dbms_java.grant_permission('<schema>','java.net.SocketP
ermission',
```

```
'my.rmi.server:1099','connect, resolve');
```

For obvious database security reasons, you probably need to ask your Oracle administrator to grant you the necessary privileges in order to be in position to grant those permissions.

5. *Publishing Call_Sap_Bapi to SQL*

Finally, create a PL/SQL wrapper in order to publish the method to SQL.

```
create or replace procedure call_sap_bapi ( rmi_server
in varchar2,
   bapi_name in varchar2, xml_request in clob,
xml_response IN OUT clob,
   sap_user in varchar2, sap_pwd in varchar2, client in
varchar2,
   language in varchar2, sapServer in varchar2,
sysNumber in varchar2 )
   as language java name
'SapBapiCallerClient.execute(java.lang.String,java.lang
.String,\

oracle.sql.CLOB,oracle.sql.CLOB[],java.lang.String,java
.lang.String,\

java.lang.String,java.lang.String,java.lang.String,java
.lang.String)';
```

This new Oracle procedure, "call_sap_bapi," can be used from SQL and any data logic that require invoking SAP BAPI.

4.5   Excel-like Expression Parser in the Database

4.5.1   Rationales for Custom Parsers in the Database

SQL is the standard language for querying, updating, inserting, and deleting data in RDBMSs. However, SQL statements can be clumsy and too verbose to construct manually for complex database applications, including analytical functions, interrow calculations, spreadsheet-like calculations, and so on. A domain-specific language such as an Excel expression evaluator can be used to generate formulas (or fragments of formulas). Storing the formulas representing complex interrow calculations in the database and then reevaluating these formulas and dynamically generating the corresponding SQL is more manageable and easier to understand than maintaining long, complex SQL statements. This model becomes particularly powerful when it is integrated with the RDBMS engine. Java in the database is a natural choice for implementing database-resident language parsers/translators/compilers and their runtimes for two reasons:

1. Desire to extend your database with additional functions and capabilities such as expression parsers.

2. Java is better suited for implementing such capability than procedural SQL extensions such as PL/SQL.

Tons of Java-based parser generators are publicly available under open source licenses—no need to reinvent. The following example describes the implementation of a basic Excel-like expression parser using Java-based "Constructor of Useful Parsers" (CUP, for short), a Java equivalent of the well-known C/C++ YACC parser generator in UNIX environments.

4.5.2   What Is the Mini-Parser?

The Mini-Parser takes an Excel-like expression, parses it, evaluates it, and produces a value. Imagine that the output of the Mini-Parser serves as input to a translator (see Figure 4.6) that emits SQL Model queries, and you get a feel for the power of the expression evaluator.

Figure 4.6
The Mini-Parser

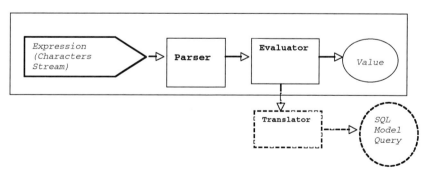

Example of Excel expression evaluator: it returns "15" when given "=sum(1,2,3,4,5)"

4.5.3 Implementing the Mini-Parser

This section explains the necessary steps to build and deploy the Excel-like expression parser in the database and expose it to SQL and PL/SQL. We'll use publicly available Java-based lexical analyzer (JLEX) and CPU parser generators, as pictured in Figure 4.7.

Figure 4.7
The Architecture of the Mini-Parser

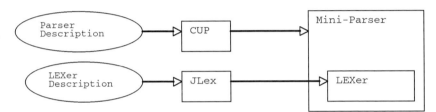

The entire process consists of five steps.

Step 1: Describing the Mini-Parser

A full explanation of the various translation and parser concepts, such as LALR, YACC, and Lex CUP,[10] is beyond the scope of this book. However, I'll describe the role of the implementation files.

The Functional Structure of the Mini-Parser

Figure 4.8 illustrates the functional structure of the Mini-Parser.

Code Outline

A description of the parser is expressed in a Java lex (Lisp-EXpression) file (formula.lex) and a CUP file (formula.cup) outlined as follows:

```
formula.lex
===========

package example.parser;
```

---

10.   http://www.cs.princeton.edu/~appel/modern/java/CUP/manual.html#code_part.

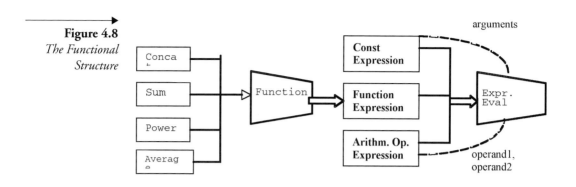

Figure 4.8
The Functional Structure

```
import java_cup.runtime.Symbol;

%%

%{
  private int comment_count = 0;
%}
%line
%char
%state COMMENT
%cup

ALPHA=[A-Za-z]
DIGIT=[0-9]
WHITE_SPACE_CHAR=[\n\ \t\b\012]
STRING_TEXT=(\\\"|[^\n\"]|\\{WHITE_SPACE_CHAR}+\\)*
DOT=[.]
%%

<YYINITIAL> "," { return (new Symbol(sym.COMMA,yytext())); }
<YYINITIAL> "(" { return (new Symbol(sym.OPAREN,yytext())); }
<YYINITIAL> ")" { return (new Symbol(sym.CPAREN,yytext())); }
<YYINITIAL> "+" { return (new Symbol(sym.PLUS,yytext())); }
<YYINITIAL> "-" { return (new Symbol(sym.MINUS,yytext())); }
<YYINITIAL> "*" { return (new Symbol(sym.TIMES,yytext())); }
<YYINITIAL> "/" { return (new Symbol(sym.DIVIDE,yytext())); }
<YYINITIAL> "=" { return (new Symbol(sym.EQUAL,yytext())); }

<YYINITIAL> {WHITE_SPACE_CHAR}+ { }

<YYINITIAL> \"{STRING_TEXT}\" {
```

```
String str =  yytext().substring(1,yytext().length() - 1);
return (new Symbol(sym.STR,str));
}
<YYINITIAL> {DIGIT}*{DOT}?{DIGIT}+ {
  Double d = new Double(yytext());
  return (new Symbol(sym.NUM,d));
}
<YYINITIAL> {ALPHA}({ALPHA}|{DIGIT}|_)* {
  String str = yytext();
  return (new Symbol(sym.SYM,str));
}
<YYINITIAL,COMMENT> . {
  System.out.println("Illegal character: <" + yytext() + ">");
}


formula.cup
===========
// {: and :} delimit strings containing code to be executed.

package example.parser;

// CUP specification for our mini expression evaluator with actions
import example.formula.*;
import java_cup.runtime.*;
import java.io.Reader;

parser code {:
  public parser(Reader r) {
    this(new Yylex(r));
  }
:}

/* Terminals (tokens returned by the scanner). */

terminal PLUS, TIMES, OPAREN, CPAREN, COMMA, MINUS,
         DIVIDE, EQUAL, UMINUS;
terminal Double NUM;
terminal String STR, SYM;

/* Non terminals */
```

```
non terminal ExprList expr_list;
non terminal String add_op, mul_op;
non terminal Expr expr, term, factor, top_level_expr;
non terminal FunctionExpr function;
non terminal StringConstantExpr literal_string_expr;


/* Precedences */
precedence left TIMES, DIVIDE;
precedence left PLUS, MINUS;
precedence left EQUAL;
precedence left UMINUS;


/* The grammar */

top_level_expr ::= EQUAL expr:e {: RESULT = e; :} |
        | literal_string_expr:e {: RESULT = e; :}
 | NUM:n {: RESULT = new ConstantExpr(n.toString()); :};
literal_string_expr ::=
        SYM:s {: RESULT = new StringConstantExpr(s); :};
expr   ::= term:t add_op:a expr:e
      {:
      RESULT = new ArithOpExpr(a, t, e);
:}
        | term:t {:
        RESULT = t;
:}
        | STR:s {: RESULT = new StringConstantExpr(s); :};


term      ::= factor:f mul_op:m term:t
              {:
RESULT = new ArithOpExpr(m, f, t);:}
            | factor:f
        {:
RESULT = f; :};
factor    ::= NUM:n
            {:
    RESULT = new ConstantExpr(n.toString()); :}
        | MINUS expr:e
      {: RESULT = new ArithOpExpr("*", new ConstantExpr("-1"), e); :}
       %prec UMINUS
        | OPAREN expr:e CPAREN {:
```

```
              RESULT = e;  :}
            |  function:f {:
   RESULT = f;  :}  ;


   function    ::= SYM:name OPAREN expr_list:el CPAREN
                 {:
   RESULT = new FunctionExpr(name, el);  :}
                |  SYM:name OPAREN CPAREN
                 {:
   RESULT = new FunctionExpr(name, new ExprList());:};


   expr_list   ::= expr:e COMMA expr_list:el
                 {:
   el.addExprFirst(e);
   RESULT = el;
   :}
                |  expr:e
                 {:
   RESULT = new ExprList(); RESULT.addExpr(e);  :};
   add_op      ::= PLUS {:
   RESULT = "+";  :}
                |  MINUS {:
   RESULT = "-";  :}
                |  EQUAL {:
   RESULT = "=";  :};
   mul_op      ::= TIMES {:
   RESULT = "*";  :}
                |  DIVIDE {:
   RESULT = "/";  :};


   Main.java[11]
   =========


   package example;

   import example.parser.parser;
   import example.formula.Expr;
   import java.io.StringReader;
```

---

11.   Not to be confused with the classic "public static void main () {}."

```
public class Main {

  public static String eval(String spreadsheetExpr) throws Exception {
    parser p =
      new parser(new StringReader(spreadsheetExpr));
    Expr expr = (Expr)p.parse().value;
    return expr.eval();
  }

  public static void main(String[] args) throws Exception {
    System.out.println(eval(args[0]));
  }
}
```

Step 2: Generating the Mini-Parser

Generating a Lexical Analyzer

java   JLex.Main <   formula.lex will produce a lexical analyzer
(**formula.lex.java**), which breaks the formula into operators (e.g., <, =),
symbols (e.g., sum, avg), numbers, and so on.

Generating the Parser

java   java_cup.Main <   parser.cup will produce sym.java and
parser.java.

- The parser class (parser.java) implements the parser
- The sym class (sym.java) contains a series of constant declarations,
  one for each terminal symbol.

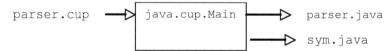

Step 3: Deploying the Mini-Parser in the Database

Compile all generated Java sources in the example directory tree, including:

Main.java, example/parser/formula.lex.java, example/

```
parser/parser.java, example/parser/sym.java, example/
formula/*.java
```

From the top-level directory of the parser, JAR-up required files in example.jar, and upload it in the database.

```
jar cvf example.jar .class */.class, *./*.class

SQL>
call dbms_java.loadjava('-f -r -v -u scott/tiger cup.jar');
/
call dbms_java.loadjava('-f -r -v -u scott/tiger
example.jar');
/
```

Step 4: Making the Mini-Parser Invocable through SQL and PL/SQL

```
CREATE OR REPLACE FUNCTION eval(p_expression IN varchar2)
 return varchar2 AS LANGUAGE JAVA name
'example.Main.eval(java.lang.String) returns
java.lang.String';
/
```

Step 5: Use It

Try this:

```
select eval('=sum(1,2,pow(2,3))') from dual;
/
```

Try more variations and combinations and have fun! Speaking of having fun, this section is a perfect transition to the next chapter about database scripting—in other words, running Python, TCL, Schema, and Groovy scripts in the database.

5

Database Scripting Using Non-Java Languages

> *"There's ways to amuse yourself while doing things and that's how I look at efficency."*
>
> *Donald Knuth*

In the previous chapters, we have seen a few examples of what you can do with Java in the database, beyond the traditional stored procedures. Oracle offers only PL/SQL and Java for database programming; however, with the emergence of Java compilers for non-Java languages (see *Programming Languages for the Java Virtual Machine*[1]), it is tempting to reuse the Java VM to run bytecode resulting from the compilation of non-Java languages in the database; the SQLJ language covered in Part III is a brilliant illustration of this approach. This is exactly what some of you did; this chapter reports basic proof of concepts running JACL (i.e., Java runtime for TCL), JYTHON (i.e., Java runtime for PYTHON), Kawa (i.e., Java runtime for Scheme), and Groovy in the database. These experimentations are foreign to Oracle and do not prefigure any plan to support any of the languages mentioned here in the Oracle database.

5.1   Why Contemplate Non-Java Languages for the Database?

Cost reduction is driving the need to improve application developer productivity (i.e., reuse skills, applications, libraries, APIs) and deployment flexibility (partitioning applications across tiers). Java fulfills such requirement by enabling the reuse of applications, libraries, and developer skills across vendors and also across the middle tier and the database. However, apart from Java, existing procedural languages[2] are not reusable across the

---

1.   http://flp.cs.tu-berlin.de/~tolk/vmlanguages.html.

middle tier and the database tier. Let's look at the offerings in this area of reusing non-Java languages in the database.

5.1.1   Common Language Runtime in RDBMS

The implementation of a Common Language Runtime (CLR) in SQL Server 2005, IBM DB2 release 8.2 and up, and Oracle Database 10*g* Release 2[3] allows programmers to use .NET-supported languages (e.g., C#, VB.NET, J#) across the Windows platform. (i.e., the middle tier and database). CRL coverage is beyond the scope of this book but is mentioned as mechanism allowing language support across tiers, beyond Java.

5.1.2   Scripting Languages Support in RDBMS

Open source databases such as MySQL and PostgreSQL offer (or are in the process of offering) basic support for popular Web scripting languages such as Perl, PHP, and Python, allowing these languages to be used across both middle tiers and databases. In section 5.2, you'll see proofs of concept of running TCL, Python, Scheme, and Groovy in the Oracle database.

Perl and PHP in MySQL

Perl is a popular scripting language backed by a large developer community, the Comprehensive Perl Archive Network (CPAN). MyPerl is a Perl interpreter for MySQL.[4] Similarly, MyPHP allows implementing PHP user-defined functions in MySQL.

Ruby Perl, Pythin, and TCL Plug-ins in PostgreSQL

According to its documentation,[5] besides its own proprietary procedural language (PL/pgSQL), the PostgreSQL database provides support for Java, as well as for popular scripting languages such as PHP, Perl, Python, TCL, Ruby, and Mono.

5.2   Database Scripting with OracleJVM—Just for Fun!

I coined the term *database scripting* to designate the ability to run scripting commands in the database, similar to SQL. How can OracleJVM help sup-

---

2.   SQL Server 2005 supports .NET languages in both the database and the middle tier.
3.   Both Oracle and IBM offer a loosely coupled CLR runtime with their databases.
4.   http://www.linuxjournal.com/article.php?sid=6841.
5.   http://techdocs.postgresql.org/guides/PLLanguages.

port non-Java languages or scripting languages? The trick is to rely on compilers that generate Java bytecode for non-Java languages and host the corresponding Java runtime of these languages in OracleJVM. You can view this as an open and broader-reach alternative to CLR; however, to my knowledge, Oracle has no plan to support such an approach. The following experiences are proofs of concept that you can implement yourself, in a nonproduction database environment; it is up to you to use the same technique in production environments if these meet your requirements.

5.2.1   Proof of Concept #1: Running TCL (JACL) Scripts in the Database

JACL is the Java implementation of the popular TCL product. The following example is a proof of concept of producing Java bytecode from non-Java languages and running the resulting bytecode in the database. It does not reflect any Oracle plan to support TCL in the database.

JACL Enable Your Database

1.   Download JACL/TCLBlend bundle jacl126-noarch.zip from:

   ```
   http://dev.scriptics.com/software/java/download.html
   ```

   jacl126-noarch.zip contains:

   ```
   lib/tcljava.jar   178583 bytes
   lib/jacl.jar      554467 bytes
   readme.jacl          147 bytes
   ```

2.   In order to simplify the manipulation (loading and ncomping) of required files in OracleJVM, unJAR/unZIP the contents of all JAR files and re-JAR everything into a single JAR (or ZIP) file.

   ```
   all_jacl.zip  341257 bytes
   ```

3.   Grant javasyspriv and java_deploy to your schema (e.g., scott):

   ```
   SQL>grant javasyspriv, java_deploy to scott;
   ```

4.   Load and NCOMP `all_jacl.zip`.

```
ncomp -u scott/tiger -load all_jacl.zip
```

Run TCL Scripts in Your Database

Using a modified variant of `StringLengthTest.java` from sourceforge.net:

```
StringLengthTest.java
=============

import tcl.lang.*;

public class StringLengthTest {
  public static void main(String[] args) {
    int thestr_len = -1;
    String thestr = "noggy";
    Interp interp = new Interp();
    try {
      interp.eval("string length \"" + thestr + "\"");
      thestr_len = TclInteger.get(interp, interp.getResult());
    } catch (TclException ex) {
      int code = ex.getCompletionCode();
      switch (code) {
      case TCL.ERROR:
        System.err.println(interp.getResult().toString());
        break;
      case TCL.BREAK:
        System.err.println(
            "invoked \"break\" outside of a loop");
        break;
      case TCL.CONTINUE:
        System.err.println(
            "invoked \"continue\" outside of a loop");
        break;
      default:
        System.err.println(
            "command returned bad error code: " + code);
        break;
      }
```

```
    } finally {
      interp.dispose();
    }

    System.out.println("string length was " + thestr_len);
  }
}
```

1.   Compile `StringLengthTest.java` on the client side, making sure to include all _jacl.zip in your classpath:

```
javac —classpath $PATH:all_jacl.zip:. $*
```

2.   Load the class file with loadjava:

```
loadjava u scott/tiger StringLengthTest.class
```

3.   Run `StringLengthTest` in the database (the text is stored in thestr string):

```
ojvmjava -u scott/tiger@
--OJVMJAVA--
--type "help" at the command line for help message
$ java StringLengthTest
string length was 5
```

Variations of `StringLengthTest` that invoke the TCL interpreter (tcl.lang.Interp described in http://www.tcl.tk/man/java1.2.6/TclJavaLib/Eval.htm) are: `TclEval`, `TclRun`, and `TclResources`.

4.   `TclEval`: takes a TCL code as a string and returns a result.

```
TclEval.java
=======

import tcl.lang.*;

public class TclEval {
  public static void main(String[] args) {
```

```
    if (args.length != 1) {
      System.out.println("pass in a tcl script");
    }
    else
      System.out.println("result: " + doit(args[0]));
  }
  public  static String doit (String tcl_code) {
    String result = "";
    Interp interp = new Interp();
      try {
        interp.eval(tcl_code);
        result += interp.getResult();
      } catch (TclException ex) {
        int code = ex.getCompletionCode();
        switch (code) {
        case TCL.ERROR:
          System.err.println(interp.getResult().toString());
          break;
        case TCL.BREAK:
          System.err.println(
                "invoked \"break\" outside of a loop");
          break;
        case TCL.CONTINUE:
          System.err.println(
                "invoked \"continue\" outside of a loop");
          break;
        default:
          System.err.println(
                "command returned bad error code: " + code);
          break;
        }
      } finally {
        interp.dispose();
      }
    return result;
  }
}
```

As usual, compile and load `TclEval.class` in the database. In order to invoke it from SQL, create a PL/SQL wrapper as follows:

```
create or replace function tcl_str (code VARCHAR2)
  return VARCHAR2 as language java name
  'TclEval.doit(java.lang.String) return
java.lang.String';
```

Store the TCL scripts in a table and then evaluate these with
tcl_str:

```
SQL> create table tcl_1 (c VARCHAR2(100), r VARCHAR2(30));

Table created.

SQL> insert into tcl_1 values ('string length "xyz"', '');

1 row created.

SQL> select tcl_str(c) from tcl_1;

TCL(C)
-----------------------------------------------------------
3
```

A more realistic variant of this would use a CLOB, LOB, or
LONG column type.

5.   TclRun.

TclRun is similar to StringLengthTest, in that it takes no args
and can be invoked from ojvmjava (ojvmjava does not understand command-line args).

```
TclRun.java
===========

public class TclRun  {
  public static void main(String[] a) {
    String code = "string length \"asdfgh\"";
    String[] args = {code};
    TclEval.main(args);
  }
}
```

Compile, load, and play!

```
% ojvmjava -u scott/tiger@
--OJVMJAVA--
--type "help" at the command line for help message
$ java TclRun
result: 6
```

6.   TclEvalResource interprets TCL scripts stored in files or Java
      resources.

```
TclEvalResource.java
=============

import tcl.lang.*;

public class TclEvalResource {
  public static void main(String[] args) {
    if (args.length != 1) {
      System.out.println("pass in a tcl script");
    }
    else
      System.out.println("result: " + doit(args[0]));
  }
  public  static String doit (String tcl_resource) {
    String result = "";
    Interp interp = new Interp();
      try {
        interp.evalFile(tcl_resource);
        result += interp.getResult();
      } catch (TclException ex) {
        int code = ex.getCompletionCode();
        switch (code) {
        case TCL.ERROR:
          System.err.println(interp.getResult().toString());
          break;
        case TCL.BREAK:
          System.err.println(
              "invoked \"break\" outside of a loop");
          break;
        case TCL.CONTINUE:
```

```
        System.err.println(
            "invoked \"continue\" outside of a loop");
        break;
      default:
        System.err.println(
            "command returned bad error code: " + code);
        break;
      }
    } finally {
      interp.dispose();
    }
  return result;
  }
}
```

TclEvalResource currently reads scripts from files but may be enhanced to read TCL script code from Java resources in the database or from CLOB. Most of these examples are borrowed from http://www.beedub.com/book/2nd/tclintro.doc.html and include simple arithmetic, such as a diagonal function, a factorial function, and callback to java.lang.String. All of these can be evaluated by TclEvalResource.

With a proper Call Spec, TclEvalResource can be invoked from SQL:

```
SQL> create or replace function tcl (code VARCHAR2)
return VARCHAR2
      as language java name
'TclEvalResource.doit(java.lang.String)
      return java.lang.String';
  2  /

  Function created.
```

Try TclEvalResource using t4.tcl, t5.tcl, and t6.tcl scripts:

<u>/tmp/t4.tcl</u>
```
set x 7; set y 9
expr $x + $y
```

```
SQL> select tcl('/temp/t4.tcl') from dual;

TCL('/TEMP/T4.TCL')
--------------------------------------------------
16
```

/temp/t5.tcl

```
proc Diag {a b} {
    set c [expr sqrt($a * $a + $b * $b)]
    return $c
}

Diag 12 34
```

```
SQL> select tcl('/temp/t5.tcl') from dual;

TCL('/TEMP/T5.TCL')
--------------------------------------------------
36.0555127546
```

/temp/t6.tcl

```
proc Factorial {x} {
    set i 1; set product 1
    while {$i <= $x} {
        set product [expr $product * $i]
        incr i
    }
    return $product
}

Factorial 10
```
```
SQL> select tcl('/temp/t6.tcl') from dual;

TCL('/TEMP/T6.TCL')
--------------------------------------------------
3628800
```

Note that SQL prints only the output from `tcl.lang.Interp`. All STD-OUT output, such as the result of TCL functions puts and putc, as well as all error messages, go to Oracle database trace files (*.trc files), but as we have seen, you can redirect standard output using `dbms_java.set_output()`.

Conclusions

These basic examples are just for fun; the integration of JACL/TCLBlends with SQL can turn it into a real database scripting solution.

5.2.2   Proof of Concept #2: Running Jython (Python) in the Database

The following example is a foreign proof of concept of hosting the Jython runtime in the database. Once again, this proof of concept does not reflect any Oracle plan to support Jython in the database.

What Is Jython?

Jython is the Java implementation of the Python runtime (`jython.jar`) that can run Python scripts. More details on Python or Jython can be easily found on the Web.

Jython Enabling Your Database

The following simple steps will install the Jython runtime in your database:

1.   Download the latest jython implementation from:

   `http://www.jython.org/download.html`

2.   Generate `jython.jar` by running jython-21:

   `java jython-21`

3.   Load `jython.jar` in your schema:

   `loadjava -v -u scott/tiger jython.jar`

Voilà! You can now run Python scripts in your database!

Running Jython Programs in the Database

A basic example:

Fib.py

=====

```python
import java

class Fib(java.lang.Object):
# Fibonacci numbers module
        def fib(self, n):    # write Fibonacci series up to n
              "@sig public void fib(int n)"
              a, b = 0, 1
              while b < n:
                    print b,
                    a, b = b, a+b
```

a.   Python is format sensitive; therefore, if you do not indent, your program will not compile. Note the location where you generate jython.jar; it should also contain jythonc, the Jython-to-Java bytecode compiler. Use the following command to generate Java source and Java class from `Fib.py`:

```
jythonc Fib.py
```

This will create a directory, **jpywork**, containing the following files:

```
Fib$_PyInner.class 3430 bytes
Fib.class 3623 bytes
Fib.java  5526 bytes
```

b.   jythonc translates all Jython methods into instance methods; however, PL/SQL can only wrap `public static java method`. We need to modify `Fib.java` and turn instance methods `Fib()` into public static ones `fib_wrapper()`, as follows:

```java
public static void fib_wrapper(int n) {
    new Fib().fib(n);
}
```

    c.   Compile the new `Fib.java` with a Java compiler (need `jython.jar` in your classpath).

    d.   Load the new Fib.class into `scott/tiger` as previously.

    e.   Write a PL/SQL wrapper to expose this to SQL and client-side JDBC:

```
create or replace procedure fib(n NUMBER) as language
java name
'Fib.fib_wrapper(int)';
/
```

    f.   Run Fib from SQL:

```
SQL> call fib(10)
*** 2003-07-17 13:07:35.448
   1
   1
   2
   3
   5
   8
```

Conclusion

Database developers and DBAs can generalize this demo by storing JYthon scripts in tables or CLOBs columns.

Hosting a JYthon runtime in the database is straightforward; its integration with SQL will make sense from a database perspective.

5.2.3 Proof of Concept #3: Running Kawa (Scheme) in the Database

Scheme belongs to the family of Lisp languages; it is also a great vehicle for implementing other languages. For example, the GNU implementation of XQuery (QEXO) is based on Kawa,[6] which is the Java-based Scheme system. Similarly, Kawa is being used to port Perl to Java. Once again, the following example is a proof of concept and does not reflect any plan to support Scheme runtime in the Oracle database.

---

6.   http://www.gnu.org/software/kawa/.

Scheme Enable Your Database (Scheme on you!)

1.   Get `kawa-1.7.jar` from http://www.gnu.org/software/kawa and put it in a directory on your file system.

2.   Load `kawa-1.7.jar` into the database with the following command:

```
loadjava -v -u scott/tiger kawa-1.7.jar
```

Voilà! You have a Scheme runtime in your database.!

Running Scheme Programs in the Database

```
prime.scm
========
;
; primes
; By Ozan Yigit
;
(define  (interval-list m n)
  (if (> m n)
        '()
        (cons m (interval-list (+ 1 m) n))))

(define (sieve l)
  (define (remove-multiples n l)
    (if (null? l)
        '()
        (if  (= (modulo (car l) n) 0) ; division test
             (remove-multiples n (cdr l))
             (cons (car l)
                   (remove-multiples n (cdr l))))))

  (if (null? l)
      '()
      (cons (car l)
            (sieve (remove-multiples (car l) (cdr
l))))))

(define (primes<= n)
  (display (sieve (interval-list 2 n))))

(primes<= 300)
```

1.   Store the program as `prime.scm` on your file system.

2.   Compile the Scheme program `prime.scm` into a Java class with the following command:

```
java -cp .:/path/to/kawa-1.7.jar kawa.repl --main -C /
path/to/prime.scm
```

This will generate a `prime.class` file in the current directory.

3.   Load the `prime.class` file into the database with the following command:

```
loadjava -v -r -u scott/tiger prime.class
```

4.   Write a PL/SQL wrapper as follows:

```
SQL> create or replace procedure primnumb(dummy
VARCHAR2)
  2  as language java name
  3  'prime.main(java.lang.String[])';
  4  /

SQL>show errors;
```

5.   Execute:

```
SQL>set serveroutput on
SQL>call dbms_java.set_output(50000);
SQL> call primnumb('test');
Call completed.
```

You will see a printout of prime numbers on your screen (or in the corresponding session trace file).

```
(2 3 5 7 11 13 17 19 23 29 31 37 41 43 47 53 59 61 67 71
73 79 83 89 97 101 103 107 109 113 127 131 137 139 149
151 157 163 167 173 179 181 191 193 197 199 211 223 227
229 233 239 241 251 257 263 269 271 277 281 283 293)
```

Conclusions

Similar to Python, hosting a Scheme runtime in the database is straightforward, but it only makes sense in the database if integrated with SQL.

5.2.4   Proof of Concept #4: Running Groovy in the Database

The following example is a foreign proof of concept of hosting the Groovy runtime in OracleJVM. Once again, it does not reflect any Oracle plan to support Groovy in the database.

What Is Groovy?

Groovy is a new scripting language candidate (JSR 241) that is derived from Java. In summary, it is a compact-syntax, dynamic object-oriented scripting language that leverages the Java language and its bytecode. Unlike Jython, JRuby, and other non-Java scripting languages, Groovy does not mix foreign language libraries or classes. However, you can mix pure Java with Groovy scripts and inherit from or use any Java code. More details on Groovy can be found at http://groovy.codehaus.org.

This section contains detailed examples of Groovy scripts running in OracleJVM, the steps needed to load the Groovy environment in the database, and a discussion of Groovy's integration with SQL. The Groovy language is not yet ready for enterprise production use, but you can already play with it on stand-alone JDK and in OracleJVM. Groovy 1.0 prerelease 2[7] has been recently made available (by the time of this writing); however, the following proof of concept is based on groovy-1.0-beta-6.

Groovy Enabling Your Database

1.   In order to run Groovy scripts in the database, we need to first upload the Groovy runtime jars in the database. The Groovy environment can be downloaded from `http://groovy.code-haus.org`.

   As listed hereafter, there are a large number of JARS and classes in the Groovy lib directory:

```
groovy-1.0-beta-6/lib/ant-1.6.1.jar
groovy-1.0-beta-6/lib/ant-junit-1.6.1.jar
groovy-1.0-beta-6/lib/ant-launcher-1.6.1.jar
groovy-1.0-beta-6/lib/asm-1.4.1.jar
groovy-1.0-beta-6/lib/asm-attrs-1.4.3.jar
groovy-1.0-beta-6/lib/asm-util-1.4.3.jar
groovy-1.0-beta-6/lib/axion-1.0-M3-dev.jar
```

7.   http://www.theserverside.com/news/thread.tss?thread_id=34587.

```
groovy-1.0-beta-6/lib/bsf-2.3.0-rc1.jar
groovy-1.0-beta-6/lib/classworlds-1.0.jar
groovy-1.0-beta-6/lib/commons-cli-1.0.jar
groovy-1.0-beta-6/lib/commons-collections-3.0-dev2.jar
groovy-1.0-beta-6/lib/commons-logging-1.0.3.jar
groovy-1.0-beta-6/lib/groovy-1.0-beta-6.jar
groovy-1.0-beta-6/lib/junit-3.8.1.jar
groovy-1.0-beta-6/lib/mockobjects-core-0.09.jar
groovy-1.0-beta-6/lib/mx4j-2.0-beta-1.jar
groovy-1.0-beta-6/lib/nekohtml-0.7.7.jar
groovy-1.0-beta-6/lib/openejb-loader-0.9.2.jar
groovy-1.0-beta-6/lib/qdox-1.3.jar
groovy-1.0-beta-6/lib/radeox-0.9.jar
groovy-1.0-beta-6/lib/radeox-oro-0.9.jar
groovy-1.0-beta-6/lib/regexp-1.2.jar
groovy-1.0-beta-6/lib/servletapi-2.3.jar
groovy-1.0-beta-6/lib/xerces-2.4.0.jar
groovy-1.0-beta-6/lib/xml-apis-1.0.b2.jar
```

2.   When you are unzipping all JARS, the number of classes reach 4,492; on UNIX/Linux it can be done using:

```
find groovy-1.0-beta-6/lib/ -name \*.jar -exec unzip -l
{} \; | wc -l
   =>   4492
```

3.   Loading all of these classes one by one will be cumbersome, will consume too many resources, and will create too many unresolved references; besides, you don't need to load all of the classes in all JARS. To simplify the loading of Groovy in the database and NCOMPing, we'll repackage the distribution by bundling only the following classes: `groovy.*`, `org.codehaus.groovy.*`, and `org.objectweb.asm.*` into `needed.zip`. This will greatly reduce the number of classes; `needed.zip` only has 529 classes and yet contains all classes needed to run Groovy in the database.

```
unzip -l tmp/needed.zip  | wc -l => 529
```

Loading the Groovy Runtime in the Database

4.   In order to meet the storage requirements of the experience, I recommend adding more space to the tablespace that will be used, indicated as follows:

```
alter tablespace <tblspace> add datafile
                '$ORACLE_HOME/../oradata/orcl/t_db2.f'
size 500M;
```

5.   The runtime could now be loaded using loadjava with the gen-missing options to avoid class resolution error messages:

```
loadjava -force -genmissing -genmissingjar gm-min.jar -
resolve
        -verbose -u  scott/tiger  needed.zip
```

6.   In order to cope with deploying the generated DLLs (upon NCOMPing), increase the storage space in the corresponding tablespace:

```
alter tablespace <tblspace> add datafile
            '$ORACLE_HOME/../oradata/orcl/t_db3.f' size
    500M;
```

7.   NCOMP it using:

```
ncomp -u scott/tiger  needed.zip
```

This will produce error messages, but the required/critical DLLs will be generated.

The following DLLs will be "installed":

```
libjox10_fe59e88f8d_sys_org_codehaus_groovy_control_messages.so
libjox10_fe59e88f8d_sys_org_codehaus_groovy_sandbox_markup.so
libjox10_fe59e88f8d_sys_groovy_model.so
libjox10_fe59e88f8d_sys_org_codehaus_groovy_sandbox_util.so
libjox10_fe59e88f8d_sys_org_codehaus_groovy_control.so
libjox10_fe59e88f8d_sys_org_codehaus_groovy_wiki.so
```

```
libjox10_fe59e88f8d_sys_groovy_swing.so
libjox10_fe59e88f8d_sys_groovy_security.so
libjox10_fe59e88f8d_sys_org_codehaus_groovy_runtime.so
libjox10_fe59e88f8d_sys_org_codehaus_groovy_classgen.so
libjox10_fe59e88f8d_sys_groovy_xml.so
libjox10_fe59e88f8d_sys_org_codehaus_groovy_syntax.so
libjox10_fe59e88f8d_sys_org_codehaus_groovy_syntax_parser.so
libjox10_fe59e88f8d_sys_org_codehaus_groovy_control_io.so
libjox10_fe59e88f8d_sys_org_codehaus_groovy.so
libjox10_fe59e88f8d_sys_groovy_xml_dom.so
libjox10_fe59e88f8d_sys_groovy_swing_impl.so
libjox10_fe59e88f8d_sys_groovy_servlet.so
libjox10_fe59e88f8d_sys_org_codehaus_groovy_syntax_lexer.so
libjox10_fe59e88f8d_sys_org_codehaus_groovy_ast.so
libjox10_fe59e88f8d_sys_org_codehaus_groovy_ant.so
libjox10_fe59e88f8d_sys_org_objectweb_asm.so
libjox10_fe59e88f8d_sys_groovy_text.so
libjox10_fe59e88f8d_sys_groovy_lang.so
libjox10_fe59e88f8d_sys_org_codehaus_groovy_ast_expr.so
libjox10_fe59e88f8d_sys_groovy_sql.so
libjox10_fe59e88f8d_sys_org_codehaus_groovy_tools_xml.so
libjox10_fe59e88f8d_sys_org_codehaus_groovy_ast_stmt.so
```

8.   Next, you need to install a Groovy shell or eval environment, in the database:

```
/// File TestGroovyShellFileX.java ////////
import java.io.*;
import groovy.lang.*;

public class TestGroovyShellFileX {

  public static void main (String[] args) {
    System.out.println("-- starting " + args[0]);

    try {
    // call groovy expressions from Java code
    Binding binding = new Binding();
    GroovyShell shell = new GroovyShell(binding);
    Object value = shell.evaluate(new File(args[0]));
    } catch (Exception e) {
      System.out.println("-- got: " + e);
```

```
        }
      }
    }
```

```
$ javac -classpath groovy-1.0-beta-6/lib/groovy-1.0-beta-6.jar
                         TestGroovyShellFileX.java
$ loadjava -resolve -verbose -u sys/<path>install
                  TestGroovyShellFileX.class
```

Voilà! Your database (schema) is Groovy enabled.

Running Groovy Scripts in the Database

Now let's see how you can run Groovy scripts in the database. Groovy scripts (*.gro) can be converted to Java code by means of groovyc, which is available in Groovy installations.

The classes generated by groovyc can be loaded with loadjava and invoked directly in the database, as in the following example:

```
//// File hellow.gro
3.times { println 'Hello World!'; x = 123; println (x * x); }
```

```
$ groovyc --classpath classes12.jar hellow.gro
$ zip hellow.zip hellow*.class
$ loadjava -resolve -verbose -u scott/tiger hellow.zip
$ ojvmjava -u scott/tiger
--OJVMJAVA--
--type "help" at the command line for help message
$ java hellow
Hello World!
15129
Hello World!
15129
Hello World!
15129
```

Running Groovy Scripts as a Dynamically Loaded Class

We can design a Java program that takes a Groovy script as input and transparently converts it into a Java class (instead of running it), upload the resulting class (with related classes), and then let the Java developer instantiate such a class and invoke it. Such operation corresponds to a dynamic invocation of the Groovy script. The following Java code snippet `TestDyn-Load.java` does just that:

```
/// File TestDynLoad.java ///////////

import java.io.*;
import groovy.lang.*;

public class TestDynLoad {

  public static void main (String[] args) {
    System.out.println("-- loading " + args[0]);

    try {

      GroovyClassLoader loader = new GroovyClassLoader();
      Class groovyClass = loader.parseClass( new File(args[0]) );
      GroovyObject groovyObject = (GroovyObject)
        groovyClass.newInstance();
      Object[] run_args = {};
      groovyObject.invokeMethod( "run",run_args );

    } catch (Exception e) {
      System.out.println("-- got: " + e);
    }
  }
}

% javac -classpath groovy-1.0-beta-6/lib/groovy-1.0-beta-6.jar
        TestDynLoad.java
% loadjava -resolve -verbose -u scott/tiger TestDynLoad.class
```

Now, any Groovy script can be dynamically uploaded as a class and invoked directly in the database using the `ojvmjava` shell:

```
% ojvmjava -u scott/tiger
--OJVMJAVA--
--type "help" at the command line for help message

$ java TestDynLoad hellow.gro
```

```
-- loading hellow.gro
Hello World!
15129
Hello World!
15129
Hello World!
15129
```

Storing Groovy Scripts in Database Columns

In the JACL proof of concept, we mentioned how TCL scripts can be stored in Oracle database table columns and executed from SQL queries. This is achieved by means of a Java driver class defining a static method that takes the TCL code as a string, evaluates it, and returns the result as a string, and a corresponding PL/SQL wrapper function, which can be called from SQL queries. Similarly, a Java driver and a PL/SQL wrapper can be provided for Groovy, as follows:

1. First, the `TestGroovyShell` driver suitable for receiving and executing code as text from main's args; we will also equip it with a static method, which takes code as a string and returns the result of the evaluation as Java string. Here is the `TestGroovyShell`:

```
/// File TestGroovyShell.java /////////////
import groovy.lang.*;

public class TestGroovyShell {
  public static void main (String[] args) {
    // System.out.println("-- starting ");

    Binding binding = new Binding();
    if (args.length > 0) {
      eval(args[0], binding);
    }
    else {
      binding.setVariable("foo", new Integer(2));
      Object value = eval("println 'Hello World!'; x = 123;\
                      return foo * 10");
      System.out.println("-- value: " + value);
      System.out.println("-- variable x: " + \
                      binding.getVariable("x"));
```

```
      }
   }

   public static Object eval (String code, Binding binding) {
      GroovyShell shell = new GroovyShell(binding);
      Object value = null;
      try {
         value = shell.evaluate(code);
      } catch (Exception e) {
         System.out.println("-- got: " + e);
      }
      return value;
   }

   public static Object eval (String code) {
      Binding binding = new Binding();
      return eval(code, binding);
   }

   public static String evalAsString (String code) {
      return eval(code, new Binding()).toString();
   }
}
```

2. Compile and load `TestGroovyShell.class` in the database:

```
% javac -classpath .:groovy-1.0-beta-6/lib/groovy-1.0-beta-
6.jar \
    TestGroovyShell.java
% loadjava -resolve -verbose -u scot/tiger \
    TestGroovyShell.class
```

3. Evaluate Groovy scriptlets interactively using the ojvmjava shell:

```
% ojvmjava -u scott/tiger
--OJVMJAVA--
--type "help" at the command line for help message

$ java TestGroovyShell "println System.currentTimeMillis();"
1096262669077
```

```
$ java TestGroovyShell " [1,2,3].each { println it}"
1
2
3

$ java TestGroovyShell " println([1,2,3].findAll { it > 0 })"
[1, 2, 3]

$ java TestGroovyShell "closure = [1,2,3].min;
println(closure());"
1
```

4.   Let's now create a PL/SQL wrapper and use SQL to store and
     retrieve Groovy scriptlets in the database :

```
SQL> create or replace function groovy_eval (code VARCHAR2)
     return VARCHAR2 as language java name
     'TestGroovyShell.evalAsString(java.lang.String)\
            return java.lang.String';
  2  /

Function created.

SQL> create table groovy_code (code VARCHAR2(200));

Table created.


SQL> insert into groovy_code values ('[10,2,3,2,1].min()');

1 row created.

SQL> insert into groovy_code values ('[10,2,3,2,1].max()');

1 row created.

SQL> insert into groovy_code values
                      ('[10,2,3,2,1].reverse()');

1 row created.
```

```
SQL> insert into groovy_code values
                    ('[10,2,3,2,1].findAll { it > 2 } ');

1 row created.

SQL> insert into groovy_code values ('[10,2,3,2,1].sort()');

1 row created.


SQL> select * from groovy_code;

CODE
------------------------------------------------------------
[10,2,3,2,1].min()
[10,2,3,2,1].max()
[10,2,3,2,1].reverse()
[10,2,3,2,1].findAll { it > 2 }
[10,2,3,2,1].sort()

SQL> select groovy_eval(code) from groovy_code;

GROOVY_EVAL(CODE)
-------------------------------------------
1
10
[1, 2, 3, 2, 10]
[10, 3]
[1, 2, 2, 3, 10]

SQL>
```

Integrating Groovy with SQL

Because we are running in the database, it makes sense to make SQL more "Groovy"! Groovy SQL performs queries and SQL statements, passing in variables easily with proper handling of statements, connections, and exception handling using closures.

Let's look at an example using Groovy SQL along with `GroovyMarkup`. The following example is a modified version of the SQL access example from the Groovy Web site. It demonstrates both SQL access and XML generation using Groovy running in the schema SCOTT. The script iterates over a result set for the table EMP, composing an XML document on the fly.

```
sqlrepdb.gro
========


import groovy.sql.Sql
import groovy.xml.MarkupBuilder;

import oracle.jdbc.OracleDriver
driver = new OracleDriver()
con   = driver.defaultConnection();

println "con = $con"
sql = new Sql( con )
print "sql = $sql"

xml = new MarkupBuilder()
print xml

xml.xul() {
  menubar( id:'MAIN' ) {
    menu( label:'Employees' )

    sql.eachRow( 'select EMPNO, ENAME from emp' ) { row |
        xml.menuitem( id:"${row.EMPNO}", name:"${row.ENAME}" )
    }
  }
}

println xml
```

Invocation with TestGroovyShellFileX:

```
$ ojvmjava -u scott/tiger
$ java TestGroovyShellFileX sqlrepdb.gro
-- starting sqlrepdb.gro
con = $con
sql = $sqlgroovy.xml.MarkupBuilder@5e8324c6<xul>
  <menubar id='MAIN'>
    <menu label='Employees' />
```

```
            <menuitem name='SMITH' id='7369' />
            <menuitem name='ALLEN' id='7499' />
            <menuitem name='WARD' id='7521' />
            <menuitem name='JONES' id='7566' />
            <menuitem name='MARTIN' id='7654' />
            <menuitem name='BLAKE' id='7698' />
            <menuitem name='CLARK' id='7782' />
            <menuitem name='SCOTT' id='7788' />
            <menuitem name='KING' id='7839' />
            <menuitem name='TURNER' id='7844' />
            <menuitem name='ADAMS' id='7876' />
            <menuitem name='JAMES' id='7900' />
            <menuitem name='FORD' id='7902' />
            <menuitem name='MILLER' id='7934' />
        </menubar>
    </xul>groovy.xml.MarkupBuilder@5e8324c6
```

Instead of dumping the XML to `System.out` (i.e., the screen) as a result of using `'println xml'` at the end of `sqlrepdb.gro`, you can direct Groovy to write to a file using the following instruction:

```
// replace println xml with
    new File("records.xml").newPrintWriter().println(xml)
```

Alternatively, if the expected/resulting XML text is large, you might instead use the XML builder with a writer in argument, as follows:

```
// replace println xml with
new MarkupBuilder(new File("records.xml").newPrintWriter());
```

Let's look at another example using Groovy to convert a SQL Result Set into XML[8] and store it in a file:

```
/// File xmlgen.gro /////////////////////

import groovy.sql.Sql
import java.io.File
```

---

8.   See Part II.

```
import java.sql.DriverManager
import oracle.jdbc.OracleDriver

def toAttr(n) { s == null ? 'NULL' : "'${s}'" }

driver = new OracleDriver()
con   = driver.defaultConnection();
sql = new Sql( con );

new File("ResultSet.xml ").withWriter() { writer |
  writer.writeLine ("<employees>");
  sql.queryEach("select * from scott.emp") { row |
    writer.writeLine (
      "  <employee>" +
      " id=" + toAttr(row.EMPNO) +
      " name=" + toAttr(row.ENAME) +
      " position=" + toAttr(row.JOB) +
      " manager=" + toAttr(row.MGR) +
      ">"
    )
  };
  writer.writeLine ("</employees>");
}
```

which would create a file ResultSet.xml containing:

```
<employees>
  <employee id='7369' name='SMITH' position='CLERK' manager='7902'>
  <employee id='7499' name='ALLEN' position='SALESMAN'
manager='7698'>
...
</employees>
```

However, OracleJVM security will not allow code to work unless the output file—in this case, ResultSet.xml—is granted java.io.FilePermission.

```
SQL>dbms_java.grant_permission("SCOTT","
java.io.FilePermission" "ResultSet.xml",  "write");
```

In addition, the schema requires `java.util.PropertyPermission` against the current/target directory.

```
SQL>dbms_java.grant_permission("SCOTT","
java.util.PropertyPermission" "<current directory>",
      "read");
```

Per OracleJVM security best practices, the permissions have been specifically granted for the script file and the current directory.

The script is invoked as:

```
$ java TestGroovyShellFileX xmlgen.gro
```

The beauty of Groovy lies in the fact that, unlike other scripting languages, it adds high-level mapping to existing Java libraries; in the SQL and XML examples, we have just mapped and used the server-side JDBC.

Conclusion

This chapter completes Part I. Now that you've learned everything you ever wanted to know about Java in the database and practical and extreme examples, Part II, III, and IV will look at programming APIs that you can use to build Java applications, which you can run in the database or in the middle tier: JDBC and SQLJ. In addition, we'll also look at magic JPublisher, the multipurpose tool for accessing the Oracle database.

Part II: Java Persistence and Java SQL Data Access

In Part I, we covered in depth Java in the database, including the rationale for using Java in the database, an overview of the Oracle implementation, and the various application types enabled by an embedded Java virtual machine in the database. However, database programming using Java goes way beyond running Java in the database; in fact, the largest part of database programming using Java happens in the middle tier (i.e., J2EE, J2SE, object to relational mapping iconified by Toplink, and database-related Java design patterns).[1]

The relational database (RDBMS) world and the Java world do not share the same model or semantics. On one hand, we have the relational technology, which includes the SQL language, the RDBMS semantics (i.e., schemas, tables, primary keys, foreign keys, views, stored procedures), and a set of proprietary and open languages for building stored procedures, functions, and packages on top of SQL. On the other hand, we have the Java technology and platform, which includes the object-oriented Java language, the design patterns, a rich set of JCP-sanctioned APIs and enterprise services, and a growing number of open source frameworks and programming models. The mapping between database semantics (SQL data) and Java semantics (i.e., Java state) is achieved through numerous Java APIs, design patterns, and frameworks.

We can group these into two categories:

1. *The do-it-yourself persistence technologies and APIs*, such as JDBC, SQLJ, and vendor-specific tools/utilities such as Oracle JPublisher. These technologies explicitly manipulate SQL statements,

---

1. There is no enterprise/transactional Java application without RDBMS data access.

stored procedures to access or persist Java states into relational tables columns, under the control of the application developer.

2. *The transparent persistence (O/R mapping) technologies,* which include frameworks such as Toplink, JavaBeans, JDO, Enterprise JavaBeans, POJOs, and so on. These technologies shield the Java developer from the hassle of doing it by transparently mapping Java objects states to database tables/columns. Ultimately, these technologies use JDBC or SQLJ or stored procedures under the covers.

In Part II, we'll focus on the do-it-yourself Java API for accessing SQL data and persisting Java states in the Oracle database, including JDBC and Oracle's implementation, SQLJ and Oracle's implementation, and Oracle's JPublisher (which complements JDBC and SQLJ for dealing with advanced/complex Oracle Database types but also enables Database Web Services, covered in Part III).

Database Programming with Oracle JDBC

Enterprise computing is not conceivable without RDBMS access. It's no surprise then that the JDBC API remains by far the most-used Java API either directly or under the covers. Part II will give you a condensed but hopefully comprehensive and pragmatic coverage of Oracle JDBC. We first introduce the JDBC technology, review the various JDBC specifications, and then look at the implementation of Oracle JDBC, including its architecture, packaging, the level of support for standard APIs, the Oracle extensions, transaction handling, security handling, manageability, and advanced JDBC connection pooling mechanisms for scalability, load balancing, failover, and troubleshooting. Most of the features described apply to the server-side JDBC, which is used by Java in the database.

Introducing the JDBC Technology and Oracle's Implementation

6.1 JDBC Primer

Before diving into the details, let's first introduce the technology. Readers who are already familiar with JDBC may want to skip this section, or revisit it!

6.1.1 First Steps in JDBC

The basic JDBC steps include loading and registering the driver, connecting to the database, creating a statement object, executing the query, processing the results, and closing the resources.

Step 1: Loading and Registering the Driver

Loading and registering the driver can be achieved in your code using either `DriverManager.registerDriver` or `Class.forName`; in case something goes wrong, the first method throws a `SQLException` and the second throws a `ClassNotFoundException`:

```
DriverManager.registerDriver (new
oracle.jdbc.OracleDriver());
```

or:

```
Class.forName ("oracle.jdbc.OracleDriver");
```

Alternatively, you can register the driver when launching the JavaVM to execute your application, as follows:

```
java -Djdbc.drivers = oracle.jdbc.OracleDriver <ClassName>;
```

Step 2: Connecting to the Database

Connecting to the database is achieved by getting a connection object from connection factories. Two methods are available: (1) the obsolete but still used DriverManager approach and (2) the more standard datasource approach.

Method 1: Using DriverManager Factory

```
Connection conn=DriverManager.getConnection(conn,uname,paswd);


Connection conn = DriverManager.getConnection(
   "jdbc:oracle:thin:@<host>:<port>:<sid>","scott","tiger");
```

Method 2: Using OracleDataSource Factory

```
OracleDataSource ods = new OracleDataSource();
 // set neccessary properties (JDBC URL, etc)
      java.util.Properties prop = new java.util.Properties();
      ...
  prop.put(....)
      ods.setURL(url);


 // get the connection
  Connection conn = ods.getConnection(); ...
```

As we will see later, datasources can be used with or without a JNDI namespace.

Step 3: Creating a Statement

Once you get a connection, you create a statement object on the connection object. A statement object can be seen as a context for executing a SQL statement.

```
Statement stmnt=conn.createStatement();
```

The `Connection` object also offers `PreparedStatement` and `CallableStatement` objects, which will be addressed later.

Step 4: Executing a SQL Statement

The statement interface provides three SQL execution methods: `executeQuery()`, `executeUpdate()`, and `execute()`.

1. The executeQuery(String sql) method is invoked on the statement object to execute a SELECT statement; it returns a ResultSet object, which is used to process the rows resulting from the query execution.

   ```
   ResultSet rs = stmt.executeQuery("SELECT empno, ename FROM
   emp");
   ```

2. The executeUpdate(String sql) method is invoked on the statement object for DML (INSERT/UPDATE/DELETE) and DDL (i.e., CREATE TABLE); it returns an int.

   Examples:

   ```
   int rowcount = stmt.executeUpdate
     ("CREATE TABLE table1 (numcol NUMBER(5,2),
   strcol VARCHAR2(30)");

   int rowcount = stmt.executeUpdate
     ("DELETE FROM emp WHERE empno = 2354");
   ```

3. The execute(String) method can be invoked on the statement object for any SQL statement (i.e., query, DML, DDL); it returns a Boolean value.

   ```
   boolean result = stmt.execute(SQLstatement);

   if (result) {// was a query - process results
     ResultSet r = stmt.getResultSet(); ...
   }
   else { // was an update or DDL - process result
    int count = stmt.getUpdateCount(); ...
   }
   ```

Step 5: Retrieving and Processing Result Sets

The result set maintains a cursor pointing to the current row. The next() method allows iterating through the rows that made the result set, and the getXXX() method is for retrieving the values of the columns. Table 6.1 is a basic and incomplete sample of a few result set methods.

```
while (rs.next() { XXXX obj=rs.getXXXX(<column name>) }
```

Table 6.1   *Sample Result Set getXXX Methods*

SQL Column Type	getXXX Method
NUMBER	getInt()
DATE	getDate()
VARCHAR2	getString()
BLOB	getBlob()
CLOB	getClob()
ARRAY	getArray()
Structured type	getObject()
REF	getRef()

Example:

```
while (rs.next()) {
   String ename = rs.getString("ENAME");
   String empno = rs.getInt("EMPNO");
   ...
}
```

Step 6: Closing Results Sets, Statements, and Connections

The JDBC best practices recommend closing explicitly Connection, Statement, and ResultSet objects, so as to release resources that are no longer needed.

```
...
// freeing up resources
rs.close();
   stmt.close();
   conn.close();
...
```

A Basic but Complete JDBC Program

Here is a basic but complete JDBC program. This program assumes that the database is on the same machine as the code (i.e., localhost), the Service name is ORCL, the PORT is 1521, and the schema is SCOTT.

```
JDBCPrimer.java
================
/*
 * A Basic/Complete JDBC program
 */

import java.sql.*;
import oracle.jdbc.*;
import oracle.jdbc.pool.OracleDataSource;

public class JDBCPrimer
{

   public static void main (String args []) throws SQLException {

       String name = null;
       Connection conn = null;
       Statement stmt = null;

       OracleDataSource ods = new OracleDataSource();

     // Set the URL (user name, and password)
       String url = "jdbc:oracle:thin:scott/tiger@//localhost:1521/
orcl";
       ods.setURL(url);

     // Get a connection object
       conn = ods.getConnection();

     // create statement
       stmt = conn.createStatement();

     // Execute SQL statement and retrieve result sets
       ResultSet rs =
           stmt.executeQuery("SELECT ENAME FROM EMP where EMPNO
='7934'");

     // Retrieve and print the result (we are only expecting 1 row)
       while (rs.next()) { name = rs.getString("ENAME");}
       System.out.println ("Employee# 7934 is " + name);

     // Close the ResultSet
```

```
        rs.close();

    // Close the Statement
        stmt.close();

    // Close the connection
        conn.close();
      }
    }


C:\>javac JDBCPrimer.java


C:\>java JDBCPrimer


Employee# 7934 is MILLER


C:\>
```

6.1.2 JDBC within J2SE and J2EE Environments

Because RDBMS access is a must in enterprise computing, JDBC is a must in J2SE and J2EE environments, heavily used explicitly or under the covers. It is used explicitly by stand-alone JDBC applications/frameworks, EJB BMP, Servlets, JSPs, JSP Tags, and Java stored procedures (see Part I) to perform SQL operations (i.e., queries, DML) and DDL directly against the database.

It is used transparently, under the covers (i.e., nonintrusive persistence), through O/R mapping frameworks such as Toplink, POJOs, and EJBs containers, which generate and execute SQL statements on behalf of their clients. Table 6.2 illustrates how JDBC is, used under the covers, by EJB CMP.

Table 6.2 *JDBC Usage under the Covers by EJB CMP*

EJB API (CMP Beans)	Container Action	SQL Operation (JDBC)
ejbCreate()	The EJB container creates a bean instance.	INSERT a database record.
EjbPostCreate()		UPDATE foreign key or INSERT (deferred write).

Table 6.2   *JDBC Usage under the Covers by EJB CMP (continued)*

EJB API (CMP Beans)	Container Action	SQL Operation (JDBC)
ejbLoad()	The EJB container loads the bean instance corresponding to the supplied primary key.	SELECT statement to retrieve database row(s).
ejbStore()	The EJB container persists the changes to the bean in the database.	UPDATE statement to apply changes to the corresponding database row(s), which persist the EJB instance.
ejbRemove()	The EJB container removes/deletes the bean instance.	DELETE the corresponding database record/rows corresponding to the EJB instance.
ejbFindBy()	The EJB container finds the beans based on a search criteria.	SELECT statement to retrieve database row(s)corresponding to the EJB instance.

6.2   Overview of JDBC Specifications

JDBC specifications are part of (associated with) both Java Standard Edition and Java Enterprise Edition specifications as follows: each new release of the JDBC specification relies on features in the corresponding Java SE— for example, the `javax.sql` extensions in JDBC 2.0 rely on the Java Naming and Directory Interface (JNDI) in Java SE—and each new release of Java EE relies on features in the corresponding JDBC specification. Similarly, each new JDBC release supports new SQL data types and relies on a minimal/common support for ANSI/SQL specifications in RDBMS. As a result, the various JDBC specifications have to accommodate the differences in RDBMS and only mandate commonly supported database interfaces and mechanisms (wonder why the specs move so slowly!).

6.2.1   Overview of JDBC 1.22 Specification (Where Things Started!)

The JDBC 1.22 specification represents the first formalization of the JDBC API.

Key Features

- `java.sql.DriverManager` handles loading of drivers and supports the creation of new database connections.

- `java.sql.Connection` represents a connection to a particular database JDBC URLs.

- `java.sql.Statement` supports the execution of a SQL statement on a given connection and furnishes the following methods:
  - `executeUpdate()`
  - `execute ()`
  - `executeQuery()`

- `java.sql.ResultSet`: for managing the results set from the execution of a given statement; forward-only and read-only modes.

- `DatabaseMetaData`: information about database objects such as catalogs, schemas, tables, and primary keys.

- `ResultSetMetaData`: information about each column of the result set, such as column name, column type, and display size.
  - `Java.sql.Date`
  - `Java.sql.Time`
  - `Java.sql.TimeStamp`

- `JDBC Escape {}` mechanism to support RDBMS-specific features.

  Examples:
  - { escape ' character ' }
  - Sored procedures: { call stproc [(arg1, arg2, ..)]}
  - Scalar Functions call: { fn function ([arg1, arg2, …argn])}
  - Outer join: { oj table ….. }

6.2.2 Overview of JDBC 2.0 Specification (A Major Spec!)

The JDBC 2.0 specification consists of two parts: (1) the JDBC 2.1 Core API part of J2SE 1.2 `java.sql` package, and (2) the JDBC 2.0 Standard Extensions (also known as Optional Package) part of the `javax.sql` package in J2EE 1.2.

Features Introduced in the JDBC 2.1 Core API

The new functionality in the core API includes scrollable result sets; batch updates; programmatic inserts, deletes, and updates; performance hints;

character streams for streams of internationalized Unicode characters, full precision for `java.math.BigDecimal` values, and support for time zones in `Date, Time,` and `Timestamp` values.

- Support for SQL3 (SQL-99) data types:

  - java.sql.Blob and java.sql.Clob interfaces
  - java.sql.Array interface
  - java.sql.Ref
  - Distinct user-defined data type
  - java.sql.Struct interface for mapping user-defined types (UDTs)

- New methods for dealing with SQL3 types:

  - `getBlob()`, `setBlob()`, `updateBlob()` for mapping a Java BLOB instance to a SQL BLOB instance
  - `getClob()`, `setClob()`, `updateClob()` for mapping a Java Clob instance to a SQL CLOB instance
  - `getArray()`, `setArray()`, `updateArray()` for mapping a Java Array instance to a SQL ARRAY
  - `getObject()`, `setObject()`, `updateObject()` for mapping a Java Struct instance to a SQL structured type instance
  - `getRef()`, `setRef()`, `updateRef()` for mapping a Java Ref instance to a SQL REF instance

- New `java.sql.Types` variables for BLOB, CLOB, Array, Ref, Distinct, and Struct

- Increased support for storing persistent objects in the Java programming language

- Scrollable and updatable result set (Insert, Update, Delete), which implements SQL-92 scrollable cursors

  - Forward-only, scroll-sensitive, scroll-insensitive result set
  - Scroll result set forward and backward
  - Move to a specific row: first, last, beforeFirst, afterLast, next, previous, relative(3), absolute(-2)
  - DatabaseMetaData.supports ResultSetType and ResultSetConcurrency

- Statement and Result Set Hints specify the direction in which result sets will be processed:

  - SetFetchDirection(<direction>):
    `ResultSet.FETCH_FORWARD,`   `ResultSet.FETCH_REVERSE,`
    `ResultSet.FETCH_UNKNOWN`

- SetFetchSize(<number>): specifies how many rows should be fetched each time

- Batching SQL Statements Execution: new statement methods for sending multiple DML or DDL statements to the database as a batch

- Programmatic inserts, deletes, and update: make DML operations to database tables using methods in the Java programming language (i.e., ResultSet updater methods) instead of using SQL commands

- Enhancements to Java Objects data types support

- java.sql.SQLData interface for SQL types customization

- Full precision for java.math.BigDecimal values

- Additional security

- Support for time zones in date, time, and timestamp values

Features Introduced in the javax.sql JDBC 2.0 Optional Package

- The javax.sql.DataSource interface is a more flexible and portable mechanism for getting a connection (an alternative to DriverManager)

  - The distributed transaction implementation: returning XA-compliant connection objects to be used for distributed transactions

- The Java Naming and Directory Interface (JNDI) for registering DataSource objects with a naming service

- Connection Pooling: A set of pooled connections that can be cached and reused. JDBC 2.0 specifies hooks that allow the connection pooling to be implemented on top of the JDBC driver layer.

- JDBC support for two-phase commit protocol allows global transactions to span multiple databases (or multiple connections to the same database)

- Rowsets: JavaBeans that encapsulate result sets, for more convenient Java data handling and passing

- Character streams for streams of internationalized Unicode characters

6.2.3   Overview of JDBC 3.0 Specification

The following java.sql and javax.sql features were introduced in the JDBC 3.0 specification:

- Transactional Savepoints: allow a transaction to be partially committed or rolled back to a designated savepoint

- Caching PreparedStatement: pooling and reusing PreparedStatement

- Standard Connection Pooling Properties (i.e., `maxStatement`, `initialPoolSize`, `minPoolSize`, `maxPoolSize`, `maxIdleTime`, `propertyCycle`): define how connections are pooled on the `ConnectionPoolDataSource` interface

- `ParameterMetaData` interface for parameters of a `PreparedStatement` object

- New methods added to the `DatabaseMetaData` interface, such as `getSQLStateType`, `getSuperTypes`, `getSuperTables`, `getAttributes`, and so on, for retrieving SQL-type hierarchies

- Retrieval of auto-generated keys: ability to retrieve values from automatically generated or incremented columns (e.g., Rowid or Sequence Numbers)

- Multiple open `ResultSet`: ability to have multiple result sets from `CallableStatement` open at the same time; added a new signature to `getMoreResults()`, which now takes a flag (i.e., `getMoreResults(int)`) for controlling how to handle previously opened result sets upon the invocation of `getResultSet()`

- Named parameters in `CallableStatements`: ability to reference parameters to `CallableStatement` objects by name as well as by index (e.g., `getXXX(column-name)`). Note: not supported for RefCursors/ResultSets.

- `ResultSet` holdability: ability to specify whether cursors should be held open or closed at the end of a transaction

- Simplify updating the values of `CLOB`, `BLOB`, `ARRAY`, and `REF` (SQL structured) types with new methods on the `ResultSet` interface

- The `java.sql.Types.DATALINK` data type: allows JDBC drivers access to objects stored outside a data source. The `DATALINK` column value is retrieved from `ResultSet` using `getURL()`.

- Mapping the JDBC interface to the J2EE Connector Architecture Service Provider Interface (SPI) allows the JDBC driver to be used as a JCA Resource Adapter for its target database.

6.2.4   Overview of Upcoming JDBC 4.0 Specification

According to the publicly available early draft,[1] the JDBC 4.0 specification will focus on Ease of Development and features for power developers, including the following:

- Ease of Development API: including JDBC Annotations (JDBC metadata for Query, Table, and Update, similar to Java 5.0 Annotation[2]), Query Interface (SQLJ in disguise!), Base Query Interface - DataSet Interface, and JDBC User Defined Class

- Automatic discovery and loading of `java.sql.Driver` , which eliminates the need to do it explicitly in your program, an alternative to the Datasource

- `java.sql.ROWID`: support for ROWID data type

- National Character Set Conversion Support: new `NCHAR`, `NVARCHAR`, `LONGNVARCHAR`, and `NCLOB` JDBC types

- Enhanced support for `BLOB` and `CLOB:` new methods to `Connection`, `PreparedStatement`, `Blob`, `Clob`, and `NClob` interfaces

- SQL/XML and XML Support: à la SQL 2003, through new APIs

- Wrapper Pattern: unwrap JDBC connections to use nonstandard vendor methods

- `SQLException` Enhancements: Support J2SE chained exception, new iterable interface, and new subcategories

- Connection Management Enhancements: new connection pool features similar to Oracle's Implicit Connection Cache (not sure this will make the first release of the spec)

- Changes to `Connection`, `CallableStatement`, `DatabaseMetaData`, `PreparedStatement`, `ResultSet`, `Statement`, `DataSource`, and `PooledConnection` APIs

Table 6.3 summarizes the relationship between the various JDBC specifications, J2SE, and J2EE.

---

1.   http://java.sun.com/products/jdbc/download.html#corespec40.
2.   Java Annotation is a new construct for associating metadata with methods, fields, and so on at design time.

Table 6.3 *JDBC, J2SE, and J2EE Relationship*

JDBC Specs	Main Interface/Features	J2SE	J2EE	SQL Types
1.22	java.sql.*—java.sql.DriverManager, java.sql.Connection, java.sql.Statement, java.sql.PreparedStatement java.sql.CallableStatement, java.sql.ResultSet, JDBC Escape Syntax, DatabaseMetaData, ResultSetMetaData java.sql.Date, java.sql.Time, java.sql.TimeStamp	1.1	1.1	SQL-92
2.1	SQL3 (SQL-99) datatypes, java.sql.Struct, Distinct, New java.sql.Types, SQL-92 scrollable cursors, Statement and Result Set Hints, Batching SQL Statements Execution, java.sql.SQL-Data, timezones in date, time, and timestamp values Javax.sql.*—javax.sql.DataSource, JNDI, Connection Pooling, RowSet, XAConnection, XADataSource	1.2 1.3	1.2 1.3	SQL:19 99 (SQL3) UDT
3.0	Transactional Savepoints, Caching PreparedStatement, Standard Connection Pooling Properties, ParameterMetaData interface, Enhanced DatabaseMetaData, Retrieval of auto-generated keys, Multiple Open ResultSet, Named parameters, ResultSet holdability, Simplify updating CLOB, BLOB, ARRAY and REF, DATALINK Data Type, JCA Resource Adapter	1.4	1.4	
4.0 (Early Draft)	Automatic loading of Driver, Ease of Development APIs, java.sql.ROWID, National Character Set Conversion Support, Enhanced Support for BLOB and CLOB, SQL/XML and XML Support, Wrapper Pattern, SQLException Enhancements, Connection Pool Enhancement, java.sql objects API changes	6.0	5.0	

6.2.5 JDBC Standards Support in the Oracle JDBC Drivers

The Oracle JDBC drivers are developed and delivered as part of the Oracle database; hence, they inherit the database version numbering. This section gives you an overview of the level of support for JDBC specifications across the Oracle database releases.

Oracle 8i Release 8.1.5 JDBC Drivers

Offered support for the following:

- JDBC 1.22 features

- A subset of JDBC 2.1 features such as structured types

- Support only JDK 1.1.x

- XA features are not supported

Oracle 8i Release 8.1.6 JDBC Drivers

Offered support for the following JDBC 2.1 features:

- Core JDBC features including structured types, LOB types, batching, and scrollable cursors (Beta quality). However, Calendar data types are not supported.
- Support for JDBC 2.1 Extensions such as Connection Pooling and JDBC-XA (excluding "xArecover()")
- Support JDK 1.1.x and 1.2.x (Use classes 1.2 for JDK 1.2)

Oracle 8i Release 8.1.7 JDBC Drivers

- Added support for JDBC XAResource.recover(), which is part of JDBC 2.1 extensions.
- Furnished a production quality support for scrollable cursors (the previous implementation was not ready for production). However, because the Oracle database does not support scrollable cursors natively, the Oracle JDBC drivers emulate these. As a result, a performance penalty may be incurred when dealing with large result sets.

Oracle 9i Release 1 (9.0.1) JDBC Drivers

- Complete support for JDBC 2.1 extensions (2.0 Optional Packages)

Oracle 9i Release 2 (9.2.0.x) JDBC Drivers

Initial support for JDBC 3.0, including the following:

- Transaction savepoints
- Reuse of *PreparedStatement*
- Using both global and local transactions on the same connection
- Support for JDK 1.4.x client

Oracle Database 10g Release 1 (10.1.0.x) JDBC Drivers

Support for most JDBC 3.0 features except the following:

- Auto-generated keys retrieval
- Result set holdability (throws an exception)
- Returning multiple result sets

- Support for JDBC RowSet (JSR-114) Public Draft Specification

Oracle Database 10g Release 2 (10.2.0.x) JDBC Drivers

In this release, Oracle JDBC completes its support for JDBC 3.0 by adding a few new features and enhancing the implementation of a few others.

- Added support for auto-generated keys retrieval; its implementation has been enabled by JDBC support for DML with RETURNING, in 10.2.

- Changes the implementation, hence behavior, of result set holdability: it no longer throws a SQL exception but returns the value of `ResultSet.HOLD_CURSORS_OVER_COMMIT`, which is the default for the Oracle RDBMS because it always keeps cursors open.

- Returning multiple result sets using the standard `getMoreResult()` is not applicable with the Oracle database however, you may retrieve multiple RefCursor (must be declared as `IN OUT` parameters).

- In addition, Oracle JDBC upgrades its implementation of JDBC RowSet (JSR 114) to the final specification, from 10.1 implementation, which was based on the public draft (see Chapter 7 for more details).

- Both client-side drivers (JDBC-Thin and JDBC-OCI) have been certified against JDK 5.0.

Table 6.4 summarizes the level of JDBC standards support in Oracle JDBC drivers releases.

Table 6.4 *JDBC Standards support in Oracle JDBC drivers*

Oracle JDBC Drivers Release	Level of JDBC Standards Support	J2SE/JDK Support
8.1.5	JDBC 1.22 and a subset of JDBC 2.0	1.1.x
8.1.6	Core JDBC 2.1 features	1.1.x 1.2.x

Table 6.4   *JDBC Standards support in Oracle JDBC drivers (continued)*

8.1.7	JDBC 2.1 Production quality support for scrollable cursors; support for JDBC-XAResource.recover()	1.1.x 1.2.x 1.3.x
9.0.1	Complete support for JDBC 2.0 Optional Packages	1.1.x 1.2.x
9.2.0	Initial JDBC 3.0 support, including transaction savepoints, sharing connection with local/global transaction, J2SE 1.4 support	1.1.x, 1.2.x, 1.3.x, 1.4.x
10.1.0	Most JDBC 3.0 features were still missing or incompletely implemented, including auto-generated keys, result set holdabilty, and returning multiple result sets. Support for Draft JDBC RowSet Spec. (JSR-114)	1.2.x, 1.3.x, 1.4.x
10.2.0	Complete support for JDBC 3.0 Spec. Support for Final JDBC RowSet Spec. (JSR-114)	1.2.x, 1.3.x, 1.4.x, 1.5.x

6.3   Architecture and Packaging of Oracle JDBC Drivers

6.3.1   Rearchitected Oracle JDBC Drivers

Starting with 9*i* releases, the rearchitecture of Oracle JDBC drivers was cemented in Oracle Database 10*g* Release 1. The primary goals were performance, reduction of the functional gap between drivers, and better integration with the Oracle Database and particularly Real Application Cluster (RAC).

Faster Features Implementation and Reduction of Functional Gap

In order to speed up the implementation of new features across all driver types, thereby reducing the features gap between driver types, the architecture of the drivers has been revamped into a common code base and lighter-weight layers for each specific driver type, as pictured in Figure 6.1 (and as some of you have already figured out by inspecting the JAR files).

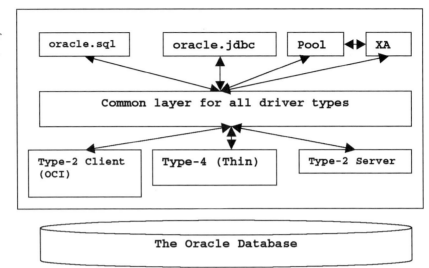

Figure 6.1
*Architecture of
Oracle JDBC 10g*

The Main Packages of Oracle JDBC

- oracle.sql: contains public and private Oracle JDBC classes, which implement java.sql interfaces (Oracle types extensions). As an example, oracle.sql.ARRAY implements java.sql.Array.

- oracle.jdbc: contains public Oracle JDBC interfaces that extend the standard java.sql and javax.sql interfaces; in addition, these interfaces define Oracle extensions. As an example, oracle.jdbc.OracleConnection extends java.sql.Connection. A JDBC application may choose to use only standard packages for portability purposes and not benefit from Oracle extensions, optimizations, and services. Notable subpackages include rowset, xa, pool, and connector.

- oracle.jdbc.rowset: contains classes that implement javax.sql.rowset JDBC RowSet (JSR-114)

- oracle.jdbc.xa: contains public and private interfaces and classes (including client.xa and server.xa), which implement distributed transaction interfaces. As an example, oracle.jdbc.xa.OracleXADataSource implements javax.sql.XADataSource.

- oracle.jdbc.pool: for JDBC connection pooling; as an example, OracleDataSource class implements javax.sql.DataSource.

- `oracle.jdbc.connector:` contains classes that implement javax.resource interfaces, allowing JDBC to be used as a JCA adapter

- `oracle.jdbc.oci:` contains OCI driver-specific public and private classes.

Performance Optimizations

The Oracle JDBC 10*g* drivers are faster than previous releases. Customers have publicly reported[3] 30 percent performance improvement by just switching to newer drivers, with no change to existing applications and databases. The performance optimizations techniques are briefly described as follows:

- Reducing the number of Java methods called for implementing a typical SQL-related JDBC operation.

- Data buffers and temporary buffers needed to satisfy a JDBC operation have been reduced through caching and reuse techniques, resulting in fewer creation of new Java objects and reduced Garbage Collection overhead.

- Reducing data movement from/to Java to/from the RDBMS, as well as the number of Java methods for mapping Java to/from SQL,[4] was achieved through a set of single data copy algorithms, which allow data type conversion to be performed in-line.

- The Type-2 JDBC driver (also known as JDBC-OCI) uses the JNI interface and callbacks to access Java and C memory spaces. In order to minimize JNI callbacks, the driver has optimized the storage of states and also the linkage between C memory structures and Java objects.

- XA operations are much faster in 10*g* Release 1, with native XA support, as opposed to stored procedures based implementation in previous releases.

6.3.2 Packaging of Oracle JDBC Drivers

Oracle JDBC drivers are produced and delivered as part of the Oracle database; more specifically, the client-side type-4 (JDBC-Thin) and type-2 (JDBC-OCI) are part of the Oracle database client. The server-side type-4 driver (identical to client-side type-4) and server-side type-2 driver (a light-

---

3.   http://download-west.oracle.com/oowsf2004/1235_wp.pdf.
4.   Customers have reported up to 30 times speed-up for conversions.

weight driver used by Java in the database, as detailed in Part I) are installed in the RDBMS when the Java option is selected. The client-side drivers[5] are also bundled with all Oracle products that require Java SQL data access, including the Oracle Application Server, the Oracle Collaboration Suite, the Oracle eBusiness Suite, and Oracle JDeveloper. The drivers are available for download from the Oracle Technology Network (OTN), under the OTN Development and Distribution License Terms at http://www.oracle.com/technology/software/tech/java/sqlj_jdbc/index.html.

Type-4 Client-side JDBC (JDBC-Thin)

The type-4 (i.e., pure Java) driver is platform independent and does not require installation of the Oracle Client. As illustrated in Figure 6.2, it comprises the JDBC layer on top of a pure Java implementation of the Oracle TTC[6], Net8, and SQL*Net protocol adapters. It supports only TCP/IP protocol. Most Oracle customers who use JDBC have adopted JDBC-Thin, mostly for ease of installation and upgrade reasons, and only use JDBC-OCI for features not available in a pure Java environment, such as the Transparent Application Fail-over (TAF) and XDB client.

Figure 6.2
Type-4 Driver
Implementation

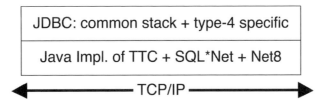

- For JDK1.4.x and JDK 1.5.x environments:
    - `ojdbc14.jar` for production and `ojdbc14_g.jar` for development and troubleshooting (debugging, tracing)
    - `ojdbc14dms.jar` and `ojdbc14dms_g.jar` represent DMS instrumented editions of `ojdbc14.jar` and `ojdbc14_g.jar` for collecting statistics and monitoring. In an Oracle application server environment, a DMS Servlet is furnished along with `dms2Server.jar` for analyzing and displaying the results
- For JDK 1.2.x and JDK 1.3.x environments:
    - `classes12.jar` for production and `classes12_g.jar` for development and troubleshooting (debugging, tracing)

---

5.   Designate client-side drivers, unless specified.
6.   Two Task Common (TTC) is the presentation layer of Oracle's SQL Net protocol.

■ `classes12dms.jar` and `classes12dms_g.jar` are similar to `ojdbc14dms.jar` and `ojdbc14dms_g.jar` (see previous discussion)

Type-4 Server-side JDBC

This driver is exactly the same as a type-4 client but runs directly in the database. It is used by Java code running in the database to connect to either another session within the same database or to a remote Oracle database.

Type-2 Client-side JDBC (JDBC-OCI)

The type-2 client driver comprises a JDBC layer on top of C/OCI based implementation, Oracle TTC, Net8, and SQL*Net protocol adapters, as illustrated by Figure 6.3. It uses Java native methods to call entry points in the underlying Oracle Call Interface (OCI) library (i.e., OCI7 in Oracle 9*i* OCI8 in Oracle Database 10*g*). It requires installation of an Oracle client of the same version as the driver. It is used mostly for OCI-only features such as transparent application fail-over (TAF).[7] See the features differences listed in Table 6.5. The JDBC-OCI driver supports all protocols supported by Oracle Net, including TCP/IP, IPC, named pipes, and IPX/SPX.

Figure 6.3
Type-2 Driver
Implementation

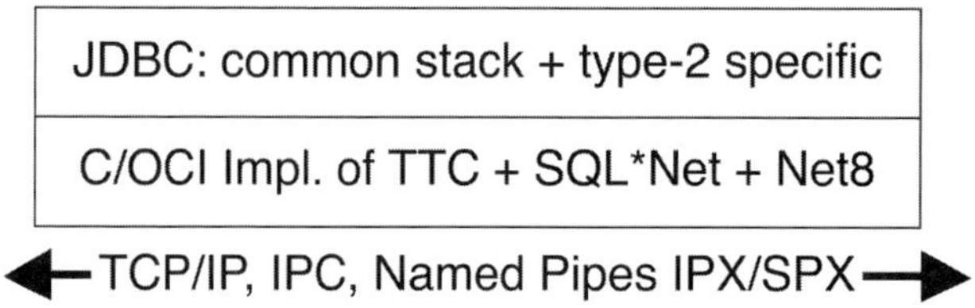

```
┌──────────────────────────────────────────────┐
│ JDBC: common stack + type-2 specific          │
├──────────────────────────────────────────────┤
│ C/OCI Impl. of TTC + SQL*Net + Net8           │
└──────────────────────────────────────────────┘
◄──TCP/IP, IPC, Named Pipes IPX/SPX──►
```

The type-2 client driver (also known as JDBC-OCI) requires the following additional libraries:

■ For Solaris environment: `libjdbcoci9.so`, `libjdbcoci10.so`

■ For Windows environments: `ocijdbc9.dll`, `ocijdbc10.dll`

Starting with Oracle JDBC 10*g* Release 1, the OCI libraries are available as part of the Oracle Instant Client download and are therefore no longer posted on the JDBC download page.

---

7.   The Oracle Database 10g offers Fast Connection Failover, a driver-type independent alternative

Type-2 Server-side JDBC

A lightweight type-2 driver runs in the OracleJVM, in the same server process address space as SQL, PL/SQL, and Java in the database, thereby incurring zero network latency. It is used exclusively by Java in the database for SQL data access within the session; in fact, the resulting JDBC connection is a mere handle to the database session itself.

Additional JARS

The following JARS are also furnished for globalization and rowsets support:

- `ora18n.jar`: part of the Globalization Developers Kit (GDK) for national languages and multibyte character support; a replacement for `nls_charset.jar` in pre-10*g* JDBC

- `demo.zip` and `demo.tar` contain code samples

- javadoc.zip

- `ocrs12.jar`: furnished in previous releases and contains classes implementing an early implementation of JDBC Rowset (JSR-114) specification. This JAR is no longer furnished starting with Oracle JDBC 10*g* Release 2; it has been folded into ojdbc14.jar, which implements the final specification of JDBC Rowset.

   * xdb.jar in $ORACLE_HOME/rdbms/jlib for XMLType support

Instant Client ("Homeless" Oracle Client)

Starting with Oracle Database 10*g* Release 1, Instant Client is a new packaging of the Oracle Client aimed at reducing the disk space requirements of a full Oracle Client (i.e., about three-quarters space reduction) and also simplifying deploying OCI, OCCI, ODBC, and JDBC-OCI applications by removing the need for an ORACLE_HOME. As of Oracle Database 10*g* Release 2, the Instant Client package for JDBC-OCI comprises the following:

For UNIX environments:

- type-4 JDBC jars (as described previously), under $ORACLE_HOME/jdbc/lib

- `libocijdbc10.so` OCI Instant Client JDBC Libraries, under $ORACLE_HOME/lib

- `libheteroxa10.so` for native XA support, to be copied under ORACLE_HOME/jdbc/lib

For Windows environments:

- `type-4` `JDBC` `jars` (as described previously), under `$ORACLE_HOME\bin`

- `oraocijdbc10.dll` OCI Instant Client JDBC Library under `$ORACLE_HOME\bin`

- `heteroxa10.dll` for native XA support, to be copied under `$ORACLE_HOME\bin`

6.3.3   **Features Differences Between Driver Types**

The $65,475 question customers ask all the time (and for good reasons) is: "Which driver type should I use: JDBC-Thin or JDBC-OCI?" The answer is that most Java developers have standardized on the pure Java driver (also known as JDBC-Thin) for ease of deployment and only use JDBC-OCI for specific features not available in a pure Java environment, such as the XDB client and transparent application fail-over (TAF). See Table 6.6, which summarizes the features differences in JDBC-Thin (client-side type-4), JDBC-OCI (type-2), and server-side type-2 JDBC (also known as JDBC-kprb). This table lists only features that were introduced in one driver and missing in the other, for a specific release. For the complete list of features and when these appear in each driver type, see Table 8.1.[8] Oracle's strategy is to reduce the functional gap between type-2 and type-4 drivers; however, some features, such as TAF and XDB client, which are C/OCI specific, won't be available in a pure Java environment (i.e., JDBC-Thin). Newer JDBC releases either consolidate features support across driver types (e.g., Proxy Authentication was first introduced in 10.1 JDBC-Thin, then in 10.2 JDBC-OCI) or offer driver-type independent alternatives (e.g., Fast Connection Failover in 10.1 instead of TAF, only applicable to OCI).

Table 6.5   *Features Differences between Driver Types per Release*

JDBC Release	JDBC-OCI Type-2 Client	JDBC-Thin Type-4	Server-Side Type-2 JDBC
As of 9*i* R2			
TNSNAMES.ORA Lookup	X		
OCI Connection Pooling	X	N/A	N/A

---

8.   http://www.oracle.com/technology/tech/java/sqlj_jdbc/index.html.

Table 6.5   *Features Differences between Driver Types per Release (continued)*

JDBC Release	JDBC-OCI Type-2 Client	JDBC-Thin Type-4	Server-Side Type-2 JDBC
OCI Optimized Fetch/Prefetching	X	N/A	N/A
XDB XMLType (via C/OCI)	X	N/A	X
TAF	X	N/A	N/A
Advanced Security: Encryption: SSL Strong authentication: Kerberos, PKI Certificates	X		
Heterogeneous XA Resource Manager	X		
Index-by-Table of PL/SQL scalars	X		
LOB Streaming (Use setXXXStream to bind to a LOB column)	X		
Service Name in URL	X		N/A
As of 10g R1			
TNSNAMES.ORA Lookup	X		
Scalar PL/SQL Index by Table	X	X	
TAF	X	N/A[*]	N/A
OCI Connection Pooling	X	N/A	N/A
OCI Optimized Fetch/Prefethcing	X	N/A	N/A
XDB XMLType (via C/OCI)	X	N/A	X
Proxy Authentication		X	N/A
Encryption: SSL, RC4_40, RC4_56, DES, DES40, AES128, AES192, AES256, 3DES112, 3DES168 (RC4_128 and RC4_256 support in domestic edition) Strong authentication: Kerberos, PKI Certificates	X	Encryption: RC4_40 RC4_56 DES40C DES56C 3DES112 3DES168	

Table 6.5   *Features Differences between Driver Types per Release (continued)*

JDBC Release	JDBC-OCI Type-2 Client	JDBC-Thin Type-4	Server-Side Type-2 JDBC
Instant Client (Removes ORACLE_HOME requirement)	X	N/A	N/A
Native XA as default (performance)	Stored Procedure	X	N/A
Service Name in URL	X		N/A
As of 10*g* R2			
JDBC 3.0 Auto-Generated Keys	X	X	
DML with RETURNING	X	X	
Scalar PL/SQL Index by Table	10.1	10.1	X
JSR 114 Rowsets	X	X	
Encryption: `RC4_40`, `RC4_56`, DES, DES40, AES128, AES192, AES256, 3DES112, 3DES168 (`RC4_128` and `RC4_256` support in domestic edition) Strong authentication: Kerberos, PKI Certificates, Radius	X	Encryption: SSL, RC4_40 RC4_56 DES40C DES56C 3DES112 3DES168	
Proxy Authentication	X	10.1	N/A
OCI Connection Pooling	X	N/A	N/A
OCI Optimized Fetch/Prefetching	X	N/A	N/A
Native XA as default (performance)	Stored Procedure	X	
TAF	X	N/A	N/A
XDB XMLType (via C/OCI)	X	N/A	X
Instant Client (Removes ORACLE_HOME requirement)	10.1	N/A	N/A
Instant Client Light (English)	X	N/A	N/A
TNSNAMES.ORA Lookup	X	X	X

*   Use newer driver-type independent solution: Fast Connection Fail-over.

6.3.4 JDBC Drivers and Database Interoperability

Oracle JDBC drivers are part of the database client and therefore comply with the Oracle database client and server interoperability, which consists of forward compatibility (i.e., older client versus newer database server) and backward compatibility (i.e., newer client versus older database server). However, JDBC features, which require server-side instrumentation, such as fast connection fail-over and runtime connection load balancing, won't work against older database releases. Table 6.6 summarizes Oracle JDBC driver forward and backward compatibility against recent database releases, up to the third digit (refer to the Oracle client compatibility matrix[9] for the complete story); see specific details on patch sets within each major release.

Table 6.6   *JDBC versus RDBMS Interoperability Matrix*

JDBC Releases versus Database Releases	Database 10.2.0.x	Database 10.1.0.x	Database 9.2.0.x
JDBC 10.2.0.x	Yes	Yes	Yes
JDBC 10.1.0.x	Yes	Yes	Yes
JDBC 9.2.0.x	Yes	Yes	Yes

I strongly recommend moving to the latest drivers—especially if you are using the pure Java drivers—as soon as possible, because you get better performance and better code quality (fewer bugs). As reported during Oracle World 2004, eBay observed 33 percent performance enhancement[10] simply by switching the Oracle JDBC driver to JDBC-Thin 10*g* Release 1, against 9*i* and even 8*i* databases.

How to Check the Version of the JDBC Drivers

Oracle JDBC drivers do not currently offer a command for identifying the version of the drivers in use. However, you can check the JDBC version by using DatabaseMetaData class and by pulling the information from the Manifest file.

---

9.   See Metalink Note# 207303.1 "Oracle Client / Server Interoperability Support."
10.   http://download-west.oracle.com/oowsf2004/1235_wp.pdf.

- The DatabaseMetaData approach is programmatic and works for all supported JDBC versions, including 9.1.0.x, 9.2.0.x, 10.1.0.x, and 10.2.0.x.

```
GetJDBCVersion.java
====================

import java.sql.*;
import oracle.jdbc.*;
import oracle.jdbc.pool.OracleDataSource;

public class GetJDBCVersion
{
 public static void main (String args[]) throws SQLException {
  OracleDataSource ds = new OracleDataSource();
     ds.setURL("jdbc:oracle:thin:scott/tiger@//localhost:1521/
orcl");
  Connection conn = ds.getConnection();
  DatabaseMetaData dbmd = conn.getMetaData();
     // gets driver info:
  System.out.println("The JDBC driver version is "
                              + dbmd.getDriverVersion()); }
}
```

- Starting with version 10*g* R1, the Manifest file also contains the version information. All you need to do is unJAR/unZIP the JDBC library (`classes12.jar` or `ojdbc14.jar`) and read the Manifest file. As an example, in UNIX environments, the following script retrieves the version:

```
Unzip –c ojdbc14.jar META_INF/MANIFEST.MF | grep –I
version
```

This concludes the introduction to the JDBC technology and Oracle's implementation. In the next chapter, I'll walk you through JDBC URLs, DataSources, JDBC Connections, and JDBC Statements.

7

URL, DataSource, Connection, and Statements

This chapter describes how the Oracle JDBC supports URL, datasources, connections, and associated services, including connection wrapping, connection caching, connection scalability/load balancing, and connection failover, proxy connection. Finally, we'll address JDBC statements (Statement, PreparedStatement, CallableStatement) and Oracle extensions, statement caching, and statement batching.

7.1 JDBC URL

A JDBC URL is the connect string used during database connection requests. It specifies the JDBC driver type, authentication information, the database instance, the host, the protocol, the port, service name, and so on. It contains either the complete authentication information or partial information plus indirections (i.e., aliases) to other mechanisms such as the TNSNAMES.ORA.

The Oracle JDBC URL format is as follows:

jdbc:oracle:<drivertype>:

[<username>/<password>]@<database_specifier>

where:

<drivertype> = "thin" | "oci[1]" | "kprb"

[<username>/<password>] = "<username>"/"<password>" | empty

---

1. For backward compatibility, oci8: is also supported.

<database_specifier> depends on driver type.

- If <driver type> = "kprb," then the database specifier is empty.
- If <driver type> = "oci" and bequeath[2] connection, then the database specifier is empty (i.e., "jdbc:oracle:oci:scott/tiger/@").
- Otherwise, the database specifier description is one of the following:
    - <Thin style service name>
    - <host>:<port>:<SID>
    - <TNSName alias>
    - <LDAp Syntax>

Note that starting with the Oracle Database 10*g* JDBC, URL connect strings using SIDs are deprecated in favor of database service name:

```
jdbc:oracle:thin:@localhost:1521:orcl  -> deprecated
jdbc:oracle:thin:@localhost:1521/myservice ->
recommended
```

In summary, the <database specifier> is the variable part of the Oracle JDBC URL and may take one of the following formats:

```
<Oracle Net descriptor> |<Thin style service name> |
 <LDAP syntax>|<bequeath>|<TNSNames alias>

<Oracle Net descriptor> =
```

- Thin:

```
"jdbc:oracle:thin:@(DESCRIPTION=
            (LOAD_BALANCE=on)
              (ADDRESS_LIST=
              (ADDRESS=(PROTOCOL=TCP)(HOST=host1)(PORT=1521))

(ADDRESS=(PROTOCOL=TCP)(HOST=host2)(PORT=1521)))
              (CONNECT_DATA=(SERVICE_NAME=service_name)))"
```

- OCI:

```
"jdbc:oracle:oci:@(DESCRIPTION=
            (ADDRESS=(PROTOCOL=TCP)(HOST=cluster_alias)
```

---

2.   The client and the database reside on the same host connection through named pipe protocol.

```
                    (PORT=1521))

            (CONNECT_DATA=(SERVICE_NAME=service_name)))"
```

\<Thin style service name\> =

`//host_name:port_number/service_name`

The full URL becomes `jdbc:oracle:thin:[<user>/<password>]@//`
`<host>[:<port>]/<service>`.

Examples:

```
    jdbc:oracle:thin:@//foo.com/customer
    jdbc:oracle:thin:scott/tiger@//mycomany.com:5521/sales
```

\<LDAP syntax\> = `"jdbc:oracle:thin:@ldap://`
`ldap.acme.com:7777/sales,cn=OracleContext,dc=com"`

or:

```
    "jdbc:oracle:thin:@ldaps://ldap.acme.com:7777/
    sales,cn=OracleContext,dc=com"
```

\<TNSNames alias\> = `String url =`
`"jdbc:oracle:thin:@tns_alias";`

In 10.2, JDBC-Thin supports TNSNAMES entries lookup in
tnsnames.ora, resulting in a much simplified and driver type–
independent Oracle Net descriptor. You must set the system property
`oracle.net.tns_admin` to the directory that contains your
tnsnames.ora file.

Example:

```
    java -Doracle.net.tns_admin=$ORACLE_HOME/network/admin
```

or:

```
    System.setProperty("oracle.net.tns_admin", "c:\oracle\net\
    admin");

    OracleDataSource ods = new OracleDataSource();
    ods.setTNSEntryName("tns_alias");
```

```
ods.setUser("scott");
ods.setPassword("tiger");
ods.setDriverType("thin");
Connection conn = ods.getConnection();
```

Examples of valid URLs:

- jdbc:oracle:thin:@mydatabase: The username and password must be provided by other mechanisms, while the following URL specifies an empty username and password.

- jdbc:oracle:thin:/@mydatabase.

- jdbc:oracle:thin:scott/tiger@//myhost:1521/orcl: connects user scott with password tiger to a database with service orcl through port 1521 of myhost, using the Thin driver.

- jdbc:oracle:oci:@myhost:1521:orcl: connects to the database using the OCI driver and the SID orcl.

- jdbc:oracle:thin:@HR: this URL connects to the database, whose alias in the tnsnames.ora file is HR, using the Thin driver. The username and password must be specifed by other means.

See the Oracle JDBC Reference Guide and the Oracle Net Administration Guide documentation for more details on JDBC URL and TNSNAMES.ORA.

Now that you have specified the JDBC URL, the next step consists of requesting a connection object from either the DriverManager or DataSource factories. DriverManager is a deprecated mechanism maintained for backward compatibility purposes only, but it is still widely used. The next section explains DataSources.

7.2 **DataSources**

The javax.sql package introduced in JDBC 2.0 Optional Packages provides the following interfaces:

- DataSource: javax.sql.DataSource

- Connection pooling: `PooledConnection`, `ConnectionPoolData-Source`

- Distributed transactions: `XAConnection`, `XADataSource`

- Rowsets: `RowSet`, `RowSetReader`, `RowSetWriter`, `RowSetMetaData`, `RowSetListener` (JSR-114 specifies further JDBc RowSet)

This section focuses on the `javax.sql.DataSource` interface, which is a Connection factory; in other words, it returns a standard Connection object. It is a more flexible alternative to `DriverManager`, as it shields application developers from hard-coding database names and other datasource properties such as username and password.

Methods include: `getConnection()`, `getConnection(java.lang.String username, java.lang.String password)`, `getLoginTimeout()`, `getLogWriter()`, `setLoginTimeout(int seconds)`, and `setLogWriter(java.io.PrintWriter out)`.

7.2.1 The OracleDataSource

The `oracle.jdbc.pool.OracleDataSource` class implements the `javax.sql.DataSource` interface with advanced connection caching extensions. Oracle's extension includes the following methods:

```
getConnection(java.util.Properties
cachedConnectionAttributes),
getConnection(java.lang.String _user, java.lang.String
_passwd, java.util.Properties cachedConnectionAttributes),
getDriverType(), getServiceName(), getTNSEntryName().
```

Listing 7.1 illustrates a basic JDBC program using OracleDataSource; see the Oracle JDBC javadoc for a complete and detailed description.

Listing 7.1   *DataSrce.java*

```
===============================
/*
 * Basic DataSrce sample
 */

import java.sql.*;
import javax.sql.*;
```

```java
import oracle.jdbc.*;
import oracle.jdbc.pool.OracleDataSource;

public class DataSrce
{
  public static void main (String args [])
    throws SQLException
  {
    // Create an OracleDataSource
    OracleDataSource ods = new OracleDataSource();

    // Set the URL (user name, and password)
    String url = "jdbc:oracle:thin:scott/tiger@//localhost:1521/
orcl";
    ods.setURL(url);

    // Retrieve a connection
    Connection conn = ods.getConnection();

    // Create a Statement
    Statement stmt = conn.createStatement ();

    // Select the USER column from the dual table
    ResultSet rset = stmt.executeQuery ("select USER from dual");

    // Get and print the contains of the Result Set
    while (rset.next ())
      System.out.println ("User name is " + rset.getString (1));

    // Close the RseultSet, the Statement and the Connection
    rset.close();
    stmt.close();
    conn.close();
  }
}
```

```
C:\My_Data\PM\Book>javac DataSrce.java

C:\>java DataSrce
User name is SCOTT
```

Using SQL*Plus

```
SQL> select USER from dual;

USER
------------------------------
SCOTT

SQL>
```

7.2.2   DataSources and JNDI

JNDI 101

The Java Naming and Directory Interface (JNDI) specification provides Java applications with a standard naming service over directories or repositories for storing configuration parameters, objects, and object factories. This uniform directory and naming service allows applications to access different naming and directory services using a common API. The main interface is the `javax.naming.Context`, which furnishes (self-explanatory) methods such as the following:

- bind(Name name, Object obj) / rebind(Name name, Object obj): for binding names to resources
- unbind(Name name)
- lookup(Name name, Object obj)
- createSubcontext(Name name)
- listBindings(Name name)
- createSubcontext(...)
- list (Name name)

The `javax,naming.InitialContext` class implements the `Context` interface; the InitialContext object is implementation specific and the starting point for JNDI operations.

The `javax.naming.spi.ContextFactory` interface is the factory for creating InitialContext objects.

Using Oracle DataSources with Stand-alone JNDI

When combined with DataSources, JNDI allows Java applications to access the database as a data source through its logical name as opposed to hard-coded or explicit URL. This has the advantage of making the application code independent of a particular database, JDBC driver, or JDBC URL and portable to other environments. In summary, the logical name is registered with a naming service; the application retrieves the `DataSource` object, looking up on the logical name previously registered (associated with it); and the application can then use the `DataSource` object to request a connection to the DataSource in question. JNDI implementation is in general furnished by middle tiers, typically J2EE containers of application servers,[3] but JNDI can also be used in J2SE (JDK) environments.

The following code sample describes how to use OracleDataSoure with a stand-alone JNDI provider (J2SE environment):

Step 1

Download a file system-based JNDI provider[4] (`fscontext-1_2-beta3.zip`).

Extract `providerutil.jar` and `fscontext.jar` and add the location to your classpath.

Create a directory with JNDI (e.g., C:\Temp\JNDI).

Step 2

Create a `Hashtable` object for holding the parameter {name, value} pairs, necessary to access the naming service and create an Oracle-DataSource object.

```
Hashtable env = new Hashtable (5);
env.put (Context.INITIAL_CONTEXT_FACTORY,
         "com.sun.jndi.fscontext.RefFSContextFactory");
env.put (Context.PROVIDER_URL, "file:C:\Temp\JNDI" );
// use the url supplied in command line or the
// following default
String url = "jdbc:oracle:oci8:@";
// import the Oracle database 10g JDBC pool package
import oracle.jdbc.pool.*;
```

---

3.   The mapping is achieved at runtime through deployment descriptors.
4.   http://java.sun.com/products/jndi/serviceproviders.html#12.

```
OracleDataSource ods = new OracleDataSource();
```

Step 3

Set the name and value of parameters, including authentication and other datasource properties.

```
/*
  * Explicit parameters setting. It is also possible, with
  * JDKs, to load
  * parameter values from a file or XML document.
  */
ods.setURL(url);
ods.setUser("Scott");
ods.setPassword("tiger");
```

Step 4

Obtain an initial JNDI naming context for storing the DataSource parameters in the naming space and bind the DataSource object to JNDI.

```
/*
   * Create an InitialContex object and bind the logical name
   * "MyDS" with
   * the previously created Oracle dataSource
   */
Context ctx = new IntialContext(env);
ctx.bind("MyDS", ods);
```

Step 5

Since the datasource object has been registered with JNDI, application code can retrieve it from the JNDI context.

```
ods =(OracleDataSource) ctx. lookup("MyDS");   // lookup
DataSource
```

Step 6

Get the JDBC connection object from the DataSource object factory:

```
Connection conn = ods.getConnection();
```

Here is a portable code sample, adapted from an Oracle JDBC code sample:

```
datasoure.properties
====================
url=jdbc:oracle:thin:scott/tiger@//localhost:1521/orcl
```

Listing 7.2   *DataSrceJNDI.java*

```
=================================
/*
 *
 * Portable Application Using OracleDatasSource with JNDI
 */

import java.sql.*;
import javax.sql.*;
import oracle.jdbc.*;
import oracle.jdbc.pool.OracleDataSource;
import javax.naming.*;
import javax.naming.spi.*;
import java.util.Hashtable;
import java.util.*;
import java.io.*;

public class DataSrceJNDI
{
  public static void main (String args [])
    throws SQLException, NamingException, java.io.IOException
  {
    if ( args.length != 1 )
    {
      System.out.println("usage: java DataSrceJNDI <dir>");
      System.exit(0);
    }

    // initialize the Context
    Context ctx = null;
    try {
      Hashtable env = new Hashtable (5);
      env.put (Context.INITIAL_CONTEXT_FACTORY,
```

```
                    "com.sun.jndi.fscontext.RefFSContextFactory");
          env.put (Context.PROVIDER_URL, "file:" + args[0]);
          ctx = new InitialContext(env);
        } catch (NamingException ne)
        {
          ne.printStackTrace();
        }
        // Create a OracleDataSource instance explicitly
        OracleDataSource ods = new OracleDataSource();

      /*
       * Get URL from datasource.properties
       */

        InputStream is    = null;
        is =
ClassLoader.getSystemResourceAsStream("datasource.properties"
);
        Properties p = new Properties();
        p.load(is);
        is.close();
        String url = p.getProperty("url");
        System.out.println ("url in config file: " + url);
        ods.setURL(url);

        // Bind
        System.out.println ("Binding the logical name: jdbc/
oracle");
        ctx.bind ("jdbc/oracle", ods);

        // Lookup
        System.out.println ("Looking with the logical name: jdbc/
oracle");
        ods = (OracleDataSource) ctx.lookup ("jdbc/oracle");

        // Retrieve a connection
        Connection conn = ods.getConnection();

        // Create a Statement
        Statement stmt = conn.createStatement ();

        // Select the name of employee #7934 from EMP table
```

```
        ResultSet rset =
            stmt.executeQuery ("select ename from emp where empno
    ='7934'");

        // Iterate through the result and print the employee names
        while (rset.next ())
          System.out.println ("User name is " + rset.getString
    (1));

        // Close the RseultSet
        rset.close();
        // Close the Statement
        stmt.close();
        // Close the connection
        conn.close();


      }
    }
```

Compile and execute:

```
C:\>javac DataSrceJNDI.java

C:\>java DataSrceJNDI C:\Temp\JNDI
url in config file: jdbc:oracle:thin:scott/tiger@//
localhost:1521/orcl
Binding the logical name: jdbc/oracle
Doing a lookup with the logical name: jdbc/oracle
User name is MILLER


C:\>
```

Look at the contents of the .bindings file under the JNDI directory
(i.e., C:\Temp\JNDI).

After this overview of JDBC URL, OracleData sources with and without JNDI, the next step is to request a database connection. As we will see, there are many concepts and features around database connections.

7.3   Connections and Connection Services

Establishing a physical database connection is one of the most expensive database operations; sharing and reusing connections shields Java applications from paying such high cost, every time. This section describes the JDBC connection, as well as the services that the Oracle JDBC drivers furnish around it, and how these services help JDBC applications and Java/J2EE components scale and be reliable when accessing either a single database instance or a cluster of database instances (i.e., RAC). The Oracle Database 10*g* JDBC drivers furnish a range of connection services on top of standard/basic connection pooling, including implicit connection caching, connection tagging, connection searching/retrieval, fast connection fail-over, runtime connection load balancing, connection proxy, and connection wrapping. Furthermore, all of these capabilities[5] are driver-type independent; in other words, these are available in both client-side drivers (i.e., JDBC-Thin and JDBC-OCI). Last, we'll touch on JDBC and Grid computing. Grid computing is the buzzword du jour, a savant term for "resources consolidation and virtualization in order to reduce costs." What does this have to do with JDBC? As we will see, there are new issues and requirements for Java/J2EE applications running against database grids.[6]

7.3.1   JDBC Connections and Oracle Extensions

The `java.sql.Connection` interface defines the JDBC Connection object, which is obtained from DataSources. The Connection object furnishes the following methods:[7] `clearWarnings`, `close`, `commit`, `createStatement`, `createStatement`, `getAutoCommit`, `getCatalog`, `getHoldability`, `getMetaData`, `getTransactionIsolation`, `getTypeMap`, `getWarnings`, `isClosed`, `isReadOnly`, `nativeSQL`, `prepareCall`, `prepareStatement`, `releaseSavepoint`, `rollback`, `setAutoCommit`, `setCatalog`, `setHoldability`, `setReadOnly`, `setSavepoint`, `setTransactionIsolation`, `setTypeMap`.

The `oracle.jdbc.OracleConnection` interface defines an Oracle JDBC Connection object (i.e., `OracleConnection`). It is Oracle's extension to `java.sql.Connection`. The extensions include support for connection wrapping and services such as implicit connection cache, fast connection fail-over, and runtime connection load balancing, which are described later.

---

5.   Notice that I did not mention the Transparent Application Failover (TAF) but will talk about it.
6.   A set of clustered databases (e.g., Oracle database RAC) over hardware grids (i.e., blades).
7.   As of JDBC 3.0 specification, see the javadoc for more details on the methods and their signatures.

In addition, it supports Oracle Statements objects, associated caching, and so on.

Methods such as _getPC(), applyConnectionAttributes(connAttr), close(connAttr), close(OracleConnection.INVALID_CONNECTION), getConnectionAttributes(), and so on have been added to support the extension features that will be described hereafter.

7.3.2   Connection Caching: Implicit Connection Cache

As already mentioned, establishing a physical database connection is one of the most expensive database operations. It involves creating and authenticating a database session through several message exchanges between the requester and the RDBMS. Connection pooling is a well-known technique for sharing a pool of physical database connections among a larger number of consumers, as illustrated by Figure 7.1. For example, a pool of 100 database connections can be satisfactorily shared by 1,000 concurrent users. As a result, the cost of connection establishment is eliminated. Java applications—including stand-alone JDBC applications, O/R mapping frameworks, Servlets, JavaServer Pages, Session Beans, BMP Beans, J2EE/EJB containers, and persistence frameworks—typically get preestablished connections from the pool. Connection pooling is transparent from an application's viewpoint, although it traditionally involves calling a specific API (i.e., getPooledConnection()). The javax.sql.ConnectionPoolData-Source interface defines a factory for PooledConection objects (i.e., javax.sql.PooledConnection), which can participate in connection pooling (i.e., caching and reusing physical connections). As of Oracle JDBC 10*g*, an application simply invokes the DataSource.getConnection method to get a Pooled Connection object (i.e., javax.sql.Pooled-Connection) and uses it the same way it would use a physical Connection object (i.e., java.sql.Connection), hence the name Implicit Connection Cache. How does it work?

Figure 7.1
*Connection
Caching: the Big
Picture*

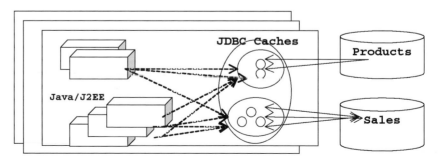

The Implicit Connection Cache is an extended JDBC-3.0-compliant[8] connection cache, which, beyond the standard, addresses some of the shortcomings in the JDBC connection cache specification, such as the requirement for all cached connections to belong to the same database, be authenticated by the same user, and the lack of a mechanism to either resize or refresh the cache or search for and reclaim abandoned connections.

As summarized in Table 7.1, the new connection cache in Oracle Database 10*g* JDBC, called Implicit Connection Cache has been designed to overcome limitations in previous implementations (i.e., `OracleConnectionCacheImpl`) by providing transparent access to the cache, support for multiple identities, and the ability to retrieve connections based on user-defined attributes and weights. In addition, it supports the ability to refresh or recycle stale connections from the cache. The base principle in Implicit Connection Cache is to only enable features explicitly requested by setting or changing connection cache properties and/or connection attributes. Middle-tier containers or frameworks such as the Oracle Application server, which integrates Implicit Connection Cache, allow enabling these features declaratively through deployment descriptors.

Table 7.1   *Comparing Connection Caching in Oracle JDBC Drivers*

Features	Pre-10*g* Connection Pooling	10*g* Connection Pooling
Transparent Cache Access	No	Yes
Refresh Stale Connections	No	Yes
Attributes-based Connection Retrieval	No	Yes
Reclaim and Reuse Abandoned Connections	No	Yes
Cache Heterogeneous Pairs of User/Password	No	Yes
Centralized Cache Management	No	Yes
Integration with RAC Events	No	Yes
Caching XA Connections	No	Yes (10.2)*

* Not exposed to end users.

8.   The oracle.jdbc.pool.OracleConnectionPoolDataSource implements javax.sql.ConnectionPoolDataSource, and the oracle.jdbc.pool.OraclePooledConnection class implements javax.sql.PooledConnection.

Implicit Access to the Cache

By default, the getConnection() method in the standard DataSource API creates a new database session and a physical connection to a database, thus incurring performance and scalability penalties. With the Implicit Connection Cache, once the DataSource property `ConnectionCachingEnabled` has been set to *true*, `getConnection()` will service connection requests from the cache.

```
ods.setConnectionCachingEnabled(True);


public void setConnectionCacheProperties(java.util.Properties
cp)
        throws java.sql.SQLException
```

Where `cp` – is a list of key/value pairs properties. If a null value is set for a property, the default values will take effect.

Following is the list of furnished properties to configure and fine tune the behavior of your connection cache (the keys are case sensitive):

- `MinLimit`: Specifes the low watermark or the minimum number of physical connections to remain in the cache. Defaults to 0.

- `MaxLimit`: Specifies the high watermark or the maximum number of physical connections in the cache. Default to `Integer.MAX_VALUE`.

- `InitialLimit`: Specifies the number of initial physical connections to be created when the cache is initialized. Defaults to 0.

- `MaxStatementsLimit`: Sets the maximum number of statements that each physical connection keeps open in its cache. Defaults to 0.

- `InactivityTimeout`: Sets the maximum time, in seconds, that a physical connection <u>in the cache</u> can remain idle (i.e., not checked out) before being closed. Defaults to 0 (i.e., disabled).

- `TimeToLiveTimeout`: Sets the maximum time, in seconds, that a <u>checked-out</u> physical connection can remain idle. Defaults to 0 (i.e., disabled).

- `AbandonedConnectionTimeout`: Sets the maximum inactivity time between two JDBC calls before regarding the connection as abandoned and reclaimed back to the cache. Note that in early implementation, the inactivity heartbeat starts at the beginning of a query but is not reset when the query completes so each operation must happen within the specified inactivity time since the begining of the previous one; check that you have the latest implementation or related patch. Defaults to 0 (i.e., disabled).

- `ConnectionWaitTimeout`: Specifies the time limit to wait when a new connection request arrives and there are no connections to check out. Defaults to 0.

- `PropertyCheckInterval`: A timeout daemon thread is associated with each cache to enforce the various timeouts listed previously; this parameter sets the time interval for the daemon thread to kick in and enforce timeout limits. Defaults to 900 seconds (15 minutes).

- `ValidateConnection`: Verifies each physical connection for validity (by issuing a dummy query to the database) before a checked-out connection is returned to the caller. Defaults to false.

- `ClosestConnectionMatch`: Causes the connection cache to retrieve the connection with the closest approximation to the specified connection attributes. Defaults to false.

- `AttributeWeights`: Sets the weight (integer) for each connection attribute. This is used when `ClosestConnectionMatch` is set to true and enables retrieval of a connection with the highest combined weight of all its connection attributes. Defaults to a weight of 1.

- `LowerThresholdLimit`: Sets the lower threshold limit on the cache. This is used when the `releaseConnection()` cache callback method is registered. Defaults to 20% (of `MaxLimit`).

The various timeout properties ensure that stale or abandoned connections are reclaimed back to the cache. However, to find out that a specific connection is invalid (i.e., dead server process or failed node), upon a SQL exception, the JDBC application must invoke `isFatalConnectionError(java.sql.SQLException se)`. In the current implementation, the application has to explicitly let the Cache Manager know that a connection is invalid by closing it with `INVALID_CONNECTION` flag (i.e., `myconn.close(INVALID_CONNECTION)`).

In addition, the Oracle JDBC drivers also furnish/support the following timeouts at TCP socket, SQL*Net, JDBC driver, and SQL Query levels:

1. The following timeouts abort a hung query once the specified timeout has been reached (i.e., no data received from the server within the specified amount of time):

    ```
    // conn property — n seconds
    prop.put ("oracle.net.READ_TIMEOUT", n);


    // SQL Net Timeout -- n second
    prop.put (oracle.net.ns.SQLnetDef.TCP_CONNTIMEOUT_STR,
    "" + (n * 1000));
    ```

2. sqlnet.recv_timeout: a new SQL*Net 10*g* parameter, which can be set on client and server sides in sqlnet.ora, as follows:

    ```
    # for 100 second timeout
    sqlnet.recv_timeout=100
    ```

3. setQueryTimeout(): this is a standard JDBC timeout, which sets the number of seconds the driver will wait for a Statement to execute; it can be set at a SQL statement (Statement, Prepared-Statement) level, as follows:

    ```
    stmt.setQueryTimeout(10);
    ```

a) setLoginTimeout(): sets the maximum time in seconds that this datasource will wait while attempting to connect to a database:

    ```
    ods.setLoginTimeout(10) ;
    ```

The connection cache is created either explicitly using the Cache Manager API or implicitly by the first invocation of the getConnection() method. The cache is populated either by preinitializing it using the Cache Manager APIs or, incrementally, upon the release of connections back to the cache. The Cache Manager API, which is described in the next section, is not intended for use by JDBC applications but rather by middle-tier containers and frameworks.

Based on the following settings, the first call to getConnection() will create the cache MyCache, create a physical connection to the MyDS datasource, and the handle to the connection will be returned to the requester:

```
ods.setConnectionCacheName("MyCache"); // optional
ods.setConnectionCacheProperties(cp);  // optional
ctx.bind("MyDS", ods);
ods =(OracleDataSource) ctx.lookup("MyDS");  // lookup
// DataSource

// create a database session (physical connection)
    conn = ods.getConnection();
```

The following code snippet shows a skeleton of a complete JDBC program, which will create a `MyCache` cache and a connection associated to the `SalesDS` datasource, authenticated by "SCOTT":

```
// look up the datasource object from the Context
   OracleDataSource ds = (OracleDataSource) ctx.lookup("SalesDB");
   java.util.Properties prop = new java.util.Properties ();
// setting the cache size to at least 2
   prop.setProperty("MinLimit", "2");

// create the cache and populate with 4 connections
   prop.setProperty("InitialLimit", "4");
   prop.setProperty("MaxStatementsLimit", "1");
   prop.setProperty("InactivityTimeout", "10");     // 10 seconds
   prop.setProperty("PropertyCheckInterval", "5"); // 5 seconds

// Setting cache properties on the datasource object
   ds.setConnectionCacheProperties (prop);

// 1st invocation of getConnection creates the
// Cache with 4 connections
   Connection conn = ds.getConnection();
```

Subsequent invocations of `getConnection()` will simply retrieve available connections from the cache or create new ones (within the value of MaxLimit). Once the connection is retrieved, the requesting application can proceed with statement(s) creation:

```
// Create a Statement
    Statement stmt = conn.createStatement ();
```

```
...

// Do some work

...

// Close the Statement
    stmt.close();
    stmt = null;
```

Saving the Values of Connection Attributes

In order to make persistent the values assigned to the connection attributes for future use, JDBC applications may use one of two methods described in the following text.

Caching Heterogeneously Authenticated Connections

While a database does not impose any restriction on the connection authentication, a traditional cache might impose such a limitation on pairs of user/passwords. The Implicit Connection Cache can handle any user-authenticated connection. For example, the *joe.blow* connection can coexist very well with the *bobo.lafleur* connection in the same connection cache.

Connection Retrieval Based on User-Defined Attributes

One of the cool new features in the Implicit Connection Cache is the notion of *connection striping*. Connection striping or labeling consists of applying user-defined attributes to a connection and persisting the state of the attributes when the connection is returned back to the cache. These attributes can then be used later to retrieve the same connection from the cache; furthermore, cached connections do not have to restate attributes.

Retrieving a connection based on NLS_LANG attribute:

```
// a connection that matches with NLS_LANG attribute
    java.util.Properties connAttr = null;
    connAttr.setProperty("NLS_LANG", "ISO-LATIN-1");
    conn = ds.getConnection(connAttr);
...
```

Retrieving a connection based on isolation-level attribute:

```
// retrieve a connection that matches Transaction Isolation
   java.util.Properties connAttr = null;
   connAttr.setProperty("TRANSACTION_ISOLATION",
"SERIALIZABLE");
   conn = ds.getConnection(connAttr);
…

   conn.close(connAttr); // save settings for this connection
```

Retrieving a connection based on connection tag attribute:

```
…
java.util.Properties connAttr = null;
connAttr.setProperty("CONNECTION_TAG", "Rita'S_CONNECTION");
conn = ds.getConnection(connAttr); // retrieve Rita's
// connection
conn.close(connAttr); // Save connection_tag  for future
// retrieval
conn = ds.getConnection(connAttr); // retrieve Rita's
// connection
```

Applying Connection Attributes to a Cached Connection

A connection attribute can be applied to a cached connection using one of the following two approaches:

1. Setting the attributes on the connection object by calling `apply-ConnectionAttributes(java.util.properties    connAttr`. Connection attribute settings can be done incrementally/cumulatively through multiple calls. For example, the `NLS_LANG` attribute may be set in module M1, then module M2 sets the `TXN_ISOLATION` attribute, and so on.

    ```
    conn.applyConnectionAttributes(conAttr);
    ```

2. Calling the `close(java.util.properties connAttr)` method on the connection object. This method closes the logical connection and then applies the connection attributes on the underlying physical connection (i.e., PooledConnection). Attributes setting via close() overrides other approaches.

    ```
    conn.close(connAttr); // apply the supplied
    // attributes to the connection object
    ```

Setting Unmatched Attribute Values

A JDBC application may set the values for the unmatched attributes before returning the connection to the cache. This ensures that this connection object will match subsequent connection requests with the same search attributes.

```
// Connection request
   java.util.properties connAttr = null;
   connAttr.setProperty("NLSLANG", "ISO-LATIN-1");
   conn = ds.getConnection(connAttr); // request connection
   java.util.properties unmatchedAttr =
                 conn.getUnMatchedConnectionAttributes();
...
//Apply unmatched attributes before using the connection.
...

// Save the attributes settings
conn.close(connAttr);
```

Connection Retrieval Based on Attributes and Weights

Connections may be selectively retrieved from the connection cache based on a combination of `ConnectionAttributes` and attribute weights. Weights are assigned to each key in a `ConnectionAttribute` in a one-time operation that also changes cache properties. The cache property `CacheAttributeWeights` is a `java.util.Properties` that allows setting attribute weights. Each weight is a user-defined integer value that specifies how expensive the key is in terms of resources. Once the weights are set on the cache, connection requests are made on the DataSource by calling `getConnection(connectionAttributes)`. The `connectionAttributes` argument refers to keys and their associated values. Retrieving the connection from the cache involves searching for a connection that satisfies a combination of the following:

- A key/value match on a connection from the cache
- The maximum total weight of all the keys of the `connectionAttributes` that were matched on the connection

Here is an example using the `CacheAttributeWeights` property:

```
// Define cache weights properties
   java.util.properties cacheProps = new Properties();
   java.util.properties cacheWeights = null;

   cacheWeights.setProperty("NLSLANG", "10");
   cacheWeights.setProperty("SecurityGroup", "8");
   cacheWeights.setProperty("Application", "4");
 ...
// Apply the weight setting to the CacheAttributeWeights
// property
   cacheProps.put(CacheAttributeWeights, cacheWeights);
 ...
// Specify Connection Attributes
   java.util.properties connAttr = null;
   connAttr.setProperty("NLSLANG", "ISO-LATIN-1");
   connAttr.setProperty("SecurityGroup", "1");
   connAttr.setProperty("Application", "HR")

//
   ds.setCacheName("MyCache");

// First retrieval of the connection from myCache
   conn = ds.getConnection(connAttr);
 ...
// Release the connection and Save attribute settings
   conn.close(connAttr);
 ...
// Subsequent retrieval of the connection from the cache
   conn = ds.getConnection(connAttr);
 ...
```

This getConnection() request tries to match and retrieve a connection from the *MyCache* cache. One of the following two things can happen:

1. *An exact match is found.* As in the previous example, an exact match is a connection that satisfies the same attribute values and all the keys defined by Keys (NLS_LANG, SECURITY_GROUP).

    ```
    private void listProperties(java.util.Properties prop)
       {
          java.util.Enumeration enum = prop.propertyNames();
    ```

```
String key = null;
while ( enum.hasMoreElements() )
{
    key = (String)enum.nextElement ();
    System.out.print(key + ": ");
    System.out.println (prop.getProperty(key));
}
System.out.print("\n");
}
```

```
// List the matched properties
    connProp =
```

```
((OracleConnection)conn).getConnectionAttributes();
    System.out.println("\nThe Properties of the
connection:");
    listProperties (connProp);
```

2.   *An exact match is not found.* In this case, a closest match
      based on the attribute key/value and their associated weights
      are used (but only if the `ClosestConnectionMatch` property
      is set).

```
// List the unmatched properties
    connProp =
```

```
((OracleConnection)conn).getUnMatchedConnectionAttribut
es ();
    System.out.println("The Unmatched properties:");
listProperties (connProp);
```

For example, a closest match may be a connection that matches the
attributes of NLS_LANG and APPLICATION but not SECURITY_GROUP. It is
also possible to find connections that match some keys of the original list,
but their combined weights are different. For example, connection1 could
have a match of NLS_LANG with its associated weight of 10, whereas
connection2 may have an attribute match of SECURITY_GROUP and
APPLICATION with their combined weight of 12. In this case, it is desired
that connection2 is returned. In other words, connection2 is the closest
match and is more expensive to reconstruct (from the caller's perspective) as

opposed to connection1. When none of the `connectionAttributes` matches, a new connection is returned. The new connection is created using the user and password set on the DataSource.

Once the connection is returned, the user can invoke the `getUn-MatchedConnectionAttributes()` method on the connection object to get the list of attributes (`java.util.Properties`) that did not match the criteria. The caller can use the list of unmatched attributes to set the unmatched/missing values before using the connection.

List of System and Connection Properties

`Driver.getPropertyInfo()` // returns the list of all available properties. The following code fragment lists the driver and/or connection properties that the Oracle JDBC drivers support, as summarized in Table 7.2.

```
String url =
"jdbc:oracle:thin:@(DESCRIPTION=(ADDRESS_LIST=(ADDRESS=(PROTO
COL=tcp)(HOST=<host>)(PORT=<port>)))(CONNECT_DATA=(SID=<sid>)
))";
DriverPropertyInfo[] dpi =
            new OracleDriver().getPropertyInfo(url,new
Properties());
for (int i=0; i<dpi.length; i++) {
 String dp_name = dpi[i].name; // get the name of property
 String value = dpi[i].value; // get the current value
  String dp_desc = dpi[i].description; // get the description
 }
```

Table 7.2   *Connection Properties (from the Oracle JDBC Users Guide)*

Key	Value	Comment
User	String	The value of this property is used as the user name when connecting to the database.
password	String	The value of this property is used as the password when connecting to the database.
database	String	The value of this property is used as the SID of the database.
server	String	The value of this property is used as the host name of the database.

Table 7.2 *Connection Properties (from the Oracle JDBC Users Guide) (continued)*

Key	Value	Comment
internal_logon	String	The value of this property is used as the user name when performing an internal logon. Usually this will be SYS or SYSDBA.
defaultRowPrefetch	int	The value of this property is used as the default number of rows to prefetch.
defaultExecuteBatch	int	The value of this property is used as the default batch size when using Oracle-style batching.
processEscapes	boolean	If the value of this property is "false," then the default setting for Statement.setEscapeProccessing is false.
disableDefineColumnType	boolean	When this connection property has the value "true," the method defineColumnType has no effect. This is highly recommended when using the Thin driver, especially when the database character set contains four-byte characters that expand to two UCS2 surrogate characters (e.g., AL32UTF8). The method defineColumnType provides no performance benefit (or any other benefit) when used with the 10.x.x Thin driver. This property is provided so that you do not have to remove the calls from your code. This is especially valuable if you use the same code with a Thin driver and either the OCI or Server Internal driver.
DMSName	String	Set the name of the DMS Noun that is the parent of all JDBC DMS metrics.
DMSType	String	Set the type of the DMS Noun that is the parent of all JDBC DMS metrics.
AccumulateBatchResult	boolean	When using Oracle-style batching, JDBC determines when to flush a batch to the database. If this property is "true," then the number of modified rows accumulated across all batches is flushed from a single statement. The default is to count each batch separately.

Table 7.2 *Connection Properties (from the Oracle JDBC Users Guide) (continued)*

Key	Value	Comment
oracle.jdbc.J2EE13Compliant	boolean	If the value of this property is "true," JDBC uses strict compliance for some edge cases. In general, Oracle's JDBC drivers will allow some operations that are not permitted in the strict interpretation of J2EE 1.3. Setting this property to "true" will cause those cases to throw SQLExceptions. This can be either a system property or a connection property. The default value of this property is "false" in classes12.jar and ojdbc14.jar. The default value is "true" in classes12dms.jar and ojdbc14dms.jar.
oracle.jdbc.TcpNoDelay	boolean	If the value of this property is "true," the TCP_NODELAY property is set on the socket when using the Thin driver. See java.net.SocketOptions.TCP_NODELAY. This can be either a system property or a connection property.
defaultNChar	boolean	If the value of this property is "true," the default mode for all character data columns will be NCHAR.
useFetchSizeWithLongColumn	boolean	If the value of this property is "true," then JDBC will prefetch rows even though there is a LONG or LONG RAW column in the result. By default, JDBC fetches only one row at a time if there are LONG or LONG RAW columns in the result. Setting this property to true can improve performance but can also cause SQL Exceptions if the results are too big.
remarksReporting	boolean	If the value of this property is "true," Oracle-DatabaseMetaData will include remarks in the metadata. This can result in a substantial reduction in performance.
includeSynonyms	boolean	If the value of this property is "true," JDBC will include synonyms when getting information about a column.

Table 7.2   *Connection Properties (from the Oracle JDBC Users Guide) (continued)*

Key	Value	Comment
restrictGetTables	boolean	If the value of this property is "true," JDBC will return a more refined value for DatabaseMetaData.getTables. By default, JDBC will return things that are not accessible tables. These can be nontable objects or accessible synonymns for inaccessible tables. If this property is true, JDBC will return only accessible tables. This has a substantial performance penalty.
fixedString	boolean	If the value of this property is "true," JDBC will use the FIXED CHAR semantic when setObject is called with a String argument. By default, JDBC uses VARCHAR semantics. The difference is in blank padding. With the default there is no blank padding, so, for example, "a" does not equal "a" in a CHAR(4). If true, these two will be equal.
oracle.jdbc.ocinativelibrary	String	Set the name of the native library for the oci driver. If not set, the default name, libocijdbcX (X is a version number), is used.
SetBigStringTryClob	boolean	Setting this property to "true" forces the PreparedStatement.setString method to use setStringForClob if the data is larger than 32,765 bytes. Please note that using this method with VARCHAR and LONG columns may cause large data to be truncated silently or cause other errors differing from the normal behavior of setString.
oracle.jdbc.StreamBufferSize	int	Set size of the buffer for the InputStream/Reader obtained from getXXXStream/getXXXReader. The default size is 16K. The size passed should be at least 4,096, or else 4,096 is assumed.
OCINewPassword	String	Pass the value of new password to be set during logon. This could typically be used for resetting the password when the password has expired or when the account is in the grace period.

Key	Value	Comment
`oracle.jdbc.FreeMemoryOnEnter` `ImplicitCache`	`boolean`	Clear the define buffers before caching the statement when Implicit statement caching is enabled. Setting the value to true would enable the clearing of define buffers before caching of Statements in the Statement cache. False is the default value, and this would behave in the same way as statement caching worked in prior releases.
`oracle.jdbc.ReadTimeout`	`int`	Read timeout while reading from the socket. This affects Thin driver only. Timeout is in milliseconds.

Implicit Connection Cache Code Sample

Listing 7.3 is a code sample taken from the Oracle JDBC code samples; it is made up of a set of code fragments that show how MinLimit, Inactivity timeout, TimeToLive timeout, AbandonedConnection timeout, and Max-Statement limit work.

Listing 7.3 *ImplicitCache.java*

```
/*
 *  ImplicitCache.java
 */

import java.sql.*;
import javax.sql.*;
import java.util.*;
import javax.naming.*;
import javax.naming.spi.*;
import oracle.jdbc.*;
import oracle.jdbc.pool.*;

class ImplicitCache extends Thread
{
```

```java
  Context ctx = null;

  public static void main (String args [])
       throws SQLException
  {
    ImplicitCache icc = new ImplicitCache();
    icc.start();
  }

  public void run ()
  {
    try
    {
      setods ();
      // See each procedure below for more details
      InactivityTimeout();
      TimeToLiveTimeout();
      AbandonedConnectionTimeout();
      MaxStatementsLimit();
    } catch (Exception e)
    {
       e.printStackTrace();
       System.exit(1);
    }
  }

/*
 * Show InactivityTimeOut
 */

  private void InactivityTimeout() throws Exception
  {
    Connection conns[] = new OracleConnection[8];
    int i = 0;
    ResultSet rs = null;
    Statement stmt = null;

  // look up the datasource object from the Context
    OracleDataSource ds = (OracleDataSource) ctx.lookup("SalesDS");

  // setting cache properties
```

```
// set PropertyCheckInterval to a value lower than InactivityTimeout
// to allow the deamon to kick-in during the inactivity period

   java.util.Properties prop = new java.util.Properties ();
   prop.setProperty("MinLimit", "2");        // low watermark is  2
   prop.setProperty("InitialLimit", "4"); // create cache with 4 conn
   prop.setProperty("InactivityTimeout", "10");    // 10 seconds
   prop.setProperty("PropertyCheckInterval", "5"); //  5 seconds
   ds.setConnectionCacheProperties (prop);

// Call getConnection to create the Cache
   Connection conn = ds.getConnection();
   conn.close();

   System.out.println("\n*** Show Inactivity timeout ***");

   Thread.sleep(2000); // wait 2 second for the warming up
// check the number of sessions after initialization
   System.out.println("The initial connections in the cache: "
      + checkNoSessions(ds)); // expect 4 as the InitialLimit

// retrieve 8 connections, then check the number of
// sessions.
   for ( i = 0; i < 8; ++i )
   {
     conns[i] = ds.getConnection();
   }
   System.out.println("expect 8 cached connections,  got:  "
        + checkNoSessions(ds)); // 8 is the number of connections

// close all the connections, then check the number of
// sessions to see whether it goes below the MinLimit
   for (i=0; i<8; ++i )
   {
     conns[i].close();
   }

   System.out.println("Sleep 15 sec to enable Inactivity Timeout");
   Thread.sleep(15000);
   System.out.println("number of cached connections "
        + checkNoSessions(ds)); // 1 = MinLimit - System's session
```

```
   for ( i = 0; i < 8; ++i )
   {
      if ( conns[i] != null )
      {
         conns[i].close();
         conns[i] = null;
      }
   }

   ds.close();// close the DataSource and clean the cache
} // end of InactivityTimeout()


/*
 * Show TimeToLiveTimeout
 */
private void TimeToLiveTimeout () throws Exception
{
   Connection conns[] = new Connection[15];
   Statement stmts[] = new Statement[15];
   int  i = 0;

   // look up the datasource object
   OracleDataSource ds = (OracleDataSource)ctx.lookup("SALESDB");

   // set cache properties
   java.util.Properties prop = new java.util.Properties();
   prop.setProperty("TimeToLiveTimeout", "10");     // 10 seconds
   prop.setProperty("PropertyCheckInterval", "5");   // 5 seconds
   ds.setConnectionCacheProperties(prop);

   System.out.println("\n*** Show TimeToLive timeout ***");

   // create 15 connections and 15 statements
   System.out.println("Get 15 connections and statements from the cache");
   for ( i = 0; i < 15; ++i )
   {
      conns[i] = ds.getConnection();
      if ( conns[i] == null )
         System.err.println("conns[" + i + "] is bad");
      else
```

```
      stmts[i] = conns[i].createStatement();
}


// sleep 15 seconds longer than 10 sec TimeToLive
// so as to enable TimeToLive timeout
System.out.println("Sleeping 15 sec enables TimeToLive timeout");
Thread.sleep (15000);


// check all the statements and conn. should be claimed
  for ( i = 0; i < 15; ++i )
  {
   // check whether all those 15 stmts get canceled out
   try
   {
      ResultSet rs = stmts[i].executeQuery("select USER from DUAL");
      System.err.println("statement " + i + " still alive");
   } catch (Exception e)
   {
      System.out.print("Statement " + i + " is successfully canceled. ");
   }


   // check whether all those 15 conns get canceled out
   try
   {
      stmts[i] = conns[i].createStatement();
      System.err.println("connection " + i + "is still alive");
   } catch (Exception e)
   {
      System.out.println("connection " + i + " is successfully canceled");
   }
  }
  ds.close(); // close the datasource and clean up the cache
} // end of TimeToLiveTimeout()


/*
 * Show AbandonnedConnectionTimeout
 */
private void AbandonedConnectionTimeout() throws Exception
{
  Connection conns[] = new Connection[6];
```

```
Statement   stmts[] = new Statement[6];
int         i       = 0;
int         j       = 0;

// look up for the DataSource object
OracleDataSource ds = (OracleDataSource) ctx.lookup("SALESDB");

// set cache properties
java.util.Properties prop = new java.util.Properties();
prop.setProperty("AbandonedConnectionTimeout", "10");   // 10 seconds
prop.setProperty("PropertyCheckInterval", "5");         //  5 seconds
ds.setConnectionCacheProperties(prop);

System.out.println("\n*** Show AbandonedConnectionTimeout ***");

// create 6 connections and 6 statements
System.out.println("Get 6 conn. and statements from the cache");
for ( i = 0; i < 6; ++i )
{
   conns[i] = ds.getConnection();
   if ( conns[i] == null )
      System.err.println("conns[" + i + "] is null");
   else
      stmts[i] = conns[i].createStatement();
}

// Keep the first 3 connections active and let others inactive
// and sleep 15 seconds to enable the AbandonedConnection timeout
System.out.println("Let conns[0] ~ conns[2] be active, " +
                   "and others be inactive");
for ( i = 0; i < 6; ++i )
{
   for ( j = 0; j < 3; ++j )
   {
      stmts[j].execute("select USER from DUAL");
   }
   Thread.sleep (2500);   // each thread sleep 2.5 seconds
}

// check which connections are closed, which statements
// are canceled, and which are still alive
```

```
System.out.println("15 seconds later, conns[0] ~ conns[2] " +
                   "should still there");
System.out.println("inactive conns[3] ~ conns[5] and their " +
                   "stmts should be canceled");
for ( i = 0; i < 3; ++i )
{
   try
   {
      ResultSet rs = stmts[i].executeQuery("select USER from DUAL");
      stmts[i].close();
   } catch (Exception e)
   {
      System.err.print("Statement handle " + i + " is canceled. ");
   }

   try
   {
      stmts[i] = conns[i].createStatement();
      System.out.println("conns[" + i +
               "] and its statement handle is good");
   } catch (Exception e)
   {
      System.err.println("conns[" + i + "] is canceled");
   }
}

for ( i = 3; i < 6; ++i )
{
   try
   {
      ResultSet rs = stmts[i].executeQuery("select USER from DUAL");
      System.err.println("Statement handle " + i + " is not canceled");
   } catch (Exception e)
   {
      System.out.print("statement handle " + i + "
        is successfully canceled. ");
   }

   try
   {
      stmts[i] = conns[i].createStatement();
```

```
          System.err.println("conns[" + i + "] is not canceled");
       } catch (Exception e)
       {
          System.out.println("conns[" + i + "] is successfully canceled");
       }
    }


    for ( i = 0; i < 6; ++i )
    {
       if ( conns[i] != null )
       {
          conns[i].close();
          conns[i] = null;
       }
    }
    ds.close(); // close the DataSource and clean up the cache
 } // end of AbandonedConnectionTimeout()
/*
 * Show Statement caching
 */
 private void MaxStatementsLimit () throws Exception
 {
    Connection conns[] = new Connection[4];
    Statement  stmts[] = new Statement[8];
    int  i = 0;

    OracleDataSource ds = (OracleDataSource)ctx.lookup("SALESDB");

    // set the Datasource with maxium cache size as 4,
    // maximum statement size per connection as 1
    java.util.Properties cacheProp = new java.util.Properties();
    cacheProp.setProperty("MaxLimit", "4");
    cacheProp.setProperty("MaxStatementsLimit", "1");
    ds.setConnectionCacheProperties(cacheProp);

    System.out.println("\n*** demo MaxStatementsLimit ***");
    for ( i = 0; i < 4; ++i )
    {
       conns[i] = ds.getConnection();
       if ( conns[i] == null )
          System.err.println("conns[" + i + "] is bad");
```

```
        else
        {
            System.out.print("conns[" + i +"].getStatementCacheSize(): "
                + ((OracleConnection)conns[i]).getStatementCacheSize());
            stmts[2*i] = conns[i].prepareStatement("select user from dual");
            ((PreparedStatement)stmts[2*i]).execute();
            stmts[2*i].close();

            stmts[2*i+1] = conns[i].prepareStatement("select user from dual");
            ((PreparedStatement)stmts[2*i+1]).execute();

            if ( stmts[2*i+1] == stmts[2*i] )
                System.out.println(". Get the cached statement for additional
request");
            else
                System.err.print("we get a different statement. ");
        }
    } // end of for loop
    for ( i = 0; i < 4; ++i )
    {
        if ( conns[i] != null )
        {
            conns[i].close();
            conns[i] = null;
        }
    }
    ds.close();
    ds = null;

} // end of MaxStatementsLimit()

/*
 * Utility to Create a JNDI-based Data Source
 */
private void setods() throws Exception
{
    // create a context for holding name-to-object bindings
    Hashtable env = new Hashtable (5);
    env.put (Context.INITIAL_CONTEXT_FACTORY,
            "com.sun.jndi.fscontext.RefFSContextFactory");
    env.put (Context.PROVIDER_URL, "file:./JNDI" );
    ctx = new InitialContext (env);
```

```
    // use the url supplied in command line or the default
    String url = "jdbc:oracle:thin:@";
    try {
      String url1 = System.getProperty("JDBC_URL");
      if (url1 != null)
        url = url1;
    } catch (Exception e) {
      // If there is any security exception, ignore it
      // and use the default
    }

    // create a DataSource
    OracleDataSource ods = new OracleDataSource();

    // set DataSource properties
    ods.setURL(url);
    ods.setUser("hr");
    ods.setPassword("hr");
    ods.setConnectionCachingEnabled(true);
    ods.setConnectionCacheName("ImplicitCache03");

    // set DataSource object to JNDI
    try {
        ctx.bind("SALESDB", ods);
    } catch (Exception e) { }
  } // end of setods()


/*
 * Utility to check the number of active sessions
 * uses system account (and password)
 */
private int checkNoSessions ( OracleDataSource ods)
{
    Connection conn = null;
    PreparedStatement pstmt = null;
    ResultSet rs = null;
    int sessions = 0;

    try
    {
```

```
        conn = ods.getConnection("system", "manager");
        pstmt = conn.prepareStatement (
                    "SELECT COUNT(username) " +
                    "FROM v$session " +
                    "WHERE type != \'BACKGROUND\'");
        rs = pstmt.executeQuery ();
        rs.next ();
        sessions = rs.getInt (1);
        // subtracting the entry of system/manager from the actual
        // entry
        --sessions;

        rs.close();
        rs = null;
        pstmt.close();
        pstmt = null;
        conn.close ();
        conn = null;
    } catch (SQLException e)
    {
        e.printStackTrace();
    }

    return sessions;
  } // end of private int checkNoSessions ()


}
```

7.3.3 The Connection Cache Manager

In order to centrally manage all caches associated with all datasources within a Java VM, the Oracle JDBC driver furnishes a Mister Cache Manager.

Managing and Maintaining Caches

The Oracle JDBC uses one instance of Connection Cache Manager per JVM to manage all of the connection caches used by applications running on that JVM. The Connection Cache Manager is responsible for creating caches, maintaining their states, and terminating them. Each cache is identified by a unique name and is tightly bound to a datasource. Each cache is created either transparently when getConnection() requests are made on a cache-enabled datasource or explicitly via the Connection Cache Manager

API. Once a cache is created, it is terminated either explicitly via the Connection Cache Manager API or implicitly when the datasource is closed.

The Connection Cache Manager API

The Cache Manager API allows programmatic management of caches and access to information such as the number of connections checked out, the number of connections available in each cache, and so on. This API is intended for use by middle-tier containers or frameworks, not by the Java applications (however, when processing SQL exceptions, applications or containers should invoke the isFatalConnectionError() method. The oracle.jdbc.pool.OracleConnectionCacheManager javadoc provides the following methods:

- createCache(OracleDataSource   ods,java.util.Properties cacheProperties): Creates a connection cache using an auto-generated cache name and the supplied properties.

- createCache(java.lang.String   cacheName, OracleData-Source ods, java.util.Properties cacheProperties): Creates a connection cache using the supplied cache name and the properties.

- disableCache(java.lang.String cacheName): Disables a given connection cache.

- enableCache(java.lang.String cacheName): Activates a given connection cache.

- existsCache(java.lang.String cacheName): Checks if a given connection cache exists.

- getCacheNameList(): Gets all the cache names managed by this Connection Cache Manager; remember, there is one instance of Connection Cache Manager per Java VM (JDK).

- getCacheProperties(java.lang.String cacheName): Gets the connection cache properties corresponding to the given cache.

```
// list the connection cache properties
System.out.println("\nConn. Cache's properties ");
listProperties (occm.getCacheProperties("MyCache"));
```

- getConnectionCacheManagerInstance(): Returns the instance of ConnectionCacheManager.

- `getConnectionErrorCodes()`: Retrieves pre-defined + user-added Fatal Error codes.

- `getNumberOfActiveConnections(java.lang.String    cacheName)`: Gets the number of connections already in use.

- `getNumberOfAvailableConnections(java.lang.String cacheName)`: Gets the number of connections in the cache that are available for use.

- `isFatalConnectionError(java.sql.SQLException se)`: Returns true if the SQL exception is one of ORA-3113, ORA-3114, ORA-1033, ORA-1034, ORA-1090, ORA-17008, plus user-defined fatal exceptions

- `purgeCache(java.lang.String    cacheName, boolean    cleanupCheckedOutConnections)`: Purges the connections in the cache (cleans the cache by removing connections).

- `refreshCache(java.lang.String    cacheName, int    mode)`: Refreshes the connections in the cache.

- `reinitializeCache(java.lang.String    cacheName, java.util.Properties cacheProperties)`: Reinitializes a connection cache using the new supplied set of properties.

- `removeCache(java.lang.String    cacheName, long    waitTimeout)`: Removes the connection cache associated with the given name.

- `setConnectionErrorCodes(int[]    fatalErrorCodes)`: Use this for adding user-defined exceptions to the list of fatal SQL Exceptions.

- `setConnectionPoolDataSource(java.lang.String    cacheName, javax.sql.ConnectionPoolDataSource ds)`: Sets the ConnectionPoolDataSource that may be used to create the implicit connection cache.

Connection Cache Manager Callback

The `OracleConnectionCacheCallback` interface lets the JDBC application control the handling of abandoned or released connections. It must be implemented by the JDBC applications and registered with an `OracleConnection` before checking out the connection from the cache. This section explains how a datasource layer or a stand-alone JDBC application can take avantage of the callback mechanism.

```
package oracle.jdbc.driver;
```

```
public interface OracleConnectionCacheCallback
{
    public boolean handleAbandonedConnection(OracleConnection conn,
                                          Object userObject);
    public void releaseConnection(OracleConnection conn,
                                          Object userObject);
}


// Callback implementation Skeleton
public class UserConnectionCacheCallback implements
OracleConnectionCacheCallback
{
     public boolean handleAbandonedConnection(OracleConnection conn,
        Object userObject)
    {
      … implementation …
    }

     public void releaseConnection(OracleConnection conn, Object
userObject)
    {
        … implementation …
    }
}
```

The callback mechanism is expected to work as follows:

`handleAbandonedConnection`

If registered on an OracleConnection, it is invoked upon the expiration of the `AbandonedConnectionTimeout`, which it overrides, as follows:

- Must return FALSE if the user wants to hold on to the connection longer; in this case the connection is not relaimed, it remains active.
- Otherwise, it must return TRUE if the user wants to return the connection back to the cache (i.e., wants JDBC to reclaim this abandoned connection) but wants to handle the necessary cleanup and close the connection.

Note: JDBC returns a `StaleConnectionException` if the user attempts to use this connection later.

---

releaseConnection

By default, connections are released back to the cache by the JDBC user upon the invocation of `conn.close()`. The `releaseConnection()` callback method is used to override this default behavior, based on the following priorities set on the connection object:

- `OracleConnection.CONNECTION_RELEASE_LOCKED`
- `OracleConnection.CONNECTION_RELEASE_LOW`
- `OracleConnection.CONNECTION_RELEASE_HIGH`

A setter and getter method is provided on the connection object to set the connection release priorities.

```
public void setConnectionReleasePriority(int priority) throws
java.sql.SQLException;

where priority takes one of the following value
    CONNECTION_RELEASE_LOCKED
    CONNECTION_RELEASE_LOW
    CONNECTION_RELEASE_HIGH

public int getReleasePriority();
```

If a `releaseConnection()` callback is registered on a connection, and the cache is empty, then:

1. For every connection with a `CONNECTION_RELEASE_HIGH` priority, invoke the callback method.

2. If the number of connections released back to the cache is below the `MaxThresholdLimit` (the default is 80 percent of `MaxLimit`):

    a. If all the connections with a CONNECTION_RELEASE_HIGH priority have been processed, then process the connections with CONNECTION_RELEASE_LOW priority.

    b. Stop releasing connections either when the cache is below the MaxThresholdLimit or when all the connections with CONNECTION_RELEASE_LOW and CONNECTION_RELEASE_HIGH priorities have been processed.

    c. Skip all connections that have the release priority set to CONNECTION_RELEASE_LOCKED.

registerConnectionCacheCallback

```
registerConnectionCacheCallback(OracleConnectionCacheCallback
                callbackImpl, Object userObj, int callbackFlag)
-- callbackImpl user's implementation of the
                   OracleConnectionCacheCallback interface.
-- userObj any user object which is passed back, unmodified, when
                   the callback method is invoked.
-- callbackFlag specifies which callback method should be invoked.
   It must be one of the following values:
   OracleConnection.ABANDONED_CONNECTION_CALLBACK - calls only
                 the handleAbandonedConnection() method
   OracleConnection.RELEASE_CONNECTION_CALLBACK - calls only
                 the releaseConnection() method (see below)
   OracleConnection.ALL_CALLBACKS - calls all the connection cache
                 callback methods
```

For example, you can register a callback to invoke all callback methods, as follows:

```
((OracleConnection)conn).registerConnectionCacheCallback( new
UserConnectionCacheCallback(), new <userObject>,
                   OracleConnection.ALL_CALLBACKS);


conn.registerConnectionCacheCallback(new
UserConnectionCacheCallback(),
           this, OracleConnection.ABANDONED_CONNECTION_CALLBACK);
```

Here is a code snippet for testing the `AbandonedConnectionTimeout` callback:

```
public void cachecallback(String dsName)
{
  // Look up the datasource object
  OracleDataSource ds = (OracleDataSource) ctx.lookup(dsName);

  // Set Cache properties
  java.util.Properties prop = new java.util.Properties();
  prop.setProperty("AbandonedConnectionTimeout", "4"); // 4 seconds
  prop.setProperty("PropertyCheckInterval", "1");

  // Apply the new properties to test the callback mechanism
  ds.setConnectionCacheProperties(prop);

  // get a connection from the cache
  OracleConnection conn = (OracleConnection) ds.getConnection();
  ds.getConnectionCacheProperties());

  public boolean abandonedFlag = false;
  public boolean ConnOk = false;

  conn.registerConnectionCacheCallback(new
UserConnectionCacheCallback(),
                    this,
OracleConnection.ABANDONED_CONNECTION_CALLBACK);

  System.out.println("sleep 8 sec to kick-in
AbandoonedConnectionTimeout");
  Thread.sleep(8000);
  try {
      Statement stmt = conn.createStatement();
      stmt.executeQuery("Select USER from dual");
      System.out.println("The connection is not abandoned");
      stmt.close();
  } catch (Exception e){
      System.out.println("The connection is abandoned");
      System.out.println(e.getMessage());
  }
}
```

```
class UserConnectionCacheCallback implements
                            OracleConnectionCacheCallback
{
    public boolean handleAbandonedConnection(OracleConnection conn,
                                      Object userObject)
    {
Statement stmt = null;
cachecallback snipet = (cachecallback) userObject;
snipet.abandonedFlag = true;
try {
stmt = conn.createStatement();
stmt.executeQuery("Select USER from dual");
stmt.close();
snipet.ConnOk = true;
        } catch (SQLException e) {
        snipet.ConnOk = false;
snipet.System.out.println("SQLException: " + e.getMessage());
        }

    if (snipet.abandonedFlag == true) {
      try {
conn.close();
    } catch (SQLException e) {
snipet.logErr(e);
    }
return true;
    } else
return false;

    } // end handleAbandonedConnection


    public void releaseConnection(OracleConnection conn,
                                   Object userObject)
    {
    cachecallback snipet = (cachecallback) userObject;
    String prioritySetting = "";
    prioritySetting = snipet.getPriority(conn);
    snipet.System.out.println("priority of connection is: " +
                                       prioritySetting);
    try {
```

```
snipet.System.out.println("Release connection with close()");
conn.close();
   } catch (SQLException e) {
snipet.logErr(e);
   }


  snipet.System.out.println("Exiting releaseConnection()");
   } // end releaseConnection

 }// end UserConnectionCacheCallback

}// end cachecallback
```

7.3.4 RAC Events and Fast Application Notification

When a new instance is added to a database cluster, when a new service is enabled on a database instance, or when an instance is retrenched from a cluster (i.e., instance stopped, service stopped, or node dies), the Oracle Database 10*g* RAC generates events that indicate what happened, including: SERVICE, SERVICE_MEMBER, DATABASE, INSTANCE, NODE, ASM, SRV_PRECONNECT, with the following possible status: UP, DOWN, NOT_RESTARTING, PRECONN_UP, PRECON_DOWN, and UNKNOWN.

The Oracle JDBC 10*g* drivers subscribe to the following RAC events and status:

- Service Up: The connection pool starts establishing connections in small batches.

- Instance (of Service) Up: The connection pool gradually releases idle connections associated with existing instances and reallocates these onto the new instance.

- Instance (of Service) Down: The connections associated with the instance are aborted and cleaned up, leaving the connection pool with sound and valid connections.

- Node Down: The connections associated with the instance are aborted and cleaned up, leaving the connection pool with good connections.

For reliability purposes, those events must be propagated to interested parties as fast as possible. Unfortunately, the timeout mechanisms (tcp_keepalive, tcp_ip_interval, and so on) are unreliable, because these may take a long (tens of minutes) to indefinite time to be kick-in. Fast Application Notification (FaN) is a new Oracle Database 10*g* RAC feature that uses more reliable publish and subscribe notification mechanisms such as Oracle Streams Advanced Queue and the Oracle Notification Service (ONS), which detects and propagates quasi-instantaneously (few seconds) those events to components that have subscribed to these mechanisms. The Oracle JDBC subscribes to RAC events through the ONS mechanism. The following steps describe how to configure the Fast Application Notification through ONS.

1. Set up a multinstance Oracle Database 10*g* RAC database (see RAC documentation).

2. Virtualize the database host through a service name (see JDBC URL in section 7.1).

3. Enable the Implicit Connection Cache.

4. Configure ONS on each RAC server node.

5. Configure ONS on each client node (10*g* Release 1) or use remote subscription (10*g* Release 2).

Step 4: Configure ONS on Each RAC Server Node

The onsctl utility lets you check that ONS is running on each RAC node:

```
$ onsctl ping
ONS Is Running
```

If you receive "ONS is running," you can skip the rest of this step and go to step 5.

The easier approach for server-side configuration consists in using the RACGONS utility. The following command makes the RAC aware of your client/application tier:

```
racgons.bin add_config <hostname1>:<port> [<hostname2>:<port>
...]
```

Otherwise, here it goes.

The ONS configuration is controlled by the ONS configuration file, *ORACLE_HOME*/opmn/conf/ons.config. Three values should always be configured within ons.config:

- Localport: Specifies the port that ONS binds to on the local host for talking to local clients:

    localport=4100

- remoteport: Specifies the port that ONS binds to on all interfaces for talking to other ONS daemons:

    remoteport=4200

- nodes: Specifies a comma-separated list (hostnames or IP_addresses:port) of other ONS daemons to talk to: a remote port that each ONS instance is listening on. In order to maintain an identical file on all nodes, the host:port of the current ONS node can also be listed in the nodes list. It will be ignored when reading the list. The list corresponds to the nodes in the RAC cluster. Listing the nodes ensures that the middle-tier node can communicate with the RAC nodes. There is no need to list every cluster and middle-tier node in the ONS config file on each RAC node. As long as one middle-tier node and one node in the RAC cluster are configured to see each other, all nodes are visible.

    nodes=myhost.example.com:4200,123.123.123.123:4200

Three additional options—loglevel, logfile, and walletfile—can be provided in ons.config:

- loglevel: Specifies the level of messages that should be logged by ONS. This value is an integer that ranges from 1 (least messages logged) to 9 (most messages logged, use only for debugging purposes). The default value is 3.

    loglevel=3

- `logfile`: Specifies a log file for logging messages. The default value is *$ORACLE_HOME*/opmn/logs/ons.log.

    ```
    logfile=/private/oraclehome/opmn/logs/myons.log
    ```

- `walletfile`: Specifies an Oracle wallet[9] file to be used to store SSL certificates. If a wallet file is specified to ONS, it will use SSL when communicating with other ONS instances and will require SSL certificate authentication from all ONS instances that try to connect to it. You cannot turn SSL on for one ONS instance independently. The wallet file should point to the directory where your `ewallet.p12` file is located.

    ```
    walletfile=/private/oraclehome/opmn/conf/ssl.wlt/default
    ```

```
$ORACLE_HOME/opmn/conf/ons.config
localport=6100 # This is the port ONS is writing to
remoteport=6200 # This is the port ONS is listening on
loglevel=3
# This is the list of hosts and ports ONS is poting to.
# Include RAC and client nodes.
nodes=node-1.country.company.com:6200,node-
2.country.company.com:6200,
node-3.country.company.com:6200,node-4.country.company.com:6200,
node6-1.country.company.com:6200
```

Note: If RAC is installed on a shared file system, the *$ORACLE_HOME*/opmn/ conf directory might need to be created locally on each node.

For example, a symbolic link can be created to a directory under `$HOME` with the following `UNIX` commands, on each node:

```
$ mv $ORACLE_HOME/opmn/conf $ORACLE_HOME/opmn/conf.orig
$ mkdir $HOME/opmn/conf
$ cp ORACLE_HOME/opmn/conf.orig/* $HOME/opmn/conf
$ ln -s $HOME/opmn/conf $ORACLE_HOME/opmn/conf
```

---

9.   A wallet is a password-protected storage for authentication and signing credentials (i.e., private keys, certificates, and trusted certificates). See the Oracle Database Advanced Security Administrator's Guide for more details.

With Oracle Database 10*g* Release 2, an additional option "useocr" simplifies the configuration file `$ORACLE_HOME/opmn/conf/ons.config`:

```
localport=6100    # This is the port ONS is writing to
remoteport=6200   # This is the port ONS is listening on
loglevel=3
useocr=on $ populate OCR
```

With useocr=on, the Cluster Ready Services (CRS) automatically populate the list of RAC nodes.

Step 5: Configuring/Subscribing ONS Clients

An `ONSException` is thrown at the first `getConnection()` if ONS is not correctly set up. The JVM in which your JDBC instance is running must have `oracle.ons.oraclehome` set to point to your `ORACLE_HOME`.

Here is how to configure ONS on client/application tiers:

- If you are using the Oracle Application Server 10*g*, the OPMN process handles client registration for you; otherwise, proceed as follows:

- If you are using Oracle Database 10*g* Release 2, the Oracle JDBC integrates the pure Java ONS client for remote subscriptions. The C-based client (10.1) is still delivered, though. Make sure that `ons.jar` is in CLASSPATH and then invoke `setONSConfiguration(String remoteONSConfig)` on an `OracleDataSource` where `remoteONSConfig` is a list of name/value pairs of the form name=value, separated by a new line character (\n).

  Here is an example of setting `setONSConfiguration`, without and with security wallet:

  ```
  setONSConfiguration("nodes=host1:port1,host2:port2 ");
  setONSConfiguration("nodes=host1:port1,host2:port2\
  nwalletfile=wfile");
  ```

  See the Oracle Database 10.2 JDBC and RAC documentation for more details.

- If you are using Oracle Database 10*g* Release 1, the ONS client is C-based and must be installed on every client (even if you are using JDBC-Thin). The ONS client libraries are included on the client CD. See the Oracle Database 10*g* RAC and JDBC documentation.

ONS is controlled through the `onsctl` utility located in *ORACLE_HOME/* bin. This command-line utility accepts the following commands:

```
ORACLE_HOME/bin/onsctl start|stop|ping|reconfig|debug|help|detailed
```

These are described in Table 7.3.

Table 7.3   *Command Descriptions*

Command	Effect	Output
start	Starts the ONS daemon.	onsctl: ons started
stop	Stops the ONS daemon.	onsctl: shutting down ons daemon...
ping	Verifies whether the ONS daemon is running.	ons is running ...
reconfig	Triggers a reload of the ONS configuration without shutting down the ONS daemon.	
debug	Displays debug information for the ONS daemon.	
help	Prints a help summary message for onsctl.	
detailed	Prints a detailed help message for onsctl.	

Testing ONS Operations

The java class `onc_subscriber.java` is provided to test ONS functionality.[10] The class is an ONS client. It subscribes to the ONS daemon and listens for events.

```
/*
 * Copyright (c) 2001, 2004 by Oracle. All Rights Reserved
 * ONC Subscription client. This client listens for all events ONS receives
 * Based on the event type decisions are made on how and whether to print the
 * event body
 */

import oracle.ons.*;
import java.util.*;
import java.io.*;
```

---

10.   All required files are in the ONCdemoClient.zip available on the book's code sample page.

```
import java.nio.*;

public class onc_subscriber
{

  public static void main(String args[])
  {
    boolean debug = false;
    // Set ONC-required System property for oracle.ons.oraclehome:
    //System.setProperty("oracle.ons.oraclehome", "<your ons home>");

    //Subscriber s = new Subscriber("\"oraDb/myProdCluster\"",
     "database/event/*");
    //Subscriber s = new Subscriber("", "database/event/*");
    Subscriber s = new Subscriber("", ""); // subscribe to all events
    Notification e;

    System.out.println("ONC subscriber starting");

    boolean shutdown = false;
    while (!shutdown)
    {
      e = s.receive(true);   // blocking wait for notification receive

      System.out.println( "** HA event received -- Printing header:" );
      e.print();
      System.out.println( "** Body length = " + e.body().length);
      System.out.println( "** Event type = " + e.type());

      /* Test the event type to attempt to determine the event body format.
         Database events generated by the racg code are "free-format" events -
         the event body is a string. It consists of space delimited key=value
         pairs. Events constructed using the ONC Java API have an event body
         that is a byte array (byte []) which have a terminating character.
         The Java API call to read the body waits on this character to
         terminate the read.
         Attempting to read a free-form event using the Java API can cause the
         reading thread to hang waiting on the byte array terminator.

         The following test only looks for database events, and events
         generated by the program onc_publisher.java. Other events will be
```

```
        received, but their bodies will not be displayed.
    */

    if (e.type().startsWith("database")) {
        if (debug) { System.out.println( "New print out"); }
        evtPrint myEvtPrint = new evtPrint(e);
    } else if (e.type().startsWith("javaAPI")){
        oncPrint myPrint = new oncPrint(e);
    } else {
        System.out.println("Unknown event type. Not displaying body");
    }

    try
    {
        if (e.type().equals("onc/shutdown")) {
            System.out.println("Shutdown event received.");
            shutdown = true;
        }
        else {
            java.lang.Thread.currentThread().sleep(100);
            System.out.println("Sleep and retry.");
        }
    }
    catch (Exception te)
    {
        te.printStackTrace();
    }
}

s.close();

System.out.println(" ONC subscriber exiting!");
    }
}
```

Using JDK 1.4.2, edit the script Jmake_onc to reflect the JAVA_HOME containing JDK 1.4.2 and the ORACLE_HOME containing the client libraries:

- Edit Jmake_onc

  Replace JHOME with a full path to JDK 1.4.2.

  Replace ORACLE_HOME with a full path to client libraries.

```
JHOME=/net/myclient/private/myuser/java/SUNWappserver/jdk/
export JHOME
ORACLE_HOME=/myclient/myuser/product/oracle/10gClient
export ORACLE_HOME
```

- Save Jmake_onc
- To build and run the classes, execute the following:

Step 1

```
$ Jmake_onc sub -c
>> Recompiling onc_subscriber ...
>> Executing onc_subscriber ...
ONC subscriber starting
```

Step 2

Perform an action on a RAC cluster that will cause an event to be generated. Stop an instance, start a service, start an instance, kill an instance, and so on.

Output

```
** HA event received -- Printing body:
Notification Type:          database/event/service
Affected Components:        null
Affected Nodes:             null
Delivery Time:              1095793164948
Generating Component:       oraDb/myProdCluster
Generating Node:            dlsun1344.us.oracle.com
Generating Process:         1095793164651
Notification ID:            109579316465111
Notification Creation Time:1095793164766
Cluster ID:                 databaseClusterId
Cluster Name:               databaseClusterName
Instance ID:                databaseInstanceId
Instance Name:              databaseInstanceName
Local Only Flag:            FALSE
Cluster Only Flag:          FALSE
Body:                       [B@1888759
```

The correct generation and receipt of these events will demonstrate that ONS is configured correctly. It is possible to subscribe to and generate events from different machines, provided that the nodes list for both ONS daemons contains entries corresponding to the separate hosts. RAC events propagated to the ONS daemon being subscribed to by the onc_subscriber class will also be printed out.

7.3.5 High Availability: Fast Connection Failover

High availability is a major requirement in enterprise computing. This section will help you understand how JDBC 10*g* ensures high-availabilty for database connections. The unexpected node failure, planned database instance, or service shutdown in a clustered Oracle Database RAC environment generates a DOWN event, which automatically triggers a detect-and-fix reaction. Processing the event consists of quickly removing connections belonging to the failed instance and preventing invalid connections from being handed out on connection request. Oracle JDBC processes Instance, Service, and Node down events through the Fast Connection Fail-over (FCF) mechanism. FCF is implemented on top of the Implicit Connection Cache and works only in RAC environments. When a service/instance/ node goes down, a DOWN event is sent, which leads JDBC to clean up the cache from the orphan's connections and redistribute the workload over surviving nodes only.

This section describes how Fast Connection Fail-over works, how it is enabled, and which steps the Java/JDBC developer must take to use it through the application.

How Fast Connection Fail-over Works

Each cached connection is mapped to a service, an instance, a database, and a hostname. Fast Connection Fail-over is bound to the OracleDataSource and the cache, but it cannot be enabled when reinitializing a connection cache and cannot be disabled as long as the cache lives.

When a RAC instance fails:

- The database automatically rolls back in-flight (local) transactions; the applications do not have to do this.

- The Fast Application Notification (FAN) mechanism (see ONS above) allows the rapid detection of "Instance DOWN" or "Node DOWN" events and propagates this event to the cache manager (event handler).

- The event handler thread (one per JVM) and the Fast Connection Fail-over worker thread help the cache manager invalidate and remove all connections associated with the failed instance from the corresponding cache.

- All connections/sessions and in-flight transactions associated with the failed instance will be lost.

- The JDBC application realizes that an instance has failed when it receives a fatal SQL Exception (i.e., `connectionCacheManager.isFatalConnectionError(e)` returns "true") upon an attempt to interact with the RDBMS. It must then retry to get a new connection (i.e., `getConnection()`), in order to be reconnected to another instance of the same database, and either replay the entire transaction or replay only from the last savepoint (if enabled). A J2EE container such as the Oracle Application Server Containers for J2EE (OC4J) may intersperse and transparently handle the retry/reconnection. *Note:* The Oracle Application Server Release 10.1.3 transparently handles the retry for CMP EJBs.

Configuring Fast Connection Fail-over

1. Configure ONS and Fast Application Notification as described previously.

2. Enable Fast Connection Fail-over.

3. Code your application to catch `SQLExceptions` and retry connection requests.

Step 2: Enabling Fast Connection Fail-over

Once you have enabled Implicit Connection Cache on a datasource, you can enable Fast Connection Fail-over by setting the `FastConnectionFailoverEnabled` property to `true`, either through a datasource property object or by setting system properties (runtime flag) when launching the JDK VM.

Using DataSource Property (Programmatic):

```
// In this code snippet, OracleDataSource are bound to JNDI
// and cache properties are set on the datasource.

import oracle.jdbc.pool.*;
Context ctx = new IntialContext(ht);
OracleDataSource ods = new OracleDataSource();
```

```
// Set Datasource properties
   ods.setUser("Scott");
   ods.setPassword("tiger");
   ods.setConnectionCacheName("MyCache");
   ods.setConnectionCacheProperties(cp);
   ods.setURL("jdbc:oracle:thin:@(DESCRIPTION= (LOAD_BALANCE=on)
   (CONNECT_DATA=(SERVICE_NAME=SalesDS)))");

// Enable Connection Caching First
   ods.setConnectionCachingEnabled(True);

// Enable Fast Connection Failover programmatically
   ods.setFastConnectionFailoverEnabled(true);
   ctx.bind("MyDS", ods);
…
// lookup datasource
   ds = lookup("MyDS");

// Create a Failover Enabled Connection Cache
   conn = ds.getConnection();

// do some work…

// return the connection to the cache
   conn.close();
…

// close datasource and cleanup the cache
   ods.close()
```

Using System Property (No Code Change):

Set the following system property:

```
java -D oracle.jdbc.FastConnectionFailover=true
```

Fast Connection Fail-over Status:

An application determines whether Fast Connection Fail-over is enabled by calling   OracleDataSource.getFastConnectionFailoverEnabled(), which returns true if failover is enabled and false otherwise.

There is one cache per datasource per VM; in the absence of a middle-tier-container to enable FCF and create caches, you may have one special program (i.e., a Java Servlet) to do that. Alternatively, each bean may first invoke get-ConnectionFailoverEnabled() to check whether FCF has been enabled, so as to avoid enabling it several times (this won't hurt though).

Step 3: Catching and Retrying Connection Request

The following code fragment shows how a JDBC application can detect node failure and retry getConnection().

```
// declare datasource
ods.setUrl("jdbc:oracle:oci:@(DESCRIPTION=
    (ADDRESS=(PROTOCOL=TCP)(HOST=cluster_alias)
    (PORT=1521))
    (CONNECT_DATA=(SERVICE_NAME=SalesDB)))");

ods.setUser("scott");
// Enable Implicit Connection Cache
ods.setConnectionCachingEnabled(true);
// Enable and Fast Connection FailOver
ods.setFastConnectionFailoverEnabled(true):
//  Bind and lookup the data source
ctx.bind("myDS",ods);
ds =(OracleDataSource) ctx.lookup("MyDS");
// The first getConnection will create the cache:
try {
     ods.getConnection();
     // do some work
} catch (SQLException e) {
    handleSQLException(e);
}
...
handleSQLException (SQLException e)
{
   if (connectionCacheManager.isFatalConnectionError(e))
      ConnRetry = true;  // Fatal Connection error detected
}
```

The following complete code sample loops over getConnection() in a RAC environment with FCF enabled. For the code to be effective, you have to generate instance UP and DOWN events.

```
FCFConnectionTest.java
======================

/*
 * FCFConnectionTest
 * Adapted from JDBC code sample with additional contributions
 *
 */
package FCFTest;
import java.io.IOException;
import java.sql.Connection;
import java.sql.ResultSet;
import java.sql.SQLException;
import java.sql.Statement;
import java.text.DateFormat;
import java.text.SimpleDateFormat;
import java.util.Properties;
import oracle.jdbc.pool.OracleDataSource;

public class Main  {
  public Main() {
    try {
      OracleDataSource ods = new OracleDataSource();
      String url = "jdbc:oracle:thin:@" +

"(DESCRIPTION=(ADDRESS=(PROTOCOL=TCP)(HOST=sturachh1vip)(PORT=1521))"
+
        "(ADDRESS=(PROTOCOL=TCP)(HOST=sturachh2vip)(PORT=1521))" +
        "(LOAD_BALANCE=yes)" +
        "(CONNECT_DATA=(SERVICE_NAME=FCF)))";

      Boolean retryConnection = false;

      Properties prop = new Properties();
      prop.setProperty("MinLimit", "100");
      prop.setProperty("MaxLimit", "200");
      prop.setProperty("InitialLimit", "100");

      ods.setURL(url);
      ods.setUser("SCOTT");
      ods.setPassword("TIGER");
      ods.setConnectionCachingEnabled(true);
```

```
ods.setConnectionCacheProperties(prop);
ods.setFastConnectionFailoverEnabled(true);
ods.setConnectionCacheName("ImplicitConnectionCache");

SimpleDateFormat formatTime =
(SimpleDateFormat)DateFormat.getTimeInstance(DateFormat.LONG);
formatTime.applyPattern("dd.MM.yy HH:mm:ss");
Connection conn = null;
Statement stmt = null;
ResultSet rset = null;
long curTime = 0;
long startTime = 0;

for (int i=0; i<50; i++) {
  try {
    startTime = System.currentTimeMillis();
    System.out.println(formatTime.format(new Long(startTime))+
        ": Connecting with FCF Enabled" );
    if (retryConnection)
    {
     // This is a retry;
     // You migh want to do additional processing beforehand
       System.out.println ("getConnection retry");
    }
    conn = ods.getConnection();
    stmt = conn.createStatement();
    rset = stmt.executeQuery("select * from v$instance");
    while (rset.next()) {
      curTime = System.currentTimeMillis();
      System.out.println(formatTime.format(new Long(curTime))+":
" +
        rset.getInt("INSTANCE_NUMBER") + " " +
rset.getString("HOST_NAME"));
    }
    rset.close();
    stmt.close();
    conn.close();
    curTime = System.currentTimeMillis();
    System.out.println(formatTime.format(new Long(curTime))+
        ": Connection Closed");
    byte[] input = new byte[10];
    System.out.println("Enter to continue");
```

```
                System.in.read(input);
              } catch (SQLException sqle) {
                  handleSE(sqle);
          }
        } catch (Exception e) {
          System.out.println("Caught an Exception" + e.getMessage());
          e.printStackTrace();
        }
      }

  handleSE (SQLException e)
  {
      e.getMessage();
      e.printStackTrace();
      if (connectionCacheManager.isFatalConnectionError(e)) {
          System.out.println("Caught a Fatal SQLException, must retry");
          retryConnection = true;   // Retry getConnection()
          Thread.sleep(30000);       // Wait few seconds before retry
      }

  /**
    *
    * @param args
    */
    public static void main(String[] args) {
      Main main = new Main();
    }
  }
```

7.3.6 Scalability: Connection Load Balancing

Scaling up is also a key requirement in enterprise computing. Adding new database instances to an Oracle Database RAC cluster generates an UP event. The Oracle JDBC drivers proactively and automatically (i.e., without waiting for application connection retries/requests) spread the existing connections over all active RAC instances, including the newly added ones. Let's consider a basic example where we have:

- A database service SalesDB deployed over a two-node RAC cluster, one database instance per node.

- An Oracle JDBC driver instance/node, part of a middle-tier container or stand-alone, holds a pool of 180 connections relative to the SalesDB service in two caches, hence 90 connections per datasource (instance).

Adding a new node to the service will trigger an UP event, which is detected and propagated via ONS. As a result, the connection cache manager will automatically split the pool of 180 connections over the three instances (or caches), resulting in 60 connections being established per database instance (or per cache). This process involves removing some connections from the former two caches and creating new ones to the new (third) cache.

Prior to Oracle Database 10g Release 2, load balancing was done using traditional load-balancing techniques, including random, round-robin, and FIFO load, which potentially lead to unbalanced workload distribution.

The Listerner config should contain:

```
PREFER_LEAST_LOADED_NODE_[listener]=OFF
```

Run-time connection load balancing is a new JDBC feature made possible by the new SERVICE_METRIC event from Oracle Database 10g RAC Release 2. The JDBC drivers susbcribe to service metrics advisory events through ONS and exploit these to achieve a well-balanced dynamic distribution of connection requests.

Service metrics are new RAC event types posted every 30 seconds or so and include the following:

- A service flag, which indicates the state or health of the service or its metrics: GOOD (metrics are valid), UNKNOWN (no data for the service), VIOLATING (thresholds or event-level agreements violated), NO_DATA (no metric from this instance)

- The percentage of work that should be directed to this service on this instance

- Event retrieval and propagation to subscribers by various Oracle background processes, including MMON (retrieves and sends advice to AQ), IMON (retrieves and sends advice to ONS), EMON (retrieves and sends advice to `OCI` and `ODP.NET` clients), and `PMON` (retrieves and sends advice to Listener)

The routing of connection requests is based on flags and percentage idle; in addition, JDBC uses other algorithms (i.e., the Monte Carlo) for selecting the right connection cache. When a service comes up on an instance, or either newly added or rejoined after a crash, an `UP` event is sent, which leads JDBC to redistribute connections over the existing and the new instance. The redistribution of connections over nodes depends on the load-balancing goals.

See the *Real Application Clusters Administration and Deployment Guide* for more details on setting service goals.

The good news is that runtime connection load balancing is transparent to your JDBC application provided the RDBMS and the listener have been properly configured.

Enabling Runtime Connection Load Balancing

The following steps are required for enabling runtime connection load balancing:

Step 1

Set a goal for each service on the RDBMS side, using either `dbms_service.create_service` or `dbms_service.modify_service`, with one of the following values:

- `NONE`: The default value uses the traditional load-balancing techniques for this service.

- `GOAL_SERVICE_TIME`: Best response time overall, the load balancing is done based on weighted moving average elapsed time:

      DBMS_SERVICE.CREATE_SERVICE
      ('SERVICE1','SERVICE1.company.com',
          goal => DBMS_SERVICE.GOAL_SERVICE_TIME)

- `GOAL_THROUGHPUT`: Best throughput overall, the load balancing is done using weighted moving average throughput.

      DBMS_SERVICE.CREATE_SERVICE
      ('SERVICE2','SERVICE2.company.com',

```
goal => DBMS_SERVICE.GOAL_THROUGHPUT)
```

Alternatively, the service goal can be set using the `goal` parameter in init.ora.

Step 2

Set a goal to the connection load balancing (`CLB_GOAL`) using either `dbms_service.create_service` or `dbms_service.modify_service`:

- `CLB_GOAL_SHORT`: For applications that have short-lived connections (i.e., online shopping) or workloads where the rate of connections exceeds the number of connections to an instance.

```
DBMS_SERVICE.MODIFY_SERVICE
('SERVICE1','SERVICE1.company.com',
    clb_goal => DBMS_SERVICE.CLB_GOAL_SHORT)
```

- `CLB_GOAL_LONG`: For applications that have long-lived connections (i.e., connection pools, batch jobs) or workloads where the rate of work completion is equal to the rate new request.

```
DBMS_SERVICE.MODIFY_SERVICE
('SERVICE2','SERVICE2.company.com',
    clb_goal => DBMS_SERVICE.CLB_GOAL_LONG)
```

Alternatively, the connection listener's load-balancing goal can be set using the `clb_goal` parameter in init.ora.

Step 3

Enable Fast Connection Fail-over either programmatically or using system property; the rest is transparent to the JDBC application. A Runtime Connection Load-Balancing (RCLB) Event Handler thread is started to listen to RCLB events.

7.3.7 JDBC Support for Transparent Application Fail-over

Transparent Application Fail-over (TAF) is an OCI feature (it should have been called "OCI fail-over") that is exposed to Java through JDBC-OCI.

Certain TAF features work well, but others are either misunderstood or do not work as expected.

What Usually Works with TAF

- Database Connection Fail-over: TAF can fail over the physical connection either to a backup instance or to the same instance, transparently to the application. TAF can detect failures and reestablish failed sessions in a single-instance environment (on the same database) and in a RAC environment (see the preconnect option).

- `Query Resubmit` or `Query Failover`: TAF can fail-over active cursors—in other words, SQL queries (prepared statements) that have begun to return results by reissuing the prepared statement (reopening the cursors) and discarding rows that have already been returned; then the application can continue fetching the remaining rows as if the failure never happened, at the price of performance drop, though.

What Does Not Work with TAF

- TAF is an OCI8 feature; therefore, applications that are not using OCI8 libraries (i.e., via JDBC-OCI in Java case) cannot leverage it.

- Rolling Back Active Transactions: If a failure occurs in the middle of a transaction, TAF requires that the application rolls back the transaction by issuing a ROLLBACK command, then lets TAF know by issuing an acknowledgment (that a rollback has been performed).

- TAF does not protect or fail-over codes that have server-side states such as Java or PL/SQL packages; however, the application can register a callback function that will be called upon failure to reestablish the session states.

```
// register TAF callback function "cbk"
   ((OracleConnection) conn).registerTAFCallback(cbk,
msg);
```

TAF Configuration

TAF Configuration consists of specifying the following attributes of `TNSNAMES.ORA`:

- Method = {`BASIC` | `PRECONNECT`} determines how fast fail-over occurs from the primary node to the backup node.

BASIC: Establish connections at fail-over time only, in the mean time no work request is routed to the backup server.

PRECONNECT: Preestablished connections eliminate the need to reconnect to a surviving instance upon failure and thus speed up fail-over. However, PRECONNECT pre-allocates resources awaiting the fail-over event, which requires the backup instance to be able to support all connections from every failed instance.

- Recovery Type = {NONE|SESSION| SELECT}

  - NONE: Is the default; no fail-over functionality is used. This can also be explicitly specified to prevent fail-over from happening.
  - SESSION: The user session can reauthenticate; a new session is automatically created for the user on the backup node. This type of fail-over does not attempt to recover queries.
  - SELECT: Queries in progress by the time of the failure are reissued and processed from the beginning, discarding any rows that have already been returned to the application; the user session can continue fetching from the point of failure. However, this mode involves overhead on the client side in normal select operations.

- BACKUP: If specified, the client will automatically connect to the backup node immediately; otherwise, the client will attempt to reconnect to the failed node and experience tcp_ip_abort_cinterval_delay. This is required when using PRECONNECT to preestablish connections.

- DELAY: Number of seconds to wait between retries; defaults to one second if RETRIES is specified.

- RETRIES: Number of retries; defaults to five attempts if DELAY is specified.

Examples of TNSNAMES.ORA entry; see *Net8 Administrator's Guide* for more details.

```
primary=(DESCRIPTION=
              (ADDRESS=(PROTOCOL=tcp)(Host=hostname)(Port=1521))
              (CONNECT_DATA=(SERVICE_NAME=payrol)
                 (FAILOVER_MODE=(TYPE=SELECT)(METHOD=BASIC))
```
Example of URL:
```
String url =
"jdbc:oracle:oci8:@(DESCRIPTION=(ADDRESS=(PROTOCOL=tcp)(HOST=
```

```
"myhosy")(PORT="5521"))(CONNECT_DATA=(SID="ORCL")(FAILOVER_MO
DE=(TYPE=SELECT)(METHOD=BASIC)(RETRIES=10000)(DELAY=2))))";
```

Customizing TAF Using OCI Callback and Fail-over Events

TAF allows developers to register callback functions that can be used to reestablish session state after the failure.

```
CallBack  callbck = new CallBack();
...
// register TAF callback function
   ((OracleConnection) conn).registerTAFCallback(callbck,
msg);
```

The Java application captures the failure status and provides a function that the OCI callback mechanism will automatically call during fail-over. Here are the fail-over events defined in the OCI API:

`FO_BEGIN` = 1 indicates a lost connection has been detected and fail-over is starting.

`FO_END` = 2 indicates a successful completion of fail-over.

`FO_ABORT` = 3 indicates an unsuccessful fail-over with no option of retrying.

`FO_REAUTH` = 4 indicates that a user handle has been reauthenticated.

`FO_ERROR` = 5 indicates that a fail-over was temporarily unsuccessful, but the application has the opportunity to handle the error and retry.

`FO_RETRY` = 6 indicates retry fail-over.

`FO_EVENT_UNKNOWN` = 7 indicates a bad/unknown fail-over event.

OCI Fail-over Interface

The `OracleOCIFailover` interface includes the `callbackFn` method, supporting the following types and events:

```
public interface OracleOCIFailover{

// Possible Failover Types
public static final int FO_SESSION = 1;
public static final int FO_SELECT  = 2;
```

```
public static final int FO_NONE  = 3;
public static final int;

// Possible Failover events registered with callback
public static final int FO_BEGIN   = 1;
public static final int FO_END     = 2;
public static final int FO_ABORT   = 3;
public static final int FO_REAUTH  = 4;
public static final int FO_ERROR   = 5;
public static final int FO_RETRY   = 6;
public static final int FO_EVENT_UNKNOWN = 7;

public int callbackFn (Connection conn,
                 Object ctxt, // Anything the user wants to save
                 int type, // One of the possible Failover Types
                 int event ); // One of the possible Failover
                             // Events

class CallBack implements OracleOCIFailover {
  public int callbackFn (Connection conn, Object ctxt, int type, int
event) {

    String failover_type = null;

    switch (type) {
      case FO_SESSION:
          failover_type = "SESSION";
          break;
      case FO_SELECT:
          failover_type = "SELECT";
          break;
      default:
          failover_type = "NONE";
    }

    switch (event) {

      case FO_BEGIN:
          testCase.begin_called++;
          break;
      case FO_END:
          testCase.end_called++;
```

```
              break;
       case FO_ABORT:
              testCase.abort_called++;
              break;
       case FO_REAUTH:
              testCase.reauth_called++;
              break;
       case FO_ERROR:
              testCase.error_called++;
              // Sleep for a while
              try {
                 Thread.sleep(100);
              }
              catch (InterruptedException e) {
                 System.out.println ("Thread.sleep Issue: " +
e.toString());
              }
              return FO_RETRY;
       default:
              System.out.println (ctxt + ": Unknown failover event.");
              break;


   }
.}
```

Graceful Shutdown

For planned downtime, the DBA can configure TAF to transparently reconnect users to the backup instance as soon as the transactions complete,
thereby achieving a graceful shutdown.

FCF versus TAF

Fast Connection Fail-over and TAF differ from each other in the following
ways:

- *Application-Level Connection Retries*: Fast Connection Fail-over supports application-level connection retries. You may see this as giving
   more control and flexibility to the application in how to process the
   fail-overs. In other words, with FCF, the application might choose to
   retry the connection or to rethrow the exception. TAF on the other

hand retries connection transparently at the OCI/Net layer, out of the application's control you may see this as a usability advantage.

- *Integration with the Connection Cache*: Fast Connection Fail-over is integrated with the Implicit Connection Cache. Subsequently, failed connections are automatically invalidated. TAF, on the other hand, works on a per-connection basis at the network level; therefore, it currently does not notify the connection cache of failures.

- *Event-Based*: Fast Connection Fail-over is based on the RAC event mechanism, so it detects failures quickly for both active and inactive connections. TAF, on the other hand, is based on the network call mechanism. Starting with Oracle Database 10*g* Release 2, TAF also subscribes to RAC events and Fast Application Notification, similar to JDBC FCF; however, TAF is not integrated with JDBC connection cache and does not furnish runtime connection load balancing. TAF can now send notifications to the OCI clients in the event of a failure to interrupt clients that are blocked waiting on a server acknowledgment.

- *Load Balancing*: Fast Connection Fail-over and runtime connection load balancing support UP event load-balancing of connections and runtime work request distribution across active RAC instances.

- *Transaction Management*: FCF automatically rolls back in-flight transactions; TAF, on the other hand, requires the application to roll back the transaction and send an acknowledgment to TAF to proceed with the failover.

7.3.8 Proxy Authentication

In a multitier architecture, the end users typically authenticate and connect to a middle tier through various middle-tier authentication mechanisms. The middle tier in its turn authenticates against the database through various database authentication mechanisms. Proxy authentication is the ability for the middle tier to create a database session on its own behalf (i.e., mid-tier session) and then create a lightweight end-user session (i.e., client session) on behalf of the end user through the mid-tier session. The middle tier acts as a proxy to the client (end user), hence the name proxy session.

How Proxy Authentication Works

1. Create middle-tier and client database schemas with appropriate database privileges. Be aware that granting coarse-grained roles

such as "connect" and "resource" is not advised, so you should select which authorizations you'd like to grant and grant only these.

```
create user midtier identified by midtier;
grant create session, <+ selected privileges> to
midtier;

create user client identified by client;
grant create session, <+ selected privileges> to
client;
```

2. By default, the middle tier cannot create connections on behalf of any client. The client must first allow it by granting "connect through" priveleges to the proxied used.

```
ALTER USER client GRANT CONNECT THROUGH midtier;
```

See the following different options.

3. Specify the proxy properties that are passed to getConnection(). See the following JDBC. The end-user session is created through the proxy session (middle tier)—in reality the proxy session takes the identity of the end user—based on the following options:

    ■ USER_NAME: Supply only the username (default authentication) or username and password:

```
ALTER USER client GRANT CONNECT THROUGH midtier;

ALTER USER client GRANT CONNECT THROUGH midtier
AUTHENTICATED USING password;
```

    ■ DISTINGUISHED_NAME: A global name in lieu of the user being proxied:

```
CREATE USER client IDENTIFIED GLOBALLY AS

'CN=client,OU=americas,O=oracle,L=redwoodshores,ST=ca,C
=us';
```

```
ALTER USER client GRANT CONNECT THROUGH midtier
AUTHENTICATED USING
            DISTINGUISHED NAME;
```

- CERTIFICATE: Encrypted credentials of the user to be proxied:

```
ALTER USER jeff GRANT CONNECT THROUGH scott
AUTHENTICATED USING
            CERTIFICATE;
```

- ROLE: The following SQL command grants permission to the middle tier (the proxy session) to initiate a connection on behalf of the client, using the client's database roles (i.e., proxyquery, proxyinsert, proxyupdate, proxydelete):

```
Pre-Requisite

Connect system/<password>
create role proxyquery;
create role proxyinsert;
create role proxyupdate;
create role proxydelete;

grant select on tab1 to proxyquery;
grant insert on tab1 to proxyinsert;
grant update on tab1 to proxyupdate;
grant delete on tab1 to proxydelete;

grant proxyquery, proxyinsert, proxyupdate, proxydelete
to client;

commit;

Then

ALTER USER client GRANT CONNECT THROUGH midtier
      WITH ROLE proxyquery,proxyinsert, proxyupdate,
proxydelete;
```

JDBC Support for Proxy Authentication

The Oracle JDBC drivers support proxy authentication in JDBC-Thin as of 10.1 and in JDBC-OCI as of 10.2, through the following methods.

```
public void openProxySession(int type,
java.util.Properties prop)
                              throws java.sql.SQLException
```

Opens a new proxy session with the username provided in the prop argument and switches to this new session where type can take one of the following values:

```
- OracleConnection.PROXYTYPE_USER_NAME  ->
   a java.lang.String object PROXY_USER_NAME needs to be set in prop.

- OracleConnection.PROXYTYPE_DISTINGUISHED_NAME  ->
   a java.lang.String object PROXY_DISTINGUISHED_NAME has to be set
   in prop.

- OracleConnection.PROXYTYPE_CERTIFICATE ->
   a bytep[] which contains the certificate PROXY_CERTIFICATE needs to be
   set in prop. Properties prop = new Properties();
   prop.put(OracleConnection.PROXY_CERTIFICATE, cert);
   oraConn.openProxySession(OracleConnection.PROXYTYPE_CERTIFICATE, prop);

- OracleConnection.PROXY_ROLES ->
   Roles can also be set in the property argument, the value is a String[]
   which contains the roles.
   prop.put(OracleConnection.PROXY_ROLES, roles);
   oraConn.openProxySession(OracleConnection.PROXY_ROLES, prop);
```

```
public boolean isProxySession(): returns true if the session
   associated with this connection is a proxy session.

public void close(int OracleConnection.PROXY_SESSION) throws
   java.sql.SQLException closes the proxy session.
```

The following code sample illustrates Proxy Authentication:

```
ProxyAuten.java
================
/*
 * Pre-Requisite: create the database users (client, proxy)
 * or use existing database schemas: HR (client), and SCOTT (proxy)
 * See "How proxy Authentication Works"
 *
 * connect system/<password>
 * create role proxyquery;
 * create role proxyinsert;
 * create role proxyupdate;
 * create role proxydelete;
 * grant select on regions to proxyquery;
 * grant insert on regions to proxyinsert;
 *       grant proxyquery, proxyinsert to hr;
 *       ALTER USER hr GRANT CONNECT THROUGH scott WITH ROLE
 *                proxyquery,proxyinsert;
 *
 */

import java.util.*;
import java.sql.*;
import oracle.jdbc.OracleConnection;
import oracle.jdbc.pool.OracleDataSource;

class ProxyAuthen
{
  public static void main (String args [])
        throws SQLException
  {
    OracleConnection conn = null;
    Statement stmt = null;
    ResultSet rset = null;
    OracleDataSource ods = new OracleDataSource();
    String url = "jdbc:oracle:thin:scott/tiger@//localhost:1521/
orcl";
    ods.setURL(url);

    // get a proxy connection
    conn = (OracleConnection)ods.getConnection();

    // Check if the connecton is a proxy session, should return false
```

```
System.out.println("isProxySession? " + conn.isProxySession());


// open a proxy session of type "connect through with role".
Properties prop = new Properties();
prop.put(OracleConnection.PROXY_USER_NAME, "HR");
String[] roles = {"proxyquery", "proxyinsert"};
prop.put(OracleConnection.PROXY_ROLES, roles);
conn.openProxySession(OracleConnection.PROXYTYPE_USER_NAME,
prop);

// Check if the connecton is a proxy session, should return true
System.out.println("isProxySession? " + conn.isProxySession());


// Check the Current Id of the Session
stmt = conn.createStatement();
rset = stmt.executeQuery("select user from dual");
while (rset.next())
  {
      System.out.println("This Session is associated with: " +
      rset.getString(1));
  }
  rset.close();

// Performing authorized activities on behalf of the client
rset = stmt.executeQuery("select count(*) from regions");
while (rset.next())
  {
    System.out.println("# of existing Regions: " + rset.getInt(1));
  }
  rset.close();

System.out.println("Adding a new Region and Printing the whole
table");
  stmt.execute("insert into regions values (5, 'New Region')");

  rset - stmt.executeQuery("select * from regions");
  while (rset.next())
  {
      System.out.println("Region id: " + rset.getInt(1) + "  Region
Name: "
```

```
               + rset.getString(2));
       }
       rset.close();

      // Attempt to perform unauthorized activities/roles must fail

       try
       {
        stmt.execute("delete from regions where region_id = 1");

       } catch (SQLException e)
       {
           System.out.println("Proxy user attempts to delete from
HR.Regions");
       }
       stmt.close();
       conn.close();
       ods.close();


    }
}

C:\>javac ProxyAuthen.java

C:\>java ProxyAuthen
isProxySession? false
isProxySession? true
This Session is associated with: HR
# of existing Regions: 4
Adding a new Region and Printing the whole table
Region id: 1 Region Name: Europe
Region id: 2 Region Name: Americas
Region id: 3 Region Name: Asia
Region id: 4 Region Name: Middle East and Africa
Region id: 5 Region Name: New Region
Proxy user attempts to delete from HR.Regions

C:\>
```

Caching Proxy Sessions

...

```
java.util.Properties connAttr = null;
...
//obtain connection from a cache enabled DataSource
OracleConnection conn = ds.getConnection("scott","tiger");
conn.openProxySession(proxyType, proxyProps);
...
connAttr.setProperty("CONNECTION_TAG","JOE'S_PROXY_CONNECTION");
conn.applyConnectionAttributes(connAttr); //apply attributes to the
// connection
conn.close(); //return the tagged connection to the cache
...
//come back later and ask for Joe's proxy connection
conn=ds.getConnection(connAttr); //This will retrieve Joe's proxy
// connection
```

7.3.9   Connection Wrapping

Wrapping a Java class is a common object-oriented programming technique, which consists of creating entirely new classes that implement the same interfaces as the original classes. In general, the wrapped classes forward to the original classes, but special codes can be added to the former. J2EE containers use this technique to intercept JDBC calls and intersperse transaction management, exception handling, connection management, performance enhancements, and logging services on top of the original conection object. Since Oracle 9i Release 2, the Oracle JDBC drivers support connection wrapping through the `oracle.jdbc.OracleConnectionWrapper` class, which implements `java.sql.Connection` and `OracleConnection`.

```
// Wrap
Connection conn = ds.getConnection();
Connection w = new OracleConnectionWrapper(conn);

// Unwrap
Connection orig = ((OracleConnection)w).unwrap
```

The following example is adapted from the ConnectionWrapperSample.java in Oracle JDBC demos:

```
ConnWrapper.java
=================
/*
```

```
 * Demo wrapping and  unwrapping a JDBC  connection
 */

import java.sql.*;
import oracle.jdbc.*;
import oracle.jdbc.pool.OracleDataSource;

public class ConnWrapper
{
  public static void main (String args [])
       throws SQLException
  {
    // Create an OracleDataSource
    OracleDataSource ods = new OracleDataSource();

    // Set the URL, user name, and password
    String url = "jdbc:oracle:thin:scott/tiger@//localhost:1521/
orcl";
    ods.setURL(url);
    OracleConnection conn = (OracleConnection)ods.getConnection();

    // Wrap the connection
    OracleConnectionWrapper wrappedConn =
        new OracleConnectionWrapper( conn );
    System.out.println(" **** Wrapped Connection ***");

    // Print employee names
    Statement stmt = wrappedConn.createStatement ();
    ResultSet rset = stmt.executeQuery ("select ENAME from EMP");

    while (rset.next ())
      System.out.print(rset.getString(1) + " ");
    rset.close();
    stmt.close();
    System.out.println();

   // Get a standard connection by unwrapping the wrapped Connection

    OracleConnection orig = ((OracleConnection)wrappedConn).unwrap();
    System.out.println(" **** UnWrapped Connection ***");

    // Print employee names
```

```
      stmt = orig.createStatement ();
      rset = stmt.executeQuery ("select ENAME from EMP");
      while (rset.next ())
        System.out.print(rset.getString(1) + " ");
      rset.close();
      stmt.close();
      System.out.println();

      conn.close();
  }
}


C:\>javac ConnWrapper.java


C:\>java ConnWrapper
 **** Wrapped Connection ***
SMITH ALLEN WARD JONES MARTIN BLAKE CLARK SCOTT KING TURNER ADAMS
JAMES FORD MILLER
 **** UnWrapped Connection ***
SMITH ALLEN WARD JONES MARTIN BLAKE CLARK SCOTT KING TURNER ADAMS
JAMES FORD MILLER


C:\>
```

Assume you need to augment/tweak getXXX() in ResultSet across all your JDBC applications. You can generalize the wrapper technique to OracleDataSource, OracleConnection, OracleStatement, and OracleResultSet, so that the new behavior is implemented at the driver level and not across your applications. Each of these classes and interfaces may have an instance variable, which stores an instance implementing the corresponding interface and a constructor that lets you create the wrapped instance by passing in the wrapper.

7.3.10 JDBC Connections in Grid Environment

Unless you have been living in a cave the last two years, you probably have heard about the grid. Leaving aside the marketing hype and whatever it is called (i.e., utility computing, on-demand computing, autonomic computing), grid computing aims at substantially cutting costs by consolidating IT resources, virtualizing their location, allocating/provisioning, and managing resources based on policies. Why should you care about the grid at the

JDBC level? Cost cutting is a compelling value proposition galvanized by a new generation of blade servers and network-attached storage; as such, all layers of enterprise computing must adapt and support these new platforms. In principle, application servers and their containers, such as the Oracle Application Server, shield Java/J2EE developers from the direct impact of grid platform. If you've read this book so far, you are already aware of the mechanisms in Oracle JDBC that address these requirements. To summarize:

- Most JDBC applications use "connect strings" that explicitly specify the hostname or IP address of the target database. This won't work in enterprise grid computing, where nodes are dynamically added to or retrenched from the cluster of database servers. The solution consists of virtualizing the database host and instance by connecting to a service and not to an actual physical server; as a result, clients (i.e., JDBC applications, middle tier, and so on) are insulated from changes made to the physical elements of the cluster (add/remove nodes), as well as from node failures.

- Caching only identically authenticated connections is useless in an enterprise grid environment, where you need to serve thousands of arbitrarily authenticated customers. The solution here is the ability to cache heterogeneously authenticated connections and proxy connections.

- Application servers (and J2EE containers) that rely on unpredictable timeout mechanisms will not be able to provide a reliable, guaranteed service in an enterprise grid environment. The solution is an event-based mechanism, which can notify susbscribers as the event happens, so that appropriate action can be taken in a timely manner. The Oracle Notification Services do just that by notifying the Oracle JDBC drivers of RAC events (e.g., Instance Up, Instance Down, Node) instantaneously, and processing these so as to provide a fast and reliable fail-over and connection load balancing.

- In order to manage and service database resources on demand, a mechanism for dynamically creating, resizing, and terminating connection caches is required.

- A feature-rich connection cache, which lets you search, retrieve, reclaim, and allocate connections based on user-defined criteria.

Virtualizing the Database as a Service

Grid computing materializes itself at every level of computing infrastructure, including the storage grid, disk and network grid, database grid, and application server grid. A grid of Oracle databases is made of a set of clustered databases (RAC), in which each clustered database is hosted on shared networked storage and concurrently accessed and managed by multiple database server instances. The traditional Oracle datasource URL attribute or connect string is in the form of the following: `jdbc:oracle<type>@<host>:<port>:<sid>`

```
String connString="jdbc:oracle:thin:@prodHost:1521:ORCL";
```

In an Oracle Database RAC environment, the hosts and database server instances that make up the cluster are represented as a single logical entity known as a service. A client application connects to the logical database service without any real knowledge of the actual host or database server instance that's used in the cluster. By connecting to the service, and not to an actual physical server, clients can be insulated from changes made to the physical elements of the cluster, as well as insulated from node failures.

As we have seen, in the Oracle Database RAC model, services are represented as "/<service-name>.

```
String connString = "jdbc:oracle:thin:scott/tiger@//
mycomany.com:5521/sales"
```

Fast Event Notification, Connection Fail-over, and Load Balancing

The dynamic nature of an enterprise grid environment leads to a constantly changing system configuration in terms of node allocations/deallocations. To allow JDBC applications to meet these requirements a mechanism must be provided to rapidly propagate changes occurring at service, node, and database level. Upon receipt of the changes, the subscriber must take the appropriate action. The combination of Oracle Notification Services and Oracle JDBC Connection Cache Manager allows the following:

- Monitoring of events

- Rerouting of connection requests to surviving instances on failure events (Instance Down)

- Repartitionning of the pool of connections across all active instances

7.4   JDBC Statements and Oracle Extensions

In the previous section, we looked at JDBC connections and Oracle extensions. Once you've got a connection object, you want to access and manage data through SQL statements. In this section, we look at the various JDBC statement types, statement caching, and statement batching.

7.4.1   JDBC Statement Types

As illustrated by Figure 7.2, the JDBC specification furnishes three types of statements that address different requirements:

- `Statement`: For submitting basic and adhoc SQL statements to the RDBMS.

- `PreparedStatement`: Derived from Statement, used for submitting (parameterized) SQL statements that are parsed once and executed many times; methods are furnished to replace input parameter placeholders with the actual values at runtime.

- `CallableStatement`: Derived from `PreparedStatement` for calling stored procedures; methods are furnished for retrieving the values returned by output parameters.

Figure 7.2
JDBC Statement Types

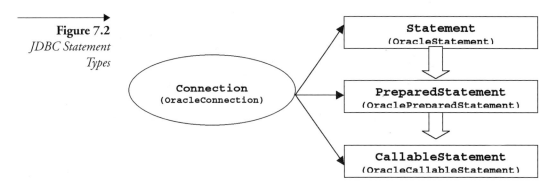

Let's look at each statement type in greater detail.

7.4.2 **Statement**

In a Nutshell

An instance of a statement object is obtained through the invocation of the
`createStatement()` method on the Connection object.

```
Statement stmt = null;
ResultSet rs = null;
// assume conn refers to a connection object
stmt = conn.createStatement();
```

Once you get an instance of the `Statement` object, you invoke either
the `execute()`, `executeQuery()`, or `executeUpdate()` methods:

- `executeQuery(String)`: For SQL queries, which return a `Result-Set` object (described later)

```
try {

// assume the statement is a SELECT...
rs = stmt.executeQuery("SELECT ename FROM emp");
} finally {…}
```

- `execute(String)`: For unknown, dynamic, adhoc SQL statements;
  it returns true if the SQL query was a `SELECT` or false if the SQL
  statement was a DML (i.e., UPDATE, INSERT, or DELETE). For DML,
  you retrieve the number of affected rows by invoking `getUpdate-Count()` on the Statement instance; `getUpdateCount` returns −1 for
  queries (i.e. `SELECT`).

```
if (stmt.execute("SELECT ename FROM emp")) {
        rs = stmt.getResultSet();
   }
 } finally {…}
```

- `executeUpdate`: For DDL (i.e., `create table`) and DML state-ments (i.e., `insert`, `update`, `delete`), it returns the number of rows
  affected by the update statement.

```
stmt.executeUpdate("update emp set ename = 'FOOBAR'
              where empno = '7934' ")
```

`JDBCPrimer.java`, in section 6.1, is a basic use of Statement.

Standard Statement API and Oracle Extensions

The `oracle.jdbc.OracleStatement` interface captures both the standard Statement API as well as Oracle extensions.

The `java.sql.Statement` interface specifies methods supporting the execution of SQL statements, including `addBatch`, `cancel`, `clearBatch`, `clearWarnings`, `close`, `execute`, `executeBatch`, `executeQuery`, `executeUpdate`, `getConnection`, `getFetchDirection`, `getFetchSize`, `getGeneratedKeys`, `getMaxFieldSize`, `getMaxRows`, `getMoreResults`, `getQueryTimeout`, `getResultSet`, `getResultSetConcurrency`, `getResultSetHoldability`, `getResultSetType`, `getUpdateCount`, `getWarnings`, `setCursorName`, `setEscapeProcessing`, `setFetchDirection`, `setFetchSize`, `setMaxFieldSize`, `setMaxRows`, and `setQueryTimeout`.

- `execute`, `executeQuery`, `executeUpdate` were addressed previously.

- The `addBatch`, `clearBatch`, and `executeBatch` methods are discussed later.

- Result Set–related methods (e.g., `getFetchDirection`, `getFetchSize`, `getMaxFieldSize`, `getMaxRows`, `getMoreResults`, `getQueryTimeout`, `getResultSet`, `getResultSetConcurrency`, `getResultSetType`, `getUpdateCount`, `setCursorName`, `setFetchDirection`, `setFetchSize`, `setMaxFieldSize`, `setMaxRows`) are discussed in the next chapter.

- `cancel` sends a message to the RDBMS and waits for a reply. If, for whatever reason, the RDBMS is not responding, then the cancel will hang until the socket read times out.

- `setQueryTimeout` sends `Statement.cancel` when it times out; it guarantees that it will not cancel the statement in less than the supplied number of seconds. A Statement timeout thread is started in each JVM to enforce timeouts.

Note: The `cancel()` and `setQueryTimeout` methods are not supported in Oracle's server-side driver types.

- The `setEscapeProcessing(true|false)` method, when invoked with "true," instructs the driver to translate an RDBMS-independent format into Oracle RDBMS SQL format and data representations. The Oracle JDBC supports the following SQL 92 escape syntaxes:

    - Time and Date Literals: `{d 'yyyy-mm-dd'}` and `{t 'hh:mm:ss'}`

```
// Select ename from the emp where the hiredate is Nov-25-1995
    ResultSet rset = stmt.executeQuery
    ("SELECT ename FROM emp WHERE hiredate = {d '1995-11-25'}");
    or
    ("SELECT ename FROM emp WHERE hiredate = {t '12:00:00'}");
```

    - Timestamp Literals: `{ts 'yyyy-mm-dd hh:mm:ss.f...'}`
```
        ResultSet rset = stmt.executeQuery
        ("SELECT ename FROM emp WHERE hiredate = {ts '1995-11-
        25 12:00:00'}");
```
    - Scalar Functions: The Oracle JDBC drives support only the scalar function escape syntax: `{fn <scalar function>}`;
    - LIKE escape characters

```
    // Select empno from the emp where ename starts with '_'
    ResultSet rset = stmt.executeQuery
    ("SELECT empno FROM emp WHERE ename LIKE '&_%' {escape '&'}");
```

    or:

```
("SELECT empno FROM emp WHERE ename LIKE '\\_%' {escape '\\'}");
```

    - Outer Joins: The Oracle JDBC drivers do not support the standard outer join syntax.

```
        ResultSet rset = stmt.executeQuery
            ("SELECT ename, dname
                    FROM {OJ dept LEFT OUTER JOIN emp ON
        dept.deptno = emp.deptno}
                ORDER BY ename");
```

    use Oracle's own outer join syntax instead
```
        ResultSet rset = stmt.executeQuery
            ("SELECT ename, dname
```

```
                        FROM emp a, dept b WHERE a.deptno =
     b.deptno(+)
                        ORDER BY ename");
```

- Function Call Syntax: See section 7.4.4.

The `oracle.jdbc.OracleSql` class furnishes the `parse()` method to translate the SQL92 syntax into an Oracle-supported syntax (See the *SQL92 to SQL Syntax Example* in the Oracle JDBC documentation).

The `oracle.jdbc.OracleStatement` interface extends the standard `java.sql.Statement` with additional methods, including `clearDefines()`, `closeWithKey()`, `creationState()`, `defineColumnType()`, `defineColumnTypeBytes()`, `defineColumnTypeChars()`, `getRowPrefetch()`, `isNCHAR()`, `setResultSetCache()`, and `setRowPrefetch()`. These extensions mostly address performance optimizations.

- `defineColumnType()` defines the data type to be used for retrieving values from a column. Without `defineColumnType`, JDBC might require additional roundtrip(s) to the database to get the definition from metadata in system tables. As of release 10.2, this method is no longer needed or recommended when using JDBC-Thin.

Example:

```
//
((OracleStatement)stmt).defineColumnType(1,Types.INTEGER);
((OracleStatement)stmt).defineColumnType(2,Types.VARCHAR,10);
ResultSet rset = stmt.executeQuery();
 while (rset.next())
 System.out.println("INTEGER " + rset.getInt(1)+
   ", VARCHAR " + rset.getString(2));
stmt.close();
rset.close();
```

- `defineColumnTypeBytes()`: Similar to `defineColumnType` but specifies the maximum size in bytes. The values for this column will not exceed the maximum.

- `defineColumnTypeChars()`: Similar to `defineColumnTypeBytes` but instead specifies the maximum size in characters.

See the Oracle JDBC javadoc for more details on the various signatures.

For each SQL statement execution, a new cursor is created, then the statement is parsed and (if query) optimized, then executed; there is no bind phase because there is no parameter. However, the overhead incurred by a systematic parse might become expensive, so the JDBC specification defines PreparedStatement, our next topic.

7.4.3 PreparedStatement

In a Nutshell

PreparedStatement addresses the requirement of preparsing/preparing SQL statements that can be parameterized ahead of the execution phase. Most RDBMSs including Oracle, process SQL statements through four steps: parse, bind, execute, and, optionally, "fetch" for getting result sets. In the Statement object, there is no bind step; in the Prepared-Statement case, the parse and bind steps are explicitly delineated. The bind step consists of replacing the placeholders of input parameters, which are represented by "?" in the SQL string, by the actual parameter values at runtime using either constant values or bind variables. Unlike Statement object, the cursor associated with the instance of the preparsed statement is not reinitialized/rebuilt after execution, which allows multiple executions of the same statement without reparsing.

Typical PreparedStatement SQL statements:

- UPDATE emp SET deptno=? WHERE empno=?
- INSERT INTO footab (id, code, descr) VALUES (?, ?, ?)
- DELETE footab WHERE id = ?
- SELECT col1, ?, job FROM tab WHERE col 2 = ? ORDER by ?

Note that the Oracle RDBMS does not support bind parameters as part of the IN clause of SELECT statements. In other words, the following syntax is not supported:

```
SELECT prod_id, prod_name from prod_tab where prod_id
in ( ?, ?, );
```

However, the following syntax, which uses a nested table as part of the IN clause works:

```
SELECT prod_id, prod_name
FROM prod_tab
WHERE prod_id IN (SELECT column_value FROM TABLE(?))
```

The following steps describe the typical use of `PreparedStatement`.

Steps 1 and 2

Initialize the `PreparedStatement` and set the value of the input parameters using

```
pstmt.setXXX(<column index>, <constant value>|<bind
variable>)
```

where:

<XXX> = standard Java types and Oracle Java types, addressed in the next chapter

<column index> = the index of the column (i.e., 1 for col 1, 2 for col 2, etc.)

<bind variable> = the name of a variable containing the input value

Example #1:

```
int empnum = 7934


PreparedStatement pstmt =
  conn.prepareStatement
("SELECT empno, ename FROM emp WHERE empno = ? ");
pstmt.setInt(1, empnum);
...


-------
```

Example #2:

```
int empnum = 7934


PreparedStatement pstmt =
  conn.prepareStatement("UPDATE emp
  SET ename = ? WHERE empno = ? ");
pstmt.setString(1, "FOOBAR");
```

```
pstmt.setInt(2, empnum);
...
```

Step 3

Execute the prepared statement using `executeQuery()` or executeUp-
date() methods; however, in the `PreparedStatement` case, these methods have no parameters. The discussion on executeQuery() or
executeUpdate() (See section 7.4.2) applies here too.

```
pstmt.executeUpdate();
...
```

Step 4

Dealing with Results, see Chapter 8 for more details on Result Set.

See Chapter 3 for a basic but complete example of using Prepared-
Statement.

The Standard PreparedStatement API and OraclePreparedStatement

The `oracle.jdbc.PreparedStatement` interface captures both standard
API as well as Oracle extensions.

The `java.sql.PreparedStatement` interface specifies standard methods for using prepared SQL statements, mostly for setting parameter values.
These methods include addBatch, clearParameters, execute, execute-
Query, executeUpdate, getMetaData, getParameterMetaData, setArray, setAsciiStream, setBigDecimal, setBinaryStream, setBlob,
setBoolean, setByte, setBytes, setCharacterStream, setClob, set-
Date, setDouble, setFloat, setInt, setLong, setNull, setObject,
setRef, setShort, setString, setTime, setTimestamp, setUnicode-
Stream, and setURL.

- The clearParameters() method has been defined for clearing the
  values that have been set for the parameter placeholders; by default,
  these values are not reset through execution (unless new values are set).

- The ParameterMetaData interface is new in JDBC 3.0 and provides information about the number, type, and properties of parameters to PreparedStatement (i.e., getParamaterMetaData()). It

also specifies the ability to cache and reuse a `PreparedStatement` associated with a physical connection (see section 7.4.6).

To set the values of input parameters (i.e., bind data for input), the Oracle JDBC driver uses three approaches depending on the data size (see Tables 7.4 and 7.5) and whether the input parameter is for SQL or PL/SQL operations. For example, LOB binding is applied for LOB parameter for PL/SQL when the data size is greater than 32,767:

- `direct binding`: Where the data is placed in a bind buffer; it is fast and supports batching (statement batching is discussed later).
- `stream binding`: Where the data is streamed; it is slower, because it may require roundtrips, and it does not support batching (it turns it off).
- `LOB binding`: Consists of creating a temporary LOB to hold the input data using the LOB APIs, and the bytes of the LOB locator are placed in the bind buffer; it is very slow because it requires many roundtrips to the RDBMS. Batching is supported but not recommended.

Prior to 10*g* Release 2, the Oracle JDBC implementation of `setString`, `setCharacterStream`, `setAsciiStream`, `setBytes`, and `setBinaryStream` methods for setting the value(s) of input parameter(s) worked as follows:

setBytes: performs a `direct` bind of bytes

setBinaryStream: performs a `stream` bind of bytes

In 10*g* Release 2, the implementation has changed as follows:

- The switching between binding modes is fully automatic, contrary to 10*g* Release 1, where a SQL exception is thrown if the parameter size is larger than the threshold of the bind method, listed in Tables 7.4 and 7.5, and based on the type of the SQL statement:
- `setBytes` switches to `setBinaryStream` (i.e., stream bind of bytes) for SQL operations (i.e., PreparedStatement) on data larger than 2,000 bytes.

- `setBytes` switches to `setBinaryStream` for PL/SQL operations (i.e., CallableStatement) on data larger than 2,000 bytes and to `setBytesForBlob` for data larger than 32,512 bytes.
- `setString` switches to `setCharacterStream` (i.e., stream bind of characters) for SQL operations on data larger than 32,766 characters.
- `setString` switches to `setStringForClob` for string data larger than 32,512 bytes in the database character set or national character set, depending on whether `setFormOfUse` has been used for NCLOB parameters.

For fixed-length character sets, data byte length is equal to the length of the Java character data multiplied by the character size in bytes.

For variable-length character sets, data byte length is computed as follows:

- Direct bind is used if the length of the character set is less than 32,512 divided by the maximum character size.

- LOB bind is used if the length of the character set is greater than 32,512 divided by the minimum character size.

- Direct bind is used if the length of the character set is between and if the actual length of the converted bytes is less than 32,512; otherwise, LOB bind is used.

Table 7.4 describes the size limits and the bind approach used by `setString`, `setCharacterStream` and `setAsciiStream`, according to the size of data.

Table 7.5 describes the size limits and the bind approach used by `setBytes` and `setBinaryStream`, according to the size of data.

Table 7.4   *Size Limits and Bind Mechanisms*

Form	Stmt	Driver Type	Lower Limit	Upper Limit	Bind Mechanism
All	All	All	0	0	Null
All	SQL	Client	1 char	32,766 chars	Direct

Table 7.4 *Size Limits and Bind Mechanisms (continued)*

Form	Stmt	Driver Type	Lower Limit	Upper Limit	Bind Mechanism
All	SQL	Client	32,767 chars	2,147,483,647 bytes	Stream
All	SQL	Client	2,147,483,648 bytes	2,147,483,647 chars	Temp Clob
CHAR		Server	1 char	65,536 bytes	Direct
NCHAR			1 char	4,000 bytes	Direct
NCHAR			4,001 bytes	2,147,483,647 chars	Temp Clob
CHAR			65,537 bytes	2,147,483,647 bytes	Stream
			2,147,483,647 bytes	2,147,483,647 chars	Temp Clob
All	PL/SQL	All	1 char	32,512 chars	Direct
All	PL/SQL	All	32,513 chars	2,147,483,647 chars	Temp Clob

Table 7.5 *Size Limits and Bind Mechanisms*

Stmt	Driver Type	Lower Limit	Upper Limit	Bind Mechanism
SQL	Client	32,767 bytes	2,147,483,648 bytes	Stream
All	All	0	0	Null
SQL	All	1	2,000 bytes	Direct
SQL	All	2,000 bytes	2,147,483,647 bytes	Stream
PL/SQL	All	1	32,512 bytes	Direct

Table 7.5   *Size Limits and Bind Mechanisms (continued)*

Stmt	Driver Type	Lower Limit	Upper Limit	Bind Mechanism
PL/SQL	All	32,513 bytes	2,147,483,647 bytes	Temp blob

Methods inherited from the `java.sql.Statement` interface: `addBatch`, `cancel`, `clearBatch`, `clearWarnings`, `close`, `execute`, `executeBatch`, `executeQuery`, `executeUpdate`, `getConnection`, `getFetchDirection`, `getFetchSize`, `getGeneratedKeys`, `getMaxFieldSize`, `getMaxRows`, `getMoreResults`, `getMoreResults`, `getQueryTimeout`, `getResultSet`, `getResultSetConcurrency`, `getResultSetHoldability`, `getResultSetType`, `getUpdateCount`, `getWarnings`, `setCursorName`, `setEscapeProcessing`, `setFetchDirection`, `setFetchSize`, `setMaxFieldSize`, `setMaxRows`, `setQueryTimeout`.

Methods inherited from the `oracle.jdbc.OracleStatement` interface: `clearDefines`, `closeWithKey`, `creationState`, `defineColumnType`, `defineColumnTypeBytes`, `defineColumnTypeChars`, `getRowPrefetch`, `isNCHAR`, `setResultSetCache`, `setRowPrefetch`

The Oracle extensions consist of the following methods: `defineParameterType`, `defineParameterTypeBytes`, `defineParameterTypeChars`, `getExecuteBatch`, `getReturnResultSet`, `OracleGetParameterMetaData`, `registerReturnParameter`, `setARRAY`, `setArrayAtName`, `setARRAYAtName`, `setAsciiStreamAtName`, `setBfile`, `setBFILE`, `setBfileAtName`, `setBFILEAtName`, `setBigDecimalAtName`, `setBinaryDouble`, `setBinaryDoubleAtName`, `setBinaryFloat`, `setBinaryFloatAtName`, `setBinaryStreamAtName`, `setBLOB`, `setBlobAtName`, `setBLOBAtName`, `setBooleanAtName`, `setByteAtName`, `setBytesForBlob`, `setBytesForBlobAtName`, `setCHAR`, `setCHARAtName`, `setCheckBindTypes`, `setCLOB`, `setClobAtName`, `setCLOBAtName`, `setCursor`, `setCursorAtName`, `setCustomDatum`, `setCustomDatumAtName`, `setDATE`, `setDateAtName`, `setDATEAtName`, `setDisableStmtCaching`, `setDoubleAtName`, `setFixedCHAR`, `setFixedCHARAtName`, `setFloatAtName`, `setFormOfUse`, `setIntAtName`, `setINTERVALDS`, `setINTERVALDSAtName`, `setINTERVALYM`, `setINTERVALYMAtName`, `setLongAtName`, `setNullAtName`, `setNUMBER`, `setNUMBERAtName`, `setObjectAtName`, `setOPAQUE`, `setOPAQUEAtName`, `setOracleObject`, `setOracleObjectAtName`, `setORAData`, `setORADataAtName`, `setPlsqlIndexTable`, `setRAW`, `setRAWAtName`, `setREF`, `setRefAtName`, `setREFAtName`, `setRefType`, setRefTypeAtName, setROWID, setROWIDAtName, setShortAtName, set-StringAtName, setStringForClob, setStringForClobAtName, set-STRUCT, setSTRUCTAtName, setStructDescriptor, setStructDescriptorAtName, setTimeAtName, setTIMESTAMP, set-TimestampAtName, setTIMESTAMPAtName, setTIMESTAMPLTZ, setTIMES-TAMPLTZAtName, setTIMESTAMPTZ, setTIMESTAMPTZAtName, setUnicodeStreamAtName, setURLAtName.

Most of these methods deal with binding java.sql.* and ora-cle.sql.* types to either parameter indexes (i.e., setXXX()) or parameter names (i.e., setXXXAtName()) and statement batching (i.e., getExecute-Batch()).

registerReturnParameter(): See DML with Returning section, below.

```
defineParameterType (<col index>, <Type constant>, <max-size>
);
```
where:

```
<Type constant> = java.sql.Types or oracle.sql.OracleTypes
<max-size> = the maximum size of data to bind in
```

Example:

```
SQL> CREATE TABLE pstmttab ( iname NUMBER, cname
VARCHAR2(1096));

OraclePreparedStatement pstmt =
(OraclePreparedStatement) conn.prepareStatement("INSERT INTO"
        "+ pstmsttab(iname, cname) VALUES (?, ?)");

pstmt.defineParameterType(2, OracleTypes.VARCHAR, 1096);
```

setXXX(int, XXX): Standard and Oracle-specific methods for binding java.sql.* and oracle.sql.* types to RDBMS SQL types. In Chapter 3, Tables 3.2 and 3.3 summarize the mapping of SQL and PL/SQL types to Java/JDBC types. Table 7.6 summarizes the setXXX() method to use per Java input parameter type.

setNull(parameterIndex, sqlTYpe), setNull(parameterIndex, sqlTYpe, sql_type_name): For setting an object to NULL.

setCHAR(): Because CHAR SQL type is right-padded with spaces to the column width, setCHAR performs a padded comparison when used to bind character data in a WHERE clause; use setFixedCHAR() instead; it performs a nonpadded comparison.

Assume a table, pstmttab, with columns col 1 to col 18 corresponding to the various oracle.sql.* data types. The following code snippet illustrates the invocation of the various setXXX methods:

Table 7.6 *setXXX Method versus Input Parameter Types*

Input Parameter Type	setXXX method(s)
int	setInt()
short	setShort()
float	setFloat()
double	setDouble()
long	setLong()
byte	setByte()
byte[]	setBytes()
oracle.sql.NUMBER	setNUMBER()
java.sql.Array	setArray()
oracle.sql.ARRAY	setARRAY()
java.io.InputStream	setAsciiStream(), setBinaryStream(), setUnicodeStream()
java.io.Reader	sSetCharacterStream()
oracle.sql.BFILE	setBFILE(), setBfile()
BigDecimal	setBigDecimal()
oracle.sql.BINARY_FLOAT	setBinaryFloat()
oracle.sql.BINARY_DOUBLE	setBinaryDOuble()
java.sql.Blob	setBlob()
oacle.sql.BLOB	setBLOB()

Table 7.6 *setXXX Method versus Input Parameter Types (continued)*

Input Parameter Type	setXXX method(s)
java.sql.Clob	setClob()
oracle.sql.CLOB	setCLOB()
Boolean	seBoolean()
java.lang.String	setString(), setFixedCHAR()
oracle.sql.CHAR	setCHAR(), setFixedCHAR()
java.sql.Date	setDate()
oracle.sql.DATE	setDATE()
java.sql.Time	setTime()
java.sql.Timestamp	setTimestamp()
oracle.sql.TIMESTAMP	setTIMESTAMP()
oracle.sql.TIMESTAMPTZ	setTIMESTAMPTZ()
oracle.sql.TIMESTAMPLTZ	setTIMESTAMPLTZ()
oracle.sql.RAW	setRAW()
java.sql.Ref	setRef()
oracle.sql.REF	setREF()
oracle.sql.ROWID	setROWID()
oracle.sql.STRUCT	setSTRUCT()
java.net.URL	setURL()

```
String stmt = "insert into pstmttab values (?, ?, ?, ?, ?." +
    "?,?,?,?,?,?,?,?,?,?)";;

OraclePreparedStatement opstmt =
        (OraclePreparedStatement)con.prepareStatement(stmt);

opstmt.setInt(1, index);
opstmt.setString(2, "This is a String");
opstmt.setShort(3, (short)12);
```

```
opstmt.setLong(4, (long)12345);
opstmt.setFloat(5, (float)123.456);
opstmt.setDouble(6, (double)12345.678);
opstmt.setBigDecimal(7, new BigDecimal(12.34));
opstmt.setBoolean(8, true);
opstmt.setDATE(9, date);
opstmt.setTIMESTAMP(10, xts);
opstmt.setTIMESTAMPTZ(11, xtstz);
opstmt.setTIMESTAMPLTZ(12, xtsltz);
opstmt.setCLOB(13, xclb);
opstmt.setBLOB(14, xblb);
opstmt.setAsciiStream(15, is, xlength);
opstmt.setRAW(16, new RAW((Object)rawString));
opstmt.setBFILE(17, xbfile);
opstmt.setObject(18, xobject);
```

setOracleObject: A generic set*XXX* method for binding oracle.sql.*
data as an oracle.sql.Datum object. The oracle.sql.Datum is the root
class of Oracle's native data type classes, including BINARY_DOUBLE,
BINARY_FLOAT, CHAR, DATE, ARRAY, NUMBER, REF, INTERVALDS, INTERVA-
LYM, NUMBER, RAW, ROWID, TIMESTAMP, TIMESTAMPLTZ, TIMESTAMPTZ. It may
be used to bind any data type.

setFormOfUse(): Because the NCHAR SQL data type is similar to the
SQL CHAR data type (i.e., CHAR, VARCHAR2, and CLOB) and has no separate
corresponding classes defined in the oracle.sql.* package, JDBC programs that manipulate the NCHAR SQL data type must call the
setFormOfUse() method to specify that the data will be bound to the SQL
NCHAR data type.

```
setFormOfUse(int parameterIndex, short formOfUse)
```

formOfUse: Sets the form to use and takes two values: FORM_CHAR and
FORM_NCHAR.

- FORM_CHAR for CHAR, VARCHAR2, and CLOB data; it is the default
  value.
- FORM_NCHAR for NCHAR, NVARCHAR2, and NCLOB data; JDBC will
  represent the data in the national character set of the server
  internally.

Example:

```
int empno = 12345;
String ename = "\uFF2A\uFF4F\uFF45";
String job = "Manager";
oracle.jdbc.OraclePreparedStatement pstmt =
(oracle.jdbc.OraclePreparedStatement)
conn.prepareStatement
    ("INSERT INTO emp (empno, ename, job) VALUES(?, ?, ?)");
pstmt.setFormOfUse(2, FORM_NCHAR);
pstmt.setFormOfUse(3, FORM_NCHAR);
pstmt.setInt(1, 1);
pstmt.setString(2, ename);
pstmt.setString(3, job);
pstmt.execute();
```

setXXXAtName(String, XXX): An Oracle extension similar to setXXX(), which allows binding by name, as illustrated below.

```
opstmt.setIntAtName ("col1", 12);
opstmt.setStringAtName("col2", "string");
opstmt.setFloatAtName("col3", (float)1.2);
opstmt.setBooleanAtName("col4", true);
opstmt.setShortAtName("col5", (short)7);
opstmt.setBigDecimalAtName("col7", new BigDecimal(123));
opstmt.setDoubleAtName("col8", 1.23);
opstmt.setIntAtName("col9", 12);
opstmt.setLongAtName("col10", (long)123);
```

Working with Oracle data types is covered in Chapter 8.

Performance

The PreparedStatement implementation is much more efficient and faster in Oracle Database 10*g* than in previous releases; see the eBay testimonial[11] on the average performance gain when moving to 10*g* JDBC. However, the very first PreparedStatement object since the creation of the Java VM instance pays a one-time and barely noticeable price to load a few helper classes (one class loader per JVM).

---

11. http://download-west.oracle.com/oowsf2004/1235_wp.pdf.

7.4.4   CallableStatement (Calling Stored Procedures)

CallableStatements are designed for invoking stored procedures in JDBC. The Oracle JDBC drivers support Java and PL/SQL stored procedures. There is an abundant PL/SQL literature. Java in the database is traditionally invoked through a PL/SQL wrapper, using CallableStatement, which is the topic of this section; however, as described previously, Java in the database can also be invoked using a client-side stub. Defining PL/SQL wrappers for Java in the database was covered earlier.

In a Nutshell

Processing a CallableStatement involves the following five steps:

Step 1

Create and initialize a CallableStatement object using the prepare-Call(String) method of the Connection object. The parameters are specified using the same placeholder notation as in PreparedStatement. The prepareCall method in Oracle JDBC drivers supports both the SQL92 and the anonymous PL/SQL block syntaxes.

- In the SQL 92 syntax, the string has two forms. The first form invokes a stored function with a result parameter, while the second form invokes a stored procedure:

```
// {? = call func (…) } -- A result is returned to a
// variable
CallableStatement cstmt1 =
    conn.prepareCall("{? = call func1(?, ?)}");
...

// {call proc (…) }    -- Does not return a result
CallableStatement cstmt2 =
    Conn.prepareCall("{call proc2 (?, ?)}");
```

- Similarly, the anonymous PL/SQL block syntax also has two forms:

```
// begin ? := func (?, ?); end; -- a result is
// returned to a variable
CallableStatement cstmt3 =
```

```
                        conn.prepareCall("begin ? := func3(?, ?); end;");
          ...


          // begin proc(?, ?); end;  -- Does not return a result
          CallableStatement cstmt4 =
                Conn.prepareCall("begin proc4(?, ?); end;");
```

Step 2

In order to retrieve the values from the `CallableStatement` object when the stored procedures successfully return, you must register the data type of the `OUT` and `IN/OUT` parameters using the `registerOutParameter` (index, parameter type) method of `CallableStatement`. The OraTypes (oracle.jdbc.OracleTypes) entry in the javadoc of the Oracle JDBC defines the valid SQL types that can be used as parameter types, including ARRAY, BFILE, BIGINT, BINARY, BINARY DOUBLE, BINARY FLOAT, BIT, BLOB, BOOLEAN, CHAR, CLOB, CURSOR, DATE, DOUBLE, FIXED_CHAR, INTEGER, INTERVALDS, INTERVALYM, JAVA_OBJECT, JAVA_STRUCT, LONGVARBINARY, LONGVARCHAR, NULL, NUMBER, OPAQUE, REF, RAW, ROWID, STRUCT, TIMESTAMP, TIMESTAMPLTZ, TIMESTAMPTZ, VARCHAR, and so on.

The following instruction assumes a VARCHAR is returned:

```
          cstmt1.registerOutParameter(1,Types.VARCHAR);
          ...
```

Step 3

Similar to `PreparedStatement`, you must set the value(s) for input parameters:

```
          cstmt1.setString(2, "aadfadfad");
          cstmt1.setInt(3, 125);
          ...
```

Step 4

Execute the `CallableStatement`. While `CallableStatement` supports calling any of the `Statement` execute methods (i.e., `executeUpdate()`, `executeQuery()`, or `execute()`), `execute()` is the most flexible method because it does not require you to know ahead of time if the stored procedure returns result sets or not.

```
          cstmt1.execute();
          ...
```

Step 5

Get the Output value(s) using the getXXX() method corresponding to the previously registered type (in step 2). See more details on getXXX() in the following text.

```
// var = cstmt.getXXX(index);
String outParam = cstmt1.getString(1);
```

Examples:

```
// Calling a procedure which has no parameter
try (
  cstmt = conn.prepareCall("{call p0}");
  cstmt.execute();
} catch (SQLException ex) {
}


// Calling a function which has no parameter but returns
// a VARCHAR
try (
cstmt2 = conn.prepareCall("{? = call f0o}");
cstmt.registerOutParameter(1, Types.VARCHAR);
cstmt.execute();
String res = cstmt.getString(1);
} catch (SQLException ex) {
}



// Calling a procedure which has one IN parameter
try (
cstmt = conn.prepareCall("{call pli(?)}");
cstmt.setString(1, "foo");
cstmt.execute();
} catch (SQLException ex) {
}

/*
 * Calling a stored procedure with no parameters
 *
 */
```

```
{
  CallableStatement proc0 = conn.prepareCall
  ("begin foo; end;");
  proc0.execute ();
}

/*
 * Calling a procedure with an IN parameter
 *
 */
{
  CallableStatement p1in =
            conn.prepareCall ("begin proc1 (?);
end;");
  p1in.setString (1, "foobar");
  p1in.execute ();
}
†

/*
 * Calling a procedure with an OUT parameter
 *
 */
{
    CallableStatement p1out =
          conn.prepareCall ("begin ocstmt (?); end;");
    p1out.registerOutParameter (1, Types.CHAR);
    p1out.execute ();
    System.out.println ("Out argument is: "+
p1out.getString (1));
}

 /*
  * Calling a procedure with an IN/OUT prameter
  *
  */
  {
    CallableStatement p1inout =
              conn.prepareCall ("begin procinout (?);
end;");
    p1inout.registerOutParameter (1, Types.VARCHAR);
    p1inout.setString (1, "foobar");
```

```
    plinout.execute ();
    System.out.println ("Out argument is: " +
plinout.getString (1));
  }


/*
 * Calling a function with no parameters
 *
 */
 {
  CallableStatement f0 =
                conn.prepareCall ("begin ? := funcnone;
end;");
    f0.registerOutParameter (1, Types.CHAR);
    f0.execute ();
      System.out.println ("Return value is: "+
f0.getString (1));
  }


/*
 * Calling a function with an IN parameter
 *
 */
 {
   CallableStatement f1in =
                conn.prepareCall ("begin ? := funcin (?);
end;");
    f1in.registerOutParameter (1, Types.CHAR);
    f1in.setString (2, "aaaaaaaaaa");
    f1in.execute ();
    System.out.println ("Return value is: " +
f1in.getString (1));
  }



/*
 * Calling a function with an OUT parameter
 *
 */
 {
     CallableStatement f1out =
                conn.prepareCall ("begin ? := funcout (?);
```

```
end;");
        flout.registerOutParameter (1, Types.CHAR);
        flout.registerOutParameter (2, Types.CHAR);
        flout.execute ();
        System.out.println ("Return value is: " +
flout.getString (1));
        System.out.println ("Out argument is: " +
flout.getString (2));
    }
```

The Standard API and OracleCallableStatement

The java.sql.CallableStatement interface extends java.sql.Prepared-Statement (see the corresponding javadoc for the list of inherited methods) and specifies the following methods: getArray, getBlob, getBoolean, getByte, getBytes, getClob, getDate, getDouble, getFloat, getInt, getLong, getObject, getRef, getShort, getString, getTime, get-Timestamp, getURL, registerOutParameter, setAsciiStream, setBig-Decimal,   setBinaryStream,   setBoolean,   setByte, setCharacterStream, setDate, setDouble, setFloat, setInt, setLong, setNull, setObject, setShort, setString, setTime, setTimestamp, setURL, wasNull.

- The JDBC 3.0 API specifies multiple open ResultSet as the ability to have multiple ResultSet open at the same time, from a Call-ableStatement. A new signature to getMoreResults(), which now takes a flag (i.e., getMoreResults(int)), allows controlling how to handle previously opened ResultSet upon the invocation of getRe-sultSet().

- The JDBC 3.0 API also specifies Named Parameters in CallableStatements as the ability to reference parameters to CallableStatement objects by name as well as by index (e.g., getXXX(column-name)).

Note: Named Parameter is not supported for RefCursors/ResultSets.

Methods inherited from oracle.jdbc.OraclePreparedStatement:

The oracle.jdbc.Callable interface extends the oracle.jdbc.Ora-clePreparedStatement interface and inherits the following methods (addressed in section 7.4.3):

```
defineParameterType, defineParameterTypeBytes,
defineParameterTypeChars, getExecuteBatch,
getReturnResultSet, OracleGetParameterMetaData,
registerReturnParameter, setARRAY, setArrayAtName,
setARRAYAtName, setAsciiStreamAtName, setBfile, setBFILE,
setBfileAtName, setBFILEAtName, setBigDecimalAtName,
setBinaryDouble, setBinaryDoubleAtName, setBinaryFloat,
setBinaryFloatAtName, setBinaryStreamAtName, setBLOB,
setBlobAtName, setBLOBAtName, setBooleanAtName,
setByteAtName, setBytesForBlob, setBytesForBlobAtName,
setCHAR, setCHARAtName, setCheckBindTypes, setCLOB,
setClobAtName, setCLOBAtName, setCursor, setCursorAtName,
setCustomDatum, setCustomDatumAtName, setDATE, setDateAtName,
setDATEAtName, setDisableStmtCaching, setDoubleAtName,
setFixedCHAR, setFixedCHARAtName, setFloatAtName,
setFormOfUse, setIntAtName, setINTERVALDS,
setINTERVALDSAtName, setINTERVALYM, setINTERVALYMAtName,
setLongAtName, setNullAtName, setNUMBER, setNUMBERAtName,
setObjectAtName, setOPAQUE, setOPAQUEAtName,
setOracleObject, setOracleObjectAtName, setORAData,
setORADataAtName, setPlsqlIndexTable, setRAW,
setRAWAtName, setREF, setRefAtName, setREFAtName,
setRefType, setRefTypeAtName, setROWID, setROWIDAtName,
setShortAtName, setStringAtName, setStringForClob,
setStringForClobAtName, setSTRUCT, setSTRUCTAtName,
setStructDescriptor, setStructDescriptorAtName,
setTimeAtName, setTIMESTAMP, setTimestampAtName,
setTIMESTAMPAtName, setTIMESTAMPLTZ,
setTIMESTAMPLTZAtName, setTIMESTAMPTZ,
setTIMESTAMPTZAtName, setUnicodeStreamAtName,
setURLAtName.
```

OracleCallableStatement Extensions to java.sql.CallableStatement

```
getAnyDataEmbeddedObject, getARRAY, getAsciiStream, getBFILE,
getBinaryStream, getBLOB, getCHAR, getCharacterStream,
getCLOB, getCursor, getDATE,  getINTERVALDS, getINTERVALYM,
getNUMBER, getOPAQUE, getOracleObject,
getOraclePlsqlIndexTable, getORAData, getPlsqlIndexTable,
getRAW, getREF, getROWID, getSTRUCT, getTIMESTAMP,
getTIMESTAMPLTZ, getTIMESTAMPTZ, getUnicodeStream,
registerIndexTableOutParameter, registerOutParameter,
sendBatch, setBinaryDouble, setBinaryFloat, setBytesForBlob,
setExecuteBatch, setStringForClob.
```

getXXX(): Similar to setXXX(), these methods return Java data types, as illustrated in Table 7.7.

Table 7.7 *getXXX() and Returned Object*

getXXX()	Returned Object Type
getInt()	int
getShort()	short
getFloat()	float
getDouble()	double
getLong()	long
getByte()	byte
getBytes()	byte[]
getNUMBER()	oracle.sql.NUMBER
getArray()	java.sql.Array
getARRAY()	oracle.sql.ARRAY
getAsciiStream(), getBinaryStream(), getUnicodeStream()	java.io.InputStream
getCharacterStream()	java.io.Reader
getBFILE(), getBfile()	oracle.sql.BFILE
getBigDecimal()	BigDecimal
getBinaryFloat()	oracle.sql.BINARY_FLOAT
getBinaryDOuble()	oracle.sql.BINARY_DOUBLE
getBlob()	java.sql.Blob
getBLOB()	oacle.sql.BLOB
getClob()	java.sql.Clob
getCLOB()	oracle.sql.CLOB
getBoolean()	Boolean
getString(), getFixedCHAR()	java.lang.String

Table 7.7   *getXXX() and Returned Object (continued)*

getXXX()	Returned Object Type
getCHAR(), getFixedCHAR()	oracle.sql.CHAR
getDate()	java.sql.Date
getDATE()	oracle.sql.DATE
getTime()	java.sql.Time
getTimestamp()	java.sql.Timestamp
getTIMESTAMP()	oracle.sql.TIMESTAMP
getTIMESTAMPTZ()	oracle.sql.TIMESTAMPTZ
getTIMESTAMPLTZ()	oracle.sql.TIMESTAMPLTZ
getRAW()	oracle.sql.RAW
getRef()	java.sql.Ref
getREF()	oracle.sql.REF
getROWID()	oracle.sql.ROWID
getSTRUCT()	oracle.sql.STRUCT
getURL()	java.net.URL

getObject: Generic method for retrieving any java.sql.* data into an java.lang.Object object.

getOracleObject: Generic method for retrieving any oracle.sql.* data into an oracle.sql.Datum object.

Examples:

```
/* Example#1
 * Basic CallableStatement using Cursor
 *
 */

OracleCallableStatement cstmt =
   (OracleCallableStatement) conn.prepareCall
        ("begin select cursor(select 1 from dual) into ? from dual;
end;");
```

```
cstmt.registerOutParameter(1, OracleTypes.CURSOR);

ResultSet rs = cstmt.executeQuery();

// returns true if the column is of type NCHAR/NVARCHAR/NCLOB
cstmt.isNCHAR(1);

while(rs.next())
System.out.println ("column1 = " + rs.getString(1));
cstmt.close();


/* Example#2
 * CallalableStatement with TIMESTAMP dtatypes OUT parameters
 * Assume a procedure timeproc (?, ?, ?, ?)
 */


String dateStr = "2005-09-03 12:31:56.78";
Timestamp tss = Timestamp.valueOf(dateStr);
TimeZone tz = TimeZone.getDefault();
tz.setID("US/Pacific");
greg_cal = new GregorianCalendar(tz);

tsltz = new oracle.sql.TIMESTAMPLTZ(conn, tss, gcal);
tstz = new oracle.sql.TIMESTAMPTZ(conn, tss, gcal);
ts = new oracle.sql.TIMESTAMP(tss);
date = new oracle.sql.DATE(tss);
long longTime = tss.getTime();
time = new Time(longTime);
dateTime = new java.sql.Date(longTime);

CallableStatement ocstmt = null;

((oracle.jdbc.OracleConnection) conn).setSessionTimeZone("GMT");

ocstmt = conn.prepareCall ("begin timeproc (?, ?, ?, ?); end;");

((OracleCallableStatement)ocstmt).setTIMESTAMPLTZ(1, tsltz);
((OracleCallableStatement)ocstmt).registerOutParameter
                                (1, OracleTypes.TIMESTAMPLTZ);
```

```
((OracleCallableStatement)ocstmt).setTIMESTAMPTZ(2, tstz);
((OracleCallableStatement)ocstmt).registerOutParameter
                                (2, OracleTypes.TIMESTAMPTZ);

((OracleCallableStatement) ocstmt).setTIMESTAMP(3, ts);
((OracleCallableStatement) ocstmt).registerOutParameter
                                    (3, Types.TIMESTAMP);

((OracleCallableStatement) ocstmt).setTimestamp(4, tss, greg_cal);
((OracleCallableStatement) ocstmt).registerOutParameter
                                (<index>, Types.TIMESTAMP);
ocstmt.executeUpdate();
ocstmt.close();
```

Performance

`Connection.prepareCall()` requires metadata retrieval for processing output parameters and is therefore an expensive method; reusing instances of `CallableStatement` reduces such cost (see section 7.4.6). See more on performance and best practices in Chapter 9.

7.4.5 Retrieval of Auto-Generated Keys and DML with Returning

JDBC 3.0 Auto-Generated Keys

In release 10.2, the Oracle JDBC drivers support the JDBC 3.0 *Retrieval of Auto-Generated Key*. To illustrate this feature, let's take a J2EE BMP entity bean instance, which is uniquely identified by the primary key associated with the newly inserted data as the result of *ejbCreate()*. Inserting the data and retrieving the value of the primary key within *ejbCreate()* usually involves two database operations: (1) an INSERT statement, and then (2) the retrieval of the key of the newly inserted row, which in the Oracle RDBMS case could be the *ROWID* or a sequence number. Using the standard JDBC 3.0 Retrieval of the Auto-Generated Key feature, these two database operations are combined into one, resulting in performance optimization. The following interfaces have been extended to support auto-generated keys:

java.sql.DatabaseMetaData:

■ `Public Boolean supports GeneratedKeys();`

java.sql.Statement:

- `Public Boolean execute(String sql, int autoGeneratedKeys)`

        `throws SQLException;`

- `Public Boolean execute(String sql, int[] columnIndexes)`

        `throws SQLException;`

- Public `Boolean execute(String sql, int[] columnNames)`

        `throws SQLException;`

- `Public Boolean executeUpdate(String sql, int autoGener-
  atedKeys)`

        `throws SQLException;`

- `Public Boolean executeUpdate(String sql, int[] columnIn-
  dexes)`

        `throws SQLException;`

- `Public Boolean executeUpdate(String sql, int[] column-
  Names)`

        `throws SQLException;`

`java.sql.Connection:` Methods that extend PreparedStatement objects:

- `Public PreparedStatement preparedStatement`

        `(String sql, int autoGeneratedKeys) throws
        SQLException;`

- `Public PreparedStatement preparedStatement`

        `(String sql, int[] columnIndexes) throws SQLException;`

- `Public PreparedStatement preparedStatement`

        `(String sql, String[] columnNames) throws SQLException;`

- `Public ResultSet getGeneratedKeys() throws SQLException;`

Specifying `Statement.RETURN_GENERATED_KEYS` tells executeUpdate to return the generated key(s):

```
ResultSet rset = null;
Statement stmt = conn.createStatement();

int countrows stmt.executeUpdate("INSERT INTO prodtab " +
```

```
                    "(prodid, prodname) " +
                    "VALUES (12345,'abdcefghi')",
                    Statement.RETURN_GENERATED_KEYS);

// Obtain the result set object from the query.
rs = stmt.getGeneratedKeys();

// Retrieve the auto generated key.
while (rset.next())
    int key = rs.getInt(1);
rset.close();
```

Use the `DatabaseMetaData.supportsGetGeneratedKeys` method to check that a JDBC driver and underlying RDBMS support the retrieval of auto-generated keys.

The Oracle JDBC implementation of the retrieval of auto-generated keys is based on the JDBC support for "*DML with the RETURNING clause*"; it works only for the `INSERT` statement and is not supported in server-side drivers.

DML with RETURNING

In Release 10.2, the Oracle JDBC drivers support `DML with RETURNING`, which is an Oracle RDBMS feature that lets you combine a query (in the `RETURNING` clause) with a DML into a single statement. It is more general purpose than the JDBC 3.0 Auto-Generated Keys, because it allows you to return any columns. However, it is not currently supported by server-side drivers. The following Oracle JDBC methods support `DML with RETURNING`:

`registerReturnParameter()`: Registers the return parameter for *DML with Returning*; it can only be used with `CHAR` or `RAW` types.

- registerreturnparameter(int paramIndex, int externalType)
        throws SQLException;
- registerreturnparameter(int paramIndex, int externalType,
- int maxSize) throws SQLException;
- registerReturnParameter(int paramIndex, int intsqlType,

        String typeName) throws SQLException;

getReturnResulSet(): Fetches the data returned from *DML with Returning* as a ResultSet object.

```
// Same example as above, using DML with RETURNING

OracleResultSet orset = null;
OraclePreparedStatement opstmt = null;

opstmt = (OraclePreparedStatement) conn.prepareStatement(
    "insert into prodtab (prodid, prodname)
values(12345,'abdcefghi') returning "
                    + "prodid, prodname into ?, ?");
opstmt.registerReturnParameter(1, OracleTypes.NUMBER);
opstmt.registerReturnParameter(2, OracleTypes.CHAR);

int countrows = opstmt.executeUpdate();

orset = (OracleResultSet) opstmt.getReturnResultSet();

while (orset.next())
  System.out.println("Product Id: " + orset.getInt(1)+
    ", Product Name:  " + orset.getString(2));

orset.close();
```

DML with RETURNING has the following limitations:

- It cannot be used with batch update.
- It does not support streams.
- It is used under the covers for implementing auto-generated keys; therefore, these two features cannot be used in the same statement.
- The returned ResultSet objects do not support ResultSetMetaData.

7.4.6 Statement Caching

This section explains the concept of statement caching, the various flavors of statement caching supported by the Oracle JDBC drivers, and how to enable and disable these features.

In a Nutshell

JDBC 3.0 introduces statement pooling or statement caching. Statement caching consists of caching the cursors associated with statement objects. Statement caching improves performance by caching executable statements for search and reuse if there is a match.

Statement caching does the following:

- Eliminates the overhead of repeated cursor creation
- Prevents repeated statement parsing and creation
- Reuses metadata and/or data structures on the client side

A statement cache is associated with a physical connection (pooled or not); consequently, and contrary to what Java developers would expect, statement caching cannot cross the boundary of the physical connection. In other words, statement objects cannot be shared across physical connections; logical connections will share the same statement cache only if they share the same physical connection.

The Oracle JDBC drivers support both implicit and explicit statement caching schemes; both can be simultaneously enabled against the same cache.

Implicit Statement Caching

Implicit statement caching is Oracle's implementation of JDBC 3.0 statement pooling; it is managed by the driver and hence transparent to the application code (at least caching operations). The Oracle JDBC driver automatically caches the `PreparedStatement` or the `CallableStatement` objects upon the invocation of the `close()` method. As stated in section 7.4.2, a new cursor is created for each execution of a Statement object (i.e., the cursor is not maintained upon `Statement.close()`). On the other hand, for `PreparedStatements` (`OraclePreparedStatement`) and `CallableStatement` (`OracleCallableStatement`) objects, the cursors are kept after the closing of these objects and not recreated for each new execution of the prepared or callable statements.

Implicit statement caching is enabled using one of the two following approaches:

1. Invoke `((OracleConnection)conn).setImplicitCachingEn-abled(true);` on the connection object.

2. Set the `ImplicitCachingEnabled` property to true and invoke `OracleDataSource.getConnection()`.

    - `OracleDataSource.setImplicitCachingEnabled(true);`

    - `OracleDataSource.getConnection();`

    To check whether implicit statement caching has been enabled or not, use the following Boolean method: `getImplicitCachingEnabled();`

    The cache size—for both implicit and explicit statement caching—can be set:

    - Either at the data source level (for all pooled connections):

    ```
    // Set the statement cache size at the pooled connection
    // level
    ((OraclePooledConnection)pc).setStmtCacheSize(10);
    ```

    - Or at each pooled connection level:

    ```
    // Set & Get the statement cache size at the data source
    // level
    OracleConnectionCacheImpl ods =
            new OracleConnectionCacheImpl(ocpds);
    ods.setStmtCacheSize(12);
    ```

A cache entry is automatically allocated to a new SQL statement—if not already in the cache—upon the invocation of `preparedStatement()` and `prepareCall()` methods. The Oracle JDBC driver transparently searches the cache for a match using the following criteria:

- The SQL string must be identical.

- The statement type must be identical `PreparedStatement` or `CallableStatement`.

- The type of scrollable result sets `FORWARD-ONLY` or `SCROLLABLE` must be the same.

If a match is found, then the cached statement is returned; otherwise, a new statement is created and returned. When a cached statement is retrieved, its cursor and state are automatically reinitialized to their default values, while the metadata is preserved.

In either case, the statement, its cursor, and any associated states are cached upon the invocation of the `close()` method of the `Prepared-Statement` or `CallableStatement` object(s). Statement objects can be removed from the cache when the maximum cache size is reached using a Least Recently Used (LRU) algorithm.

The implicit statement cache is disabled:

- either by invoking `setImplicitCachingEnabled(false)` on the connection object
- or by setting the `ImplicitStatementCachingEnabled` property to false

The Implicit cache can be purged by invoking the `OracleConnection.purgeImplicitCache()` method on the connection object. It closes all of the implicitly cached statements in the cache, freeing the database cursors and removing all references to JDBC objects. It does not purge the explicitly cached statements.

A Complete Example: ImplStmtCache.java

```
/*
 *    Implicit Statement Caching
 *
 */
// import the java.sql package
import java.sql.*;
import javax.sql.*;
import oracle.jdbc.*;
import oracle.jdbc.pool.OracleDataSource;

class ImplStmtCache
{
 public static void main (String args [])
 throws SQLException
 {
  long  start;
  long end;
```

```
long elapsed;

String name = null;
OracleConnection conn = null;
OraclePreparedStatement pstmt = null;
OracleDataSource ods = new OracleDataSource();
// Set the URL (user name, and password)
String url = "jdbc:oracle:thin:scott/tiger@//localhost:1521/orcl";
ods.setURL(url);


String query = "select EMPNO, ENAME from EMP";
System.out.println("PredStmt is " + query);

//
// Phase 1 - NO caching
//
// Get a connection object
conn = (OracleConnection)ods.getConnection();
// Set the start time
   start = System.currentTimeMillis();
// Loop, prepare and execute the query 10 times
for (int i = 1; i <= 10; i++) {
  pstmt = (OraclePreparedStatement)conn.prepareStatement (query);
  ResultSet rset = pstmt.executeQuery ();
  // Do not process ResultSet
  rset.close();
  pstmt.close();

}
// Set the End time
   end = System.currentTimeMillis();
   elapsed = end - start ;
// Print the time taken to prepare and execute query
   System.out.println
    (" Time to prepare and execute NON CACHED query 10 times is: " +
     elapsed);
// Close the connection
conn.close();
//
// Phase 2 - Implicit Statement Caching
```

```
//
// Get a connection object
    conn = (OracleConnection)ods.getConnection();
// Set the Statement cache size to 1
    conn.setStatementCacheSize(1);
// Enable Implicit caching
    conn.setImplicitCachingEnabled(true);
// Set the start time
    start = System.currentTimeMillis();
// Loop, prepare and execute the query 10 times
for (int i = 1; i <= 10; i++) {
    pstmt = (OraclePreparedStatement)conn.prepareStatement (query);
    ResultSet rset = pstmt.executeQuery ();
// Do not process ResultSet
    rset.close();
    pstmt.close();
 }
// Set the End time
    end = System.currentTimeMillis();
    elapsed = end - start;
// Print the time taken to prepare and execute query
    System.out.println
        (" Time to prepare and execute CACHED query 10 times is: "
        + elapsed);
// Close the connection
  conn.close();
 }
}


C:\>javac ImplStmtCache.java
C:\>java ImplStmtCache
PredStmt is select EMPNO, ENAME from EMP
 Time to prepare and execute NON CACHED query 10 times is: 611
 Time to prepare and execute CACHED query 10 times is: 20
```

Explicit Statement Caching

Unlike implicit statement caching, explicit statement caching is managed by the application, because it requires explicit instructions for caching and searching, using a user-defined key.

To enable explicit statement caching, you must first set the application cache size (note that the same cache can be shared by both implicit and explicit statement caching schemes, but it needs to be set only once) by:

- Either by invoking `setStatementCacheSize()` on the physical connection:

```
((OracleConnection)conn).setStatementCacheSize(20);
```

- Or by invoking `OracleDatasource.setMaxStatements()` (a size of zero disables the statement caching)

Explicit statement caching is enabled by invoking `setExplicitStatementCaching(true)` on the connection object.

Determining whether explicit caching is enabled is achieved by invoking `getExplicitStatementCachingEnabled()`, which returns `true` if explicit caching is enabled, or `false` otherwise.

A cache entry is allocated to a new SQL statement—if not already in the cache—upon the invocation of `createStatement()`, `prepareStatement()`, and `prepareCall()` methods. It is up to the application to search the cache for a match using the user-defined key (a Java string) specified during the `closeWithKey(String)`, using the following:

- `getStatementWithKey(String);`
- `getCallWithKey(String);`

If a match is found, then the cached statement with the parameter and metadata defined in the last usage is returned; otherwise, a `null` value (not an exception) is returned to the application. Statement objects can be removed from the cache when the maximum cache size is reached using a Least Recently Used (LRU) algorithm.

The statements are cached upon the invocation of `closeWithKey(String)`.

```
pstmt.closeWithKey("Stmt1");
```

Explicit statement caching is disabled by invoking the `setExplicit-StatementCaching(false)` method on the connection object.

The explicit cache can be purged by invoking the `OracleConnection.purgeExplicitCache ()` method on the connection object.

It closes all of the explicitly cached statements in the cache, freeing the database cursors and removing all references to JDBC objects. It does not purge the implicitly cached statements.

A Complete Example: ExplStmtCache.java

```
/*
 *    Explicit Statement Caching
 *
 */
// import the java.sql package
import java.sql.*;
import javax.sql.*;
import oracle.jdbc.*;
import oracle.jdbc.pool.OracleDataSource;

class ExplStmtCache
{
 public static void main (String args [])
 throws SQLException
 {
   long  start;
   long end;
   long elapsed;

   String name = null;
   OracleConnection conn = null;
   OraclePreparedStatement pstmt = null;
   OracleDataSource ods = new OracleDataSource();
   // Set the URL (user name, and password)
   String url = "jdbc:oracle:thin:scott/tiger@//localhost:1521/orcl";
   ods.setURL(url);
   String query = "select EMPNO, ENAME from EMP";
   System.out.println("PredStmt is " + query);


   //
   // Phase 1 - NO caching
```

```
//
// Get a connection object
conn = (OracleConnection)ods.getConnection();
// Set the start time
   start = System.currentTimeMillis();
// Loop, prepare and execute the query 10 times
for (int i = 1; i <= 10; i++) {
  pstmt = (OraclePreparedStatement)conn.prepareStatement(query);
  ResultSet rset = pstmt.executeQuery ();
  // Do not process ResultSet
  rset.close();
  pstmt.close();
 }
  // Set the End time
  end = System.currentTimeMillis();
  elapsed = end - start ;
  // Print the time taken to prepare and execute query
  System.out.println
  (" Time to prepare and execute NON CACHED query 10 times is : "
  + elapsed);

// Close the connection
conn.close();
//
// Phase 2 - Explicit Statement Caching
//
// Get a connection object
   conn = (OracleConnection)ods.getConnection();
// Set the Statement cache size to 1
   conn.setStatementCacheSize(1);

// Enable Explicit caching
   conn.setExplicitCachingEnabled(true);

// Set the start time
   start = System.currentTimeMillis();
// Loop, search/find or prepare and execute the query 10 times

for (int i = 1; i <= 10; i++) {
// Look first in the cache
  pstmt =
(OraclePreparedStatement)conn.getStatementWithKey("Stmt1");
```

```
    if (pstmt == null) { //If not in the cache then prepare again
        pstmt = (OraclePreparedStatement)conn.prepareStatement(query);
    }

    ResultSet rset = pstmt.executeQuery ();
    // Do not process ResultSet
    rset.close();
    pstmt.closeWithKey("Stmt1"); ;
    }
  // Set the End time
    end = System.currentTimeMillis();
    elapsed = end - start;
  // Print the time taken to prepare and execute query
    System.out.println
      (" Time to prepare and execute EXPLICITLY CACHED query 10 times
is " +
        elapsed);
  // Close the connection
    conn.close();
  }
}
```

```
C:\>javac ExplStmtCache.java
C:\>java ExplStmtCache
PredStmt is select EMPNO, ENAME from EMP
 Time to prepare and execute NON CACHED query 10 times is : 581
 Time to prepare and execute EXPLICITLY CACHED query 10 times is 10
```

7.4.7 DML Batching

The JDBC 2.0 specification defines "batch updates" as the ability to group and send a batch of DML operations to the database, in one roundtrip, resulting in optimized performance. The Oracle JDBC drivers implement the standard batch update and furnish in addition Oracle's own "update batching."

Standard Batch Updates

In a nutshell, the application manually builds up the batch using the addBatch() method and then explicitly sends the array of operations by invoking the executeBatch() method. All statement types, including Statement, PreparedStatement, and CallableStatement (without OUT parameter), are supported. However, in the Oracle JDBC implementation, only `PreparedStatement` will see a performance benefit.

Example I

```
PreparedStmt pstmt =
       conn.preparedStatement("INSERT INTO PRODUCT VALUES (?,
?)");

pstmt.setInt(1, 1234);
pstmt.setString(2, "Product #1");
pstmt.addBatch();
...
pstmt.setInt(1, 1234);
pstmt.setString(2, "Product #1");
pstmt.addBatch();
...
pstmt.setInt(1, 1234);
pstmt.setString(2, "Product #1");
pstmt.addBatch();
...
int [] batchCount = pstmt.executeBatch();
```

Example 2: syntax

```
Statement stmt = conn.createStatement();
...
// First batch set
stmt.addBatch("INSERT INTO product VALUES( 1111, 'Prod1')");
stmt.addBatch("INSERT INTO product VALUES( 2222, 'Prod2')");
stmt.addBatch("INSERT INTO product VALUES( 3333, 'Prod3')");
stmt.addBatch("INSERT INTO product VALUES( 4444, 'Prod4')");
executeBatch();

//Second batch set
stmt.addBatch("insert into product values (5555,'Prod5')");
stmt.executeBatch();

// Explicit Commit
conn.commit();
ps.close();
```

There is no defined batch size; it is up to the application to explicitly send the batched statements to the database.

An array of int is returned to the caller; according to the JDBC specification, each entry in the array may have the following values:

1. If the value of an array entry is greater than or equal to zero, then the batch element was processed successfully and the value is an update count indicating the number of rows in the database that were affected by the element's execution.

2. A value of minus 2 indicates that an element was processed successfully, but the number of affected rows is unknown.

   For PreparedStatement, upon successful execution, the Oracle JDBC implementation conforms to option 2, because the Oracle database does not currently return the number of rows updated per each array element (i.e., update count). Option 1 could be implemented at the cost of additional roundtrips.

For the generic/plain Statement, upon successful execution, the batch array contains the number of rows affected by each operation, which corresponds to option 1.

For CallableStatement, upon successful execution, the RDBMS always returns −1.

Stream types (LOB) are not supported as bind values.

Oracle Update Batching

In a nutshell, the application manually builds up the batch using the executeUpdate() method (similar to addBatch() method); however, unlike the standard update batching, Oracle's update batching automatically sends the batch set to the RDBMS when the number of entries in the array reaches a defined batch value (defaults to 1). In other words, executeUpdate() usually queues the operations for later shipment—in this case, it returns 0—but also triggers the shipment to the RDBMS when the batch value is reached—in this case, it returns the total number of rows affected by the batch processing (all operations in the array).

Only PreparedStatements are supported. Batch values between 5 and 30 (typically 10) yield the best performance; the value is specified using:

- setDefaultExecuteBatch(value) on the connection object for all statements

- setExecuteBatch(value) for a PreparedStatement

Similar to the executeBatch() method in the standard update batching, the sendBatch() method on PreparedStatement may be used to manually ship the array of operations to the RDBMS; it returns the total number of rows affected by the batch processing. The Oracle *update batch* also ships the array to the RDBMS on statement close, connection close, and commit operations.

The getDefaultExecuteBatch() method on OracleConnection returns the batch value of a connection instance. The getExecuteBatch() method on OraclePreparedStatement returns the batch value of a specific statement.

Example:

```
Connection conn = ds.getConnection();

//Always disable auto-commit when using update batching
conn.setAutoCommit(false);


PreparedStmt pstmt =
      conn.preparedStatement("INSERT INTO PRODUCT VALUES (?,
?)");

//Set Batch value for this statement to 3
((OraclePreparedStatement)pstmt).setExecuteBatch (3);

pstmt.setInt(1, 1234);
pstmt.setString(2, "Product #1");
pstmt.executeUpdate();
...
pstmt.setInt(1, 1234);
pstmt.setString(2, "Product #1");
pstmt.executeUpdate();


...
pstmt.setInt(1, 1234);
```

```
pstmt.setString(2, "Product #1");
pstmt.executeUpdate(); // This one triggers the shipment

conn.commit();  // Explicit Commit
pstmt.close();
```

Note: Don't mix the standard and Oracle update batching.

This concludes this chapter on the essentials of JDBC connections and statements. The next chapter addresses data access and retrieval, including, access and conversion (mapping) of various data types, result sets, rowsets, and much more.

8

SQL Data Access and Manipulation

In the previous chapter, we covered the essentials of JDBC programming, including connect string URL, data sources, connections, and statements. In this chapter, we'll look at the JDBC API for accessing and manipulating SQL data, including the key metadata, the built-in SQL data types, LOBs, user-defined collections, Oracle object data types, XML type, Result Sets (scrollable, updatable), and rowsets (`JdbcRowSet`, `CachedRowSet`, `WebRowSet`, `JoinRowSet` and `FilteredRowSet`).

8.1 Key Metadata in JDBC

JDBC metadata is an umbrella name for a set of metadata objects that provide information about the database entities, including the database itself (`DatabaseMetaData`); the parameters of a PreparedStatement (`Paramater-MetaData`); the ResultSet (`ResultSetMetaData`); the number, name, and type of each column; and so on. Let's look at the main standard JDBC metadata as well as Oracle extensions.

8.1.1 DatabaseMetaData: OracleDatabaseMetaData

The `DatabaseMetaData` object contains more than 100 methods, which allow you to dynamically (i.e., at runtime) find out the environment of the database your JDBC application is running against, as well as the supported features. The `oracle.jdbc.OracleDatabaseMetaData` class implements the standard `java.sql.DatabaseMetaData` interface. You need first to get the `DatabaseMetaData` object from the connection object and then invoke its methods. The method names are self-explanatory; each method returns either a metadata or whether or not the database supports such feature/capability.

```
DatabaseMetaData dbmd = conn.getMetaData ();

System.out.println("Database Name? " +
                dbmd.getDatabaseProductName() );

System.out.println("Database Version? " +
                dbmd.getDatabaseProductVersion() );

System.out.println("Default Transaction Isolation?  " +
                dbmd.getDefaultTransactionIsolation() );

System.out.println("Supports Savepoints?  " +
                dbmd.supportsSavepoints());

System.out.println("Driver Name? " +
                dbmd.getDriverName() );
System.out.println("Driver Major Version? " +
                dbmd.getDriverMajorVersion() );
System.out.println("DriverVersion? " +
                dbmd.getDriverVersion() );
System.out.println("Driver Minor Version? " +
                dbmd.getDriverMinorVersion() );
...
```

See the `java.sql.DatabaseMetaData` javadoc for a complete list of standard methods.

In addition, this class also furnishes Oracle's JDBC specific extensions; a few of these are highlighted as follows:

```
OracleDatabaseMetaData odbmd = new
oracle.jdbc.OracleDatabaseMetaData((OracleConnection)conn);

System.out.println("Supports Statement Pooling() = " +
                odbmd.supportsStatementPooling());
System.out.println ("locatorsUpdateCopy() = " +
                odbmd.locatorsUpdateCopy());
System.out.println("Supports Auto GeneratedKeys is : " +
                odbmd.supportsGetGeneratedKeys());
...
```

See the `oracle.jdbc.OracleDatabaseMetaData` javadoc for a complete list of methods.

8.1.2 ResultSetMetaData: OracleResultSetMetaData

The Result Set metadata interface allows you to dynamically (i.e., at runtime) find the number of columns in a result set (covered later), the table's catalog name, the name of each column, its SQL type, whether it is NULLable, and so on. The standard `java.sql.ResultSetMetaData` interface furnishes the following methods: `getCatalogName`, `getColumnClassName`, `getColumnCount`, `getColumnDisplaySize`, `getColumnLabel`, `getColumnName`, `getColumnType`, `getColumnTypeName`, `getPrecision`, `getScale`, `getSchemaName`, `getTableName`, `isAutoIncrement`, `isCaseSensitive`, `isCurrency`, `isDefinitelyWritable`, `isNullable`, `isReadOnly`, `isSearchable`, `isSigned`, `isWritable`.

The `oracle.jdbc.OracleResultSetMetaData` interface extends the standard `java.sql.ResultSetMetaData` interface and furnishes the `isNCHAR` method, which returns true if the column is of type NCHAR/NVARCHAR/NCLOB, and false otherwise.

The Oracle JDBC implements the `OracleResultSetMetaData` interface but the `getSchemaName()` and `getTableName()` methods. The `ResultSetMetaData` object is returned upon the invocation of the `getMetaData()` method on a `ResultSet` object, and then its methods can be invoked as follows:

```
pstmt =
    conn.prepareStatement("SELECT ename, empid, job FROM
emp");
rs = (OracleResultSet)pstmt.executeQuery ();

ResultSetMetaData rsmd = rs.getMetaData ();

rsmtdt.getColumnCount();
rsmtdt.getColumnType (i);
rsmd.getColumnTypeName (i);
rsmtdt.getPrecision(i);
...
rsmtdt.isAutoIncrement(i);
rsmtdt.isNullable(i);
```

Listing 8.1 retrieves the `ResultSetMetaData` object and then prints the total column count, and for each column prints the column name, the column type, and the column value (with provision for dealing with NCHAR, NVARCHAR, and NCLOB data types).

Listing 8.1   *Result7MtDt.java*

```
================================

import java.sql.*;
import oracle.jdbc.*;
import oracle.sql.*;
import oracle.jdbc.pool.OracleDataSource;
import java.io.*;

public class Result7MtDt
{
  public static void main (String args [])throws SQLException
  {
    try
    {
    // Create an OracleDataSource
    OracleDataSource ods = new OracleDataSource();
    // Set the URL (user name, and password)
    String url =
            "jdbc:oracle:thin:scott/tiger@//localhost:1521/orcl";
    ods.setURL(url);

    // Retrieve a connection
    Connection conn = ods.getConnection();
    // Create a Statement
    Statement stmt = conn.createStatement();
    // Get a Result Set object
    ResultSet rs =
        stmt.executeQuery("select * from EMP Where ename = 'SMITH'");
    while(rs.next()){
      ResultSetMetaData mtdt = rs.getMetaData ();
      int count = mtdt.getColumnCount ();
      System.out.println("Column Count = " + count);
      for (int i=1; i<=count; i++){
            String colName = mtdt.getColumnName(i);
          String colType = mtdt.getColumnTypeName(i);
```

```
            System.out.println("*** Col. name = " + colName +
                                ", col type = " + colType);
            printCol(mtdt,rs,i);
            }
          }

    rs.close();
    stmt.close();
    conn.close();
    } catch (SQLException sqle) {
   System.out.println(sqle.getMessage());
   sqle.printStackTrace();
    }
}// end main

private static void
          printCol(ResultSetMetaData mtdt, ResultSet rs, int col)
{
 try
 {
  String str = rs.getString(col);
  if(!((OracleResultSetMetaData)mtdt).isNCHAR(col))
  {
    //The column is not of type NCHAR/NVARCHAR/NCLOB
    System.out.println("Col. length = "+ str.length() +
                       ",rs.getString(" + col +")=" + str);
  }
  else
  {
    //The column is of type NCHAR/NVARCHAR/NCLOB
    char[] bytarr = str.toCharArray();
    if (bytarr == null)
      System.out.println("<Null char array!>");
    else
    {
     int n = bytarr.length;
       for (int i = 0; i < n; i++)
       System.out.println("\\u" +
                   Integer.toHexString(bytarr [i] & 0xFFFF));
    }
  }
```

```
  } catch (Exception e) {} //Note NULL column exception ignored
} //end printCol

} // end Result7MtDt

C:\>javac Result7MtDt.java

C:\>Java Result7MtDt

Column Count = 8
*** Col. name = EMPNO, col type = NUMBER
Col. length = 4,rs.getString(1)=7369
*** Col. name = ENAME, col type = VARCHAR2
Col. length = 5,rs.getString(2)=SMITH
*** Col. name = JOB, col type = VARCHAR2
Col. length = 5,rs.getString(3)=CLERK
*** Col. name = MGR, col type = NUMBER
Col. length = 4,rs.getString(4)=7902
*** Col. name = HIREDATE, col type = DATE
Col. length = 21,rs.getString(5)=1980-12-17 00:00:00.0
*** Col. name = SAL, col type = NUMBER
Col. length = 3,rs.getString(6)=800
*** Col. name = COMM, col type = NUMBER
*** Col. name = DEPTNO, col type = NUMBER
Col. length = 2,rs.getString(8)=20
```

8.1.3 ParameterMetaData

ParameterMetaData is a new interface in JDBC 3.0, which allows you to find the types and properties of the parameters in a PreparedStatement object. In Oracle Database 10*g* Release 2, Oracle Database 10*g* Release 10.1.0.3, and Oracle 9*i* Release 9.2.0.6 the JDBC drivers furnish a limited implementation of the standard java.sql.ParameterMetaData interface for JDK 1.4.x and above; only getParameterCount()is supported, while most of the other methods, such as getParameterType() and getParameterClassName(), currently throw an "Unsupported Operation" exception. An application running on a pre-JDK 1.4 JVM must use the oracle.jdbc.OracleParameterMetaData.interface, which is functionally identical to the java.sql.ParameterMetaData.

Listing 8.2 gets a `PreparedStatement` object, then a `Parameter-`
`Metadata` from it, and finally invokes the `getParameterCount()` method
on the `ParameterMetaData` object.

Listing 8.2   *ParamMtDt.java*

```
================================

import java.sql.*;
import oracle.jdbc.*;
import oracle.sql.*;
import oracle.jdbc.pool.OracleDataSource;
import java.io.*;
/*
 * 1 get the PreparedStatement object
 * 2 get the getParameterMetaData
 * 3 Invoke getParameterCount() on the parametermetadata
 *
 */

public class ParamMtDt
{
  public static void main (String args [])throws SQLException
  {
   ParameterMetaData pmd=null;
   ResultSetMetaData rsmd=null;
   String stmt = "insert into EMP values (?,?,?,?,?,?,?,?)";
   // Create an OracleDataSource
   OracleDataSource ods = new OracleDataSource();
   // Set the URL (user name, and password)
   // String url = "jdbc:oracle:thin:scott/tiger@//localhost:5521/
orcl";
   String url = "jdbc:oracle:thin:scott/tiger@tns_alias";

   ods.setURL(url);
   // Retrieve a connection
       Connection conn = ods.getConnection();
   // get the PreparedStatement objects
   PreparedStatement pstmt = conn.prepareStatement(stmt);
   try
   {
      pmd = pstmt.getParameterMetaData(); // get ParameterMetaData
```

```
        // get the Number of Parameters
        System.out.println(" Number of Parameters: " +
            pmd.getParameterCount());
    } catch(SQLException sqle){
        System.out.println("SQL Exception" + sqle.getMessage());
        sqle.printStackTrace();
    }

    pstmt.close();

  }
}


$ javac ParamMtDt.java
$ java -Doracle.net.tns_admin=$TNS_ADMIN ParamMtDt

Number of Parameters: 8
```

8.1.4   StructMetaData

The `java.sql.Struct` and `oracle.sql.STRUCT` are covered later in section 8.2. The `oracle.jdbc.StructMetaData` interface lets you get the metadata of structured column types (i.e., user-defined types) through the following methods:

- `getAttributeJavaName(int   column)`: Gets a `JAVA_STRUCT` attribute's external name
- `getOracleColumnClassName(int column)`: Returns the fully qualified name of the datum class
- `isInherited`(int column): Indicates whether the attribute is inherited from its supertype
- `getLocalColumnCount()`: Gets the number of local attributes (i.e., not inherited from supertype)

In addition, StructMetaData inherits the following methods from the java.sql.ResultSetMetaData interface: getCatalogName, getColumnClassName, getColumnCount, getColumnDisplaySize, getColumnLabel, getColumnName, getColumnType, getColumnTypeName, getPrecision, getScale, getSchemaName, getTableName, isAutoIncrement, isCaseSensitive, isCurrency, isDefinitelyWritable, isNullable, isReadOnly, isSearchable, isSigned, isWritable.

It also inherits the isNCHAR() method from the oracle.jdbc.OracleResultSetMetaData interface.

Assume a user-defined type STUDENT:

```
create type student as object (id number, name varchar2(20),
height float, dob date, picture BLOB, address1 address_t,
address2 ref address_t)
```

A JDBC program can retrieve the following metadata:

```
StructDescriptor strdesc =
StructDescriptor.createDescriptor("STUDENT", conn);
StructMetaData strmd = (StructMetaData)strdesc.getMetaData();

int count = strmd.getLocalColumnCount();
for(int i = 1; i < count; i++) {
  strmd.getColumnType (i);
  strmd.getColumnTypeName (i);
  strmd.getOracleColumnClassName (i);
  strmd.isSearchable (i);
}
```

8.2 Manipulating Oracle Data Types with JDBC

This section discusses the methods for storing and persisting Java types, standard JDBC types, Oracle JDBC types, as well as methods for manipulating SQL types, PL/SQL types, user-defined object types, user-defined collections, and references in Java.

The oracle.sql.* package contains the oracle.sql.XXX wrapper classes (i.e., the oracle.sql.CHAR wraps the SQL CHAR type). The oracle.jdbc.* package contains the OracleStatement, OraclePreparedStatement, OracleCallableStatement, and OracleResultSet classes, which furnish the corresponding getXXX(), setXXX(), and updateXXX(), as well as the standard setxxx(), getxxx(), and updatexxx() methods defined in the standard Statement, PreparedStatement, CallableStatement, and ResultSet interfaces. Underneath the API, as shown in Figure 8.1, the Oracle JDBC drivers use the following internal conversion mechanisms for storing Java data and retrieving SQL data:

- A set of *binders* for converting[1] the Java parameters into SQL types. Underneath the setXXX and updateXXX methods, these binders store the target data type and the payload (i.e., the UCS2 bytes) into staging JDBC buffers; then upon the execution of the statement, the staging buffer is sent to the server (once for all parameters). The operation succeeds if the server can convert the payload into the target data type, but otherwise it fails.

- A set of *accessors* for converting the SQL types into Java/JDBC types. Underneath the getXXX methods, these accessors know how to turn Java byte arrays (i.e., bytes[ ]) and/or Java char arrays (i.e., char [ ]) into values.

- A set of *character set converters* for converting UCS2 bytes (the standard Java character set) into the database character set; for JDBC-OCI, this step is perfomed in the OCI layer.

- For data that can be streamed over the wire, such as LOBs, LONG, and LONG RAW types, the *stream binding* approach bypasses the JDBC staging buffers.

In 10*g*, these conversion functions have been rewritten (as part of the entire rearchitecture of the drivers) and account largely for the huge performance improvement.

Example:

Assume a table T1 (x number, y varchar2[120], z clob), and the following prepared statement:

```
pstmt = conn.prepareStatement( "insert into T1 values( ?, ?, ?
)" );
The following setXXX methods perform  the binding as described
above.
pstmt.setInt( 1, 123 );
pstmt.setString( 2, "abcdefg" );
pstmt.setString( 3, "wxyz" );
pstmt.execute();
```

This code snippet utilizes *direct binding*, described in section 7.3.

---

1.   In fact, in 10g, the conversion happens in the server, so the binders only prepare all needed information.

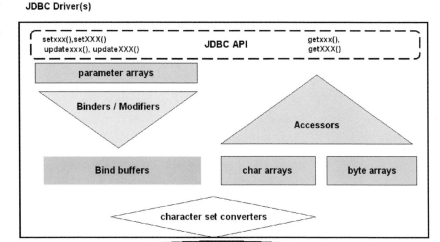

Figure 8.1
Conversion Mechanisms

The `oracle.sql` package contains the following Java classes that wrap the Oracle database SQL data types: NUMBER, CHAR, DATE, TIMESTAMP, TIMESTAMPTZ, TIMESTAMPLTZ, STRUCT, REF, ARRAY, BLOB, CLOB, BFILE, RAW, ROWID, and OPAQUE.[2]

These wrapper classes have the following features in common:

- To be subclasses of the `oracle.sql.Datum` class and inherit the following methods: `asciiStreamValue`, `bigDecimalValue`, `binaryStreamValue`, `booleanValue`, `byteValue`, `characterStreamValue`, `dateValue`, `doubleValue`, `equals`, `floatValue`, `getBytes`, `getLength`, `getStream`, `intValue`, `longValue`, `setBytes`, `setShareBytes`, `shareBytes`, `stringValue`, `timestampValue`, `timeValue`, etc.

- A set of constructors (not for all types) that take either the raw bytes or a Java type as input; the `getBytes` method returns the raw bytes as received from the database.

- Methods to convert SQL data into Java bytes (UCS2 character set)

---

2. There is no corresponding class for LONG, LONGRAW, and REF CURSOR.

- Direct access to the data in SQL format, which avoids the conversion in Java format
- Math operations on the data in SQL format, which avoids the loss of precision that can occur during the conversion between Java and SQL formats
- To implement the `java.sql.Struct` interface (i.e., `getAttributes()`, `getSQLTypeName()` methods)

Table 3.2 (duplicated here) illustrates the mapping between SQL or PL/SQL types and standard Java types or Oracle JDBC types.

SQL Types, and PL/SQL Types	Oracle JDBC Mapping[*]	Standard Java Mapping
CHAR, CHARACTER, LONG, STRING, VARCHAR, VARCHAR2	Oracle.sql.CHAR	java.lang.String, java.sql.Date, java.sql.Time,java.sql.Timestamp, java.lang.Byte, java.lang.Short, java.lang.Integer, java.lang.Long, java.sql.Float, java.lang.Double, java.math.BigDecimal, byte, short, int, long, float, double
NUMBER	Oracle.sql.NUMBER	java.lang.Byte, java.lang.Short, java.lang.Integer, java.lang.Long, java.sql.Float, java.lang.Double, java.math.BigDecimal, byte, short, int, long, float, double
DATE	Oracle.sql.DATE	java.sql.Date, java.sql.Time, java.sql.Timestamp,java.lang.String
NCHAR, NVARCHAR2	Oracle.sql.NCHAR (note 1)	n/a
RAW, LONG RAW	oracle.sql.RAW	byte[]

SQL Types, and PL/SQL Types	Oracle JDBC Mapping[*]	Standard Java Mapping
BINARY_INTEGER, NATURAL, NATURALN, PLS_INTEGER, POSITIVE, POSITIVEN, SIGNTYPE, INT, INTEGER	oracle.sql.NUMBER	int, java.lang.Integer
DEC, DECIMAL, NUMBER, NUMERIC	oracle.sql.NUMBER	java.math.BigDecimal
DOUBLE PRECISION, FLOAT	oracle.sql.NUMBER	Double, java.lang.Double
SMALLINT	oracle.sql.NUMBER	short, Int
REAL	oracle.sql.NUMBER	Float, Float
TIMESTAMP TIMESTAMP WITH TZ TIMESTAMP WITH LOCAL TZ	oracle.sql.DATE, oracle.sql.TIMESTAMP oracle.sql.TIMESTAMPTZ oracle.sql.TIMESTAMPLTZ	java.sql.Date, java.sql.Time, java.sql.Timestamp, byte[]
INTERVAL YEAR TO MONTH INTERVAL DAY TO SECOND	String (note 2)	oracle.sql.INTERVALDS oracle.sql.INTERVALYM String (note 2)
URITYPE DBURITYPE XDBURITYPE HTTPURITYPE	java.net.URL (note 3)	java.net.URL (note 3)
ROWID	oracle.sql.ROWID, oracle.sql.CHAR	java.sql.String
BOOLEAN	boolean (note 4)	boolean (note 4)
CLOB LOCATOR	oracle.sql.CLOB	java.sql.Clob
BLOB LOCATOR	oracle.sql.BLOB	java.sql.Blob
BFILE LOCATOR	oracle.sql.BFILE	n/a
NCLOB LOCATOR	oracle.sql.NCLOB (note 1)	n/a
User-defined objects types	oracle.sql.STRUCT, oracle.sql.ORAData	java.sql.Struct, java.sql.SqlData
User-defined collection	oracle.sql.ARRAY, oracle.sql.ORAData	java.sql.Array

SQL Types, and PL/SQL Types	Oracle JDBC Mapping[*]	Standard Java Mapping
OPAQUE types	oracle.sql.OPAQUE	Generated or predefined class (note 5)
RECORD types	Through mapping to SQL object type (note 5)	Through mapping to SQL object type (note 5)
Nested table, VARRAY	oracle.sql.ARRAY, oracle.sql.ORAData	java.sql.Array
Reference to SQL object type	oracle.sql.REF, oracle.sql.SQLRef, oracle.sql.ORAData	java.sql.Ref
REF CURSOR	oracle.jdbc.OracleResultSet	java.sql.ResultSet
Indexed-by tables	Through mapping to SQL collection (note 6)	Through mapping to SQL collection (note 6)
Scalar Indexed-by tables (numeric or character)	Through mapping to java array (note 7)	Through mapping to java array (note 7)
User-defined subtypes	Same as base type	Same as base type

[*]   The `oracle.sql.*` datatypes let you store and retrieve data without losing information/precision.

1. `oracle.sql.NCHAR`, `oracle.sql.NCLOB`, and `oracle.sql.NString` are not part of JDBC but are distributed with the JPublisher runtime (see Part IV) to represent the NCHAR form of `oracle.sql.CHAR`, `oracle.sql.CLOB`, and `java.lang.String`.

2. See JPublisher "JPublisher User Type Map and Default Type Map" in Part IV.

3. See JPublisher: SQL URI types, also known as *data links*, are mapped to `java.net.URL`.

4. Mapping of PL/SQL BOOLEAN to SQL NUMBER and Java `boolean` is defined in the default JPublisher type map.

5. Java classes implementing the `oracle.sql.ORAData` interface.

6. See JPublisher "Type Mapping Support for PL/SQL RECORD and Indexed-by Table Types" in Part IV of this book.

7. See JPublisher "Type Mapping Support for Scalar Indexed-by Tables" in Part IV of this book.

Tables 8.1 and 8.2 summarize the getXXX(), getxxx(), setXXX(), and setxxx() methods.

Table 8.1   *Return Types of getXXX Methods*

Method	Return Type (method signature)	Type of Returned Object
getArray	java.sql.Array	oracle.sql.ARRAY
getARRAY	oracle.sql.ARRAY	oracle.sql.ARRAY
getAsciiStream	java.io.InputStream	java.io.InputStream
getBfile	oracle.sql.BFILE	oracle.sql.BFILE
getBFILE	oracle.sql.BFILE	oracle.sql.BFILE
getBigDecimal	java.math.BigDecimal	java.math.BigDecimal
getBinaryStream	java.io.InputStream	java.io.InputStream
getBlob	java.sql.Blob	oracle.sql.BLOB
getBLOB	oracle.sql.BLOB	oracle.sql.BLOB
getBoolean	boolean	boolean
getByte	byte	byte
getBytes	byte[]	byte[]
getCHAR	oracle.sql.CHAR	oracle.sql.CHAR
getCharacterStream	java.io.Reader	java.io.Reader
getClob	java.sql.Clob	oracle.sql.CLOB
getCLOB	oracle.sql.CLOB	oracle.sql.CLOB
getDate	java.sql.Date	java.sql.Date
getDATE	oracle.sql.DATE	oracle.sql.DATE
getDouble	double	double
getFloat	float	float
getInt	int	int
getINTERVALDS	oracle.sql.INTERVALDS	oracle.sql.INTERVALDS
getINTERVALYM	oracle.sql.INTERVALYM	oracle.sql.INTERVALYM
getLong	long	long

Table 8.1　*Return Types of getXXX Methods (continued)*

Method	Return Type (method signature)	Type of Returned Object
getNUMBER	oracle.sql.NUMBER	oracle.sql.NUMBER
getOracleObject	oracle.sql.Datum	subclasses of oracle.sql.Datum
getRAW	oracle.sql.RAW	oracle.sql.RAW
getRef	java.sql.Ref	oracle.sql.REF
getREF	oracle.sql.REF	oracle.sql.REF
getROWID	oracle.sql.ROWID	oracle.sql.ROWID
getShort	short	short
getString	String	String
getSTRUCT	oracle.sql.STRUCT	oracle.sql.STRUCT.
getTime	java.sql.Time	java.sql.Time
getTimestamp	java.sql.Timestamp	java.sql.Timestamp
getTIMESTAMP	oracle.sql.TIMESTAMP	oracle.sql.TIMESTAMP
getTIMESTAMPTZ	oracle.sql.TIMESTAMPTZ	oracle.sql.TIMESTAMPTZ
getTIMESTAMPLTZ	oracle.sql.TIMESTAMPLTZ	oracle.sql.TIMESTAMPLTZ
getUnicodeStream	java.io.InputStream	java.io.InputStream
getURL	java.net.URL	java.net.URL

Table 8.2　*Input Types for setXXX Methods*

Method	Input Parameter Type
setArray	java.sql.Array
setARRAY	oracle.sql.ARRAY
setAsciiStream	java.io.InputStream
setBfile	oracle.sql.BFILE
setBFILE	oracle.sql.BFILE

Table 8.2   *Input Types for setXXX Methods (continued)*

Method	Input Parameter Type
setBigDecimal	BigDecimal
setBlob	java.sql.Blob
setBinaryStream	java.io.InputStream
setBinaryDouble	double or oracle.sql.BINARY_DOUBLE
setBinaryFloat	float or oracle.sql.BINARY_FLOAT
setBLOB	oracle.sql.BLOB
setBoolean	boolean
SetByte	byte
setBytes	byte[]
setCHAR	oracle.sql.CHAR
setCharacterStream	java.io.Reader
setClob	java.sql.Clob
setCLOB	oracle.sql.CLOB
setDate	java.sql.Date
setDATE	oracle.sql.DATE
setDouble	double
setFixedCHAR	java.lang.String
setFloat	float
setInt	int
setINTERVALDS	oracle.sql.INTERVALDS
setINTERVALYM	oracle.sql.INTERVALYM
setLong	long
setNUMBER	oracle.sql.NUMBER
setRAW	oracle.sql.RAW
setRef	java.sql.Ref

Table 8.2	*Input Types for setXXX Methods (continued)*

Method	Input Parameter Type
setREF	oracle.sql.REF
setROWID	oracle.sql.ROWID
setShort	short
setString	String
setSTRUCT	oracle.sql.STRUCT
setTime	java.sql.Time
setTimestamp	java.sql.Timestamp
setTIMESTAMP	oracle.sql.TIMESTAMP
setTIMESTAMPTZ	oracle.sql.TIMESTAMPTZ
setTIMESTAMPLTZ	oracle.sql.TIMESTAMPLTZ
setUnicodeStream	java.io.InputStream
setURL	java.net.URL

## 8.2.1	Manipulating SQL Null Data

When no value is assigned to a column during Insert/Update, the Oracle database automatically and by default assigns a NULL value, unless the target column has been declared NOT NULL; in this case, a value must be assigned to it. As summarized in Table 3.3, primitive Java types such as boolean, byte, short, int, long, float, and double cannot represent or retrieve SQL NULL columns. However, the corresponding reference Java types, also called *wrapper classes,* including java.lang.Boolean, java.lang.Byte, java.lang.short, java.lang.Integer, java.lang.Long, java.lang.Float, and java.lang.Double, must be used to map table columns that may return SQL NULL. These wrapper classes furnish getters and setters methods (see the java.lang package in any Java book for more details). As illustrated in the following code snippet, the combination of getters methods and wasNull() method of ResultSets allows you to determine if the retrieved value was Null and deal with it.

```
int deptno = rset.getInt("deptno");
if (rset.wasNull()) {
      … // Deal with null value
}
```

Conversely, the standard `PreparedStatement` method `setNull ()` and `OraclePreparedStatement setNullAtName()` methods can be used to set a parameter to `SQL NULL`.

Signatures:

- `setNull(int index, int sqlType);`
- `setNull(int index, int sqlType, String sql_name);`

Examples:

- `psmt.setNull(1, OracleTypes.FIXED_CHAR);`
- `pstmt.setNull(1, java.sql.Types.VARCHAR);`
- `pstmt.setNull(1, OracleTypes.NUMERIC);`
- `pstmt.setNull(1, OracleTypes.STRUCT, "ADDRESS");`

8.2.2 Manipulating Character Data Types

CHAR, CHAR(n), CHAR(n BYTE), CHAR(n CHAR)

`SQL CHAR` types are fixed-length character data of maximum 2,000 bytes or characters and minimum 1 byte or character. If you insert a value that is shorter than the specified column length, Oracle will blank-pad to match the length. The Oracle JDBC furnishes the `oracle.sql.CHAR` wrapper class and the corresponding `getCHAR()`, `setCHAR()`, `setCHARAtName`, and `updateCHAR()` methods in `OraclePreparedStatement`, `OracleCallableStatement`, and `OracleResultSet` classes. The `oracle.sql.CHAR` class furnishes `getString()`, `toString()`, and `getStringWithReplacement()` methods for converting character data into Java strings.

As Table 3.2 indicates, a `CHAR` column can also be mapped to and from the following standard Java types using the corresponding `setxxx()`, `updatexxx()`, and `getxxx()` methods defined in `PreparedStatement`, `CallableStatement`, and `ResultSet` interfaces: `java.lang.String`, `java.sql.Date`, `java.sql.Time`, `java.sql.Timestamp`, `java.lang.Byte`, `java.lang.Short`, `java.lang.Integer`, `java.lang.Long`, `java.sql.Float`, `java.lang.Double`, `java.math.BigDecimal`, `byte`, `short`, `int`, `long`, `float`, and `double`.

The following code snippet excerpted from the complete code sample in Chapter 3 illustrates retrieving and updating CHAR columns:

```
/*
 * Update SQL CHAR column with oracle.sql.CHAR
 */
  OraclePreparedStatement ops = (OraclePreparedStatement)
    conn.prepareStatement("UPDATE TypesTab SET xchar = ?");
  ops.setCHAR (1, c);
  ops.execute();
  ops.close();



 /*
  * Retrieve SQL CHAR column as oracle.sq.CHAR
  */
  OracleStatement ostmt = (OracleStatement)
conn.createStatement();
    String ochar = null;
    OracleResultSet ors =
     (OracleResultSet) ostmt.executeQuery("SELECT xchar FROM
TypesTab");
    while (ors.next())
    {
      ochar = ors.getString(1);
    }
    ostmt.close();
    // construct an oracle.sql.CHAR object
    return new CHAR(ochar, null);
```

Because of the automatic blank-padding of CHAR columns, setCHAR() might not give the right result when comparing a CHAR column with character data in a WHERE clause; use the setFixedCHAR() method of the OraclePreparedStatement object instead.

VARCHAR2 (n), VARCHAR2(n BYTE), VARCHAR2 (n CHAR)

The SQL VARCHAR2 data type defines a variable-length (nonblank-padded) character data type. The size, which is between 1 and 4,000, must be specified. There is no oracle.sql.VARCHAR2 class; as Table 3.2 indicates, the Oracle JDBC maps SQL VARCHAR2 to and from oracle.sql.CHAR, java.lang.String, java.sql.Date, java.sql.Time, java.sql.Timestamp, java.lang.Byte, java.lang.Short, java.lang.Integer, java.lang.Long, java.sql.Float, java.lang.Double, java.math.BigDecimal, byte, short, int, long, float, and double.

Apart from setFixedCHAR, the same methods as CHAR (i.e., setString, getString, etc.) apply for manipulating VARCHAR.

VARCHAR2 (as well as CHAR) columns can also be streamed using getAsciiStream by redefining it as a LONGVARCHAR using defineColumn-Type of OracleStatement. In fact, the data is fetched into a staging buffer, from which getAsciiStream returns an InputStream.

Assume a database with a UTF-8 character set, a VARCHAR2(4000) column, and the following code snippet:

```
char[] ch = new char[4000];
// fill up ch[1..4000] = 'a'
setString (1, new String (ch));
```

- Pre-10*g* JDBC-Thin sends the actual byte length after conversion (i.e., 4,000 bytes) to the server and lets you bind up to 4000 ASCII characters (single-byte characters) against such a column.

- 10*g* JDBC-Thin sends the predicted max length after conversion (i.e., 4,000 × 3 = 12,000 bytes) to the server; as a result, the server throws ORA-1461 because you cannot insert 12,000 bytes in VARCHAR2(4000).

- Using 10*g* JDBC and setting the retain_v9_bind_behavior_string flag to true tells JDBC that the byte length after conversion will always be less than 4,000. JDBC sends 4,000 to the server, thus simulating the Oracle 9i JDBC behavior for ASCII binding to a UTF-8 database.

NCHAR, NCHAR(n), NVARCHAR2 (n)

NCHAR specifies a fixed-length Unicode data type; the actual maximum column length (2,000 bytes) is determined by the width (in bytes) of the national character set, defined at database creation.

NVARCHAR specifies a variable-length Unicode data type; the maximum size (less or equal to 4,000 bytes) must be specified.

JDBC does not currently offer standard APIs to deal with NCHAR/NVARCHAR data types in a way different from CHAR. The application must unwrap the connection to get an Oracle Connection (if not already) in order to map to and from `oracle.sql.NCHAR`.

The `OracleConnection` provides an `isNCHAR` method for checking if the column is of type `NCHAR`, and the `OraclePreparedStatement` object furnishes the `setFormOfUse` method to direct JDBC to treat the column as either SQL `NCHAR` or SQL `CHAR`.

```
pstmt.setFormOfUse(2, FORM_NCHAR); // NCHAR column
pstmt.setString(2, UnicodeString);
```

If the system property `oracle.jdbc.defaultNChar` or the connection property `defaultNChar` is set to `true` (default is `false`), then there is no need to specify `setFormOfUse`. JDBC treats all character columns as being national language (the database will convert all `CHAR` data into `NCHAR`/`NVARCHAR2`).

Notes:

- Pre-10.2 JDBC does not support **NCHAR** literal (n'...') containing Unicode characters that cannot be represented in the database character set.

- Using 10.2 JDBC against 10.2 RDBMS, **NCHAR** literals (n'...') are converted to Unicode literals (u'...'); non-ASCII characters are converted to their corresponding Unicode escape sequence.

- Using 10.2 JDBC against pre-10.2 RDBMS, NCHAR literals (n'...') are not converted and generate undetermined content for characters that cannot be represented in the database character set.

The upcoming JDBC 4.0 specification is said to provide standard support for NCHAR, NVARCHAR, LONGNVARCHAR, and NCLOB data types.

8.2.3   Oracle JDBC Support for Number Data Types

NUMBER , NUMBER(p), NUMBER(p, s)

SQL NUMBER columns store positive and negative fixed numbers with absolute values from 1.0×10^{-130} to 1.0×10^{126} (but not including 1.0×10^{126} itself). A SQL NUMBER data types represent numbers with precision p between 1 and 38 and scale s between -84 and 127.

Examples:

- A NUMBER with p = 4 stores values between −9999 and +9999.

- A NUMBER with p = 5 stored values between −99999 and +99999.

The Oracle JDBC furnishes the `oracle.sql.NUMBER` wrapper class and the corresponding `getNUMBER()`, `setNUMBER()`, `setNUMBERAtName`, and `updateNUMBER()` methods in `OraclePreparedStatement`, `OracleCallableStatement`, and `OracleResultSet` classes. In fact, the `oracle.sql.NUMBER` is a wrapper class for all ANSI SQL92 data types, including `INTEGER`, `SMALLINT`, `NUMERIC`, `DECIMAL`, `FLOAT`, `DOUBLE`, and `REAL`.

Depending on the Java type that you use to receive the data, you may lose the precision information, `oracle.sql.NUMBER` preserves the precision.

Per Table 3.2, a SQL `NUMBER` can also be mapped to and from the following standard Java types using the corresponding `setxxx()`, `updatexxx()`, and `getxxx()` methods defined in `PreparedStatement`, `CallableStatement`, and `ResultSet` interfaces: `java.lang.Byte`, `java.lang.Short`, `java.lang.Integer`, `java.lang.Long`, `java.sql.Float`, `java.lang.Double`, `java.math.BigDecimal`, `byte`, `short`, `int`, `long`, `float`, and `double`.

Here is a code snippet excerpted from Listing 3.5:

```
/*
 * Update SQL NUMBER column with java.lang.Integer
 */
  PreparedStatement ps =
    conn.prepareStatement("UPDATE TypesTab SET num = ?");
  int n = x.intValue();
  ps.setInt (1, n);
  ps.execute();
  ps.close();

/*
 * Retrieve SQL NUMBER column as int
 */
  Statement stmt = conn.createStatement();
  int n = 0;
```

```
    ResultSet rs = stmt.executeQuery("SELECT num FROM
TypesTab");
    while (rs.next())
    {
      n = rs.getInt(1);
    }
    stmt.close();
    return n;
```

Here is a code snippet excerpted from Listing 3.6:

```
/*
 * Map oracle.sql.NUMBER to SQL NUMBER
 */
  OraclePreparedStatement ops = (OraclePreparedStatement)
      conn.prepareStatement("UPDATE TypesTab SET num = ?");
  ops.setNUMBER (1, n);
  ops.execute();
  ops.close();


 /*
  * Map SQL NUMBER column to oracle.sq.NUMBER
  */
   OracleStatement ostmt = (OracleStatement)
conn.createStatement();
   NUMBER onb = new NUMBER();
   OracleResultSet ors =
     (OracleResultSet) ostmt.executeQuery("SELECT num FROM
TypesTab");
   while (ors.next())
   {
     onb = ors.getNUMBER(1);
   }
   ostmt.close();
   return onb;
```

BINARY_FLOAT and BINARY_DOUBLE

A `SQL BINARY_FLOAT` is a 32-bit, single-precision, floating-point number data type; its values vary between `1.17549E–38F` and `3.40282E+38F`. A

SQL BINARY_DOUBLE is a 64-bit, double-precision, floating-point number data type; its values vary between 2.22507485850720E-308 and 1.79769313486231E+308.

Since Oracle Database 10*g* Release 1, the JDBC drivers support the SQL BINARY_FLOAT and SQL BINARY_DOUBLE data types, respectively, through the oracle.sql.BINARY_FLOAT and oracle.sql.BINARY_DOUBLE classes. The JDBC mapping is compatible with IEEE754 float and IEEE754 double, but with the following restrictions:

- −0 is coerced to +0.

- Comparison with NaN (i.e., Not a Number) is not supported.

- All NaN values are coerced to either BINARY_FLOAT_NAN or BINARY_DOUBLE_NAN.

- Nondefault rounding modes are not supported.

- Nondefault exception handling modes are not supported.

The following methods have been added to the OraclePrepared-Statement and OracleCallableStatement objects: setBinary-Float(int, float), setBinaryDouble(int, double), setBinaryFloat(String, float), and setBinaryDouble(String, double).

```
BINARY_FLOAT bf = new BINARY_FLOAT((float)789.669);
BINARY_DOUBLE bd = new BINARY_DOUBLE((double)897.9999);

OraclePreparedStatement opstmt = (OraclePreparedStatement)
   oconn.prepareStatement("insert into binary_tab
values(?,?)");

pstmt.setBinaryFloat (1, bf);
pstmt.setBinaryDouble (2, bd);
pstmt.executeUpdate();

pstmt.registerReturnParameter(1, OracleTypes.BINARY_FLOAT);
pstmt.registerReturnParameter(2, OracleTypes.BINARY_DOUBLE);

OraclePreparedStatement pstmt = (OraclePreparedStatement)
```

```
oconn.prepareStatement("SELECT bfcol, bdcol FROM binary_tab
where ...);
ResultSet rs = pstmt.executeQuery ();

float bfcol= 0;
double bdcol = 0;
while (rs.next()) {
col2 = rs.getFloat (2);
col3 = rs.getDouble (3);
```

8.2.4   JDBC Support for Long and Raw Data Types

SQL RAW(s)

The SQL RAW data type stores raw binary data such as graphics, sound, documents, or arrays of binary data. The variable size, between 1 and 2,000, must be specified. Oracle recommends to use SQL BLOB instead (you can view the RAW data type as a small-sized BLOB but without the locator). The Oracle JDBC maps SQL RAW to and from oracle.sql.RAW and Java bytes[]. SQL RAW can be manipulated using the setRAW, setRAWAtName, getRAW, and updateRAW methods of OraclePreparedStatement, OracleCallableStatement, and OracleResultSet classes. The oracle.sql.RAW class furnishes the newRAW method for creating instances of RAW data type compatible with Oracle Database 10*g*, and oldRAW constructors for creating instances of RAW data type compatible with pre-10*g* releases. The following code snippet excerpted from Listing 3.8 illustrates the mapping of a RAW column to oracle.sql.RAW:

```
/*
 * Update a SQL RAW column with oracle.sql.RAW data
 */
   byte[] bytearr = new byte[600]; // Max size of SQL RAW data
   RAW oraw = new RAW(bytearr);
   OraclePreparedStatement ops = (OraclePreparedStatement)
      conn.prepareStatement("UPDATE TypesTab SET xraw = ?");
   ops.setRAW (1, oraw);
   ops.execute();
   ops.close();

/*
 * Retrieve a SQL RAW column as oracle.sq.RAW
 */
   OracleStatement ostmt = (OracleStatement) conn.createStatement();
```

```
// construct an oracle.sql.RAW object

OracleResultSet ors =
   (OracleResultSet) ostmt.executeQuery("SELECT xraw FROM
TypesTab");
   while (ors.next())
   {
      oraw = ors.getRAW(1);
   }
   ostmt.close();
return oraw;
```

RAW columns can also be redefined as LONGVARBINARY using defineColumnType of OracleStatement, then streamed using getBinaryStream. In fact, the data is fetched into a staging buffer, from which getBinaryStream returns an InputStream.

LONG and LONG RAW

LONG columns store variable-length character strings containing up to 2 gigabytes −1, (i.e., $2^{31}−1$) bytes. LONG columns have many of the characteristics of VARCHAR2 columns. A LONG RAW data type is a variable-length raw binary data, up to 2 gigabytes data, and the storage is allocated dynamically.

LONG and LONG RAW data types are maintained for backward compatibility only; Oracle recommends to use VARCHAR2 or LOBs instead. Still, the Oracle JDBC maps LONG to oracle.sql.RAW and java.lang.String, while LONG RAW data is mapped to oracle.sql.RAW and byte[].

LONG and LONG RAW columns can be manipulated using one of the following three approaches:

1.   The setRAW, setRAWAtName, getRAW, and updateRAW methods

```
byte[] buf = { 00, 01, 02, 03, 04, 05, 00, 01, 02, 03,
04, 05,
00, 01, 02, 03, 04, 05, 00, 01, 02, 03, 04, 05,
00, 01, 02, 03, 04, 05, 00, 01, 02, 03, 04, 05 };

OraclePreparedStatement opstmt =
(OraclePreparedStatement)
   oconn.prepareStatement("insert into raw_tab
values(?)");
```

```
ps.setRAW (1, new RAW(buf));
ps.executeUpdate();
```

2.   The `setString`, `setBytes`, and `getBytes` methods perform
     "direct binding" (i.e., the entire content is fetched into a staging
     buffer), which is fast, allows statement batching, but is restricted to
     32,766 characters/bytes. In Oracle JDBC 10*g* Release 2, for data
     larger than 32,766, these methods switch automatically (under the
     covers) to streaming mode (i.e., `setCharacterStream` or `setBi-`
     `naryStream`, described hereafter):

```
ResultSet rs = stmt.executeQuery ("SELECT RAWCol FROM
raw_ab";);
 ResultSetMetaData rsm = rs.getMetaData();
 int index = rsm.getColumnCount();
 while (rs.next()) {
      for (int i = 1; i <= index; i++) {
      rs.getBytes(i)); // do something about this output
 }
 rs.close ();
```

3.   `LONG` and `LONG RAW` data types are by default (or most of the
     time) manipulated in "streaming" mode using `setCharacter-`
     `Stream`, `setAsciiStream`, `setBinaryStream`, `getBina-`
     `ryStream`, `getCharacterStream`, and `getUnicodeStream`
     methods. These methods return the bytes of the data as a stream
     (i.e., `InputStream` object) of RAW bytes, ASCII bytes, or Uni-
     code bytes (with the `UTF-16` encoding). In fact, the data is
     fetched into a staging buffer, from which it is streamed. In addi-
     tion, such `stream` binding is slower than the `direct` binding
     (i.e., `setString`, `getString`) and does not support statement
     batching.

```
// Insert  a LONG column
File if = new File("Ascii.dat");
InputStream is = new FileInputStream(if);
PreparedStatement pstmt =
     conn.prepareStatement("INSERT INTO LONGTAB VALUES (?)");
pstmt.setAsciiStream(1, is, (int)if.length());
pstmt.execute();
```

```
// retrieve a LONG Column
ResultSet rs =
      stmt.executeQuery("SELECT LongCol FROM TAB");
 if (rs.next())
 {
   InputStream longdata = rs.getAsciiStream(1);
   FileOutputStream fos = new FileOutputStream("Long.log");
   // Read from the stream and write to log file
   int count;
   while ((count = longdata.read()) != -1) fos.write(c);
   ...
   fos.close ();
 }


// Insert a LONG RAW column
OraclePreparedStatement ps = (OraclePreparedStatement)
      conn.prepareStatement ("insert into LONGRAWTAB values (?)");
byte[] bytearr = new byte[200]; // byte array
InputStream is = new ByteArrayInputStream (bytearr);
ps.setBinaryStream (1, is, 200);
pstmt.executeUpdate ();
is.close ();


// Retrieve  a LONG RAW column
ResultSet rs =
  stmt.executeQuery ("SELECT LongRawCol FROM Tab");
if (rs.next ())
 {
   InputStream in = ((OracleResultSet)rset).getBinaryStream (1);
   //process input stream as above (retrieve LONG)
   ...
 }
```

Note: When retrieving a LONG data with getBinaryStream, the returned data stream, depending on the driver type (i.e., JDBC-Thin or JDBC-OCI), the client character set, or the server character set, is summarized in Table 8.3.

Table 8.3   *Returned Data Stream for LONG column*

Driver Type	JDBC Client Character Set	Database Character Set	Returned Data Stream
Thin	Not regarded	US7ASCII or WE8ISO8859P1	*US7ASCII*
Thin	Not regarded	Other	*UTF-8*
OCI	US7ASCII or WE8ISO8859P1	Not regarded	*US7ASCII*
OCI	Other	Not regarded	*UTF-8*

In Oracle JDBC 10*g* Release 2, for data smaller than 32,766 bytes, the getXXXStream methods switch automatically to setString or setBytes. You may also explicitly disable the automatic streaming of LONG and LONG RAW columns by redefining these respectively as VARCHAR2 and VARBINARY using the defineColumnType() method of OracleStatement, and then manipulating it using setString/setBytes.

8.2.5   JDBC Support for SQL Datetime Data Types

DATE

The SQL DATE data type stores date and time information, including century, year, month, date, hour, minute, and second; it is equivalent to SQL99 TIMESTAMP[0], meaning without the fractional part of second. The Oracle JDBC supports SQL DATE through the oracle.sql.DATE wrapper class. SQL DATE data types can be manipulated using the setDATE, setDATEAtName, getDATE, and updateDATE methods of OraclePreparedStatement, OracleCallableStatement, and OracleResultSet classes. In addition, DATE data types can also be mapped to standard java.sql.Date, java.sql.Time, java.sql.Timestamp, and java.lang.String; however, doing so may lead to precision loss (i.e., the time component of java.sql.Date is zeroed, and the behavior differs throughout releases), as explained later.

The following code snippets, excerpted from Listing 3.2, illustrates the mapping of SQL DATE to java.sql.Date, and vice versa:

```
/*
 * Update SQL DATE column with java.sql.Date
 */
   PreparedStatement ps =
       conn.prepareStatement("UPDATE TypesTab SET xdat = ?");
   ps.setDate (1, x);
   ps.execute();
   ps.close();

/*
 * Retrieve SQL DATE column as java.sql.Date
 */
   Statement stmt = conn.createStatement();
   Date dat = null;
   ResultSet rs = stmt.executeQuery("SELECT xdat FROM
TypesTab");
   while (rs.next())
   {
      dat = rs.getDate(1);
   }
   stmt.close();
   return dat.toString();
```

The following code snippet, excerpted from Listing 3.3, shows mapping `oracle.sql.DATE` to SQL DATE:

```
/*
 * Update SQL DATE with oracle.sql.DATE
 */
   OraclePreparedStatement ops = (OraclePreparedStatement)
       conn.prepareStatement("UPDATE TypesTab SET xdat = ?");
   ops.setDATE (1, x);
   ops.execute();
   ops.close();
/*
 * Retrieve SQL DATE column as oracle.sq.DATE
 */
   OracleStatement ostmt = (OracleStatement)
conn.createStatement();
   DATE dat = new DATE();
```

```
OracleResultSet ors =
  (OracleResultSet) ostmt.executeQuery("SELECT xdat FROM
TypesTab");
  while (ors.next())
  {
    dat = ors.getDATE(1);
  }
  ostmt.close();
  return dat;
```

TIMESTAMP, TIMESTAMPTZ, TIMESTAMPLTZ

Starting with Oracle 9i Release 2, the Oracle database furnishes the SQL99 TIMESTAMP data type (i.e., precision up to nanosecond). The SQL TIMES-TAMP data type is an extension of the DATE data type, since it stores year, month, day, hour, minute, second, and fractional seconds; these fractional seconds are not stored by the DATE data type.

```
TIMESTAMP'1997-01-31 09:26:50.124'
```

The Oracle JDBC supports SQL TIMESTAMP through the oracle.sql.TIMESTAMP class and can be manipulated using the setTIMESTAMP, setTIMESTAMPAtName, getTIMESTAMP, and updateTIMESTAMP methods of OraclePreparedStatement, OracleCallableStatement, and OracleResultSet classes. In addition, the TIMESTAMP data can also be mapped to oracle.sql.DATE, java.sql.Date, java.sql.Time, java.sql.Timestamp, java.lang.String, and byte[]. In these cases, the corresponding setxxx, getxxx, and updatexxx methods of the PreparedStatement, CallableStatement, and ResultSet interfaces can be used.

- Mapping a SQL TIMESTAMP column into java.sql.Date, using setDate(), will lose the time precision, since java.sql.Date only stores up to milliseconds.

- 8.1.7 JDBC: Retrieving a SQL DATE column using getObject() returns a java.sql.Timestamp.

- In Oracle 9i JDBC, retrieving a SQL DATE column using getObject() returns either java.sql.Date (9.0.1) or java.sql.Timestamp (9.2).

- In Oracle 10g JDBC, retrieving a SQL DATE column using getObject() returns a java.sql.Date.

- JDBC applications can preserve the behavior they are accustomed to (i.e., retrieve `java.sql.Timestamp` or `java.sql.Date`) using the `oracle.jdbc.V8Compatible` flag (setting to true returns `java.sql.Timestamp`).

```
properties.put ("oracle.jdbc.V8Compatible", "true");
```

The `TIMESTAMPTZ` data type (i.e., `TIMESTAMP WITH TIME ZONE data type ()`) is a `TIMESTAMP` data type "with a time zone offset, which is the difference (in hours and minutes) between the local time and the UTC (Coordinated Universal Time.)"

```
TIMESTAMP '1997-01-31 09:26:56.66 +02:00'
TIMESTAMP '1999-04-15 8:00:00 -8:00'
TIMESTAMP '1999-04-15 8:00:00 US/Pacific'
```

The Oracle JDBC supports SQL `TIMESTAMPTZ` through the `oracle.sql.TIMESTAMPTZ` class and corresponding `setTIMESTAMPTZ`, `setTIMESTAMPTZATName`, `getTIMESTAMPTZ`, `updateTIMESTAMPTZ` in `OraclePreparedStatement`, `OracleCallableStatement`, and `OracleResultSet` classes. Similar to `TIMESTAMP`, it can also be mapped to `oracle.sql.DATE`, `java.sql.Date`, `java.sql.Time`, `java.sql.Timestamp`, `java.lang.String`, and `byte[]`, with the corresponding manipulation methods.

The `TIMESTAMPLTZ` data type is a `TIMESTAMP WITH TIME ZONE` data type; however, "the data stored in the database is normalized to the database time zone, and the time zone offset is not stored as part of the column data."

The Oracle JDBC supports `TIMESTAMPLTZ` through the `oracle.sql.TIMESTAMPLTZ` class and corresponding `setTIMESTAMPLTZ`, `setTIMESTAMPLTZATName`, `getTIMESTAMPLTZ`, and `updateTIMESTAMPLTZ` in `OraclePreparedStatement`, `OracleCallableStatement`, and `OracleResultSet` classes..

Similar to `TIMESTAMPTZ`, it can also be mapped to `oracle.sql.DATE`, `java.sql.Date`, `java.sql.Time`, `java.sql.Timestamp`, `java.lang.String`, and `byte[]`.

```
// Assume a TIMESTAMP_TAB with the various Timestamp types
// as columns
```

```
String my_date = "2005-12-04 12:23:47.66";
oracle.sql.TIMESTAMPLTZ     my_tsltz = null;
GregorianCalendar           my_gcal  = null;
Timestamp my_tss = Timestamp.valueOf(my_date);

TimeZone my_tz = TimeZone.getDefault();
my_tz.setID("US/Pacific");
my_gcal = new GregorianCalendar(my_tz);
my_tsltz = new oracle.sql.TIMESTAMPLTZ(conn, my_tss, my_cal);
my_tstz = new oracle.sql.TIMESTAMPTZ(conn, my_tss, my_cal);
my_ts = new oracle.sql.TIMESTAMP(my_tss);
String query = "update timestamp_tab set c1 = ?, c2 = ?, c3 =
?";
OraclePreparedStatement ops =
  (OraclePreparedStatement)  con.prepareStatement(sql);
ops.setTIMESTAMPLTZ(1, my_ts);
ops.setTIMESTAMPLTZ(2, my_tstz);
ops.setTIMESTAMPLTZ(3, my_tsltz);

ops.executeUpdate ();
```

INTERVAL YEAR TO MONTH and INTERVAL DAY TO SECOND

The SQL INTERVALYM data type (i.e., INTERVAL YEAR TO MONTH) stores
a period of time in YEAR and MONTH; it is used to measure time differences. The Oracle JDBC supports this data type through the
oracle.sql.INTERVALYM class and the setINTERVALYM, setINTERVALY-
MATName, getINTERVALYM, and updateINTERVALYM methods.

The SQL INTERVALDS (i.e., INTERVAL DAY TO SECOND) stores a period
of time in days, hours, minutes, and seconds; it is used to measure time differences. The Oracle JDBC supports this data type through the
oracle.sql.INTERVALDS   class,   and   the   setINTERVALDS,
setINTERVALDSATName, getINTERVALDS, and updateINTERVALDS methods.

```
INTERVALDS ids = new INTERVALDS ("15 08:12:42.0");
OraclePreparedStatement ops = (OraclePreparedStatement)
    oconn.prepareStatement("INSERT INTO idstab VALUES (?)");
ops.setINTERVALDS (1, ds);
...
opst.executeUpdate ();
```

```
ops = (OraclePreparedStatement) conn.prepareStatement
        ("SELECT ids1 FROM idstab");
OracleResultSet ors = pstmt.executeQuery ();
ids = new INTERVALDS;
while (rs.next ()) {
   col2 = rs.getINTERVALDS (1);
}
```

8.2.6 JDBC Support for LOB Datatypes

Overview

Large Object data types (LOBs) is an umbrella name for the Binary LOB (BLOB), the Character LOB (CLOB), the Unicode LOB (NCLOB), and the Binary File (BFILE) data types. These are used for storing large and unstructured data such as text, image, video, and spatial data. The BLOB, CLOB, and NCLOB data types can store unlimited data size (the physical storage is the limit). CLOB data is in the database character set, which may be single or multibytes, while NCLOB data is in the national language character set. LOB data types larger than 4 K are not stored within the table column; in all cases, the column contains a locator, which points to the actual LOB data (inside or outside of the database). See the Oracle Database SQL Reference documentation for more details on the features and restrictions of SQL LOB data types. How does JDBC support LOB manipulation?

1. *Using LOB API*

    The LOB API designates standard and Oracle's proprietary LOB methods furnished by the locator and PreparedStatement (OraclePreparedStatement), CallableStatement (OracleCallableStatement), and ResultSet (OracleResultSet); it allows random read and/or write (if SELECT ... FOR UPDATE) access. You can start anywhere in the LOB, read as much data as you want, and then start again at a different offset. Assume a CLOB containing a table of contents or index; you can read a chunk, then select another chunk based on the previously retrieved data, and update the LOB, if you had selected the column with the FOR UPDATE clause.

    LOB manipulation through the LOB API is done in two steps:

Step 1: Retrieve, insert, and update the LOB locator using the standard setBlob, setClob, getBlob, getClob, update-Blob, updateClob, and the proprietary setBLOB, setBLOBAT-Name, setBFILE, seBFILEATName, setBfile, setBfileAtName, setBloabATName, setCLOB, setCLOBATName, setClobAtName, getBFILE, getBLOB, getCLOB, updateBFILE, updateBfile, updateBLOB, and updateCLOB methods of the OraclePre-paredStatement, OracleCallableStatement, and OracleRe-sultSet classes. The LOB wrapper classes (i.e., oracle.sql.BLOB, oracle.sql.CLOB, oracle.sql.BFILE, oracle.sql.NCLOB) do not have public constructors; therefore, in order to create a new LOB, you must use the createTempo-rary, getEmptyCLOB, or getEmptyBLOB methods.

```
ResultSet rs = stmt.executeQuery("SELECT
blobcol,bfilcol clobcol from XobTab";

While (rs.next())
{
  BLOB BlobLoc = ((OracleResultSet)rs).getBLOB(1);
  CLOB ClobLoc = ((OracleResultSet)rs).getCLOB(2);
  BFILE BfileLoc = ((OracleResultSet)rs).getBFILE(3);
}
```

Alternatively, the getOracleObject method can be used to retrieve an oracle.sql.Datum object, which can then be cast appropriately to CLOB, BLOB, or BFILE.

```
BLOB BlobLoc = (BLOB)
((OracleResultSet)rs).getOracleObject (1);
```

Step 2: Manipulate the LOB content

- To read the LOB content:
    - Stream the content out, using getBinaryStream, get-String, getCharacterStream, and getAsciiStream.

    ```
    byte[] bytarr = new byte[20]; // 20 bytes chunk
    ```

```
BLOB LOBLoc = ps.getBLOB (1);
InputStream is = LOBLoc.getBinaryStream();
while ((length = stream.read(bytarr)) != -1)
{
    // process the chunk
        bytarr = new byte[10];
}
is.close();
```

- Use getString, getSubString, and getBytes methods.

```
String ClobData = ClobLoc.getSubString(1,12);
```

- To write, update, and append the LOB content:
  - Use putBytes, setString

```
BLOB tempBlob = BLOB.createTemporary (conn, false,
                    BLOB.DURATION_SESSION);
byte[] bytarr = { ... };
tempLob.putBytes (1, bytarr);
PreparedStatement pstmt = conn.prepareStatement (
    "insert into XobTab values (?)";
((OraclePreparedStatement)ps).setBLOB (1, tempLob);
ps.execute ();
ps.close ();
```

  - Streaming the data in by invoking : getBinaryOutput-
    Stream, getAsciiOutputStream(), or getCharacter-
    OutputStream methods on the locator; then write on the
    output stream.

```
OutputStream os = LobLoc.getBinaryOutputStream();
FileInputStream is = new FileInputStream(…);
int bufsiz = LobLoc.getBufferSize();
byte[] bytarr = new byte[bufsiz];
int count = -1;
while((count = is.read(bytarr)) != -1) {
  os.write(bytarr, 0, len);
}
is.close();
os.close();
```

Notes:

- Explictly demarcating LOB operations by open() and close() allows reading and writing the LOB content without firing associated triggers; however, upon close(), the trigger is fired.

- In pre-10*g* releases, the JDBC-Thin driver uses the PL/SQL DBMS_LOB package under the covers for manipulating LOB data in the RDBMS. Starting with 10*g* releases, the JDBC-Thin is on par with JDBC-OCI and uses the more efficient native LOB functions for most operations (certain operations such as hasPattern and isSub-Lob are still done via the dbms_lob package, though).

2.   *Using Optimized LOB Access*

In Oracle Database 10*g*, for LOBs of size less than 2 gigabytes (i.e., 2,147,483,648 bytes),[3] which is a limit imposed by Java int on array sizes, the manipulation has been simplified by removing the need to explicitly manage the locator. In fact, the appropriate getBLOB, setBLOB, getCLOB, setCLOB, getBFILE, and so on are invoked under the covers.

- The standard getBytes, getBinaryStream, getString, get-CharacterStream, getAsciiStream setBytes, setBina-ryStream,   setString,   setCharacterStream,   and setAsciiStream methods of PreparedStatement, Result-Set, and CallableStatement have been extended to take BLOB, CLOB, and BFILE columns as parameters. Note that in Oracle JDBC 10*g* Release 2, getBytes now returns the LOB data instead of the unusable bytes of the LOB locator.

- Oracle JDBC 10*g* Release 2 implements the standard JDBC 3.0 setBytes, setString, setBinaryStream, setCharac-terStream, setAsciiStream, and truncate methods using ojdbc14.jar; for classes12.jar with JDK 1.2/1.3, the LOB variable must be cast to java.sql.Blob or java.sql.Clob. As a result, the behavior of setString, setCharacterStream, setAsciiStream, setBytes, and setBinaryStream methods has changed between 10*g* Release 1 and Release 2, as described later (and discussed in Chapter 7).

---

3.   For server-side JDBC, this limit is **4,000** bytes for SQL operations, as opposed to PL/SQL operations.

- setBytes switches to setBinaryStream for SQL operations (i.e., PreparedStatement) on data larger than 2,000 bytes.
- setBytes switches to setBinaryStream for PL/SQL operations (i.e., CallableStatement) on data larger than 2,000 bytes and to setBytesForBlob for data larger than 32,512 bytes.
- setString switches to setCharacterStream for SQL operations on data larger than 32,766 characters.
- setString switches to setStringForClob for string data larger than 32,512 bytes in the database character set or national character set, depending on whether setFormOfUse has been used for NCLOB parameters.

See Tables 7.4 and 7.5 for more details.

- In Oracle JDBC 10*g* Release 1, for CLOB data larger than 32,765 bytes, setting the connection property SetBigStringUseClob to true causes the standard setString method (of PreparedStatement) to switch to Oracle's setStringForClob (of OraclePreparedStatement), under the covers.

```
props.put("SetBigStringTryClob", "true");
...
ps.setString(1, str);
ps.executeUpdate();
```

In Oracle JDBC 10*g* Release 2, this property is no longer necessary for large data, the driver automatically (and under the covers) switches setString to setStringForClob; otherwise, it uses setCharacterStream.

3.   *Using LONG Streaming for LOBs (10g JDBC only)*

If you don't need the flexibility offered by the LOB locator (and corresponding APIs), you can use defineColumnType(nn, Types.LONGVARBINARY) or defineColumn-

Type(nn,Types.LONGVARCHAR) to redefine the LOB as LONG or LONG RAW and then stream the LOB column as if it were a LONG or LONG RAW (i.e., the data is fetched into a staging buffer, from which getXXXStream returns an InputStream) column. However, unlike the traditional LOB streaming and LOB locator APIs, "LONG streaming" always starts at the beginning of the LOB, allows only one single access, and can read as much data as desired.

```
// Claim that these columns are of LONG and LONG RAW
types
(OracleStatement)stmt.defineColumnType(1,
Types.LONGVARBINARY);
(OracleStatement)stmt.defineColumnType(2,
Types.LONGVARCHAR);
 ...
ResultSet rs = stmt.executeQuery("select LOBCOL from
XOBTab");

// Retrieving a Clob with getString");
    ocrs.setCommand ("SELECT lobcol FROM XOBTab");
    ocrs.execute ();
    while (ocrs.next ())
    {
        bytarr = stmt.getString (1));
    }
    ocrs.close ();
// Retrieving a Clob with getString");

    ocrs.execute ();
    while (ocrs.next ())
    {
        ocrs.getBytes (2).length);
    }
}
```

Table 8.4 summarizes the various methods offered by the various LOB interfaces/mechanisms.

Temporary LOB

Temporary LOBs (BLOB, CLOB, NCLOB) are created either implicitly or explicitly in temporary tablespace (as opposed to regular tablespace) for

Table 8.4   *LOB Interfaces/Mechanisms and Methods*

	BLOB	**CLOB/NCLOB**	**BFILE**
Locators	`oracle.sql.BLOB` `java.sql.Blob`	`oracle.sql.CLOB` `java.sql.Clob`	`oracle.sql.BFILE`

Locator Methods	`getBinaryStream`
	`setBinaryStream`
	`getBytes`
	`setBytes`
	`getChunkSize`
	`opwn, close`
	`position, truncate`
		`getAsciiStream`
		`setAsciiStream`
		`getCharacterStream`
		`setCharacterStream`
		`getChars`
		`setString`
		`putChars`
		`getSubString`
		`getChunkSize`
		`open, close`
		`position, truncate`
			`getBinaryStream`
			`setBinaryStream`
			`getBytes`
			`openFile`
			`closeFile`
			`getDirAlias`
			`isFileOpen`

PrepdStmt Methods	`setBlob`
	`setBLOB`
	`setBloabAtName`
	`setBLOBAtName`
	`setOracleObject`
		`setClob`
		`setCLOB`
		`setClobAtName`
		`setCLOBAtName`
		`setOracleObject`
			`setBFile`
			`setBFILE`
			`setBfileAtName`
			`setBFILEAtNAme`
			`setOracleObject`

Additional CallblStmt Methods	`getBLOB`
	`getBinaryStream`
	`setBytesForBlob`
		`getCLOB`
		`getAsciiStream`
		`getCharacterStream`
		`setStringForClob`
			`getBFILE`
			`getObject`
			`getOracleObject`

ResultSet Methods	`getObject`
	`getOracleObject`
	`updateBLOB`
	`updateBytes`
	`upddateBinaryStream`
		`getObject`
		`getOracleObject`
		`updateCLOB`
		`updateAsciiStream`
		`updateCharacterStream`
			`getObject`
			`getOracleObject`

Temporary LOB methods	`createTemporary`
	`isTemporary`
	`freeTemporary`
		`createTemporary`
		`isTemporary`
		`freeTemporary`	

storing transient data. In Oracle JDC 10g Release 2, the `setBytesFor-Blob` and `setStringForClob` methods implicitly create temporary LOBs, which are automatically freed when the statement is executed or closed before execution.

You can explicitly create a temporary `LOB` with the `createTempo-rary(Connection, boolean, int)` method, which is defined in both the `oracle.sql.BLOB` and `oracle.sql.CLOB` classes.

- `createTemporary(java.sql.Connection   conn,   boolean cache, int _duration);`

   The duration takes either `DURATION_SESSION` or `DURATION_CALL` values defined in the `oracle.sql.BLOB` or `oracle.sql.CLOB` classes, although currently, the only usable value is `DURATION_SESSION`.

```
CLOB tempClob =
    CLOB.createTemporary(conn, true, CLOB.DURATION_SESSION);
 java.io.Writer iow = tempClob.getCharacterOutputStream();
 iow.write(s3);
 iow.flush();
 iow.close();
```

   For `NCLOB`, the `createTemporary` method has a slightly different signature:

- `createTemporary (Connection  conn,  boolean  cache,  int duration, short form);`

   where the short form must take one of the following values:

   ```
   oracle.jdbc.OraclePreparedStatement.FORM_NCHAR
   oracle.jdbc.OraclePreparedStatement.FORM_CHAR
   ```

   For very large `LOB`s, `createTemporary` may be slower than the traditional LOB operations (i.e., creating the LOB Locator, retrieving it, and filling the content).

The `freeTemporary()` method frees a temporary `LOB`:

- `freeTemporary(BLOB temp_lob)`

   The `isTemporary` method returns `true` if the `LOB` was created by calling the `createTemporary` method.

Examples of BLOBs Manipulation

Reading BLOBs

The `getBinaryStream` method of `oracle.sql.BLOB` retrieves the entire content of a `BLOB` as an input stream (`java.io.InputStream`) from the locator.

```
// Retrieve blob data as binary output stream
 InputStream ibs= myBlob.getBinaryStream();
 byte[] barr = new byte[20];
 int count = 0;
 while ((length = ibs.read(barr)) != -1)
   {
     for (int i=0; i<length; i++)
     // process barr[i]
   }
 ibs.close();
```

Writing BLOBs

The `setBinaryStream` method of `oracle.sql.BLOB` retrieves the `BLOB` as an output stream (`java.io.OutputStream`) to be written back to the `BLOB`.

```
PreparedStatement pstmt =
   conn.prepareStatement ("INTO XobTab (ID, blob_col)
 VALUES(?, ?)");

 ps.setNUMBER (1, id);

 File binaryFile = new File("c:\\BLOBTest.jpg");
 long flength = binaryFile.length();
 FileInputStream fis = new FileInputStream(binaryFile);
 byte[] bytes = new byte[(int)flength];
 fis.read(bytes);
 ps.setBinaryStream(2,new
 ByteArrayInputStream(bytes),bytes.length);
 fis.close();
 ps.execute();
 ps.close();
```

See Listing 3.10 for a basic example of Java stored procedure manipulating BLOB, and the Oracle *inter*Media case study in Chapter 17 for an advanced use of BFILE.

Examples of CLOB Manipulation

Reading CLOB Data

The getAsciiStream method of oracle.sql.CLOB retrieves the entire content of a CLOB as an input stream (java.io.InputStream).

```
Inputstream is = myClob.getAsciiStream();
byte[] acarr = new byte [20];
int count = is.read(acarr, 0, 20);
```

The getSubString method retrieves a subset of the CLOB as a character string (java.lang.String).

```
String mySubstr = myClob.getSubString(1,10)).toCharArray());
```

The getCharacterStream method returns a Unicode input stream in a java.io.Reader object.

```
// Assume myClob contains the CLOB Locator
// Read from Clob as a character stream
   Reader istream = myClob.getCharacterStream();
   char[] buf = new char[20];
   int count = 0;
   while ((count = istream.read(buf)) != -1)
   {
        for (int i=0; i<count; i++)
        // process chararr[i]);
   }
   istream.close();
```

Writing CLOB Data

The setAsciiStream method of oracle.sql.CLOB retrieves the CLOB as an output stream (java.io.OutputStream) to be written back to the CLOB.

```
InputStream is = new FileInputStream ( fis );
int flength = (int)fis.length ();
```

```
                      ps.setAsciiStream (1, fis, flength);
```

With JDBC 3.0, the standard `java.sql.Clob` interface furnishes the `setCharacterStream` method, which returns a Unicode output stream in a `java.io.Writer` object.

```
         OraclePreparedStatement ps =
             (OraclePreparedStatement) conn.prepareStatement
               ("INTO XobTab (clob_col1) VALUES(?)");
             java.io.StringReader sr = new StringReader (myString);
               ps.setCharacterStream (2, sr, 1);
               ps.executeUpdate ()

         // Explicit use of setStringForClob

         String ClobString = "sdsdfsdfsdsdsdfsdsdsfsdfsdf";
         pst.setStringForClob (3, ClobString);
         pst.executeUpdate ();

         // Using setString
            OraclePreparedStatement ps = (OraclePreparedStatement)
               conn.prepareStatement ("insert into ClobTab values
         (?)");
         String ClobString = "sdsdfsdfsdsdsdfsdsdsfsdfsdf";
               ps.setString (3, ClobString);
               pst.executeUpdate ();
```

See Listing 3.9 for a basic example of Java stored procedure manipulating CLOB, and the Oracle *inter*Media case study in Chapter 17 for an advanced use of CLOB.

Examples of BFILE Manipulation

Prerequisites

In order to manipulate an external file through the Oracle SQL (and JDBC):

1.   The schema must have the Oracle Database ANY DIRECTORY privilege, which is required to create an alias, or the external directory containing the external file.

2.   Create the alias using the following SQL DDL:

```
create or replace directory bfiledir as 'C:\TEMP';
```
or the following JDBC statement
```
stmt.execute ("CREATE DIRECTORY bfiledir AS 'C:\
Temp'");
```

3.   Insert the name of the external file, as follows:

```
insert into BFILETab values (bfilename('BFILEDIR',
'Filename'));
```

Reading BFILE Data

- Retrieve the locator:

```
OracleResultSet rs = (OracleResultSet)
stmt.executeQuery("SELECT Bfile_col FROM BFILETab WHERE ID =
...");

BFILE bfil = null;
while (rs.next())
{
bfil = rs.getBFILE(1);
}
stmt.close();
return bfil;
```

- Read the file content, using the   getBinaryStream() method
  retrieves the file as an input stream:

```
myBfile.openFile();
long count = myBfile.length();
int lump = 20;
InputStream is = myBfile.getBinaryStream();
byte[] buf = new byte[lump];
while ((count = is.read(buf)) != -1)
{
  for (int i=0; i<length; i++)
  // process buffer[i]
}
is.close();
myBfile.closeFile()
```

Creating BFILE Data

- Create the Locator:

```
Statement stmt = conn.createStatement();
    OraclePreparedStatement ps = (OraclePreparedStatement)
     conn.prepareStatement
            ("INSERT INTO XobTab (ID, Bfile_col) VALUES(?,
?)");
    ps.setNUMBER (1, id[0]);
    ps.setBFILE (2, bf[0]);
    ps.execute ();
    ps.close();
```

- That's all—BFILEs are read-only existing files/media.

See Listing 3.11 for a basic example of Java stored procedure manipulating BFILE, and the Oracle *inter*Media case study in Chapter 17 for an advanced BFILE use case.

8.2.7 JDBC Support for ROWID

The ROWID is a pseudocolumn of database rows. The oracle.sql.ROWID is the wrapper class for the Oracle proprietary ROWID data type. The OraclePreparedStatement, Oracle CallableStatement, and OracleResultSet classes furnish the getROWID, setROWID, setROWIDAtName, and updateROWID methods. However, applications cannot change it. As explained in Chapter 7, using the JDBC 3.0 *Retrieval of Auto-Generated Key,* the newly generated ROWID can be retrieved using stmt.getGeneratedKeys().

```
stmt = (OracleStatement)conn.createStatement();
stmt.execute ("insert into <Table> values (.,.,.)
                        OracleStatement.RETURN_GENERATED_KEYS);

rset = (OracleResultSet)stmt.getGeneratedKeys();
while (rset.next())
    {
       ROWID r = rset.getROWID(1);
    }
```

JDBC 4.0 is expected to provide support for a standard `java.sql.Rowid` type and make this a supported parameter for `PreparedStatement`, `CallableStatement`, `ResultSet`, and `DatabaseMetaData`.

8.2.8   JDBC Support for OPAQUE Type

OPAQUE

The `SQL OPAQUE` type acts as a black box, which hosts custom binary data types. The `oracle.sql.OPAQUE` class wraps the `SQL OPAQUE` data type, and the drivers retrieve the bytes from the server, but the consumer must turn the bytes into a meaningful type (e.g., `XMLType`). It is used mainly internally by Oracle to support complex built-in types.

The `oracle.sql.OPAQUE` extends the `oracle.sql.DatumWithConnection` class and furnishes the following methods: `getBytesValue()`, `getDescriptor()`, `getJavaSqlConnection()`, `getMap()`, `getSQLTypeName()`, `getValue()`, `isConvertibleTo()`, and `toJdbc()`. The `OraclePreparedStatement`, `OracleResultSet` furnish the `setOPAQUE()`, `setOPAQUEAtNAme()`, and `getOPAQUE()` methods.

See the following XMLType code fragments that use the OPAQUE type.

OPAQUE Descriptor

The `oracle.sql.OpaqueDescriptor` class furnishes the following methods for describing the OPAQUE data type: `createDescriptor()`, `descType()`, `getMaxLength()`, `getTypeCode()`, `hasFixedSize()`, `hasUnboundedSize()`, `isModeledInC()`, and so on.

See the Oracle JDBC javadoc for more details on the signatures.

8.2.9   JDBC Support for XMLType

XML DB and XML Type

The Oracle XML Database (also known as XDB) furnishes a native XMLType data type for managing XML documents directly in the database. As well explained in the Oracle XML DB Developer's Guide and white paper,[4] XDB stores XML in XMLType columns and/or tables, using either a structured or an unstructured format. In summary:

---

4.   http://download-west.oracle.com/otndocs/tech/xml/xmldb/TWP_XML_DB_10gR2_long.pdf.

- In the *unstructured format*, the XML document is stored in a LOB. The structure of the XML document is maintained byte for byte; however, it must be retrieved entirely, updated, and written back. Xpath operations are expensive, and SQL constraints are not enforced.

- In the *structured format*, the XML document is stored as an XML Object. This allows b-tree indexing, query rewrite, in-place and piece-wise updates, and optimized memory and storage, but the original document formatting is lost. Xpath operations are fast and cheap. SQL constraints are enforced.

XDB furnishes a comprehensive Java API, including a Java DOM API and JDBC support for XMLType. Full coverage of XML DB will require an entire book, but the use case in Chapter 17 is an example of a complete open-source framework leveraging XML DB.

The upcoming JDBC 4.0 specification is expected to define a standard `XMLType` data type.

JDBC Support for XMLType

JDBC supports the `SQL XMLType` data type through the `oracle.xdb.XML-Type` wrapper class in `xdb.jar` (located under $ORACLE_HOME/rdbms/jlib). It extends `oracle.sql.OPAQUE` and furnishes a constructor `XML-Type()`, which can build an `XMLType` object from `BLOB`, `CLOB`, `String`, `OPAQUE Descriptor`,[5] `InputStream`, and `DOM` documents, using the corresponding signature. It also furnishes the following APIs: `createXML()`, `close()`, `createContext()`, `existsNode()`, `extract()`, `getClobVal()`, `getBlobVal()`, `getConnType()`, `getDocument()`, `getDocumentFragment()`, `getDOM()`, `getErrorHandle()`, `getInputStream()`, `getNameSpace()`, `getNumberVal()`, `getRootElement()`, `getSChemaURL()`, `getServiceHandle()`, `getStringVal()`, `isFragment()`, `isSchema-Based()`, `isSChemaValid()`, `transform()`, and `WriteToOutputStream()`.

`XMLType` is based on the `OPAQUE` type. All Oracle JDBC driver types are capable of transporting `OPAQUE` data types (hence `XMLType`) to and from the database; however, because most or all SQL XMLTypes operations are implemented in C and available in the C libraries, only JDBC-OCI can access the C layer of the Oracle client, similarly the server-side type 2 driver

5. A type descriptor of OPAQUE data type.

can access the C layer of the RDBMS, and understand `XMLType` and its various storage formats. See Part IV for a driver-independent workaround.

Code fragments:

1.   Prerequisites:

add xdb.jar to CLASSPATH

```
// Set the URL, using TNS Alias with JDBC-OCI
String url = "jdbc:oracle:oci:scott/tiger@inst1";
  ods.setURL(url);
// Retrieve a connection
Connection conn = ods.getConnection();

// import the XMLTYype class
import oracle.xdb.XMLType;
            ...
```

2.   Retrieve XMLType data from OPAQUE type:

```
  OraclePreparedStatement pstmt =
(OraclePreparedStatement)
    conn.prepareStatement("select x.xmlDoc from XMLtab
x");

  OracleResultSet ors = (OracleResultSet)
pstmt.executeQuery();
  while(ors.next())
  {
    // get the XMLType
    XMLType xmldat =
XMLType.createXML(ors.getOPAQUE(1));
    // retrieve the XMLDocument
    Document xmldoc = (Document)xmldat.getDOM();
    // or, alternatively
    // Retrieve the XML as a String
    String xmlString = xmldat.getStringVal();
  }
```

3.   Retrieve the XML document as a CLOB:

```
OraclePreparedStatement pstmt =
    (OraclePreparedStatement) conn.prepareStatement
        ("select x.xmlDoc.getClobVal() xmlDoc from XMLtab
x");

OracleResultSet ors = (OracleResultSet)
pstmt.executeQuery();
    while(ors.next())
    {
        // get the XMLType as a CLOB
        oracle.sql.CLOB xmldat = ors.getCLOB(1);
    }
```

4.   Update XMLType data:

```
OraclePreparedStatement pstmt =
    (OraclePreparedStatement) conn.prepareStatement
        ("update XMLtab set xmlDoc = XMLType(?) ");

    // approach #1 using setString

    String xmlString =
        "<PO><PONO>200</PONO><PNAME>PO_2</PNAME></PO>";
    // bind the string..
    pstmt.setString(1,xmlString);
    pstmt.execute();

    // aproach #2 using setObject
    String xmlString =
        "<PO><PONO>200</PONO><PNAME>PO_2</PNAME></PO>";
    XMLType xmldat = XMLType.createXML(conn,
xmlString);
        // bind the string..
pstmt.setObject(1,xmldat);
        pstmt.execute();
```

See more code fragments and DOM document manipulation techniques in the online XDB documentation.[6]

---

6.   http://download-west.oracle.com/docs/cd/B19306_01/appdev.102/b14259/xdb11jav.htm#sthref1429.

8.2.10   JDBC Support for SQL Object Types and References Types

The Object types designate user-defined SQL types and SQLJ Object types created using the "CREATE TYPE ..." SQL syntax. See the *Oracle Database SQL Reference 10g Release 2* and the *Oracle Database Application Developer's Guide: Object-Relational Features 10g Release 2.*

The SQL Objects can be mapped to Java, either automatically by the driver using `java.sql.Struct` or `oracle.sql.STRUCT` approach—also called *weak type mapping*—or using the custom Java classes approach (i.e., `SQLData or ORAData`)—also called *strong type mapping.* The SQLJ Object type is a special Object type, built using a Java class in the database, and is covered later in this section.

Type Map

As we have seen, built-in SQL types are mapped to Java through the classes furnished by the `oracle.sql.*` package. For user-defined SQL types, a type-map object (`java.util.Map`) allows defining the mapping between a SQL user-defined type and the associated Java class. A type-map object is a class (i.e., `java.util.Hashtable`) that implements a `java.util.Map` interface and is associated with each `Connection` object.

The `getTypeMap()` and `setTypeMap()` methods of the `java.sql.Connection` and `oracle.jdbc.OracleConnection` interfaces allow "installing" and retrieving the `TypeMap` object associated with a Connection object.

```
java.util.Map map = con.getTypeMap();
```

The following code snippet maps the SQL type `Address_t` to the class `AddressObj`:

```
map.put("Address_t",Class.forName("AddressObj"));
oconn.setTypeMap((Map)map);
```

When retrieving data from the result set, you use the default type-map of the connection object, unless you specify a type-map, as follows:

```
rs.getObject(int columnIndex, Map map);
rs.getObject(String colName, Map map);
```

A type-map is required for the `getObject()`, `getAttribute()`, `getAR-RAY()`, and `getValue()` methods of the `ResultSet`, `CallableStatement`, `Struct`, `java.sql.Array`, and `oracle.sql.REF` interfaces. However, when there is none specified for the method in question, the default connection type-map is checked, and, if undefined, the JDBC driver materializes the Oracle object as an instance of `oracle.sql.STRUCT`.

Weak Type Mapping: Struct and STRUCT

The `java.sql.Struct` interface defines methods for custom mapping and processing of a user-defined type (i.e., Object type) and its attributes. It furnishes the following methods:

- `getAttributes()` or `getAttributes(map)`: Materializes the attributes of a `Struct` (or Oracle `STRUCT`) as an array of `java.lang.Object` (i.e., `java.lang.Object[]`) using either the default connection type-map or the one furnished in the parameter, as if `getObject` is invoked on each attribute, and then returns a Java array containing the result.

- `getSQLTypeName`: Returns the fully qualified name of the SQL object type that this `Struct` (or Oracle `STRUCT`) represents (i.e., `SCOTT.ADDRESS_T`).

The `oracle.sql.STRUCT` class is Oracle's implementation of `java.sql.Struct` and extends the `oracle.sql.Datum`. It wraps the "raw bytes" of an instance of an Oracle Object type and contains its SQL type name and an array of `oracle.sql.Datum` objects that hold the value of each attribute in SQL format. This is the default mapping of Oracle objects when a custom mapping through `SQLData` or `ORAData` interfaces is not provided.

In addition to the `java.sql.Struct` methods discussed previously, it furnishes the following methods:

- `getOracleAttributes`: Materializes the attributes of a `STRUCT` as an array of `oracle.sql.Datum` objects (i.e., `oracle.sql.Datum[]`)

- `getDescriptor`: Retrieves the `StructDescriptor`. Oracle Objects are structured data; in order for a data stream containing those objects to be parsed and interpreted, a descriptor of the structure (one descriptor per SQL type) must be present within the driver.

- The `oracle.sql.StructDescriptor` class and its methods help describe, create, and convert objects to and from `STRUCT`.

```
STRUCT str1 = new STRUCT(<connection>,
<structDescriptor>, <attributes>);
// Example
StructDescriptor strdesc =
     StructDescriptor.createDescriptor(sql_type,
strdescc);
     Object [] attrib = { new(ssn), name, address };
     return new STRUCT(strdesc, conn, attrib);
```

Note: When retrieving the Oracle object as `STRUCT`, the driver constructs the `STRUCT` descriptor; the application must furnish it when creating values for use with `setObject()`.

- `toJdbc()` and `toJdbc(map)`: Retrieves the target class in the default map or in the specified type-map.

To access a `STRUCT` or a `Struct` object, the JDBC application invokes either the standard `getObject()` method or the Oracle proprietary `getSTRUCT ()` methods.

```
// retrieving the object as a java.sql.Stuct
ResultSet rset = stmt.executeQuery("SELECT * from
AddressTab");
Struct struct = (Struct)rset.getObject(1);

// retrieving the object as an oracle.sql.STRUCT
STRUCT struct =(oracle.sql.STRUCT) rset.getObject(1);
or
STRUCT struct = rset.getSTRUCT(1);
```

To retrieve the attributes, the JDBC application invokes either `getAttributes()` or `getOracleAttributes()`.

```
// using getAttributes()
Struct struct = (Struct)rset.getObject(1);
```

```
Object[] attrarr = struct.getAttributes();

// using getOracleAttriutes()
oracle.sql.STRUCT strct =(oracle.sql.STRUCT)
rset.getObject(1);
System.out.println("SQL Object type: " +
strct.getSQLTypeName());
Object[] attrarr = strct.getOracleAttributes();
```

To bind the `oracle.sql.STRUCT` or the `java.sql.Struct` instance to an IN parameter, use the `setObject ()`, `setSTRUCT()`, `setSTRUCTAtName()`, `setObject()`, `setOBjectAtName()`, `setOracleObject()`, and `setOracleObjectATName()`methods of `OraclePreparedStatement`, `OracleCalableStatement`, and `OracleResultSet`.

```
STRUCT strct new STRUCT (...);
pstmt.setObject(<index>, strct, Types.STRUCT);
```

or:

```
((OraclePreparedStatement)pstmt).setOracleObject(<index>,
strct);
```

The `updateSTRUCT()`, `updateOracleObject()`methods of `OracleResultSet` can be used to update a `STRUCT` object.

Code Snippet

Assume a user-defined object type, ADTTYP2, and then a table, ADTTAB2 of ADT TYP2 objects:

```
create type ADTTYP2 as object (n1 number, n2 varchar2(30), n3
date)
/
create table ADTTAB2 (id number, adtcol ADTTYP2)
/
insert into ADTTAB2 values (1, ADTTYP2(101, 'Row One', '01-
JAN-2001'));
commit;

 // inserts an oracle.sql.STRUCT object into an Object Type
table
```

```
//
    OraclePreparedStatement ps =
        (OraclePreparedStatement) conn.prepareStatement
            ("INSERT INTO ADTTAB2 (ID, ADTCOL) VALUES(?, ?)");

    ps.setNUMBER (1, id);
    ps.setSTRUCT (2, adt);
    ps.execute ();
    ps.close();


//retrieves a user-defined type as oracle.sql.STRUCT
//
    OraclePreparedStatement ps =
        (OraclePreparedStatement) conn.prepareStatement
            ("SELECT ADTCOL FROM ADTTAB2 WHERE ID = ?");

    ps.setNUMBER (1, id);
    OracleResultSet rs = (OracleResultSet) ps.executeQuery();

    STRUCT st = null;
    while (rs.next())
    {
      st = (STRUCT) rs.getObject(1);
    }
    ps.close();
    return st;
```

See a complete code sample in Chapter 3.

Strong Type Mapping: SQLData and ORAData

SQLData

The `java.sql.SQLData` interface allows custom mapping of a user-defined SQL type to a Java class that implements this interface. The Java class must define the mapping in a type-map; it must also define a field for each attribute of the structured SQL type, and finally it must contain the following methods:

- `getSQLTypeName()`: Returns the fully qualified name of the user-defined SQL type that this object represents.

- `readSQL()`: Retrieves the state of the Java object with data read from the database, using a `SQLInput` stream. It calls the appropriate `readXXX()` methods (i.e., `readInt`, `readLong`, `readFloat`, `readString`, `readBlob`, `readObject`, etc.) of the `SQLInput` object.

```
public void readSQL(SQLInput stream, String
sql_type_name) throws SQLException
```

- `writeSQL()`: Stores the state of the Java object back to the database using a `SQLOutput` stream. It calls the appropriate `writeXXX()` methods (i.e., `writeInt`, `writeLong`, `writeString`, `writeObject`) of the `SQLOutput` object.

```
public void writeSQL(SQLOutput stream) throws
SQLException
```

To read data from an Oracle object, the driver determines the Java class to use for converting the data from SQL format to Java attributes by looking up the type-map.

```
ResultSet rset =
          stmt.executeQuery ("select value(t) from
ClientTab t");
    while (rset.next ())
    {
      System.out.println(rset.getObject(1));
    }
```

The `ResultSet.getObject()` method maps the user-defined type to an instance of the implementation class. If the type-map is not specified, the Oracle object is materialized as an `oracle.sql.STRUCT`.

Conversely, for storing the Java class attributes into an Oracle object, the driver gets the SQL type name from the Java class by calling the `getSQLTypeName()` method of the `SQLData` interface. The `SQLData` object must be assigned the `OracleTypes.STRUCT` typecode.

```
pstmt.setObject(<index>, <SQLData object>,
OracleTypes.STRUCT);
```

The driver furnishes the `SQLInput` implementation class, which is an input stream passed to `readSQL()`, and the `SQLOutput` implementation class, which is an output stream passed to `writeSQL()`. These classes are used by the `SQLData` methods, not by the application code.

Assume the following object type:

```
CREATE or REPLACE TYPE Client_t AS OBJECT
  (
   ssn NUMBER(10),
   name   VARCHAR2(30),
   address     VARCHAR2(100)
);
/
```

The following Java class manually implements SQLData for mapping the SQL `CLIENT_T` Object type; the JPublisher utility covered later generates this for you.

```
import java.sql.*;

public class jClient_t implements SQLData
{
  private String sql_type;
  public int ssn;
  public String name;
  public String address;

  public jClient_t () {}

  public jClient_t (String sql_type, int ssn, String name,
String address)
    {
      this.sql_type = sql_type;
      this.ssn = ssn;
      this.name = name;
      this.address = address;
    }
```

```
    public String getSQLTypeName() throws SQLException
    {
      return sql_type;
    }

    public void readSQL(SQLInput stream, String typeName)
  throws SQLException {
        sql_type = typeName;
        ssn = stream.readInt();
        name = stream.readString();
        address = stream.readString();
    }
    public void writeSQL(SQLOutput stream) throws SQLException
  {
        stream.writeInt(ssn);
        stream.writeString(name);
        stream.writeString(address);
    }

    public String toString ()
    {
      return sql_type + " = " + ssn + ", " + name + ", " +
  address;
    }
}
```

A JDBC application would use this as follows:

1.   Create the `Client_t` type and the corresponding Object table
     either directly through SQL or programmatically, as follows:

```
    // Create the SQL object type "Client_t".
        stmt.execute ("CREATE TYPE Client_t AS OBJECT     "+
                        "(  ssn NUMBER,                    "+
                        "   name VARCHAR2(30),             "+
                        "   address VARCHAR2(100))         ");

        stmt.execute ("CREATE TABLE ClientTab of Client_t");
```

2.   Specify the mapping and insert instances of `Client_t`:

```
// Map jClient_t class to Oracle object Client_t type
   map.put ("SCOTT.Client_t", Class.forName
   ("jClient_t"));

PreparedStatement pstmt =
     conn.prepareStatement ("insert into ClentTab
values (?)");


   // Insert a Client_t object into the database
     Object client = new jClient_ ("SCOTT.Client_t",
981, "Adam", " 203 Chapms Elysses - Paris France");
     pstmt.setObject (1, client, OracleTypes.STRUCT);
     pstmt.executeUpdate ();
```

The `setObject()` method invokes `writeSQL()`, which in turn invokes the `writeXXX()` per the `SQLData`.

3.   Retrieve instances of Client_t:

```
Statement stmt = conn.createStatement ();
ResultSet rset =
     stmt.executeQuery ("select value(o) from
ClientTab o");
   while (rset.next ())
   {
     System.out.println(rset.getObject(1));


   }
```

The `getObject()` method invokes `readSQL()`, which in turn invokes the `readXXX()` per the `SQLData`.

ORAData and ORADataFactory

The `oracle.sql.ORAData` interface, which is a replacement for the `oracle.sql.CustomDatum` interface, is a more flexible, optimized, but proprietary alternative to `SQLData`. It allows custom mapping and processing of Oracle Objects as well as any other Oracle SQL type (i.e., any data type available in the Oracle database).

For example, beyond custom type-mapping, you can use `ORAData` to implement custom processing such as data encryption, decryption, validation, logging, Java object serialization and deserialization, character conversion and formatting, and so on. It does not require a type-map because it uses `oracle.sql.Datum` directly. The Java class, which implements the `oracle.jdbc.ORAData` interface, contains the following static fields and methods:

```
public static final String _SQL_NAME = "<schema>.<Object type>";
public static final int _SQL_TYPECODE = OracleTypes.STRUCT;
public static ORADataFactory getFactory() { ... }
```

Note: The public static final field `_SQL_TYPECODE` is an alternative

```
way of specifying the type map.
```

```
public Datum toDatum(java.sql.Connection c)
          throws java.sql.SQLException
```

The `oracle.sql.Datum` type is the internal format used by the driver to hold Oracle objects (it was introduced at the beginning of this long section). The `toDatum()` method retrieves the corresponding `Datum` object from the `ORAData` object.

The `ORADataFactory` interface acts as a constructor of `ORAData` instances. It provides the following methods for creating customized `ORAData` from a `Datum`:

```
public ORAData create(Datum d,
                      int sqlType)
            throws java.sql.SQLException
```

The following Java class manually implements `ORAData` and `ORADataFactory` for mapping the SQL `CLIENT_T` Object type; the JPublisher utility covered later generates this for you.

```
import java.sql.*;
import oracle.sql.*;

public class Client_t implements ORAData, ORADataFactory
{
```

```
static final Client_t factory = new Client_t ();
String sql_type = "SCOTT.CLIENT_T";
public int ssn;
public String name;
public String address;

public static ORADataFactory getFactory()
{
  return _factory;
}

public Client_t () {}

public Client_t (int ssn, String name, String address)
{
  this.ssn = ssn;
  this.name = name;
  this.address = address;
}

public Datum toDatum(Connection conn)
  throws SQLException
{
  StructDescriptor strdesc =
   StructDescriptor.createDescriptor(sql_type, conn);
  Object [] attribs = {  new Integer(ssn), name, address };
  return new STRUCT(strdesc, conn, attribs);
}
public ORAData create(Datum datm, int sqlType) throws SQLException
{
  if (datm == null) return null;
  Datum[] attribs = ((STRUCT) datm).getOracleAttributes();
  return new Address (attribs[0].intValue (),
                      attribs[1].stringValue (),
                      attribs[2].stringValue ());
}

public String toString ()
{
  return sql_type + " = " + ssn + ", " + name + ", " + address;
}
}
```

To read data from an Oracle object, the JDBC application may use the getORAData() or getObject() methods; however, getObject() requires a type-map, similar to the SQLData approach.

```
// Using getORAData()
OraleResultSet  rset = (OracleResultSet)stmt.executeQuery
                        ("SELECT value(o) from ClientTab o");
Client_t client =
        (Client_t)rset.getORAData(1, Client_t.getFactory());
```

To write data into an Oracle object, the JDBC application may use the setORAData() or setObject() methods.

```
PreparedStatement pstmt =
    conn.prepareStatement ("insert into ClentTab values (?)");

Object client = new jClient_ ("SCOTT.Client_t", 1343, "Julie",
        " 203 Fillmore St — 92 xxx San Francisco USA");
pstmt.setORAData(1, client);
pstmt.executeUpdate ();
```

The setObject() method in ORAData works similar to the SQLDAta counterpart.

SQLJ Object Types

The SQLJ Object type is a special Object type specified by ANSI SQLJ Part II. It allows constructing user-defined SQL types, using Java classes that implement the SQLData or ORAData interfaces.

```
CREATE TYPE <SQLJ object>  AS OBJECT
  [ EXTERNAL NAME '<Class name>'  LANGUAGE JAVA ]
    USING SQLData|ORAdata (...);
```

The attributes, the setters, and the getters of the Java class can be mapped to SQL through the EXTERNAL NAME clause; more specifically, public class methods (i.e., public static) map to STATIC FUNCTION or STATIC PROCEDURE, and public instance methods (i.e., public) map to MEMBER FUNCTION or MEMBER PROCEDURE.

The SQLJ object type may also be created as a usual SQL object type (i.e., without a base Java class), but the "externalized" methods must be implemented by Java methods.

The `oracle.sql.JAVA_STRUCT` class, which extends the `oracle.sql.STRUCT`, and the `OracleTypes.JAVA_STRUCT` typecode represent such object types.

Here are the required steps for creating a SQLJ Obect type, as illustrated by Listing 8.3:

1. Create a Java class implementing the `ORAData` and `ORADataFactory` interfaces.

2. Load the Java class into the database.

3. Issue the SQL `CREATE TYPE` command.

Listing 8.3   *Paymaster.java*

=================================

```
import java.sql.*;
import java.io.*;
import oracle.sql.*;
import oracle.jdbc.*;
import java.math.*;
public class Paymaster implements SQLData {
  // Implement the attributes and operations for this type.
  private BigDecimal empno;
  private String ename;
  private String job;
  private BigDecimal mgr;
  private Date hiredate;
  private BigDecimal sal;
  private BigDecimal comm;
  private Ref dept;

  public BigDecimal wages() {
    BigDecimal pay = sal;
    if (comm != null) pay = pay.add(comm);
    return pay;
  }
```

```
public void raiseSal(BigDecimal amount) {
  //
  sal = sal.add(amount);
  System.out.println(sal);
}



// Implement SQLData interface.
String sql_type;

public String getSQLTypeName() throws SQLException {
  return sql_type;
}

public void readSQL(SQLInput stream, String typeName)
  throws SQLException {
  sql_type = typeName;
  empno = stream.readBigDecimal();
  ename = stream.readString();
  job = stream.readString();
  mgr = stream.readBigDecimal();
  hiredate = stream.readDate();
  sal = stream.readBigDecimal();
  comm = stream.readBigDecimal();
  dept = stream.readRef();
}

public void writeSQL(SQLOutput stream) throws SQLException
{
  stream.writeBigDecimal(empno);
  stream.writeString(ename);
  stream.writeString(job);
  stream.writeBigDecimal(mgr);
  stream.writeDate(hiredate);
  stream.writeBigDecimal(sal);
  stream.writeBigDecimal(comm);
  stream.writeRef(dept);
}
}

$ javac Paymaster.java
$ loadjava -u user/pass Paymaster.class
```

Paymaster.sql

```
----------------
drop table employee_tab;
drop table dept_tab;
drop type employee;
drop type department;

CREATE TYPE Department AS OBJECT (
  deptno NUMBER(2),
  dname  VARCHAR2(14),
  loc    VARCHAR2(13)
);
/
CREATE or replace TYPE Employee AS OBJECT (
  empno    NUMBER(4),
  ename    VARCHAR2(10),
  job      VARCHAR2(9),
  mgr      NUMBER(4),
  hiredate DATE,
  sal      NUMBER(7,2),
  comm     NUMBER(7,2),
  deptno   REF Department,
  MEMBER FUNCTION wages RETURN NUMBER
    AS LANGUAGE JAVA
    NAME 'Paymaster.wages() return java.math.BigDecimal',

  MEMBER PROCEDURE raise_sal (r NUMBER)
    AS LANGUAGE JAVA
    NAME 'Paymaster.raiseSal(java.math.BigDecimal)'

);
/
create table employee_tab of employee;
create table dept_tab of department;
insert into dept_tab values (department(1, 'physics',
'sample'));
insert into employee_tab values (employee(1, 'kuassi', 'sw',
10 , '13-dec-2005', 1000, 1000, (select rof(d) from dept_tab
d)));

select value(a).wages() from employee_tab a;
$ sqlplus user/pass @Paymaster
```

REF

The SQL REF type represents references (pointer) to objects of a specified type such as REF of ADT types, REF of X. In SQL and PL/SQL, REF of X can be created in SQL by querying the X object and applying the REF operator. Similarly, to access the object referenced by a REF, you dereference the REF, using the Oracle-supplied DEREF operator.

The Oracle JDBC oracle.sql.REF class wraps the SQL REF data type and implements the java.sql.Ref interface. The java.sql.Ref interface furnishes the following methods:

- getBaseTypeName(): Retrieves the fully qualified SQL name of the SQL structured type that this Ref object references

- getObject(): Retrieves the SQL structured type instance referenced by this Ref object

- getObject(Map): Retrieves the referenced object and maps it to a Java type using the given type-map

- setObject(Object): Sets the structured type value that this Ref object references to the given instance of Object

The OraclePreparedStatement, OracleCallableStatement, and OracleResultSet furnish the getREF, getRef, setREF, setRef, setREFAtName, setRefType, setRefTypeAtName, updateREF, getObject, and setObject methods. Unlike SQL, in JDBC, application codes cannot create an instance of oracle.sql.REF, only the driver may.

Manipulating REF of ADT Table Types

Assume a user-defined object type ADTtyp, a table ADTtab of ADTtyp objects, and a table of REF of ADTtyp:

```
create type ADTtyp as OBJECT (a1 number, a2 varchar2(20), a3
date)
/
create table ADTtab of ADTtyp
/
create table REFtab (id number, refcol REF ADTtyp)
/
```

Prepopulated as follows:

```
insert into ADTtab values (ADTtyp(1, 'One', '01-JAN-2001'));
insert into REFtab select 1, REF(R2) from ADTtab R2 where
R2.a1 = 1;
commit;
```

The following code snippet inserts an `oracle.sql.REF` into the REFtab table:

```
OraclePreparedStatement ps = (OraclePreparedStatement)
    conn.prepareStatement("INSERT INTO REFTAB (ID, REFCOL)
VALUES(?, ?)");

    ps.setNUMBER (1, id);
    ps.setREF (2, rf);
    ps.execute ();
```

The following code snippet retrieves and returns an instance of REF ADTTyp as `oracle.sql.REF`:

```
OraclePreparedStatement ps = (OraclePreparedStatement)
    conn.prepareStatement ("SELECT REFCOL FROM REFTAB WHERE
ID = ?");

    ps.setNUMBER (1, id);
    OracleResultSet rs = (OracleResultSet) ps.executeQuery();

    REF r = null;
    while (rs.next())
    {
      r = (REF) rs.getObject(1);
    }
    ps.close();
    return r;
```

REF Cursors

Cursors contain query results and metadata. A `REF Cursor` (or cursor variable) data type contains a reference to a cursor. It can be passed between the RDBMS and the client, or between PL/SQL and Java in the database; it can also be returned from a query or a stored procedure. The Oracle JDBC furnishes the `getCursor` and `setCursorAtName` methods for manipulating `Ref Cursor` as `ResultSet` and `OracleResultSet`. Setting `setCreateStatementAsRefCursor()` to true turns any statements created from this connection into a `REF CURSOR`.

Returning a `REF Cursor` as a `java.sql.ResultSet`:

...

```
((OracleConnection)conn).setCreateStatementAsRefCursor(true);
    Statement stmt = conn.createStatement();
    ((OracleStatement)stmt).setRowPrefetch(1);

    ResultSet rset =
        stmt.executeQuery("select * from EMP order by empno");
        rset = ((OracleResultSet)rset).getCursor(i);
    return rset;
```

For `CallableStatement`, the `RefCursor` must be declared as an `OUT` parameter with the `CURSOR` typecode:

```
cstmt.registerOutParameter(1,OracleTypes.CURSOR);
...
```

See a complete example in Chapter 3.

8.2.11 JDBC Support for User-Defined Collections

User-defined collections include `VARRAYs`, `Nested Tables`, and `PL/SQL Associative Arrays`.

ARRAY, VARRAYs, and ArrayDescriptor

The Oracle database furnishes only variable-length arrays (i.e., `VARRAYs`) as part of the user-defined SQL collection types. They represent an ordered set of elements of the same type (scalar or complex types) and are used to map array data types in other languages. `VARRAY` data are stored in line in table columns; however, when their size is larger than 4 K, or when a storage clause is specified, these are stored outline, as `BLOB` data. The maximum number of elements in a `VARRAY` must be specified at creation time.

The Oracle JDBC drivers support the SQL VARRAY through the ora-cle.sql.ARRAY wrapper class (which implements the standard java.sql.Array interface) and the oracle.sql.ArrayDescriptor class.

The oracle.sql.ARRAY furnishes the following methods: getArray() with various signatures (see the Oracle JDBC javadoc), getBaseType(), getBaseTypeName(), getDescriptor(), getDoubleArray(), getFloa-tArray(), getIntArray(), getLongArray(), getResultSet(), getJav-aSQLConnection(), toJdbc(), and so on

The oracle.sql.ArrayDescriptor furnishes the following methods: createDescriptor(), dscType(), getArrayType(), getBaseName(), getBaseType(), getTypeCode(), getMaxLength(), getArrayType() (i.e., TYPE_VARRAY and TYPE_NESTED_TABLE), toResultSet(), and so on.

The OraclePreparedStatement, OracleCallableStatement, and OracleResultSet furnish the setArray, setArrayAtName, setARRAY, setARRAYAtName, getArray, getARRAY, updateArray, and updateARRAY methods. These methods can be used directly to manipulate arrays of scalar (built-in) SQL types. However, if the elements of the SQL Array are user-defined types, the java.sql.SQLData or oracle.sql.ORAData classes and a type-map must be used to manipulate the elements of the Java array, similar to SQL Object types, covered earlier.

The following snippets excerpted from Chapter 3 illustrate the manipulation of VARRAY of scalar types, including VARRAY of NUMBER, VARRAY of VARCHAR2, and VARRAY of DATE.

VARRAY of NUMBER

Assume the following NVARRAY type and instance:

```
create or replace type NVARRAY as VARRAY(10) of number;
 NVARRAY(1, 2, 3, 4, 5, 6, 7, 8, 9, 10)


// The following code snippet inserts a java.sql.Array into
// VarrayTab table as NVARRAY

    Statement stmt = conn.createStatement();


    OraclePreparedStatement ps = (OraclePreparedStatement)
    conn.prepareStatement("INSERT INTO VarrayTab (ID, NVA)
VALUES(?, ?)");
```

```
        ps.setNUMBER (1, id[0]);
        ps.setARRAY (2, (ARRAY)va[0]);
        ps.execute ();


    // The following code snippet retrieves and returns an NVARRAY
    // as a java.sql.Array

        OraclePreparedStatement ps = (OraclePreparedStatement)
        conn.prepareStatement ("SELECT NVA FROM VarrayTab WHERE ID
    = ? ");
        ps.setNUMBER (1, id[0]);
        OracleResultSet rs = (OracleResultSet) ps.executeQuery();
        Array a = null;
        while (rs.next())
        {
           a = (Array) rs.getObject(1);
        }
        ps.close();
        return a;
```

See the complete code sample in Chapter 3.

VARRAY of VARCHAR2

Assume the following VC2VARRAY type and instance:

```
    create or replace type VC2VARRAY as VARRAY(10) of
    varchar2(30);
    VC2VARRAY('Thirty One', 'Thirty Two', 'Thirty Three',
                'Thirty Four', 'Thirty Five', 'Thirty Six',
                'Thirty Seven', 'Thirty Eight')


    // The following code snippet inserts a java.sql.Array row
    // into VC2VARRAY as a java.sql.Array

        Statement stmt = conn.createStatement();

        OraclePreparedStatement ps = (OraclePreparedStatement)
        conn.prepareStatement("INSERT INTO VarrayTab(ID, VC2VA)
    VALUES(?, ?)");


        ps.setNUMBER (1, id[0]);
```

```
ps.setARRAY (2, (ARRAY)va[0]);
ps.execute ();
ps.close();



// The following code snippet retrieves and returns a
// VC2VARRAY as a java.sql.Array

OraclePreparedStatement ps = (OraclePreparedStatement)
conn.prepareStatement ("SELECT VC2VA FROM VarrayTab WHERE
ID = ? ");
ps.setNUMBER (1, id[0]);
OracleResultSet rs = (OracleResultSet) ps.executeQuery();
Array a = null;
while (rs.next())
{
  a = (Array) rs.getObject(1);
}
ps.close();
return a;
```

See the complete code sample in Chapter 3.

VARRAY of DATE

Assume the following DATVARRAY and instance:

```
create or replace type DATVARRAY as VARRAY(10) of date;
DATVARRAY('01-JAN-2005', '02-JAN-2005', '03-JAN-2005', '04-
JAN-2005',
             '05-JAN-2005', '06-JAN-2005', '07-JAN-2005',
             '08-JAN-2005','09-JAN-2005', '10-JAN-2005')

// The following code snippet inserts a java.sql.Array
// row into VarrayTab table as DATVARRAY

Statement stmt = conn.createStatement();

OraclePreparedStatement ps = (OraclePreparedStatement)
    conn.prepareStatement ("INSERT INTO VarrayTab (ID,
DATVA)
       VALUES(?, ?)");
```

```
ps.setNUMBER (1, id[0]);
ps.setARRAY (2, (ARRAY)va[0]);
ps.execute ();
ps.close();
conn.commit();

// The following code snippet retrieves and returns
// a DATVARRAY as a java.sql.Array

OraclePreparedStatement ps = (OraclePreparedStatement)
conn.prepareStatement ("SELECT DATVA FROM VarrayTab WHERE
ID = ? ");

ps.setNUMBER (1, id[0]);
OracleResultSet rs = (OracleResultSet) ps.executeQuery();
Array a = null;
while (rs.next())
{
   a = (Array) rs.getObject(1);
}
ps.close();
return a;
```

See the complete code sample in Chapter 3.

Nested Tables

Nested Tables, or tables within a table, are part of the user-defined SQL collection types. They define a type, which represents an unordered set of elements of the same type and are used to map sets and bag data types in other languages. The nested table columns of a table are stored out of line from the rows of the parent table, using the "store as" clause (see the Oracle SQL Reference Guide). Unlike VARRAYs, which have fixed boundaries, Nested Tables are more flexible because the size can dynamically grow or shrink; however, there is no such thing as a free lunch, so the size change will be at the expense of more storage. If the elements of the Nested Tables are user-defined types, the java.sql.SQLData or oracle.sql.ORAData classes and a type-map must be used to manipulate the elements of the Java arrays, similar to SQL Object types, covered earlier.

The following snippets excerpted from Chapter 3 illustrate the manipulation of NESTED TABLE of scalar types, including NESTED TABLE of NUMBER, NESTED TABLE of VARCHAR2, and NESTED TABLE of DATE.

NESTED TABLE of NUMBER

Assume NTab_Num a nested table of type numnt store as NSTabNum and an instance declared as follows:

```
NTab_Num(1, 2, 3, 4, 5, 6, 7, 8, 9, 10)


// The following code snippet inserts a java.sql.Array row
// into NSTableTab as NTab_Num

    Statement stmt = conn.createStatement();
    OraclePreparedStatement ps = (OraclePreparedStatement)
        conn.prepareStatement ("INSERT INTO NSTableTab (ID,
NUMNT)
          VALUES(?, ?)");

    ps.setNUMBER (1, id[0]);
    ps.setARRAY (2, (ARRAY) nt[0]);
    ps.execute ();
    ps.close();


// The following code snippet retrieves and returns a NTab_Num
// as a java.sql.Array

    OraclePreparedStatement ps = (OraclePreparedStatement)
        conn.prepareStatement ("SELECT NUMNT FROM NSTableTab
                WHERE ID = ?");
    ps.setNUMBER (1, id[0]);
    OracleResultSet rs = (OracleResultSet) ps.executeQuery();
    Array a = null;
    while (rs.next())
    {
      a = (Array) rs.getObject(1);
    }
    ps.close();
    return a;
```

See the complete code sample in Chapter 3.

NESTED TABLE of VARCHAR2

Assume `NTab_Vc2` a nested table of type `vc2nt` store as `NSTabVc2` and an instance declared as follows:

```
NTab_Vc2('One', 'Two', 'Three', 'Four', 'Five', 'Six',
'Seven',
                'Eight', 'Nine', 'Ten')


// The following code snippet inserts a java.sql.Array row
// into NSTableTab as NTab_Vc2

Statement stmt = conn.createStatement();

 OraclePreparedStatement ps = (OraclePreparedStatement)
 conn.prepareStatement("INSERT INTO NSTableTab(ID,VC2NT)
VALUES(?, ?)");

    ps.setNUMBER (1, id[0]);
    ps.setARRAY (2, (ARRAY) nt[0]);
    ps.execute ();
    ps.close();

 // The following code snippet retrieves and returns a
 // NTab_Vc2 as a java.sql.Array

    OraclePreparedStatement ps = (OraclePreparedStatement)
        conn.prepareStatement ("SELECT VC2NT FROM NSTableTab
WHERE ID = ?");

    ps.setNUMBER (1, id[0]);
    OracleResultSet rs = (OracleResultSet) ps.executeQuery();
    Array a = null;
    while (rs.next())
    {
      a = (Array) rs.getObject(1);
    }
    ps.close();
    return a;
```

See the complete code sample in Chapter 3.

NESTED TABLE of DATE

Assume `NTab_Dat` a nested table of type datnt store as `NSTabDat` and an instance declared as follows:

```
NTab_Dat('01-JAN-2003', '02-JAN-2003', '03-JAN-2003', '04-
JAN-2003',
          '05-JAN-2003', '06-JAN-2003', '07-JAN-2003', '08-
JAN-2003',
          '09-JAN-2003', '10-JAN-2003')


// The following code snippet inserts a java.sql.Array row
// into NSTableTab as NTab_Dat

 Statement stmt = conn.createStatement();

 OraclePreparedStatement ps = (OraclePreparedStatement)
 conn.prepareStatement("INSERT INTO NSTableTab(ID,DATNT)
VALUES(?, ?)");
    ps.setNUMBER (1, id[0]);
    ps.setARRAY (2, (ARRAY) nt[0]);
    ps.execute ();
    ps.close();

    id[0] = new NUMBER(id[0].intValue() + 1000);
    nt[0] = nt2;
  }


// The following code snippet retrieves and returns a NTab_Dat
// as a java.sql.Array

 Statement stmt = conn.createStatement();

 OraclePreparedStatement ps = (OraclePreparedStatement)
   conn.prepareStatement ("SELECT DATNT FROM NSTableTab WHERE
ID = ?");

   ps.setNUMBER (1, id[0]);
   OracleResultSet rs = (OracleResultSet) ps.executeQuery();

   Array a = null;
```

```
while (rs.next())
{
  a = (Array) rs.getObject(1);
}
ps.close();
id[0] = new NUMBER(id[0].intValue() + 1000);
nt[0] = nt2;

return a;
```

See the complete code sample in Chapter 3.

Alternatively to mapping NESTED TABLE to oracle.sql.VARRAY and java.sql.Array, you may perfom custom mapping of NESTED TABLEs, using classes that implement ORAData.

- The custom collection must have a String constant _SQL_TYPECODE initialized to OracleTypes.ARRAY:

```
public static final int _SQL_TYPECODE = OracleTypes.ARRAY;
```

- The custom collection class must have the constant _SQL_NAME initialized to the SQL name of the user-defined collection:

```
public static final String _SQL_NAME = "ADT_VARRAY";
```

PL/SQL Associative Array

The PL/SQL Associative Array type (previously PL/SQL Index-by Table) is a hash table of key/value pairs, which models unordered lists, trees, maps, dictionaries, and lookup tables found in other languages (e.g., a phone book of name/phone numbers, a dictionary of words, definition).

- The keys have unique values that locate the element in the array; it can be of type number, string values, even user-defined subtypes, positive, negative, nonsequential, and expressed by the INDEX BY clause, including INDEX BY BINARY_INTEGER PLS_INTEGER, VARCHAR2(<size>), POSITIVE, NEGATIVE, NATURAL, and so on. However, the Oracle JDBC currently supports only number keys.

- The values (elements of table) can be of all valid SQL or PL/SQL types. The Oracle JDBC currently supports only number and character as value elements. RAW, DATE, CLOB, BLOB, TIMESTAMP[[L]TZ] , INTEVALYM/INTERVADS, PL/SQL Records, and ADTs are currently not supported as element types.

PL/SQL Associative Arrays are similar to Nested Tables in terms of their structure (i.e., unbound, single dimension, all elements must be of the same type), but unlike nested tables, the former can only be used in PL/SQL, are sparse, have no storage clause, and are easily extensible. They are constructed in memory each time the corresponding package is initialized or at the invocation of corresponding procedure(s).

The following PL/SQL methods are available: COUNT, DELETE, EXISTS(n), FIRST, LAST, PRIOR(n), and NEXT(n). See the PL/SQL Users Guide for more details.

The Oracle JDBC allows applications to bind PL/SQL Associative Array types as IN, OUT, and IN/OUT parameters. Prior to Oracle JDBC 10g Release 2, PL/SQL Associate Arrays were supported by JDBC-OCI only, but with 10g Release 2, both driver types support these.

The Oracle JDBC supports PL/SQL Associative Array through the set-PlsqlIndexTable(), registerIndexTableOutParameter(), getOraclePlsqlIndexTable(), and getPlsqlIndexTable() methods in OraclePreparedStatement and OraleCallableStatement.

- setPlsqlIndexTable(): In OraclePreparedStatement and OracleCallableStatement for binding a PL/SQL associative array as IN parameter:

```
setPlsqlIndexTable(int parameterIndex,
        java.lang.Object arrayData,
        int maxLen,
        int curLen,
        int elemSqlType,
        int elemMaxLen)

// bind IN parameter
proc.setPlsqlIndexTable (1, values,
        maxLen, currentLen,
        elemSqlType, elemMaxLen);
```

- `registerIndexTableOutParameter()`: In `OracleCallableStatement` for registering the OUT parameter:

```
registerIndexTableOutParameter(int paramIndex,
        int maxLen,
        int elemSqlType,
        int elemMaxLen)

// register OUT parameter
    proc1.registerIndexTableOutParameter (2, maxLen,
                                            elemSqlType,
elemMaxLen);
```

The following methods return elements of associative arrays using either JDBC default mapping, Oracle mapping, or Java primitive type-mapping:

- `public java.lang.Object getPlsqlIndexTable(int paramIndex)`: Returns the elements of a PL/SQL index table as Java array using the JDBC default mappings.

    ```
    NUMERIC elements -> BigDecimal array (BigDecimal[] )
    VARCHAR elements  -> String array (String[])

    // retrieve the elements using JDBC default mapping
        BigDecimal[] elements =
            (BigDecimal[]) proc1.getPlsqlIndexTable (2);
    ```

- `public Datum[] getOraclePlsqlIndexTable(int paramIndex)`: JDBC-OCI driver specific; returns the elements of a PL/SQL index table as an oracle.sql.Datum array.

    ```
    NUMBER elements -> oracle.sql.Datum array (Datum[])
        VARCHAR elements -> oracle.sql.Datum array (Datum[])

    // retrieve the elements using Oracle JDBC mapping
    Datum[] elements = proc2.getOraclePlsqlIndexTable (2);
    ```

- synchronized   public   Object   `getPlsqlIndexTable(int paramIndex, Class primitiveType)`: Returns the elements of index-by-table as array of Java primitive types. The possible `primi-`

tiveType   values   are   `java.lang.Integer.TYPE`, `java.lang.Long.TYPE`,   `java.lang.Float.TYPE`, `java.lang.Double.TYPE`, and `java.lang.Short.TYPE`.

```
java.lang.Integer.TYPE -> int array (int[])
java.lang.Float.TYPE   -> double array (double[])
java.lang.Short.TYPE   -> short array (short[])

    // retrieve the elements  as a Java primitive array.
    int[] element = (int[])
        func1.getPlsqlIndexTable (2,
java.lang.Integer.TYPE);
```

In order to use PL/SQL associative arrays, the following prerequisite steps must be performed either in a separate SQL session or directly within JDBC (see following example):

Step 1. Create a PL/SQL package and the PL/SQL associative array of the scalar type:

```
TYPE <index-by-table-type> IS TABLE OF <scalar>
            INDEX BY BINARY_INTEGER

  CREATE OR REPLACE PACKAGE mypkg AS TYPE plsqldxtyp IS
      TABLE OF VARCHAR2(20) INDEX BY BINARY_INTEGER;
  END;
```

Step 2. Create PL/SQL procedures and/or functions, which take the new type as IN and/or OUT and/or IN/OUT parameter(s) and manipulate the associative array (e.g., update the elements):

```
CREATE TABLE plsqlidxtab (col VARCHAR2(30));

create or replace procedure proc1
(feedback OUT VARCHAR2(30),  p1 in mypkg.plsqlidxtyp) is
    begin
        for i in p1.FIRST..p1.LAST loop
        insert into plsqlidxtab (plsqlidxtyp(i));
        end loop;
       feedback := 'PLSQL ASSOC ARRAY ROCKS';
    end;
```

Listing 8.4 illustrates PL/SQL Associative Array.

Listing 8.4   *myPLSQLIndexTab.java*
==

```java
import java.sql.*;
import java.util.*;
import java.io.*;
import oracle.jdbc.*;
import oracle.sql.*;
import oracle.jdbc.pool.*;
import oracle.jdbc.pool.OracleDataSource;

public class myPLSQLIndexTab
{
  public static void main(String[] args) throws SQLException
  {
   //Create an OracleDataSource
   OracleDataSource ods = new OracleDataSource();
   // Set the URL, using TNS Alias with JDBC-Thin
   String url = "jdbc:oracle:thin:scott/tiger@inst1";
   ods.setURL(url);
   // Retrieve a connection
   OracleConnection conn = (OracleConnection)ods.getConnection();
   Statement stmt = conn.createStatement ();
   try {

     // define PL/SQL Index by table
     stmt.execute ("create or replace package mypkg as type plsidxtyp "+
                 " is table of varchar2(20) index by binary_integer; "+
                 "end;");

     // create procedure p1
     stmt.execute ("create or replace procedure proc1 "+
             "(p1 in out mypkg.plsidxtyp) is " +
             "begin "+
             " for i in p1.FIRST..p1.LAST loop "+
             " p1(i) := p1(i)|| ' out'; "+
             " end loop; "+
             "end;");
```

```
stmt.close();
 // set the table values
 String [] plsqlidxarr1 =
   { "element1","element2","element3", "element4" };

 // prepare the invocation of the stored procedue
 OracleCallableStatement cstmt = (OracleCallableStatement)
   conn.prepareCall ("begin proc1 (?); end;");

 // actual size of the index-by table bind value
 int currentLen = plsqlidxarr1.length;
 int maxLen = currentLen;

 // index-by table element type
 int elemSqlType =  OracleTypes.VARCHAR;

 // index-by table element length
 int elemMaxLen = 20;

 // Bind the IN parameter
 cstmt.setPlsqlIndexTable (1, plsqlidxarr1,
                     maxLen, currentLen,
                     elemSqlType, elemMaxLen);
 // Register OUT parameter
 // cstmt.registerOutParameter (1, Types.CHAR);
 // register the OUT parameter
 cstmt.registerIndexTableOutParameter (1, maxLen,
                   elemSqlType, elemMaxLen);
 // execute the call
 cstmt.execute ();

 // retrieve the elements using JDBC default mapping
 String[] elements =
   (String[]) cstmt.getPlsqlIndexTable (1);

 // print the elements
 for (int i=0; i<elements.length; i++)
  System.out.println(" " + elements[i]);

  cstmt.close();
```

```
      } catch (SQLException ea) {
        ea.printStackTrace();
      }
    }
  }
}
$ javac myPLSQLIndexTab.java
$ java -Doracle.net.tns_admin=$TNS_ADMIN myPLSQLIndexTab
 element1 out
 element2 out
 element3 out
 element4 out
$
```

PL/SQL Record and PL/SQL Boolean

These data types are not currently supported by Oracle JDBC; for example, you cannot call a PL/SQL procedure that has a Record parameter. However, using JPublisher (covered later), a Java wrapper is generated that calls the procedure in question.

8.2.12 JDBC Support for Spatial Types

The SDO_Geometry, SDO_Topo_Geometry, and SDO_GeoRaster data types are not currently supported natively by the Oracle JDBC drivers; however, the Oracle *inter*Media and JPublisher furnish ways to manipulate these types (see the *inter*Media Case Study in Part VI).

8.2.13 Unsupported Types

As of Oracle Database 10g Release 2, the Oracle JDBC does not currently expose the following Oracle database supplied types to end users:

- Media types
- Expression filter types
- URIType
- Any types: SYS.AnyData, SYS.AnyType, and SYS.Any-DataSet

8.3   Result Set Support in Oracle JDBC

With connections and statements, result sets are one of the key JDBC features. In the previous section, we covered (among other things) the set of getXXX() methods for retrieving column data types that made a result set row. This section focuses on the result set types, their implementation in Oracle JDBC drivers, and methods for retrieving data and navigating through rows.

8.3.1   The Result Set API in a Nutshell

Result sets are Java objects that contain the set of rows and columns that result from the execution of a SQL query. The getXXX() and updateXXX() methods allow the retrieval, updating, and inserting of rows from/in the result set. A cursor controls positioning and how the rows are being returned/consumed by the requester. First, let's look at the chronological evolution of the Result Set API.

The Evolution of the Result Set API

Since its introduction in JDBC 1.22, result sets have evolved into various types with additional capabilities. As discussed in the overview of the JDBC specifications in Chapter 6:

- JDBC 1.22 specifies java.sql.ResultSet forward-only and read-only modes for managing the result set from the execution of a given JDBC statement.

- JDBC 2.0 (core API) specifies scrollable and updatable result set (supports insert, update, and delete), which implements SQL-92 scrollable cursors. The result set maintains a positional cursor, which points to the current row. The movements of the cursor are controlled by the following methods on the result set object: first(), last(), beforeFirst(), afterLast(), next(), previous(), relative(), absolute(), and Hints, which specify the direction in which result sets will be processed (FETCH_FORWARD, FETCH_REVERSE), and fetch size.

- JDBC 3.0 specifies the getMoreResults() method for controlling how to handle a previously opened result set upon the invocation of getResultSet(); in addition, JDBC 3.0 also introduces Result-Set Holdability as the ability to specify whether cursors should be held open or closed at the end of a transaction using CLOSE_CURSORS_AT_COMMIT or HOLD_CURSORS_OVER_COMMIT.

Methods Specified by the java.sql.ResultSet Interface

Methods for navigation and row manipulation include: `absolute`, `afterLast`, `beforeFirst`, `getFetchDirection`, `isAfterLast`, `isBeforeFirst`, `isFirst`, `isLast`, `last`, `moveToCurrentRow`, `moveToInsertRow`, `next`, `previous`, `refreshRow`, `relative`, `rowDeleted`, `rowInserted`, `rowUpdated`, `getRow`, `cancelRowUpdates`, `clearWarnings`, `close`, `deleteRow`, `findColumn`, `first`, `setFetchDirection`, `setFetchSize`.

Methods for retrieving and updating Oracle database SQL types to and from Java types (i.e., `java.sql.*`) include: `getArray`, `getAsciiStream`, `getBigDecimal`, `getBinaryStream`, `getBlob`, `getBoolean`, `getBytes`, `getCharacterStream`, `getClob`, `getConcurrency`, `getCursorName`, `getDate`, `getDouble`, `getFetchSize`, `getFloat`, `getFloat`, `getInt`, `getInt`, `getLong`, `getLong`, `getMetaData`, `getObject`, `getRef`, `getShort`, `getShort`, `getStatement`, `getString`, `getString`, `getTime`, `getTime`, `getTime`, `getTime`, `getTimestamp`, `getTimestamp`, `getTimestamp`, `getTimestamp`, `getType`, `getUnicodeStream`, `getUnicodeStream`, `getURL`, `updateArray`, `updateArray`, `updateAsciiStream`, `updateBigDecimal`, `updateBinaryStream`, `updateBlob`, `updateBoolean`, `updateByte`, `updateBytes`, `updateCharacterStream`, `updateClob`, `updateDate`, `updateDouble`, `updateFloat`, `updateInt`, `updateLong`, `updateNull`, `updateObject`, `updateRef`, `updateRow`, `updateShort`, `updateShort`, `updateString`, `updateTime`, `updateTimestamp`, `wasNull`.

Depending on its requirement, a JDBC application must specify the scrollability of the result set (i.e., forward-only vs. scrollable), the sensitivity of the result set to underlying data changes (i.e., scroll insensitive vs. scroll sensitive), and the updatability or concurrency mode (i.e., read-only vs. updatable). Table 8.5 summarizes the six result set types.

Table 8.5   *Result Set Types and Modes*

Result Set Type	Concurrency (Mode)
Forward Only	Read Only
Forward Only	Updatable
Scroll Insensitive	Read Only
Scroll Insensitive	Updatable
Scroll Sensitive	Read Only
Scroll Sensitive	Updatable

The result set type and concurrency mode are specified on statement objects during the invocation of `CreateStatement()`, `preparedStatement()`, and `prepareCall()` methods using the following ResultSet static constants:

- Result Set Types: `TYPE_FORWARD_ONLY`, `TYPE_SCROLL_INSENSITIVE`, `TYPE_SCROLL_SENSITIVE`
- Result Set Concurrency: `CONCUR_READ_ONLY`, `CONCUR_UPDATABLE`

Examples:

```
Statement stmt =
con.createStatement(ResultSet.TYPE_SCROLL_INSENSITIVE,
      ResultSet.CONCUR_READ_ONLY);

PreparedStatement pstmt = conn.preparedStatement ("SELECT
ename, empno, sal, job FROM emp WHERE ename = ?",
ResultSet.TYPE_SCROLL_SENSITIVE, ResultSet.CONCUR_UPDATABLE);
CallableStatement cs = con.prepareCall("{ ? = call
stproc.queyr1()}",
      ResultSet.TYPE_SCROLL_INSENSITIVE,
ResultSet.CONCUR_READ_ONLY);
```

The result set type and result set concurrency can be obtained by invoking the following methods:

- On `Statement`, `PreparedStatement`, or `CallableStatement` objects: All result sets produced will inherit the statement property.

  `getResultSetType()`: Returns the result set type property of this statement object.

  `getResultSetConcurrency()`: Returns the result set concurrency property of this statement object.

- On the result set object upon the execution of the query:

  `ResultSet.getType`: Returns the type of the result set object
  `ResultSet.getConcurrency`: Returns the concurrency mode of the result set object.

Fetch Direction

In the JDBC 2.0 specification, the result set API furnishes the following hints and methods for presetting the *fetch direction* for scrollable result sets:

- Fetch Direction Hints (int): `ResultSet.FETCH_FORWARD`, `Result-Set.FETCH_REVERSE`, and `ResultSet.FETCH_UNKNOWN`.

Note: The Oracle JDBC driver supports only `FETCH_FORWARD` (`FETCH_REVERSE` or `FETCH_UNKNOWN` are ignored, and a SQL Warning is issued).

- The following methods, which can be invoked either on the statement object (including plain `Statement`, `PreparedStatement`, and `CallableStatement`) or on the result set object, allow presetting and retrieving the fetch directions:

```
void setFetchDirection (int) throws SQLException
int getFetchDirection()throws SQLException
```

Code snippet:

```
ResultSet rs = null;
Statement stmt =

con.createStatement(ResultSet.TYPE_SCROLL_INSENSITIVE,
            ResultSet.CONCUR_READ_ONLY);
rs.setFetchDirection(ResultSet.FETCH_FORWARD);
rs = stmt.executeQuery("SELECT empn, sal, job FROM emp");
```

Fetch Size

In the JDBC 2.0 specification, the result set API furnishes the following methods, which can be invoked either on the statement object (i.e., `Statement`, `PreparedStatement`, and `CallableStatement`) or on the result set object, for setting (and retrieving) the *fetch size*; in other words, the number of rows to be fetched at each database roundtrip:

```
void setFetchSize (int) throws SQLException
int getFetchSize() throws SQLException
```

Code snippet:

```
ResultSet rs = null;
Statement stmt = con.createStatement();
// set fetch size on the Statemnt object
stmt.setFetchSize(15);
rs = stmt.executeQuery("SELECT empn, sal, job FROM emp");
```

The fetch size is set by default to 10 in the Oracle JDBC drivers.

8.3.2   The Oracle Result Set Interface

The `oracle.jdbc.OracleResultSet` interface extends the standard result set interface, mainly with methods for retrieving and mapping Oracle database SQL types to Oracle JDBC types (i.e., `oracle.jdbc.*`). These methods include `getARRAY`, `getBfile`, `getBFILE`, `getBLOB`, `getCHAR`, `getCLOB`, `getOPAQUE`, `getINTERVALYM`, `getINTERVALDS`, `getTIMESTAMP`, `getTIMES-TAMPTZ`, `getTIMESTAMPLTZ`, `getCursor`, `getCustomDatum`, `getORAData`, `getCustomDatum`, `getDATE`, `getNUMBER`, `getOracleObject`, `getRAW`, `getREF`, `getROWID`, `getSTRUCT`, `updateARRAY`, `updateBfile`, `updateBLOB`, `updateCHAR`, `updateCLOB`, `updateORAData`, `updateDATE`, `updateINTER-VALYM`, `updateINTERVALDS`, `updateTIMESTAMP`, `updateTIMESTAMPTZ`, `updateTIMESTAMPLTZ`, `updateNUMBER`, `updateOracleObject`, `update-eRAW`, `updateREF`, `updateROWID`, and `updateSTRUCT`.

Implementation History

In Chapter 6, the historical trail of JDBC specifications support by Oracle JDBC drivers was briefly outlined. Result set support started with forward-only/read-only result set support in Oracle 8i release 8.1.5, which implements JDBC 1.22 API. Then, in Oracle 8*i* Release 8.1.6, a "Beta-quality"[7] support was made available for scrollable cursors; the "production quality" support was delivered in Oracle 8*i* Release 8.1.7. Result set holdability was finally supported in Oracle database 10g Release 2 (i.e., `Result-Set.HOLD_CURSORS_OVER_COMMIT` is the default and only holdability is supported). As mentioned in Chapter 6, the Oracle database does not allow returning multiple result sets; therefore, the `OracleDatabaseMeta-Data.supportsMultipleOpenResults` will return `false`.

---

7.   In other words, "Not Production Quality"!

Forward-only result sets (i.e., `Forward-Only/Read-Only` and `Forward-Only/Updatable`) reside within the RDBMS, while the rows and columns that make up scrollable result sets are cached on the client side within the driver. The next section describes the implementation and navigation within scrollable result sets, updating the result sets, inserting in the result sets, sensitivity and insensitivity to changes, and refetching rows.

8.3.3 Oracle JDBC Support for Scrollable Result Sets

Scrollable result sets (scroll insensitive and scroll sensitive) are more complicated to manage than forward-only result sets, because the former allow scrolling (i.e., random navigation) within the result set. The Oracle JDBC driver currently implements and stores a scrollable result set within a cache in the JDBC driver. Cursor positioning and movement within scrollable result sets were illustrated in Listing 8.1. From a performance perspective, because the entire set of rows that made up the result set is cached on the client side (i.e., in the JDBC driver), scrolling through a large result set will incur significant performance overhead, while a small result set will benefit from the client-side caching. This section explains the scrollable result set functionality and by the same token highlights the specifics of Oracle's implementation. Scroll-sensitive result sets will be specifically addressed later.

Scrollable Result Set Retrictions

The following restrictions apply to Oracle JDBC implementation of scrollable result sets:

- "`SELECT  *  FROM ...`" queries are not allowed; as workaround you can either use table aliases "`SELECT alias.* from <your table> alias`" or explicitly select all the columns of the table.
- The query can only apply to a single table, no join.
- Calling `getSTRUCT()` on an ADT in a scrollable result set may result in a `NullPointerException`.
- `setFetchDirection()` does not do anything.

Scrolling the Result Sets

In order to navigate within the scrollable result set, applications must position the cursor by invoking its positioning methods: `beforeFirst()`, `first()`, `next()`, `previous()`, `last()`, `afterLast()`, `absolute(int`

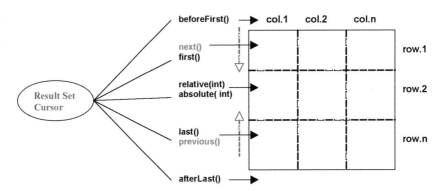

Figure 8.2
Navigating the
Result Set Rows

row), and relative(int row). At the creation of the result set object, the cursor is positioned *beforeFirst*, as illustrated by Figure 8.2, and then moves forward to the first row upon the invocation of the next() method. Conversely, when the last row has been retrieved, the cursor is positioned *afterLast*; it then may move backward using either previous() or relative() methods. Listing 8.5 illustrates this navigation.

Listing 8.5   *NavigResSet*

```
=============================
import java.sql.*;
import oracle.jdbc.*;
import oracle.sql.*;
import oracle.jdbc.pool.OracleDataSource;
import java.io.*;
/*
 *Exercise the various Result Set Navigation Methods
 *
 */

public class NavigResSet
{
 public static void main (String args [])throws SQLException
 {
   // Create an OracleDataSource
   OracleDataSource ods = now OracleDataSource();

   // Set the URL, using TNS Alias with JDBC-Thin
   String url = "jdbc:oracle:thin:scott/tiger@inst1";
   ods.setURL(url);
```

```
      // Retrieve a connection
      Connection conn = ods.getConnection();
      // Create a Statement
      Statement stmt = conn.createStatement
              (ResultSet.TYPE_SCROLL_INSENSITIVE,
                    ResultSet.CONCUR_READ_ONLY);
      // Set the statement fetch size to 1
      stmt.setFetchSize (1);

      // Query EMP Table
      ResultSet rset =
          stmt.executeQuery ("select EMPNO, ENAME, SAL from EMP");

      /*
       *  rs.next()
       */
      RsNext(rset);

      /*
       *  rs.previous()
       */
      RsPrevious(rset);

      /*
       *  rs.absolute()
       */
      RsAbsolute(rset);

      /*
       *  rs.relative()
       */
      RsRelative(rset);

      // Close RseultSet, statement and Connection
      rset.close();
      stmt.close();
      conn.close();
    }


    private static void RsNext(ResultSet rset) throws SQLException
```

```
{
  System.out.println
      ("**** Forward Navig using ResultSet.next():");

  // Ensure the cursor is before the first row
  if (!rset.isBeforeFirst()) rset.beforeFirst ();

  // Iterate through the rows using next()
  while (rset.next())
     System.out.println ("Employee Id: " + rset.getString (1));
}

private static void RsPrevious(ResultSet rset) throws SQLException
{
  System.out.println
      ("**** Backward Navig using ResultSet.previous():");
  // Ensure the cursor is after the last row
  if (!rset.isAfterLast()) rset.afterLast();

  // Iterate through the rows using previous()
  while (rset.previous())
     System.out.println ("Employee Id: " + rset.getString (1));
}

private static void RsAbsolute(ResultSet rset) throws SQLException
{
  System.out.println
      ("**** Forward Navig using  ResultSet.absolute():");

  // Place the cursor at the first row
  int pos = 1;
  // Loop through rows
  while (rset.absolute(pos))
  {
    System.out.println ("Employee Id: " + rset.getString (1));
    pos ++;
  }
}
```

```
      private static void RsRelative(ResultSet rset) throws SQLException
      {
      System.out.println
             ("**** Backward Navig using ResultSet.relative():");

        // Make sure the cursor is on the last row
        if (rset.getRow () == 0 || !rset.isLast())
             rset.last ();

        // relative(-1) is similar to previous()
        do
        {
          System.out.println ("Employee Id: " + rset.getString (1));
        }
        while (rset.relative (-1));
      }
}
$ javac NavigResSet.java
$ java -Doracle.net.tns_admin=$TNS_ADMIN NavigResSet
```

The Oracle Result Set Cache Interface

For various reasons, you may want to bypass the default (i.e., Oracle-supplied) result set cache. The Oracle JDBC driver furnishes the `OracleRe-`
`sultSetCache` interface, which allows you to implement your own result
set cache.

```
/*
 *  OracleResultSetCache interface.
 */
public interface OracleResultSetCache
{

  /*
   * Store the data in row r and column c
   */
  public void put(int r, int c, Object value) throws IOException;


  /*
   * Retrieve the data in row r and column c.
   */
```

```
      public Object get(int row, int column) throws IOException;


      /*
       * Remove row r.
       */
      public void remove(int row) throws IOException;


      /*
       * Remove the data in row r and column c.
       */
      public void remove(int row, int column) throws IOException;


      /*
       * Clear/Purge the cache (remove all cached data).
       */
      public void clear() throws IOException;


      /*
       * Close the cache.
       */
      public void close() throws IOException;
   }



   import oracle.jdbc.*;
   ...
   public class MyOracleResultSetCache implements OracleResultSetCache
   {
    // OracleResultSetCache methods implementation

   }
```

Once you have implemented your own cache, you can use the setResultSetCache() method to instruct OracleStatement, OraclePreparedStatement, or OracleCallableStatement objects—before the execution of these statements—to use the specified instance of your cache object.

```
      public void
      setResultSetCache(oracle.jdbc.OracleResultSetCache cache)
          throws SQLException;
```

Code Snippet:

```
============

OracleStatement stmt = conn.createStatement
        (ResultSet.TYPE_SCROLL_INSENSITIVE,
                ResultSet.CONCUR_READ_ONLY);

// Instantiate the cache and assign the instance
// to the statement
    MyOracleResultSetCacheImpl rscache = new
    MyOracleResultSetCache();
    stmt.setResultSetCache(rscache);

// execute the statement
OracleResultSet rs = stmt.executeQuery(" SELECT col1, col2
FROM table1)
```

At this stage, you can navigate the result set from within the user-supplied cache, exactly as you would do with the Oracle-supplied cache.

8.3.4 Oracle JDBC Support for Updatable Result Sets

Unlike read-only result sets, rows in updatable result sets (i.e., concurrency type equal `ResultSet.CONCUR_UPDATABLE`) may be updated, inserted, and deleted. However, unlike the regular SQL DML operations (i.e., update, insert, delete) that can be performed as single operations directly on the target table(s), updatable result sets require additional steps, precautions, and restrictions.

Updatable Result Set Restrictions

The following restrictions apply to Oracle JDBC implementation of updatable result sets:

- "SELECT * FROM ..." queries are not allowed; as a workaround you can either explicitly select all the columns of the table or table aliases, as follows:

    ```
    SELECT alias.* from <your table> alias
    ```

- The query can only apply to a single table (no join) and must select all nonnullable columns for the result insert to work.

- The query cannot contain/select aggregate or derived columns (i.e., SUM, MAX, set).

Updating Result Sets

Performing an UPDATE operation in a result set requires the following four steps:

1. For Scrollable result sets, move the cursor to the row to be updated, using the navigation/positioning methods of scrollable cusrors described earlier in this section. The position must be valid, not located by beforeFirst() or afterLast(). For Forward-Only result sets, iterate over the next() method until you locate the row in question.

2. Invoke the updateXXX() methods corresponding to the data types of the columns to be updated (see section 8.2) with the new values.

    Example:

    ```
    rs.updateString(1, "20" );
    rs.updateBoolean(5, false);
    rs.updateShort(6, (short)53);
    rs.updateInt(7, index);
    rs.updateLong(8, (long)893932);
    rs.updateDouble(9, (double)930.932);
    rs.updateDouble(10, (double)99302.3945);
    ...
    rs.updateDATE(11, date);
    ```

    At this stage, you have updated the columns of a specific row in the result set. If I may paraphrase Alfred Korzybski,[8] "the result set is not the table." You need to propagate the changes to the table, which is what the next step does.

3. Invoke the updateRow() method on the result set object to copy and save the changes to the table:

    ```
    rs.updateRow();
    ```

---

8.   Alfred Korzybski, "The map is not the territory"; the analogy is not accurate but I like the formula.

If, instead of saving the changes, you want to revert to the original values (before the updateXXX()), you can do so by invoking cancelRowUpdate() instead:

```
rs.cancelRowUpdate();
```

Note: If, between steps 2 and 3, you change the position of the cursor, then the changes are discarded, which is equivalent to a cancelRowUpdate() invocation.

4.   At this stage, assuming you have invoked updateRow(), then you can either COMMIT or ROLLBACK the changes as part of the ongoing transaction.

Note: In Listing 8.6, I used SELECT ... FOR UPDATE because the JDBC driver does not handle potential update conflicts; also, auto-commit has been disabled.

Listing 8.6   *UpdateRSet.java*

=================================

```
import java.sql.*;
import oracle.jdbc.*;
import oracle.sql.*;
import oracle.jdbc.pool.OracleDataSource;
import java.io.*;
/*
 * Result Set Update Test.
 */
public class UpdateRSet
{
  public static void main (String args [])throws SQLException
  {
   // Create an OracleDataSource
   OracleDataSource ods = new OracleDataSource();

   // Set the URL, using TNS Alias with JDBC-Thin
```

```
String url = "jdbc:oracle:thin:scott/tiger@inst1";
ods.setURL(url);
Connection conn = ods.getConnection(); // Retrieve a connection
conn.setAutoCommit(false); // Disable Auto Commit
Statement stmt = null;
try
{
  stmt = conn.createStatement( ResultSet.TYPE_SCROLL_SENSITIVE,
  ResultSet.CONCUR_UPDATABLE );

  String sql =
   "SELECT deptno, dname, loc FROM dept WHERE deptno = 10 FOR
        UPDATE";
  ResultSet rs = stmt.executeQuery(sql);
  while (rs.next())
    System.out.println("** Result Set " + rs.getString(1) + " " +
        rs.getString(2) + " " + rs.getString(3) );

  // The result set has only 1 row
  rs.first();
  System.out.println("*** updating LOC column in row #1 of result
        set ...");
  rs.updateString(3, "LAS VEGAS " ); // change this the next time
  System.out.println("*** saving changes to the table and
        commiting...");
  rs.updateRow();
  conn.commit();
  rs.close();
  System.out.println("Display the table  After Update");
  rs = stmt.executeQuery("select deptno, dname, loc from dept");
  while (rs.next ())
  System.out.println (rs.getString(1) + " "
               + rs.getString(2) + " "+ rs.getString(3));
} catch (SQLException e) {
  System.out.println( " Exception = " + e.getMessage() +
                  " SQLState = " + e.getSQLState() +
                  " ErrorCode = " + e.getErrorCode() );
  }
 }
 }
```

```
$ javac UpdateRSet.java
$ java -Doracle.net.tns_admin=$TNS_ADMIN UpdateRSet

** Result Set 10 ACCOUNTING LOS ANGELES
*** updating LOC column in row #1 of result set ...
*** saving changes to the table and commiting...
Display the table  After Update
10 ACCOUNTING LAS VEGAS
20 RESEARCH DALLAS
30 SALES CHICAGO
40 OPERATIONS BOSTON
$
```

Deleting Result Sets

Performing a DELETE operation in a result set req:ires the following three steps:

1. For Scrollable result sets, move the cursor to the row to be deleted, using the navigation/positioning methods of scrollable result sets described earlier. The position must be valid, not located by beforeFirst() or afterLast(). For Forward-Only result sets, iterate over the next() method until you locate the row in question.

2. Invoke the deleteRow() method on the result set to remove the row from the table:

    ```
    rs.deleteRow();
    ```

3. At this stage, you can either COMMIT or ROLLBACK the deletion as part of the ongoing transaction. *Note:* The JDBC driver does not handle potential delete conflict.

    Code snippet:
    ```
    rs.absolute(12);
    rs.deleteRow();
    ...
    COMMIT
    ```

Inserting Result Sets

Performing an INSERT operation in a result set requires the following five steps:

1.   For insert operations, each result set provides a virtual row (or staging area) called *insert-row*, which has a specific position. The result set method moveToInsertRow() saves the current position of the cursor (for later restoraton) and then moves it to the *insert-row*.

```
rs.moveToInsertRow();
```

2.   Populate (i.e., assign value to) all of the nonnullable columns of the *insert-row* using the appropriate updateXXX() methods (nullable columns will be set to NULL, if not populated).

```
rs.updateStrig("loc" "San Francisco"); //using column name
rs.updateFloat("sal", 999.2f); //using column name
rs.updateBoolean(5, false);
rs.updateShort(6, (short)53);
rs.updateInt(7, index);
...

rs.updateLong(8, (long)893932);
rs.updateDouble(9, (double)930.932);
rs.updateDouble(10, (double)99302.3945);
```

3.   Similar to UPDATE result set, you need to insert the new row (i.e., the *insert-row*) to the database table using the insertRow() method. Positioning to a different row before the invocation of insertRow() will cancel the insert operation.

```
rs.insertRow();
```

4.   Restore the cursor position saved in step 1, using the moveToCurrentRow() method.

```
rs.insertRow();
```

5.   COMMIT or ROLLBACK as part of your ongoing transaction.

> **Note:** The current Oracle JDBC implementation of the `insertRow()` method does not insert the new row into the result set itself, but, as illustrated in Listing 8.7, it does insert the new row in the database.

Listing 8.7 *InsertRSet.java*

```
================================

import java.sql.*;
import oracle.jdbc.*;
import oracle.sql.*;
import oracle.jdbc.pool.OracleDataSource;
import java.io.*;
/*
 * Result Set Insert
 */
public class InsertRSet
{
  public static void main (String args [])throws SQLException
  {
    // Create an OracleDataSource
    OracleDataSource ods = new OracleDataSource();

    // Set the URL, using TNS Alias with JDBC-Thin
    String url = "jdbc:oracle:thin:scott/tiger@inst1";
    ods.setURL(url);
    Connection conn = ods.getConnection(); // Retrieve a connection
    conn.setAutoCommit(false); // Disable Auto Commit
    Statement stmt = null;
    try
    {
      stmt = conn.createStatement( ResultSet.TYPE_SCROLL_SENSITIVE,
      ResultSet.CONCUR_UPDATABLE );
      ResultSet rs = stmt.executeQuery("SELECT deptno, dname, loc FROM
dept");

      // Print the result set before the insert
      System.out.println("*** Printing Result Set *** ");
      while (rs.next())
         System.out.println(rs.getString(1) + " " +
```

```
                    rs.getString(2) + " " + rs.getString(3) );

         System.out.println("*** Insert new row");
         // Step#1 save cursor position and move to insert-row
         rs.moveToInsertRow();

         // Step#2 populate the columns
         rs.updateString(1, "50");
         rs.updateString("dname", "MARKETING");
         rs.updateString(3, "San Diego" );



         // Step#3 save changes to the table
         System.out.println("*** saving changes to the table and
                 commiting...");
         rs.insertRow();

         // Step#4 restore cursor position
         rs.moveToCurrentRow();

         // Step#5 Commit
         conn.commit();
         rs.close();

         System.out.println("*** Printing the table  After Insert");
         rs = stmt.executeQuery("select deptno, dname, loc from dept");
         while (rs.next ())
         System.out.println (rs.getString(1) + " "
                         + rs.getString(2) + " "+ rs.getString(3));
      } catch (SQLException e) {
        System.out.println( " Exception = " + e.getMessage() +
                       " SQLState = " + e.getSQLState() +
                       " ErrorCode = " + e.getErrorCode() );
      }
  }
}

$ vi InsertRSet.java
$ javac InsertRSet.java
$ java -Doracle.net.tns_admin=$TNS_ADMIN InsertRSet
```

```
*** Printing Result Set ***
10 ACCOUNTING LAS VEGAS
20 RESEARCH DALLAS
30 SALES CHICAGO
40 OPERATIONS BOSTON
*** Insert Result Set
*** saving changes to the table and commiting...
*** Printing the table  After Insert
10 ACCOUNTING LAS VEGAS
20 RESEARCH DALLAS
30 SALES CHICAGO
40 OPERATIONS BOSTON
50 MARKETING San Diego
$
```

8.3.5   Prefetching and Auto Refresh

Row Prefetching

Row prefetching consists of anticipating forward fetching by fetching multiple rows at a time. This improves performance, because the application can consume the prefetched rows without a database roundtrip. This is obviously a common requirement, but there is no standard API yet. The Oracle JDBC furnishes the following proprietary API for retrieving a window of rows, starting with the current row. The window size or fetch size can be set at statement or connection levels.

- `OracleConnection.setDefaultRowPrefetch`: Sets the value of row prefetch for all statements associated with this connection. The statements retrieve this setting at creation time; subsequent changes to the connection's default row prefetch won't alter their settings.

- `OracleConnection.getDefaultRowPrefetch()`:   Retrieves   the value of row prefetch for this connection object.

- `OracleStatement.setRowPrefetch()`: Sets the row prefetch value for this statement and therefore for all result sets created from it.

- `OracleStatement.getRowPrefetch()`: Retrieves the value of row prefetch for this statement.

The optimal `Row Prefetching` value is 10. Starting with JDBC 10g Release 1, the driver allocates a fixed amount of memory to hold all column values of each row; therefore, setting `Row Prefetching` to a value larger than 50 will result in allocating a too large amount of memory for minimal to no additional peformance (compared with `Row Prefetching` value of 10). You need to trade/tune the number of columns versus the number of rows.

When retrieving data (typically `LONG`, `LONG RAW`, or `LOBs` data types or other data types redefined using `defineColumnType(nn, Types.LONG-VARXXX)`) via the `LONG` streaming approach (i.e., the data is fetched into a staging buffer, from which `getXXXStream` returns an `InputStream`), the driver sets the window size to 1 (i.e., disable row prefetching).

```
Code Snippet
============

Connection conn = ds.getConnection();
//Connection level row-prefetch  -- default for all statements
((OracleConnection)conn).setDefaultRowPrefetch(10);

Statement stmt = conn.createStatement();

ResultSet rset = stmt.executeQuery("SELECT dname FROM dept");
System.out.println( rset.next () );
while( rset.next () )
System.out.println( rset.getString (1) );

//Statement level row-prefetch overrides the default value

( (OracleStatement)stmt ).setRowPrefetch (5);

ResultSet rset = stmt.executeQuery("SELECT ename FROM emp");
System.out.println( rset.next () );
while( rset.next() )
System.out.println( rset.getString (1) );
stmt.close();
...
```

Auto Refetch

During the processing of a result set, changes may have occurred to rows that are part of the result set in question. The values of columns in the `ResultSet` set by the `updateXXX()` calls may not be in sync with the state/

values of the columns in the database table (e.g., a database trigger may have modified the column values). Auto-Refresh consists of automatically refetching the column values during `updateRow()`. The JDBC API specified the `refreshRow()` method on result set objects for obtaining the latest copies of the result rows from the RDBMS tables.

The Oracle JDBC implementation of `refreshRow()`only supports result sets that are implemented with a `ROWID` pseudo column: namely, the following result set types: `Scroll-Insensitive/Updatable`, `Scroll-Sensitive/Read-Only`, and `Scroll-Sensitive/Updatable`. However, `auto-refetch` incurs a database roundtrip during the `updateRow()`. Disabling `auto-refresh` avoids such a roundtrip, resulting in performance improvement.

- `OracleStatement.setAutoRefetch(boolean)`: Sets the default value of ResultSet's auto-refetch mode for the statement.

- `OracleResultSet.setAutoRefetch(boolean)`: Sets the default value of ResultSet's auto-refetch mode for the result set object.

- `OracleConnection.setAutoRefetch(boolean)`: Sets the default state of ResultSet's auto-refetch mode for the connection object and corresponding statements. The default value is `true`.

8.3.6 Changes Detection and Visibility

Visibility of Internal and External Changes

Change visibility refers to the ability to see a new value of the same data when calling `ResultSet.getXXX()` following a (previous) call to `Result-Set.updateXXX()`. Internal changes refer to changes made by the result set itself through `DML` (i.e., `INSERT`, `UPDATE`, `DELETE`) and are summarized in Table 8.6.

Table 8.6 *Result Set, Internal Changes*

	Internal UPDATE	Internal DELETE	Internal INSERT
Forward-Only	No	No	No
Scroll-Sensitive	Yes	Yes	No
Scroll-Insensitive	Yes	Yes	No

The `DatabaseMetaData` (and `OracleDatabaseMetaData`) API furnish the following methods for checking the response:

```
public boolean ownUpdatesAreVisible(int type)
                         throws java.sql.SQLException
public boolean ownDeletesAreVisible(int type)
                         throws java.sql.SQLException
public boolean ownInsertsAreVisible(int type)
                         throws java.sql.SQLException
```

Where type stands for the result set type (i.e., `ResultSet.TYPE_XXX`).

```
OracleDatabaseMetaData odmd;
...
if (odmd.ownUpdatesAreVisible(ResultSet.TYPE_SCROLL_INSENSITIVE))
{
// changes are visible
}
```

External changes refer to committed changes (the Oracle database does not allow seeing uncommitted changes, anyway) made by external sources in other database sessions, or changes incurred by a trigger as a result of internal change. There is a nuance between the visibility of external changes and the awareness that the changes happened (changes detection). The `OracleDatabaseMetaData` implements the `deletesAreDetected()`, `updatesAreDetected()`, and `insertsAreDetected()`; however, these methods will always return false because the Oracle JDBC does not detect row change.

Table 8.7 summarizes external changes visibility:

Table 8.7   *Result Set, External Visibility*

	External UPDATE	External DELETE	External INSERT
Forward-Only	No	No	No
Scroll-Sensitive	Yes	No	No
Scroll-Insensitive	No	No	No

The `DatabaseMetaData` (and `OracleDatabaseMetaData`) API furnish the following methods for checking the response:

```
public boolean othersUpdatesAreVisible(int type)
                              throws java.sql.SQLException
public boolean othersDeletesAreVisible(int type)
                              throws java.sql.SQLException
public boolean othersInsertsAreVisible(int type)
                              throws java.sql.SQLException
```

Where type stands for the result set type (i.e., `ResultSet.TYPE_XXX`).

```
OracleDatabaseMetaData odmd;
...
if (odmd.othersUpdatesAreVisible(ResultSet.TYPE_SCROLL_SENSITIVE))
{
// changes are visible
}
```

8.4   RowSet

In the previous section, we looked at result sets and their capabilities; however, there are Java SE, Java EE, and Web services requirements that are not addressed by the result set interface when interacting with relational databases and tabular data. This section explains the RowSet API and Oracle JDBC implementation of JDBC Rowset, CachedRowSet, WebRowSet, JoinRowSet, and FilteredRowSet.

8.4.1   Introducing the RowSet API

The goal of the RowSet API is to address the following shortcomings: (1) associating a set of properties and a listener to a rowset; (2) making a result set scrollable and updatable when the JDBC driver does not offer these capabilities; (3) allowing manipulating data and making changes while disconnected and synchronizing the changes back to the data source; (4) making a result set object serializable and movable across JVM or the Web; (5) shipping result set to thin clients, handheld devices, or PDAs, which are not always connected and do not have a full-fledged JDBC driver stack; (6) consuming rowset in chunks; (7) turning rowset into an XML document;

(8) producing a rowset from an XML document; and (9) joining rowset objects (while disconnected from the data source).

So, what are RowSets? The `javax.sql.Rowset` interface extends the `java.sql.ResultSet` interface; similarly, the `RowSetMetaData` interface extends the `java.sql.ResultSetMetaData` interface. Simply put, RowSets encapsulate ResultSets (and other tabular data) through a set of properties, including `datasource`, `datasourcename`, `url`, `username`, `password`, `typeMap`, `maxFiedSize`, `maxRows`, `queryTimeout`, `fetchsize`, `transactionisolation`, `escapeProcessing`, `command`, `concurrency`, `readOnly`, `fetchDirection`, as well as events and an event listener mechanism.

A listener for a RowSet object is a component that implements the following methods from the RowSetListener interface:

- `cursorMoved`: What the listener will do, if anything, when the cursor in the RowSet object moves
- `public void cursorMoved(javax.sql.RowSetEvent event)`
- `rowChanged`: What the listener will do, if anything, when one or more column values in a row have changed, a row has been inserted, or a row has been deleted (OracleRowSet maintains attributes to let users know if the row is changed, deleted, or inserted)

    `public void rowChanged(javax.sql.RowSetEvent event)`
- `rowSetChanged`: What the listener will do, if anything, when the RowSet object has been populated with new data

    `public void rowSetChanged(javax.sql.RowSetEvent event)`

The `OracleRowSetListenerAdapter` implements `RowSetListener`.

The Java Specification Request (JSR) 114[9] formalizes the RowSet API and defines five models, including `JdbcRowSet`, `CachedRowSet`, `WebRowSet`, `JoinRowSet`, and `FilteredRowSet`. The relationship between the various RowSet models and their key differentiators is depicted in Figure 8.3. With 10g Release 1, the Oracle JDBC furnished the RowSets implementation based on the public draft of the JSR-114 specification, which is what was available by the time the product development was done; in 10g Release 2, the implementation is based on the final specification. All Oracle rowset implementations are by default serializable, read-only (i.e.,

9.   http://www.jcp.org/aboutJava/communityprocess/mrel/jsr114/

ResultSet.CONCUR_READ_ONLY),   and   scrollable   (Result-
Set.TYPE_SCROLL_SENSITIVE).

The JSR-114 furnishes a reference implementation of each rowset type,
as part of Java SE 5 (i.e., JDK 5.0), or as stand-alone JARS (i.e., rowset-
jsr114.jar)[10] that can be used on top of any standard JDBC driver.
JDBC providers such as Oracle provide their own implementation as part
of their JDBC drivers (i.e., ojdbc14.jar).

Figure 8.3
*How the RowSet
Interface Stacks Up*

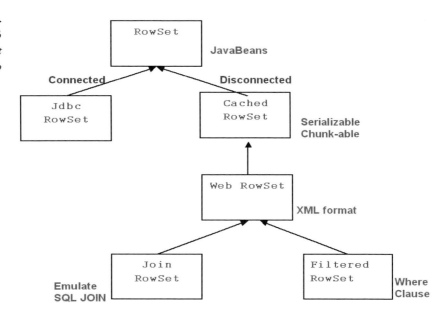

8.4.2 **JDBCRowSet and OracleJDBCRowSet**

A JDBCRowSet object can be viewed as a ResultSet disguised as a Java-
Bean. It maintains a connection to its datasource, has a set of properties,
and a listener notification mechanism. Its contents are identical to those in
a ResultSet object, and it inherits all of the row manipulation methods, the
cursor movement methods, the data type manipulation methods (i.e.,
getXXX(), setXXX(), and updateXXX()) of a ResultSet; hence, as illustrated by the code sample in Listing 8.8, operating on the JDBCRowSet
object is equivalent to operating on the ResultSet object.

---

10.   http://java.sun.com/products/jdbc/download.html#rowset1_0_1.

Listing 8.8   *myJDBCRowSet.java*
================================

```java
import java.sql.*;
import java.io.*;
import oracle.sql.*;
import oracle.jdbc.*;
import javax.sql.*;
import oracle.jdbc.rowset.*;

public class myJDBCRowSet
{
  public static void main (String[] args) throws SQLException
  {
    RowSet rowset = new OracleJDBCRowSet ();
    try
    {
      rowset.setUrl("jdbc:oracle:thin:scott/tiger@inst1");
      //rowset.setUrl("jdbc:oracle:thin:@inst1");
      rowset.setUsername("scott");
      rowset.setPassword("tiger");
      rowset.setCommand ("SELECT empno, ename, sal, hiredate FROM emp");
      rowset.execute();

      for (int i = 0; rowset.next() ; ++i)
         System.out.println ("*** RowSet(" +(i+1) +") "
          +rowset.getInt (1) +" : " + rowset.getString (2)
         +" : " + rowset.getFloat (3) +" : " +rowset.getDate(4));
    } catch (SQLException sqle) {
      System.out.println( " SQL Exception = " + sqle.getMessage() +
                    " SQLState = " + sqle.getSQLState() +
                    " ErrorCode = " + sqle.getErrorCode() );
    }
  }
}

$ javac myJDBCRowSet.java
$ java -Doracle.net.tns_admin=$TNS_ADMIN myJDBCRowSet

*** Row(1) 7369 : SMITH : 800.0 : 1980-12-17
```

```
*** Row(2)  7499 : ALLEN  : 1600.0 : 1981-02-20
*** Row(3)  7521 : WARD   : 1250.0 : 1981-02-22
*** Row(4)  7566 : JONES  : 2975.0 : 1981-04-02
*** Row(5)  7654 : MARTIN : 1250.0 : 1981-09-28
*** Row(6)  7698 : BLAKE  : 2850.0 : 1981-05-01
*** Row(7)  7782 : CLARK  : 2450.0 : 1981-06-09
*** Row(8)  7788 : SCOTT  : 3000.0 : 1987-04-19
*** Row(9)  7839 : KING   : 5000.0 : 1981-11-17
*** Row(10) 7844 : TURNER : 1500.0 : 1981-09-08
*** Row(11) 7876 : ADAMS  : 1100.0 : 1987-05-23
*** Row(12) 7900 : JAMES  : 950.0  : 1981-12-03
*** Row(13) 7902 : FORD   : 3000.0 : 1981-12-03
*** Row(14) 7934 : MILLER : 1300.0 : 1982-01-23
$
```

According to the specification, the resulting objects are by default scrollable (i.e., `ResultSet.TYPE_SCROLL_SENSITIVE`) and read-only (i.e., `ResultSet.CONCUR_READ_ONLY`) but can be made updatable by calling `setReadOnly (false)`. Changes made to the rowset using `updateXXX()` methods will be reflected in the corresponding database rows and columns. However, it is not clear how exactly a JDBCRowSet can be made updatable if the result set is not updatable.

The `OracleJDBCRowSet` class implements the `javax.sql.rowset.JdbcRowSet` interface. However, the OracleJDBCRowSet object is serializable, as are all Oracle's implementations of the five rowset types.

Let's look at the disconnected rowset models, which are more interesting.

8.4.3 CachedRowSet and OracleCachedRowSet

A `CachedRowSet` object is the most well known and probably the most used type of the RowSet family. It caches its rows in memory and allows operating on these without being connected to the datasource. The `OracleCachedRowSet` object is Oracle's implementation of the `javax.sql.rowset.CachedRowSet` interface. Unlike `JDBCRowSets`, discussed in the previous section, a `CachedRowSet` object turns any result set object (even the read-only ones) into scrollable and updatable rowsets. This capability is interesting if the JDBC driver does not support scrollable and updatable result sets. There are many other interesting features but, in my opinion, the most interesting and immediate benefit of `CachedRowSet` is the scalabilty and performance provided by the ability to be disconnected from the datasource; typically, fewer database connections will accommodate a larger number of clients.

Creating and Populating CachedRowSets

An instance of CachedRowSet object is created by invoking a constructor (i.e., new CachedRowSet() or new OracleCachedRowSet()). It is then populated (i.e., gets its data) primarily from a result set, using either the populate() method, as illustrated by Listing 8.9, or the execute() method, discussed later.

Listing 8.9   *myCachedRowSet.java*
======================================

```
import oracle.jdbc.rowset.*;
import javax.sql.*;
import java.sql.*;
import oracle.sql.*;
import java.io.*;
import oracle.jdbc.pool.OracleDataSource;
public class myCachedRowSet
{
 public static void main (String[] args) throws SQLException
 {
    OracleCachedRowSet crset = new OracleCachedRowSet ();
    try
    {
      // Get a connection from data source
      OracleDataSource ods = new OracleDataSource();
      String url = "jdbc:oracle:thin:scott/tiger@inst1";
      String sql = "SELECT empno, ename, sal, hiredate FROM emp";
      ods.setURL(url);
      Connection conn = ods.getConnection();
      Statement stmt = conn.createStatement ();

      // Execute the statement and produce a result set
      ResultSet rs = stmt.executeQuery ( sql);
      // set cached row set properties
      crset.setUrl(url);
      crset.setCommand (sql);
      crset.setUsername("scott");
      crset.setPassword("tiger");
```

```
    // populate the CachedRowSet with the data in the result set
    crset.populate (rs);

    // release the result set, the statement and the connection
    rs.close ();
    stmt.close ();
    conn.close ();
    System.out.println ("*** Connection  Closed *** ");

    // loop through the cached rowset and retrieve data
    for (int i = 0; crset.next () ; ++i)
      System.out.println ("*** Cached RowSet(" +(i+1) +") "
        + crset.getInt (1) +" : " + crset.getString (2)
        +" : " + crset.getFloat (3) +" : " + crset.getDate(4));
      crset.close ();

    } catch (SQLException sqle) {
      System.out.println( " SQL Exception = " + sqle.getMessage() +
                    " SQLState = " + sqle.getSQLState() +
                    " ErrorCode = " + sqle.getErrorCode() );
    }
  }
}

$ javac myCachedRowSet.java
$ java -Doracle.net.tns_admin=$TNS_ADMIN myCachedRowSet

*** Connection  Closed ***

*** Cached RowSet(1) 7369 : SMITH : 800.0 : 1980-12-17
*** Cached RowSet(2) 7499 : ALLEN : 1600.0 : 1981-02-20
*** Cached RowSet(3) 7521 : WARD : 1250.0 : 1981-02-22
*** Cached RowSet(4) 7566 : JONES : 2975.0 : 1981-04-02
*** Cached RowSet(5) 7654 : MARTIN : 1250.0 : 1981-09-28
*** Cached RowSet(6) 7698 : BLAKE : 2850.0 : 1981-05-01
*** Cached RowSet(7) 7782 : CLARK : 2450.0 : 1981-06-09
*** Cached RowSet(8) 7788 : SCOTT : 3000.0 : 1987-04-19
*** Cached RowSet(9) 7839 : KING : 5000.0 : 1981-11-17
*** Cached RowSet(10) 7844 : TURNER : 1500.0 : 1981-09-08
*** Cached RowSet(11) 7876 : ADAMS : 1100.0 : 1987-05-23
*** Cached RowSet(12) 7900 : JAMES : 950.0 : 1981-12-03
```

```
*** Cached RowSet(13) 7902 : FORD : 3000.0 : 1981-12-03
*** Cached RowSet(14) 7934 : MILLER : 1300.0 : 1982-01-23
```

In this example, the cached rowset is populated through the invocation of the `populate()` method, which takes a result set as parameter; this approach populates the cached rowset, starting with the first row of the result set. Another form of `populate()` takes an additional parameter representing the starting row within the result set from which to populate the cached rowset; this approach is used for chunking large result sets data to the cached rowset.

```
OracleCachedRowSet ocrs = new OracleCachedRowSet();
ocrs.setPageSize(8); // chunk size
ocrs.populate(rset, 2);  // populate cached row set, 8 rows at a time
                         // starting with row #2
// consume
ocrs.populate(rset, 10); // populate cached row set, 8 rows at a time
                         // starting with row #10
```

The `nextPage()` method on the cached rowset, combined with `setPageSize()`, also allows you to populate and consume the result sets, iteratively, in chunks, as cached rowset.

```
ocrs.setPageSize(8);
while (ocrs.nextPage())
{
 //consume
}
```

A `CachedRowset` may also be populated using the following methods:

- `CachedRowSet.execute()`
- `CachedRowSet.execute(conn)`

The parameterless form uses the connection defined in the rowset properties, while the second form uses the connection object furnished in parameter and then closes it afterward.

A `CachedRowSet` object may also get its data from any tabular datasource such as flat files or spreadsheets. The reference implementation supports only getting data from a `ResultSet` object, and so does `OracleCachedRowSet` (the `OracleCachedRowSetReader` class simply implements `javax.sql.RowSetReader`), but Java developers can associate an alternative `SyncProvider` implementation, which can furnish access to other forms of tabular data sources:

1. Either by invoking the `setSyncProvider` method on the CachedRowSet.

    ```
    crs.setSyncProvider("foo.bar.xxx.ExcelProvider ");
    ```

2. Or by invoking the cached rowset constructor with the Syncprovider implementation as parameter.

    ```
    OracleCachedRowSetImpl ocrs =
        new
    OracleCachedRowSetImpl("com.foo.xxx.ExcelProvider");
    ```

Manipulating and Making Changes to Disconnected Data

`CachedRowsets` make a result set object serializable and, therefore, movable across JVM, movable across the Web, and shipable to thin clients and handheld devices or PDAs, which are not always connected and do not have a full-fledged JDBC driver stack (e.g., Java Micro Edition stack). As a result, the cached rowset can be populated with chunks (pages) of data from the result set, updated or changed, and then synchronized back to the datasource. How does it work?

The `SyncProvider` furnishes a `RowSetReader` interface (implemented by the `OracleCachedRowSetReader` class) for reading from a datasource to populate the `CachedRowSet`, and a `RowSetWriter` interface (implemented by the `OracleCachedRowSetWriter` class) to synchronize the changes back to the datasource. During the propagation of changes, and depending on the implementation, the `SyncProvider` can detect conflicts between changes in the rowset and changes to the datasource. The `CachedRowSet` keeps track of the original state of the underlying datasource and the states in the rowset. In case of conflict, it invokes the `restoreOriginal()` method to resore the datasource to its state before the changes. Depending on the `SyncProvider`, the `CacheRowSet` performs an optimistic concurrency control (i.e., no lock used) or a pessimistic concurrency control (i.e., use locks). The Reference Implementation furnishes an optimistic concurrency control (`RIOptimisticProvider`), so does Oracle's implementation.

```
// set cached row set properties
ocrs.setUrl(url);
ocrs.setCommand (sql);
ocrs.setUsername("scott");
ocrs.setPassword("tiger");

ocrs.beforeFirst();   // Navigate
ocrs..next();

pid = ocrs.getInt(1); // Get Value

// Make the rowset updatable
rowset.setReadOnly(false);
ocrs.updateInt(1,1721); // Update columns
ocrs.updateShort(2, 35);
ocrs.updateString(2, "Making Changes");

...
ocrs.updateRow();   // apply changes to the Cached Row

// Batch multiple rowset updates and
// optimize the invocation of accepChanges
...

// Assume another JDBC thread/client makes changes to the
// underlying rows at this stage → conflict
//

// Done with changes, connect to the data source ...
conn = ods.getConnection();

try
{
 // ... and propagate the changes to the data source
 ccrs.setTableName("<table>"); // the originating table
 ccrs.acceptChanges(conn);
} catch (SyncProviderException spe) {
```

```
// Oops, conflict, restore the data source to its original state
ccrs.restoreOriginal);
}
```

Event Listeners

Similar to other rowsets, CachedRowSet objects may have consumers (i.e., displaying the data in the rowset) that want to be notified when a change happens, so as to refresh their own state (i.e., display). The interested parties must implement the `javax.sql.RowSetListener` interface and then register as a listener for the cached rowset in question, using the `addRowSetListener()` method.

```
ocrs.addRowSetListener(consumer1);
...
ocrs.addRowSetListener(consumern);
```

The interested parties will be notified when any `CachedRowSet` method moves the cursor (`cursorMoved`), changes rows (`rowChanged`), or when the entire rowset has changed (`rowSetChanged`).

Let's now look at the other members of the RowSet family, which are more complex disconnected rowsets built on top of CachedRowSet and include: the `WebRowSets`, the `JoinRowSets`, and the `FilteredRowSets`.

8.4.4 WebRowSet and OracleWebRowSet

A `WebRowSet` object is a `CachedRowSet` object, augmented with a default `WebRowSetXmlReader`, which reads an XML document into the rowset, and a default `WebRowSetXmlWriter`, which writes the rowset as an XML document. The XML format of the WebRowSet makes it suitable for shipment across the Web (hence the name). As a result, Web services or Java components can receive data from a database, through Web protocols.

The `oracle.jdbc.rowset.OracleWebRowSet` class is an Oracle JDBC implementation of `WebRowSet` and furnishes the following features:

- Supports JAXP 1.2–compliant XML parsers; SAX 2.0 and DOM parsers are supported by default.
- Supports `getXXX`, `setXXX`, and `updateXXX` methods for JDBC 3.0 standard complex types for disconnected RowSets.
- Supports Blob/Clob data types.

- `OracleWebRowSetXmlReader`.

- `OracleWebRowSetXmlWriter`.

Understanding the WebRowSet XML Schema

The XML Schema Definition (XSD) is a W3C recommendation[11] for describing "the structure, content, and semantics of XML documents"; it allows all parties involved to have a common and exact understanding of the document based on the schema in question. The W3C XML schema for WebRowSet defined by Sun, and the corresponding schema definition, is available at the following URL: http://java.sun.com/xml/ns/jdbc/webrowset.xsd.

The `WebRowSet` schema also uses SQL/XML schema annotations, which are available at the following URL: http://standards.iso.org/iso/9075/2002/12/sqlxml.xsd.

The `WebRowSet XSD` describes the structure of a `WebRowSet` in the following areas: properties, metadata, and data.

```
<xs:element name="webRowSet">
<xs:complexType>
<xs:sequence>
  <xs:element ref="wrs:properties" />
  <xs:element ref="wrs:metadata" />
  <xs:element ref="wrs:data" />
  </xs:sequence>
  </xs:complexType>
  </xs:element>
```

Let's look at the structure of each area of the `WebRowSet.XSD` and illustrate with the XML document `deptWRS.xml` corresponding to the output of the WebRowSet created from the dept table.

```
$ sqlplus scott/tiger

SQL*Plus: Release 10.2.0.1.0 - Production on Fri Nov 11 21:53:06 2005

Copyright (c) 1982, 2005, Oracle.  All rights reserved.
```

---

11.   http://www.w3.org/XML/Schema#dev.

```
Connected to:
Oracle Database 10g Enterprise Edition Release 10.2.0.1.0 - Production
With the Partitioning and Data Mining options

SQL> desc dept
 Name                                          Null?    Type
 --------------------------------------------- -------- --------------------
 DEPTNO                                        NOT NULL NUMBER(2)
 DNAME                                                  VARCHAR2(14)
 LOC                                                    VARCHAR2(13)

SQL> select * from dept
  2  /

    DEPTNO DNAME          LOC
---------- -------------- -------------
        10 ACCOUNTING     LAS VEGAS
        20 RESEARCH       DALLAS
        30 SALES          CHICAGO
        40 OPERATIONS     BOSTON
        50 MARKETING      San Diego

SQL>
```

The Properties section: Describe the RowSet properties and the synchronization provider properties. Here is the corresponding section in the WebRowSet.XSD:

```
<xs:element name="properties">
<xs:complexType>
<xs:sequence>
  <xs:element name="command" type="xs:string" />
  <xs:element name="concurrency" type="xs:string" />
  <xs:element name="datasource" type="xs:string" />
  <xs:element name="escape-processing" type="xs:string" />
  <xs:element name="fetch-direction" type="xs:string" />
  <xs:element name="fetch-size" type="xs:string" />
  <xs:element name="isolation-level" type="xs:string" />
<xs:element name="key-columns">
<xs:complexType>
  <xs:sequence minOccurs="0" maxOccurs="unbounded">
```

```
                    <xs:element name="column" type="xs:string" />
                  </xs:sequence>
                  </xs:complexType>
              </xs:element>
              <xs:element name="map">
              <xs:complexType>
              <xs:sequence minOccurs="0" maxOccurs="unbounded">
                <xs:element name="type" type="xs:string" />
                <xs:element name="class" type="xs:string" />
                </xs:sequence>
                </xs:complexType>
              </xs:element>
                <xs:element name="max-field-size" type="xs:string" />
                <xs:element name="max-rows" type="xs:string" />
                <xs:element name="query-timeout" type="xs:string" />
                <xs:element name="read-only" type="xs:string" />
                <xs:element name="rowset-type" type="xs:string" />
                <xs:element name="show-deleted" type="xs:string" />
                <xs:element name="table-name" type="xs:string" />
                <xs:element name="url" type="xs:string" />
               <xs:element name="sync-provider">
               <xs:complexType>
              <xs:sequence>
                <xs:element name="sync-provider-name" type="xs:string" />
                <xs:element name="sync-provider-vendor" type="xs:string" />
                <xs:element name="sync-provider-version" type="xs:string" />
                <xs:element name="sync-provider-grade" type="xs:string" />
                <xs:element name="data-source-lock" type="xs:string" />
              </xs:sequence>
               </xs:complexType>
               </xs:element>
               </xs:sequence>
               </xs:complexType>
               </xs:element>
```

Here is an example based on Web RowSet XSD created for the DEPT table:

```
<properties>
    <command></command>
    <concurrency>1007</concurrency>
```

```
<datasource></datasource>
<escape-processing>true</escape-processing>
<fetch-direction>1002</fetch-direction>
<fetch-size>10</fetch-size>
<isolation-level>2</isolation-level>
<key-columns>
</key-columns>
<map>
   <type>SYS.XMLTYPE</type>
   <class>oracle.xdb.XMLTypeFactory</class>
</map>
<max-field-size>0</max-field-size>
<max-rows>0</max-rows>
<query-timeout>0</query-timeout>
<read-only>false</read-only>
<rowset-type>1005</rowset-type>
<show-deleted>false</show-deleted>
<table-name></table-name>
<url>jdbc:oracle:thin:scott/tiger@inst1</url>
<sync-provider>
   <sync-provider-name>com.sun.rowset.providers.RIOptimisticProvider</
sync-provider-name>
   <sync-provider-vendor>Sun Microsystems Inc.</sync-provider-vendor>
   <sync-provider-version>1.0</sync-provider-version>
   <sync-provider-grade>2</sync-provider-grade>
   <data-source-lock>1</data-source-lock>
</sync-provider>
</properties>
```

The Metadata section: Describes the metadata of the WebRowSet and is aligned with the metadata of the underlying `java.sql.ResultSet` interface.

```
<xs:element name="metadata">
<xs:complexType>
<xs:sequence>
 <xs:element name="column-count" type="xs:string" />
<xs:choice>
<xs:element name="column-definition" minOccurs="0"
maxOccurs="unbounded">
<xs:complexType>
<xs:sequence>
```

```
<xs:element name="column-index"   type="xs:string" />
<xs:element name="auto-increment" type="xs:string" />
<xs:element name="case-sensitive" type="xs:string" />
<xs:element name="currency" type="xs:string" />
<xs:element name="nullable" type="xs:string" />
<xs:element name="signed" type="xs:string" />
<xs:element name="searchable" type="xs:string" />
<xs:element name="column-display-size" type="xs:string" />
<xs:element name="column-label" type="xs:string" />
<xs:element name="column-name" type="xs:string" />
<xs:element name="schema-name" type="xs:string" />
<xs:element name="column-precision" type="xs:string" />
<xs:element name="column-scale" type="xs:string" />
<xs:element name="table-name" type="xs:string" />
<xs:element name="catalog-name" type="xs:string" />
<xs:element name="column-type" type="xs:string" />
<xs:element name="column-type-name" type="xs:string" />
</xs:sequence>
</xs:complexType>
</xs:element>
</xs:choice>
</xs:sequence>
</xs:complexType>
</xs:element>
```

Here is an example based on Web RowSet XSD created for the DEPT table:

```
<metadata>
    <column-count>3</column-count>
    <column-definition>
      <column-index>1</column-index>
      <auto-increment>false</auto-increment>
      <case-sensitive>false</case-sensitive>
      <currency>true</currency>
      <nullable>0</nullable>
      <signed>true</signed>
      <searchable>true</searchable>
      <column-display-size>22</column-display-size>
      <column-label>DEPTNO</column-label>
      <column-name>DEPTNO</column-name>
```

```
                  <schema-name></schema-name>
                  <column-precision>2</column-precision>
                  <column-scale>0</column-scale>
                  <table-name></table-name>
                  <catalog-name></catalog-name>
                  <column-type>2</column-type>
                  <column-type-name>NUMBER</column-type-name>
              </column-definition>
              <column-definition>
                  <column-index>2</column-index>
                  <auto-increment>false</auto-increment>
                  <case-sensitive>true</case-sensitive>
                  <currency>false</currency>
                  <nullable>1</nullable>
                  <signed>true</signed>
                  <searchable>true</searchable>
                  <column-display-size>14</column-display-size>
                  <column-label>DNAME</column-label>
                  <column-name>DNAME</column-name>
                  <schema-name></schema-name>
                  <column-precision>0</column-precision>
                  <column-scale>0</column-scale>
                  <table-name></table-name>
                  <catalog-name></catalog-name>
                  <column-type>12</column-type>
                  <column-type-name>VARCHAR2</column-type-name>
              </column-definition>
              <column-definition>
                  <column-index>3</column-index>
                  <auto-increment>false</auto-increment>
                  <case-sensitive>true</case-sensitive>
                  <currency>false</currency>
                  <nullable>1</nullable>
                  <signed>true</signed>
                  <searchable>true</searchable>
                  <column-display-size>13</column-display-size>
                  <column-label>LOC</column-label>
                  <column-name>LOC</column-name>
                  <schema-name></schema-name>
                  <column-precision>0</column-precision>
                  <column-scale>0</column-scale>
```

```
      <table-name></table-name>
      <catalog-name></catalog-name>
      <column-type>12</column-type>
      <column-type-name>VARCHAR2</column-type-name>
    </column-definition>
  </metadata>
```

The Data section: Describes the original data and the current data, so as to track the delta between these. Tracking the changes will enable the WebRowSet to detect and resolve conflicts when synchronizing changes back to the data source.

```
<xs:element name="data">
<xs:complexType>
<xs:sequence minOccurs="0" maxOccurs="unbounded">
<xs:element name="currentRow" minOccurs="0"
maxOccurs="unbounded">
<xs:complexType>
<xs:sequence minOccurs="0" maxOccurs="unbounded">
 <xs:element ref="wrs:columnValue" />
 </xs:sequence>
 </xs:complexType>
 </xs:element>
<xs:element name="insertRow" minOccurs="0"
maxOccurs="unbounded">
<xs:complexType>
<xs:choice minOccurs="0" maxOccurs="unbounded">
 <xs:element ref="wrs:columnValue" />
 <xs:element ref="wrs:updateValue" />
 </xs:choice>
 </xs:complexType>
 </xs:element>
<xs:element name="deleteRow" minOccurs="0"
maxOccurs="unbounded">
<xs:complexType>
<xs:sequence minOccurs="0" maxOccurs="unbounded">
 <xs:element ref="wrs:columnValue" />
 <xs:element ref="wrs:updateValue" />
 </xs:sequence>
 </xs:complexType>
 </xs:element>
```

```
<xs:element name="modifyRow" minOccurs="0"
maxOccurs="unbounded">
<xs:complexType>
<xs:sequence minOccurs="0" maxOccurs="unbounded">
 <xs:element ref="wrs:columnValue" />
 <xs:element ref="wrs:updateValue" />
 </xs:sequence>
 </xs:complexType>
 </xs:element>
 </xs:sequence>
 </xs:complexType>
 </xs:element>
 </xs:schema>
```

This is a Web RowSet XSD entry based on the DEPT table:

```
<data>
    <currentRow>
      <columnValue>10</columnValue>
      <columnValue>ACCOUNTING</columnValue>
      <columnValue>LAS VEGAS </columnValue>
    </currentRow>
    <currentRow>
      <columnValue>20</columnValue>
      <columnValue>RESEARCH</columnValue>
      <columnValue>DALLAS</columnValue>
    </currentRow>
    <currentRow>
      <columnValue>30</columnValue>
      <columnValue>SALES</columnValue>
      <columnValue>CHICAGO</columnValue>
    </currentRow>
    <currentRow>
      <columnValue>40</columnValue>
      <columnValue>OPERATIONS</columnValue>
      <columnValue>BOSTON</columnValue>
    </currentRow>
    <currentRow>
      <columnValue>50</columnValue>
      <columnValue>MARKETING</columnValue>
```

```
          <columnValue>San Diego</columnValue>
        </currentRow>
      </data>
```

Creating a WebRowSet Object and Dumping Its Contents to an XML Document

The `oracle.jdbc.rowset.OracleWebRowSetXmlWriter` class extends the `javax.sql.rowset.spi.XmlWriter`. It furnishes the `writeXml()` method for populating the `OracleWebRowSet` with XML data from the given resultset, and also for writing the content of the rowset to the supplied `java.io.Writer` or `java.io.OutputStream` objects. The structure of the XML data must be compatible with the standard WebRowSet XML schema definition (i.e., <data>, <properties>, and <metadata>, described later).

Here are the various signatures of `writeXml()`:

```
writeXml(java.io.OutputStream ostream)
writeXml(java.sql.ResultSet rset, java.io.OutputStream ostream)
writeXml(java.sql.ResultSet rset, java.io.Writer writer)
writeXml(java.io.Writer writer)
```

Listing 8.10 creates a `WebRowSet` object, populates it with the result set obtained from querying all rows of the DEPT table, and then outputs the WebRowSet into the `deptWRS.xml` file.

Listing 8.10   *deptWebRowSet.java*

===================================

```
import java.sql.*;
import java.io.*;
import oracle.sql.*;
import oracle.jdbc.*;
import oracle.jdbc.pool.OracleDataSource;
import javax.sql.*;
import oracle.jdbc.rowset.*;
public class deptWebRowSet
{
  public static void main (String[] args) throws SQLException
  {
    // Create an OracleDataSource
```

```
OracleDataSource ods = new OracleDataSource();

// Set the URL, using TNS Alias with JDBC-Thin
String url = "jdbc:oracle:thin:scott/tiger@inst1";
ods.setURL(url);
Connection conn = ods.getConnection(); // Retrieve a connection
conn.setAutoCommit(false); // Disable Auto Commit

Statement stmt = conn.createStatement();
ResultSet rset = stmt.executeQuery ("select * from dept");

// Create and populate an OracleWebRowSet with the ResultSet
System.out.println ("*** Create and populate WebRowSet");
OracleWebRowSet wrset = new OracleWebRowSet();
wrset.populate(rset);

// close the statement, connection and result set
System.out.println("*** Close Connection and other resources");
stmt.close();
conn.close();
rset.close();

// RowSet still contains values...
wrset.first();
String  dname = wrset.getString(2);
System.out.println("*** Retrieve Department Name from Web Row Set: " +
dname);

// Create a FileWriter (i.e., a java.io.Writer)
try {
   FileWriter printXml = new FileWriter("deptWRS.xml");
   // Write the WebRowSet as XML
   wrset.writeXml(printXml);
   System.out.println("*** Output Web RowSet as XML");
  } catch (IOException exc) {
    System.out.println("......Couldn't create a FileWriter");
  }
System.out.println ("*** WebRowSet created and XML outputted.");

  }
}
```

```
$ javac deptWebRowSet.java
$ java -Doracle.net.tns_admin=$TNS_ADMIN deptWebRowSet
*** Create and populate WebRowSet
*** Close Connection and other resources
*** Retrieve Department Name from Web Row Set: ACCOUNTING
*** Output Web RowSet as XML
*** WebRowSet created and XML outputted.
$
```

The deptWRS.xml file is created in the current directory; notice that its structure maps the WebRowSet XML Schema Definition (XSD).

Reading an XML Document into a WebRowSet Object

The oracle.jdbc.rowset.OracleWebRowSetXmlReader class extends the javax.sql.rowset.spi.XmlReader. It furnishes the readXml() method for populating the OracleWebRowSet object either from an XML document file (i.e., java.io.Reader) or an XML stream (i.e., java.io.InputStream), as reflected in the following signatures:

```
readXml(java.io.Reader reader)
readXml(java.io.InputStream istream)
```

The readXml requires the JDBC application to specify the XML parser either programmatically or through a system property.

For the Oracle SAX parser:

```
java -Djavax.xml.parsers.SAXParserFactory=oracle.xml.jaxp.JXSAXParserFactory
```

```
System.setProperty("javax.xml.parsers.SAXParserFactory",
              "oracle.xml.jaxp.JXSAXParserFactory");
```

For the Oracle DOM parser:

```
java -Djavax.xml.parsers.DocumentBuilderFactory =oracle.xml.jaxp.
DocumentBuilderFactory
```

```
System.setProperty("javax.xml.parsers.DocumentBuilderFactory ",
              "oracle.xml.jaxp.DocumentBuilderFactory ");
```

Here is a code snippet for creating a new OracleWebRowSet reading an XML document:

```
OracleWebRowSet wrset = new OracleWebRowSet();
// Use Oracle JAXP SAX parser
System.setProperty("javax.xml.parsers.SAXParserFactory",
    "oracle.xml.jaxp.JXSAXParserFactory");
try
{
  FileReader freadr = new FileReader("inWRS.xml");
  // Now read XML stream from the FileReader
  wrset.readXml(freadr);
  close(freadr);
}
```

Listing 8.11 constructs a WebRowSet in memory without any database connection, from an XML document (empWRS.xml; for ease of demo purpose, the XML document was previously created from a WebRowSet constructed by querying the EMP table). The readXml method of the WebRowSet object populates the rowset with the content of the file given as input to the java.io.FileReader object. Notice that the parser validates the structure of the document against the WebRowSet XSD (comment out http.proxyHost and http.proxyPort settings if you are not running the example behind a firewall).

Listing 8.11   *empWebRowSet.java*

================================

```
import java.sql.*;
import java.io.*;
import oracle.sql.*;
import oracle.jdbc.*;
import javax.sql.*;
import oracle.jdbc.rowset.*;
public class inWebRowSet
{
 public static void main (String[] args) throws SQLException
 {
  // Create and populate an OracleWebRowSet from an XML document
```

```
// Use Oracle JAXP SAX parser
System.setProperty("javax.xml.parsers.SAXParserFactory",
        "oracle.xml.jaxp.JXSAXParserFactory");
System.setProperty("http.proxyHost", "www-proxy.us.oracle.com");
System.setProperty("http.proxyPort", "80");

OracleWebRowSet wrset = new OracleWebRowSet();
try
{
 System.out.println ("*** Create and populate WebRowSet");
  FileReader fr = new FileReader("empWRS.xml");
  // populate the Web RowSet from the FileReader
  wrset.readXml(fr);
  fr.close();
  System.out.println("*** Print the Web RowSet constructed from XML file");

  // loop through the Web rowset and print
  wrset.beforeFirst();
  for (int i = 0; wrset.next () ; ++i)
  System.out.println ("*** EMPNO: " + wrset.getInt (1)
          + " ENAME: " + wrset.getString (2)
          + "JOB: " + wrset.getString(3)+ " MGR ID: " + wrset.getInt(4)
          + " HIREDATE: " + wrset.getDate(5)
          + " SAL: " + wrset.getFloat(6) + " COMM" + wrset.getFloat(7)
          + " DEPTNO: " +  wrset.getInt(8) );
   wrset.close ();
  } catch (IOException exc){
    System.out.println("Couldn't construct a FileReader becoz: "
      + exc.getMessage());
  }
 }
}


$ javac inWebRowSet.java
$ java -Doracle.net.tns_admin=$TNS_ADMIN inWebRowSet
*** Create and populate WebRowSet
*** Print the Web RowSet constructed from XML file


*** EMPNO: 7369 ENAME: SMITHJOB: CLERK MGR ID: 7902 HIREDATE: 1980-12-17 SAL: 800.0
COMM0.0 DEPTNO: 20
*** EMPNO: 7499 ENAME: ALLENJOB: SALESMAN MGR ID: 7698 HIREDATE: 1981-02-20 SAL:
1600.0 COMM300.0 DEPTNO: 30
```

```
*** EMPNO: 7521 ENAME: WARDJOB: SALESMAN MGR ID: 7698 HIREDATE: 1981-02-22 SAL:
1250.0 COMM500.0 DEPTNO: 30
*** EMPNO: 7566 ENAME: JONESJOB: MANAGER MGR ID: 7839 HIREDATE: 1981-04-02 SAL:
2975.0 COMM0.0 DEPTNO: 20
*** EMPNO: 7654 ENAME: MARTINJOB: SALESMAN MGR ID: 7698 HIREDATE: 1981-09-28 SAL:
1250.0 COMM1400.0 DEPTNO: 30
*** EMPNO: 7698 ENAME: BLAKEJOB: MANAGER MGR ID: 7839 HIREDATE: 1981-05-01 SAL:
2850.0 COMM0.0 DEPTNO: 30
*** EMPNO: 7782 ENAME: CLARKJOB: MANAGER MGR ID: 7839 HIREDATE: 1981-06-09 SAL:
2450.0 COMM0.0 DEPTNO: 10
*** EMPNO: 7788 ENAME: SCOTTJOB: ANALYST MGR ID: 7566 HIREDATE: 1987-04-19 SAL:
3000.0 COMM0.0 DEPTNO: 20
*** EMPNO: 7839 ENAME: KINGJOB: PRESIDENT MGR ID: 0 HIREDATE: 1981-11-17 SAL: 5000.0
COMM0.0 DEPTNO: 10
*** EMPNO: 7844 ENAME: TURNERJOB: SALESMAN MGR ID: 7698 HIREDATE: 1981-09-08 SAL:
1500.0 COMM0.0 DEPTNO: 30
*** EMPNO: 7876 ENAME: ADAMSJOB: CLERK MGR ID: 7788 HIREDATE: 1987-05-23 SAL: 1100.0
COMM0.0 DEPTNO: 20
*** EMPNO: 7900 ENAME: JAMESJOB: CLERK MGR ID: 7698 HIREDATE: 1981-12-03 SAL: 950.0
COMM0.0 DEPTNO: 30
*** EMPNO: 7902 ENAME: FORDJOB: ANALYST MGR ID: 7566 HIREDATE: 1981-12-03 SAL: 3000.0
COMM0.0 DEPTNO: 20
*** EMPNO: 7934 ENAME: MILLERJOB: CLERK MGR ID: 7782 HIREDATE: 1982-01-23 SAL: 1300.0
COMM0.0 DEPTNO: 10

$
```

Changing a WebRowSet Object and Synchronizing Back to the Datasource

Similar to `CachedRowSet` object, you can make changes locally to a WebRowSet object (i.e., delete/update existing rows or add/insert new rows) and then synchronize the changes back to the underlying datasource, and you have the same ability to detect and resolve potential conflicts with changes performed by other threads/clients. But unlike `CachedRowSet`, the XML document representing the `WebRowSet` captures the details of the changes. Let's look in greater detail at each case (i.e., insert, update, delete) and their corresponding code snippet(s).

Inserting a New Row in a WebRowSet Object

Similar to inserting a row in a `CachedRowSet`, inserting a new row in a WebRowSet object consists of saving the current position of the cursor (for later restoration), setting the cursor to the pseudo insertRow position, setting a value for columns, inserting the new row in the rowset, restoring the cursor position (saved earlier), and finally synchronizing the changes back to the datasource. The following code snippet illustrates the main steps. See Listing 8.12 for a complete Java example of `WebRowSet` modification.

```
// save current cursor position then move to insertRow
wrset.moveToInsertRow();

// set values to columns
wrset.updateString(1, "DEPT1 ");
wrset.updateString(2, "1234");

// insert the new row in the rowset
wrset.insertRow();

// set the cursor to the saved position
wrset.moveToCurrentRow();

// later, synchronize the changes back to the data source
 wrset.acceptChanges();
```

Here is the insertRow tag entry of the standard webrowset.xsd:

```
<xs:element name="insertRow" minOccurs="0"
maxOccurs="unbounded">
 <xs:complexType>
  <xs:choice minOccurs="0" maxOccurs="unbounded">
    <xs:element ref="wrs:columnValue" />
    <xs:element ref="wrs:updateValue" />
  </xs:choice>
 </xs:complexType>
</xs:element>
```

And here is the insertRow entry when inserting a new row into the DEPT table–based WebRowSet:

```
<insertRow>
  <columnValue>60</columnValue>
  <columnValue>DEPT 60</columnValue>
  <columnValue>CYRACUSE</columnValue>
</insertRow>
```

See Listing 8.12 for a complete example of WebRowSet modification.

Deleting a Row in a WebRowSet Object

Similar to deleting a row in a `CachedRowSet`, deleting a row in a `WebRowSet` object consists of navigating to the row in question (i.e., position the cursor), marking it as "deleted" using `deleteRow` method, and then synchronizing the changes back to the datasource using the `acceptChanges()` method of the rowset object. The following code snippet deletes the fourth row in the object referenced by `wrset`. See Listing 8.12 for a complete Java example of `WebRowSet` modification.

```
// Move the cursor to the row to be deleted
wrest.absolute(4); // 4th row

// Mark Row as "deleted"
wrset.deleteRow();

// later, synchronize changes to the data source
wrest.acceptChanges();
```

Here is the `deleteRow` tag entry of the standard `webrowset.xsd`:

```
<xs:element name="deleteRow" minOccurs="0" maxOccurs="unbounded">
  <xs:complexType>
    <xs:sequence minOccurs="0" maxOccurs="unbounded">
      <xs:element ref="wrs:columnValue" />
      <xs:element ref="wrs:updateValue" />
    </xs:sequence>
  </xs:complexType>
</xs:element>
```

And here is the `deleteRow` entry when deleting a row in the DEPT table–based WebRowSet:

```
<deleteRow>
  <columnValue>50</columnValue>
  <columnValue>MARKETING</columnValue>
  <columnValue>San Diego</columnValue>
</deleteRow>
```

Updating a Row in a WebRowSet

Similar to updating a CachedRowSet, modifying a row in a WebRowSet consists of navigating to the row in question and making changes to columns using the appropriate updateXXX() method(s), then applying the changes to the row using the updateRow() method on the rowset, and finally synchronizing back the changes to the datasource by invoking the acceptChanges() method. However, the last step could be delayed and batched with other changes (batch updates). The following code snippet moves the cursor to a specific row, performs changes to columns, and applies the changes to the rowset. See the complete example in Listing 8.12.

```
// Navigate to the row to be modified (1st row in this case)
wrset.beforeFirst();
wrset.next();
id = wrset.getInt(1);    // Get Value
wrset.updateInt(1,4545); // Update Int column
wrest.updateDouble("comm.", 1.19d);
wrest.updateString(3, "blahblah");

// Confirm changes in the Web RowSet object first
wrset.updateRow();

// Get a connection and persist the changes to the data source
conn = ods.getConnection(); // Retrieve a connection
wrset.acceptChanges(conn);
```

Here is the modifyRow tag entry of the standard webrowset.xsd.

```
<xs:element name="modifyRow" minOccurs="0"
maxOccurs="unbounded">
  <xs:complexType>
    <xs:sequence minOccurs="0" maxOccurs="unbounded">
      <xs:element ref="wrs:columnValue" />
      <xs:element ref="wrs:updateValue" />
    </xs:sequence>
  </xs:complexType>
</xs:element>
```

And here is the modifyRow entry when updating an existing row in the DEPT table–based WebRowSet:

```
              <currentRow>
                <columnValue>40</columnValue>
                <columnValue>OPERATIONS</columnValue>
                <updateValue>NEW OPERATION</updateValue>
                <columnValue>BOSTON</columnValue>
                <updateValue>BANGALORE</updateValue>
              </currentRow>
```

Notice that `columnValue` and `updateValue` elements help the rowset keep track of the original values in the datasource when the rowset was created and the new values (i.e., changes applied to the rowset by this client). See the complete code sample in Listing 8.12.

Listing 8.12   *modWebRowSet.java*

```
=================================
import java.sql.*;
import java.io.*;
import oracle.sql.*;
import oracle.jdbc.*;
import oracle.jdbc.pool.OracleDataSource;
import javax.sql.*;
import oracle.jdbc.rowset.*;
public class modWebRowSet
{
  public static void main (String[] args) throws SQLException
  {
    // Create an OracleDataSource
    OracleDataSource ods = new OracleDataSource();

    // Set the URL, using TNS Alias with JDBC-Thin
    String url = "jdbc:oracle:thin:scott/tiger@inst1";
    ods.setURL(url);
    Connection conn = ods.getConnection(); // Retrieve a connection
    conn.setAutoCommit(false); // Disable Auto Commit

    Statement stmt = conn.createStatement();
    ResultSet rset = stmt.executeQuery ("select * from dept");

    // Create and populate the OracleWebRowSet with the ResultSet
    System.out.println ("*** Create and populate WebRowSet");
    OracleWebRowSet wrset = new OracleWebRowSet();
```

```
wrset.populate(rset);

// close the statement, connection and result set
System.out.println("*** Close Connection and other resources");
stmt.close();
conn.close();
rset.close();

/*
 * Delete a row in WebRowSet where Deptno=50
 */
  System.out.println("*** Delete Row #50 ");
  // Move the cursor to the row to be deleted
  wrset.absolute(5); // 5th row
  // Mark Row as "deleted"
  wrset.deleteRow();

/*
 * Update a row in WebRowSet where Deptno=40
 */
  System.out.println("***  Update  Row #40 ");
  // Set the cursor to 4th row and update DNAME and LOCATIN
  wrset.absolute(4); // 4th row
  wrset.updateString(2, "NEW OPERATION");
  wrset.updateString(3, "BANGALORE");
  // Confirm changes in the Web RowSet object first
  wrset.updateRow();

/*
 * Insert a new row in WebRowSet with Deptno=60
 */
System.out.println("*** Insert New Row #60");
  // save current cursor position then move to insertRow
  wrset.moveToInsertRow();
  // set values to columns
  wrset.updateInt(1, 60);
  wrset.updateString(2, "DEPT 60");
  wrset.updateString(3, "CYRACUSE");
  // insert the new row in the rowset
  wrset.insertRow();
  // set the cursor to the saved position
```

```
wrset.moveToCurrentRow();
 try {
   // Dump the WebRowSet before synchronizing with data source
   FileWriter printXml = new FileWriter("modWRS_before.xml");
   wrset.writeXml(printXml);
  } catch (IOException exc) {
    System.out.println("......Couldn't create a FileWriter");
  }
/*
 * Synchronize changes back to the data source.
 */
System.out.println("***  Synchronize changes to DS");
wrset.setUrl("jdbc:oracle:thin:scott/tiger@inst1");
wrset.setUsername("scott"); // working around a bug
wrset.setPassword("tiger");
conn = ods.getConnection(); // Retrieve a connection
wrset.setTableName("dept"); // Needed for accaptChanges()
// Synchrronize changes back to the data source
wrset.acceptChanges(conn);
conn.close();
try {
   // Dump the WebRowSet after synchronizing with data source
   FileWriter printXml = new FileWriter("modWRS_after.xml");
   wrset.writeXml(printXml);
   // Print the Web rowset
   System.out.println("*** Output Web RowSet as XML");
   wrset.beforeFirst();
   for (int i = 0; wrset.next () ; ++i)
   System.out.println ("*** DEPTPNO: " + wrset.getInt (1)
       + " DNAME: " + wrset.getString (2)
       + " LOCATION: " + wrset.getString(3));
   wrset.close ();
  } catch (IOException exc) {
    System.out.println("......Couldn't create a FileWriter");
  }
 }
}
```

Notice the wrest.setTableName("dept"); this is required before invoking wrest.acceptChanges(...), which can't update more than one table.

Let's query the DEPT Table, before the execution of modWebRowSet.java:

```
SQL> select * from dept
  2  /

    DEPTNO DNAME          LOC
---------- -------------- -------------
        10 ACCOUNTING     LAS VEGAS
        20 RESEARCH       DALLAS
        30 SALES          CHICAGO
        40 OPERATIONS     BOSTON
        50 MARKETING      San Diego

SQL> exit
Disconnected from Oracle Database 10g Enterprise Edition Release
10.2.0.1.0 — Production With the Partitioning and Data Mining options

$ javac modWebRowSet.java
$ java -Doracle.net.tns_admin=$TNS_ADMIN modWebRowSet
*** Create and populate WebRowSet
*** Close Connection and other resources
*** Delete Row #50
***  Update  Row #40
*** Insert New Row #60
***  Synchronize changes to DS
*** Output Web RowSet as XML
*** DEPTPNO: 10 DNAME: ACCOUNTING LOCATION: LAS VEGAS
*** DEPTPNO: 20 DNAME: RESEARCH LOCATION: DALLAS
*** DEPTPNO: 30 DNAME: SALES LOCATION: CHICAGO
*** DEPTPNO: 40 DNAME: NEW OPERATION LOCATION: BANGALORE
*** DEPTPNO: 60 DNAME: DEPT 60 LOCATION: CYRACUSE
```

Let's query the DEPT Table, after the execution of modWebRowSet.java:

```
$ sqlplus scott/tiger

SQL*Plus: Release 10.2.0.1.0 - Production on Wed Nov 16
14:34:47 2005
```

Copyright (c) 1982, 2005, Oracle. All rights reserved.
Connected to:
Oracle Database 10g Enterprise Edition Release 10.2.0.1.0 –
Production
With the Partitioning and Data Mining options

```
SQL> select * from dept;

    DEPTNO DNAME          LOC
---------- -------------- -------------
        10 ACCOUNTING     LAS VEGAS
        20 RESEARCH       DALLAS
        30 SALES          CHICAGO
        40 NEW OPERATION  BANGALORE
        60 DEPT 60        CYRACUSE

SQL>exit
```

And here is the <data> section of modWRS_after.xml:

```
<data>
   <currentRow>
     <columnValue>10</columnValue>
     <columnValue>ACCOUNTING</columnValue>
     <columnValue>LAS VEGAS </columnValue>
   </currentRow>
   <currentRow>
     <columnValue>20</columnValue>
     <columnValue>RESEARCH</columnValue>
     <columnValue>DALLAS</columnValue>
   </currentRow>
   <currentRow>
     <columnValue>30</columnValue>
     <columnValue>SALES</columnValue>
     <columnValue>CHICAGO</columnValue>
   </currentRow>
   <currentRow>
     <columnValue>40</columnValue>
     <columnValue>NEW OPERATION</columnValue>
     <columnValue>BANGALORE</columnValue>
   </currentRow>
```

```
<currentRow>
  <columnValue>60</columnValue>
  <columnValue>DEPT 60</columnValue>
  <columnValue>CYRACUSE</columnValue>
</currentRow>
</data>
```

8.4.5 FilteredRowSet and OracleFilteredRowSet

In the SQL world, a `WHERE` clause allows you to specify a filtering criterion, which, if true, returns only rows that meet the criterion in question. What if you need to filter disconnected rows of a `CachedRowSet` or `WebRowSet` object? A `FilteredRowSet` object simulates a `SQL WHERE` clause by allowing you to apply user-defined filtering criteria on rows in a disconnected rowset; in other words, it returns/retrieves only rows that meet the defined criteria, and inserts/updates only rows that meet the constraints defined in the filter(s). The trick is to define constraints within a predicate class, which implement the `javax.sql.rowset.Predicate` interface, and then assign this predicate to the `FilteredRowSet` object; as a result, the constraints defined in the predicate class will be evaluated against each row in the rowset object.

The Oracle JDBC implements the standard `javax.sql.rowset.FilteredRowSet` and `javax.sql.rowset.Predicate` interfaces in `ojdbc14.jar` and furnishes the `oracle.jdbc.rowset.OracleFilteredRowSet` class and `oracle.jdbc.rowset.OraclePredicate` interface for `classes12.jar`.

In order to use filtered rowsets (i.e., `FilteredRowSet` or `OracleFilteredRowSet`), the JDBC applications must:

1.   Define and implement the `Predicate` interface.

2.   Create an instance of `FilteredRowSet` object and set properties.

3.   Populate the `FilteredRowSet`.

4.   Set/enable filters.

5.   Retrieve the filtered rows.

The following sections describe these steps individually, and at the end a complete example is given (Listings 8.13 and 8.14).

Define and Implement the Predicate Interface

The JSR-114 (RowSet) does not currently furnish standard filters; the JDBC application must implement the `javax.sql.rowset.Predicate` or `oracle.jdbc.rowset.OraclePredicate` interfaces.

The filtering criterion within a `Predicate` object is materialized by the implementations of the Boolean `evaluate` method, which has the following signatures:

```
evaluate(javax.sql.RowSet rowSet);
evaluate(java.lang.Object value, int columnIndex);
evaluate(java.lang.Object value, java.lang.String
columnName);
```

The evaluate method returns `true` or `false`, depending on whether the rows in the rowset meet the defined constraint. One commonly used type of constraint consists of defining a range of values that the filtering column must match:

low boundary <= `columnName` <= *high boundary*

or:

low boundary <= `columnIndex` <= *high boundary*

with:

- The (inclusive) high boundary of the range of values that meet the criterion

- The (inclusive) low boundary of the range of values that meet the criterion

- The column index or column name of the set of values that must fall between these boundaries (e.g., `salary`, `job`)

Listing 8.13 is an example of a `Predicate` class implementation using the type of constraint described previously.

Listing 8.13   *Predicate1.java*

==============================

```
import java.util.*;
import java.sql.*;
```

```java
import javax.sql.*;
import javax.sql.rowset.Predicate;

public class Predicate1 implements Predicate {

    private int  low;
    private int high;
    private String columnName;
    private int columnIndex;

    public Predicate1 (int low, int high, int colIndex) {
        this.low = low;
        this.high= high;
        this.columnIndex = colIndex;
        columnName = new String("");
    }

    public Predicate1 (int low, int high, String colName) {
        this.low = low;
        this.high= high;
        this.columnName = colName;
        columnIndex = 0;
    }

    public boolean evaluate(RowSet rs){
      int colvalue = 0;
      try{
         colvalue = rs.getInt(columnIndex);
         if (colvalue >= low && colvalue <= high ){
            return true;
         } else {
            return false;
         }
       } catch(SQLException sqle){
           return false;
       }
     }

    public boolean evaluate(java.lang.Object obj, int colIndex)
    {
         // cast Object to Integer then get it's value
```

```
        int colvalue = ((Integer)obj).intValue();

        if (colvalue >= low && colvalue <= high ){
          return true;
        } else {
          return false;
        }
    }

    public boolean evaluate(java.lang.Object obj, String colName)
    {
        // cast Object to Integer then get it's value
        int colvalue = ( (Integer)obj).intValue();

        if (colvalue >= low && colvalue <= high) {
          return true;
        } else {
          return false;
        }
    }

}
```

Creating a FilteredRowSet Object and Setting Properties

Now that we have defined the filering criteria, we need to create an empty filtered rowset object and set some properties, as shown in the following code snippet:

```
// Create an OacleFilteredRowSet
OracleFilteredRowSet ofrs = new OracleFilteredRowSet();

// set properties
ofrs.setComand(" SELECT * from emp");
ofrs.setUrl (<URL>); // could also be set on the data source object
ofrs.setUsername("SCOTT");
ofrs.setPassword("TIGER");

// set ResultSet type (optional)
// ofrs.setType(ResultSet.TYPE_FORWARD_ONLY);
// ofrs.setType(ResultSet.TYPE_SCROLL_INSENSITIVE);
```

```
// Set concurrenty control (optional)
// ofrs.setConcurrency(ResultSet.CONCUR_UPDATABLE);
```

Populating the FilteredRowSet

FilteredRowset objects are populated using either execute() or populate() methods, with the same semantics as CachedRowSet and WebRowSet objects.

```
ofrs.execute(conn); // alternatively ofrs.populate();
```

At this stage, the filtered rowset has been prepopulated from the datasource using a query command; we can disconnect from the datasource and enable the filter.

Enabling Filters

```
// This Filter retrieves rows with col1 in (50,100) and col2
in (100,200)
int low[] = {50, 100};
int high[] = {100, 200};
int indexes[] = {1, 2};
ofrs.setFilter(new Predicate1(low, high, indexes));

// Retrieve the active predicate
Predicate p = ofrs.getFilter();
System.out.println("The active predicate: " +
p.getClass().getName());
```

Retrieving Filtered Rows and Closing the FilteredRowSet Object

The usual rowset navigation applies here:

```
ofrs.beforeFirst();

for (int i = 0; ofrs.next () ; ++i) {...}
```

Good programming practice recommends to close/release objects when you no longer need them:

```
        // clode the FilteredRowSet object
        ofrs.close();
```

Rows that do not meet the filtering criteria cannot be modified; also, only "filtered" rows can be synchronized with the datasource. A new filter (with different criteria) may be applied to an existing `FilteredRowSet` object, which will result in retrieving a different set of rows.

Listing 8.14   *myFilteredRowSet.java*

```
=====================================
import java.sql.*;
import java.util.*;
import javax.sql.RowSet;
import javax.sql.rowset.Predicate;
import oracle.sql.*;
import oracle.jdbc.rowset.*;
import oracle.jdbc.pool.OracleDataSource;

public class myFilteredRowSet
{
  public static void main(String[] args) throws SQLException
  {
      // Create an OracleDataSource
      OracleDataSource ods = new OracleDataSource();

      // Set the URL, using TNS Alias with JDBC-Thin
      String url = "jdbc:oracle:thin:scott/tiger@inst1";
      ods.setURL(url);
      Connection conn = ods.getConnection(); // Retrieve a connection

      conn.setAutoCommit(false); // Disable Auto Commit
      System.out.println ("*** Create and populate FilteredRowSet");
      OracleFilteredRowSet ofrs = new OracleFilteredRowSet();
      ofrs.setUsername("SCOTT");
      ofrs.setPassword("TIGER");
      ofrs.setCommand("select * from emp");
      // populate the FilteredRowSet
      ofrs.execute(conn);

      // close the connection and result set
      System.out.println("*** Close Connection and other resources");
```

```
        conn.close();

        // Let employees with deptno in (10, 20) pass through
        Predicate1 predic1 = new Predicate1 ( 10, 20, 8);
        ofrs.setFilter(predic1);

        // Retrieve the active predicate
        Predicate p2 = ofrs.getFilter();
        System.out.println("*** The active predicate is: " +
                                    p2.getClass().getName());

        // loop through the FilteredRowset and print
        ofrs.beforeFirst();
        for (int i = 0; ofrs.next () ; ++i)
        System.out.println ("*** EMPNO: " + ofrs.getInt (1)
            + " ENAME: " + ofrs.getString (2)
            + " JOB: " + ofrs.getString(3)+ " MGR ID: " +
ofrs.getInt(4)
            + " HIREDATE: " + ofrs.getDate(5)
            + " SAL: " + ofrs.getFloat(6) + " COMM" + ofrs.getFloat(7)
            + " DEPTNO: " +  ofrs.getInt(8) );
        ofrs.close ();
    }
}

$ javac myFilteredRowSet.java
$ java -Doracle.net.tns_admin=$TNS_ADMIN myFilteredRowSet

*** Create and populate FilteredRowSet
*** Close Connection and other resources
*** The active predicatei is: Predicate1
*** EMPNO: 7369 ENAME: SMITHJOB: CLERK MGR ID: 7902 HIREDATE: 1980-12-
17 SAL: 800.0 COMM0.0 DEPTNO: 20
*** EMPNO: 7566 ENAME: JONESJOB: MANAGER MGR ID: 7839 HIREDATE: 1981-
04-02 SAL: 2975.0 COMM0.0 DEPTNO: 20
*** EMPNO: 7782 ENAME: CLARKJOB: MANAGER MGR ID: 7839 HIREDATE: 1981-
06-09 SAL: 2450.0 COMM0.0 DEPTNO: 10
*** EMPNO: 7788 ENAME: SCOTTJOB: ANALYST MGR ID: 7566 HIREDATE: 1987-
04-19 SAL: 3000.0 COMM0.0 DEPTNO: 20
*** EMPNO: 7839 ENAME: KINGJOB: PRESIDENT MGR ID: 0 HIREDATE: 1981-11-
17 SAL: 5000.0 COMM0.0 DEPTNO: 10
```

```
*** EMPNO: 7876 ENAME: ADAMSJOB: CLERK MGR ID: 7788 HIREDATE: 1987-05-
23 SAL: 1100.0 COMM0.0 DEPTNO: 20
*** EMPNO: 7902 ENAME: FORDJOB: ANALYST MGR ID: 7566 HIREDATE: 1981-
12-03 SAL: 3000.0 COMM0.0 DEPTNO: 20
*** EMPNO: 7934 ENAME: MILLERJOB: CLERK MGR ID: 7782 HIREDATE: 1982-
01-23 SAL: 1300.0 COMM0.0 DEPTNO: 10
$
```

8.4.6   JoinRowSet and OracleJoinRowSet

In the SQL world, a JOIN operation is a query involving at least two tables in the FROM clause and one or multiple JOIN predicate(s) in the WHERE clause, as in the following join query:

```
SELECT * from EMP, DEPT WHERE EMP.DEPTNO = DDEPT.DEPTNO;
```

In order for the JOIN predicate to evaluate to true, values of columns in one table must match values of column(s) in the other table; these columns are called the *matching columns* (e.g., EMP.DEPTNO and DDEPT.DEPTNO).

Similarly, the javax.sql.rowset.JoinRowSet interface lets you simulate a SQL JOIN operation between disconnected RowSet objects. A JoinRowSet object combines data from multiple rowsets. The Oracle JDBC implements the standard javax.sql.rowset.JoinRowSet interface in ojdbc14.jar and furnishes the oracle.jdbc.rowset.OracleJoinRowSet class for classes12.jar. In addition, for all rowset types, ojdbc14,jar also implements the javax.sql.rowset.Joinable interface, while classes12.jar implements the oracle.jdbc.rowset.Joinable interface.

In order to use Join rowsets (i.e., JoinRowSet or OracleJoinRowSet), the JDBC applications must:

- Create an empty instance of JoinRowSet object and set properties.
- Create and add RowSets objects to the JoinRowSet.
- Define the match column (similar to SQL matching columns).
- Navigate and consume the JoinRowSet Object.

The following sections describe these steps individually, and at the end a complete example is given (Listing 8.15).

Creating an Empty Instance of JoinRowSet Object and Setting Properties

```
// Set the URL, using TNS Alias with JDBC-Thin
String url = "jdbc:oracle:thin:scott/tiger@inst1";
ods.setURL(url);
Connection conn = ods.getConnection(); // Retrieve a
connection
conn.setAutoCommit(false); // Disable Auto Commit
 ...
OracleJoinRowSet ojrs = new OracleJoinRowSet();
```

Creating and Adding RowSet Objects to the JoinRowSet

- The addRowSet () method has the following signatures and allows you to add RowSet objects to the JoinRowSet or OracleJoin-RowSet object:

```
addRowSet(Joinable rowSet)
addRowSet(javax.sql.RowSet rowSet, int matchColumnIndex)
addRowSet(javax.sql.RowSet rowSet,
      java.lang.String matchColumnName)
addRowSet(javax.sql.RowSet[] rowSets,
      int[] matchColumnIndexes)
addRowSet(javax.sql.RowSet[] rowSets,
      java.lang.String[] matchColumnNames)
```

- The getRowSets() method allows you to retrieve a java.util.Collection object containing all rowset objects that have been added to this JoinRowSet object.

- The getRowSetNames() method allows you to retrieve a String array containing the names of all RowSet objects that have been added to this JoinRowSet object.

Defining the Match Column(s)

Many of the aforementioned addRowSet() methods have either a matchColumnIndex or a matchColumnName parameter, which allows you to specify the match column.

```
ojrs.addRowSet(emprs, "DEPTNO");
ojrs.addRowSet(deptrs, 1);
```

The first rowset added to the join rowset imposes the match column to other rowsets that will be added later.

The setMatchColumn() method, inherited from the Joinable interface, is an alternative approach for setting the *match column* on a rowset object before adding it to the JoinRowSet object.

```
ocrs.setMatchColumn(3);
    ...
ojrs.addRowSer(ocrs);
```

The Joinable interface furnishes, in addition, the getMatchColumn() and unsetMatchColumn() methods for retrieving and unsetting the match column(s).

Multiple match columns may be specified as an array of int:

```
int[] matchcolint = {2, 3, 4};
    ...
ocrs.setMatchColumns(matchcolint);
ojrs.addRowSet(ocrs);
```

or an array of String objects:

```
String [] matchcolstr = {"DEPTNO", "LOCATION"};
    ...
ocrs.setMatchColumns(matchcolint);
ojrs.addRowSet(ocrs);
```

The JOIN types include INNER JOIN, CROSS JOIN, and OUTER JOINS (FULL JOIN, LEFT JOIN, RIGHT JOIN). The following methods are specific to each JOIN type and return a Boolean indicating whether the type in question is supported or not:

- supportsInnerJoin(): Returns only rows that satisfy the join condition; this is the default and only JOIN type currently supported in OracleJoinRowSet.

- supportsCrossJoin(): Returns the combination of each row from the first table with each row from the second table.

- supportsLeftOuterJoin(): Returns inner join results plus rows from the left table in the from clause list, for which no row from the right table satisfies the join condition.

- supportsRightOuterJoin(): Returns inner join results plus rows from the right table (in the from clause list), for which no row from the left table satisfies the join condition.

- supportsFullJoin(): This is a two-sided outer join, because it returns the results of both left join and right join.

See the Oracle Database SQL reference doc for more details on JOIN types.

- The setJoinType() method allows you to define the JOIN type to be assigned to the JoinRowSet object. INNER JOIN is currently the default and the only supported type; therefore, you can ignore this method for now.

- The getJoinType() method returns the JOIN type of the Join-RowSet object; it can be ignored for now.

- The getWhereClause() method returns a description of the pseudo-WHERE clause.

```
ojrs.getWhereClause()
```

Navigating and Consuming the JoinRowSet Objects

The usual rowset navigation applies here:

```
ojrs.beforeFirst();
...
for (int i = 0; ojrs.next () ; ++i) {...}
```

Listing 8.15   *myoinRowSet.java*

```
==============================
import java.sql.*;
import java.util.*;
import javax.sql.RowSet;
import oracle.sql.*;
import oracle.jdbc.rowset.*;
```

```
import oracle.jdbc.pool.OracleDataSource;
/*
 * Create an OracleJoinRowSet corresponding to
 * SELECT * FROM EMP, DEPT WHERE EMP.DEPTNO = DEPT.DEPTNO
 *
 */
public class myJoinRowSet
{
  public static void main(String[] args) throws SQLException
  {
      // Create an OracleDataSource
      OracleDataSource ods = new OracleDataSource();

      // Set the URL, using TNS Alias with JDBC-Thin
      String url = "jdbc:oracle:thin:scott/tiger@inst1";
      ods.setURL(url);
      Connection conn = ods.getConnection(); // Retrieve a connection
      conn.setAutoCommit(false); // Disable Auto Commit

      OracleCachedRowSet ocrs1 = new OracleCachedRowSet();
      ocrs1.setCommand("SELECT * FROM DEPT");
      ocrs1.setUrl(url);
      ocrs1.setUsername("scott");
      ocrs1.setPassword("tiger");
      System.out.println ("*** Populate CRowSet #1 with rows from DEPT
table");
      ocrs1.execute();

      OracleCachedRowSet ocrs2 = new OracleCachedRowSet();
      ocrs2.setCommand("SELECT * FROM EMP");
      ocrs2.setUrl(url);
      ocrs2.setUsername("scott");
      ocrs2.setPassword("tiger");
      System.out.println ("*** Populate CRowSet #2 with rows from EMP table");
      ocrs2.execute();

      System.out.println("*** Close the Connection");
      conn.close();

      System.out.println ("*** Create an empty JoinRowSet");
      OracleJoinRowSet ojrs = new OracleJoinRowSet();
```

```
        System.out.println ("*** Adding CRowSet#1 with DEPTNO as Match Column");
        ojrs.addRowSet(ocrs1, "DEPTNO");
        System.out.println ("*** Adding CRowSet#2 with DEPTNO as Match Column");
        ojrs.addRowSet(ocrs2, "DEPTNO");

        System.out.println ("*** WHERE Clause: " + ojrs.getWhereClause());
        // loop through the JoinRowset and print
        ojrs.beforeFirst();
        System.out.println ("DEPTNO DNAME   LOCATION ENAME    JOB     EMPNO" +
                                                   "HIRED   MGR ");
        System.out.println ("****** ****** ******** ****   ******** ******* " +
                                                   " **** ******** ");
        for (int i = 0; ojrs.next () ; ++i)
       System.out.println (ojrs.getString(1) + " " + ojrs.getString(2) + " " +

          ojrs.getString(3) + " " + ojrs.getString(4) + " "  + ojrs.getString(5)
   +
          " " + ojrs.getString(6) + " " + ojrs.getString(7) + " " +
          ojrs.getString(8));

        ojrs.close ();
   }
}


$ javac myJoinRowSet.java
$ java -Doracle.net.tns_admin=$TNS_ADMIN myJoinRowSet

*** Populate Cached RowSet #1 with rows from DEPT table
*** Populate Cached RowSet #2 with rows from EMP table
*** Close the Connection
*** Create an empty JoinRowSet
*** Adding CRowSet#1 with DEPTNO as Match Column
*** Adding CRowSet#2 with DEPTNO as Match Column
*** WHERE Clause: WHERE
(null.DEPTNO = null.DEPTNO);
DEPTNO DNAME   LOCATION ENAME  JOB       EMPNO    HIRED    MGR
****** ****** ******** ****   ******** *******i   **** ********
10 ACCOUNTING LAS VEGAS CLARK MANAGER 7839 1981-06-09 2450
10 ACCOUNTING LAS VEGAS KING PRESIDENT null 1981-11-17 5000
10 ACCOUNTING LAS VEGAS MILLER CLERK 7782 1982-01-23 1300
20 RESEARCH DALLAS SMITH CLERK 7902 1980-12-17 800
20 RESEARCH DALLAS JONES MANAGER 7839 1981-04-02 2975
```

```
20 RESEARCH DALLAS SCOTT ANALYST 7566 1987-04-19 3000
20 RESEARCH DALLAS ADAMS CLERK 7788 1987-05-23 1100
20 RESEARCH DALLAS FORD ANALYST 7566 1981-12-03 3000
30 SALES CHICAGO ALLEN SALESMAN 7698 1981-02-20 1600
30 SALES CHICAGO WARD SALESMAN 7698 1981-02-22 1250
30 SALES CHICAGO MARTIN SALESMAN 7698 1981-09-28 1250
30 SALES CHICAGO BLAKE MANAGER 7839 1981-05-01 2850
30 SALES CHICAGO TURNER SALESMAN 7698 1981-09-08 1500
30 SALES CHICAGO JAMES CLERK 7698 1981-12-03 950
$
```

Further Considerations

The `toCachedRowSet()` method allows dumping the data of a `JoinRowSet`, which has been applied to the acceptChanges method, into a `CachedRowSet` for presumably further synchronization back to the datasource.

8.5 Conclusion

Throughout this long chapter, you have learned (or refreshed your memory on) how to: (1) use key metadata in JDBC, (2) manipulate Oracle SQL data types in JDBC, and (3) use Result Sets and RowSet (`JSR-114`). The next chapter discusses some of the quality of services in JDBC, such as transaction management, security management, and some best practices.

9

JDBC Quality of Services and Best Practices

Quality of service refers to transaction services, security services, connection caching, and other infrastructure services. Connection caching was addressed in Chapter 7. This chapter looks at transaction services in JDBC, including local transaction, distributed transactions, and transaction savepoint, and then looks at security services such as SSL/JSSE support. Finally, we'll look at some programming tips and logging/tracing.

9.1 Transaction Services

9.1.1 Transactions

A transaction is a unit of work, which has the generally defined and well-known ACID properties (i.e., Atomicity, Consistency, Isolation, and Durability). In the Oracle database environment, a transaction begins at the first SQL statement that follows the most recent commit, rollback, or connect statement; however, even though a SELECT statement may follow a COMMIT or ROLLBACK, only DML (Insert, Update, Delete, SELECT FOR UPDATE) and SET statements are regarded as starting point(s) of a new database transaction. The javax.sql.Connection provides commit and rollback methods for demarcating local transactions.

9.1.2 AutoCommit

Autocommit mode is a Boolean value (i.e., false/true), which instructs the database whether or not to automatically commit after every SQL operation. By default, autocommit is set to true for new connection objects. For better application performance, disable autocommit mode by invoking setAutoCommit() method on the connection object and use the explicit commit() or rollback() methods.

```
// It's faster when auto commit is off
conn.setAutoCommit (false);
```

Note that DDL statements (e.g., `CREATE TABLE`) are systematically auto-committed.

9.1.3 Transaction Isolation Levels

JDBC defines the following transaction isolation levels: `TRANSACTION_NONE`, `TRANSACTION_READ_UNCOMMITTED`, `TRANSACTION_READ_COMMITTED`, `TRANSACTION_REPEATABLE_READ`, and `TRANSACTION_SERIALIZABLE`, but ultimately the JDBC driver can only expose what the underlying datasource supports.

Table 9.1 summarizes the isolation levels defined by ANSI SQL 92 and the ones supported by the Oracle database. However, the Oracle database furnishes multilevel read consistency and ensures nonblocking reads, which is the goal of `READ UNCOMMITTED`.

Table 9.1   *ANSI SQL 92 Isolation Levels*

ANSI SQL 92 Isolation Levels	Dirty Read	Non Repeatable Read	Phantom Insert Possible	Oracle Database
READ UNCOMMITTED	Yes	Yes	Yes	
READ COMMITTED	No	Yes	Yes	X
REPEATABLE READ	No	No	Yes	READ-ONLY
SERIALIZABLE	No	No	No	X

The Oracle JDBC drivers support only `TRANSACTION_READ_COMMITTED` and `TRANSACTION_SERIALIZABLE` isolation levels.

```
connAttr.setProperty("TRANSACTION_ISOLATION",
"TRANSACTION_SERIALIZABLE");
...
oconn = ods.getConnection(connAttr); // retrieve connection
```

The default RDBMS isolation is returned by the `getDefaultTransactionIsolation` method.

```
oconn.getMetaData().getDefaultTransactionIsolation ();
```

Similarly, the isolation level of an OracleConnection can be set and retrieved by the `getTransactionIsolation` and `setTransactionIsolation` methods.

```
oconn.getTransactionIsolation ();
```

9.1.4 Transaction SavePoint Support

Transaction savepoint is a well-known RDBMS mechanism, which allows setting intermediate control points (partial commit or rollback points) within a local transaction (not supported for global/distributed transactions). JDBC 3.0 now specifies a standard interface for exposing transaction savepoint to Java developers.

The Oracle JDBC furnishes the standard `java.sql.Savepoint` for JDK 1.4 and up environments and `oracle.jdbc.OracleSavepoint` for pre-JDK 1.4 environments.

A savepoint is created using either `Connection.setSavepoint()`, which returns `java.sql.Savepoint` object, or `OracleConnection.oracleSetSavepoint()`, which returns `oracle.jdbc.OracleSavepoint` object. A savepoint is either named by a string provided during its creation or automatically assigned an integer id.

```
Savepoint svpt1 = conn.setSavepoint("SVPT1");
Savepoint svpt3 = conn.setSavepoint();
```

The following methods retrieve the name or the id of the savepoint. Retrieving a name from an unnamed savepoint or retrieving an id from a named savepoint throws a SQL Exception.

```
svpt.getSavepointName();
svpt.getSavepointId();
```

Once a savepoint has been set, the transaction can be rolled back to that savepoint using either `Connection.rollback (Savepoint svpt)` or `OracleConnection.oracleRollback (OracleSavepoint svpt)`.

```
conn.rollback(svpt1);
```

Rolling back to a savepoint that has been released throws a SQL Exception.

The JDBC standard also specifies a method to explicitly release/cancel savepoints by using `Connection.releaseSavepoint(Savepoint svpt)`. The Oracle JDBC does not currently offer proper support for explicit savepoint releasing; however, when a transaction is committed or rolled back, all savepoints created as part of the transaction are implicitly/automatically released (i.e., become invalid). (See Listing 9.1.)

Listing 9.1   *TransSavepoint.java*

```
===================================
```

```java
/*  Transaction SavePoint Sample Code
 *
 * The program uses the "DEPT" table and performs
 * following operations
 *    checks Savepoint support
 *    insert a new dept row
 *    set a first named Savepoint
 *    insert another dept row
 *    set a second named Savepoint
 *    set an unamed Savepoint
 *    rollback to first named Savepoint
 *    commit ==> the DEPT table should only show one new row
 *
 */
import java.sql.*;
import oracle.sql.*;
import oracle.jdbc.*;
import oracle.jdbc.pool.OracleDataSource;
public class TransSavepoint
{
  public static void main(String args[]) throws SQLException
  {
    Connection conn = null;
    Statement  stmt = null;
    ResultSet  rset = null;
    int        rows = 0;
    try
    {
    // Create an OracleDataSource
```

```
 OracleDataSource ods = new OracleDataSource();
 // Set the URL, using TNS Alias with JDBC-Thin
 String url = "jdbc:oracle:thin:scott/tiger@inst1";
 ods.setURL(url);
conn = ods.getConnection(); // Retrieve a connection

 // Disable Auto Commit for Transaction Savepoint
 conn.setAutoCommit(false);
 // Create a Statement
 stmt = conn.createStatement();
 // Cleanup changes by previous executions
 stmt.execute("DELETE FROM dept WHERE deptno >= 90");

 // Check Savepoint support
 DatabaseMetaData dbmd = conn.getMetaData();
 print("Checking savepoint support ...");
 if (dbmd.supportsSavepoints()) print("Savepoint supported");
 else
   print("Savepoint not supported");

 // Insert a new record into the "dept" table
 print("Insert dept(91, 'DEPT91''Tumbuctou') ...");
 rows =
 stmt.executeUpdate("insert into dept values (91,
     'DEPT91','Tumbuctou')");

 // Establish first named savepoint
 print("Establish svpt1 ...");
 Savepoint svpt1 = conn.setSavepoint("SVPT1");

 // Insert second record into the "dept" table
 print("Insert record(92, 'DEPT92', 'New York') ...");
 rows =
 stmt.executeUpdate("insert into dept values (92, 'DEPT92','New
     York')");

 // Establish second named savepoint
 print("Establish named savepoint svpt2 ...");
 Savepoint svpt2 = conn.setSavepoint("SVPT2");

 // Establish an unamed savepoint
 print("Establish svpt3 ...");
```

```
Savepoint svpt3 = conn.setSavepoint();

// Insert a third record into the "dept" table
print("Insert dept(93, 'DEPT93', 'Paris') ...");
rows =
stmt.executeUpdate("insert into dept values (93, 'DEPT93',
    'Istanbul')");

// Check names and ids of established Savepoints
print("The name of txn savepoint #1 is: " +
    svpt1.getSavepointName());
print("The name of txn savepoint #2 is: " +
    svpt2.getSavepointName());
print("The id of txn savepoint #3 is: " +
    svpt3.getSavepointId());

// Rollback to the first savepoint
print("Rollback to SVPT1...");
conn.rollback(svpt1);

// Commit the transaction
print("Commit the transaction ...");
conn.commit();

print("Checking changes to Dept ...");
rset =
  stmt.executeQuery ("select * from dept where deptno >= 90");

// Print the result
while (rset.next ())
{
  print ("DeptNo: " + rset.getString (1));
  print ("DeptName: " + rset.getString (2));
  print ("DeptLoc: " + rset.getString (3));
}

// Close the ResultSet
rset.close();

// Cleanup table to original state
stmt.execute("DELETE FROM dept WHERE deptno >= 100");
```

```
          // Close the Statement
           stmt.close();

          // Close the Connection
           conn.close();
        } catch(SQLException sqle) {
         print("Unexpected SQL Exception " + sqle.getMessage());
         sqle.printStackTrace();
        } catch(Exception exc) {
         print("Unexpected Exception " + exc.getMessage());
         exc.printStackTrace();
        }
     }

   static void print(String mesg)
   {
      System.out.println(mesg);
   }
}

$ javac TransSavepoint.java
$ java -Doracle.net.tns_admin=$TNS_ADMIN TransSavepoint

Checking savepoint support ...
Savepoint supported
Insert dept(91, 'DEPT91''Tumbuctou') ...
Establish svpt1 ...
Insert record(92, 'DEPT92', 'New York') ...
Establish named savepoint svpt2 ...
Establish svpt3 ...
Insert dept(93, 'DEPT93', 'Paris') ...
The name of txn savepoint #1 is: SVPT1
The name of txn savepoint #2 is: SVPT2
The id of txn savepoint #3 is: 1
Rollback to SVPT1...
Commit the transaction ...
Checking changes to Dept ...
DeptNo: 91
DeptName: DEPT91
DeptLoc: Tumbuctou
```

9.1.5   **Global/Distributed Transaction**

The X/Open Distributed Transaction Model

The X/Open Distributed Transaction Processing (DTP) specifies a standard model for distributed/global transactions, which includes the following components:

- *Application Component*, which implements transactional operations and programmatically demarcates transactions using the TX interface.

- *Resource Manager*, which is an X/Open XA-compliant component such as RDBMS; it manages persistent and stable data storage systems.

- *Transaction Manager*, which implements the two-phase commit protocol. This protocol allows the transaction manager and the resource manager to preserve the ACID properties (i.e., "all or nothing"); in other words, either all the resource managers commit the transaction ("all") or they all rollback ("nothing").

- *Communication Resource Manager*, which allows interoperability between transaction managers in different transaction processing domains.

Figure 9.1 illustrates the key components within a single DTP domain.

Figure 9.1
The Distributed Transaction Processing Model

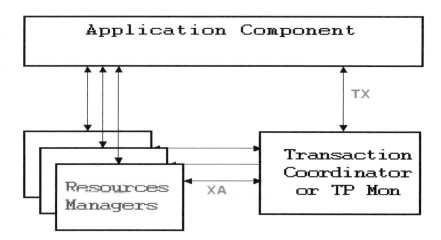

JDBC Support for Global Transactions

JTA is a high-level transaction management API, used in Java EE DTP environments by resource managers and transactional applications, the JTA libraries are also built into JDK 1.4 and JDK 1.5 (for pre-1.4 JDK, you need supplemental `jta.jar` and `jndi.jar`). JTA defines `UserTransaction`, `TransactionManager`, `XAResource`, and `Transaction` interfaces.

- The `javax.transaction.UserTransaction` interface provides methods for the user application to demarcate transactions programmatically, including `begin()`, `commit()`, `rollback`, `getStatus()` `setTransactionTimeout()`, and `setRollbackOnly()`.

- The `javax.transaction.TransactionManager` interface provides methods that allow an application server to manage transaction boundaries, including `begin()`, `commit()`, `rollback`, `getStatus()` `setTransactionTimeout()`, `setRollbackOnly()`, `suspend()`, `resume()`, and `getTransaction()`.

- The `javax.transaction.xa.XAResource` interface is the Java mapping of the X/Open XA interface. It provides the following methods: `commit()`, `end()`, `forget()`, `getTransactionTimeout()`, `isSameRM()`, `prepare()`, `recover()`, `rollback()`, `setTransactionTimeout()`, and `start()`. These methods are used by resource managers and transaction managers to associate a global transaction and a database connection (or a message service connection). JDBC (or a JMS provider) implements this interface to provide the underlying Java XA support necessary for JTA transactions. The `oracle.jdbc.xa.OracleXAResource` class implements the `javax.transaction.xa.XAResource` interface.

- The `javax.transaction.xa.Xid` interface is the Java mapping of the X/Open transaction identifier `XID` structure. The Xid must be globally unique and contains the `formatId`, the global transaction id (`gtrid`), and branch qualifier id (`bqual`). It provides the following methods: `getBranchQualifier()`, `getFormatId()`, and `getGlobalTransactionId()`. The `oracle.jdbc.xa.OracleXid` class implements the `javax.transaction.xa.Xid` interface, in addition to the `isLocalTransaction()` method. See the "Distributed Transaction" chapter in the Oracle JDBC Users Guide for more details on the `XAResource` flags and Xids.

- The `javax.transaction.xa.XAException` interface defines an exception thrown by the resource manager for consumption/processing by the transaction coordinator/manager when it encounters an error specific to the transaction involved. The `oracle.jdbc.xa.OracleXAException` extends the `javax.transaction.xa.XAException` and furnishes the `getOracleError()`, `getXAError()`, and `getXAErrorMessage()` methods.

```
try{
...
// XA operations
...
} catch(OracleXAexception oraxae){
   int oraerr = oraxae.getOracleError();
   System.out.println("Oracle XA Exception" + oraerr);
} catch (XAException xae) {
 // generic XA Exceptions
}
```

See Table 29-2 in the Oracle JDBC 10*g* reference guide for a mapping between `Oracle XA Error codes` and `XA Errors`.

JDBC XADataSource and XAConnection Interfaces

The `javax.sql.XADataSource` interface defines a factory for `XAConnection` objects. The `oracle.jdbc.xa.OracleXADataSource` class in both `oracle.jdbc.xa.client` (for client-side JDBC) and `oracle.jdbc.xa.server` (for RDBMS-side JDBC) packages implement `javax.sql.XADataSource`.

The `javax.sql.XAConnection` interface defines the `getXAResource()` method. The `XAConnection.getXAResource()`method returns an `XAResource` object, which is used to associate and enlist the `XAConnection` object with the current transaction. The `oracle.jdbc.xa.OracleXAConnection` class implements the `javax.sql.XAConnection` interface and extends `oracle.jdbc.pool.OraclePooledConnection` (which implements the `javax.sql.PooledConnection` interface). However, although the Oracle JDBC may cache `OracleXAConnection` objects, as of Oracle Database 10*g* Release 2, this feature is not publicly available. Consequently, when connection caching is enabled on an `OracleXADataSource`, invoking `OracleXADataSource.getXAConnection(...)` will fail; to get an

XAConnection object Java applications should call OracleXAData-
Source.getConnection(...) instead.

Native XA Support in Oracle JDBC

In pre-10*g* releases of the Oracle JDBC, XA operations were sent to the
RDBMS using stored procedures. Starting with Oracle Database 10*g*
Release 1, Oracle JDBC furnishes a more efficient/direct or native XA
mechanism, thereby improving performance. Native XA is the default
mode for JDBC-Thin (pure Java) drivers, while native XA has to be explicitly enabled for JDBC-OCI using the datasource property tnsEntry (the
property is set to the value of the TNS entry name).

```
ods.setTNSEntryName("tnsalias");
```

```
ods.getTNSEntryName();
```

Two-Phase Commit Optimization

Upon initiating the prepare() phase of the two-phase commit, if two or
more branches of a distributed transaction use the same Oracle database
instance—that is, the OracleXAResource instances are associated to the
same Resource Manager (i.e., the Oracle database)—and all but one branch
return XA_RDONLY, and only one branch returns XA_OK or a failure, then the
Oracle JDBC XA performs Commit or Rollback only on the branch, which
returns XA_OK or a failure. The transaction coordinator uses the
isSameRM() method on the OracleXAResource object (it also takes an
OracleXAResource as parameter) to make such a determination.

Listing 9.2 summarizes the required steps for performing a distributed
transaction with an optimized two-phase commit.

Listing 9.2   *JdbcXa.java*

```
==========================
/*
 * XA 2PC code sample (mix application and TM dialogs with RM)

 */
import java.sql.*;
import javax.sql.*;
import oracle.jdbc.*;
import oracle.jdbc.pool.*;
```

```java
import oracle.jdbc.xa.*;
import javax.transaction.xa.*;
import oracle.jdbc.xa.client.OracleXADataSource;

public class JdbcXa
{
  public static void main (String args [])throws SQLException
  {
   try
   {

   // Create a XADataSource instance
   OracleXADataSource oxads = new OracleXADataSource();

   // Set the URL, using TNS Alias with JDBC-Thin
   String url = "jdbc:oracle:thin:scott/tiger@inst1";
   oxads.setURL(url);

   // Set User/Pass, not currenrly retrieved from URL
   // for XADataSources
    oxads.setUser("SCOTT");
    oxads.setPassword("TIGER");

   // XA Connection Caching is not yet exposed publicly
   // oxads.setConnectionCachingEnabled(true);
   // get XA connection from XADataSource

   XAConnection xaconn1 = oxads.getXAConnection();
   XAConnection xaconn2 = oxads.getXAConnection();

   // Get the pysical connections
   OracleConnection conn1 =
(OracleConnection)xaconn1.getConnection();
   Statement stmt1 = conn1.createStatement ();

   // Get another physical conn. from the same data source
   OracleConnection conn2 =
(OracleConnection)xaconn2.getConnection();
   Statement stmt2 = conn2.createStatement ();

   // Get the XA Resources
   XAResource oxar1 = xaconn1.getXAResource();
```

```
XAResource oxar2 = xaconn2.getXAResource();

// Create the Xids With the Same Global Ids
Xid xid1 = createXid(1);
Xid xid2 = createXid(2);

// Start the Resources
oxar1.start (xid1, XAResource.TMNOFLAGS);
oxar2.start (xid2, XAResource.TMNOFLAGS);

// DO some work through xacon1
  stmt1.executeUpdate("insert into dept values (91, 'DEPT91',
'Tumbuctou')");

// Do some work through xacnn2
  stmt2.executeUpdate("insert into emp values (9999, 'XA EMP',
'XATEST', 7566, '29-OCT-05', 99, 0, 10)");

// END both the branches
oxar1.end(xid1, XAResource.TMSUCCESS);
oxar2.end(xid2, XAResource.TMSUCCESS);

// Prepare the RMs
int xaprp1 = oxar1.prepare (xid1);
int xaprp2 = oxar2.prepare (xid2);
System.out.println("Return value for prepare 1 is " + xaprp1);
System.out.println("Return value for prepare 2 is " + xaprp2);
boolean xa_commit = true;

//  Check the return from the prepare phase
  if (!((xaprp1 == XAResource.XA_OK) || (xaprp1 ==
XAResource.XA_RDONLY)))
  xa_commit = false;
  if (!((xaprp2 == XAResource.XA_OK) || (xaprp2 ==
XAResource.XA_RDONLY)))
  xa_commit = false;
  System.out.println("xa_commit is " + xa_commit);

// If both branches are from same RM, the TM does XA optimization
  System.out.println("Is oxar1 same as oxar2 ? " +
oxar1.isSameRM(oxar2));
```

```
    // Determine which branch to commit or rollback
    if (xaprp1 == XAResource.XA_OK)
     if (xa_commit)
       oxar1.commit (xid1, false);
     else
       oxar1.rollback (xid1);
    if (xaprp2 == XAResource.XA_OK)
     if (xa_commit)
       oxar2.commit (xid2, false);
     else
       oxar2.rollback (xid2);

    // Close the XA connections and resources
     stmt1.close(); conn1.close();
     stmt2.close(); conn2.close();

    /*
     * Print the changes to the tables and clean up
     */

      // Create an OracleDataSource
      OracleDataSource ods = new OracleDataSource();
      // Set the URL, using TNS Alias with JDBC-Thin
      ods.setURL(url);

      // Retrieve a connection <<-- Naive approach,
     // see connection sharing b/w local and global transaction, next

      conn1 = (OracleConnection) ods.getConnection();

      stmt1 = conn1.createStatement();
      // Print the newly added row in dept table
    ResultSet
         rset1 = stmt1.executeQuery ("select * from dept where deptno
>= 91");
      while (rset1.next ())
      {
        print ("\nDeptNo: " + rset1.getString (1));
        print ("DeptName: " + rset1.getString (2));
        print ("DeptLoc: " + rset1.getString (3));
      }
       rset1.close();
```

```
        // Clean up our changes
        stmt1.execute("DELETE FROM dept WHERE deptno >= 91");

        // Print the newly added row in emp table
        rset1 = stmt1.executeQuery ("select * from emp where empno >=
9999");
        while (rset1.next ())
        {
          print ("\nEmpNo: " + rset1.getString (1));
          print ("EmpName: " + rset1.getString (2));
          print ("EmpJob: " + rset1.getString (3));
          print ("Manager: " + rset1.getString (4));
          print ("HireDate: " + rset1.getString (5));
        }
        rset1.close();
        // Clean up our changes
        stmt1.execute("DELETE FROM emp WHERE empno >= 9999");
        conn1.commit(); // commit deletions in both tables
        rset1.close();
        stmt1.close();

    } catch (SQLException sqe){
       sqe.printStackTrace();
    } catch (XAException xae){
       if (xae instanceof OracleXAException) {
       System.out.println("XA Error is " +
       ((OracleXAException)xae).getXAError());
       System.out.println("SQL Error is " +
       ((OracleXAException)xae).getOracleError());
       }
    }
  }

static Xid createXid(int bids)
 throws XAException
 {
  byte[] gid = new byte[1]; gid[0]= (byte) 9;
  byte[] bid = new byte[1]; bid[0]= (byte) bids;
  byte[] gtrid = new byte[64];
  byte[] bqual = new byte[64];
  System.arraycopy (gid, 0, gtrid, 0, 1);
  System.arraycopy (bid, 0, bqual, 0, 1);
```

```
  Xid xid = new OracleXid(0x1234, gtrid, bqual);
  return xid;
}


static void print(String mesg)
  {
    System.out.println(mesg);
  }
}


$ javac JdbcXa.java
$ java -Doracle.net.tns_admin=$TNS_ADMIN JdbcXa


Return value for prepare 1 is 3
Return value for prepare 2 is 0
xa_commit is true
Is oxar1 same as oxar2 ? true


DeptNo: 91
DeptName: DEPT91
DeptLoc: Tumbuctou


EmpNo: 9999
EmpName: XA EMP
EmpJob: XATEST
Manager: 7566
HireDate: 2005-10-29 00:00:00.0
```

9.1.6 Connection Sharing between Local and Global Transactions

JDBC 3.0 specifies the ability to alternatively share the same connection between a local and a global transaction. A JDBC connection can only be in one of three states or modes: NO_TXN, LOCAL_TXN, or GLOBAL_TXN.

- NO_TXN: At creation, every connection is in this state, and then it transitions to either LOCAL_TXN or GLOBAL TXN.

- LOCAL_TXN: The connection is being used by a local transaction; autocommit is disabled.

- GLOBAL_TXN: The connection being used by a global transaction.

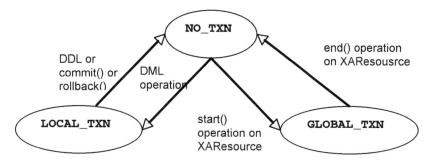

Figure 9.2
State Transition

A connection can participate alternatively in local and global transactions, as illustrated by Figure 9.2. The first thing to notice is that there is no direct transition to and from LOCAL_TXN mode from and to GLOBAL_TXN.

NO_TXN -> LOCAL_TXN and LOCAL_TXN-> NO_TXN

- The connection state changes into LOCAL_TXN when AutoCommit is set to false and DML operations (i.e., Insert, Update, Delete) are performed.

- The connection returns to NO_TXN state when DDL (i.e., Create, Alter), commit(), or rollback() operations are performed.

```
// Transition: NO_TXN -> LOCAL_TXN
xconn.setAutoCommit(false);

// Create a Statement and do some work
Statement stmt = xconn.createStatement ();
stmt.executeUpdate("insert into dept values (91,
'DEPT91', 'Tumbuctou')");

// Transition: LOCAL_TXN-> NO_TXN
xconn.commit();
```

NO_TXN -> GLOBAL_TXN and GLOBAL_TXN -> NO_TXN

- The connection goes in GLOBAL_TXN state when a start() operation is performed on an XAResource object.

- The connection returns to NO_TXN when an end() operation is performed on an XAResource object.

```
// Transition NO_TXN -> GLOBAL_TXN
XAResource oxar = pc.getXAResource();
Xid xid = createXid ();
oxar.start (xid, XAResource.TMNOFLAGS);

// Create a Statement and do some work
stmt = xconn.createStatement ();
stmt2.executeUpdate("insert into emp values (9999, 'XA
EMP', 'XATEST', 7566, '29-OCT-05', 99, 0, 10)");

// Transition GLOBAL_TXN -> NO_TXN
oxar.end(xid, XAResource.TMSUCCESS);
oxar.commit (xid, true);
```

9.2   **Security Services**

9.2.1   **Oracle JDBC Support for SSL**

SSL in a Nutshell

The Secure Socket Layer (SSL) is a protocol for secure client/server communications in connected and Web environments (i.e., unconnected). SSL works on top of the TCP/IP protocol and uses various cryptography mechanisms to achieve strong authentication (beyond traditional username/password), data privacy, and ensure integrity. These mechanisms include secret key cryptology (i.e., DES, 3DES, RC2, RC4), public-key cryptography (i.e., RSA, DH), public-key certificates (i.e., VeriSign, Entrust, GTE Cyber-Trust), cryptographic hash functions (i.e., MD5, SHA), and message authentication code (MAC).

For starters, here is some lexicon:

- *Certificate:* A digitally signed document that binds a public key with an entity. The certificate can be used to verify that the public key belongs to that individual.

- *Certificate authority (CA):* An entity that issues digitally signed certificates.

- *Certificate signing request (CSR):* Contains the identity of the certificate requester, as well as the public key of the server on which the certificate will be installed.

- *Cipher suite:* A set of cryptographic algorithms (public-key exchange algorithm, key agreement algorithms, and cryptographic hash functions) and key sizes used to encrypt data sent over the network.

- *Private key:* A secret key, used to decrypt a message that has been encrypted using the corresponding public key. It is also used to sign certificates. The certificate is verified using the corresponding public key.

- *Public key:* A public key used for encrypting the message sent over SSL. It is also used to verify that a certificate has been signed by the corresponding private key.

- *Root certificate:* A trusted root certificate or self-signed certificate that identifies a CA.

- *Session key:* A pair of public_key/private_key for the duration of a session. The public key is provided by the receiver and used by the sender to encrypt sent messages, while the private key is not shared and used by the receiver to decrypt received messages.

- *Wallet:* A password-protected container for storing private keys, certificates, and trusted certificates used by SSL for authentication and signing

During the establishment of secure communication, the client and the server perform a one-time SSL handshake, during which both parties negotiate and agree on the cipher suite and the encryption algorithm to use. At 20,000-feet view, the handshake process can be described as follows:[1]

1. The client requests a secure communication with the server.

2. The server sends back its public key to the client. Optionally, the server also sends its certificate and root certificate (for verification by the client), and requests the client's certificate for authentication purposes.

3. The client sends its public key to the server. Optionally, the client verifies that the server's certificate and root certificate are signed by a trusted certificate authority, and if requested, the client also sends its certificate and root certificate back to the server for verification.

---

1. http://java.sun.com/j2se/1.5.0/docs/guide/security/jsse/JSSERefGuide.html#HowSSLWorks.

4.   The client and the server each generate a session key using public-key/private-key cryptography.

5.   At this stage, all subsequent communications between the client and the server are encrypted and decrypted using this set of session keys and the negotiated cipher suite.

Java Support for SSL (JSSE)

JSSE is a Java implementation of Secure Socket Layer (SSL) and Transport Layer Security (TLS); it furnishes classes and interfaces for creating and configuring key managers, trust managers, secure socket factories, and so on. Since release 1.4 of Java Standard Edition (i.e., JDK 1.4), JSSE has been an integral part of the Java security arsenal (it was optional before), along with the Java Cryptography Extension (JCE) and the Java Authentication and Authorization Service (JAAS).

The `JSSE` API is available in the `javax.net`, `javax.net.ssl`, and `java.security.cert` packages. It defines the following properties (i.e., system properties or security properties) for configuring `SSL`:

- `javax.net.ssl.keyStore`: Location of the certificate container (no default value) `prop.put("javax.net.ssl.keyStore", "<file_location>| NONE");`

- `javax.net.ssl.keyStoreType`: The type of keystore (default value = `KeyStore.getDefaultType()`).
  `prop.put("javax.net.ssl.keyStoreType", "JKS");`

- `javax.net.ssl.keyStorePassword`: Protects the content of a keystore (no default). `prop.put("javax.net.ssl.keyStorePassword", "<password>");`

- `javax.net.ssl.trustStore`: A set of certificates that the SSL client uses to validates the received certificate the default value is either:

    `$JAVA_HOME/lib/security/jssecacerts`

  if it exists, otherwise:

    `$JAVA_HOME/lib/security/cacerts).`

    `prop.put("javax.net.ssl.trustStore", "<valid location>");`

- `javax.net.ssl.trustStoreType`: The type of trustStore (default value = `KeyStore.getDefaultType()`).

  `prop.put("javax.net.ssl.trustStoreType", "JKS");`

- `javax.net.ssl.trustStorePassword`: Used to protect the trust-store

  `prop.put("javax.net.ssl.trustStorePassword", "<password>");`

These properties can be set at the launch of the JDK VM, as follows:

```
$java -Djavax.net.ssl.keyStore=~/keystore
      -Djavax.net.ssl.keyStorePassword=key123456 JdbcApp
```

These properties can also be set at the connection object level, overriding the settings through system properties.

```
ods.setConnectionProperties(info);
```

Configuring and Using the Oracle JDBC Drivers with SSL

The Oracle Advanced Security (ASO) option provides data privacy, data integrity, strong authentication, and single sign-on. Table 9.2 summarizes the ASO security mechanisms supported in Oracle JDBC drivers, as of 10*g* Release 2. Various data encryption and data integrity algorithms over SSL are supported for both drivers (see algorithms supported in JDBC-Thin versus JDBC-OCI in Table 9.2), while SSL authentication is only supported for JDBC-OCI through third-party digital certificates (`Entrust-PKI`).

Table 9.2 *Oracle Advanced Security Support in JDBC*

	Data Encryption Algorithms	Strong Authentication (Third-Party Adapters)	Data Integrity Algorithms
JDBC-Thin	DES, 3DES, RC4		MD5
JDBC-OCI	DES, 3DES, RC4, AES	Kerberos, Radius, DCE, SSL (digital certificates)	MD5, SHA-1

How does SSL work with the Oracle JDBC and the Oracle database?

1.   The JDBC code seeks a connection to the Oracle database, using SSL.

2.   JDBC and the database perfom a handshake, during which the server authenticates itself to the driver and both agree on the cipher suite to use.

3.   Once the SSL handshake is successfully completed, JDBC can access the database using SSL.

4.   The Oracle database server authenticates the user in the JDBC URL through a non-SSL authentication method,[2] such as password authentication (all driver types). For JDBC-OCI, a strong authentication mechanism such as `Kerberos, RADIUS, DCE,` or `SSL (digital certificates)` can be used to authenticate the user.

5.   Upon authentication, the Oracle database server grants access and authorization to the user, and then the user can access the database securely through JDBC, using SSL.

As of 10*g* Release 2, the Oracle JDBC drivers support two SSL implementations:

-   Standard JSSE, which can be used with standard client-side certificates stored in truststored

-   Oracle's own JavaSSL implementation, which can be used with client-side Oracle wallets

In the rest of this section, we'll only look at how the Oracle JDBC-Thin works with JSSE; see the Oracle JDBC documentation[3] and/or white paper on the Oracle JDBC portal[4] regarding the configuration of JDBC-OCI with JSSE and also using Oracle JavaSSL with both JDBC-Thin and JDBC-OCI.

The steps for configuring JDBC Thin with SSL consist of (1) creating and storing the server certificates within an Oracle wallet, (2) configuring the

---

2.   SSL authentication is not currently supported in Oracle JDBC-Thin.
3.   http://download-west.oracle.com/docs/cd/B19306_01/network.102/b14268/asossl.htm#CIHCBIEG.
4.   http://www.oracle.com/technology/tech/java/sqlj_jdbc/index.html.

database for SSL, (3) creating and storing client certificates in a keystore, (4) configuring JDBC-Thin for SSL, and (5) using JDBC-Thin with SSL.

Creating and Storing Server Certificates in an Oracle Wallet

This step consists of the following operations: create an Oracle wallet, create a certificate request, obtain the corresponding certificate and a trusted certificate from a CA, and, finally, store the certificates in the Oracle wallet. If you already have your certificates, you can just use the command-line utility `orapki` to create the wallet, store the certificates, save the wallet in a convenient location (i.e., `$TNS_ADMIN/jdbcssl`), and export the certificates as well under the same directory tree.

```
orapki wallet create —wallet ~/jdbcssl —auto-login
```

`auto-login` avoids furnishing the password at each operation; however, operations that make changes to the content of the wallet still require keying in the password.

```
...
orapki wallet add —wallet ~/jdbcssl —trusted_cert —cert ~/
root_cert.txt
```

The rest of this step gives examples of accomplishing the various operations listed previously.

Start the `Oracle Wallet Manager GUI tool`:

- On Windows, select `Start`, `Programs`, `Oracle—HOME_NAME`, `Integrated Management Tools`, `Wallet Manager`
- On UNIX, enter `owm`.

Creating a Wallet

- Select `New` from the `Wallet` menu.
- If it displays "`Your default wallet directory does not exist. Do you want to create it?`" Click `Yes`.
- Provide a password and confirm in the `New Wallet` dialog box.
- The default Wallet type is "`Standard`." Click OK.

- "A new empty wallet has been created. Do you want to create a certificate request at this time?"

  If you choose **Yes**, then go to the next section, step 2.

  If you choose **No**, then go to the next section, step 1.

Creating a Certificate Request

Assume the following distinguished name (DN):

```
'CN=myserver,OU=america,O=oracle,L=redwood
shores,ST=ca,C=US'
```

- Select Add Certificate Request in the Operations menu.
- Fill in the Create Certificate Request dialog box, and click OK.
  Use the default Key Size of 1024.
- On Success, click OK.

Obtaining and Importing a Certificate

Obtain a free valid certificate for test purposes from a CA. In this example, we went to Thawte, but you can get it from your preferred/alternate CA.

- Point your browser to: www.thawte.com/cgi/server/test.exe.
- Fill in the required information, and click **Submit**.
- On "The Test CA Root Certificate is available in text format here."

  Click "here" to land in a new browser window.
- Provide the required information on this page, and **Accept**.
- Save the thawte-roots.zip file on your disk.
- Extract and rename the **Thawte Test** Root_TEXT.txt file to root_cert.txt.
- Select **Import Trusted Certificate** from the **Operations** menu.
- Select **Paste** the certificate, and click OK.
- Paste the contents of the root_cert.txt file in the **Import Trusted Certificate** dialog box, and click OK.

  A new trusted certificate called "Thawte Test CA Root" is added to the Trusted Certificates node.

- Go to the first browser window, and click **next**.

- Accept the default values and click **next**.

- Select the certificate request, and copy the text in the **Certificate Request** field.

- Paste the text in the text area in the browser, and click **next**. The certificate is displayed.

- Select **Import User Certificate** from the **Operations** menu.

- Select **Paste the certificate**, and click OK.

- Copy the certificate text displayed on the browser window, paste it into the **Import Certificate** dialog box, and click OK. The certificate you requested will now show a Ready status.

Saving the Wallet and Certificate

Save your newly created wallet and the certificate, as follows:

- Create the following directory tree (`myserver` is the common name [CN] of the distinguished name [DN])

      $TNS_ADMIN/jdbcssl/wallet
      $TNS_ADMIN/jdbcssl /wallet/myserver

- Copy the `root_cert.txt` file to the `wallet` directory.

- From the Wallet menu, select the **Wallet** node on the Oracle Wallet Manager, and **Save As**.

- Traverse to the `wallet` directory in the `Select Directory` dialog box or provide the wallet path, as suggested in step 1, in the **Directory field** in the dialog box, and click **OK**.

- Select the user certificate with status equals `Ready`, and **Save As** from the **Wallet** menu.

- Browse the myserver directory in the **Select Directory** dialog box or provide the path, as suggested in step 1, in the **Directory** field in the dialog box, and click **OK**.

- Select **Auto Login** from the **Wallet** menu.

- Select **Save** from the **Wallet** menu.

  The directory structure will look like this:

```
$TNS_ADMIN/jdbcssl
$TNS_ADMIN/jdbcssl/root_cert.txt
$TNS_ADMIN/jdbcssl/myserver
$TNS_ADMIN/jdbcssl/myserver/cwallet.sso
$TNS_ADMIN/jdbcssl/myserevr/ewallet.p12
```

Configure the Oracle Database for SSL

The database certificate is contained in a server-side wallet; you need to make a few changes to RDBMS configuration files (sqlnet.ora and lis-tener.ora) to reflect the wallet location, protocol (tcps), SSL authentication, and port.

Setting ssl_client_authentication to true in both configuration files will instruct the RDBMS to authenticate the client, during the SSL handshake.

Perform the following steps to configure the database:

- Stop the Net listener:

```
$ lsnrctl stop listener
```

- Edit the sqlnet.ora file in $ORACLE_HOME/network/admin/ by adding the following lines and save:

```
SSL_VERSION=3.0
ssl_client_authentication=true
WALLET_LOCATION=
  (SOURCE=
     (METHOD=FILE)
     (METHOD_DATA=
        (DIRECTORY=jdbcssl/myserver)))
```

- Edit the listener.ora file in $ORACLE_HOME/network/admin/ by adding a new entry as shown and save:

```
secure_lsnr=
  (DESCRIPTION=
    (ADDRESS=
      (PROTOCOL=tcps)
      (HOST=<hostname.company.com>)
```

```
                (PORT=<port>)))
           ssl_client_authentication=false
           WALLET_LOCATION=
             (SOURCE=
                (METHOD=FILE)
                (METHOD_DATA=
                    (DIRECTORY=jdbcssl/myserver)))
           SID_LIST_secure_lsnr=
             (SID_LIST=
             (SID_DESC=
                 (SID_NAME=<sid>)
                 (ORACLE_HOME=<ORACLE_HOME_PATH>)))
```

Restart the listener:

```
> lsnrctl start secure_lsnr
LSNRCTL for Linux: Version 10.2.0.1.0 - Production on 05-NOV-2005
20:21:48
Copyright (c) 1991, 2005, Oracle.  All rights reserved.
Starting /kmensah_lab/oracle/bin/tnslsnr: please wait...
TNSLSNR for Linux: Version 10.2.0.1.0 - Production
System parameter file is /kmensah_lab/oracle/work/listener.ora
Log messages written to /kmensah_lab/oracle/network/log/
secure_lsnr.log
Listening on:
(DESCRIPTION=(ADDRESS=(PROTOCOL=tcps)(HOST=stadp15.us.oracle.com)(POR
T=13333)))
Connecting to
(DESCRIPTION=(ADDRESS=(PROTOCOL=tcps)(HOST=stadp15.us.oracle.com)(POR
T=13333)))
STATUS of the LISTENER
-----------------------
Alias                     secure_lsnr
Version                   TNSLSNR for Linux: Version 10.2.0.1.0 -
Production
Start Date                05-NOV-2005 20:21:48
Uptime                    0 days 0 hr. 0 min. 0 sec
Trace Level               off
Security                  ON: Local OS Authentication
SNMP                      OFF
Listener Parameter File   /kmensah_lab/oracle/work/listener.ora
```

```
Listener Log File          /kmensah_lab/oracle/network/log/
secure_lsnr.log
Listening Endpoints Summary...

(DESCRIPTION=(ADDRESS=(PROTOCOL=tcps)(HOST=stadp15.us.oracle.com)(POR
T=13333)))
Services Summary...
Service "lab" has 1 instance(s).
  Instance "lab", status UNKNOWN, has 1 handler(s) for this service...
The command completed successfully
```

The following listener security checklist is excerpted from the Oracle Security Users Guide:

- Restrict the privileges of the listener, so that it cannot read or write files in the database or the Oracle server address space.

- Protect the listener with a password.

- Prevent online administration.

- Use SSL when administering the listener.

- Remove the external procedure configuration from the listener.ora file if you do not intend to use such procedures.

- Use the same port(s) on firewalls for secure (SSL) communication. The Oracle Advanced Security supports two types of firewalls:
  - Application proxy-based firewalls, such as Network Associates Gauntlet or Axent Raptor
  - Stateful packet inspection firewalls, such as Check Point Firewall-1 or Cisco PIX Firewall

Some firewall vendors furnish an Oracle Net Firewall Proxy kit to optimize the network traffic.

Creating and Storing Client Certificates in a Truststore

On the client side (i.e., JDBC), unlike Oracle's JavaSSL, JSSE does not recognize Oracle wallets, so you need to create a truststore and optionally a client-side certificate (if SSL_CLIENT_AUTHENTICATION has been set to TRUE).

- Create a subdirectory `myclient` under `$TNS_ADMIN/`jdbcssl.

- Copy the `root_cert.txt` file to `$TNS_ADMIN/`jdbcssl on the client machine.

- Create a truststore using the `keytool` utility (part of the JDK). The truststore will contain the root certificate and the user certificate that will be used during the SSL handshake.

The following command uses a keytool to import the CA trusted certificate into the keystore:

```
$ cd $TNS_ADMIN/jdbcssl

$ keytool -import -v -alias trustroot -file ./root_cert.txt -
keypass <password> -keystore truststore -storepass <password>

Owner: CN=Thawte Test CA Root, OU=TEST TEST TEST, O=Thawte
Certification, ST=FOR TESTING PURPOSES ONLY, C=ZA
Issuer: CN=Thawte Test CA Root, OU=TEST TEST TEST, O=Thawte
Certification, ST=FOR TESTING PURPOSES ONLY, C=ZA
Serial number: 0
Valid from: Wed Jul 31 17:00:00 PDT 1996 until: Thu Dec 31
13:59:59 PST 2020
Certificate fingerprints:
        MD5:  5E:E0:0E:1D:17:B7:CA:A5:7D:36:D6:02:DF:4D:26:A4
         SHA1:
39:C6:9D:27:AF:DC:EB:47:D6:33:36:6A:B2:05:F1:47:A9:B4:DA:EA
Trust this certificate? [no]:  yes
Certificate was added to keystore
[Storing truststore]
$
```

Creating the Client Certificate (Optional)

This step is needed only if `SSL_CLIENT_AUTHENTICATION` has been turned on, on the server.

- Use `keytool` to create a new pair of private/public keys with the following DN:

```
CN=myclient, OU=america, O=oracle, L=redwood shores,
ST=ca, C=US.
$ keytool -genkey -v -alias myclient -keyalg RSA
```

```
-dname 'CN=myclient,OU=america,O=oracle,
L=redwood shores,ST=ca,C=US' -keypass <password>
-keystore <keystore> -storepass <password>
```

- Create a certificate request as `certreq.txt`.

```
$ keytool -certreq -alias myclient
  -file certreq.txt —keypass <password>
  -keystore <keystore>   -storepass <password>
```

- Get a signed certificate from a CA using the same steps used in the server case.

  (Note that the certificate must be in PKCS #7 format.)

  Save it in `response.txt`.

- Import the certificate into your keystore. Note that if the certificate was obtained through Thawte, `keytool` does not recognize it as a trusted source. Answer Yes to the following question: "`Do you want to install it anyway?`"

```
$ keytool -import -v -alias myclient
  -file response.txt -keypass <password>
  —keystore <keystore> -storepass <password>
```

- Import the trusted certificate into the keystore:

```
> keytool -import -v -noprompt -alias trustroot
  -file ./root_cert.txt -keypass <password>
  -keystore keystore -storepass <password>
```

- Use the –list option to verify:

```
> keytool -list -storepass <password>
  -keystore keystore
```

Configuring the JDBC-Thin Driver for SSL

SSL is automatically used for JDBC-Thin when the connection description contains "`(PROTOCOL=tcps)`."

1. Confirm `ojdbc14.jar` in the `CLASSPATH`.

2. Modify the `tnsnames.ora` file as follows, to ensure database connection over SSL:

```
secure_client=
 (DESCRIPTION=
   (ADDRESS=
     (PROTOCOL=tcps)
     (HOST==<hostname.company.com>)
     (PORT=<port>))
   (CONNECT_DATA=(SERVICE_NAME=lab))
   (SECURITY=

   (SSL_SERVER_CERT_DN="CN=myserver,OU=america,O=oracle,L=
   redwood shores,
       ST=ca,C=US)))
```

Using JDBC-Thin with SSL

At this stage, we are in a position to use JDBC with SSL; however, it is highly recommended to always get SSL working in SQLPlus first (using the secure TNS alias), before getting it to work in JDBC. Notice the following connection properties:

- `oracle.net.ssl_version`: Specifies the SSL version to be used by the driver; default value is `ANY`.

  ```
  prop.put("oracle.net.ssl_version", "3.0")
  ```

- `oracle.net.wallet_location`: If set, it overrides the standard JSSE properties `javax.net.ssl.keyStore` and `javax.net.ssl.trustStore`; no default value.
  ```
  prop.put("oracle.net.wallet_location", "<location>");
  ```

- `oracle.net.cipher_suites`: A comma-separated list of strings, which controls the algorithm and key sizes for data integrity and encryption between the SSL implementation and the RDBMS; no default value.

  ```
  prop.put("oracle.net.cipher_suites",
  "SSL_DH_DSS_WITH_DES_CBC_SHA");
  ```

- `oracle.net.ssl_server_dn_match`: Matches the distinguished name (DN) with the service name; the possible values are TRUE/FALSE/ON/OFF/YES/NO

```
prop.put("oracle.net.ssl_server_dn_match", "TRUE");
```

```
JdbcSSL.java
============
/* sample using JSSE SSL
 * This sample shows how to call a PL/SQL function that opens
 * a cursor and get the cursor back as a Java ResultSet.
 *
 * sqlType CURSOR corresponds to "ref cursor". open the cursor
 * by specifying CURSOR type at register method. retrieve the
 * value by getObject method.
 */

import java.sql.*;
import java.io.*;
import oracle.jdbc.*;
import oracle.jdbc.pool.OracleDataSource;
import java.security.*;

class JdbcSSL
{
  public static void main (String args [])
        throws SQLException
  {
    String url = "jdbc:oracle:thin:@secure_client";

    //set properties
    java.util.Properties info = new java.util.Properties();
    System.setProperty("oracle.net.tns_admin", "<your
$TNS_ADMIN>");
    info.put ("javax.net.ssl.keyStore",<$TNS_ADMIN>/jdbcssl/
keystore");
    info.put ("javax.net.ssl.keyStoreType","JKS");
    info.put ("javax.net.ssl.keyStorePassword","<password>");

    // if you have a trustStore (SSL_CLIENT_AUTHENTICATION on)
    String trustStore = "/home/kmensah/jdbcssl/truststore";
    info.setProperty("javax.net.ssl.trustStore", trustStore);
```

```
      info.setProperty("javax.net.ssl.trustStorePassword",
"<password>");

    // optional settings

    //Cipher suite        //
info.put("oracle.net.ssl_cipher_suites","SSL_DH_DSS_WITH_DES_
CBC_SHA"// );

  // Force dn to match service name
  // info.put("oracle.net.ssl_server_dn_match","TRUE");

   // Create a OracleDataSource instance and set properties
  OracleDataSource ods = new OracleDataSource();
   ods.setUser("hr");
   ods.setPassword("hr");
   ods.setURL(url);
   ods.setConnectionProperties(info);

   // Connect to the database
   Connection conn = ods.getConnection();
   ...
   ...

   stmt.close();
   conn.close();

  }
 }
```

To conclude this section, please note that state regulations in countries such as the United States prohibit the use of SSL authentication concurrently with non-SSL authentication, as well as the use of SSL encryption concurrently with non-SSL encryption.

9.3   **Tips and Best Practices**

This section is a list of tips for understanding common error messages and performance optimizations. This section also describes end-to-end tracing, common errors, optimizing result set retrieval, and logging service.

9.3.1 End-to-End Tracing

The Oracle database and the Oracle Application Server have been instrumented to allow gathering metrics for tracking and correlating all operations performed by a session or a module (i.e., a browser, a thread). The following metrics are supported: `Action`, `Module`, `ClientId`, and `ExecutionContextId` (also known as ECID).

- `Client ID (i.e., thread-id)`: For tracking which client invoked work on a connection
- `The Service Module or Service Action`: Used to tag and trace units of work (transaction blocks) for a given session
- `The Execution Context Id (also known as ECID)`: A unique identifier associated with a thread of execution

The following SQL statement retrieves the current module (i.e., `SQL*Plus`):

```
$ sqlplus system/xxxxx

SQL*Plus: Release 10.2.0.1.0 - Production on Sat Nov 26 19:18:00 2005
Copyright (c) 1982, 2005, Oracle.  All rights reserved.

Connected to:
Oracle Database 10g Enterprise Edition Release 10.2.0.1.0 -
Production
With the Partitioning and Data Mining options

SQL> col module format a12
SQL> col client_identifier format a20
SQL> select action, module, client_identifier from V$SESSION where
username ='SYSTEM'

ACTION                               MODULE       CLIENT_IDENTIFIER
------------------------------------ ------------ --------------------
                                     SQL*Plus
SQL>
```

The Oracle JDBC 10*g* drivers expose the database metrics to Java applications and Java containers, such as the Oracle Application server, which complement the database metrics through the DMS framework.

JDBC supports these metrics at the connection level with the following methods:

- getEndToEndECIDSequenceNumber(): Gets the current end-to-end tracing context id sequence number. As you can observe in Listing 9.3, the sequence number is incremented by the database, allowing the requestor to sort the call sequence (and/or the error sequence) in the order they occurred. Its value could be:
- The value passed in the most recent call to setEndToEndMetrics
- The value returned by the database after the most recent statement execution
- The value incremented by JDBC diagnostic messages

```
short seqnum =
((OracleConnection)conn).getEndToEndECIDSequenceNumber();
```

End-to-end metrics are enabled in JDBC by invoking the setEnd-ToEndMetrics method.

- setEndToEndMetrics(java.lang.String[]   metrics,   short sequenceNumber): It sets the values of the tracing metrics. The indices of the array of metrics are defined in the OracleConnection class.
- END_TO_END_STATE_INDEX_MAX: The size of the string array containing the metrics values.

```
short seqnum = 100;
String[] metric =
new String[OracleConnection.END_TO_END_STATE_INDEX_MAX];
```

- END_TO_END_ACTION_INDEX: The index of the ACTION metrics; the maximum length of these metrics is 32 bytes/characters.

```
metric[OracleConnection.END_TO_END_ACTION_INDEX] =
"ActionMetrics";
```

```
                          conn.setEndToEndMetrics(metric,seqnum);
```

- **END_TO_END_MODULE_INDEX**: The index of the MODULE metrics; the
  maximum length of these metrics is 48 bytes/characters.

```
          metric[OracleConnection.END_TO_END_MODULE_INDEX] =
          "ModuleMetrics";

          conn.setEndToEndMetrics(metric,seqnum);
```

- **END_TO_END_CLIENTID_INDEX**: The index of the CLIENTID metrics;
  the maximum length of these metrics is 64 bytes/characters.

```
          metric[OracleConnection.END_TO_END_CLIENTID_INDEX] =
          "ClientIdMetrics";

          conn.setEndToEndMetrics(metric,seqnum);
```

- **END_TO_END_ECID_INDEX**: The index of the ECID metrics; the maximum length of these metrics is 64 bytes/characters.

```
          metric[OracleConnection.END_TO_END_ECID_INDEX] =
          "ECIDMetrics";

           conn.setEndToEndMetrics(metric,seqnum);
```

- **getEndToEndMetrics( )**: Gets the values of the end-to-end metrics,
  if any. Does not include the sequence number.

Listing 9.3   *myEnd2EndMetrcis.java*

```
==================================
import java.sql.*;
import java.util.*;
import oracle.jdbc.*;
import oracle.jdbc.pool.OracleDataSource;

public class myEnd2EndMetrics
{
  public static void main(String[] args) throws SQLException
```

```
   {
     //Create an OracleDataSource
     OracleDataSource ods = new OracleDataSource();
     // Set the URL, using TNS Alias with JDBC-Thin
     // Use a schema, which can see/read V$SESSION
     String url = "jdbc:oracle:thin:<user>/<password>@inst1";
     ods.setURL(url);
     // Retrieve a connection
     OracleConnection conn = (OracleConnection)ods.getConnection();
     short seqnum = 20;
     String[] metric = new
String[OracleConnection.END_TO_END_STATE_INDEX_MAX];
     metric[OracleConnection.END_TO_END_ACTION_INDEX] =
"ActionMetrics";
     metric[OracleConnection.END_TO_END_MODULE_INDEX] =
"ModuleMetrics";
     metric[OracleConnection.END_TO_END_CLIENTID_INDEX] =
"ClientIdMetrics";
     metric[OracleConnection.END_TO_END_ECID_INDEX] = "ECIDMetrics";

     conn.setEndToEndMetrics(metric,seqnum);

     try {
       Statement stmt = conn.createStatement();
       ResultSet rs = stmt.executeQuery
       ("select ACTION,MODULE,CLIENT_IDENTIFIER from V$SESSION where
USERNAME=\'SYSTEM\'");

       seqnum =
((OracleConnection)conn).getEndToEndECIDSequenceNumber();
       System.out.println("*** Sequence Number = " + seqnum);
       while (rs.next()) {
         System.out.println("*** Action = " + rs.getString(1));
         System.out.println("*** Module = " + rs.getString(2));
         System.out.println("*** Client_identifier = " +
rs.getString(3));
       }

       stmt.close();
       String[] metrics =
((OracleConnection)conn).getEndToEndMetrics();
       System.out.println("*** End-to-end Metrics: "+metrics[0]+",
"+metrics[1]+
```

```
                 ", "+metrics[2]+", "+metrics[3]);
        } catch (SQLException sqle) {
          sqle.printStackTrace();
        }
    }
}
```

```
$javac myEnd2EndMetrics.java
$java -Doracle.net.tns_admin=$TNS_ADMIN myEnd2EndMetrics
*** Sequence Number = 22
*** Action = ActionMetrics
*** Module = ModuleMetrics
*** Client_identifier = ClientIdMetrics
*** End-to-end Metrics: ActionMetrics, ClientIdMetrics, ECIDMetrics,
ModuleMetrics
$
```

9.3.2   Common Errors

```
"No more data to read from socket."
```

This message happens when the JDBC-Thin driver times out while
waiting to get more bytes from the server (and the server is finished!). This
is usually a result of the crash of a server process; see the server logs for more
details.

```
"Bigger type length than expected."
```

This message happens when using older JDBC-Thin drivers with newer
RDBMS releases; it indicates that the driver is expecting a UB2 but got a
UB4. Check that such a bug has not already been fixed for the version of
the driver in question.

9.3.3   Optimizing Result Set Retrieval

- Result sets are usually retrieved using a while loop:

```
while (rs.next()) {
   // retrieve and process the row/columns
}
```

Such a while loop is generic enough to accommodate the retrieval of 0 or <n> rows. If Row-Prefetch has not been set (i.e., defaults to 1), then the driver sends a FETCH(1) command per roundtrip until it gets an error; however, if you know you will be retrieving only a single row, setting the Row-Prefetch size to 2 (see Chapter 8) will save the extra roundtrip.

- Alternatively, using an if statement with a default Row-Prefetch does not incur an additional roundtrip.

```
if (rs.next()) {
// retrieve and process the row/columns
}
```

- If you are using JDBC-Thin, and retrieving 0 or 1 row, by setting the useFetchSizeWithLongColumn connection property to true, the driver will perform PARSE, EXECUTE, and FETCH all together in a single roundtrip.

9.3.4 Logging Service

Since Oracle JDBC 10*g*, you can initiate JDBC logging using the java.util.logging package, which comprises the following objects: Logger, LogRecord, Handler, Level, Filter, and Formatter. See the java.util.logging[5] for more details.

Logging Levels

The tracing levels are represented by java.util.logging.Level. The user controls the tracing by setting specific levels on one or more loggers.

The most useful predefined levels are the following:

- OFF: Disables logging
- CONFIG: SQL statements, low data volume
- INFO: JDBC API level tracing, low data volume
- SEVERE: SQLExceptions, unrecoverable error conditions, low data volume

---

5.   http://java.sun.com/j2se/1.4.2/docs/api/java/util/logging/package-summary.html.

- WARNING: SQLWarnings, recoverable error conditions, low data volume

- FINE: Public JDBC APIs, function entry/return, medium data volume

---

Note: Not all levels are listed. Java developers may define additional levels using a distinct integer value (each level is uniquely identified by an integer value).

Loggers

A *logger* is associated with every JDBC package; as of version 10.2.0.1, some of the tracing loggers are as follows:

- oracle.jdbc
- oracle.jdbc.driver
- oracle.jdbc.thin
- oracle.jdbc.pool
- oracle.jdbc.xa
- oracle.jdbc.oci
- oracle.jdbc.datum
- oracle.jdbc.adt
- oracle.jdbc.conversion
- oracle.jdbc.sqlj
- oracle.jdbc.jpub
- oracle.jdbc.level

A *logger handler* exports the log messages from the logger in question

A *formatter* is associated with the logger handler for writing log records. The SimpleFormatter and XMLFormatter are available by default.

- The simple formatter prints a summary of the LogRecord in a human-readable format.

- The XML formatter outputs a LogRecord into a standard XML format.

Tracing JDBC Using System Properties

Here are the steps for enabling logging through system properties and a sample properties file:

1. Use JDK 1.4 and the debug version of the driver (i.e., ojdbc14_g.jar). You may also use ojdbc14dms.jar, which lets you trace SQL execution, connections, and public JDBC methods.

2. Edit the OracleLog.properties file with the following contents:

    ```
    # Handler
    # default output file location = user's home directory.
    handlers= java.util.logging.ConsoleHandler,
    java.util.loggingFileHandler
    .level= INFO
    java.util.logging.FileHandler.pattern = jdbc.log
    java.util.logging.FileHandler.limit = 50000
    java.util.logging.FileHandler.count = 1
    java.util.logging.FileHandler.formatter =
    java.util.logging.XMLFormatter

    # Speficy the trace/debug level for targeted packages
    # Predefined levels are: ALL, SEVERE, WARNING, INFO,
    CONFIG, FINE, FINER,
    # OFF
    # Setting ConsoleHandler level to SEVERE avoids
    duplicate output from logger
    java.util.logging.ConsoleHandler.level = SEVERE
    java.util.logging.ConsoleHandler.formatter =
    java.util.logging.SimpleFormatter
    oracle.jdbc.level = CONFIG# Uncomment and/or change the
    levels for more detail
    oracle.jdbc.level = FINE
    oracle.jdbc.driver.level = FINE
    #oracle.sql.level = FINE
    #oracle.jdbc.pool.level = FINE
    ```

3. Set the oracle.jdbc.Trace property, as follows:

    ```
    java -Doracle.jdbc.Trace=true -
    Djava.util.logging.config.file=<properties file
    location> <program name>
    ```

9.4   Conclusion

This chapter concludes the JDBC part of the book. At this stage, you have a better understanding of Oracle database programming using Java in the database (with server-side JDBC) and client-side JDBC. However, you might feel that the JDBC API is too fine grained and would love to have a coarse-grained API; this is exactly the purpose of SQLJ, our next topic.

Part III: Oracle Database Programming with SQLJ

JDBC furnishes a call-level API, modeled after ODBC, and similar to the Oracle Call-level Interface (OCI). Some people find it easy to use, while others find it not concise and even painful. SQLJ furnishes a coarser-grained API modeled after the ANSI/ISO Embedded SQL Languages (C, COBOL). SQLJ has been adopted by many developers, mostly database developers, as proven by the avalanche of reaction triggered by the announcement of its desupport by Oracle. Fortunately, after a brief absence in early releases of Oracle Database 10*g* and Oracle Application Server 10*g*, SQLJ is back for good, as part of the Oracle Database, starting with 10*g* Release 10.1.0.4 and later.

Part III gives you an overview of the SQLJ technology (definition, rationale, translator, runtime) and then looks at the Oracle SQLJ packaging and SQLJ in the database. In Chapter 11, we'll look at the elements of SQLJ programming, including connection, statements, execution contexts, iterators, and dynamic SQL support (Oracle extension). Finally, in Chapter 12, we'll look at SQL data manipulation and best practices.

10

Introducing the SQLJ Technology and Oracle's Implementation

10.1 Overview

This section looks at what exactly SQLJ is and why you should consider using it. Readers who are familiar with the SQLJ technology and Oracle SQLJ may skip this overview.

10.1.1 What Is SQLJ?

In 1997, a group of engineers from IBM Tandem and Oracle started a project to allow embedding of SQL statements in Java. Sun, Sybase, and Informix joined the group, which gave birth to the "JSQL" specifications that were submitted to ANSI; as they say, the rest is history!

The SQLJ Specification

SQLJ is an umbrella name for an `ANSI SQL-1999 (SQL3 or SQL-99)` multipart specification, which comprises:

- *Part 0—Embedded SQL in Java*: Specifies the ability to embed SQL statements in Java, similar to Pro*C and a more productive alternative to JDBC for both client-side and server-side Java. Oracle's implementation, which is the purpose of this part of the book, is called "SQLJ" and furnishes many extensions, such as support for dynamic SQL, beyond the standard specification.

- *Part 1—SQL Routines Using Java*: Specifies the ability to invoke static Java methods from SQL as procedures and functions. Oracle's implementation of Java stored procedures and functions was covered in Part I.

■ *Part 2—SQL Types Using Java*: Specifies the ability to use Java classes as wrappers for user-defined data types in SQL. Oracle's implementation, called SQLJ object types, covered in both Part I and Part II.

In the rest of this part of the book, "SQLJ" will refer to "SQLJ Part 0." The Oracle SQLJ environment comprises the JDK (i.e., stand-alone Java compiler and runtime), the OracleJVM (i.e., Java compiler and runtime in the database), the Oracle JDBC drivers, the SQLJ translator (stand-alone and in the database), the SQLJ runtime (stand-alone and in the database), and the SQLJ profiler.

The SQLJ Translator

The SQLJ translator takes SQLJ sources files (`.sqlj`), Java sources files (`.java`), Java classes (`.class`), and Java resources (`.ser`) as input and performs the following operations (detailed later): SQLJ-to-Java parsing, online/offline type checking, customization of code generation (optional), and compilation of Java source(s) (can be deferred).

The Oracle SQLJ translator is a pure Java code for use as stand-alone on the client side, in the middle tier, as part of a Java application server, and also in the database.

The `sqlj` command, which is in fact a shell script, invokes the translator, more precisely the `sqlj.tools.Sqlj` class in `$ORACLE_HOME/sqlj/lib/translator.jar`.

It carries its own options as well as the options for the Java VM, the compiler, and the profiler.

```
sqlj   <-J-javavm-options>
       <-P-profiler-options>
       <-C-compiler-options>
       <-sqlj-options> <*.java, *.sqlj, *.jar and *.ser files>
```

The SQLJ Runtime

The SQLJ runtime is launched by the Java VM during the execution of the resulting Java class (i.e., `java <sqlj class>`). It handles SQLJ runtime operations and delegates the execution of SQL operations to a JDBC driver. The Oracle SQLJ runtime requires the Oracle JDBC drivers; it is a pure Java code for use as stand-alone on the client side, in the middle tier, as part of a Java application server, and also in the database.

SQLJ Profiler

SQLJ profiles are serialized Java resources (`.ser` file) or Java classes (`.class` file), which contain metadata that allows vendor customization in various areas, such as SQL operations, specific data types support, and performance optimization.

Now that you have a glimpse of SQLJ, your next legitimate question is (should be): "Why?" or, "What for?"

10.1.2   Why SQLJ?

SQLJ allows embedding SQL statements directly into Java sources, similar to embedding SQL in C programs (i.e., Pro*C). SQLJ is a multivendor ISO/ANSI standard, defined and implemented mainly by RDBMS vendors (e.g., IBM, Sybase, Oracle)—you now understand why it is not part of the J2EE specification. Here are a few quotes from the publicly available JDBC/SQLJ forum[1] of the Oracle Technology Network:

- "Most of our developers were comfortable with Pro*C, and SQLJ allowed a smooth transition to Java."

- "SQLJ provides several benefits, but perhaps the most significant to us in terms of software development is the compile time checking of SQL statements."

- "I began using SQLJ. It is very good. I am in the process of converting all of my JDBC programs to SQLJ/JDBC combination. The result is much simpler code and more powerful."

In summary, the key benefit is increased Java/database developers' productivity through simplicity, strong translation-time type checking (both syntax and semantic), and interoperability with JDBC. Additional benefits brought by the Oracle SQLJ implementation are support for dynamic SQL, enhanced runtime performance through optimized JDBC code generation, and the use of the JPublisher utility (covered later) to automatically map complex user-defined SQL types and PL/SQL types to Java. Sounds like an interesting value proposition, so let's look at the benefits in greater details.

---

1.   http://forums.oracle.com/forums/forum.jspa?forumID=99.

Benefits Brought by the Standard ISO SQLJ

Simplicity

SQLJ is a developer-friendly alternative to JDBC.

Example 1: Assume the following JDBC code fragment updating DEPT table:

```
PreparedStatement st =
conn.prepareStatement("UPDATE dept SET location   = "San
Francisco" WHERE dname = ? ");
st.setString(1, dName);
st.executeUpdate();
st.close();
```

The corresponding SQLJ code fragment is:

```
#sql { UPDATE dept SET location = "San Francisco"  WHERE dname
= :dName };
```

Example 2: Consider the following JDBC code fragment, which queries the EMP table and retrieves the result set:

```
Statement st = conn.createStatement("SELECT ename, empid FROM
emp");
ResultSet rs = st.executeQuery();
while (rs.next()) {
   x = rs.getString(1);
   y = rs.getInt(2);
}
rs.close();
```

Here is the SQLJ equivalent:

```
sqlj.runtime.ResultSetIterator rsi;

#sql rsi = { SELECT ename, empid FROM emp };
while (rsi.next()) {
   #sql { FETCH CURRENT FROM :rsi INTO :x, :y };
}
rsi.close();
```

Here is a highlight of simplicity features that SQLJ brings compared with JDBC:

- Host variables are embedded, while JDBC uses parameter markers.
- No need to cast data types.
- No need to programmatically register output parameters.
- No need to explicitly handle the NULL value.
- Support for SELECT INTO statements.
- Support for PL/SQL anonymous blocks makes it easy to embed PL/SQL in Java.
- No need for String concatenation for long SQL statements

Concise code is easier to write and debug, resulting in greater productivity. Simply put, SQLJ is to JDBC what JavaServer Pages (JSP) are in some respect for Java servlets; in other words, SQLJ is "JDBC made simpler."

Translation-Time Type Checking

Here is a highlight of controls that the SQLJ translator performs:

- Syntax checking of SQLJ constructs: A SQLJ parser checks the grammar, according to the SQLJ language specification.
- Syntax checking of Java instructions: A Java parser (invoked under the covers) checks the syntax of Java host variables and expressions within SQLJ executable statements.
- Semantics checking: Depending on the option settings, this includes the following:
  - Syntax of SQL statements by a SQL semantics checker
  - SQL offline parser
- Validation of schema objects (i.e., tables name, columns name).
- Validation of the mapping between Java types and SQL types.

These translation checks reduce run-time errors/exceptions and result in more robust and faster to deploy applications.

Interoperability with JDBC

Even though you can write pure SQLJ or pure JDBC code, these two programming models work well together. As described later, JDBC connections can be used by SQLJ as a connection context and vice versa. Similarly, JDBC `ResultSet` can be passed to a SQLJ application as a SQLJ `Iterator`, and vice versa.

Benefits Brought by Oracle SQLJ Extensions

You can generate pure ISO SQLJ code with the Oracle SQLJ translator and execute it with the Oracle SQLJ runtime; however, like JDBC, if you are deploying primarily against the Oracle database, you can uptake and benefit from the following extensions.

Support for Dynamic SQL

Even though the ANSI/ISO specification supports only static SQL, Oracle's implementation allows dynamic SQL statements (constructed at runtime), so as to be on par with JDBC, as illustrated by the following code fragments:

```
// dynamic SQL support directly in SQLJ
//
#sql { insert into :{table_name :: emp} (ename,empno,sal)
                       values(:ename, :empno, :sal) };


// dynamic SQL support through Anonymous PL/SQL block
//
#sql { begin
          execute immediate
                  'insert into ' || :table_name ||
                  '(ename, empno, sal) values( :1, :2, :3)'
          using :ename, :empno, :sal;
          end;
       };
```

And here is the JDBC equivalent:

```
String dml = "insert into "+ table_name +"(ename,empno,sal)
values(?,?,?)";
```

```
PreparedStatement ps =
DefaultContext.getDefaultContext().getConnection().prepareSta
tement(dml);
ps.setString(1,ename);
ps.setInt(2,empno);
ps.setDouble(3,sal);
ps.executeUpdate();
ps.close();
```

Dynamic SQL support allows you to write entire SQLJ applications without the need to switch back and forth to JDBC, just to work around a limitation in the SQLJ specification.

Compile-Time Performance Optimizations

The Oracle SQLJ furnished the following performance optimizations, covered in the next chapters and including: row prefetching, SQLJ statement caching, update batching, column type(s) definition, and parameter size definition.

The Architecture and Packaging of Oracle SQLJ

This section describes the SQLJ translator options, the Oracle customizer, the SQLJ runtime and environment setup, and, finally, your first SQLJ program. Figure 10.1 summarizes the various steps and pieces of the Oracle SQLJ architecture.

Figure 10.1
The Architecture of Oracle SQLJ

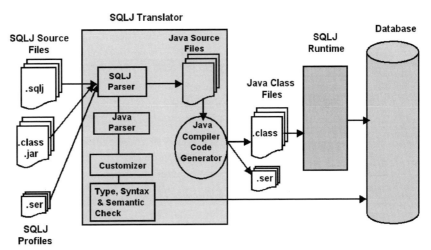

10.1.3 The Oracle SQLJ Translator

The SQLJ Parser, the Java Parser, and the SQL Parsers

A SQLJ parser and a Java parser are used to process all the source code and check the syntax. As the SQLJ translator parses the `.sqlj` file, it invokes the following:

- The SQLJ parser, which checks the syntax of SQLJ constructs (#sql ...) and the grammar against the SQLJ language specification
- The Java parser, which checks the syntax of Java statements, Java host variables, and expressions within SQLJ statements

When you invoke the SQL command without any argument, it displays a short summary of its options, as follows:

```
$ sqlj
Usage:  sqlj [options] file1.sqlj [file2.java] ...
   or   sqlj [options] file1.ser  [file2.jar]  ...
where options include:
    -d=<directory>          root directory for generated binary files
    -encoding=<encoding>    Java encoding for source files
    -user=<user>/<password> enable online checking
    -url=<url>              specify URL for online checking
    -status                print status during translation
    -compile=false         do not compile generated Java files
    -linemap               instrument compiled class files from sqlj source
    -profile=false         do not customize generated *.ser profile files
    -ser2class             convert generated *.ser files to *.class files
    -P-<option> -C-<option> pass -<option> to profile customizer or compiler
    -P-help  -C-help       get help on profile customizer or compiler
    -J-<option>            pass -<option> to the JavaVM running SQLJ
    -version               get SQLJ version
    -help-alias            get help on command-line aliases
    -help-long             get full help on all front-end options

Note:  place -<key>=<value> in sqlj.properties as sqlj.<key>=<value>

$
```

Table 10.1 furnishes a comprehensive and explanatory list of the translation options; these can be grouped into four categories, including the basic options, the Javac options, environment options, and advanced options.

Basic Options

- *Command-line only options:* The following options can only be specified on the command line (not in properties files) or in the SQLJ_OPTIONS environment variable: -props, -classpath, -help, -help-long, -help-alias, -P-help, -C-help, -version, -version-long, -n

- *Connection options*: The following database connections are used to enable/disable online semantics checking: -user, -password, -url, -default-url-prefix, -driver

- *Reporting options*: The following options specify the conditions to monitor, including real-time errors, status messages, and whether to explain the cause and action: -warn, -status, -explain.

- *Line-mapping options*: The following options enable tracing runtime errors from the generated Java .class file back to the original .sqlj source file: -linemap, -jdblinemap (-jdblinemap should be used in conjunction with the Sun Microsystems jdb debugger; otherwise, use -linemap).

- *Output files and directories options*: The following options specify the location for SQLJ output files for encoding .ser, .class, and .java files: -d, -dir.

- *Oracle's Dynamic Monitoring System (DMS) options*: -instrument, -components.

- *Code generation, optimizations, CHAR comparison, and bind options*: -codegen, -optcols, -optparams, -optparamdefaults, -fixedchar, -ncharconv.

Environment and Customizer Options

The Oracle Database 10g SQLJ is by default configured to work with Sun Microsystems JDK (compiler and runtime). You can alter this environment using the the following options: -vm, -compiler-executable, -compiler-encoding-flag, -compiler-output-file, and -compiler-pipe-output-flag.

In addition, the -checkfilename option prevents SQLJ from verifying that the souce file name matches the public class.

The –passes option instructs SQLJ to perfom SQLJ parsing and Java parsing in two distinct steps.

Compiler or Java VM options can be passed through the SQLJ translator, using the –J and –C prefixes.

Note: The –vm and –passes options and the –J prefix can only be used on the command line or in the SQLJ_OPTIONS environment variable, not in a properties file.

For ISO-specific code generation (no profile is generated for Oracle-specific code generation), the Oracle SQLJ is also configured to work with the default Oracle profile customizer (`oracle.sqlj.runtime.util.OraCustomizer`), but an alternative customizer can be specified using the –default-customizer option.

```
-default-customizer=sqlj.mypav=ckage.Customizer
```

The profiler options can be passed directly using the –P prefix.

Javac Options

The Oracle SQLJ supports Java compiler options using -C-bootclass-path, -classpath, -d, -depend, -deprecation, -encoding, -C-extdirs, -g, -nowarn, -O, -C-target, -verbose.

```
$ sqlj -vm=/usr/local/packages/jdk1.4.1/bin/java
-compiler-executable=/usr/local/packages/jdk1.4.1/bin/javac
-C-bootclasspath=/usr/local/packages/jdk1.4.1/jre/lib/rt.jar
-C-extdirs="" -C-target=1.3.1 Demo.sqlj
```

Advanced Options

For ISO code generation, the –profile option enables/disables the processing of the generated profile files (.ser) by the SQLJ profile customizer.

```
-profile=false
```

The -ser2class optionconverts .ser files into .class files.

```
-ser2class=true
```

The -checksource flag instructs SQLJ to examine source files in the classpath for Java types that appear in SQLJ statements.

```
-checksource=false
```

Semantics Checking and Offline Parsing

The -offline option enables the offline checker or parser, while the -online option specifies the online checker. The Oracle SQLJ furnishes OracleChecker, a default front-end, which chooses the appropriate checker to use, depending on whether or not you have enabled online checking and which Java Database Connectivity (JDBC) driver you are using.

As summarized in Table 10.1, the offline parser performs syntax checking of all SQL and PL/SQL statements without connecting to the database (prior to Oracle 9*i*, syntax checking required a database connection). However, it does not perform verification of operations against the database

Table 10.1 *Offline Parsing versus Online Semantics Checking*

Feature	By Offline Parser?	By Online Checker?
Verify data manipulation language (DML), SELECT, and PL/SQL syntax.	Yes	Yes
Verify data definition language (DDL) syntax.	Yes	No
Verify DML, SELECT, and PL/SQL semantics (comparison against database schema).	No	Yes
Verify DDL semantics (comparison against database schema).	No	No

schema. Setting the -parse option to true enables the offline parser. Also, as summarized in Table 10.1, the online parser performs the following operations:

- Validates SQLJ FETCH, CAST, CALL, SET TRANSACTION, VALUES, and SET statements.

- Checks Java expressions in SQLJ statements against SQL types of table columns, of IN and OUT parameters of stored procedures/functions.

- Verifies that tables, views, and stored procedures actually exist in the database.

- Checks the NULLability of table columns used in iterators.

Code Generation

SQLJ code generation is governed by the codegen option; the generated code will differ depending on the specified option (iso or oracle).

1.   –codegen=iso: Generates a standard ISO SQLJ code, along with profile file(s).

   - Profile files as serialized resource files (i.e., Class_SJProfile0.ser, Class_SJProfile1.ser), which can be further customized

   - If the –ser2class is set to true, the profile files are generated as Java classes files (i.e., Class_SJProfile0.class, Class_SJProfile1.class); however, these class files cannot be customized.

      There is a mapping between SQLJ executable statements in the application and SQL operations in the profile. The SQLJ runtime reads the profiles and creates *connected profiles*, with database connections. Then for each database access by the application:

      - The runtime uses methods in a SQLJ-generated profile-keys class to access the connected profile and read the relevant SQL operations.
      - The runtime reads the SQL operation from the profile and passes it to the JDBC driver along with input parameters
      - The JDBC driver executes the SQL operations and transmits returned data, if any, to the SQLJ runtime, which, in turn, passes the returned data to the application.

2.   –codegen=oracle: Generates Oracle-specific code, which supports Oracle extensions; no profile file is generated/needed. The SQLJ runtime performs the following operations:

   - Executes the Oracle-specific APIs for statement batching, creates and closes Oracle JDBC statements

   - Directs invocation of Oracle JDBC APIs for registering, passing, and retrieving parameters and result sets

Table 10.2   *SQLJ Translator Options*

-bind-by-identifier	Flag to treat multiple appearances of the same host variable in a given SQLJ statement as a single bind occurrence.	False	Advanced
-C	Prefix that marks options to pass to the Java compiler.	NA	Advanced
-cache	Enables caching of online semantics-checking results (to reduce trips to database).	False	Advanced
-checkfilename	Specifies whether a warning is issued during translation if a source file name does not correspond to the name of the public class (if any) defined there.	True	Environment
-checksource	Instructs SQLJ type resolution to examine source files in addition to class files in certain circumstances.	True	Advanced
-classpath	Specifies the CLASSPATH to the JVM and Java compiler; also passed to javac. Use this on the command line only.	None	Basic
-codegen	Specifies mode of code generation: oracle for Oracle-specific code generation with direct Oracle Java Database Connectivity (JDBC) calls; iso for ISO standard SQLJ code generation.	Oracle	Basic
-compile	Enables or disables the Java compilation step, either for .java files generated during the current SQLJ run or for previously generated or other .java files specified on the command line.	True	Advanced
-compiler-executable	Specifies the Java compiler to use.	javac	Environment
-compiler-encoding- flag	Instructs SQLJ whether to pass the -encoding setting, if set, to the Java compiler.	true	Environment

Table 10.2   *SQLJ Translator Options (continued)*

-compiler-output-file	Specifies a file to which the Java compiler output should be written. If this option is not set, then SQLJ assumes that compiler output goes to standard output.	None	Environment
-compiler-pipe-output-flag	Instructs SQLJ whether to set the javac.pipe.output system property, which determines whether the Java compiler prints errors and messages to STDOUT instead of STDERR.	true	Environment
-components	Specifies the components (packages and classes) to instrument for use with Oracle Dynamic Monitoring Service (DMS). This assumes instrumentation is enabled through the -instrument option. Use all to instrument all components being translated.	all	Basic
-d	Specifies the output directory for .ser profile files, if applicable, generated by SQLJ, and .class files generated by the compiler; also passed to javac.	Empty*	Basic
-default-customizer	Determines the profile customizer to use. Specify a class name.	oracle. sqlj. runtime. util. OraCustomizer	Environment
-default-url-prefix	Sets the default prefix for URL settings.	jdbc:oracle: thin:	Basic
-depend	Passed to javac; enables -check-source. This option requires the -C compiler prefix if set in a properties file.	NA	javac
-deprecation	Passed to javac only. This option requires the -C compiler prefix if set in a properties file.	NA	javac

Table 10.2   *SQLJ Translator Options (continued)*

-dir	Sets the output directory for SQLJ-generated .java files.	Empty (Use directory of .sqlj input file.)	Basic
-driver	Determines the JDBC driver class to register. Specify a class name or comma-delimited list of class names.	oracle.jdbc. OracleDriver	Basic
-encoding	Specifies the encoding that SQLJ and the compiler will use in globalization support; also passed to javac. You can use -e on the command line.	JVM file.encoding setting	Basic
-explain	Flag to request cause and action information to be displayed with translator error messages.	false	Basic
-fixedchar	Flag to account for blank padding when binding a string into a WHERE clause for comparison with CHAR data.	false	Basic
-g	Passed to javac; enables -linemap. This option requires the -C compiler prefix if set in a properties file.	NA	javac
-help-help-long-help-alias	Flags to display different levels of information about SQLJ option names, descriptions, and current values. Use these on the command line only. You can use -h instead of -help.	Disabled	Basic
-instrument	Specifies whether to instrument translated files for use with Oracle DMS.	false	Basic
-jdblinemap	Variant of -linemap option for use with the Sun Microsystems jdb debugger.	false	Basic

Table 10.2 *SQLJ Translator Options (continued)*

-J	Prefix that marks options to pass to the JVM. Use this on the command line only.	NA	Advanced
-linemap	Enables mapping of line numbers between the generated Java class file and the original SQLJ code.	false	Basic
-n	Instructs the sqlj script to echo the full command line as it would be passed to the SQLJ translator, including settings in SQLJ_OPTIONS, without having the translator execute it. This is equivalent to -vm=echo. Use this on the command line only.	Disabled	Basic
-ncharconv	Performs bind to NCHAR columns for String host variables.	false	Basic
-nowarn	Passed to javac; sets -warn=none. This option requires the -C compiler prefix if set in a properties file.	NA	javac
-O	Passed to javac; disables -linemap. This option requires the -C compiler prefix if set in a properties file.	NA	javac
-offline	Determines the offline checker to use for semantics-checking. Specify a list of fully qualified class names.	oracle.sqlj. checker. OracleChecke r	Advanced
-online	Determines the online checker to use for semantics-checking. Specify a fully qualified class name. (You must also set -user to enable online checking.)	oracle.sqlj. checker. OracleChecker	Advanced

Table 10.2   *SQLJ Translator Options (continued)*

`-optcols`	Enables iterator column type and size definitions to optimize performance. It is used directly by the translator for Oracle-specific code generation, or forwarded to the Oracle customizer along with user, password, and URL settings for ISO code generation.	false	Basic
`-optparams`	Enables parameter size definitions to optimize JDBC resource allocation (used with -optparamdefaults). This is used directly by the translator for Oracle-specific code generation, or forwarded to the Oracle customizer for ISO code generation.	false	Basic
`-optparamdefaults`	Sets parameter size defaults for particular data types (used with -optparams). This is used directly by the translator for Oracle-specific code generation, or forwarded to the Oracle customizer for ISO code generation.	false	Basic
`-P`	Prefix that marks options to pass to the SQLJ profile customizer.	NA	Advanced
`-parse`	Option to enable the offline SQL parser. Possible settings: both, online-only, offline-only, none, or the name of a Java class that implements an alternative parser. **Note**: Some settings for this option will also disable online semantics-checking, overriding the effect of the -user option.	both	Advanced
`-passes`	Instructs the sqlj script to run SQLJ in two separate passes, with compilation in between. Use this on the command line only.	false	Environment

Table 10.2 *SQLJ Translator Options (continued)*

-password	Sets the user password for the database connection for online semantics-checking. You can use -p on the command line.	None	Basic
-profile	For ISO code generation, enables or disables the profile customization step for profile files generated during the current SQLJ run.	true	Advanced
-props	Specifies a properties file, an alternative to the command line for setting options. (The sqlj.properties is also still read.) Use this on the command line only.	None	Basic
-ser2class	For ISO code generation, instructs SQLJ to translate generated .ser profiles to .class files.	false	Advanced
-status	Requests SQLJ to display status messages as it runs. Instead of -status, you can use -v on the command line.	false	Basic
-url	Sets the URL for the database connection for online semantics-checking.	jdbc:oracle: oci:@	Basic
-user	Enables online semantics-checking and sets the user name (and optionally password and URL) for the database connection. You can use -u on the command line.	None (no online semantics-checking)	Basic
-verbose	Passed to javac; enables -status. This requires the -C compiler prefix if set in a properties file.	NA	javac
-version-version-long	Flag to display different levels of SQLJ and JDBC driver version information. Use these settings on the command line only.	Disabled	Basic
-vm	Specifies the JVM to use for running the SQLJ translator. Use this on the command line only.	java	Environment

Table 10.2 *SQLJ Translator Options (continued)*

–warn	Comma-delimited list of flags to enable or disable different SQLJ warnings. Individual flags are cast/ nocast precision/noprecision, nulls/nonulls, portable/noport- able, strict/nostrict, and verbose/ noverbose. The global flag is all/ none.	`cast`
		`precision`
		`nulls`
		`noportable`
		`strict`
		`noverbose`
			Basic

*   Use directory of `.java` files to place generated `.class` files; use directory of .sqlj files to place generated .ser files.

The Oracle Customizer

If this is your first contact with SQLJ, you may want to skip this topic and come back to it later when you really need it. (All of the code samples were run with the default settings.)

The role of the SQLJ customizer is to allow applications to use any vendor-specific database types or features. The SQLJ translator invokes a Java front end called the customizer harness, which acts as a command-line utility. The harness invokes either the default Oracle customizer or a customizer specified through SQLJ option settings (see Table 10.2).

The translator creates a profile as follows:

1.   As an instance of the `sqlj.runtime.profile.Profile` class.

2.   It inserts information about embedded SQL operations into the profile.

3.   It serializes the profile object (in its original nonserialized state) into a Java resource file (`.ser`).

A customizer is a JavaBeans, which implement the `sqlj.runtime.profile.util.ProfileCustomizer` interface (which specifies a `customize()` method). The Oracle customizer is defined in the `oracle.sqlj.runtime.OraCustomizer` class.

The Oracle customizer implements the following options:

■   `compat`: Displays the version-compatibility information.

■   `force`: Customizes even if a valid customization already exists.

- `optcols`: Enables iterator column type and size definitions to optimize performance.

- `optparams`: Enables parameter size definitions to optimize JDBC resource allocation (used in conjunction with `optparamdefaults`).

- `optparamdefaults`: Sets parameter size defaults for particular data types (used in conjunction with `optparams`).

- `fixedchar`: Enables CHAR comparisons with blank padding for WHERE clauses.

- `showSQL`: Displays SQL statement transformations.

- `stmtcache`: Sets the statement cache size (the number of statements that can be cached for each connection during runtime) for performance optimization, or set it to zero to disable statement caching.

- `summary`: Displays a summary of Oracle features used in your application.

The profile information can be printed using the `-P-print` option. Any output is written to the standard output. See the Oracle SQLJ documentation for more details.

Translator Exit Codes

The following exit codes are returned by the SQLJ translator:

0: No error in execution

1: Error in SQLJ execution

2: Error in Java compilation

3: Error in profile customization

4: Error in class instrumentation, the optional mapping of line numbers from `.sqlj` source file to `.class` file

5: Error in `ser2class` conversion, the optional conversion of profile files from `.ser` files to `.class` files

10.1.4 The Oracle SQLJ Runtime

Runtime Packaging

The Oracle SQLJ runtime is certified against JDK 1.2.x, 1.3.x, or 1.4.x, and delivered through the following JARS:

- `runtime12.jar`:[2] For use in all environments including Oracle 9*i* or Oracle 10*g* JDBC drivers against Oracle database 9*i* Release 2 and Oracle database 10*g* Releases 1 and 2, and middle-tier environment.

- `runtime12ee.jar`: Was furnished in previous releases for middle-tier environments (i.e., Java Enterprise Edition containers/servers); has been deprecated and subsummed by `runtime12.jar`.

- The database-resident runtime for running SQLJ in the database

It supports any standard JDBC driver; however, the Oracle JDBC driver is required by your application whenever you use the Oracle customizer during translation, even if you do not use Oracle extensions in your code. It furnishes full ISO SQLJ functionality if your application has no customizations.

The following packages are used internally by the runtime:

`sqlj.runtime.profile:` Contains interfaces that define SQLJ ISO profiles

`sqlj.runtime.profile.ref:` Contains classes that implement the ISO profiles interfaces

`sqlj.runtime.error:` For generic/standard ISO SQLJ error messages

`oracle.sqlj.runtime.error:` For Oracle SQLJ specific error messages

---

2. `runtime.jar` is furnished for older Oracle JDBC drivers against Oracle 8i Release 8.1.7; it does not provide all ISO SQLJ functionality or Oracle extensions.

Runtime Packages That Support the SQLJ API

Packages That Support Standard SQLJ API

- `sqlj.runtime`: Contains standard interfaces such as `Connection-Context`, `ConnectionContextFactory`, `ResultSetIterator`, `ScrollableResultSetIterator`, and Java wrapper classes or SQL types

- `sqlj.runtime.ref`: Contains classes that implement standard SQLJ interfaces (iterator, connection contexts, etc.)

Package(s) That Support Oracle SQLJ Extensions APIs

- `oracle.sqlj.runtime`: Contains classes that handle Oracle types and extensions

The runtime generates SQLJ, JDBC, and RDBMS errors as instances of `java.sql.SQLException`.

10.1.5 Environment Setup

SQLJ and JPublishr are part of the Oracle Database 10*g* Client (from the client CD or downloaded from OTN). See Chapter 13 "Installing JPublisher" for SQLJ install. It creates the `$ORACLE_HOME/sqlj` directory with `lib`, `doc`, and `demo` subdirectories.

The following command checks the status of SQLJ in your environment:

```
$ sqlj -version
Oracle SQLJ Release 10.2.0.1.0 Production
Copyright (c) 1997, 2005, Oracle Corporation. All Rights
Reserved.
$
```

In addition, Oracle furnishes the following code samples under `$ORACLE_HOME/sqlj/demo/` to check your environment:

- `connect.properties // to be customized to your environment`

- `TestInstallCreateTable.java`

- `TestInstallJDBC.java`

- TestInstallSQLJ.sqlj

- TestInstallSQLJChecker.sqlj

And here is how to use them to check your environment:

```
// create a table for test purposes
$ javac TestInstallCreateTable.java
$ java -Doracle.net.tns_admin=$TNS_ADMIN
TestInstallCreateTable
SALES table created
$


// Check JDBC install
$ javac TestInstallJDBC.java
$ java -Doracle.net.tns_admin=$TNS_ADMIN TestInstallJDBC
Hello JDBC!
$


// Check the SQLJ translator, runtime, and the application
$ sqlj TestInstallSQLJ.sqlj
$ java -Doracle.net.tns_admin=$TNS_ADMIN TestInstallSQLJ
Hello, SQLJ!
$
```

Otherwise, ensure that your environment meets the following requirements:

- The executables (script and binaries) are available under $ORACLE_HOME/bin.

- The PATH environment variable must include $ORACLE_HOME/bin.

- The CLASSPATH environment variable must include the following:
  - The JDBC jars (ojdbc14.jar, or classes12.jar)
  - *ORACLE_HOME*/sqlj/lib/translator.jar
  - *ORACLE_HOME*/sqlj/lib/runtime12.jar

- The connect.properties file (a sample is located at $ORACLE_HOME/sqlj/demo/) allows configuring and customizing the connection to the Oracle database for the runtime.

```
$ cat connect.properties

# Users should uncomment one of the following URLs or add
their own.
# (If using Thin, edit as appropriate.)
sqlj.url=jdbc:oracle:thin:@localhost:1521/myservice
#sqlj.url=jdbc:oracle:oci:@

# Uncommenting User name triggers the onlike checking
sqlj.user=scott
sqlj.password=tiger

$
// And here is how it is referenced in a SQLJ source code
Oracle.connect(mySQLJ.class, "connect.properties");
```

10.1.6 SQLJ Primer

Listing 10.1 is the SQLJ version of the JDBCPrimer.java in Chapter 6:

Listing 10.1   *SqljPrimer.sqlj*

```
================================

import java.sql.SQLException;
import sqlj.runtime.ref.*;
import oracle.sqlj.runtime.*;

// specify the iterator for the query
#sql iterator EnameIter (String ENAME);

class SqljPrimer
{
 public static void main (String args[])
   {
    try
    {
      Oracle.connect(SqljPrimer.class, "connect.properties");
      EnameIter iter;
      #sql iter =  {SELECT ENAME FROM EMP where EMPNO ='7934'};
      if (iter.next()) {
          System.out.println("Employee# 7934 is " + iter.ENAME());
```

```
        }
      } catch (SQLException e){
        System.err.println("Exception: " + e);
      }
    }
  }
}
connect.properties
==================
# Users should uncomment one of the following URLs or add their own.
#
#sqlj.url=jdbc:oracle:thin:@localhost:1521:sid
sqlj.url=jdbc:oracle:thin:@inst1
#sqlj.url=jdbc:oracle:oci8:@

# User name and password here (edit to use different user/password)
sqlj.user=scott
sqlj.password=tiger
~


$ sqlj SqljPrimer.sqlj
$ java -Doracle.net.tns_admin=$TNS_ADMIN SqljPrimer
Employee# 7934 is MILLER
$
```

Contrast this with the JDBC equivalent and you'll get a feel for the conciseness and simplicity of SQLJ.

10.2 SQLJ in the Database

Chapter 5 showed you how to run non-Java languages in the database using the embedded Java VM;[3] SQLJ is one of these languages. This section looks at translating and running SQLJ directly in the database.

Loading, Translating, and Publishing SQLJ in the Database

The database-resident Java VM (also known as OracleJVM) embeds a SQLJ translator and runtime. You can translate your SQLJ source on the client side and then load the resulting class and resource file(s) in the database using loadjava; however, the Java VM in the database is J2SE 1.4

---

3.   http://www.robert-tolksdorf.de/vmlanguages.html.

compatible as of Oracle Database 10g Releases 1 and 2. Alternatively, the embedded SQLJ translator automatically translates SQLJ source files directly in the database upon loading. Note that the –codegen option is not supported in the database; therefore, only Oracle-specific code can be generated in the server. However, ISO standard code can be generated on the client side and then loaded in the database. See the next section on the differences in behavior of SQLJ in the database versus SQLJ on the client side.

Environment Check

The following command checks that the SYS.SQLJUTL package is loaded in the database :

```
SQL> describe sys.sqljutl
FUNCTION BOOL2INT RETURNS NUMBER(38)
 Argument Name                  Type                     In/Out Default?
 ------------------------------ ------------------------ ------ --------
 B                              BOOLEAN                  IN
FUNCTION CHAR2IDS RETURNS INTERVAL DAY TO SECOND
 Argument Name                  Type                     In/Out Default?
 ------------------------------ ------------------------ ------ --------
 CH                             CHAR                     IN
FUNCTION CHAR2IYM RETURNS INTERVAL YEAR TO MONTH
 Argument Name                  Type                     In/Out Default?
 ------------------------------ ------------------------ ------ --------
 CH                             CHAR                     IN
PROCEDURE GET_TYPECODE
 Argument Name                  Type                     In/Out Default?
 ------------------------------ ------------------------ ------ --------
 TID                            RAW                      IN
 CODE                           NUMBER                   OUT
 CLASS                          VARCHAR2                 OUT
 TYP                            NUMBER                   OUT
FUNCTION HAS_DEFAULT RETURNS NUMBER
 Argument Name                  Type                     In/Out Default?
 ------------------------------ ------------------------ ------ --------
 OID                            NUMBER                   IN
 PROC                           CHAR                     IN
 SEO                            NUMBER                   IN
 OVR                            NUMBER                   IN
FUNCTION IDS2CHAR RETURNS CHAR
```

```
Argument Name                   Type                      In/Out Default?
----------------------------    ----------------------    ------ --------
IV                              INTERVAL DAY TO SECOND    IN
FUNCTION INT2BOOL RETURNS BOOLEAN
Argument Name                   Type                      In/Out Default?
----------------------------    ----------------------    ------ --------
I                              NUMBER(38)                IN
FUNCTION IYM2CHAR RETURNS CHAR
Argument Name                   Type                      In/Out Default?
----------------------------    ----------------------    ------ --------
IV                              INTERVAL YEAR TO MONTH    IN
FUNCTION URI2VCHAR RETURNS VARCHAR2
Argument Name                   Type                      In/Out Default?
----------------------------    ----------------------    ------ --------
URI                            URITYPE                   IN

SQL>
```

Otherwise, run the `sqljutl.sql` script to install it.

The following query checks the availability of the SQLJ translator in the database (using system or a DBA account)

```
SQL> select object_type, status from all_objects where
  2  dbms_java.longname(object_name) ='oracle/sqlj/checker/
JdbcVersion';

OBJECT_TYPE          STATUS
-------------------  -------
JAVA CLASS           VALID
SYNONYM              VALID

SQL>
```

Loading SQLJ Sources, Classes, and Resources in the Database

Similar to Java in the database (covered in Part I), the `loadjava` utility can be used to load `.sqlj` file(s), as well as SQLJ-related `.class`, `.jar`, and `.ser` files. (See Listing 10.2.)

The `-resolve` option of loadjava performs the translation and compilation of the SQLJ application as it is loaded.

Listing 10.2   *SqljDb.sqlj*

```
============================
import java.sql.Date;
import java.sql.SQLException;

class SqljDb
{
  public static void main (String argv[])
  {
   // use the default context and the default connection
    try {

        dbprint("Hello from SQLJ in the Database!");
        Date today;
        #sql {select sysdate into :today from dual};
        dbprint("Today is " + today);

      } catch (java.sql.SQLException e) {
        dbprint("Got this error: " + e);
      }
    }
    static void dbprint(String s) {
      try {
        #sql { call dbms_output.put_line(:s)};
      } catch (SQLException e) {}
    }
}
~
$ loadjava -u scott/tiger -r -f -v SqljDb.sqlj

arguments: '-u' 'scott/tiger' '-r' '-f' '-v' 'SqljDb.sqlj'
creating : source SqljDb
loading  : source SqljDb
resolving: source SqljDb
Classes Loaded: 0
Resources Loaded: 0
Sources Loaded: 1
Published Interfaces: 0
Classes generated: 0
Classes skipped: 0
```

```
Synonyms Created: 0
Errors: 0
$

sqljdb.sql
==========

create or replace procedure sqljdb as language java
 name 'SqljDb.main (java.lang.String[])';
/
set serveroutput on
call sqljdb()
/
exit

$ sqlplus scott/tiger @sqljdb

SQL*Plus: Release 10.2.0.1.0 - Production on Fri Dec 30 17:08:59 2005
Copyright (c) 1982, 2005, Oracle.  All rights reserved.

Connected to:
Oracle Database 10g Enterprise Edition Release 10.2.0.1.0 -
Production
With the Partitioning and Data Mining options


Procedure created.

Hello from SQLJ in the Database!
Today is 2005-12-30

Call completed.

Disconnected from Oracle Database 10g Enterprise Edition Release
10.2.0.1.0 — Production
With the Partitioning and Data Mining options
$
```

Conversely, the dropjava utility allows removing SQLJ sources, Java sources, Java classes, and resource files that have been previously loaded by loadjava.

Setting Compiler Options

Before running loadjava, however, you may set SQLJ translator options. The translator and compiler options are maintained in a schema-specific JAVA$OPTIONS table (see Chapter 3 for more details). The get_compiler_option(), set_compiler_option(), and reset_compiler_option() in dbms_java let you manipulate the options:

```
sql> execute dbms_java.set_compiler_option('x.y', 'online', 'true');
sql> execute dbms_java.set_compiler_option('x.y', 'encoding',
'SJIS');
```

However, the encoding option can be set on the loadjava command line, as follows:

```
$ loadjava -user scott/tiger -resolve -encoding SJIS mySQLJ.sqlj
```

Publishing SQLJ to SQL, PL/SQL, and JDBC

Similar to Java in the database, in order for SQL, PL/SQL, and JDBC to invoke your SQLJ application, the top-level methods and their signature(s) must be "published" to the RDBMS catalog. Chapter 3 provided extensive coverage of call specs for Java in the database, and the same mechanisms work for SQLJ. Alternatively, for smart-but-lazy developers, JPublisher (covered later) does this for you!

Differences in Code and Behavior

You need to be aware of the following differences when developing and deploying SQLJ applications in the database.

- As mentioned in Part I, auto-commit is not supported (i.e., false) in the server-side JDBC driver(s). You must explicitly commit or roll back your changes, as follows:

```
#sql { COMMIT };
#sql { ROLLBACK };
```

- A default connection is automatically initialized for SQLJ programs; therefore, setting the default connection context to `null`, as follows, only restates the default connection context:

    ```
    (i.e.,  DefaultContext.setDefaultContext(null)) :
    ```

- For standard ISO code, unlike client-side SQLJ, closing the JDBC connection object does *not* reclaim statement handles. In order to clean up the statements cache, you must close the connection context instance, as follows:

    ```
    DefaultContext ctx = new DefaultContext(conn);
    // Use JDBC connection
    #sql [ctx] { SQL operation };
    ...
    // release the connection context instance
    ctx.close(sqlj.runtime.ConnectionContext.KEEP_CONNECTIO
    N);
    ...
    ```

- For Oracle-specific code, the statements are cached within the JDBC statement cache and are automatically reclaimed when you "close" the default JDBC connection (even though the connection handles remain active). In order for Oracle-specific code to interoperate with ISO SQLJ code, you must use an explicit `Execution-Context` as follows:

    ```
    public static ExecutionContext exec = new
    ExecutionContext();
    ...
    #sql [exec] { SQL operation };
    ```

- In the server, the `online` option is only a flag that enables online checking using a default checker. On a client, the `-online` option specifies which checker to use, but the `-user` option enables online checking.

- Both online semantics checking and offline parsing are enabled in the server by default, equivalent to the default `-parse=both` setting on a client. You can override this to disable online semantics checking through the online option, but you cannot disable offline parsing.

- Similar to Java, the same SQLJ code can be used both on the server side and the client side; to determine where the code is running, use the following code fragment:

```
if (System.getProperty("oracle.server.version") != null

{
    // (running in server)
}
...
```

- In general, when a statement tries to use an execution context that is already in use by another statement, that statement will be blocked until the other statement completes. However, in the server, SQLJ allows recursive calls to use the same execution context.

- Similar to Java error reporting, SQLJ errors are reported in the USER_ERRORS table in the user schema. The TEXT column can be retrieved to get the text of the error message. However, with load-java you can log the error messages originating from from the server-side translator using the -fileout <file> option.

Now that we have seen the rationales for SQLJ in general, the additional benefits of Oracle extensions, the architecture of Oracle's implementation, a review of the translator options, the runtime configuration, and SQLJ in the database, it's time to look at the key structures of a SQLJ program, in the next chapter.

The SQLJ Language and Oracle Extensions

A SQLJ program contains Java/JDBC code, SQLJ declaration statements, and SQLJ executable statements, as illustrated by Figure 11.1.

Figure 11.1
Elements of a SQLJ program

```
Java & JDBC code

    +

SQLJ Declaration Statements

    +

SQLJ Executable Statements
```

This chapter covers SQLJ declarations, SQLJ executable statements, interoperability between SQLJ and JDBC, and, finally, Expressions in SQLJ.

11.1 Declaration Statements

This category contains import statements, connection contexts declaration, execution contexts declarations, and iterators declarations.

11.1.1 Import Statements

```
import java.sql.SQLException;
import sqlj.runtime.ref.DefaultContext;
import oracle.sqlj.runtime.*;
...
```

11.1.2 Connection Contexts

A connection context is not tied to a schema but is associated with a well-scoped set of tables, views, and stored procedures that have the same names and data types—called exemplar schema—and that are validated during translation time. Using the same connection context with the occurences of the "exemplar schema" through different databases (e.g., development databases versus deployment databases) preserves the validity of the translation-time checking. It is up to the developer to maintain a valid connection context versus exemplar schema association.

The `sqlj.runtime.ConnectionContext` interface specifies the following public methods:

- `getConnection()`: Returns the underlying JDBC connection object associated with this context instance.

- `getExecutionContext()`: Returns the default execution context used by this connection context (execution context will be covered later).

- `close(boolean closeConnection)`: Releases the connection context and all associated resources, including the underlying JDBC connection, unless the Boolean constant `KEEP_CONNECTION` is furnished in parameter and the connection is left open (default is `CLOSE_CONNECTION`; in this case, the JDBC connection is closed).

A SQLJ application can create a new connection context class by just declaring it as follows (the translator takes care of implementing the class):

```
#sql context <Context Name> [<implements_clause>]
[<with_clause>];
```

Here is an example of a context declaration and the implementation class generated by the translator under the covers (the implementation class is transparent to the SQLJ developer):

```
#sql context myConCxt;

// and here is the generated class

class myConCxt implements sqlj.runtime.ConnectionContext
      extends ...
  {
    public myConCxt(String url, Properties info, boolean autocommit)
        throws SQLException {...}
```

```
public myConCxt(String url, boolean autocommit)
        throws SQLException {...}
public myConCxt(String url, String user, String password,
        boolean autocommit) throws SQLException {...}
public myConCxt(Connection conn) throws SQLException {...}
public myConCxt(ConnectionContext other) throws SQLException {...}

public static myConCxt getDefaultContext() {...}
public static void setDefaultContext(myConCxt ctx) {...}
}
```

Here is how the application creates instances of the previously declared context:

```
myConCtx Ctx1 = new myConCtx
    (Oracle.getConnection(myClass.class, "connect.properties"));
myConCtx Ctx2 = new myConCtx
    ("jdbc:oracle:thin:@localhost:1521/service", "foo","bar",
false);
```

The SQLJ runtime furnishes a special `sqlj.runtime.ref.Default-Context` class that applications can use just to create instances of default connection context as follows:

```
DefaultContext defConCtx = new DefaultContext
    ("jdbc:oracle:thin:@localhost:1521/service", "scott",
"tiger", false);
```

The Oracle SQLJ runtime furnishes the `oracle.sqlj.runtime.Oracle` class to simplify `DefaultContext` class management, as follows:

- Upon the invocation of the `Oracle.connect()` method, a default connection context is initialized (if not already) along with an underlying JDBC connection (setting auto-commit to `false`); it takes the following signatures:

```
Oracle.connect(myClass.class, "connect.properties");
Oracle.connect(getClass, "connect.properties");
Oracle.connect("URL");
```

```
Oracle.connect("jdbc:oracle:thin@host:port:sid",
                "user", "passwd");
Oracle.connect("URL",  flag); // auto-commit true|false
```

- The `Oracle.getConnection()` creates and returns an instance of `DefaultContext` object (`auto-commit` is set to `false`, by default).
- The `Oracle.close()` closes only the default connection context.

SQLJ allows managing connections at the statement level. In order to issue executable statements against the database, a connection context is required; however:

- When not specified, all executable statements will use the default connection context.

```
#sql { SQL operation };  // a short form for the
                         // following
#sql [DefaultContext.getDefaultContext()] { SQL
operation };
```

- Alternatively, an executable statement can explicitly specify the connection context, as follows:

```
#sql [conctx] {SQL Operation};
```

As Figure 11.2 illustrates, each instance of a connection context class is tied to a JDBC connection; however:

- Different instances of a connection context class (`DefaultContext` class or user-defined context class) may share the same JDBC connection, as follows:

```
myCtx myConCtx1 = new
myCtx(DefaultContext.getDefaultContext().getConnection(
));
    myCtx myConCtx2 = new
myCtx(DefaultContext.getDefaultContext().getConnection(
));
```

- Different instances of a connection context class (`DefaultContect` or user-defined context) may use different JDBC connections, as follows:

```
DefaultContext defConCtx1 = Oracle.getConnection
    ("jdbc:oracle:thin:@localhost1:1521/service1",
"scott", "tiger");

DefaultContext defConCtx2 = Oracle.getConnection
    ("jdbc:oracle:thin:@localhost1:1521/myservice2",
"foo", "bar");
```

The default connection context can be overridden using the `sqlj.runtime.ref.DefaultContext.setDefaultContext` method to set a different connection context as the default:

```
DefaultContext.setDefaultContext(defConCtx1);

// The following execution statememts will use myCtx1
#sql { SQL operation };
...
DefaultContext.setDefaultContext(defConCtx2);
// The following execution statements will use myCtx2

#sql { SQL operation };
#sql { SQL operation };
...



// Save the current default context
DefaultContext savedCtx = DefaultContext.getDefaultContext();
// Assign new context as default
DefaultContext.setDefaultContext( new DefaultContext(
   ("jdbc:oracle:thin:@localhost:1521/service", "scott",
"tiger", false)
));
// use the newly assigned default context

#sql {SQL peration};
```

Figure 11.2
Connection
Context Classes
and Instances

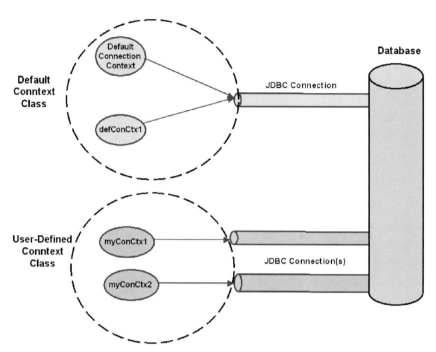

User-Defined Connection Context Interface

You may use your own custom connection context interface instead of the standard ConnectionContext interface using the IMPLEMENTS clause during the declaration step:

```
#sql public context myInterfCtx implements myCtxInterface;
```

where myCtxInterface contains your interface definition, which may be a more restrictive version (i.e., hide some functions) of ConnectionContext, and then instantiate it as follows:

```
myInterfCtx myConCtx1 =
    new myInterfCtx(("jdbc:oracle:thin:@localhost:1521/
myservice", <user>, <pass>, <autocommit>);
```

DataSource

DataSource is the standard/recommended mechanism for establishing a JDBC connection. Similarly, SQLJ supports the datasource mechanism in two ways: associate a connection context with a JDBC datasource, and use SQLJ-specific datasources.

1. *Associating a SQLJ connection context with a JDBC datasource in the connection context declaration.* Additional constructors are generated within the connection context class when it is declared with a `dataSource` property; consequently, the `DriverManager`-based constructors are not generated. The SQLJ runtime looks up the datasource object in JNDI contexts; you need an `Initial-Context` provider. Also, the `javax.sql.*` and `javax.naming.*` packages must be available in your environment (`CLASSPATH`).

    The following declaration associates a context with a datasource and generates additional constructors (listed as bullet items) in the generated class (i.e., `DSCtx`):

    ```
    #sql context DSCtx with (dataSource="jdbc/myDSource");
    ```

    ■ `DSCtx()`: Looks up the datasource for `jdbc/myDSource`, and then calls the `getConnection()` method on the datasource to obtain a connection.

    ■ `DSCtx(String user, String password)`: Looks up the datasource for `jdbc/myDSource,` and then calls the `getConnection(user,password)` method on the datasource to obtain a connection.

    ■ `DSCtx(ConnectionContext ctx)`: Delegates to `ctx` to obtain a connection.

    ■ When the default SQLJ context is not set, the SQLJ runtime will use the default data source—bound to the `jdbc/defaultDataSource`—to establish the connection.

    Listing 11.1, is based on the JDBC JNDI example `DataSrceJNDI.java` in Chapter 7; you need to install the file system–based JNDI as explained in Chapter 7 (your CLASSPATH must contain `fscontext.jar` and `providerutil.jar`). The file system–based JNDI machinery does not do justice to SQLJ simplicity; the code would be much simpler in a middle-tier environment, where containers have their own namespace and initial context provider; see #2, which follows.

Listing 11.1   *myDataSource.sqlj*

```
=====================================
import java.sql.*;
```

```
import javax.sql.*;
import oracle.jdbc.*;
import oracle.jdbc.pool.OracleDataSource;
import javax.naming.*;
import javax.naming.spi.*;
import java.util.*;
import java.io.*;
import sqlj.runtime.*;
import sqlj.runtime.ref.DefaultContext;
import oracle.sqlj.runtime.*;

public class myDataSource
{

  public static void main(String[] args) throws
java.sql.SQLException,
                          NamingException, java.io.IOException
  {

    try {
      // Initialize the Context
      Context ctx = null;
       Hashtable env = new Hashtable (5);
       env.put (Context.INITIAL_CONTEXT_FACTORY,
              "com.sun.jndi.fscontext.RefFSContextFactory");
       env.put (Context.PROVIDER_URL, "file:" + args[0]);
       ctx = new InitialContext(env);
      // Create a JDBC OracleDataSource instance explicitly
      OracleDataSource ods = new OracleDataSource();
      // Get URL from datasource.properties
      InputStream is     = null;
      is =
      ClassLoader.getSystemResourceAsStream("datasource.properties");
      Properties p = new Properties();
      p.load(is);
      is.close();
      String url = p.getProperty("url");
      String user = p.getProperty("user");
      String passw = p.getProperty("passw");
      System.out.println ("Config file: url = " + url + " User = " +
user + " Password = " + passw);
      ods.setURL(url);
```

```
        ods.setUser(user);
        ods.setPassword(passw);


        // Bind the SQLJ default data source to the JNDI name
        // jdbc/defaultDataSource
        System.out.println ("Binding the logical name: jdbc/
defaultDataSource");
        ctx.bind ("jdbc/defaultDataSource", ods);


        // The SQLJ runtime will use the default JDBC connection
        // to connect
        Connection conn = ods.getConnection();
        DefaultContext.setDefaultContext(new DefaultContext(conn));


        int i;
        #sql { select empno into :i from emp where ename = 'SCOTT' };
        System.out.println("SCOTT's emp# is : "+i);
        ods.close();
        Oracle.close();
      } catch (NamingException ne)
      {
        ne.printStackTrace();
      }
    }
}


$ sqlj myDataSource.sqlj
$ java -Doracle.net.tns_admin=$TNS_ADMIN myDataSource ~/jndi
Config file: url = jdbc:oracle:thin:@inst1 User = scott Password =
tiger
Binding the logical name: jdbc/defaultDataSource
SCOTT's emp# is : 7788
$
```

2.   *SQLJ-specific datasources extend a JDBC datasource and return SQLJ connection context instances.* The Oracle SQLJ supports SQLJ-specific datasources in the runtime12ee library for use with middle-tier containers (these are not available with runtime12.jar).

SQLJ datasources are based on the corresponding JDBC datasource interface or class. With Oracle JDBC 10g drivers, use the OracleSqljDataSource and OracleSqljConnectionPool-

DataSource classes available in oracle.sqlj.runtime and oracle.sqlj.runtime.client packages.

- The oracle.sqlj.runtime package includes the OracleSqljDataSource class, which extends oracle.jdbc.pool.OracleDataSource and implements ConnectionContextFactory.

- The oracle.sqlj.runtime.client package includes the OracleSqljXADataSource class, which extends oracle.jdbc.xa.client.OracleXADataSource and implements ConnectionContextFactory.

The sqlj.runtime.ConnectionContextFactory interface acts as a base interface for SQLJ datasource and specifies getDefaultContext() and getContext() methods:

getDefaultContext() returns a sqlj.runtime.ref.DefaultContext instance for the SQLJ default context (with signatures that enable you to specify auto-commit setting, user, and password for the underlying JDBC connection):

- DefaultContext getDefaultContext()

- DefaultContext getDefaultContext(boolean autoCommit)

- DefaultContext getDefaultContext(String user, String password)

- DefaultContext getDefaultContext(String user, String password, boolean autoCommit)

getContext() returns a sqlj.runtime.ConnectionContext instance of the user-declared connection context class (with signatures that enable you to specify auto-commit setting, user, and password for the underlying JDBC connection):

- ConnectionContext getContext(Class aContextClass)

- ConnectionContext getContext(Class aContextClass, boolean autoCommit)

- ConnectionContext getContext(Class aContextClass, String user, String password)

- `ConnectionContext getContext(Class aContextClass,`
  `String user, String password, boolean autoCommit)`

When a parameter is not specified, it is obtained from the underlying datasource that generates the connection (*Note:* auto-commit defaults to `false` when not set to `true` for the underlying datasource).

The `oracle.sqlj.runtime.client` package contains the `OracleSql-jXADataSource` class.

Here is a code fragment using SQLJ datasources:

```
//Initialize the data source
SqljXADataSource sqljDS = new OracleSqljXADataSource();
sqljDS.setUser("scott");
sqljDS.setPassword("tiger");
sqljDS.setServerName("myserver");
sqljDS.setDatabaseName("ORCL");
sqljDS.setDataSourceName("jdbc/OracleSqljXADS");

//Bind the data source to JNDI
Context ctx = new InitialContext();
ctx.bind("jdbc/OracleSqljXADS");

int i;
#sql [ctx] { select empno into :i from emp where ename =
'SCOTT' };
System.out.println("SCOTT's emp# is : "+i);
```

Statement Caching

For Oracle SQLJ code, statement caching of the underlying connection is enabled through methods on the connection context interface and classes.

The following static methods in the `sqlj.runtime.ref.DefaultContext` class and user-defined context classes set the default statement cache size for all connection contexts classes and their instances:

- `setDefaultStmtCacheSize(int)`
- `int getDefaultStmtCacheSize()`

The following instance methods in the `sqlj.runtime.ref.Default-Context` class and user-defined context classes set the cache size for the current connection context instance; this setting overrides the default setting.

- `setStmtCacheSize(int)`

- `int getStmtCacheSize()`

11.1.3   Execution Contexts

Similar to connection context, an instance of the execution context class (i.e., `sqlj.runtime.ExecutionContext`) must be associated with each executable SQLJ statement, either implictly (using the default execution context instance associated with every connection context) or explictly. The applications create new instances by invoking the constructor of the class (i.e., `new ExecutionContext()`).

The association of an execution context with an executable statement is specified in the following ways:

- #sql [<execution context>] {<SQLJ clause>}
- #sql [<connection context>, <execution context>] {<SQLJ clause>}

The following code fragment creates a new execution context and assigns it to the SQLJ statement:

```
Example
=======
import sqlj.runtime.ExecutionContext;
...

ExecutionContext ec = new ExecutionContext();
#sql [ec] { SQLJ clause};
```

The execution context associated with a context can be retrieved using the `getExecutionContext()` method of the `ConnectionContext` interface. Consequently, you can retrieve the static default execution context of each connection context class using the `DefaultContext.getDefault-Context.getExecutionContext()` method:

```
Example #1
==========

  import sqlj.runtime.ExecutionContext;

  ...
  exCtx =
DefaultContext.getDefaultContext().getExecutionContext();
  #sql [exCtx] { SQLJ clause};


Example #2
==========

  #sql static context Contx;

  ...
  Contx myCtx = new
Contx(DefaultContext.getDefaultContext().getConnection());


  #sql [ myctx.getDefaultContext(),
myctx.getExecutionContext() ] {SQLJ clause};


  ...
  #sql [ myctx.getExecutionContext()] { SQLJ Clause};
```

As Figure 11.3 illustrates, each instance of execution context class must be assigned a connection context; if not explicitly done, it is attached to the default context.

Methods of the ExecutionContext Class

- Describing the status and result of the most recent SQL operations:

  `SQLWarning   getWarnings()`: Returns a `java.sql.SQL-Warning`

  Use `getWarnings()` of the execution context to get the first warning, then `getNextWarning()` method of each `SQLWarning` object to get the next warning.

```
  Example #1
  SQLException sqle =
  contxt.getExecutionContext().getWarnings();

  Example #2
  SQLWarning sqlwarn = iter1.getWarnings();
  while (true) {
```

Figure 11.3
*Execution Contexts
and Connection
Contexts*

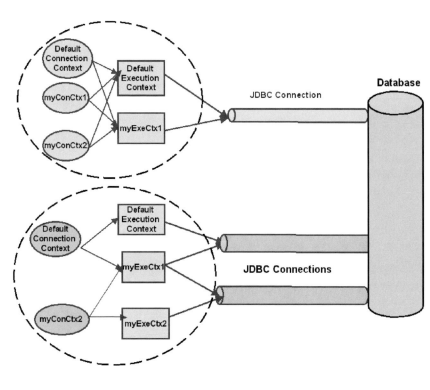

```
if (sqlwarn == null) {
    System.out.println ("No more Warning");
        break;
    } else {
        System.out.println ("Warning: " +
        sqlwarn.getMessage());
    }
    sqlwarn = sqlwarn.getNextWarning();
    }
```

int getUpdateCount(): Returns the number of rows updated by the last SQL operation that used this execution context instance.

```
Example
    System.out.println("Update cnt: " +
        conCtx.getExecutionContext().getUpdateCount());
```

■ Managing the semantic of subsequent SQL operations:

int getMaxFieldSize(): Returns the maximum amount of data (in bytes) that would be returned from a subsequent SQL operation for BINARY, VARBINARY, LONGVARBINARY, CHAR, VARCHAR, or LONGVARCHAR columns (default value is 0, i.e., no limit).

Example:

```
System.out.println ("MaxFieldSize: " +
conCtx.getExecutionContext().getMaxFieldSize());
```

setMaxFieldSize(int): sets the maximum field-size.

int getMaxRows(): Returns the maximum number of rows that can be contained in   SQLJ iterators or JDBC result sets created using this execution context instance (default is 0, i.e., no limit).

setMaxRows(int): Sets the maximum rows.

int getQueryTimeout(): Returns the timeout interval, in seconds, for any SQL operation that uses this execution context instance. A SQL exception is thrown if a SQL operation exceeds this limit (default is 0, i.e., no timeout limit).

setQueryTimeout(int): Sets the query timeout limit.

int getFetchSize(): Retrieves the current fetch size (previously set using setFetchSize()), for iterator objects generated from this ExecutionContext object.

setFetchSize(int): Sets the number of rows that should be fetched when more rows are needed from iterators.

int getFetchDirection(): Retrieves the default fetch direction for scrollable iterator objects that are generated from this Execution-Context object (default is sqlj.runtime.ResultSetIterator.FETCH_FORWARD).

setFetchDirection(int): Sets the direction in which rows of scrollable iterator objects are processed (default is sqlj.runtime.ResultSetIterator.FETCH_FORWARD).

Notes:

getNextResultSet(int): is not implemented in Oracle SQLJ.

ResultSets in Oracle SQLJ are always bound as explicit arguments.

- Terminating the SQL operations currently executing:

`cancel()`: To be used in a multithreading environment, from one thread to cancel a SQL operation currently executing in another thread.

- Enabling/disabling update batching:

`int[] executeBatch()`: Executes the pending statement batch and returns an array of `int` update counts.

`int getBatchLimit()`: Returns the current batch limit (default `UNLIMITED_BATCH`). If set, then a pending batch is implicitly executed once it contains that number of statements.

`int[] getBatchUpdateCounts()`: Returns an array of `int` update counts for the last batch executed.

`boolean isBatching()`: Returns a Boolean value indicating whether update batching is enabled. The `getUpdateCount()` method indicates whether a batch has been newly created, added to, or executed.

`setBatching(boolean)`: Boolean value to enable update batching (disabled by default).

`setBatchLimit(int)`: Takes a positive, nonzero `int` value as input to set the current batch limit. Special values are `UNLIMITED_BATCH` and `AUTO_BATCH` (lets the SQLJ runtime dynamically determine a batch limit).

Example:

```
sqlj.runtime.ExecutionContext exectx =
sqlj.runtime.ref.DefaultContext.getDefaultContext().get
ExecutionContext();
exectx.setBatching(true);
exectx.setBatchLimit(6);
```

- Managing JDBC 3.0 savepoint operations (i.e., set a savepoint, roll back to a savepoint, and release a savepoint):

`Object oracleSetSavepoint(ConnectionContextImpl, String)`: Registers a savepoint and returns it as an `Object` instance. It takes an instance of the `sqlj.runtime.ref.ConnectionContextImpl` class and a string that specifies the savepoint name. The Oracle SQLJ savepoint is an instance of the `oracle.jdbc.OracleSavepoint` class, which extends the `java.sql.Savepoint` interface. Also, the Oracle

Object does not require JDK 1.4, unlike the standard `java.sql.Savepoint` interface.

`void oracleRollbackToSavepoint (ConnectionContextImpl, Object)`: Rolls back changes to the specified savepoint. It takes the connection context as an instance of `ConnectionContextImpl` and the savepoint as an `Object` instance.

`void oracleReleaseSavepoint(ConnectionContextImpl, Object)`: Releases the specified savepoint.

- Closing the execution context:

    `close()`: To be used if (1) Oracle-specific code generation, and (2) using explicitly created `ExecutionContext,` and (3) not using an explicit execution context with `COMMIT/ROLLBACK`, and (4) not calling `executeBatch()` on the `ExecutionContext` instance.

```
Execution Context eCtx = new ExecutionContext();
...
try {
    ...
    #sql [eCtx] { SQL operation };
    ...
} finally { eCtx.close(); }
```

Execution Contexts and Multithreading

Multithreading in SQLJ depends on the multithreading support in the underlying JDBC driver. In Oracle JDBC, methods are synchronized on the connection (i.e., the driver sends a command to the server on behalf of a thread and then waits for its completion before the connection/socket can be used by another thread. Simultaneous multithreading is possible when threads are not sharing the same connection—in other words, it is not recommended!

11.1.4 Iterators

Iterators are similar to JDBC result sets in that these are used for retrieving multiple rows upon a query execution; for queries that return a single row, use the `SELECT` clause (see executable statements below). However, unlike result sets, iterators can be weakly typed (i.e., instances of `sqlj.runtime.ResultSetIterator` or `sqlj.runtime.ScrollableResultSetIt-`

erator classes furnished by the runtime) or strongly typed (i.e., instances of user-declared classes).

Weakly Typed Iterators

Weakly typed iterators are interoperable/compatible with JDBC result sets (hence, familiar to JDBC aficionados); however, they do not benefit from the SQLJ semantics and type checking (see strongly typed iterators next).

ResultSet Iterators are instances of the `sqlj.runtime.ResultSetIterator` class, which implements the `ResultSetIterator` interface; this interface specifies the following methods:

- `close()`: Closes the iterator.

- `ResultSet getResultSet()`: Extracts the underlying JDBC result set from the iterator.

- `boolean isClosed()`: Determines if the iterator has been closed.

- `boolean next()`: Moves to the next row of the iterator; it returns true if there remains a valid next row.

- `boolean endFetch()`: Returns true if the last fetch failed, false otherwise.

- `int getFetchSize()`: Retrieves the current fetch size for this iterator object.

- `setFetchSize(int rows)`: Sets the default fetch size (in parameter) for result sets generated from this iterator object.

ResultSet iterators are mainly used in Oracle SQLJ as host expressions, cursors in FETCH statements, and for accessing the JDBC ResultSet, as follows:

```
sqlj.runtime.ResultSetIterator RSetIter;
ResultSet JdbcRs;

#sql RSetIter = { SELECT ename FROM emp };
JdbcRs = RSetIter.getResultSet();
while (JdbcRs.next()) {
    System.out.println("ename: " + JdbcRs.getString(1));
}
RSetIter.close();
```

> **Note:** Closing the ResultSet iterator will also close the result set (the opposite is not true).

Scrollable iterators are another flavor of weakly typed iterators.

Strongly Typed Iterators

Like many things in SQLJ, strongly typed iterators enforce semantics checking of the queries; however, the minor downside is that these are not interoperable with JDBC. In order to define a strongly typed iterator, you must declare: its class, the names of the columns, and/or the Java types of the columns. Declaring both the name and the Java type of each column defines a "named iterator," while declaring just the column types defines a "positional iterator."

Named iterators are instances of user-declared classes; the SQLJ translator generates the corresponding classes implementing the `ResultSetIterator` and `sqlj.runtime.NamedIterator` interfaces. The beauty of named iterators, in contrast to JDBC `getxxx()`/`getXXX()`, reside, in the fact that the column names serve as getters or accessors for the retrieval of the value in the columns; in addition, the order of appearance of the column names in the *SELECT* statement and the iterator declaration does not matter.

The following code fragments illustrate named iterator declaration and usage:

```
//Fragment #1
#sql iterator namedIter1 (int empno, String ename, Double
sal, float comm);

namedIter1 nIter1
#sql nIter1 = { SELECT ename, empno, sal, comm FROM
employees};

...
while (nIter1.next()) {
...
}
nIter1.close();
```

```
//Fragment #2

#sql iterator namedIter2 (int empno, String ename);
#sql context Context;

namedIter2    nIter2;
Context ctx;
...
#sql [ctx] nIter2 = { select ename, empno from employees } ;
while (nIter2.next()) {
...
};
nIter1.close();
```

Positional iterators are instances of user-declared classes; at translation
time, the SQLJ translator generates classes that implement the
ResultSetIterator and sqlj.runtime.PositionedIterator interfaces. With positional iterators, the column names are not specified, only
the types are. The data is retrieved using FETCH INTO, in the same order as
the columns appear in the SELECT statement; however, the data types of
the table columns must match the types of the iterator columns.

The PositionedIterator interface specifies the endFetch() method
for determining if the last row has been reached.

The following code fragments define positional iterators:

```
// Fragment#3

#sql iterator posIter2 (int, String);
#sql context Context;
posIter2  pIter2;
Context ctx;
String ename;
int empno;
#sql [ctx] pIter2 = { select ename, empno from emp where empno = 7788}
;
while (true) {
  #sql [ctx] FETCH :pIter2 INTO :ename, :empno};
  if (pIter2.endFetch()) break;
  System.out.println("ename = " + ename + ", emp# = " + empno);
}
```

```
pIter2.close();

//Fragment #4

#sql iterator posIter1 (int, String, Double, float);

posIter1 pIter1
#sql pIter1 = { SELECT ename, empno, sal, comm FROM employees};
...
while (pIter1.next()) {

  // retrieve and process the row

};
pIter1.close();

//Fragment #5

#sql iterator posIter2 (int, String);
#sql context Context;
posIter2    pIter2;
Context ctx;
...
#sql [ctx] pIter2 = { select ename, empno from employees } ;
while (pIter2.next()) {

// retrieve and process the row

};
pIter1.close();
```

Scrollable Iterators

The ISO SQLJ supports the scrollable iterators that are similar/compatible with JDBC Scrollable ResultSet. The `sqlj.runtime.Scrollable` furnishes the following features:

- Hints about the fetch direction to scrollable iterators:

    `setFetchDirection(int)`: The direction in which rows are processed; takes one of the following `sqlj.runtime.ResultSetIterator` constants: `FETCH_FORWARD`, `FETCH_REVERSE`, or `FETCH_UNKNOWN` (default is `FETCH_FORWARD`) int getFetchDirection(): Retrieves the current fetch direction.

- Methods that provide information about the position of the iterator in the underlying result set:

boolean isBeforeFirst(): True if the iterator is before the first row in the result set.

```
if (sri.isBeforeFirst())System.out.println("Is before
first.");
```

boolean isFirst(): True if the iterator is on the first row of the result set.

```
if (sri.isFirst()) System.out.print("Is first. ");
```

boolean isLast(): True if the iterator is on the last row of the result set.

```
if (sri.isBeforeFirst())System.out.println("Is before
first.");
```

boolean isAfterLast(): True if the iterator is after the last row in the result set.

```
if (sri.isAfterLast()) System.out.println("Is after
last.");
```

The IMPLEMENTS SCROLLABLE clause is required for declaring scrollable iterators (i.e., implements sqlj.runtime.Scrollable):

```
public interface ScrollableResultSetIterator
                   extends ResultSetIterator
                   implements Scrollable
    {...}
```

Instances of sqlj.runtime.ScrollableResultSetIterator class, which extends ResultSetIterator and Scrollable interfaces, can be used with FETCH CURRENT syntax to process result set iterators with SQLJ.

```
#sql { FETCH CURRENT FROM :sri INTO :i, :name };
```

Scrollable Named Iterators

The scrollable named iterators use the following navigation methods in the Scrollable interface: next(), previous(), first(), last(), absolute(), relative(), beforeFirst(), and afterLast().

Example:

```
#sql public static iterator ScrollNamIter
                            implements sqlj.runtime.Scrollable
                            (int empno, String ename);
ScrollNamIter sni;
#sql sni = { select empno, ename from emp };
int no;
String name;
//
#sql { FETCH :sni INTO :no, :name };
//
#sql { FETCH NEXT FROM :sni INTO :no, :name };
//
#sql { FETCH PRIOR FROM :sni INTO :no, :name };
//
#sql { FETCH FIRST FROM :sni INTO :no, :name };
//
#sql { FETCH LAST FROM :sni INTO :no, :name };
//
#sql { FETCH ABSOLUTE :(6) FROM :sni INTO :no, :name };
//
#sql { FETCH RELATIVE :(-3) FROM :sni INTO :no, :name };
//
#sql { FETCH CURRENT FROM :sni INTO :no, :name };

Oracle.close();
```

Scrollable Positional Iterators

The following code fragment is similar to the previous one and illustrates the use of navigation methods with scrollable positional iterator:

```
#sql public static iterator ScrollPosIter
                            implements sqlj.runtime.Scrollable
                            (int, String);
ScrollPosIter spi;
```

```
#sql spi = { select empno, ename from emp };

int no;
String name;

#sql { FETCH :spi INTO :no, :name };
#sql { FETCH NEXT FROM :spi INTO :no, :name };
#sql { FETCH PRIOR FROM :spi INTO :no, :name };
#sql { FETCH FIRST FROM :spi INTO :no, :name };
#sql { FETCH LAST FROM :spi INTO :no, :name };
#sql { FETCH ABSOLUTE :(6) FROM :spi INTO :no, :name };
#sql { FETCH RELATIVE :(-3) FROM :spi INTO :no, :name };
#sql { FETCH CURRENT FROM :spi INTO :no, :name };

Oracle.close();
```

Subclassing Iterator Classes

Sometimes you may want to add new functionality relative to processing query results. SQLJ lets you extend the base iterator classes, as follows:

1.   Declare your iterator class:

```
#sql public static iterator <baseClassIter> (...);
```

2.   Extend the base class with new methods, as follows; notice that you must furnish a public constructor that takes an instance of sqlj.runtime.RTResultSet as input:

```
/*
 * This is a skeleton of Iterator SubClassing
 */

import java.sql.SQLException;
import sqlj.runtime.profile.RTResultSet;
import oracle.sqlj.runtime.Oracle;

public class mySubClassIter
{

  // Declare the base iterator class
```

```
#sql public static iterator baseClassIter(...);

// Declare a subclass Iterator class, which
// extends the base Iterator class

public static class subClassIter extends baseClassIter
{

  /*
   * Provide a sqlj.runtime.RTResultSet for the constructor
   */
  public subClassIter(RTResultSet rtrset) throws SQLException
  {
    super(rtrset);
  }

  /*
   ** Add your custom (public and private) methods here
   */
  public String method2() throws SQLException
  {
    ...
    while (super.next())
    ...
    super.close();
  }

 // Use the finalizer of the base class
  protected void finalize() throws Throwable {
    super.finalize();
  }

  // Use the close method of the base class
  public void close() throws SQLException {
    super.close();
  }
}

SubclassIterDemo() throws SQLException
{
  Oracle.connect(getClass(), "connect.properties");
```

```
    }

    void runit() throws SQLException
    {
      subClassIter subECtx;
     ...
     // Use it
      #sql subECtx = { SQLJ clause };
    }
}
```

Iterator Sensitivity

Similar to JDBC Scrollable ResultSets covered in Chapter 8, iterators may also be sensitive or insensitive to changes in the underlying data. Sensitivity is specified using the WITH clause during the iterator declaration, as follows:

```
#sql public static iterator SensRSetIter implements
      sqlj.runtime.Scrollable
      with (sensitivity=SENSITIVE)
      (String ename, int empno);
```

When sensitivity is not specified, it defaults to INSENSITIVE in the Oracle SQLJ implementation. However, you can use the ISO SQLJ ASENSITIVE, instead of INSENSITIVE.

```
#sql iterator AsNIter1 with (sensitivity=ASENSITIVE) (int s);
#sql iterator IsNIter2 with (sensitivity=INSENSITIVE) (String t);
#sql iterator AsNIter3 with
(sensitivity=sqlj.runtime.ResultSetIterator.ASENSITIVE) (int s);

#sql iterator IsNIter4 with
(sensitivity=sqlj.runtime.ResultSetIterator.INSENSITIVE) (String t);
```

11.1.5   IMPLEMENTS Clause in Context Declarations

We have seen the IMPLEMENTS SCROLLABLE clause in declaring scrollable iterators. The IMPLEMENTS clause can also be used during context and iterator declarations to implement user-defined interfaces and positioned update/delete iterators.

Iterator Implementing User-Defined Interfaces

User-defined interfaces let you customize the generated classes from which instances of iterators are created. Assume you want to restrict access to sensitive columns of a named iterator, such as date of birth, salary, Social Security number, and so on. By default, a named iterator class generates a getter method for every column involved in the SELECT clause. In order to achieve your goal, you just create an interface, which defines getters only for columns you want to expose. The following interface will generate a CustNamedIter class with only ename and empno accessors:

```
interface CustNamedIterInterf extends NamedIterator
{
  public String ename () throws SQLException;
  public int empno () throws SQLException;
}
```

```
#sql iterator cni implements CustNamedIterInterf (String emame, int
empno, data dob);
```

Similarly, you may want to restrict the columns returned by a positional iterator through a user-defined interface:

```
interface CustPosIterInterf extends PositionedIterator
{
  public String getString () throws SQLException;
  public int getInt () throws SQLException;
}
```

```
#sql iterator cpi implements CustPosIterInterf (String, int,
date);
```

The following instruction declares a connection context class that implements an interface named MyConnCtxtIntfc:

```
#sql public context MyContext implements
mypackage.MyConnCtxtIntfc;
```

Positioned Update/Delete Iterators

The current row of a result set can be updated or deleted using a positioned update (i.e., UPDATE ... WHERE CURRENT OF ...) or a positioned delete (i.e., DELETE ... WHERE CURRENT OF ...) statement that references the cursor name.

In Oracle Database 10*g* Release 2 (10.2), SQLJ supports positioned update and positioned delete operations; any type of iterator (a named, positional, or scrollable), which implements the `sqlj.runtime.ForUpdate` interface, can be used as a parameter to the WHERE CURRENT OF clause.

```
import sqlj.runtime.ForUpdate;
#sql iterator PUpdateIter implements ForUpdate
                              (int EMPNO, String ENAME);
PUpdateIter    pit;
#sql { UPDATE emp WHERE CURRENT OF :pit SET SAL = SAL * 1.2 }
;


#sql { DELETE FROM emp WHERE CURRENT OF :c };
```

However, the following restrictions apply on the iterators in question:

- The query used to populate the iterator should not operate on multiple tables.

- A PL/SQL procedure returning a REF CURSOR cannot be used with the iterator.

- The iterator cannot interoperate with a JDBC ResultSet; in other words, the iterator cannot be populated with data from a result set as follows:

```
    #sql iter = {cast :rs}
```

II.I.6 WITH Clause in Context Declarations

```
#sql <modifiers> context context_classname with
(var1=value1,..., varN=valueN);
```

Use the WITH clause to set values for fields in SQLJ-generated classes during connection context declaration that can be used later in host expressions.

```
#sql static context Ctx with (ENAME="SMITH");
#sql { SELECT sal INTO :sal FROM emp WHERE ename =
:(Ctx.ENAME) };
```

Similarly, during iterator declaration, you can use the WITH clause to set values for the fields in the SQLJ-generated classes:

```
#sql static iterator Iter with (SAL=3402) (String ename,
BigDecimal sal);
```

A predefined set of standard SQLJ constants can be defined in the WITH clause; however, the Oracle SQLJ implementation does not currently support all of these. Here is a description of supported versus unsupported constants.

Supported SQLJ Constants in WITH Clause

The Oracle SQLJ supports the following standard constants in connection context declarations:

- typeMap: A String literal defining the name of a type-map properties resource

  The Oracle SQLJ also supports the use of typeMap in iterator declarations, as follows:

  ```
  #sql iterator MyIterator with
       (typeMap="MyTypeMap") (Person pers, Address addr);
  ```

  In Oracle-specific code, the iterator and connection context declarations must use the same type maps.

- dataSource: A String literal defining the name under which a data-source is looked up in the InitialContext (covered previously)

It also supports the following standard constants in iterator declarations:

- sensitivity: SENSITIVE/ASENSITIVE/INSENSITIVE, to define the sensitivity of a scrollable iterator (covered previously)
- returnability: true/false, to define whether an iterator can be returned from a Java stored procedure or function

```
#sql iterator Iter2 with (returnability=false) (String s);
```

Unsupported SQLJ Constants in WITH Clause

The Oracle SQLJ does *not* support the following standard constants in connection context declarations:

- `path`: The name of a path (`String` literal) to be prepended for resolving Java stored procedures and functions
- `transformGroup`: The name of a SQL transformation group (`String` literal) that can be applied to SQL types

Nor does it support the following standard constants, involving cursor states, in iterator declarations:

- `holdability`: `Boolean`, determines SQL cursor holdability; the cursor can then be continued in the next transaction of the same SQL session.
- `updateColumns`: A comma-delimited list (a `String` literal) of column names. A `with` clause that specifies `updateColumns` must also have an `implements` clause for the `sqlj.runtime.ForUpdate` interface. The Oracle SQLJ implementation enforces this, even though `updateColumns` is currently unsupported. See the following syntax:

```
#sql iterator iter1 implements sqlj.runtime.ForUpdate
        with (updateColumns="ename, empno")
            (int empno, String ename);
```

11.2 Executable Statements

SQLJ executable statements are the most illustrative part of SQLJ simplicity (i.e., embedding SQL in Java). Executable statements must observe the following rules:

- Contain an optional SQLJ space where connection and execution contexts are explicitly specified
- Contain valid Java block statements wherever permitted
- Embed a SQL operation enclosed in curly braces: `{...}`; this is also called the SQL space
- Be terminated by a semicolon (;)

Executable statements can be grouped into two categories: *Statement clauses* and *Assignment clauses*.

11.2.1 Statement Clauses

The generic syntax of a statement clause is as follows:

```
#sql [optional SQLJ space] { Statement clause };
```

Statement clauses comprise SELECT INTO clause, FETCH clause, COMMIT clause, ROLLBACK clause, SAVEPOINT clause, SET TRANSACTION clause, Procedure clause, SQL clause, and PL/SQL clause.

SELECT INTO Clause

The SELECT clause includes valid query operations, which return exactly a single row into OUT Java host expressions (returning zero or several rows will throw an exception).

As you can see, the host expressions (covered in Chapter 12) are declared as :OUT parameters:

```
#sql { SELECT column_name1, column_name2
INTO :OUT host_exp1, :OUT host_exp2
FROM table WHERE condition };
```

However, it is a general practice to omit the :OUT qualifier because this is implied (using IN, IN/OUT qualifier for a SELECT INTO will throw an exception).

```
#sql { SELECT column_name1, column_name2
INTO host_exp1,  host_exp2
FROM table WHERE condition };
```

Examples:

```
int no;
int pay;
    #sql { SELECT empno, sal INTO :no, :pay
            FROM emp WHERE ename = 'SMITH' } ;
```

```
int count;
#sql { SELECT COUNT(*) INTO    :count  FROM    EMP };
```

FETCH Clause

The FETCH clause designates the operations of fetching data from a positional iterator (iterators are covered later).

```
#sql positer = { SELECT empno, sal FROM EMP
                   WHERE ENAME = 'SMITH' OR EMPNO = 7788 ORDER
                   BY EMPNO
               };
while (true) {
   #sql { FETCH :positer INTO :empno, :sal };
   if (positer.endFetch()) break;
   System.out.println("empno = " + empno + ", sal = " + sal);
}
positer.close();
```

COMMIT or ROLLBACK Clause

The JDBC semantics for manual COMMIT/ROLLBACK (i.e., for DML when auto-commit is disabled) apply here.

```
#sql { COMMIT };
#sql { ROLLBACK};
```

Note that COMMIT and ROLLBACK operations do *not impact* open result sets and iterators (unless the iterator sensitivity is set to SENSITIVE).

SAVEPOINT Clause

The SAVEPOINT clause designates the ISO SQLJ SAVEPOINT syntax and the Oracle SQLJ SAVEPOINT syntax.

The ISO SQLJ SAVEPOINT syntax takes string literals. As seen previously, execution context store savepoint and furnish methods, which parallel the following methods:

```
#sql { SAVEPOINT savepoint1 };
#sql { ROLLBACK TO savepoint1 };
#sql { RELEASE SAVEPOINT savepoint1 };
```

The Oracle SAVEPOINT syntax differs from the ISO SAVEPOINT in three ways: it takes string variables instead of string literals; it uses SET SAVEPOINT instead of SAVEPOINT; and it uses RELEASE instead of RELEASE SAVEPOINT.

```
#sql { SET SAVEPOINT :savepoint };
#sql { ROLLBACK TO :savepoint };
#sql { RELEASE :savepoint };
```

SET TRANSACTION Clause

The SET TRANSACTION clause allows setting the access mode and/or the isolation level. Like JDBC, the SET TRANSACTION instruction must be the first statement preceding any DML statements.

Syntax:

```
#sql { SET TRANSACTION <access_mode>, <ISOLATION LEVEL
isolation_level> };
#sql [context] { SET TRANSACTION <access_mode>,
                  <ISOLATION LEVEL isolation_level> };
```

- When the connection context is not specified, the setting applies to the default context.

- The access mode can take two values: READ ONLY or READ WRITE.

    - READ ONLY: SELECT is allowed, but DML (i.e., INSERT, UPDATE, DELETE, and SELECT FOR UPDATE) are not.
    - READ WRITE (default): SELECT and DML are allowed.

- The SQLJ transaction isolation levels are semantically identical to the JDBC transaction isolation levels covered in Chapter 9 (see following examples).

Examples:

```
#sql { SET TRANSACTION READ WRITE };
#sql { SET TRANSACTION READ ONLY};

#sql { SET TRANSACTION ISOLATION LEVEL SERIALIZABLE };
#sql [Ctxt] { SET TRANSACTION ISOLATION LEVEL SERIALIZABLE };
#sql { SET TRANSACTION READ WRITE, ISOLATION LEVEL
SERIALIZABLE };
```

```
#sql { SET TRANSACTION ISOLATION LEVEL READ COMMITTED READ
ONLY};
#sql { SET TRANSACTION ISOLATION LEVEL READ COMMITTED, READ
WRITE };

#sql {SET TRANSACTION READ ONLY,ISOLATION LEVEL READ
UNCOMMITTED};
#sql {SET TRANSACTION READ WRITE,ISOLATION LEVEL READ
UNCOMMITTED};
```

Procedure Clause

The procedure clause is used for calling a stored procedure (PL/SQL, Java, or SQLJ). You can think of it as JDBC `CallableStatement/OracleCall-ableStatement` made simple, and here is the syntax:

```
#sql { CALL PROC(<PARAM_LIST>) };
```

Assume we have a basic (and stupid) Java stored procedure that returns the database date (I told you it's stupid!) as out parameter.

Here is the SQLJ code fragment:

```
java.sql.Date x;
#sql { CALL basicproc(:out x) };
System.out.println(" The Database Current date is " +
x.toString());
```

The complete code and script is shown in Listing 11.2.

```
basicProc.sql
=============
create or replace and resolve java source named basicproc as
import java.sql.Date;
public class basicProc {
  public static void foo(Date d[]) {
  d[0] = new java.sql.Date(System.currentTimeMillis());;
  }
}
/
```

```
create or replace procedure basicproc(d OUT DATE) as language java
name 'basicProc.foo(java.sql.Date[])';
/
```

```
connect.properties
===================
# Users should uncomment one of the following URLs or add their own.
# (If using Thin, edit as appropriate.)
#sqlj.url=jdbc:oracle:thin:@localhost:1521:inst1
sqlj.url=jdbc:oracle:thin:@inst1
#sqlj.url=jdbc:oracle:oci8:@
#sqlj.url=jdbc:oracle:oci7:@

# User name and password here (edit to use different user/password)
sqlj.user=scott
sqlj.password=tiger
```

Listing 11.2   *basicProc.sqlj*
```
=============================
```

```
import sqlj.runtime.ref.*;
import oracle.sqlj.runtime.*;
import java.sql.*;
public class basicProc
{
  public static void main(String[] args)
  {
    try
    {
      Oracle.connect(basicProc.class, "connect.properties");
      java.sql.Date x;
      #sql { CALL basicproc(:out x) };
      System.out.println("The Database Current date is " +
x.toString());
    }
    catch (java.sql.SQLException sqlex)
    {
      sqlex.printStackTrace();
      System.out.println(sqlex);
    }
  }
}
```

```
$ sqlj basicProc.sqlj
$ java -Doracle.net.tns_admin=$TNS_ADMIN basicProc
The Database Current date is 2006-01-04
$
```

SQL Clause

The SQL clause refers to embedding valid DML statements (i.e., UPDATE, INSERT, and DELETE). Combine this with the SELECT clause, and you can get a feel for the simplicity, in its whole simplicity: no Statement/OracleStatement or PreparedStatement/OraclePreparedStatement or the like.

```
#sql { INSERT INTO TAB1 VALUES (PMTS','Kenneth',12,'Parker',NULL) };
#sql { INSERT INTO TAB2 SELECT * FROM TAB1 } ;
// A more comprehensive code fragment
#sql public static context ConCtx;
...
ctx = new ConCtx(getConnect());
...
int count = 0;
#sql [ctx] { SELECT count(*) into :count FROM Tab1 };

// Add 100 more rows
for (int i = 0; i < 100; i++) {
#sql [ctx] { INSERT INTO Tab1 values(:(i+count)) };


#sql { UPDATE EMP SET ENAME = 'Joe Bloe' WHERE EMPNO = 7788 };
#sql [ctx] { UPDATE EMP SET SAL=4500.0 WHERE EMPNO = 7788 } ;
```

PL/SQL Clause

The PL/SQL clause consists of using anonymous PL/SQL blocks such as BEGIN...END, or DECLARE ... BEGIN ... END, within SQLJ statements.

```
// Example #1
char name ;
#sql { BEGIN SELECT ename INTO :out name FROM emp
           WHERE ename='KING'; END; };
System.out.printlm("Name: " + name);
```

```
// Example #2
String pay;
#sql { BEGIN EXECUTE IMMEDIATE
        :("update emp set sal=3500 where ename='KING'"); END;
};
    #sql { SELECT sal into :pay FROM emp WHERE ename='KING' };

// Example #3

    a = 0;
    b = 0;
    c = 0;

    #sql
    {
      BEGIN
        :OUT a := 45345;
        :OUT b := 676;
        :OUT c := 9999;
      END;
    };

    System.out.println("a = " + a + ", b = " + b + ", c = "
+ c + "."  );
```

This is a very powerful technique. If you are familiar with PL/SQL, you can use this technique as a smooth transition to database programming with Java; JDBC might be a little bit intimidating. If you are unfamiliar, you can still use this same technique as a wrapper to anonymous PL/SQL block, provided you know what this block is doing.

11.2.2 Assignment Clauses

Assignment clauses comprise: Query clause, Function clause, and Iterator conversion clause.

Query Clause

The query clause consists of selecting data into a SQLJ iterator, covered in section 11.2.1.

```
#sql iter = { SQLJ clause };
```

```
#sql [conctx, exectx]  iter = { SQLJ clause };
```

Function Clause

A function clause is used for calling a stored function. The standard syntax is shown as follows:

```
#sql result = { VALUES (<Function> (<paramlist>))};
```

The Oracle-SQLJ also supports the following alternative syntax:

```
#sql result = { VALUES <Function> (<paramlist>)};
```

Assume a stored function, which is a modified version of the basic Java stored procedure (just for the sake of calling a function from SQLJ):

```
SQL> create or replace and resolve java source named basicfunc as
  2  import java.sql.Date;
  3  public class basicFunc {
  4
  5    public static String foo(Date d) {
  6      return d.toString();
  7    }
  8  }
  9  /

Java created.

SQL>
SQL> create or replace function basicfunc(d DATE) return VARCHAR2 as
language java
  2  name 'basicFunc.foo(java.sql.Date) return java.lang.String';
  3  /

Function created.
```

In SQL*Plus you invoke the function as follows:

```
SQL> select basicfunc(sysdate) from dual;
```

```
BASICFUNC(SYSDATE)

-----------------------------------------

2006-01-04


SQL>
```

Here is the equivalent SQLJ code fragment:

```
java.sql.Date x = new
java.sql.Date(System.currentTimeMillis());
#sql datstr = { VALUES basicfunc(:x) };
System.out.println(" The Curent  date is " + datstr);
```

The complete code and script are shown in Listing 11.3.

```
connect.properties
===========
# Users should uncomment one of the following URLs or add their own.
# (If using Thin, edit as appropriate.)
#sqlj.url=jdbc:oracle:thin:@localhost:1521:inst1
sqlj.url=jdbc:oracle:thin:@inst1
#sqlj.url=jdbc:oracle:oci8:@
#sqlj.url=jdbc:oracle:oci7:@

# User name and password here (edit to use different user/password)
sqlj.user=scott
sqlj.password=tiger
```

Listing 11.3   *basicFunc.sqlj*
```
===============================

import sqlj.runtime.ref.*;
import oracle.sqlj.runtime.*;

import java.sql.*;
public class basicFunc
{
   public static void main(String[] args)
    {
```

```
     try
     {
       Oracle.connect(basicFunc.class, "connect.properties");
       String datstr;
       java.sql.Date x = new java.sql.Date(System.currentTimeMillis());
       #sql datstr = { VALUES basicfunc(:IN x) };
       System.out.println("The System Curent date is " + datstr);
     }
     catch (java.sql.SQLException sqlex)
     {
       sqlex.printStackTrace();
       System.out.println(sqlex);
     }
   }
 }
$ sqlj basicFunc.sqlj
$ java -Doracle.net.tns_admin=$TNS_ADMIN basicFunc
The System Curent date is 2006-01-04
$
```

Iterator Conversion Clause

The iterator conversion clause consists of converting a JDBC result set into an iterator using the CAST operator:

```
   #sql iter = { CAST :rset };
```

Ths simple statement performs the following operations:

- Binds the JDBC result set object (i.e., rset) into the SQLJ executable statement
- Converts the result set
- Populates the SQLJ iterator (i.e., iter) with the result set data

This is yet another illustration of SQLJ conciseness.

11.2.3 Dynamic SQL

Even though the SQLJ specification only supports static SQL statements, the Oracle implementation allows dynamic SQL expressions that are only fully defined at runtime, avoiding the obligation to switch to JDBC for dynamic SQL operations. The dynamic expressions replace parts of the SQL expression, which is fully materialized only at runtime.

Meta Bind Expressions

The dynamic expressions are called meta bind expressions. These are Java `Strings`, or `String`-valued Java expressions, optionally appended with a constant or static SQL expression, which is used during translation for syntax and semantics checking.

```
:{ Java_bind_expression }
```

or:

```
:{ Java_bind_expression :: SQL_replacement_code }
```

Meta bind expressions may be used as substitutes for the following:[1]

- Table name:

```
int x = 10;
int y = x + 10;
int z = y + 10;
String table = "new_Dept";
#sql { INSERT INTO :{table :: dept} VALUES (:x, :y, :z) };
```

At translation time, using the static replacement code, it will become:
```
INSERT INTO dept VALUES (10, 20, 30);
```

At runtime it will be evaluated as:
```
INSERT INTO new_Dept VALUES (10, 20, 30);
```

- All or part of a WHERE clause condition:

```
String table = "new_Emp";
String query = "ename LIKE 'S%' AND sal>1000";
#sql myIter = { SELECT * FROM :{table :: emp2}
                    WHERE :{query :: ename='SCOTT'} };
```

---

1.   All examples come from the Oracle SQLJ 10g Release 2 documentation.

At translation time, using the static replacement code, it becomes:

```
SELECT * FROM emp2 WHERE ename='SCOTT';
```

At runtime, it becomes:

```
SELECT * FROM new_Emp WHERE ename LIKE 'S%' AND sal>1000;
```

- Column name in a SELECT statement (without the column alias, if specified):

```
double raise = 1.12;
String col = "comm";
String whereQuery = "WHERE "+col+" IS NOT null";
for (int i=0; i<5; i++)
{
    #sql { UPDATE :{"emp"+i :: emp}
           SET :{col :: sal} = :{col :: sal} * :raise
:{whereQuery ::} };
}
```

At translation time, using the static replacement code, it becomes:

```
UPDATE emp SET sal = sal * 1.12;
```

At runtime it becomes (with the for loop):

```
UPDATE emp0 SET comm = comm * 1.12 WHERE comm IS NOT null;
UPDATE emp1 SET comm = comm * 1.12 WHERE comm IS NOT null;
UPDATE emp2 SET comm = comm * 1.12 WHERE comm IS NOT null;
UPDATE emp3 SET comm = comm * 1.12 WHERE comm IS NOT null;
UPDATE emp4 SET comm = comm * 1.12 WHERE comm IS NOT null;
```

- Role, schema, catalog, or package name in a data definition language (DDL) or DML statement
- SQL literal value or SQL expression

However, in order for the SQLJ translator to figure out the nature of the SQL operation and perform syntactic analysis of the SQLJ statement, the following restrictions apply:

- A meta bind expression cannot be the first noncomment of the SQLJ clause.

- A meta bind expression cannot contain the INTO token of a SQLJ SELECT INTO statement and cannot expand to become the INTO-list of a SELECT INTO statement.

- A meta bind expression cannot appear in CALL, VALUES, SET, COMMIT, ROLLBACK, FETCH INTO, or CAST.

Other Dynamic SQL Mechanisms

In the previous descriptions, we've embedded the meta bind expressions directly into the SQL clause that is submitted to the SQL Translator; this is the usual way. You may also use anonymous PL/SQL block and JDBC for implementing dynamic SQL.

- Anonymous PL/SQL block:

```
//
#sql { begin
        execute immediate
                'insert into ' || :table_name ||
                '(ename, empno, sal) values( :1, :2, :3)'
        using :ename, :empno, :sal;
        end;
};
```

- Dynamic SQL in JDBC:

```
String stmt = "select count(*) from " + table;
PreparedStatement ps =
DefaultContext.getDefaultContext().getConnection().prepareSta
tement(stmt);
        ResultSet rs = ps.executeQuery();
        rs.next();
        count = rs.getInt(1);
        rs.close();
        ps.close();
```

11.3 Expressions in SQLJ

SQLJ lets you exploit Java expressions in SQLJ statements; this section details host expressions, context expressions, and result expressions. Here is the generic syntax:

```
#sql [connctxt_exp, execctxt_exp] result_exp =
            { SQL with host expression };
```

Host Variables

In SQLJ, host variables are Java variables prefixed by a colon (i.e., " :") and optionally coupled with the usage mode (i.e., :IN, :OUT, :INOUT, the default mode is OUT).

Examples:
```
//
int hvar;
#sql { SELECT 3 INTO :hvar FROM dual };

//
BigDecimal bdvar = new BigDecimal(8);
#sql bdvar = { VALUES(Fn(:IN bdvar, :OUT bdvar, :INOUT bdvar)
};
```

Note: A simple host variable can appear multiple times in the same SQLJ statement provided these are all input variables, or at least one of these occurrences is an output variable in a stored procedure/function call, SET statement, or INTO-list. By default, Oracle SQLJ creates a unique name for each reference of the variable; however, the -bind-by-identifier flag when set to true allows SQLJ to evaluate all occurences of the same host variable to the same value.

```
//
int raise = 250;
#sql { UPDATE EMP SET SAL = SAL + :raise WHERE ENAME = 'KING' };
```

```
//
class BaseClass
{
   static class Inner
   {
         static BigDecimal bdvar = null;
   }
   public void run() {}
   static public int i = 1;
}


public class SubClass extends BaseClass
{
   int j = 2;
   public void run()
   {
     BigDecimal bdvar = null;
     try {
         #sql { select  sal into :bdvar from emp where ENAME='KING' };
         #sql { select  sal into :(Inner.bdvar) from emp where ENAME='KING' };
         System.out.println("sal is : " + Inner.bdvar);
     } catch (SQLException e) {
       e.printStackTrace();
     }
    System.out.println("bdvar is " + bdvar);
   }
   private int l = 0;
}
```

Host Expressions

More general and more versatile than host variables, SQLJ host expressions let you use any valid Java expressions, including simple Java host variables, simple Java class field values, simple Java array elements, complex Java arithmetic expressions, Java method calls with return values, Java conditional expressions (a ? b : c), Java logical expressions, and Java bitwise expressions. Host expressions can be used in lieu of host variables, within the curly braces of a SQLJ executable statement (i.e., within the SQL space) either as OUT parameter (the default), or IN parameter, or INOUT parameter.

Host expressions are specified by enclosing them within ":(" and and ")"; optionally coupled with the mode: ":IN(" or ":OUT(" or ":INOUT(".

Examples (code fragments):

```
BigDecimal hvar;
static final double d = 0.0;
int instanceMeth(int a, int b){return 1;}
static int staticMeth(int a, int b) {return 2;}

// arithmetic  expressions (assume variable i, j, and k)
#sql { set :hvar = :(1/i) };
#sql { select :(0) from dual };
#sql { select :(i+j*k) from dual into :(m) };
#sql { select :(x[1].j[0] += -33 ) from dual };
#sql { select :( -2.71f) from dual into :(y) };
#sql { SELECT :(j+=i) into :k from dual};
#sql { select :(j + i ) from dual into :(i) };
//
public static final int FOO = 111 * 4 + 666 / 2;
#sql { select :(111 * 4 + 666 / 2) from dual into :FOO};
//
#sql {set :hvar = :(1/(true?0:3)) }; // conditional
expression
#sql {set :hvar = :(staticMeth(1, 2)) }; // ref to static
method
#sql {set :hvar = :(instanceMeth(1, 2)) }; // ref to instance
method
#sql { select :(fib(n-1)) + :(fib(n-2)) into :res from dual };

 int salary = -32;
 #sql { SELECT SAL into :salary from emp where EMPNO = 7788 };
 System.out.println("Salary = " + salary );
```

11.3.1 Context and Result Expressions

Unlike host expressions, which are used in the SQL space (i.e., within the curly braces), connection context expressions, execution context expressions, and result expressions are used in the SQLJ space, meaning outside the curly braces.

Context Expressions

A context expression is a valid Java expression, including local variables, declared parameters, class fields, and array elements, that defines the name of a connection context instance or an execution context instance.

```
#sql [context_array[thread]]  result = {
VALUES(foo(:bar,:baz)) };
```

Code fragment:

```
#sql context myCtx;
#sql iterator myCurs (Double sal, int ename, String ename);
// array of connection context
myCtx [] ctx — new myCtx[2];
ctx[0] = new Ctx(getConnect());
// get an instance of iterator
myCurs [] c = new myCurs[ 2 ];
#sql [ctx[0]] c[0] = { SELECT SAL, EMPNO, ENAME FROM EMP
WHERE EMPNO = 7788 };
```

Result Expressions

A result expression is any legal Java expression, including local variables, declared parameters, class fields, and array elements, that can receive query results or function return (i.e., appears on the left side of an equals sign).

```
#sql [context]  result_array[i] = { VALUES(foo(:bar,:baz)) };
```

Code fragment:

```
#sql context myCtx;
#sql iterator myCurs (Double sal, int ename, String ename);

myCtx ctx = new Ctx(getConnect());
// array of iterator instances
myCurs [] c = new myCurs[ 2 ];
#sql [ctx] c[0] = { SELECT SAL, EMPNO, ENAME FROM EMP WHERE
EMPNO = 7788 };
```

11.3.2   **Expressions Evaluation**

Unlike PL/SQL, where host espressions are all evaluated together in the order of their appearance before any statements within the block are executed, host expressions in SQLJ are evaluated by Java from left to right, once and only once, before being sent to SQL. Upon execution, the OUT and INOUT host expressions are assigned values in order from left to right, and then result expressions are assigned values last.

For standard ISO-SQLJ code, the following rules apply:

- Connection context expressions are evaluated immediately, before any other Java expressions.

- Execution context expressions are evaluated after connection context expressions, but before result expressions.

- Result expressions are evaluated after context expressions, but before host expressions.

11.4   **Interoperability: Using SQLJ and JDBC Together**

Chapter 10 introduced SQLJ as JDBC made simpler; however, because these API come from different standard bodies (JCP versus ISO), SQLJ does not support every JDBC features and vice versa. The good news is that you can mix the two APIs within the same application. This section briefly covers interoperability in terms of connection (i.e., how to use JDBC connection in SQLJ, how to use SQLJ connection context with JDBC) and also in terms of data retrieval (i.e., converting JDBC Result Set into SQLJ iterators and converting SQLJ iterators into JDBC ResultSet).

11.4.1   **JDBC to SQLJ Interoperability**

Listing 11.4 illustrates using JDBC connection as SQLJ connection context and converting JDBC Result Set into SQLJ Named Iterator.

Note: You should access the iterator only; avoid retrieving data from the result set, either before or after the conversion. Upon completion, close the iterator, not the result set.

Listing 11.4 *Jdbc2Sqlj.sqlj*

```
=============================
import sqlj.runtime.ref.DefaultContext;
import java.sql.*;
import oracle.sqlj.runtime.*;
import oracle.jdbc.pool.OracleDataSource;

public class Jdbc2Sqlj
{
  #sql static public iterator NameIter (double sal, int empno);

 public static void main(String[] args) throws java.sql.SQLException
 {
   try {
     // Create an OracleDataSource
     OracleDataSource ods = new OracleDataSource();
     // Set the URL, using TNS Alias with JDBC-Thin
     String url = "jdbc:oracle:thin:scott/tiger@inst1";
     ods.setURL(url);
     Connection conn = ods.getConnection(); // Retrieve a connection
     conn.setAutoCommit(false); // Disable Auto Commit
     DefaultContext.setDefaultContext(new DefaultContext(conn));
      PreparedStatement s =
DefaultContext.getDefaultContext().getConnection().prepareCall
        ("UPDATE EMP SET SAL = 4350 WHERE EMPNO = 7788");
     s.executeUpdate();
     s.close();


     s =
DefaultContext.getDefaultContext().getConnection().prepareCall
        ("SELECT SAL, EMPNO  FROM EMP WHERE EMPNO = 7788");
     ResultSet rs = s.executeQuery();
     NameIter niter;
     #sql niter = { CAST :rs };
     while (niter.next()) {
        System.out.println("SAL = " + niter.sal() + ", EMPNO = " +
niter.empno());
      }
     s.close();
     niter.close();
```

```
        } catch (SQLException e) {
            e.printStackTrace();
        }
    }
}
$sqlj Jdbc2Sqlj.sqlj
$java -Doracle.net.tns_admin=$TNS_ADMIN Jdbc2Sqlj
SAL = 4350.0, EMPNO = 7788
$
```

Leveraging Oracle JDBC Connection Services

As we have seen when discussing JDBC, the Oracle JDBC brings extraordinary connection services in RAC/Grid environments, including implicit connection caching, fast connection fail-over, and runtime connection load balancing. SQLJ can benefit from all of these by just delegating connection concerns to JDBC. Listing 11.5 illustrates this point:

Listing 11.5   *myInterop.sqlj*

```
================================

import sqlj.runtime.ref.DefaultContext;
import java.sql.*;
import oracle.sqlj.runtime.*;
import oracle.jdbc.pool.OracleDataSource;

public class myInterop
{
 public static void main(String[] args) throws java.sql.SQLException
 {
    try {
      // Create an OracleDataSource
      OracleDataSource ods = new OracleDataSource();

      // Set the URL, using TNS Alias with JDBC-Thin
      String url = "jdbc:oracle:thin:scott/tiger@inst1";
      ods.setURL(url);
      Connection conn = ods.getConnection(); // Retrieve a connection
      conn.setAutoCommit(false); // Disable Auto Commit

      // Create/Set SQLJ context from JDBC connection
      // From here let's speak SQLJ
```

```
        DefaultContext.setDefaultContext(new DefaultContext(conn));
        System.out.println("Create a dummy function.");
        #sql { CREATE OR REPLACE FUNCTION R(dummy integer) RETURN INTEGER AS
                i INTEGER;
              BEGIN
                    SELECT SAL INTO i FROM EMP WHERE ENAME = 'SMITH';
                    RETURN i;
              END; };

        int start_sal;
        #sql start_sal = { VALUE R(100) };
        System.out.println("Starting pay: " + start_sal );

        int raise = 300;
        #sql { UPDATE EMP SET SAL = SAL + :raise WHERE ENAME = 'SMITH' };
        System.out.println(" Giving Raise to  SMITH ");
        int end_sal;
        #sql end_sal = { VALUE R(100) };
        System.out.println("Ending pay: " + end_sal +
                        "  - Raise amt is "+ (end_sal-start_sal));
      conn.close();
    } catch (SQLException e) {
          e.printStackTrace();
    }
   }
  }
}
```

```
$ sqlj myInterop.sqlj
$ java -Doracle.net.tns_admin=$TNS_ADMIN myInterop
Create a dummy function.
Starting pay: 800
Giving Raise to SMITH
Ending pay: 1100  - Raise amt is 300
$
```

11.4.2   SQLJ to JDBC Interoperability

Remember that ResultSet Iterators are more suitable for conversion into JDBC Result Set. Listing 11.6 illustrates using SQLJ connection context with JDBC and converting SQLJ iterator into JDBC Result Set:

Listing 11.6 *Sqlj2Jdbc.sqlj*

```
================================

import sqlj.runtime.ref.DefaultContext;
import java.sql.SQLException;
import java.sql.PreparedStatement;
import java.sql.ResultSet;
import oracle.sqlj.runtime.*;

public class Sqlj2Jdbc
{

  public static void main(String[] args) throws java.sql.SQLException
  {
    try {
    java.sql.ResultSet rs;
    sqlj.runtime.ResultSetIterator sri;

    Oracle.connect(Sqlj2Jdbc.class, "connect.properties");
    #sql sri = { SELECT ename, empno FROM EMP };
    rs = sri.getResultSet();
    while (rs.next())
    {
    System.out.println (" *** Emp Name: " + rs.getString(1) + I
                          " -- Emp #: " + rs.getInt(2));
    };
    sri.close();
    Oracle.close();
    } catch (SQLException e) {
      e.printStackTrace();
    }
  }
}


$ sqlj Sqlj2Jdbc.sqlj
$ java -Doracle.net.tns_admin=$TNS_ADMIN Sqlj2Jdbc
 *** Emp Name: SMITH -- Emp #: 7369
 *** Emp Name: ALLEN -- Emp #: 7499
 *** Emp Name: WARD -- Emp #: 7521
```

```
*** Emp Name: JONES -- Emp #: 7566
*** Emp Name: MARTIN -- Emp #: 7654
*** Emp Name: BLAKE -- Emp #: 7698
*** Emp Name: CLARK -- Emp #: 7782
*** Emp Name: SCOTT -- Emp #: 7788
*** Emp Name: KING -- Emp #: 7839
*** Emp Name: TURNER -- Emp #: 7844
*** Emp Name: ADAMS -- Emp #: 7876
*** Emp Name: JAMES -- Emp #: 7900
*** Emp Name: FORD -- Emp #: 7902
*** Emp Name: MILLER -- Emp #: 7934
$
```

The same technique can be used for converting Named and Positional iterators into JDBC Result Sets.

11.5 Conclusion

Now that we have seen the essential elements of a SQLJ program, let's tackle the last part of this abridged SQLJ coverage: SQL data access and manipulation using SQLJ, in the next chapter.

12

SQLJ Data Access and Best Practices

In this chapter, we'll look at Oracle SQL data manipulation using SQLJ and then best practices with SQLJ.

12.1 Manipulating Oracle SQL and PL/SQL Data Types with SQLJ

SQL and PL/SQL data are manipulated in SQLJ through SQLJ host variables/expressions, result expressions, and iterator accessors. This section explains the SQLJ mechanisms to manipulate SQL data, using frequent references to the corresponding sections in Chapter 8.

12.1.1 Oracle SQLJ Type-Mapping Summary

Because Oracle SQLJ leverages the Oracle JDBC drivers and its wrapper classes, the mapping of SQL data types in SQLJ is almost identical to JDBC mapping, as summarized in Table 3.2. However, there are additional SQLJ-specific mappings. See Table 12.1, which summarizes the SQLJ type mapping.

Table 12.1 *SQLJ Type Mapping*

Oracle SQL Data Types	Standard Java and ISO SQLJ Mapping	Oracle SQLJ Extended Mapping
CHAR, CHARACTER, LONG, STRING, VARCHAR, VARCHAR2	java.lang.String, java.sql.Date, java.sql.Time, java.sql.Timestamp, java.lang.Byte, java.lang.Short, java.lang.Integer, java.lang.Long, java.sql.Float, java.lang.Double, java.math.BigDecimal, byte, short, int, long, float, double	oracle.sql.CHAR

Table 12.1   *SQLJ Type Mapping (continued)*

Oracle SQL Data Types	Standard Java and ISO SQLJ Mapping	Oracle SQLJ Extended Mapping
Globalization LONG, NCHAR, NVARCHAR2	n/a	oracle.sql.NCHAR (see note 1) oracle.sqlj.runtime.Nchar CharacterStream oracle.sqlj.runtime.Nchar AsciiStream (Deprecated; use NcharCharacterStream) oracle.sqlj.runtime.Nchar UnicodeStream (Deprecated; use NcharCharacterStream)
NUMBER, DEC, DECIMAL, NUMERIC	java.lang.Byte, java.lang.Short, java.lang.Integer, java.lang.Long, java.sql.Float, java.lang.Double, java.math.BigDecimal, byte, short, int, long, float, double	oracle.sql.NUMBER
DOUBLE PRECISION, FLOAT	double, java.lang.Double	oracle.sql.NUMBER
SMALLINT	short, int, java.lang.Integer	oracle.sql.NUMBER
REAL	float, java.sql.Float	oracle.sql.NUMBER
DATE	java.sql.Date, java.sql.Time, java.sql.Timestamp, java.lang.String	oracle.sql.DATE
TIMESTAMP TIMESTAMP WITH TZ TIMESTAMP WITH LOCAL TZ	java.sql.Date, java.sql.Time, java.sql.Timestamp, byte[]	oracle.sql.DATE, oracle.sql.TIMESTAMP oracle.sql.TIMESTAMPTZ oracle.sql.TIMESTAMPLTZ
RAW, LONG RAW	byte[]	oracle.sql.RAW
INTERVAL YEAR TO MONTH INTERVAL DAY TO SECOND	String (see note 2)	oracle.sql.INTERVALDS oracle.sql.INTERVALYM (see note 2)

Table 12.1   *SQLJ Type Mapping (continued)*

Oracle SQL Data Types	Standard Java and ISO SQLJ Mapping	Oracle SQLJ Extended Mapping
URITYPE DBURITYPE XDBURITYPE HTTPURITYPE	`java.net.URL` (see note 3)	
ROWID	`java.sql.String`	`oracle.sql.ROWID,` `oracle.sql.CHAR`
BOOLEAN	`boolean` (see note 4)	`boolean` (see note 4)
CLOB LOCATOR	`java.sql.Clob`	`oracle.sql.CLOB`
BLOB LOCATOR	`java.sql.Blob`	`oracle.sql.BLOB`
BFILE LOCATOR	`n/a`	`oracle.sql.BFILE`
NCLOB LOCATOR	`n/a`	`oracle.sql.NCLOB` (note 1)
SQLJ Streams		
LONG RAW	`sqlj.runtime.BinaryStream`	

LONG	`sqlj.runtime.CharacterStream`
	`sqlj.runtime.AsciiStream`
	(<u>Deprecated; use</u>
	<u>CharacterStream</u>.)
	`sqlj.runtime.UnicodeStream`
	(<u>Deprecated; use</u>
	<u>CharacterStream</u>.)	

User-defined objects types	`java.sql.Struct,` `java.sql.SqlData`	`oracle.sql.STRUCT,` `oracle.sql.ORAData`
User-defined collection	`java.sql.Array`	`oracle.sql.ARRAY,` `oracle.sql.ORAData`
OPAQUE types	`Generated or predefined` `class` (note 5)	`oracle.sql.OPAQUE`
RECORD types	`Through mapping to SQL` `object type` (note 5)	`Through mapping to SQL` `object type` (note 5)
Nested table, VARRAY	`java.sql.Array`	`oracle.sql.ARRAY,` `oracle.sql.ORAData`

Table 12.1   *SQLJ Type Mapping (continued)*

Oracle SQL Data Types	Standard Java and ISO SQLJ Mapping	Oracle SQLJ Extended Mapping

Reference to SQL object type	`java.sql.Ref`	`oracle.sql.REF,`
		`oracle.sql.SQLRef,`
		`oracle.sql.ORAData`

`REF CURSOR`	`java.sql.ResultSet`	`oracle.jdbc.OracleResultS` `et`
`Indexed-by tables`	Through mapping to SQL collection (see note 2)	Through mapping to SQL collection (see note 2)
`Scalar Indexed-by tables (numeric or character)`	Through mapping to java array (see note 2)	Through mapping to java array (see note 2)
`User-defined subtypes`	Same as base type	Same as base type
`Query Results Objects` `CURSOR`	SQLJ iterator objects	

Notes:

1. `oracle.sql.NCHAR,`   `oracle.sql.NCLOB,`   and   `oracle.sql.NString` are distributed with the SQLJ runtime to represent the NCHAR form of `oracle.sql.CHAR, oracle.sql.CLOB,` and `java.lang.String`.

2. See the JPublisher Type Map in Part III of this book.

3. See JPublisher: SQL URI types, also known as data links, are mapped to `java.net.URL`.

4. Mapping of PL/SQL BOOLEAN to SQL NUMBER and Java Boolean is defined in the default JPublisher type-map.

5. Java classes implementing the `oracle.sql.ORAData` interface

Also, here is a description of the EMP table in the SCOTT schema.

```
SQL> desc emp
 Name                                      Null?    Type
 ----------------------------------------- -------- ----------------------
 EMPNO                                     NOT NULL NUMBER(4)
```

ENAME	VARCHAR2(10)
JOB	VARCHAR2(9)
MGR	NUMBER(4)
HIREDATE	DATE
SAL	NUMBER(7,2)
COMM	NUMBER(7,2)
DEPTNO	NUMBER(2)

SQL>

12.1.2   Column Definitions

The Oracle SQLJ implementation leverages Oracle JDBC support for column type and size definitions.

Automatic Registration of Column Types and Sizes

When column definition is enabled, the Oracle SQLJ automatically registers OUT column types and sizes as follows:

- During translation (Oracle-specific code generation), SQLJ connects to a specified database schema to determine types and sizes of columns being retrieved.

- During ISO standard SQLJ code generation, customization of source code translation, or customization of an existing profile, the column defaults become part of the SQLJ profile.

- At runtime, the SQLJ runtime will use the column information to register the column types and sizes with the JDBC driver, using defineColumnType() method.

Enabling Column Definition

- For Oracle-specific code generation, use the SQLJ translator -optcols option. For ISO standard code generation, use either the translator option or the Oracle customizer option (-P-Coptcols on the SQLJ command line).

- Set the user, password, and URL for the database connection using either the user, password, and url options of the SQLJ translator or the -P-user, -P-password, and -P-url options of the customizer on the SQLJ command line.

■ If you are not using the default `OracleDriver` class, then set the JDBC driver class using `-P-driver` on the SQLJ command line.

12.1.3 Manipulating SQL Null Data with SQLJ

The discussion in Chapter 8 about the use of Java reference classes instead of primitive classes for handling `null` values also applies to SQLJ host and result expressions/variables.

```
// Using a Double variable to pass a null value to
// the database
int empno = 7499;
Double sal = null;

#sql { UPDATE emp SET sal = :sal WHERE empno = :empno };
```

A `sqlj.runtime.SQLNullException` is thrown when a null value is retrieved into a host Java primitive type. JDBC retrieves NULL as 0 or false, while SQLJ retrieves SQL NULL as Java null, which allows testing null consistently (e.g., if (host_var != null)) or if (iter.accessor_name != null)), as illustrated in Listing 12.1.

Listing 12.1   *testNull.sql*
=================================

```
import java.sql.*;
import sqlj.runtime.ref.*;
import oracle.sqlj.runtime.*;
import sqlj.runtime.SQLNullException;

public class  testNull
{
#sql static public iterator NamedIterRef (Double sal, String ename);
#sql static public iterator NamedIterPrim (double sal, String ename);

  public static void main(String[] args) throws java.sql.SQLException
  {
    try {
      Oracle.connect(testNull.class, "connect.properties");
      /*
```

```
           * Retrieve a NULL value into a Java reference typed accessor
           */
          NamedIterRef niterref;
          System.out.println("Retrieving null value with Java reference type");
          #sql niterref = {select NULL as sal, ename from emp where empno = 7788 };
          if (niterref.next()) {
            System.out.println
                ("Employee " + niterref.ename() + " earns " + niterref.sal());
          }
          niterref.close();


          /*
           * Retrieve NULL value into Java primitive type accessor
           */
          NamedIterPrim niterprim;
          System.out.println
        ("Retrieving null value with Java primitive type, must throw an
      exception");
          #sql niterprim = {select NULL as sal, ename from emp where empno = 7788
      };
          if (niterprim.next()) {
            System.out.println("Employee: " + niterprim.ename()  + " earns ..");
            try {
              System.out.println (" earns:" +  niterprim.sal());
             } catch (SQLNullException e) {
              System.out.println (" ...  well, null! Exception caught!");
             }
            }
          niterprim.close();


        } catch (java.sql.SQLException sqlex) {
          sqlex.printStackTrace();
          System.out.println(sqlex);
        }
      }
    }
  }
$ sqlj testNull.sqlj
$ java -Doracle.net.tns_admin=$TNS_ADMIN testNull


  Retrieving null value with Java reference type
  Employee SCOTT earns null
  Retrieving null value with Java primitive type, must throw an exception
```

```
Employee: SCOTT earns ..
... well, null! Exception caught!
$
```

12.1.4   Manipulating Character Data Types with SQLJ

CHAR, CHAR(n), CHAR(n BYTE), CHAR(n CHAR)
VARCHAR2 (n), VARCHAR2(n BYTE), VARCHAR2 (n CHAR)

Refer to Chapter 8 for a description of the SQL CHAR and VARCHAR2 types. As Table 12.1 indicates, SQL CHAR and VARCHAR2 columns can be mapped, among other possibilities, to and from Java String and oracle.sql.CHAR.

```
// Example #1
int num = 1331;
String name = "EMPLOYE";
#sql [ctx] { insert into  emp (empno, ename, hiredate, sal)
             values (:i, :(name+"_"+num), sysdate, 3500 )
           };

// Example #2
oracle.sql.CHAR   char_in = new CHAR("This is a CHAR", null);
oracle.sql.CHAR   char_out = null;
#sql { select :char_in INTO :char_out FROM dual };
```

Similar to JDBC, SQLJ does not support Java char types. The following code fragment, which declares the host variable ename as Java char, will fail and a "Java type char for column ename is illegal" exception will be thown.

```
char ename;
  #sql { SELECT ename INTO :ename FROM emp
               WHERE ename ='KING' };
```

Instead, the following code fragment, which maps a VARCHAR2 column (i.e., ename) to a Java String (the host variable is declared as Java String) will succeed.

```
String ename;
  #sql { SELECT ename INTO :ename FROM emp
               WHERE ename ='KING' };
```

SQLJ furnishes the `-fixedchar` option for `CHAR` comparisons in a `WHERE` clause. When set to `true`, `SQLJ` behaves like the JDBC `setFixed-CHAR()` method; during `WHERE` clause comparisons. This option works with both Oracle-specific and ISO standard code generations.

```
% sqlj -fixedchar MyProgram.sqlj ...
```

Notice that similar to JDBC, SQLJ treats zero-length strings (i.e., "") as `null`.

NCHAR, NCHAR(n), NVARCHAR2 (n)

The `oracle.sql.NString` class is a wrapper for `java.lang.String`, distributed with the SQLJ runtime, which ensures that the national language character form of use is registered with the JDBC driver. It furnishes the following methods:

- `NString(String)`: Creates an `NString` instance from an existing `String` instance.

- `String toString()`: Returns the underlying `String` instance; it enables you to use the `NString` instance in `String` concatenation expressions (such as `"a"+b`, where b is a string).

- `String getString()`: Returns the underlying `String` instance, similarly to `toString()`.

However, in order to use the `String` host variable to bind to `NCHAR` columns, you must translate the SQLJ file with the `-ncharconv` SQLJ translator option. Starting with Oracle Database 10g Release 2, Oracle SQLJ furnishes the `-ncharconv` option, which instructs the translator[1] to use the `SetFormOfUse` method to bind to `NCHAR` columns to `String` host variables.

```
% sqlj —ncharconv=true myNCHAR.sqlj
```

Then you can use the `String` variables to bind `NCHAR` columns, as follows:

---

1.   For codegen=iso, this option is passed to the Oracle SQLJ run time, which internally uses SetFormOfUse at run time.

```
...
String v_a = "\uFF5E";
String v_nb = "\uFF5E";
#sql {INSERT INTO Tbl1 (ColA, NColB) VALUES (:v_a, :v_nb)};
...
```

12.1.5   Oracle SQLJ Support for Number Data Types

NUMBER , NUMBER(p), NUMBER(p, s)

Refer to Chapter 8 for a description of SQL NUMBER. All numeric types in Oracle Database 10*g* are stored as NUMBER. Per Table 12.1, SQLJ can map SQL NUMBER to oracle.sql.NUMBER, Short, Integer, Long, short, int, long, and so on. However, mapping to types other than oracle.sql.NUMBER, you may lose the precision information during the mapping.

```
// Mapping SQL NUMBER to oracle.sql.NUMBER
oracle.sql.NUMBER com;
oracle.sql.NUMBER enum = new oracle.sql.NUMBER(7902);
#sql { SELECT COMM INTO :com FROM EMP WHERE EMPNO = :enum };

int rowNum = 2232
oracle.sql.NUMBER numb = new oracle.sql.NUMBER(rowNum/
1000.0));
#sql [ctx] {  INSERT INTO TAB VALUES (:numb)};

// Mapping SQL NUMBER to java.lang.Integer
java.lang.Integer sal;
#sql { select SAL into :sal from emp WHERE ENAME = 'SMITH' };
```

BINARY_FLOAT and BINARY_DOUBLE

Refer to Chapter 8 for a description of SQL BINARY_FLOAT and BINARY_DOUBLE. These types can be mapped, respectively, to oracle.sql.BINARY_FLOAT and oracle.sql.BINARY_DOUBLE.

Assume a binary_tab table with SQL BINARY_FLOAT and BINARY_DOUBLE columns. The following code fragment maps an oracle.sql.BINARY_FLOAT value and an oracle.sql.BINARY_FLOAT value to the corresponding SQL columns.

```
BINARY_FLOAT bf = new BINARY_FLOAT((float)789.669);
```

```
BINARY_DOUBLE bd = new BINARY_DOUBLE((double)897.9999);

#sql ( insert into binary_tab values(:bf, :bd)};
```

12.1.6   SQLJ Streams, LONG, and RAW Data Types

SQL RAW(s)

Refer to Chapter 8 for a description of SQL RAW data types. Similar to JDBC, the Oracle SQLJ can map SQL RAW to/from `oracle.sql.RAW` and Java `bytes[]`.

```
import oracle.sql.*;

...

byte[] bytearr = {
2,3,5,7,11,13,17,19,23,29,31,37,41,43,47,53,59,61 };
RAW oraw = new RAW(bytearr);

// Update a SQL RAW column withto oracle.sql.RAW data
#sql { update TypesTab set xraw = :oraw);

// Retrieve a SQL RAW column as oracle.sq.RAW
#sql oraw = {SELECT xraw FROM TypesTab};
```

LONG, LONG RAW

Refer to the corresponding JDBC section in Chapter 8 for a description of SQL LONG and SQL LONG RAW data. Similar to JDBC, SQLJ may map SQL LONG to `oracle.sql.RAW` or `java.lang.String`, and maps SQL LONG RAW to `oracle.sql.RAW`, or `byte[]`.

Basic Example:

```
byte[] buf = { 00, 01, 02, 03, 04, 05, 00, 01, 02, 03, 04, 05,
00, 01, 02, 03, 04, 05, 00, 01, 02, 03, 04, 05,
00, 01, 02, 03, 04, 05, 00, 01, 02, 03, 04, 05 };

#sql {INSET INTO raw_tab VALUES (:buf)};
```

However, as with JDBC, LONG and LONG RAW data types are by default (or most of the time) manipulated in SQLJ, in *streaming* mode, which is the topic of the next section.

SQLJ Streams

SQLJ supports binary and character streams through the `BinaryStream` and `CharacterStream` classes.

The `sqlj.runtime.BinaryStream` class allows mapping and streaming of binary streams, including LONG RAW and RAW data in SQLJ. It is a wrapper for an `InputStream`, which cannot be passed directly as a parameter to an executable SQL operation because of the need to specify its length and its interpretation; therefore, an instance of `BinaryStream` is passed instead.

```
public class sqlj.runtime.BinaryStream extends
sqlj.runtime.StreamWrapper
{    public sqlj.runtime.BinaryStream(java.io.InputStream);
     public sqlj.runtime.BinaryStream(java.io.InputStream,int);
     public java.io.InputStream getInputStream();
     public int getLength();
     public void setLength(int);
}
```

The `StreamWrapper` class extends `java.io.FilterInputStream` and provides the following methods:

- `InputStream getInputStream()`: Returns the underlying `java.io.InputStream` object.

- `void setLength(int length)`: Sets the length attribute of wrapped `InputStream` to the stream. Must be set before sending a SQLJ stream to the database because it controls the number of bytes read from the stream passed as an input parameter to an executable SQL operation.

- `int getLength()`: Returns the `length` in bytes of the wrapped `InputStream` (i.e., the `length` attribute of a SQLJ stream), only if the length has been explicitly set using the `setLength()` method (the `length` attribute is not set automatically).

The `java.io.FilterInputStream` class is a subclass of the `java.io.InputStream`, which furnishes the following methods to the SQLJ `BinaryStream` class:

- `int read ()`: Reads the next byte of data from the input stream; returns `-1` when it reaches the end of the stream.

- `int read (byte b[])`: Reads up to `b.length` bytes of data from the input into the specified `b[]` byte array.

- `int read (byte b[], int off, int len)`: Reads up to `len` bytes of data from the input stream, starting at the offset, `off`, and writing the data into the specified `b[]` byte array.

- `long skip (long n)`: Skips over and discards n bytes from the input stream; it returns the number of bytes actually skipped.

- `void close()`: Closes the stream and releases any associated resources.

The `sqlj.runtime.CharacterStream` class allows the manipulation of character streams in SQLJ (i.e., mapping of LONG and VARCHAR2 data). It is a wrapper for `java.io.FilterReader` and consequently for `java.io.Reader` object, which cannot be passed directly as an input parameter because of the need to specify its length; therefore, an instance of `CharacterStream` object is passed instead.

```
public class sqlj.runtime.CharacterStream extends
java.io.FilterReader
{   public sqlj.runtime.CharacterStream(java.io.Reader);
    public sqlj.runtime.CharacterStream(java.io.Reader,int);
    public int getLength();
    public java.io.Reader getReader();
    public void setLength(int);
}
```

The `java.io.Reader` class furnishes the following methods to the SQLJ `CharacterStream` class:

- `int read ()`: Reads the next character of data from the input stream; returns `-1` when it reaches the end of the stream.

- `int read (char cbuf[])`: Reads character data from the input stream into the the specified `cbuf[]` character array.

- `int read (char cbuf[], int off, int len)`: Reads up to `len` characters of data from the input stream, starting at the offset, `off`, into the specified `b[]` character array.

- ■ `long skip (long n)`: Skips over and discards n characters from the input stream; it returns the number of character actually skipped.

- ■ `void close()`: Closes the stream and releases any associated resources.

Let's see the SQLJ streams in action.

Using SQLJ Streams to Send and Retrieve Data to and from the Database

The following code sample illustrates binary SQLJ stream manipulation and performs the following operations:

1. Insert data into a `RAW` column: A `BinaryStream` is created from an `InputSream`, which is created from a `FileInputStream`, which is populated from a file.

2. Use a named iterator and a positional iterator to retrieve `String` and `RAW` column data from a table; then an `InputStream` is created from the `RAW` column and printed. (See Listing 12.2.)

```
bstream.dat
===========
$ cat bstream.dat
010203040506070809
$
```

```
myBStream.sql
=============
rem connect scott/tiger;
drop table BStreamTab ;
create table BStreamTab ( col1 number, rawcol raw(128)) ;
exit
```

Listing 12.2   *myBStream.sqlj*

```
================================
import java.sql.*;
import oracle.sqlj.runtime.*;
import sqlj.runtime.*;
import java.io.*;
```

```
import sqlj.runtime.ref.DefaultContext;

public class myBStream
{
#sql static public iterator NamedIter (String col1, BinaryStream
rawcol);
#sql static public iterator PosIter (int, BinaryStream);

  public static void main(String[] args) throws java.sql.SQLException
  {
   NamedIter nIter;
   PosIter pIter;
   try {
     Oracle.connect(testNull.class, "connect.properties");
      // Insert a row into a Binary Stream Table
      System.out.println
        ("Inserting data from bin stream file into a bin stream tab
...");
      File bsf = new File("bstream.dat");
      int size = (int)bsf.length();
      InputStream myfile = new FileInputStream(bsf);
      BinaryStream stream = new BinaryStream(myfile, size);
      #sql { insert into BStreamTab values (:size, :stream) };
      #sql { commit };
      System.out.println(" .... Done!");

      System.out.println("Retrieving data from bin stream tab ...");

      // Using the Named Iterator
      #sql nIter = { select * from BStreamTab };
      while (nIter.next()) {
        System.out.println ("col1: " + nIter.col1());
        printstream (nIter.rawcol().getInputStream());
      }
      int len1 = 0;
      BinaryStream bs1 = null;

      // Using the positional Iterator
      #sql pIter = { select * from BStreamTab };
      while ( true ) {
        #sql { fetch :pIter into :len1, :bs1 };
        if ( pIter.endFetch()) break;
```

```
        System.out.println( "size = " + len1 );
        printstream( bs1.getInputStream() );
      }


    }
    catch (FileNotFoundException ex)
    {
      ex.printStackTrace ();
    }
    catch (SQLException ex)
    {
      ex.printStackTrace ();
    }
  }


  static void printstream (InputStream s)
  {
    StringBuffer outbuf = new StringBuffer();

    try
    {
      int count;
      while ((count = s.read ()) != -1)
        outbuf.append((char)count);
        System.out.println (outbuf.toString());
    }
    catch (IOException e)
    {
      e.printStackTrace ();
    }
  }
}



$ sqlplus scott/tiger @myBStream
$ sqlj myBStream.sqlj
$ java -Doracle.net.tns_admin=$TNS_ADMIN myBStream
Inserting data from bin stream file into a bin stream tab ...
 .... Done!
Retreving data from bin stream tab ...
col1: 19
```

```
010203040506070809

size = 19
010203040506070809
$
```

SQLJ Stream Objects as Procedures Output Parameters and Function Return Values

The Oracle-specific code generation allows SQLJ stream objects to be used as OUT or INOUT host variables in a stored procedure or function call, and also as the return value from a stored function call.

Assume the following stored procedure, which takes a LONG data type column as input parameter and returns it as a VARCHAR2 data type:

```
create or replace procedure CharStrProc(
  long_col in long,
  vc2_col out varchar2)
  as begin
    vc2_col := long_col;
  end;
```

The following code fragment invokes the procedure:

```
// Note: a ByteArrayInputStream contains an
// internal buffer that
// contains bytes that may be read from the stream
CharacterStream chstr = new CharacterStream
  ( new ByteArrayInputStream("Character String".getBytes()));
String vc2 = (new String(""));
chstr.setLength(20);
#sql { call CharStrProc(:in chstr, :out vc2);
System.out.printl("VC2 is " + vc2);
```

Assume the following stored function, which takes a LONG as input parameter and returns a VARCHAR2 data:

```
create or replace function CharStrFunc(
  long_col in long) return varchar2
    as
```

```
vc2_col varchar2(32767);
begin
  vc2_col := long_col;
  return (vc2_col);
end;
```

The following code fragment invokes the function:

```
CharacterStream chstr = new CharacterStream
  ( new ByteArrayInputStream("Character String".getBytes()));
String vc2 = (new String(""));
chstr.setLength(20);
#sql vc2 =  {  values(CharStrFunc(:in chstr)) };
System.out.printl("VC2 is " + vc2);
```

12.1.7   SQLJ Support for SQL Datetime Data Types

DATE

I recommend reading the discussion on SQL DATE support in Oracle JDBC in Chapter 8 before proceeding. Per Table 12.1, SQL DATE can be mapped to java.sql.Date, java.sql.Time, java.sql.Timestamp, java.lang.String, and oracle.sql.DATE.

The following code fragment retrieves SQL DATE into a java.sql.Date host variable:

```
//
java.sql.Date hireDat = null;
String ename = null;
#sql pc = { select hiredate, ename
                   from emp order by empno};
while (true) {
    #sql { fetch :pc into :hireDat, :ename };
    if (pc.endFetch()) break;
    System.out.println("Employee " + ename + " was hired on "
+ hireDat);
  }
```

The following code fragment retrieves a SQL DATE column into an oracle.sql.DATE host variable:

```
import oracle.sql.DATE;
```

```
...
DATE date=null;
#sql date={VALUES(Sysdate)  };
```

The following code fragment inserts an `oracle.sql.DATE` value into a SQL DATE column:

```
//
oracle.sql.DATE   d_in = new DATE(new Timestamp(0L));
#sql { insert INTO  Tab VALUES(:d_in)};
```

TIMESTAMP, TIMESTAMPTZ, and TIMESTAMPLTZ

Refer to the timestamp discussion in Chapter 8. Assuming a `TIMESTAMP_TAB` table with the various timestamp type columns (i.e., `C_TIMESTAMP`, `C_TIMESTAMP`, `C_TIMESTAMP`), the following code fragment (a reuse of the JDBC timestamp-related code fragment) shows the mapping of SQL TMESTAMP data types to `java.sql.Timestamp`, `java.sql.Timezone`, and `oracle.sql.TIMESTAMPLTZ` in SQLJ:

```
import java.sql.Timestamp;
import java.util.Date;
import oracle.sql.*;
//
String my_date = "2006-01-06 12:23:47.66";
oracle.sql.TIMESTAMPLTZ    my_tsltz = null;
GregorianCalendar          my_gcal  = null;
Timestamp my_tss = Timestamp.valueOf(my_date);
TimeZone my_tz = TimeZone.getDefault();
my_tz.setID("US/Pacific");
my_gcal = new GregorianCalendar(my_tz);
my_tsltz = new oracle.sql.TIMESTAMPLTZ(conn, my_tss, my_cal);
my_tstz = new oracle.sql.TIMESTAMPTZ(conn, my_tss, my_cal);
my_ts = new oracle.sql.TIMESTAMP(my_tss);

#sql { update timestamp_tab set c_timestamp = :my_ts,
        c_timestamptz = :my_tstz, c_timestampltz = my_tsltz))};
```

INTERVAL YEAR TO MONTH and INTERVAL DAY TO SECOND

Refer to the JDBC description of this SQL data type in Chapter 8. Similar to JDBC, SQLJ can map the SQL INTERVALYM/INTERVALDS data types to

string or `oracle.sql.INTERVALDS`/`oracle.sql.INTERVALYM`, as shown
in the following code fragment:

```
import oracle.sql.*;
//
INTERVALDS ids = new INTERVALDS ("15 08:12:42.0");
#sql {INSERT INTO idstab VALUES (:ids) };
```

12.1.8   SQLJ Support for SQL LOB Data Types

Overview

Refer to Chapter 8 for a description of SQL LOB data types, including
`BLOB`s, `CLOB`s, and `BFILE`s. The Oracle SQLJ can map SQL `BLOB`,
`CLOB`, and `BFILE` as:

- `IN`, `OUT`, or `INOUT` host variables in executable SQLJ statements and in
  `INTO`-lists
- Return values from stored function calls
- Column types in iterator declarations

There are primarily three ways to manipulate LOB data: using the
`DBMS_LOB` package; using the standard JDBC LOB API (java.sql.Blob,
java.sql.Clob) and Oracle JDBC LOB wrapper classes (`oracle.sql.BLOB`,
`oracle.sql.CLOB`, `oracle.sql.BFILE`); and using SQLJ streaming.

Assume the following table with a `BLOB` and a `CLOB` column type:

```
create table XOB_tab (vc2 varchar2 (30), bcol blob, ccol
clob);
```

Using the DBMS_LOB Package

The `DBMS_LOB` package contains functions and procedures to manipulate
LOBs; however, these incur systematic roundtrip(s) to the RDBMS. The
following code fragments illustrate the steps, procedures, and functions to
use. Steps 1 to 3 are common to all LOB types; step 4 retrieves a LOB; step
5 inserts a CLOB; and step 6 opens a BFILE.

See the PL/SQL documentation for more details on the package and its methods.

1.   Declare iterators:

```
#sql public static iterator NLOBIter (String vc2, BLOB
bcol, CLOB ccol);
#sql public static iterator PLOBIter (String, BLOB,
CLOB);
```

2.   Declare LOB variable:

```
BLOB blobLoc = null;
```

3.   Inserts an empty LOB, to initialize the LOB locator:

When LOB data is smaller than 4 K, it is stored inline (within the table column); otherwise, only the locator is stored within the table column. In all cases, you need to first initialize the LOB by using the EMPTY_CLOB() and EMPTY_BLOB() methods.

```
#sql { INSERT into XOB_Tab (vc2, bcol, ccol)
            VALUEs ('one', empty_blob(), epty_clob())};
```

4.   Retrieve the locator(s) and then the LOB data:

```
// Declare Iterator and execute the query
NLOBIter nbiter;
 #sql niter = { select * from XOB_tab };

// Process result in iterator
while (niter.next ()) {

   // Get the BLOB LOcator
   blobLoc = niter.b();

   // Get the size of the BLOB
   long blobLength;
   #sql blobLength = { VALUES(dbms_lob.getLength(:blobLoc)) };

   // loop until we retrieve all data
```

```
long i = 0;
int chunk = 10;
while (i < blobLength)
{
  long readbuff = chunk;
  byte [] bytesread = null;
  // retrieve a chunk of LOB data from the database
  #sql { call dbms_lob.read(:blobLoc, :inout readbuf,
                        :i+1, :out bytesread) };
  // fill the buffer
  StringBuffer buffer = new StringBuffer();
  int j;
  for (j = 0; j < readbuf; j++) {
  buffer.append(bytesread [j] + " ");
  }
}
```

5.   Insert data into LOB columns:

```
// This time let's use CLOB methods
long i = 0;
long chunk = 10;
long length = 40;

// INSERT CLOB Data
while (i < length)
{
  String chunkStr = "CLOB Data " + i;
  #sql { call dbms_lob.write(:inout clobLoc, :chunk, :i+1,
        :chunkStr) };
  i += chunk;
  if (length - i < chunk)
  chunk = length - i;
}
```

6.   The following code fragment opens a BFILE for read access
        (BFILEs are read-only files). Refer to Chapter 8 for a description
        of directory alias.

```
BFILE bfile;
String dirAlias, fname;
```

```
        #sql { CALL dbms_lob.filegetname(:bfile, :out dirAlias, :out fname)
};
    // Print the file name
    System.out.println("fname: " + dirAlias + "/" + name);

    boolean bool;
    #sql bool = { VALUES(dbms_lob.fileisopen(:bfile)) };
    if (!bool)
    {
        #sql { CALL dbms_lob.fileopen(:inout bfile) };
    }
    // at this stage, bfile contains the reference of an openned
    // BFILE object ;
```

Using Standard JDBC LOB API and oracle.sql LOB Extensions

JDBC 2.0 specifies standard `java.sql.Blob` and `java.sql.Clob` API for manipulating LOBs. The `oracle.sql.CLOB`, `oracle.sql.BLOB`, and `oracle.sql.BFILE` wrapper classes furnish methods such as `putBytes()`, `getBytes()`, `putChars()`, `getChars()`, and so on for manipulating LOB locators and LOB data.

1.   First steps:

```
    #sql { create table XOB_Tab( vc2 VARCHAR2, bcol BLOB, ccol
    CLOB) };

    // Insert an empty LOB to initialize the locator
    #sql { insert into XOB_Tab values( 'one', null,null) };

    // Declare Standard JDBC 2.0 Locators and retrieve these
    java.sql.Blob blobLoc;
    java.sql.Clob clobLoc;
    #sql { select bcol, ccol into :blobLoc, :clobLoc from XOB_Tab
    };

    // Declare oracle.sql Locators and retrieve these
    oracle.sql.BLOB oblobLoc;
    oracle.sql.CLOB ocloLoc;
    #sql { select bcol, ccol into :oblobLoc, :oclobLoc from
    XOB_Tab };
```

2.   At this stage, the LOB data can be manipulated in chunks; the chunk size is determined by the RDBMS and must be retrieved from the locator, as follows:

```
int chunksize = blobLoc.getChunkSize();
```

3.   The data for insertion into the BLOB or CLOB must be read from a file, as follows:

```
// File and FileInputStream
File blobfile = new File("<filename>");
FileInputStream fis = new FileInputSTream(blobfile);

// create a byte array or char array buffer
byte [] bytearr = new byte[chunksize]; // for BLOBs
char [] chararr = new char[chunksize]; // for CLOBs

// read the content of the file into the byte/char
// array
long cursor = 1; // track the current position in the
                 // LOB
int readsize; // number of  bytes/char read from file
long blobsize = oblobLoc.length(); //get length in
                                   // bytes
while (readsize = fis.read(bytearr)) != -1 {
 // write bytes directly into the BLOB
 oblobLoc.putBytes(cursor, bytearr);
 cursor += readsize;
}
```

4.   Close resources and commit changes:

Using SQLJ Streaming

The SQLJ streaming classes (i.e., sqlj.runtime.BinaryStream and sqlj.runtime.CharacterStream) can be used to stream the LOB content directly to the database (or retrieve the content directly). In the previous example, we used putBytes() or putChar() to write LOB content to the database. In this case, the buffer must be written to the database, using the BinaryStream and CharacterStream approach instead (refer to the previous SQLJ stream code sample). There is no need or opportunity to commit or roll back changes when data is streamed directly into the database.

LOB and BFILE Stored Function Results

BLOB, CLOB, and BFILE host variables can be assigned the result of a stored function call.

```
CLOB clobLoc;
#sql clobLoc = { VALUES(return_clob(...)) };
```

LOB and BFILE Host Variables (SELECT INTO Targets)

Host variables of the BLOB, CLOB, and BFILE type can appear in the INTO-list of a SELECT INTO executable statement. Assume the previously created table XOB_Tab, with the following rows:

```
INSERT INTO XOB_Tab VALUES
    ('one', '010101010101010101010101010101',
'onetwothreefour');
INSERT INTO XOB_tab VALUES
  ('two', '020202020202020202020202020202',
'twothreefourfivesix');
```

The following code fragment uses a BLOB and a CLOB as host variables that receive data from the table defined, using a SELECT INTO statement:

```
...
BLOB blobLoc;
CLOB clobLoc;
#sql { SELECT t1.b, t2.c INTO :blobLoc, :clobLoc
    FROM XOB_TAb t1, XBO_Tab t2
    WHERE t1.vc2='one' AND t2.vc2='two' };
#sql { INSERT INTO XOB_Tab VALUES('three', :blobLoc,
:clobLoc) };
...
```

LOBs and BFILEs in Iterator Declarations

The BLOB, CLOB, and BFILE types can be used as column types for SQLJ positional and named iterators. Such iterators can be populated as a result of compatible executable SQLJ operations.

```
#sql iterator NamedLOBIter(CLOB ccol);
#sql iterator PositionLOBIter(BLOB);
#sql iterator NamedFILEIter(BFILE bfile);
```

LOB and BFILE Host Variables as Named Iterator

```
#sql iterator NamedLOBIter(CLOB c);


...
NamLOBIter nliter;
#sql nliter = { SELECT ccol FROM XOB_Tab };
if (nliter.next())
   CLOB clob1 = nliter.c();
if (iter.next())
   CLOB clob2 = nliter.c();
nliter.close();
//
```

LOB and BFILE Host Variables as Positional Iterator (FETCH INTO Targets)

BLOB, CLOB, and BFILE host variables can be used with positional iterators and appear in the INTO-list of the FETCH INTO statements.

```
#sql iterator PositionLOBIter(BLOB);


PosLOBIter pliter;
BLOB blobLoc = null;
#sql pliter = { SELECT bcol FROM XOB_tab };
for (long rowNum = 1; ; rowNum++)
{
    #sql { FETCH :pliter INTO :blobLoc };
    if (pliter.endFetch()) break;
    // write to Blob
}
```

12.1.9   SQLJ Support for Oracle SQL ROWID

As described in Chapter 8, the Oracle SQL ROWID uniquely identifies each row in a database table. The Oracle SQLJ maps SQL ROWID to oracle.sql.ROWID. Variables of the oracle.sql.ROWID type can be used in Oracle SQLJ applications, as follows:

- IN, OUT, or INOUT host variables in SQLJ executable statements and in INTO-lists
- Return value from a stored function call
- Column types in iterator declarations

The following code fragments illustrate these cases:

```
#sql public static iterator NamedRowidIter(String ename,
OracleRowid rowid);
#sql public static iterator PositionedRowidIter(String,
OracleRowid);

NamedRowidIter iter;
OracleRowid rowid;
int raise = 600;

#sql { select rowid into :rowid from emp where ename='KENNETH'
};
#sql { update emp set sal = sal + :raise WHERE rowid = :rowid
};

#sql { begin select rowid into :out rowid from emp where
                        ename='GARETH'; end; };

// Stored Function returning ROWID
CREATE OR REPLACE FUNCTION retrowid ( name VARCHAR2) RETURN
ROWID IS
    rowidvar ROWID;
BEGIN
    SELECT rowid INTO rowidvar FROM emp WHERE ename = name;
    RETURN rowidvar;
END retrowid;
```

Given the RETROWID stored function, the following code fragment illustrates how to use a strored function, which returns a ROWID:

```
ROWID myrowid;
#sql myrowid = { values(retrowid('GABRIELLE')) };
```

The upcoming JDBC 4.0 specification[2] is expected to furnish a standard `java.sql.ROWID` type.

12.1.10   SQLJ Support for OPAQUE Types

As described in Chapter 8, the Oracle SQL OPAQUE types are used internally by Oracle (their internal representation is not exposed) to implement other types. SQL OPAQUE can be mapped in Java to `oracle.sql` OPAQUE or to a custom class implementing the `oracle.sql.ORAData` interface (covered later).

XMLType

The most well-known example of an OPAQUE type implementation is the SQL XMLType (i.e., `SYS.XMLTYPE`) to represent and natively store XML documents (XMLType can be used as a column type in a table or view). It has a SQL API with built-in member functions to create, query, extract, and index XML data stored in an Oracle Database 10*g*.

Oracle SQLJ maps `SYS.XMLType` to `oracle.xdb.XMLType`; however, the JDBC-OCI drivers are required.

Assume a table with an XMLType column, created as follows:

```
create xmltype_tbl (xmltype_col SYS.XMLType);
insert into xmltype_tbl values(SYS.XMLType('<name>tom</name>'));
insert into xmltype_tbl values(SYS.XMLType('<name>jon</name>'));
```

It can be manipulated using the following code fragments:

```
import oracle.xdb.XMLType;
...
//
#sql iter={select xmltype_col from xmltype_tbl;}
while(iter.next()) {
   System.out.println(iter.xmltype_col().getStringVal());
}
//
while (iter.next()) {
   System.out.println(iter.xmltype_col.getClobVal());
}
```

2.   First public draft specification available at the time of this writing.

XMLType can also be used for parameters in stored procedures, and as return values. Alternatively, you can leverage the PL/SQL API for XML in the XDB documentation[3] and embed XMLType-related PL/SQL blocks within SQLJ.

12.1.11 SQLJ Support for SQL Object Types and SQL References Types

As mentioned in Chapter 8, the SQL objects can be mapped to Java using either a *weak type-mapping* approach (i.e., automatically using java.sql.Struct or a oracle.sql.STRUCT) or *strong type-mapping* approach (i.e., using the custom Java classes that implement SQLData or ORAData).

Type Map

Refer to Chapter 8 for an explanation of type-maps. SQLJ supports type-maps through connection contexts and iterators. Reusing the JDBC type map example in Chapter 8, assume you want to map the SQL type Address_t to the class AddressObj. A type map can be associated with the connection context class, as follows:

```
#sql public static context TypeMapCtx with
(typeMap="AddressObj");
```

The generated TypeMapCtx class will define a public static final String typeMap attribute that will be initialized to the value AddressObj.

A type map can also be associated with the iterator class in an iterator declaration:

```
#sql public static iterator TypeMapIterator with
(typeMap="AddressObj")
    (Person pers, Address addr);
```

For Oracle-specific code generation, the iterator and connection context declarations must be of the same type-maps.

Note: The public static final field _SQL_TYPECODE can be used as an alternative way to specify the mapping, as follows:

```
public static final int _SQL_TYPECODE = OracleTypes.STRUCT;
```

---

3. http://www.oracle.com/pls/db102/to_pdf?pathname=appdev.102%2Fb14259.pdf&remark=portal+%28Application+development%29.

Weak Type Mapping: Struct and STRUCT

SQLJ applications can perform custom mapping and processing of user-defined types (i.e., Oracle objects, references, or collections), using the following weakly typed classes: `java.sql.Struct` or `oracle.sql.STRUCT` for objects, `java.sql.Ref` or `oracle.sql.REF` for object references, and `java.sql.Array` or `oracle.sql.ARRAY` for collections. See a description of `java.sql.Struct` and `oracle.sql.STRUCT` classes and their methods in Chapter 8.

These classes can be used for:

- Iterator columns:

```
#sql public static iterator NamdStructIter ( STRUCT mySTRUCT );
#sql public static iterator PosdStructIter ( STRUCT );
```

Note: Attributes in a STRUCT object do not have names.

- Input host expressions:

```
STRUCT Struct = null;
#sql { CALL myAddress ( :IN Struct) };
```
- Output host expressions in INTO-list:
```
PosdStructIter iter;
#sql { FETCH :iter INTO :struct };
```

However, when objects or collections are written or read to and from instances of these classes, SQLJ cannot perform type checking; also, because the underlying user-defined SQL type name (i.e., `Address_t`) is not known by the Oracle JDBC driver, these classes *cannot be used in the following host expressions*:

- IN parameter if null:

```
STRUCT Struct = null;
#sql { insert into addressObjtab values(:IN Struct) }; // Wrong
```

- OUT or INOUT parameter in a stored procedure or function call:

```
STRUCT Struct = new STRUCT(strdesc, conn, attrib); // See chapt. 8
#sql { call myProc1(:INOUT Struct) }; // Wrong
```

- OUT parameter in a stored function result expression:

```
#sql ret = { VALUES(myFunc(:OUT struct)) }; // Wrong
```

Strong Type Mapping: SQLData and ORAData

Alternatively to *weak type mapping* and similar to JDBC, SQLJ can perform *strong type mapping* of a user-defined object, using classes that implement either the standard SQLData interface or Oracle-specific ORAData interface. Both interfaces are described in Chapter 8.

Custom mapping of user-defined object types using SQLData requires the following:

- A Java class implementing the SQLData interface: can be handcrafted or generated using JPublisher:

```
StudentObj.java
================
import java.sql.*;
import java.util.PropertyResourceBundle;

public class StudentObj implements SQLData
   {
   //public static final String _SQL_NAME = "STUDENT";
   private String sql_type;
   public String studName;
   public int studNo;

   //Constructors
   public StudentObj() { }

   public StudentObj (String sql_type, String studName, int studNo) {
      this.sql_type = sql_type;
      this.studName = studName;
      this.studNo = studNo;
   }

   // Implement SQLData interface
```

```
public String getSQLTypeName() throws SQLException
{
  return sql_type;
}
public void readSQL(SQLInput stream, String typeName)
    throws SQLException
{
  sql_type = typeName;
  studName = stream.readString();
  studNo = stream.readInt();
}

public void writeSQL(SQLOutput stream)
    throws SQLException
{
  stream.writeString(studName);
  stream.writeInt(studNo);
}
}
```

- A connection context and iterator of the class implementing the SQLData interface:

```
#sql public static context StudCtx with (typeMap =
"StudentObj");
#sql public static iterator StudIter with (typeMap =
"StudentObj")
          (StudentObj studobj);
```

Reminder: Oracle-specific code generation requires the same type-map for the iterator and the connection context.

- A resource file, which specifies the mapping as follows:

```
class.<class name>=STRUCT <SQL type name>
$ cat StudentObj.properties
// Student type map resource file
class.StudentObj=STRUCT SCOTT.StudentObj
$
```

- If the SQLData wrapper classes appear as OUT or INOUT parameters in SQLJ statements, then you must use the Oracle SQLJ runtime and Oracle-specific code generation or profile customization.

- The related SQLJ statements must explicitly use a connection context instance of the corresponding connection context type. (See Listing 12.3 and 12.4.)

```
StudCtx Ctx = new
StudCtx(DefaultContext.getDefaultContext());
    StudIter objiter;
    #sql [Ctx] objiter = { select studobj from Student_table
};
```

Listing 12.3   *mySqlData.sqlj*

```
=================================
import java.sql.*;
import oracle.jdbc.OracleDriver;
import sqlj.runtime.*;
import oracle.sqlj.runtime.*;
import sqlj.runtime.ref.DefaultContext;
import java.math.BigDecimal;

public class mySqlData
{

  #sql public static context StudCtx with (typeMap = "StudentObj");
  #sql public static iterator StudIter with (typeMap = "StudentObj")
                                      (StudentObj studobj);

  public static void main(String args []) throws Exception
  {
    Oracle.connect(mySqlData.class, "connect.properties");
    StudCtx Ctx = new StudCtx(DefaultContext.getDefaultContext());
    try
    {
    // Clean-up previous attempts
     #sql [Ctx] { drop table Student_TABLE };
     #sql [Ctx] { drop type Student FORCE };
    } catch (SQLException e){
     // ignore clean-up exception
    }
```

```
// Create the type and populate the table
System.out.println("Create Student type and table");
#sql [Ctx] {CREATE TYPE  StudentObj AS OBJECT
    (studName VARCHAR2(50),studNo INTEGER)};
#sql [Ctx] {CREATE TABLE Student_TABLE (studobj StudentObj)};
#sql [Ctx] {INSERT INTO  Student_TABLE
              VALUES (StudentObj('Zoe Nucci', 231))};
// Create a SQLData object
StudentObj stdobj =
      new StudentObj("SCOTT.Student", "Bobo Lafleur", 564);

// Insert the SQLData object
System.out.println("Insert new student");
#sql [Ctx] { insert into Student_table values (:stdobj) };
// Retrieve the inserted object
System.out.println("Rerieve the inserted student");
StudIter objiter;
#sql [Ctx] objiter = { select studobj from Student_table };
while(objiter.next())
{
   stdobj = objiter.studobj();
   System.out.println("Student Name: " + stdobj.studName +
                           " student #: " + stdobj.studNo );
}
objiter.close();
Oracle.close();

      }
   }
```

Strong type mapping using SQLData is restricted to user-defined objects only; however, Oracle's ORAData allows strong type mapping of object references, collections, and other SQL types.

Custom mapping of user-defined object types using ORAData requires:

- The wrapper class (in other words the Java class performing the mapping) must implement the oracle.sql.ORAData interface, including the getFactory(), create(), toString(), and toDatum() methods.

- The wrapper class must implement the getORADataFactory() method, which returns an oracle.sql.ORADataFactory object, as follows:

```
public static oracle.sql.ORADataFactory
getORADataFactory();
```

- The wrapper class must have a String constant _SQL_TYPECODE, initialized to OracleTypes.STRUCT typecode:

```
public static final int _SQL_TYPECODE =
OracleTypes.STRUCT;
```

- The wrapper class must have a _SQL_NAME initialized to the SQL name:

```
public static final String _SQL_NAME = "Student";
```

Here is a handcrafted wrapper class implementing ORAData; as already mentioned, the lazy but smart developer can use JPublisher to generate it.

```
StudentORAData.java
====================
import java.sql.*;
import oracle.sql.*;
import oracle.jdbc.OracleTypes;

public class StudentORAData implements ORAData, ORADataFactory
{
   static final StudentORAData _factory = new StudentORAData ();
   public static final String _SQL_NAME = "STUDENTORADATA";
   public static final int _SQL_TYPECODE = OracleTypes.STRUCT;

   private String sql_type = "SCOTT.STUDENTORADATA";
   public String studName;
   public int studNo;

   public static ORADataFactory getORADataFactory()
   {
```

```
      return _factory;
  }


  //Constructors
  public StudentORAData() { }

  public StudentORAData (String studName, int studNo) {
    //this.sql_type = sql_type;
    this.studName = studName;
    this.studNo = studNo;
  }
  public Datum toDatum(Connection conn)
    throws SQLException
  {
    StructDescriptor strdesc =
          StructDescriptor.createDescriptor(sql_type, conn);
    Object [] attribs = {  studName, new Integer(studNo) };
    return new STRUCT(strdesc, conn, attribs);
  }
public ORAData create(Datum datm, int sqlType) throws SQLException
  {
    if (datm == null) return null;
    Datum[] attribs = ((STRUCT) datm).getOracleAttributes();
    return new StudentORAData ( attribs[0].stringValue (),
                          attribs[1].intValue ());
  }

  public String toString ()
  {
    return sql_type + " = " + studName + ", " + studNo;
  }
}
```

$ **javac StudentORAData.java**

Listing 12.4 hereafter uses StudentORAData.

───────────────►

Listing 12.4   *myORAData.sqlj*
================================
```
import java.sql.*;
import oracle.jdbc.OracleDriver;
```

```
import sqlj.runtime.*;
import oracle.sqlj.runtime.*;
import sqlj.runtime.ref.DefaultContext;
import java.math.BigDecimal;

public class myORAData
{

   #sql public static iterator StudIter (StudentORAData studobj);

   public static void main(String args []) throws Exception
   {
     Oracle.connect(mySqlData.class, "connect.properties");
     try
     {
      // Clean-up previous attempts
       System.out.println("Drop student table and type");
       #sql { drop table Student_TABLE };
       #sql { drop type Student FORCE };
     } catch (SQLException e){
       // ignore clean-up exception
     }

     // Create the type and populate the table
     System.out.println("Create Student type and table");
     #sql {CREATE TYPE  StudentORAData AS OBJECT (studName VARCHAR2(50),studNo
INTEGER)};
     #sql {CREATE TABLE Student_TABLE (studobj StudentORAData)};
     #sql {INSERT INTO  Student_TABLE VALUES (StudentORAData('Zoe Nucci',
231))};

     // Create a ORAData object
     StudentORAData stdobj = new StudentORAData("Bobo Lafleur", 564);

     // Insert the ORAData object
     System.out.println("Insert new student");
     #sql { insert into Student_table values (:stdobj) };
     // Retrieve the inserted object
     System.out.println("Rerieve the inserted student");
     StudIter objiter;
     #sql objiter = { select studobj from Student_table };
     while(objiter.next())
```

```
      {
         stdobj = objiter.studobj();
         System.out.println("Student Name: " + stdobj.studName +
                                    " student #: " + stdobj.studNo );
      }
      objiter.close();
      Oracle.close();

   }
}

$ java -Doracle.net.tns_admin=$TNS_ADMIN myORAData
Drop student table and type
Create Student type and table
Insert new student
Rerieve the inserted student
Student Name: Zoe Nucci student #: 231
Student Name: Bobo Lafleur student #: 564
$
```

SQLJ Object Types

As described in Chapter 8, SQLJ object types are specified by ANSI SQLJ Part II and allow creating SQL types using Java classes that implement SQLData or ORAData interface. Similar to JDBC in Chapter 8, SQLJ applications may use SQLJ object types.

SQL REF

SQL REF types are explained in the corresponding section in Chapter 8. Similar to JDBC, SQLJ can automatically map SQL REF column types to and from the standard java.sql.Ref or to and from the oracle.sql.REF wrapper. Alternatively, you may use the custom mapping approach using a class that implements ORAData.

The Oracle SQLJ supports using REF:

- In iterator declaration:

```
#sql static iterator NamedRefIter (BigDecimal objid, REF
objref );
#sql static iterator PosdRefIter (BigDecimal, REF );
```

- In Query and DML statements:

```
static REF myRef = null;

#sql { select t.objref into :myRef from ref_obj_tab t
          where t.objid  = 3 };

#sql { insert into ref_obj_tab values(250, :myRef) };
NamedRefIter nriter;
#sql iter = { select ref(t) objref from ref_obj_tab t };

myObject myobj;
#sql { select DEREF(objref) into :myObj from ref_obj_tab
          where ...} ;
```

- As IN, OUT, and INOUT parameter of a stored procedure/function:

```
#sql { call InsertObjRef(303, :IN myRef ) };
REF ref = myRef;
boolean bool = true;
#sql bool = { values(ObjRefFunc(:INOUT ref)) };
```

- In PL/SQL blocks:

```
REF myRef = null;
int objnum = 1;
#sql { begin select * into :OUT myRef from ref_obj_tab p
          where p.objid  = :IN objnum; end; };
```

For custom mapping of object references using ORAData, the following requirements must be met:

- The class has a String constant _SQL_TYPECODE initialized to Ora-cleTypes.REF:

```
public static final int _SQL_TYPECODE = OracleTypes.REF;
```

- The class has a String constant, _SQL_BASETYPE, initialized to the SQL name of the user-defined type being referenced:

```
public static final String _SQL_BASETYPE = "PERSON";
```

See Chapter 8 for more elaborate examples that you can easily implement using SQLJ.

REF Cursors

REF cursors contain references to database cursors. Oracle SQLJ supports using REF CURSOR types for mapping the following:

- Result expressions for stored function returns

- Output host expressions for stored procedure or function output parameters

- Output host expressions in INTO-lists

- Output of PL/SQL anonymous blocks

- Iterator columns: you can write a REF CURSOR object to an iterator column or ResultSet column in an iterator, or write a REF CURSOR object to an iterator host variable or ResultSet host variable in an INTO-list

The following code fragment retrieves a REF CURSOR from an anonymous PL/SQL block:

```
#sql { begin
        INSERT INTO emp (ename, empno) VALUES (:name, :num);
        OPEN :out emplist FOR SELECT ename, empno FROM emp ORDER BY empno;
      end
    };
```

Listing 12.5 illustrates how to use the SQL CURSOR operator for a nested SELECT within an outer SELECT statement, to retrieve the department name of each employee.

Listing 12.5   *myRefCursor.sqlj*

```
=================================
import java.sql.*;
import sqlj.runtime.*;
import java.sql.ResultSet;
```

```
import sqlj.runtime.ref.DefaultContext;
import oracle.jdbc.driver.*;
import oracle.sqlj.runtime.*;

public class myRefCursor
{
  #sql static public iterator NameRefCursIter
                    (String ename, ResultSet deptlis);
  public static void main(String[] args)
  {
    System.out.println("**** ResultSet as Ref Cursor");
    try
    {
      Oracle.connect(basicFunc.class, "connect.properties");
      NameRefCursIter nrciter;
      #sql nrciter = { select ename,
                        CURSOR (select dname from dept
                                     where deptno = emp.deptno)
                                as deptlis
                                from emp
                      };

      System.out.println("Loop through the Iterators, print Ename and
Dname");
      while (nrciter.next ())
      {
        ResultSet deptRSet = nrciter.deptlis();
        if (deptRSet.next ())
        {
          String deptName = deptRSet.getString (1);
          System.out.println("Name: " + nrciter.ename() +
                                      " Dept: " + deptName);

        }
        deptRSet.close();
      }
      nrciter.close();
    } catch (SQLException e) {
      e.printStackTrace();
      System.out.println(e);
    }
  }
}
```

```
$ sqlj myRefCursor.sqlj
$ java -Doracle.net.tns_admin=$TNS_ADMIN myRefCursor

**** ResultSet as Ref Cursor
Loop through the Iterators and print Ename and Dname
Name: SMITH Dept: RESEARCH
Name: ALLEN Dept: SALES
Name: WARD Dept: SALES
Name: JONES Dept: RESEARCH
Name: MARTIN Dept: SALES
Name: BLAKE Dept: SALES
Name: CLARK Dept: ACCOUNTING
Name: SCOTT Dept: RESEARCH
Name: KING Dept: ACCOUNTING
Name: TURNER Dept: SALES
Name: ADAMS Dept: RESEARCH
Name: JAMES Dept: SALES
Name: FORD Dept: RESEARCH
Name: MILLER Dept: ACCOUNTING
$
```

See Chapter 3 for a Java stored procedure returning a REF cursor.

12.1.12   Serialized Java Objects

If you want to store Java objects "as is" and retrieve them later, you may use database RAW or BLOB columns along with typeMap or ORAData. You may also serialize and deserialize the Java objects on the fly (objects by value).

Serializing Java Objects Using typeMAP

The Oracle-specific code generation allows mapping a serializable Java class to RAW or BLOB columns. It uses a nonstandard extension to typeMap facility or adds a typecode field to the serializable class, so that the instances of the serializable class can be stored as RAW or BLOB.

- Declare a type-map in the connection context declaration and use this type-map to specify mappings:

```
#sql public static context SerConCtx with (typeMap="SerMap");
```

The type-map resource must provide nonstandard mappings from RAW or BLOB columns to the serializable Java classes:

```
oracle-class.java_class_name=JAVA_OBJECT RAW

oracle-class.java_class_name=JAVA_OBJECT BLOB
```

■ Alternatively, you can use the public static final field _SQL_TYPECODE to specify the mapping:

```
public final static int _SQL_TYPECODE =
oracle.jdbc.OracleTypes.RAW;

public final static int _SQL_TYPECODE =
oracle.jdbc.OracleTypes.BLOB;
```

Serializing Java Objects Using ORAData

You can also use ORAData to define a serializable wrapper class whose instances can be stored in RAW or BLOB columns. Here are the steps (from the Oracle SQLJ documentation) for achieving such mapping:

1.   Skeleton of the class:

```
public class SerializableDatum implements ORAData
{
   // Client methods for constructing and accessing the Java
   // object

   public Datum toDatum(java.sql.Connection c) throws
SQLException
   {
      // Implementation of toDatum()
   }

   public static ORADataFactory getORADataFactory()
   {
      return FACTORY;
   }

   private static final ORADataFactory FACTORY =
         // Implementation of an ORADataFactory for
         // SerializableDatum
```

```
// Construction of SerializableDatum from oracle.sql.RAW

public static final int _SQL_TYPECODE = OracleTypes.RAW;
}
```

2.   Define client methods that create a `SerializableDatum` object, populate a `SerializableDatum` object, and retrieve data from a `SerializableDatum` object:

```
private Object m_data;
public SerializableDatum()
{
   m_data = null;
}
public void setData(Object data)
{
   m_data = data;
}
public Object getData()
{
   return m_data;
}
```

3.   Implement a `toDatum()` method that serializes data from a `SerializableDatum` object to an `oracle.sql.RAW` object:

```
// Implementation of toDatum()

try {
   ByteArrayOutputStream os = new
ByteArrayOutputStream();
   ObjectOutputStream oos = new ObjectOutputStream(os);
   oos.writeObject(m_data);
   oos.close();
   return new RAW(os.toByteArray());
} catch (Exception e) {
   throw new SQLException("SerializableDatum.toDatum:
"+e.toString()); }
```

4. Implement data conversion from an `oracle.sql.RAW` object to a `SerializableDatum` object:

```
// Constructing SerializableDatum from oracle.sql.RAW

private SerializableDatum(RAW raw) throws SQLException
{
   try {
      InputStream rawStream = new
ByteArrayInputStream(raw.getBytes());
      ObjectInputStream is = new
ObjectInputStream(rawStream);
      m_data = is.readObject();
      is.close();
   } catch (Exception e) {
      throw new SQLException("SerializableDatum.create:
"+e.toString()); }
}
```

5. Implement an `ORADataFactory`:

```
// Implementation of an ORADataFactory for
SerializableDatum

new ORADataFactory()
{
   public ORAData create(Datum d, int sqlCode) throws
SQLException
   {
      if (sqlCode != _SQL_TYPECODE)
      {
         throw new SQLException
                  ("SerializableDatum: invalid SQL type
"+sqlCode);
      }
      return (d==null) ? null : new
SerializableDatum((RAW)d);
   }
};
```

The following uses a `SerializableDatum` instance as a host variable:

```
...
SerializableDatum pinfo = new SerializableDatum();
pinfo.setData (
    new Object[] {"Some objects", new Integer(51), new
Double(1234.27) } );
String pname = "MILLER";
#sql { INSERT INTO persondata VALUES(:pname, :pinfo) };
...
```

The following code fragment uses `SerializableDatum` as a named iterator column:

```
#sql iterator PersonIter (SerializableDatum info,
String name);
```

```
...
PersonIter pcur;
#sql pcur = { SELECT * FROM persondata WHERE info IS NOT
NULL };
while (pcur.next())
{
    System.out.println("Name:" + pcur.name() + " Info:" +
pcur.info());
}
pcur.close();
...
```

Serializing Java Objects by Value

The following code sample describes how to exchange serialized Java objects by value, between a client-side Java/SQLJ and server-side Java/SQLJ. The various RowSet models covered in Chapter 8 are probably more elegant approaches. The serialized Java object is passed as LONG RAW arguments to stored procedure and function using the PL/SQL interface, which limits the size of LONG RAW arguments to 32 K bytes. This example comprises the following files: `EmpObjClient.sqlj`, `EmployeeObj.java`, `EmployeeObject.sqlj`, `Util.java`, and `empobj.sql`.

- `EmployeeObjects.sqlj`: Contains methods for passing the Java object, which is serialized and passed back and forth through SQL layer as LONG RAW.

- `-byte[] getEmployeeObj (Integer empno)`: Gets an employee and all its managers by calling `getEmployee()`, then serializes and returns a Java object representing the employee and all its managers as a byte array (byte[ ]).

- -void updateEmployeeInfo (byte[] info): Deserializes the array containing a serialized EmployeeObj objects and calls updateEmployee to update the EMP table to reflect the changes to the employee and managers.

- The PL/SQL Wrappers (empobj.sql): The getEmployeeObj and updateEmployeeObj methods are wrapped as follows:

  - function getempobj (empno in number) return long raw
    as language java name
    'EmployeeByValue.getEmployeeObj (java.lang.Integer) return byte[]';

  - procedure updateempobj (info long raw)
    as language java name
    'EmployeeByValue.updateEmployeeObj (byte[])';

- EmpObjCLient.sqlj: the client program:

  - Calls the PL/SQL wrappers for entry points in EmployeeObjects to get the serialized EmployeeObj.
  - Serializes it to get the Java object instances.
  - Updates the instances (raise to the salaries of employee and its manager; Note: it is not recursive).
  - Serializes the EmployeeObj object and sends it back to the database for effective update.
  - Retrieves the employee and its hierarchy again and prints their number, name, and salary.

```
EmployeeObject.sqlj
===================
/*
 * Server-side SQLJ providing entrypoint to get
 * EmployeeObj or EmployeeObj references
 */

import java.sql.*;
import oracle.sql.RAW;

#sql iterator EmpIter (String ename, Integer mgr, int sal);
```

```
public class EmployeeObject
{
  public static byte[] getEmployeeObj (Integer empno) throws Exception
  {
    EmployeeObj empobj = getEmployee (empno);
    return Util.serializeObject (empobj);
  }

  public static void updateEmployeeObj (byte[] obj) throws Exception {
    EmployeeObj empobj = (EmployeeObj)Util.deserializeObject (obj);
    updateEmployee (empobj);
  }

  private static EmployeeObj getEmployee (Integer empno)
      throws SQLException
  {
    if (empno == null)
      return null;
    else {
      EmpIter it;
      #sql it = {select ename, sal, mgr from emp where empno =
:empno};
      if (!it.next ()) return null;
      return new EmployeeObj (empno.intValue (), it.ename (), it.sal
(), getEmployee (it.mgr ()));
    }
  }

  private static void updateEmployee (EmployeeObj empobj)
      throws SQLException
  {
    if (empobj != null) {
      updateEmployee (empobj.manager);
      if (empobj.manager != null)
        #sql {update emp set ename = :(empobj.ename),
                              mgr = :(empobj.manager.empno),
                              sal = :(empobj.salary)
                        where empno = :(empobj.empno) };
      else
        #sql {update emp set ename = :(empobj.ename),
                              sal = :(empobj.salary)
                        where empno = :(empobj.empno) };
```

```
        }
      }
    }


EmployeeObj.java
================
/* This Class represent a Java object passed by value between the
   Client and the Server.
   */


import java.io.Serializable;


public class EmployeeObj implements Serializable
{
   public int empno;
   public String ename;
   public int salary;
   public EmployeeObj manager;

   public EmployeeObj (int empno, String ename, int salary,
                       EmployeeObj manager){
      this.empno = empno;
      this.ename = ename;
      this.salary = salary;
      this.manager = manager;
   }
}


Util.java
======
/* Utility class for serializing / deserializing objects */


import java.io.*;


public class Util {

   public static byte[] serializeObject (Object obj)
       throws IOException
   {
     if (obj == null) return null;
     ByteArrayOutputStream ostream = new ByteArrayOutputStream ();
```

```
        ObjectOutputStream p = new ObjectOutputStream (ostream);
        p.writeObject (obj);
        p.flush ();
        return ostream.toByteArray ();
    }

    public static Object deserializeObject (byte[] bytes)
        throws IOException, ClassNotFoundException
    {
      if (bytes == null) return null;
      InputStream istream = new ByteArrayInputStream (bytes);
      return new ObjectInputStream (istream).readObject ();
    }
}


$ loadjava -resolve -user scott/tiger
                    EmployeeObj.java EmployeeObject.sqlj Util.java
```

You may ignore the warnings.

```
empobj.sql
==========


create or replace package empobj as
  function getempobj (empno in number) return long raw;
  procedure updateempobj (obj long raw);
end;
/

create or replace package body empobj as
  function getempobj (empno in number) return long raw
    as language java name
        'EmployeeObject.getEmployeeObj(java.lang.Integer) return
byte[]';
  procedure updateempobj (obj long raw)
    as language java name
        'EmployeeObject.updateEmployeeObj (byte[])';
end;
/

show errors;
```

```
exit

$ sqlplus scott/tiger @empobj

SQL*Plus: Release 10.2.0.1.0 - Production on Sun Jan 15 15:32:57 2006

Copyright (c) 1982, 2005, Oracle.  All rights reserved.


Connected to:
Oracle Database 10g Enterprise Edition Release 10.2.0.1.0 -
Production
With the Partitioning and Data Mining options


Package created.


Package body created.

No errors.
Disconnected from Oracle Database 10g Enterprise Edition Release
10.2.0.1.0 - Production
With the Partitioning and Data Mining options
$

EmpObjCLient.sqlj
==================
import java.sql.*;
import java.io.IOException;
import sqlj.runtime.ref.DefaultContext;
import sqlj.runtime.BinaryStream;
import oracle.sqlj.runtime.*;

public class EmpObjClient
{
  public static void main (String args[])
      throws Exception
  {
    Oracle.connect(EmpObjClient.class, "connect.properties");

    System.out.println ("Getting employee number 7788");
```

```
        EmployeeObj emp = getEmployee (7788);
        printEmp (emp);

        System.out.println ("Raising employee number 7788 and his manager
by 10%");
        emp.salary += emp.salary * 0.10;
        emp.manager.salary += emp.manager.salary * 0.10;
        updateEmployee (emp);

        System.out.println ("Getting employee number 7788 again");
        emp = getEmployee (7788);
        printEmp (emp);
    }

    public static void printEmp (EmployeeObj emp) {
      if (emp != null) {
        System.out.println (emp.empno + ": " + emp.ename +
                            " salary " + emp.salary);
        if (emp.manager != null) {
          System.out.print ("  managed by ");
          printEmp (emp.manager);
        }
      }
    }

    public static EmployeeObj getEmployee (int number)
        throws SQLException, IOException, ClassNotFoundException
    {
      byte[] serial_empobj = null;
      #sql serial_empobj = { values (empobj.getempobj (:number)) };
      return (EmployeeObj)Util.deserializeObject (serial_empobj);
    }

    public static void updateEmployee (EmployeeObj emp)
        throws SQLException, IOException
    {
      byte[] serial_empobj = Util.serializeObject (emp);
      #sql { call empobj.updateempobj (:serial_empobj) };
    }
}
```

```
$ sqlj EmpObjCLient.sqlj
$ java -Doracle.net.tns_admin=$TNS_ADMIN EmpObjClient
Getting employee number 7788
7788: SCOTT salary 4350
  managed by 7566: JONES salary 2975
  managed by 7839: KING salary 5000
Raising employee number 7788 and his manager by 10%
Getting employee number 7788 again
7788: SCOTT salary 4785
  managed by 7566: JONES salary 3272
  managed by 7839: KING salary 5000
$
```

12.1.13   SQLJ Support for User-Defined SQL Collections

VARRAYs

SQL VARRAYs are described in Chapter 8. Similar to JDBC, the Oracle SQLJ maps the SQL VARRAY to the oracle.sql.ARRAY wrapper class (which implements the standard java.sql.Array interface) or to the custom wrapper class.

VARRAY can be used for host variable, iterators, parameters for stored procedures and functions, and within anonymous PL/SQL blocks.

Beginning with Oracle Database 10g, the Oracle SQLJ supports array types in iterator columns. In other words, you can declare an iterator that uses java.sql.Array or oracle.sql.ARRAY columns.

```
#sql public static iterator NamedArrayIter (BigDecimal order,
ARRAY parts);
#sql public static iterator PositArrayIter (BigDecimal,
ARRAY);

static ARRAY myArray = null;
#sql { select t.parts into :(myArray) from VARRAY_tab t where
t.order=203};

#sql { insert into VARRAY_tab (order, parts) values (310,
:(myArray) )} ;
```

VARRAYs can be used as IN parameters for stored procedures.

```
#sql { call insertVARRAY1(204, :IN myArray ) };
```

SQL 2003 specifies `getArray()` on `RTResultSet` object, and `setArray()` on `RTStatement` for inserting and retrieving `ARRAY/MULTISET`. However, as of Oracle Database 10g Release 2 (10.2), the Oracle SQLJ does not support `getURL` on `RTResultSet` and `setURL` on `RTStatement`.

For custom mapping of user-defined collections such as VARRAYs using `ORAData`, the following requirements must be met:

- The custom collection has a `String` constant, `_SQL_TYPECODE`, initialized to `OracleTypes.ARRAY`:

```
public static final int _SQL_TYPECODE = OracleTypes.ARRAY;
```

- The custom collection class must have the constant `_SQL_NAME` initialized to the SQL name of the user-defined collection:

```
public static final String _SQL_NAME = "ADT_VARRAY";
```

Nested Tables

Nested Tables are unordered and unbound user-defined collections. See Chapter 8 for a further description and examples of nested tables. Similar to VARRAY, Nested Tables can be mapped to `java.sql.Aray`, `oracle.sql.VARRAY`, and custom wrapper classes.

Nested Tables can be used in iterator declaration, `IN` variables in select statement, `IN` and `OUT` parameter for stored procedures, and return values of stored functions.

```
#sql public static iterator NamedArrayIter(BigDecimal order,
NTab_parts parts);
#sql public static iterator PositionedArrayIter(BigDecimal,
NTab_parts );

NTab_parts myNTab = new NTab_parts();

#sql {select t.parts into :(myNTab) from NTAb_parts_tab t
where t.order=101};

NTab_parts yourNTab = new new NTab_parts();
#sql { select :myNTab into :yourNTab from dual };
```

12.1.14 PL/SQL Associative Array

Chapter 8 describes PL/SQL associative arrays. The following array types are supported in SQLJ:

- Numeric types: `int[]`, `long[]`, `float[]`, `double[]`, `short[]`, `java.math.BigDecimal[]`, `oracle.sql.NUMBER[]`

- Character types: `java.lang.String[]`, `oracle.sql.CHAR[]`

The following code fragment writes indexed-by table data to the database:

```
int[] vals = {1,2,3};
#sql { call procin(:vals) };
```

The following code fragment retrieves indexed-by table data from the database:

```
oracle.sql.CHAR[] outvals;
#sql { call procout(:OUT outvals/*[111](22)*/) };
```

The maximum length of the output array being retrieved is specified using the [**xxx**] syntax inside the /*...*/ syntax, as shown. Also, you can optionally specify the maximum length of an array element in bytes using the (**xx**) syntax, as shown.

12.1.15 Unsupported Types

DATALINK

`RTResultSet` and `RTStatement` do not support `getURL` and `setURL` methods. SQL 2003 introduced the `DATALINK` data type. Variables of `DATALINK` type can be retrieved from the database using the `getURL` method on the `RTResultSet`, and can be set using the `setURL` on `RTStatement`.

Named Parameters

JDBC 3.0 named parameters are not currently supported by Oracle SQLJ.

PL/SQL BOOLEAN and PL/SQL RECORD

Like the Oracle JDBC, the Oracle SQLJ does not support calling arguments or return values of the PL/SQL BOOLEAN type or RECORD types.

As a workaround for an unsupported type, you can create wrapper procedures that process the data using supported types. See conversion technique in JPublisher (covered later).

- You can wrap a stored procedure that uses PL/SQL Boolean values, and you can create a stored procedure that takes a character or number from JDBC and passes it to the original procedure as BOOLEAN, or for an output parameter, accepts a BOOLEAN argument from the original procedure and passes it as a CHAR or NUMBER to JDBC.

  The following code fragment utilizes a PL/SQL wrapper procedure, WRAP_BP, for a stored procedure, P, that takes a BOOLEAN as input:

```
PROCEDURE WRAP_BP (n NUMBER) IS
BEGIN
   IF n=0
      THEN BP(false);
      ELSE BP(true);
   END IF;
END;


PROCEDURE BP (b BOOLEAN) IS
BEGIN
...
END;
```

- Similarly, to wrap a stored procedure that uses PL/SQL records, you can create a stored procedure that handles scalar components of the record, such as CHAR and NUMBER.

- To wrap a stored procedure that uses PL/SQL TABLE types, you can break the data into components or perhaps use Oracle collection types.

12.2   SQLJ Best Practices

12.2.1   Row Prefetch

The `setFetchSize()` method of an `ExecutionContext` instance sets the number of rows to be prefetched during `SELECT` statement, resulting in fewer roundtrips.

```
DefaultContext.getDefaultContext().getExecutionContext().setF
etchSize(10);
```

Conversely, the `getFetchSize()` method of an `ExecutionContext` instance returns the current prefetch size as an `int` value.

12.2.2   Statement Caching

SQLJ furnishes two statement caching mechanisms:

- For Oracle-specific code generation, SQLJ statement caching uses the JDBC explicit caching mechanism controlled through connection methods and covered in Chapter 11 (statement caching). As of Oracle Database 10g Release 2, the statement cache size defaults to 5.

  The following methods of `OracleConnection` are available to SQLJ connection context instance (see Chapter 7 for more details):

  ```
  void setExplicitCachingEnabled(boolean)
  boolean getExplicitCachingEnabled()
  void setImplicitCachingEnabled(boolean)
  boolean getImplicitCachingEnabled()
  ```

- For SQLJ ISO code generation, SQLJ uses its own caching, which is controlled by the Oracle customizer `stmtcache` option.

  The Oracle Database 10g JDBC implements the `sqlj.runtime.profile.ref.ClientDataSupport` interface, resulting in a per-connection statement cache, which is shared by all instances of a connection context class that share the same underlying connection.

  You can alter the statement cache size through the Oracle customizer `stmtcache` option:

  ```
  -P-Cstmtcache=n (integer n)
  ```

A cache size of 0 disables statement caching.

12.2.3 Update Batching

JDBC update batching or DML batching is described in Chapter 7. In SQLJ, update batching is related to the execution context.

The `setBatching()` method of the execution context enables/disables update batching:

```
ExecutionContext exCtx = new ExecutionContext();

exCtx.setBatching(true); // Enabled
...
exCtx.setBatching(false); // Disabled — the default
```

The `isBatching()` method of an execution context instance determines if update batching is enabled or not:

```
boolean batching = exCtx.isBatching();
```

Chapter 7 describes and discusses implicit versus explicit update batching. The `executeBatch()` method explicitly executes an update batch:

```
int[] updateCounts = exCtx.executeBatch();
```

The `getBatchUpdateCounts()` method of an execution context returns the update count array for an implicitly executed batch:

```
int[] updateCounts = exCtx.getBatchUpdateCounts();
```

The `cancel()` method of the execution context instance cancels a pending batch:

```
if (...))
   {
      exCtx.cancel();
      throw new SQLException("Batch canceled.");
   }
```

12.3 Conclusion

This concludes the coverage of SQLJ as a simpler alternative to JDBC. Our next topic is JPublisher, which can be viewed as the Swiss Army knife for manipulating Oracle SQL data types. JPublisher complements and simplifies SQLJ, JDBC, and also enables database Web services.

Part IV: Oracle Database Programming with JPublisher

For the rest of the lazy but smart developers!

If you have ever performed custom mapping of database entities, such as user-defined SQL object types and user-defined collection types, and accessed PL/SQL types and packages, Java in the database, and so on—from JDBC and/or SQLJ, you know that this can be challenging, intimidating, time consuming, and error prone. The Oracle JPublisher utility generates the Java wrappers corresponding to database entities. The generated classes can be used in JDBC, SQLJ, stand-alone Java applications, and enterprise Java components, thereby simplifying access to the Oracle Database entities. Moreover, as we will see in Part V, JPublisher can also generate proxies that expose database operations as Web services; conversely, it can wrap external Web services for the consumption of SQL, PL/SQL, and Java DB.

Chapter 13 covers Oracle JPublisher.

Abridged Oracle JPublisher

This chapter does not purport to provide exhaustive coverage of JPublisher. Rather, it will introduce the rationale for using JPublisher, the utility, its features, its environment, the options, the mapping categories or possibilities, and some examples.

13.1 Why JPublisher?

I will use a PL/SQL RECORD type that cannot be mapped directly to or from Java. Assume you want to map the following MYPKG PL/SQL package, which contains a procedure that takes a RECORD as IN OUT parameter, into a Java class Mypkg:

```
create or replace package mypkg
as type studrec
is record (name varchar2(10),
age number);
procedure proc1 (enrold timestamp,
stud in out studrec);
end;
/
```

Assume also that you want to map SQL TIMESTAMP to java.util.Date; the signature of the corresponding Java proc1 method would be as follows:

```
public void proc1(java.util.Date enrold, StudRecSql[]
stud_inout);
```

Without JPublisher, here are the steps you would manually follow to perform the PL/SQL-to-Java mapping for the MYPKG package:

1. Create a SQL object type, STUDREC_SQL, for the PL/SQL RECORD type, STUDREC. Remember, an intermediate wrapper must be used to map a RECORD to a SQL type that JDBC supports.

2. Create a Java type for the SQL type you created (e.g., create the Java type StudRecSql for the SQL type STUDREC_SQL).

3. In the Java code, use Java Date for SQL TIMESTAMP.

4. Pass IN or IN OUT arguments (i.e.,StudRecSql and TimeStamp to proc1 via JDBC).

5. In the PL/SQL block, convert STUDREC_SQL to STUDREC.

6. Call the PL/SQL stored procedure.

7. In PL/SQL, convert OUT, IN OUT arguments, or function result, from unsupported JDBC types to the corresponding supported types (i.e., convert STUDREC to STUDREC_SQL).

8. Return each OUT, IN OUT arguments, or function result, from the PL/SQL block.

9. In Java, convert each OUT, IN OUT argument, or function result, from supported JDBC types (TimeStamp) to the unsupported types (java.util.Date).

Using JPublisher, the following command directly "publishes" the MYPKG package:

```
$ jpub -u scott/tiger -s mypkg:Mypkg -style=webservice10
-outarguments=array -plsqlfile=mypkgWrap.sql

SCOTT.MYPKG
SCOTT."MYPKG.STUDREC"
J2T-138, NOTE: Wrote PL/SQL package JPUB_PLSQL_WRAPPER to
file mypkgWrap.sql. Wrote the dropping script to file
mypkgWrap_drop.sql
```

Notice the use of –style, -outarguments, and –plsqlfile options, described later.

```
$ ls

Mypkg.class  Mypkg.java  MypkgStudrec.class
MypkgStudrec.java  MypkgStudrecRef.class
MypkgStudrecRef.java  mypkgWrap.sql  mypkgWrap_drop.sql
$
```

Here is the description of the files generated by JPublisher:

- `Mypkg.java`: The Java base class generated for the PL/SQL package `MYPKG`

- `MypkgBase.java`: The Java user subclass extended from `MypkgBase`

- `MypkgUser.java`: The Java classes extended from `MypkgBase`, for mapping `TimeStamp` to `java.util.Date`

- `MypkgStudrec.java`: The Java interface generated for `STUDREC_SQL`

- `MypkgStudrecRef.java`: The Java type for the REF type of `STUDREC_SQL`

- `MypkgWrap_drop.sql`: Cleans up type and the package

- `MypkgWrap.sql`: Contains the definition of the SQL type `STUDREC_SQL` for the PL/SQL `STUDREC` type and conversion functions between `STUDREC` and `STUDREC_SQL`. It also contains a wrapper for the PL/SQL stored procedure `proc1`. It must be executed before using the generated classes, as follows:

```
$ sqlplus scott/tiger @mypkgWrap.sql
```

Isn't that cool? Even power developers will benefit from JPublisher. Now that I have your attention, let's look deeper into JPublisher, starting with the overview.

13.2 Overview

Oracle JPublisher is a utility for generating a Java wrapper, which implements the `SQLData` or `ORAData/ORADataFactory` interfaces (i.e., *strongly typed* custom mapping) to represent the following database entities: user-defined SQL object types, object references, user-defined SQL collections, OPAQUE types, XMLType, PL/SQL Boolean, PL/SQL records, PL/SQL associative arrays, PL/SQL package, Java in the database, SQL queries, SQL DML, and streams AQ. In addition, as support to database Web services (covered in the next chapter), JPublisher also wraps PL/SQL packages, Java classes in the database, SQL queries, SQL data manipulation language (DML) statements, streams/AQ, and external Web services.

Features

JPublisher furnishes the following features in Oracle Database 9i Release 2 (9.2):

- Supports PL/SQL RECORD and INDEX-BY TABLE
- Publishes server-side Java class to PL/SQL
- Wraps external Web services for SQL, Java, and PL/SQL consumption
- Client-side stub for server-side Java invocation (also known as Native Java Interface (-java))
- Generates PL/SQL Wrapper (Call Spec) for Java in the Database (-dbjava)
- Accesses SQLJ functionality (-sqlj)
- Publishes SQL Queries and DMLs to Java

JPublisher furnishes the following features in Oracle Database 10g Release 1:

- The value of the CLASSPATH environment variable is appended to the classpath-value that is provided through the JPublisher command line.
- Implicit SQLJ translation and Java compilation. By default, in Oracle Database 10g, if SQLJ code is generated, it is automatically compiled into a Java class and then deleted (i.e., not retained). However, you have the option to instruct JPublisher to retain the intermediate SQLJ file.
- Generation of SQLJ runtime free code that only requires the Oracle JDBC drivers.
- Generation of Java interfaces.
- Style files for Java-to-Java type mappings.
- REF CURSOR returning and result set mapping.
- Filtering what JPublisher publishes.

JPublisher furnishes the following features in Oracle Database 10g Release 2:

- Support for JDBC types when calling server-side Java

- Support for publishing Oracle Streams Advanced Queue (AQ) as Web services

- Support for complex types in Web services call-outs

13.2.1 Environment Requirements

Installing JPublisher

JPublisher and SQLJ can both be installed using the following steps from the Oracle Database 10g Client (from the client CD or downloaded from OTN):

1. Insert the Oracle Database 10g Client CD or download and unzip the Oracle Database 10*g* Client.

2. Start the installer via the `setup.exe`.

3. Choose "`Custom Install.`"

4. Accept or change the `ORACLE_HOME`.

5. Select `ORACLE SQLJ` and proceed with the installation.

Environment Checklist

This section describes the environment requirements for JPublisher. Assume you have already installed an Oracle Database 10g or earlier; in order to use JPublisher, the following components must be installed:

- The Java Developer's Kit (JDK) release 1.2 or higher (i.e., JDK 1.3, and 1.4).

- The Oracle JDBC drivers either downloaded from the Oracle Technology Network (OTN) or from the Oracle Database 10g client distribution: `classes12.jar` for JDK 1.2.x /1.3.x or `ojdbc14.jar` for JDK 1.4.x, usually installed in *ORACLE_HOME*/jdbc/lib. The JPublisher runtime (i.e., `oracle.jpub.runtime` package) is included with the JDBC libraries.

- The SQLJ translator and runtime, used by JPublisher: `translator.jar` and `runtime12.jar`, typically located in in *ORACLE_HOME*/`sqlj/lib`.

- The `SQLJUTL` package installed in the database, to support PL/SQL types.

- The `SQLJUTL2` package installed in the database, to support the invocation of server-side Java classes (described later).

- The JPublisher script (`jpub`) for UNIX/LINUX environments or JPublisher executable (`jpub.exe`) for Microsoft Windows environments are typically located in *$ORACLE_HOME*/`bin` or *ORACLE_HOME*/`sqlj/bin`. It is invoked as follows:

```
$ jpub
JPub: Java Object Type Publisher, version 10.2.0.0.0 Production
Copyright (c) 1997, 2004, Oracle Corporation. All Rights Reserved.

JPub generates Java or SQLJ source code for the following SQL
entities:
   object types, collection types, and packages.

Invocation:
   jpub <options>

The following option is required:
   -user=<username>/<password>
Other options are:
   -input=<input file>
   Types and packages to be processed by JPub may be listed in the
-input file
   The contents of the -input file may be as simple as:
      SQL Person
      SQL Employee
   -sql=<sql entity list>
   Types and packages to be processed by JPub may also be listed using
the -sql option
   For example, -sql=a,b:c,d:e:f is equivalent to the -input file
entries:
      SQL a
      SQL b AS c
      SQL d GENERATE e AS f
```

• • •
• • •

Other options have been omitted; see Table 13.1 for a complete list of JPublisher options.

Table 13.1 *JPublisher Command-Line Options Summary*

Option Name	Description	Default Value	Category
-access	Determines the access modifiers that JPublisher includes in generated method definitions.	public	Java code generation
-adddefaulttypemap	Appends an entry to the JPublisher default type-map.	NA	Type maps
-addtypemap	Appends an entry to the JPublisher user type-map.	NA	Type maps
-builtintypes	Specifies the data type mappings (jdbc or oracle), for built-in data types that are not numeric or large object (LOB).	jdbc	Data type mappings
-case	Specifies the case of Java identifiers that JPublisher generates.	mixed	Java code generation
-classpath	Adds to the Java CLASSPATH for JPublisher to resolve Java source and classes during translation and compilation.	Empty	Java environment
-compatible	Specifies a compatibility mode and modifies the behavior of -usertypes=oracle.	oradata	Backward compatibility
-compile	Determines whether to proceed with Java compilation or suppress it. This option also affects SQLJ translation for backward-compatibility modes.	true	Input/output
-compiler-executable	Specifies a Java compiler version, in case you want a version other than the default.	NA	Java environment

Table 13.1   *JPublisher Command-Line Options Summary (continued)*

Option Name	Description	Default Value	Category
–context	Specifies the class that JPublisher uses for SQLJ connection contexts. This can be the DefaultContext class, a user-specified class, or a JPublisher-generated inner class.	DefaultContext	Connection
–defaulttypemap	Sets the default type-map that JPublisher uses.		Type maps
–d	Specifies the root directory for placement of compiled class files.	Empty (all files directly present in the current directory)	Input/output
–dir	Specifies the root directory for placement of generated source files.	Empty (all files directly present in the current directory)	Input/output
–driver	Specifies the driver class that JPublisher uses for Java Database Connectivity (JDBC) connections to the database.	oracle.jdbc. OracleDriver	Connection
–encoding	Specifies the Java encoding of JPublisher input and output files.	The value of the system property file.encoding	Input/output
–endpoint	Specifies a Web service endpoint. This option is used in conjunction with the -proxy-wsdl option.	NA	Web services
–filtermodes	Filters code generation according to specified parameter modes.	NA	Java code generation
–filtertypes	Filters code generation according to specified parameter types.	NA	Java code generation
–generatebean	Ensures that generated code conforms to the JavaBeans specification.	false	Java code generation

Table 13.1 *JPublisher Command-Line Options Summary (continued)*

Option Name	Description	Default Value	Category
-genpattern	Defines naming patterns for generated code.	NA	Java code generation
-gensubclass	Specifies whether and how to generate stub code for user sub-classes.	true	Java code generation
-httpproxy	Specifies a proxy URL to resolve the URL of a Web Services Description Language (WSDL) document for access through a firewall. This option is used in conjunction with the -proxy-wsdl option.	NA	Web services
-input or -i	Specifies a file that lists the types and packages that JPublisher translates.	NA	Input files/ items
-java	Specifies server-side Java classes for which JPublisher generates client-side classes.	NA	Input files/ items
-lobtypes	Specifies the data type mapping (jdbc or oracle) that JPublisher uses for BLOB and CLOB types.	oracle	Data type mappings
-mapping	Specifies the mapping that generated methods support for object attribute types and method argument types. *Note:* This option is deprecated in favor of the "*XXXtypes*" mapping options, but is supported for backward compatibility.	objectjdbc	Data type mappings

Table 13.1   *JPublisher Command-Line Options Summary (continued)*

Option Name	Description	Default Value	Category
-methods	Determines whether JPublisher generates wrapper methods for stored procedures of translated SQL objects and PL/SQL packages. This option also determines whether JPublisher generates SQLJ classes or non-SQLJ classes, and whether it generates PL/SQL wrapper classes at all. There are settings to specify whether overloaded methods are allowed.	`all`	Java code generation
-numbertypes	Specifies the data type mappings, such as jdbc, objectjdbc, bigdecimal, or oracle, that JPublisher uses for numeric data types.	`objectjdbc`	Data type mappings
-omit_schema_names	Instructs JPublisher not to include the schema in SQL type name references in generated code.	`Disabled (schema included in type names)`	Java code generation
-outarguments	Specifies the holder type, such as arrays, Java API for XML-based Remote Procedure Call (JAX-RPC) holders, or function returns, for Java implementation of PL/SQL output parameters.	`array`	Java code generation
-overwritedbtypes	Specifies whether to ignore naming conflicts when creating SQL types.	`true`	PL/SQL code generation
-package	Specifies the name of the Java package into which JPublisher generates Java wrapper classes	`NA`	Java code generation
-plsqlfile	Specifies a wrapper script to create and a dropper script to drop SQL conversion types for PL/SQL types and the PL/SQL package that JPublisher will use for generated PL/SQL code.	`plsql_wrapper .sql, plsql_dropper .sql`	PL/SQL code generation

Table 13.1 *JPublisher Command-Line Options Summary (continued)*

Option Name	Description	Default Value	Category
-plsqlmap	Specifies whether to generate PL/SQL wrapper functions for stored procedures that use PL/SQL types.	true	PL/SQL code generation
-plsqlpackage	Specifies the PL/SQL package into which JPublisher generates PL/SQL code, such as call specifications, conversion functions, and wrapper functions.	JPUB_PLSQL_WRAPPER	PL/SQL code generation
-props or -p	Specifies a file that contains JPublisher options in addition to those listed on the command line.	NA	Input files/items
-proxyclasses	Specifies Java classes for which JPublisher generates wrapper classes and PL/SQL wrappers according to the -proxyopts setting. For Web services, you will typically use -proxywsdl instead, which uses -proxyclasses behind the scenes.	NA	Web services
-proxyopts	Specifies required layers of Java and PL/SQL wrappers and additional related settings. Is used as input for the -proxywsdl and -proxyclasses options.	jaxrpc	Web services
-proxywsdl	Specifies the URL of a WSDL document for which Web services client proxy classes and associated Java wrapper classes are generated along with PL/SQL wrappers.	NA	Web services
-serializable	Specifies whether the code generated for object types implements the java.io.Serializable interface.	false	Java code generation

Table 13.1   *JPublisher Command-Line Options Summary (continued)*

Option Name	Description	Default Value	Category
-sql or -s	Specifies object types and packages, or subsets of packages, for which JPublisher generates Java classes, and optionally subclasses and interfaces.	NA	Input files/ items
-sqlj	Specifies SQLJ option settings for the JPublisher invocation of the SQLJ translator.	NA	SQLJ
-sqlstatement	Specifies SQL queries or data manipulation language (DML) statements for which JPublisher generates Java classes, and optionally subclasses and interfaces, with appropriate methods.	NA	Input files/ items
-style	Specifies the name of a style file for Java-to-Java type mappings.	NA	Data type mappings
-sysuser	Specifies the name and password for a superuser account that can be used to grant permissions to execute wrappers that access Web services client proxy classes in the database.	NA	Web services
-tostring	Specifies whether to generate a toString() method for object types.	false	Java code generation
-typemap	Specifies the JPublisher type-map.	Empty	Type maps
-types	Specifies object types for which JPublisher generates code. *Note:* This option is deprecated in favor of -sql, but is supported for backward compatibility.	NA	Input files/ items
-url	Specifies the URL that JPublisher uses to connect to the database.	jdbc:oracle: oci:@	Connection
-user or -u	Specifies an Oracle user name and password for connection.	NA	Connection

Table 13.1   *JPublisher Command-Line Options Summary (continued)*

Option Name	Description	Default Value	Category
–usertypes	Specifies the type mapping (jdbc or oracle) that JPublisher uses for user-defined SQL types.	Oracle	Data type mappings
–vm	Specifies a Java version, in case you want a version other than the default.	NA	Java environment

13.2.2   JPublisher Options

This section explains the key JPublisher options, summarized in Table 13.1. The options can be grouped into the following categories: Java environment, connection, Java code generation, runtime free code generation, style files for mapping Java in the database, type-maps, data type mapping (or type conversion), input files/items, input/output, style files, and backward compatibility. The Web services options will be covered in Part V dedicated to database Web services.

Java Environment

JPublisher shares the following options with the SQLJ environment (covered in Chapter 10):

The –classpath option specifies the CLASSPATH to be used by JPublisher during translation and compilation for resolving classes:

```
$ jpub –user=scott/tiger
-sql=PERSON:Person,EMPLOYEE:Employee
-classpath=.:$ORACLE_HOME/jdbc/lib/
    ojdbc14.jar:$CLASSPATH
```

- The –compiler-executable option can be used to specify a Java compiler other than the default for compiling the code generated by JPublisher:

```
-compiler-executable=<path to compiler executable>
```

- The -vm option can be used to specify a nondefault JVM for invoking JPublisher:

```
$ jpub -vm=$JAVA_HOME/bin/java
    -compiler-executable=$JAVA_HOME/bin/javac ...
```

Connection

JPublisher obviously requires a database connection; it also requires a datasource for Java proxies representing database entities that are deployed in the middle tier.

- The -context option specifies the SQLJ connection context class to be used by SQLJ classes generated by JPublisher (see Chapter 11 for more details on connection contexts).

    -context={generated|**DefaultContext**|user_defined}

- The -datasource option specifies the datasource to be used for publishing SQL query and DML, PL/SQL, Streams AQ, and server-side Java classes. In the absence of an explicit JDBC connection, the generated code will look up the JNDI location specified by this option in order to get a connection.

    -datasource=jndi_location

- The -driver option specifies the driver class to use for JDBC connections; the following default setting should satisfy most needs:

    -driver=oracle.jdbc.OracleDriver

- The -url option specifies the URL of the target database.

    The default is: -url=jdbc:oracle:oci:@

    For JDBC-Thin, use: -url=jdbc:oracle:thin:@host:port/servicename

■ The –user or –u option is mandatory and specifies an Oracle database user name and password:

```
-user=username/password
-u username/password
```

SQL Data Types Categories and Mapping

JPublisher shares the same mapping table with JDBC (Chapter 8) and SQLJ (Chapter 11); however, it groups SQL data types into the following four categories and, as summarized in Table 13.2, for each category, it lets you specify which style of mapping to perform.

■ *Numeric types* (-numbertypes option): Anything stored as SQL type NUMBER. The mapping choices are:

```
-numbertypes=objectjdbc|jdbc|bigdecimal|oracle
```

The default mapping is "objectjdbc." See the next section for a more detailed description of numeric data types mapping.

■ *Large object (LOB) types* (-lobtypes option): SQL BLOB and CLOB. The mapping choices are: -lobtypes=oracle|jdbc. The default mapping is "oracle."

■ *Built-in types* (-builtintypes option): Anything stored as a SQL type not covered by the preceding categories (e.g., CHAR, VARCHAR2, LONG, and RAW). The mapping choices are: -builtintypes=jdbc|oracle. The default mapping is "jdbc."

■ *User-defined types* (-usertypes option): An attribute of SQL object type. The mapping choices are: -usertypes=oracle|jdbc. The default mapping is "oracle."

Table 13.2 *JPublisher SQL Type Categories, Supported Settings, and Defaults*

SQL Type Category	JPublisher Mapping Option	Mapping Settings	Default
UDT types	-usertypes	oracle, jdbc	oracle
Numeric types	-numbertypes	oracle, jdbc, objectjdbc, bigdecimal	objectjdbc

Table 13.2   *JPublisher SQL Type Categories, Supported Settings, and Defaults*

LOB types	-lobtypes	oracle, jdbc	oracle
Built-in types	-builtintypes	oracle, jdbc	jdbc

Numeric Data Types Mapping

JPublisher defined the following mapping of numeric types: JDBC mapping, Oracle maping, Object-JDBC mapping, and Big Decimal mapping.

- *JDBC mapping* (setting jdbc): Uses Java primitive types to map SQL types. This setting is valid for the –numbertypes, –lobtypes, and –builtintypes options.

- *Oracle mapping* (setting oracle): Uses the oracle.sql types for mapping SQL types. This setting is valid for the –numbertypes, –lobtypes, and –builtintypes options.

- *Object-JDBC mapping* (setting objectjdbc): Is equivalent to JDBC mapping but uses numeric object types, or reference types (i.e., java.lang.Integer, Float, and Double), instead of primitive Java types (i.e., int, float, and double). Remember that the reference types may return null, unlike the primitive types. This setting is valid for the –numbertypes option only.

- *BigDecimal mapping* (setting bigdecimal): By default, large numeric attributes are mapped to java.math.BigDecimal. You can instruct JPublisher to map to oracle.sql.NUMBER instead, which is faster and more precise than java.math.BigDecimal.

Input Files

The JPublisher Input file lets you control the naming of the generated classes and packages and how to map them. The Input files include the INPUT files (.in) and properties files (.properties), as specified, respectively, by the following options: –input, –props.

- The general syntax of an INPUT file (.in) is as follows:

```
( SQL name_of_SQL_Type_or_PL/SQL_Package_to_be_translated
| SQL [schema_name.]toplevel  [(name_list)]
| SQLSTATEMENTS_TYPE java_name
| TYPE type_name)
```

```
[GENERATE java_name_1 [IMPLEMENTS java_interface]]
[AS java_name_2 [IMPLEMENTS java_interface]]
[TRANSLATE
     database_member_name AS simple_java_name
 { , database_member_name AS simple_java_name}*
]
(SQLSTATEMENTS_METHOD sql_statement AS java_method_name)*
   [VERSION [=] <version_name>]
```

> **Note:** AS, GENERATE, IMPLEMENTS, SQLSTATEMENTS_TYPE, SQL, TYPE, SQLSTATEMENTS_METHOD, TRANSLATE, TOPLEVEL, and VERSION are reserved words.

The VERSION clause has no specific meaning at the moment.

Examples of input files:

```
Foo.in
======
SQL foo_pkg


Rename.in
=========
SQL original as newname


Nested_Table.in
===============
TYPE module_t   as Module
TYPE moduletbl_t  as Modules
TYPE employee_t  as Employee
```

Assume the following user-defined object:

```
CREATE TYPE student AS OBJECT
(
   name        VARCHAR2(30),
   empno       INTEGER,
   deptno      NUMBER,
   enroldate   DATE,
```

```
    tuition     REAL
  );
```

And the following input file:

```
jpubinput.in
============
SQL student AS Student
TRANSLATE NAME AS Name ENROLDATE AS EnrolDate
```

Note: The input file may contain one or several TRANSLATE statements:

```
$ jpub -user=scott/tiger -input=jpubinput -numbertypes=oracle
-usertypes=oracle -dir=jpubdemo -d=jpubdemo -package=jpub
-case=same
```

This JPublisher command will perform the following mapping:

- NAME: Column name mapped to Java Name

- ENROLDATE: Column name mapped to Java EnrolDate

- STUDENT: Type mapped by Student class and written to the following files specified by the source and class directories (-dir, and -d) and the packagesettings (-package):

```
jpubdemo/jpub/Student.java
jpubdemo/jpub/Student.class
```

- The –props option (no jpub.props in properties file) furnishes an alternative to command-line options and specifies the name of a JPublisher properties file (there is no default properties file in JPublisher). Each line in the property file corresponds to one command-line option (prefixed by jpub.), with the associated value. Table 13.2 gives an explanatory summary of JPublisher options; you can take any option (but –props) and prefix it with "jpub."

Here are samples of properties files:

```
foo.properties
==============
  jpub.sql=person_t:Person,student_t:Student,
  jpub.user=scott/tiger
  jpub.compatible=CustomDatum

mapping2.properties
===================
  jpub.filtermodes=in,out,inout,return
  jpub.filtertypes=1,.INDEXBY,
       .ORACLESQL-,.BLOB,.CLOB,.STRUCT,.BFILE
  jpub.generatebean=true
  jpub.compatible=ORAData
  jpub.methods=always
  jpub.out=return
```

Items to Publish

The following options help you specify which items to publish, such as SQL objects, PL/SQL packages, SQL queries, SQL DML statements, or server-side Java classes:

```
-java, -sql, -sqlstatement.
```

- The -sql (or -s, or jpub.sql in properties file) is one of the most useful and most used options; it allows you to specify the user-defined SQL object types, user-defined SQL collection types, or PL/SQL packages (whole package or a subset) to publish. It can also be used to request the generation of interfaces or subclasses.

The generic syntax is:

```
-sql={toplevel|<object type and package translation syntax>}
```

The following command-line syntaxes apply:

```
-sql=toplevel
-sql=toplevel:MyClass
```

JPublisher generates a wrapper class named toplevel or MyClass:

```
-sql=<sql package or object type>
-sql=<sql package(<proc1>+<proc2>+<proc3>+...)>
-sql=<sql package or type>:<Java Class>
-sql=<sql package or type>:<Java Class>#<Java Interface>
-sql=<sql package or type>:<Class>:<Subclass>#<Sub Interface>
```

Alternatively, you may use the INPUT file syntax, which gives you finer-grain control:

```
SQL toplevel
SQL toplevel AS MyClass
```

The following command syntax specifies an interface for either the reference class (GENERATE) or the customizable user subclass (AS):

```
SQL name_a
[GENERATE  generated_class
          [ IMPLEMENTS intface_b] ]
[AS        user_class
          [ IMPLEMENTS intface_c ] ]
```

The −sql option can occur several times within the same command line; however, you can use a single occurrence with several items separated by commas, without any white space.

Assume a package, MYPACKAGE, object types STUDENT and LOCATION. The following command:

```
-sql=MYPACKAGE,STUDENT:Student,LOCATION:JLocation:MyLocation
```

is equivalent to the following INPUT file syntax:

```
SQL MYPACKAGE
SQL STUDENT AS Student
SQL LOCATION GENERATE JLocation AS MyLocation
```

and performs the following actions:

1. Creates a wrapper class for the MYPACKAGE; JPublisher maps a package with a single Java class (not a Java class per procedure or function).

2. The SQL STUDENT type is mapped as Student.

3. Generates an object reference class, StudentRefRef.

4. The SQL LOCATION type is mapped to JLocation; in addition, JPublisher generates a user customizable class to represent LOCATION objects by the MyLocation class.

5. A MyLocation stub is generated, which extends Jlocation; you can customize the MyLocation code.

6. Generates an object reference class, MyLocationRef.

■ The -java option (jpub.java option in properties file) creates client-side stub classes for accessing server-side classes:

```
$ jpub -u scott/tiger
  -java=<Server-side Java>:<Stub Implementation>#<Stub
interface>
```

JPublisher generates the client-side stub interface and its implementation. This option was covered in detail in Chapter 3. Depending on the database release (9.2 or 10g), it may require the sqljutl.jar library (located in $ORACLE_HOME/sqlj/lib) to be loaded in the database.

■ The -sqlstatement option lets you publish SQL statements, including SELECT, INSERT, UPDATE, or DELETE statements, as Java methods in SQLJ classes. This is mainly for Web services needs; however, you can also use the generated class in traditional JDBC and/or SQLJ programs. You can specify multiple -sqlstatement.method-Name settings. The -sqlstatement.return indicates whether a query result is returned as a result set, or an array, or both (as two methods).

Here is the generic syntax:

```
-sqlstatement.class=ClassName:UserClassName#UserInterfaceName
-sqlstatement.methodName=sqlStatement
-sqlstatement.return={both|resultset|beans}
```

The following JPublisher command will generate proxy classes that can be used in the middle tier to represent this SQL statement. See Part V for a how to publish a SQL statement as Web service.

```
$ jpub -u scott/tiger -sqlstatement.getEmpBySal="select
ename, sal, hiredate from emp where sal >:{mysal NUMBER}"
-compile=notranslate

SQLStatements
SQLStatements_getEmpBySalRow
```

JPublisher generates the following files: `SQLStatements.sqlj` and `SQLStatements_getEmpBySalRow.java`.

Alternatively, using the following properties file:

```
statement.properties
====================
jpub.sqlstatement.getEmpBySal="select ename, sal, hiredate
from emp where sal>:{mysal NUMBER}"
```

you can issue the following JPublisher command:

```
$jpub -user=scott/tiger -props=statement.props
-compile=notranslate
```

Java Code Generation

The following JPublisher options control how JPublisher performs Java code generation: -access, -case, -filtermodes, -filtertypes, -generate-bean, -genpattern, -gensubclass, -methods, -omit_schema_names, -outarguments, -package, -serializable, and -tostring.

Using these options, you can do the following:

- Filter the generated code according to parameter modes or parameter types. The -filtermodes option lets you filter generated code according to parameter modes; this is useful when not all parameter modes are supported in method signatures or attributes of the consumer of the generated code.

```
-filtermodes= <list of modes to filter out or filter in>
(i.e., in, out, inout, return)
```

```
0: exclude all by default (total filtering)
1: include all by deault (no filtering)
"-": the mode or type should be excluded
"+": the mode or type should be included
```

```
Examples:
-filtermodes=0,in+,return+
-filtermodes=1,out-,inout-
```

The `-filtertypes` option lets you filter generated code according to parameter types; this is useful when not all parameter types are supported in method signatures or attributes of the consumer of the generated code:

-filtertypes=*l<ist of types to filter out or filter in>* (i.e., `oracle.sql.XXX` types, any indexed-by table types, any SQLJ iterator types and `java.sql.ResultSet`, any types that implement `ORAData` or `SQLData`, and so on).

Examples:

Allows `ORAData` or `SQLData` types except those with a typecode of `ARRAY` or `REF`:

```
-filtertypes=0,.ORADATA+,.ARRAY-,.REF-
```

Filters all types except `.CURSOR` and `.INDEXBY`:

```
-filtertypes=0,.CURSOR+,.INDEXBY+
```

- Ensure that the generated code conforms to the JavaBeans specification (e.g., getter method must return a bean property, and so on)

```
-generatebean={true|false}   (default is false).
```

When `-generatebean=true`, the names of methods that are not JavaBean property getter and setter are changed (i.e., prefixed with "_") so as to avoid confusion.

Example:

```
     public int getBaseType() throws SQLException;
```
becomes:

```
     public int _getBaseType() throws SQLException;
```

- Specify the naming patterns. The -genpattern option can be used in conjunction with the –sql or -sqlstatement option, to define generic naming patterns:

```
-genpattern=<pattern specifications>
%1 refers to the default base names that JPublisher
generates
%2 refers to the output names if specified by -sql
```

For example, the following pattern specification:

```
-genpattern=%1Base:%1User#%1
-sql=PERSON,EMPLOYEE,EMPLOYEE_MGR
```

is equivalent to:

```
-sql=PERSON:PersonBase:PersonUser#Person
-sql=EMPLOYEE:EmployeeBase:EmployeeUser#Employee
-sql=EMPLOYEE_MGR:EmployeeMgrBase:EmployeeMgrUser#EmployeeMgr
```

- Specifying how stubs are generated for user subclasses. The -gensub-class option controls whether JPublisher generates source files for user-provided subclasses and their shape.

```
-gensubclass={true|false|force|call-super}
```

true: JPublisher generates the subclass only if it does not already exist; this is the default.

false: JPublisher does not generate any subclass.

force: JPublisher generates the subclasses, even if it already exists.

call-super: JPublisher generates only constructors and methods for implementing an interface (i.e., ORAData); getters, setters, and other methods are generated.

- The method controls the generation of wrapper methods for stored procedures in SQL object types and methods in PL/SQL packages (JPublisher generates one Java class per PL/SQL package), as well as method overloading, and connection retry.

```
-methods={all|none|named|always,overload|unique
,noretry|retry}
```

-methods=all: Generates SQLJ class if the underlying SQL object or package defines methods; otherwise a Java class. In pre-10g, SQLJ classes were always generated for this setting.

-methods=none: No wrapper method is generated, and no class is generated for the PL/SQL packages.

-methods=named: Wrapper methods are generated only for the methods explicitly named in the INPUT file.

-methods=always: SQLJ classes are generated for all SQL object types, regardless of whether the types define methods.

-methods=overload: Method in the generated code can be overloaded (i.e., same name different signatures).

Assume the following stored functions:

```
function func1 (a VARCHAR2(40)) return VARCHAR2;
function func1 ( x int, y int) return int;
```

With —methods=overload, JPublisher will generate the following method wrappers as part of the PL/SQL package mapping:

```
String func1 (String a);
java.math.BigDecimal
func1(java.math.BigDecimal x, java.math.BigDecimal y);
```

-methods=unique: No overload, and various techniques are used to generate a unique method name, such as appending a number or the first letter of the return type and argument types.

Continuing the previous example, here is how JPublisher renamed function names:

```
String func1(String a);
java.math.BigDecimal
    func1BBB(java.math.BigDecimal x, java.math.BigDecimal y);
```

-methods=retry: This option is used for Web services call-in (see next chapter). An additional constructor is generated, which takes a DataSource object as parameter to get a new connection at runtime. Extra code is gen-

erated to request a new JDBC connection and retry the method if the
method encounters a JDBC connection error during execution.

- The -outarguments option is primarily used to support Web services; it lets you specify a method to use to return PL/SQL OUT or
  IN OUT parameters (Array, JAX-RPC holder or Function
  returns).

  -outarguments={**array**|holder|return}

- Specifying whether generated code is serializable or not. The -seri-
  alizable option specifies whether the generated class (for SQL
  object types) implements the java.io.Serializable interface. The
  default is false.

  -serializable={true|**false**}

PL/SQL Code Generation

The following options let you control how JPublisher generates PL/SQL
code: -overwritedbtypes, -plsqlfile, -plsqlmap, and
-plsqlpackage.

- The -overwritedbtypes option specifies if naming conflicts are
  checked before creating new SQL types. These are generated when
  publishing PL/SQL types and PL/SQL wrappers for server-side Java
  classes. The default is true; set this option to false (overwritedb-
  types=false.) if you do not want JPublisher to overwrite the existing type. In order to always generate the same type upon multiple
  invocation of the same operation, you must run the dropperx.sql
  package before each run.

- The -plsqlfile option specifies scripts to use in creating and dropping SQL types and PL/SQL packages. The wrapper script creates
  new SQL types (to map to PL/SQL types) as well as the PL/SQL
  package that JPublisher uses for any PL/SQL wrappers or Call Specs,
  conversion functions, wrapper functions, and table functions. The
  dropper script drops these entities. JPublisher prints the following
  message on the standard output upon generating the scripts:

```
J2T-138, NOTE: Wrote PL/SQL package XXXXXXXX to
file xxxxxxxxxx.sql. Wrote the dropping script to file
zzzzzzzzzz.sql.
```

- The –plsqlmap option specifies whether PL/SQL wrapper functions
  are generated:

  -plsqlmap={**true**|false|always}

  true: Only as needed, depending on the complexity of the mapping
  of the types, arguments, parameters, and function returns.

  false: PL/SQL wrapper functions are not generated, so JPublisher
  skips this step.

  always: A PL/SQL wrapper function is generated for every stored
  procedure that uses a PL/SQL type.

- The –plsqlpackage option specifies the name of the PL/SQL package in which JPublisher generates PL/SQL call specs, conversion
  functions, wrapper functions, and table functions. By default, JPublisher uses the JPUB_PLSQL_WRAPPER *package.*

  -plsqlpackage=<*name of PLSQL package*>

Note: you must use this option to avoid erasing a previously generated
wrapper.

Style Files for Mapping Java in the Database

Style files let you specify the mapping of Java types and Oracle JDBC
types that are not supported by the target consumer (e.g., Web services
framework) into supported types; for example, java.sql.Clob and
oracle.sql.CLOB are converted into java.lang.String (see Database
Web services in Part V).

JPublisher generates client-side Java subclasses or proxies that represent
server-side Java, and the subclasses implement the mapping specified in the
style files. Table 13.3 summarizes the Java-to-Java type mapping.

As of Oracle Database 10g, the following style files are furnished as part
of translator.jar:

Table 13.3   *Summary of Key Java-to-Java Type Mappings in Oracle Style Files*

Source Type	Target Type
oracle.sql.NString	java.lang.String
oracle.sql.CLOB	java.lang.String
oracle.sql.BLOB	byte[]
oracle.sql.BFILE	byte[]
java.sql.Timestamp	java.util.Date
java.sql.ResultSet	oracle.jdbc.rowset.OracleWebRowSet org.w3c.dom.Document javax.xml.transform.Source
oracle.sql.SimpleXMLType	java.lang.String (webservices-common) org.w3c.dom.DocumentFragment (webservices9) javax.xml.transform.Source (webservices10)

```
/oracle/jpub/mesg/webservices-common.properties
/oracle/jpub/mesg/webservices10.properties
/oracle/jpub/mesg/webservices9.properties
```

The -style option specifies the base name of a style file:

```
-style=<stylename>
```

Example:

```
-style = webservices10   (i.e., webservices10.properties)
-style = local/mystyle    (i.e., local/mystyle.properties)
```

JPublisher looks for a style file as follows:

1.   It looks for the following resource in the CLASSPATH:

```
/oracle/jpub/mesg/<stylename>
```

2.   It looks for the following resource in the CLASSPATH:

    `/oracle/jpub/mesg/<stylename>.properties`

3.   It looks for the file in the current directory:

    `<stylename>`

4.   Finally, it looks for the file in the current directory:

    `<stylename>.properties`

If no style file can be found, JPublisher throws an exception.

In section 13.1, the —style=webservices10 is used to convert java.sql.Timestamp into java.util.Date.

In this example:

1.   The PL/SQL stored procedure definition includes a TIMESTAMP argument:

```
procedure proc1 (enrold timestamp, stud in out
studrec);
```

2.   JPublisher first maps this as follows in the base class:

```
public void proc1(java.sql.Timestamp enrold,
StudRecSql[] stud_inout);
```

3.   Then JPublisher maps it as follows in the user subclass:

```
public void proc1(java.util.Date enrold, StudRecSql[]
stud_inout);
```

XMLType mapping is a recurrent requirement. JPublisher takes a two-step approach in mapping XMLType into oracle.sql.SimpleXMLType:

1.   SYS.XMLTYPE is mapped to oracle.xdb.XMLType

2.   This can then be mapped to oracle.sql.SimpleXMLType using style file.

A style file has a TRANSFORMATION section and an OPTION section.

- The TRANSFORMATION section is delimited by the TRANSFORMATION and END_TRANSFORMATION tags and describes the Java-to-Java mappings, to be applied to types used for object attributes or in method signatures.

- The MAPPING subsection within the TRANSFORMATION section specifies source and target mapping, as follows:

```
MAPPING
# TIMESTAMP columns uses java.sql.Timestamp.
# For Web Services this is mapped to java.util.Date
#
SOURCETYPE java.sql.Timestamp
TARGETTYPE java.util.Date
OUT
%2 = null;
if (%1!=null) %2=new java.util.Date(%1.getTime() +
%1.getNanos()/1000000) ;
END_OUT
IN
# Converting Date to Timestamp
%1 = null;
if (%2!=null) %1 = new
java.sql.Timestamp(%2.getTime());
END_IN
END_MAPPING
```

- The OPTIONS section lets you specify additional JPublisher options and may be used in lieu of a JPublisher properties file.

Type-Maps

The JPublisher user type-map or default type-map entries to influence code generation. Type-maps are used in JPublisher for the following:

- Specifying the mappings of PL/SQL data types that are unsupported by JDBC.

- Avoiding regenerating a Java class to map to a user-defined type. For example, if you specify the EMPLOYEE:Employee mapping in the user type map, then JPublisher finds the `Employee` class and uses it without regenerating it.

JPublisher uses the following logic for mapping a given SQL or PL/SQL type to Java:

1. Checks the type-maps to see if a mapping already exists.

2. Checks the predefined Java mappings for the SQL and PL/SQL types.

3. Checks if the data type to be mapped is a PL/SQL `RECORD` or an `INDEX-BY-TABLE`.

   - If PL/SQL `RECORD` type, JPublisher generates a corresponding SQL object type that can be mapped to Java.

   - If `INDEX-BY-TABLE` type, JPublisher generates a corresponding SQL collection type that can be mapped to Java.

4. If none of these steps applies, then the data type must be a user-defined type. JPublisher generates an `ORAData` or `SQLData` class to map it accordingly.

The following options manage the type-map entries: `-addtypemap`, `-adddefaulttypemap`, `-defaulttypemap`, and `-typemap`.

- `-addtypemap` appends entries to the user-type map.
- `-typemap` replaces the existing user type-map with the specified entries.
- `-adddefaulttypemap` appends entries to the default type-map.
- `-defaulttypemap` replaces the existing default type-map with the specified entries.

These options can be specified instead in a JPublisher properties file.

A JPublisher type-map entry has one of the following formats:

```
-type_map_option=opaque_sql_type:java_type
-type_map_option=numeric_indexed_by_table:java_numeric_type[max_length]
-type_map_option=char_indexed_by_table:java_char_type[max_length](elem_size)
-type_map_option=
```

plsql_type:*java_type*:*sql_type*:*sql_to_plsql_func*:*plsql_to_sql_func*

Note: *sql_to_plsql_func* and *plsql_to_sql_func* are conversion functions between SQL and PL/SQL (conversion functions are illustrated in the next chapter).

Here are examples of default type-maps with conversion functions (e.g., INT2BOOL, BOOL2INT):

```
jpub.defaulttypemap=SYS.XMLTYPE:oracle.xdb.XMLType
jpub.adddefaulttypemap=BOOLEAN:boolean:INTEGER:
SYS.SQLJUTL.INT2BOOL:SYS.SQLJUTL.BOOL2INT
jpub.adddefaulttypemap=INTERVAL DAY TO SECOND:String:CHAR:
SYS.SQLJUTL.CHAR2IDS:SYS.SQLJUTL.IDS2CHAR
jpub.adddefaulttypemap=INTERVAL YEAR TO MONTH:String:CHAR:
SYS.SQLJUTL.CHAR2IYM:SYS.SQLJUTL.IYM2CHAR
```

Input/Output

The following options control JPublisher input and output files and their locations.

- The -compile option prevents the compilation of the generated .java files and the translation of generated .sqlj files (for backward compatibility with previous releases, since by default JPublisher now removes the .sqlj files).

  ```
  -compile={true|false|notranslate}
  ```

  true: The generated SQLJ and/or Java files are translated and compiled.

  false: The generated SQLJ files are translated; however, the Java files are not compiled.

  notranslate: The generated SQLJ files are not translated and not removed, which is the behavior of the earlier JPublisher releases.

- The -dir option specifies the directory location for .java and .sqlj source files, while the -d option specifies the directory location for .class files.

```
$ jpub -user=scott/tiger -d=classdir -dir=sourcedir ...
```

- The -encoding option specifies the Java character encoding to be used for reading the INPUT file and the output source files.

Note: This option does not apply to properties files, since these always use the 8859_1 encoding.

Backward Compatibility

The -compatible option:

```
-compatible={oradata|customdatum|both8i|8i|9i|10.1|sqlj}
```

can be used for:

Specifying the interface to implement in generated classes, for backward compatibility purposes.   If -usertypes=oracle, then -compatible=customdatum instructs JPublisher to implement the CustomDatum interface (supported for backward-compatibility purposes).

- Skipping the translation step, the .sqlj output files are kept.

     -compatible=sqlj instructs JPublisher to skip SQLJ translation of the generated .sqlj files.
- Backward-compatibility with Oracle9*i* or Oracle8*i* environments -compatibility=9i instructs JPublisher to generates .sqlj files compatible with the Oracle 9*i* release. Oracle 8i compatibility is beyond the scope of this book.

13.3   JPublisher In Action

This section describes succinctly how JPublisher maps supported database entities, including user-defined SQL object types, SQL object reference types (REF types), REF cursors, user-defined SQL collections, user-defined opaque types, XMLType, PL/SQL Boolean types, PL/SQL record types, PL/SQL associative arrays, PL/SQL packages, Java in the database, SQL queries, SQL DML, and streams AQ. The generated wrapper classes can be used as wrappers in your JDBC or SQLJ applications, as you used the handcrafted ones.

13.3.1 User-Defined SQL Object Types

For a SQL object type, FOO_T, JPublisher generates a foo_t.java class that maps the object. This includes getters and setters methods to get and set each attribute of the object type. In addition, if the object type includes methods implemented as PL/SQL stored procedures, JPublisher will generate Java wrapper methods to invoke the corresponding methods on the SQL object instances. JPublisher also generates the object reference type.

Assume a user-defined NUMBERTYPE, the ToReal, Plus, and GCD Functions, and Normalize procedure:

```
Number.sql
==========

drop table NumberTab;
drop type NumberType force;

CREATE TYPE NumberType AS OBJECT (
    num INTEGER,
    denom INTEGER,
    MAP MEMBER FUNCTION toReal RETURN REAL,
    MEMBER PROCEDURE normalize,
    STATIC FUNCTION gcd(x INTEGER,
                        y INTEGER) RETURN INTEGER,
    MEMBER FUNCTION plus ( x NumberType) RETURN NumberType
);
/
CREATE TYPE BODY NumberType AS

  MAP MEMBER FUNCTION toReal RETURN REAL IS
  -- convert rational number to real number
  BEGIN
    RETURN num / denom;
  END toReal;

  MEMBER PROCEDURE normalize IS
   g BINARY_INTEGER;
  BEGIN
```

```
    g := NumberType.gcd(num, denom);
   num := num / g;
   denom := denom / g;
 END normalize;

 STATIC FUNCTION gcd(x INTEGER,
                    y INTEGER) RETURN INTEGER IS
 -- find greatest common divisor of x and y
 ans BINARY_INTEGER;
 BEGIN
 IF x < y THEN
    ans := NumberType.gcd(y, x);
 ELSIF (x MOD y = 0) THEN
    ans := y;
 ELSE
    ans := NumberType.gcd(y, x MOD y);
 END IF;
 RETURN ans;
 END gcd;
 MEMBER FUNCTION plus (x NumberType) RETURN NumberType IS
 BEGIN
   return NumberType(num * x.denom + x.num * denom,
                 denom * x.denom);
   END plus;
END;
/

CREATE TABLE NumberTab of NumberType;
INSERT INTO NumberTab VALUES(2,3);

COMMIT;
EXIT;
/

$ sqlplus scott/tiger @Number

Number.in
=========
SQL NumberType AS NumberType

Number.properties
```

```
=================
jpub.methods=all
jpub.numbertypes=jdbc
jpub.lobtypes=jdbc
jpub.builtintypes=jdbc
jpub.usertypes=jdbc
jpub.compile=notranslate      ← do not translate/compile the
                                 sqlj file


$ jpub -u scott/tiger -input=Number.in
-props=Number.properties
SCOTT.NUMBERTYPE
```

You can look at the generated `Number.sqlj` file, and here are some highlights:

```
public class NumberType implements SQLData
{
  public static final String _SQL_NAME = "SCOTT.NUMBERTYPE";
  public static final int _SQL_TYPECODE = OracleTypes.STRUCT;
  ...


  public int gcd (int X,int Y) throws java.sql.SQLException
  ...
  #sql [getConnectionContext()] __jPt_result =
                    { VALUES(SCOTT.NUMBERTYPE.GCD(:X,:Y)) };
    ...


  public NumberType plus ( NumberType X) throws
java.sql.SQLException

  #sql [getConnectionContext()]
       { BEGIN :OUT __jPt_result := :__jPt_temp.PLUS(:X);
END;};


  public NumberType normalize ()

   NumberType __jPt_temp = this;
   #sql [getConnectionContext()]
      { BEGIN :INOUT __jPt_temp.NORMALIZE(); END;};
   return __jPt_temp;
```

```
    public float toreal ()
      #sql [getConnectionContext()]
          {BEGIN :OUT __jPt_result := :__jPt_temp.TOREAL();
END;};
```

The following test code uses the generated code (with proper environment). That's all you have to do!

```
MuNumber.java
=============


import sqlj.runtime.ref.DefaultContext;
import oracle.sqlj.runtime.Oracle;


public class MyNumber
{

  public static void main(String[] args) throws
java.sql.SQLException
    {
      int n = 5;
      int d = 10;
      NumberType r = new NumberType(5, 10);

      int g = r.gcd(n, d);
      System.out.println("gcd: " + g);

      float f = r.toReal();
      System.out.println("real value: " + f);

      NumberType s = r.plus(r);
      System.out.println("sum: " + s);

      s.normalize();
      System.out.println("sum: " + s);
    }
}
```

13.3.2   **SQL Object Reference Types (REF types)**

For a SQL object reference type, REFFOO_T, JPublisher generates a
foo_tRef.java class, which models references to the object type in Java,
along with methods for accessing the actual object value. From JPublisher's
mode of operation perspective, this mapping is similar to the previous case.
Let's reuse XREFADTtab.sql types defined in Chapter 3.

```
XREFADTTab.sql
==============
drop table REFtab;
drop table ADTtab;
drop type ADTtyp;

create type ADTtyp as OBJECT (a1 number, a2 varchar2(20), a3
date)
/
create table ADTtab of ADTtyp
/

create table REFtab (id number, refcol REF ADTtyp)
/

insert into ADTtab values (ADTtyp(1, 'One', '01-JAN-2001'));
insert into ADTtab values (ADTtyp(2, 'Two', '02-JAN-2002'));
insert into ADTtab values (ADTtyp(3, 'Three', '03-JAN-
2003'));
insert into ADTtab values (ADTtyp(4, 'Four', '04-JAN-2004'));
insert into ADTtab values (ADTtyp(5, 'Five', '05-JAN-2005'));

insert into REFtab select 1, REF(R2) from ADTtab R2 where
R2.a1 = 1;
insert into REFtab select 2, REF(R2) from ADTtab R2 where
R2.a1 = 2;
insert into REFtab values (3, NULL);
insert into REFtab select 4, REF(R2) from ADTtab R2 where
R2.a1 = 4;
insert into REFtab select 5, REF(R2) from ADTtab R2 where
R2.a1 = 5;
commit;

$ sqlplus scott/tiger @XREFADTTab
```

```
$ jpub -user scott/tiger -sql=ADTtyp:Adttyp

SCOTT.ADTTYP

$ ls Adttyp*

Adttyp.class Adttyp.java  AdttypRef.class  AdttypRef.java
```

13.3.3   REF Cursor Types and Subclassing

For a PL/SQL stored procedure or function that returns a REF CURSOR, JPublisher generates a Java class, which maps the REF CURSOR to java.sql.ResultSet. For a SQL query that returns a REF CURSOR, JPublisher maps the REF CURSOR to an array of rows, each row being represented by a JavaBean instance. Assume the following script, which declares a PL/SQL package that uses a ref cursor type:

```
Refcur.sql
==========

set serveroutput on;
create or replace package refcur as
    type curstype is ref cursor return emp%rowtype;
    FUNCTION getcurfunc RETURN curstype;
    PROCEDURE getcurproc(a curstype);
end;
/
show errors

create or replace package BODY refcur as
    FUNCTION getcurfunc RETURN curstype IS
    curs curstype;
    BEGIN
        open curs for select * from emp where ename='SCOTT';
        return curs;
    END;

    PROCEDURE getcurproc(a curstype) IS
      name emp%rowtype;
```

```
        BEGIN
           LOOP
              FETCH a INTO   name ;
              EXIT WHEN a%NOTFOUND;
              dbms_output.put_line(name.ENAME);
           END LOOP;
         close a;
        END;

END;
/
show errors
exit;



$ sqlplus scott/tiger @Refcur

SQL*Plus: Release 10.2.0.1.0 - Production on Sun Jan 22
19:00:01 2006
Copyright (c) 1982, 2005, Oracle.  All rights reserved.
Connected to:
Oracle Database 10g Enterprise Edition Release 10.2.0.1.0 -
Production
With the Partitioning and Data Mining options


Package created.

No errors.

Package body created.

No errors.
Disconnected from Oracle Database 10g Enterprise Edition
Release 10.2.0.1.0 - Production
With the Partitioning and Data Mining options
$
```

Invoke it through SQL*Plus first, as follows, for a sanity check:

```
$ sqlplus scott/tiger
```

```
SQL> set serveroutput on

SQL> declare
  2  curs refcur.curstype;
  3  begin
  4  curs := refcur.getcurfunc();
  5  refcur.getcurproc(curs);
  6  end;
  7  /
SCOTT

PL/SQL procedure successfully completed.
```

Map with JPublisher:

```
$ jpub -user scott/tiger —compile=notranslate
-sql=REFCUR:Refcur

SCOTT.REFCUR
GetcurfuncRow
```

JPublisher generates:

- `Refcur.sqlj:`

- `GetcurfuncRow.java:` containing the getters and setters for each column of the EMP table

Generated code is not nice to read, but you can notice the following method in `Refcur.sqlj` (preserved with –compile=notranslate option):

```
public java.sql.ResultSet getcurfunc () {…}
```

getcurfunc() places a SQLJ call to GETCURFUNC, which returns a Ref Cursor into a Result Set variable.

```
#sql [getConnectionContext()]
            __jPt_result_rs = {
VALUES(SCOTT.REFCUR.GETCURFUNC()) };
```

However, if you want to map Ref Cursor to String instead, for use as a Web service parameter, for example, JPublisher allows you to subclass the generated class.

The following syntax generates a base class and a subclass that can be customized by the end user:

```
jpub -sql=REFCUR:RefcurBase:MyRefcur ...
```

The following classes are generated: RefcurBase.sqlj and MyRefcur.sqlj, which extends RecurBase. You can modify MyRefcur.sqlj and add a new method, which returns the result set in the desired format, such as String:

```
public String[] readRefCursorArray(String arg1, Integer arg2)
{    java.sql.ResultSet rs = getcurfunc(arg1,arg2);
     //... create a String[] from rs and return it ... }
```

13.3.4   User-Defined SQL Collection Types

You can perform a strongly typed custom mapping of user-defined collections. For each collection type (**VARRAYs, Nested Tables**) COL_T, JPublisher generates a col_t.java class that implements ORAData and represents the collection. For Nested Tables, it generates, in addition, methods to get and set the Nested Table as an entire array and methods to get and set individual elements of the table.

Assume the following database entities definition: STUDENT_T and MODULE_T object types, MODULETBL_T as NESTED TABLE of MODULE_T, STUDENT, and PROJECT tables.

```
NTab.sql (not shown entirely)
========


DROP TABLE projects
/
drop table student
/
DROP TYPE moduletbl_t
/
DROP TYPE module_t
/
```

```
DROP TYPE student_t
/
CREATE TYPE student_t AS OBJECT (
  empno    NUMBER(4),
  ename    VARCHAR2(20),
  job      VARCHAR2(12),
  mgr      NUMBER(4),
  hiredate DATE,
  sal      NUMBER(7,2),
  deptno   NUMBER(2))
/
show errors
CREATE TYPE module_t  AS OBJECT (
  module_id  NUMBER(4),
  module_name VARCHAR2(20),
  module_owner REF student_t ,
  module_start_date DATE,
  module_duration NUMBER )
/
show errors
create TYPE moduletbl_t AS TABLE OF module_t;
/
show errors
CREATE TABLE projects (
  id NUMBER(4),
  name VARCHAR(30),
  owner REF student_t,
  start_date DATE,
  duration NUMBER(3),
  modules  moduletbl_t  ) NESTED TABLE modules STORE AS modules_tab ;

CREATE TABLE student  OF student_t ;

INSERT INTO STUDENT VALUES(
STUDENT_T(7369,'BOB SMET','ANALYST',7902,'17-DEC-95',800,20)) ;
...
INSERT INTO student VALUES (
student_t(7934,'SUE MILLER','SR ANALYST',7782,'23-JAN-02',1300,10));

INSERT INTO projects VALUES ( 111, 'P111', null, '10-JAN-02',  300,
      moduletbl_t( module_t ( 1111 , 'Physics ', null, '01-JAN-99',
100),
```

```
module_t ( 1112 , 'Advertizing', null, '05-FEB-04',20) ,
                        ...
module_t ( 1115 , 'Politics', null,'12-MAY-03',34) ) ) ;


update projects set owner=(select ref(p) from student p where p.empno
= 7839) where id=111 ;
update the(select modules from projects a where a.id = 111)   set
module_owner =
 ( select ref(p) from student p where p.empno = 7844) where module_id
= 1111 ;
update the(select modules from projects a where a.id = 111)   set
module_owner =
 ( select ref(p) from student p where p.empno = 7844) where module_id
= 1111 ;
...


INSERT INTO projects VALUES ( 444, 'P444', null, '15-FEB-03', 555,
      moduletbl_t ( module_t ( 4441 , 'Manufacturing', null, '01-MAR-
02', 120),
...
module_t ( 4447 , 'Budgets', null, '10-MAR-01',45))) ;


update projects set owner=(select ref(p) from student p where p.empno
= 7698) where id=444 ;


update the ( select modules from projects where id = 444 ) set
module_owner =
( select ref(p) from student p where p.empno = 7369) where module_id =
4441 ;
...
commit;


exit;


$ jpub -user scott/tiger -compile=false
      -sql=MODULE_T:Module,MODULETBL_T:Modules,STUDENT_T:Student


SCOTT.MODULE_T
SCOTT.MODULETBL_T
SCOTT.STUDENT_T
```

The following files are generated: `Module.java`, `Modules.java`, `ModuleRef.java`, `Student.java`, and `StudentRef.java`.

Module.java
```
public class Module implements ORAData, ORADataFactory
{
  public static final String _SQL_NAME = "SCOTT.MODULE_T";
  public static final int _SQL_TYPECODE = OracleTypes.STRUCT;
  ...
  // getters and setters
```

Modules.java

```
public class Modules implements ORAData, ORADataFactory
{
  public static final String _SQL_NAME = "SCOTT.MODULETBL_T";
  public static final int _SQL_TYPECODE = OracleTypes.ARRAY;
  ...
  public Module[] getArray(long index, int count) throws SQLException
  ...
  public void setArray(Module[] a) throws SQLException
  ...
  public Module getElement(long index) throws SQLException
  ...
  public void setElement(Module a, long index) throws SQLException
```

ModuleRef.java
```
public class ModuleRef implements ORAData, ORADataFactory
{
  public static final String _SQL_BASETYPE = "SCOTT.MODULE_T";
  public static final int _SQL_TYPECODE = OracleTypes.REF;
  ...
```

Student.java
```
public class Student implements ORAData, ORADataFactory
{
  public static final String _SQL_NAME = "SCOTT.STUDENT_T";
  public static final int _SQL_TYPECODE = OracleTypes.STRUCT;
  ...
  // getters and setters
```
StudentRef.java
```
public class StudentRef implements ORAData, ORADataFactory
```

```
{
    public static final String _SQL_BASETYPE = "SCOTT.STUDENT_T";
    public static final int _SQL_TYPECODE = OracleTypes.REF;
...
```

13.3.5 User-Defined OPAQUE Types

SQL OPAQUE types are usually used internally by other types; however, these can be exposed to Java through custom wrapper classes, which implement the oracle.sql.ORAData interface. Assume MYOPAQUE type, for which there is no associated wrapper. JPublisher will generate a MyOpaque.java wrapper class containing the following public, static fields, and methods:

```
public static String _SQL_NAME = "MYOPAQUE";
public static int _SQL_TYPECODE = OracleTypes.OPAQUE;
public static ORADataFactory getORADataFactory() { ... }
```

```
MYOPAQUE.sql
============

CREATE LIBRARY opqlib TRUSTED AS STATIC
/
CREATE OR REPLACE TYPE MYOPAQUE as OPAQUE FIXED (4)
USING library opqlib
(
        STATIC FUNCTION CONSTRUCT(str IN VARCHAR2) return MYOPAQUE,
        MEMBER FUNCTION VALUE return BINARY_INTEGER,
        MAP MEMBER FUNCTION MAPFUN return BINARY_INTEGER
)
/


CREATE OR REPLACE TYPE BODY MYOPAQUE as
STATIC FUNCTION CONSTRUCT(str IN VARCHAR2) return MYOPAQUE
...
MEMBER FUNCTION VALUE return BINARY_INTEGER
...
MAP MEMBER FUNCTION MAPFUN return BINARY_INTEGER
...
end;
/
$ jpub  -user=sys/<syspassword>    -sql=MYOPAQUE:MyOpaque
        -methods=true
```

You may associate an existing Java class to the SQL OPAQUE type using the JPublisher user type map as follows:

```
-addtypemap=MYOPAQUE:MyOpaque
```

13.3.6 XMLType

As mentioned in JDBC and SQLJ subparts, `SYS.XMLTYPE` is a named OPAQUE type that is mapped by default to the Java wrapper class `oracle.xdb.XMLType`. For simple XMLTYPE operations you may use any JDBC driver (JDBC-Thin or JDBC-OCI), however, full support for `oracle.xdb.XMLType` requires JDBC-OCI. Fortunately, JPublisher furnishes `oracle.sql.SimpleXMLType`, a driver-independent alternative wrapper for `SYS.XMLTYPE` (i.e., works for both JDBC-Thin and JDBC-OCI).

Assume `xmlobj` is an object type based on XMLtype:

```
xmltype.sql
===========
drop type xmlobj;

create type xmlobj as object (xmldoc sys.xmltype);
/
show error


exit
```

Here are the steps for generating the wrapper class `xmlobj_t` and `xmlobj_tRef`, using JPublisher:

```
Step#1: create the sql type
$ sqlplus scott/tiger

...
SQL> set echo on
SQL> @xmltype
SQL> drop type xmlobj;

Type dropped.
SQL>
SQL> create type xmlobj as object (xmldoc sys.xmltype);
  2  /
```

```
Type created.

SQL> show error
No errors.
SQL>
SQL> exit


$ jpub -u scott/tiger —compile=false -sql=xmlobj:xmlobj_t

SCOTT.XMLOBJ
```

The following files are generated, for mapping SYS.XMLTYPE to oracle.xdb.XMLType.

```
xmlobj_t.java  xmlobj_tRef.java
```

Let's glance at xmlobj_t.java:

```
xmlobj_t.java
=============
...
public class xmlobj_t implements ORAData, ORADataFactory
{
  public static final String _SQL_NAME = "SCOTT.XMLOBJ";
  public static final int _SQL_TYPECODE = OracleTypes.STRUCT;
  ...
  public static ORADataFactory getORADataFactory()
  ...


  /* ORAData interface */
  public Datum toDatum(Connection c) throws SQLException
  ...
  /* ORADataFactory interface */
  public ORAData create(Datum d, int sqlType) throws
SQLException
  ...
  protected ORAData create(xmlobj_t o, Datum d, int sqlType)
throws SQLException
  ...
```

```
/* accessor methods */
public oracle.xdb.XMLType getXmldoc() throws SQLException
...
public void setXmldoc(oracle.xdb.XMLType xmldoc) throws
SQLException
}
```

The xmlobj_tRef is not displayed.

Using a style file, we can instruct JPublisher to map SYS.XMLTYPE to oracle.sql.SimpleXMLType.

```
$ jpub -u scott/tiger -style=webservices10
                      -compile=false -sql=XMLOBJ:xmlobj_t

xmlobj_t.java  xmlobj_tBase.java  xmlobj_tUser.java
xmlobj_tUserRef.java
```

13.3.7   PL/SQL Conversion Functions

When mapping a PL/SQL type not supported by JDBC (such as BOOLEAN) as arguments or return value into a Java type, JPublisher lets you specify an intermediate supported SQL type (such as INTEGER) and the RDBMS-side conversion functions.

1.   Create a function that maps the PL/SQL type (PLTYP) to the SQL type (SQLTYP):

```
FUNCTION PL2SQL(pl PLTYP) RETURN SQLTYP
```

2.   Create a function that maps the SQL type (SQLTYP) to the PL/SQL type (PLTYP):

```
FUNCTION SQL2PL(sql SQLTYP) RETURN PLTYP
```

3.   Define a JPublisher typemap:

```
jpub -addtypemap=PLTYP:<java type>:SQLTYP:SQL2PL:PL2SQL ...
```

The SYS.SQLJUTL package is required in the database where the generated code will run (it is installed by default in Oracle Database 10g).

This technique is used for mapping PL/SQL RECORD as well as PL/SQL Index-by-Table (see section 13.3.9). Note that PL/SQL BOOLEAN typemap and conversion functions are predefined, so you don't have to implement the conversion function or define the type map.

13.3.8   PL/SQL RECORD Types

An example of PL/SQL RECORD type mapping is furnished in section 13.1. JPublisher generates the corresponding SQL objects. An intermediate wrapper (the conversion functions for mapping between PL/SQL and SQL types) is used to map a RECORD to a SQL type that JDBC supports.

13.3.9   PL/SQL Table or Scalar Index-by-Table

As we have seen in Chapter 8, JDBC now supports index-by-table (or PL/SQL associative). However, JPublisher can simplify the mapping of PL/SQL index-by-table of scalar SQL types into Java arrays or custom Java wrapper class. JPublisher generates an intermediate SQL type (i.e., VARRAY) as well as conversion functions (i.e., INDEX-BY-TABLE_to_VARRAY and VARRAY_to_INDEX-BY-TABLE) between the index-by-table type and the SQL type (i.e., VARRAY).

The following example maps a PL/SQL INDEX-BY-TABLE into a custom Java wrapper class, which implements ORAData.

Create the PL/SQL package containing the index-by-table:

```
indexbytab.sql
===============
create or replace package pkgidx is
    type plsidxtyp is table of varchar2(20) index by
binary_integer;
    procedure procidx (p1 in out plsidxtyp);
    end;
/


$sqlplus scott/tiger @indexbytab
```

The following JPublisher command generates these objects: `wrap1.sql`, `drop1.sql`, `Pkgidx.sqlj`, and `PkgidxPlsidxtyp.java` (the -notranslate option prevents it from compiling and removing the `.sqlj` files).

```
$ jpub -u scott/tiger -s PKGIDX:Pkgidx -plsqlpackage=wrap1
        -plsqlfile=wrap1.sql,drop1.sql —compile=notranslate
SCOTT.PKGIDX
SCOTT."PKGIDX.PLSIDXTYP"
J2T-138, NOTE: Wrote PL/SQL package wrap1 to file wrap1.sql.
Wrote the dropping script to file drop1.sql
$
```

The Java wrapper for the PL/SQL index-by-table type:

```
PkgidxPlsidxtyp.java
====================
public class PkgidxPlsidxtyp implements ORAData,
ORADataFactory
{
  public static final String _SQL_NAME =
"SCOTT.PKGIDX_PLSIDXTYP";
  public static final int _SQL_TYPECODE = OracleTypes.ARRAY;
...
```

The Java wrapper of the PL/SQL package (remember: JPublisher generates one Java class to map the entire PL/SQL package):

```
Pkgidx.sqlj
===========
public class Pkgidx {

/* connection management */

/* constructors */

//

  public void procidx (PkgidxPlsidxtyp P1[])
   throws java.sql.SQLException
   {
    try {
        #sql [getConnectionContext()]
```

```
                { CALL wrap1.PKGIDX$PROCIDX(:INOUT (P1[0])) };
            } catch(java.sql.SQLException _err) {…}
```

...

The conversion functions:

```
wrap1.sql
=========
-- Declare the SQL type for the PL/SQL type PKGIDX.PLSIDXTYP
CREATE OR REPLACE TYPE PKGIDX_PLSIDXTYP AS TABLE OF
VARCHAR2(20);
/
show errors
-- Declare package containing conversion functions between
SQL and PL/SQL types
CREATE OR REPLACE PACKAGE wrap1 AS
        -- Declare the conversion functions the PL/SQL type
PKGIDX.PLSIDXTYP
        FUNCTION PL2PKGIDX_PLSIDXTYP(aPlsqlItem
PKGIDX.PLSIDXTYP)
                    RETURN PKGIDX_PLSIDXTYP;
        FUNCTION PKGIDX_PLSIDXTYP2PL(aSqlItem
PKGIDX_PLSIDXTYP)
                    RETURN PKGIDX.PLSIDXTYP;
    PROCEDURE PKGIDX$PROCIDX (P1 IN OUT PKGIDX_PLSIDXTYP);
END wrap1;
/
show errors
CREATE OR REPLACE PACKAGE BODY wrap1 IS
        FUNCTION PL2PKGIDX_PLSIDXTYP(aPlsqlItem
PKGIDX.PLSIDXTYP)
        RETURN PKGIDX_PLSIDXTYP IS
        aSqlItem PKGIDX_PLSIDXTYP;
        BEGIN
            -- initialize the table
            aSqlItem := PKGIDX_PLSIDXTYP();
            aSqlItem.EXTEND(aPlsqlItem.COUNT);
          FOR I IN aPlsqlItem.FIRST..aPlsqlItem.LAST LOOP
            aSqlItem(I + 1 - aPlsqlItem.FIRST) :=
                aPlsqlItem(I);
            END LOOP;
            RETURN aSqlItem;
        END PL2PKGIDX_PLSIDXTYP;
```

```
        FUNCTION PKGIDX_PLSIDXTYP2PL(aSqlItem
PKGIDX_PLSIDXTYP)
            RETURN PKGIDX.PLSIDXTYP IS
            aPlsqlItem PKGIDX.PLSIDXTYP;
            BEGIN
                    FOR I IN 1..aSqlItem.COUNT LOOP
                            aPlsqlItem(I) := aSqlItem(I);
                    END LOOP;
                    RETURN aPlsqlItem;
            END PKGIDX_PLSIDXTYP2PL;


        PROCEDURE PKGIDX$PROCIDX (P1 IN OUT PKGIDX_PLSIDXTYP) IS
            P1_ SCOTT.PKGIDX.PLSIDXTYP;
        BEGIN
            P1_ := wrap1.PKGIDX_PLSIDXTYP2PL(P1);
            SCOTT.PKGIDX.PROCIDX(P1_);
            P1 := wrap1.PL2PKGIDX_PLSIDXTYP(P1_);
        END PKGIDX$PROCIDX;


END wrap1;
/
show errors
exit
```

You need to add the following entry into a properties file:

```
jpub.addtypemap=
SCOTT.PKGIDX.PLSIDXTYP:PkgidxPlsidxtyp:PKGIDX_PLSIDXTYP:
WRAP1.PKGIDX_PLSIDXTYP2PL:WRAP1.PL2PKGIDX_PLSIDXTYP
```

The -plsqlindextable=<table size> option has two functions:

1. On one hand, it instructs JPublisher to map PL/SQL index-by-table of scalar types into Java arrays.

2. On the other hand, this option specifies the capacity of the PL/SQL index-by-table, required by JDBC statements (see Chapter 8 for a description of JDBC methods to support PL/SQL index-by-table). In the following example, the generated Java program IndexbyTablePackage.java uses these SQL statements:

    ■ For invoking TEST_TAB:

    ```
    "BEGIN SCOTT.IDX_TAB_PKG.TEST_TAB1(\n :1 /*[32]*/) \n;
    END;";
    ```

- For invoking ECHO_IDX_TAB2:

  ```
  "BEGIN :1 := /*[32]*/ SCOTT.IDX_TAB_PKG.ECHO_IDX_TAB2(\
  n :2 /*[32]*/) \n; END;";
  ```

  and so on.

Create the PL/SQL package containing the index-by-table:

```
create or replace package idx_tab_pkg as
type idx_tab1 is table of varchar2(111) index by binary_integer;
type idx_tab2 is table of number index by binary_integer;
type varray_tab is varray(100) of varchar2(20);
type nested_tab is table of varchar2(20);
type rec1 is record (a idx_tab1, b idx_tab2);
function echo_idx_tab1(a idx_tab1) return idx_tab1;
function echo_idx_tab2(a idx_tab2) return idx_tab2;
function echo_varray_tab(a varray_tab) return varray_tab;
function echo_nested_tab(a nested_tab) return nested_tab;
function echo_rec1(a rec1) return rec1;

procedure test_tab1(xxx idx_tab1);
procedure test_tab2(yyy idx_tab2);
end;
/
show errors

create or replace package body idx_tab_pkg is
function echo_idx_tab1(a idx_tab1) return idx_tab1 is
begin return a; end;
function echo_idx_tab2(a idx_tab2) return idx_tab2 is
begin return a; end;
function echo_varray_tab(a varray_tab) return varray_tab is
begin return a; end;
function echo_nested_tab(a nested_tab) return nested_tab is
begin return a; end;
function echo_rec1(a rec1) return rec1 is
begin return a; end;
procedure test_tab1(xxx idx_tab1) is
begin null; end;

procedure test_tab2(yyy idx_tab2) is
```

```
begin null; end;
end;
/
show errors
```

And here is the JPublisher invocation and the feedback of code generation:

```
$jpub -user=scott/tiger -
sql=idx_tab_pkg:IndexbyTablePackage#IndexbyTableIntf -
plsqlindextable=32
SCOTT.IDX_TAB_PKG
SCOTT."IDX_TAB_PKG.VARRAY_TAB"
SCOTT."IDX_TAB_PKG.NESTED_TAB"
SCOTT."IDX_TAB_PKG.REC1"
SCOTT."IDX_TAB_PKG.IDX_TAB1"
SCOTT."IDX_TAB_PKG.IDX_TAB2"
J2T-138, NOTE: Wrote PL/SQL package JPUB_PLSQL_WRAPPER to
file plsql_wrapper.sql. Wrote the dropping script to file
plsql_dropper.sql
```

The following Java wrapper classes and interfaces are generated, along with the Java wrapper class for the PL/SQL package (in the absence of the -notranslate option, the intermediate .sqlj files have been compiled and removed):

```
$ls *.java
IndexbyTableIntf.java IndexbytableintfNestedTab.java
IndexbytableintfRec1Ref.java Indexbytableintfrec1IdxTab1.java
IndexbyTablePackage.java IndexbytableintfRec1.java
IndexbytableintfVarrayTab.java Indexbytableintfrec1IdxTab2.java
$
IndexbyTableIntf.java
=====================
import java.sql.SQLException;
import sqlj.runtime.ref.DefaultContext;
import sqlj.runtime.ConnectionContext;
import java.sql.Connection;

public interface IndexbyTableIntf{

  public IndexbytableintfVarrayTab echoVarrayTab (
```

```
   IndexbytableintfVarrayTab A) throws java.sql.SQLException;

public void testTab2 (
   java.math.BigDecimal[] YYY) throws java.sql.SQLException;

public void testTab1 (
   String[] XXX) throws java.sql.SQLException;

public java.math.BigDecimal[] echoIdxTab2 (
   java.math.BigDecimal[] A) throws java.sql.SQLException;

public IndexbytableintfNestedTab echoNestedTab (
   IndexbytableintfNestedTab A) throws java.sql.SQLException;

public IndexbytableintfRec1 echoRec1 (
   IndexbytableintfRec1 A) throws java.sql.SQLException;

public String[] echoIdxTab1 (
   String[] A) throws java.sql.SQLException;
}
```

Notice the plsql_dropper.sql and plsql_wrapper.sql; in the absence of –plsqlpackage option JPublisher used the default JPUB_PLSQL_WRAPPER name for the generated PL/SQL wrapper.

At this stage, the PL/SQL index-by-table type, the Java wrapper classes, the SQL collection type, and the conversion functions can be used for publishing PL/SQL packages that contain PL/SQL index-by-table types.

13.3.10   Oracle Streams AQ

Streams AQ is a robust database-backed messaging and information integration system, which comprises queues, topics, and streams. A queue is a one-to-one message pipe with a specific payload type. A topic is a one-to-many message pipe with a specific payload type. A stream is a queue or topic with SYS.ANYDATA payload type. JPublisher maps a queue, a topic, or a stream as a Java class, which uses the Java Message Service (JMS) API.

```
$ jpub -user=SCOTT/TIGER -sql=AQNAME:javaName
```

13.3.11   **Java in the Database**

Java in the database (Java DB), can be exposed by JPublisher in many ways: to client/middle-tier Java, to Web Services, and to PL/SQL.

- The —java option publishes Java DB to client-side or middle-tier Java through a client-side stub—see Chapter 3. It supports JDBC types, Java Beans, arrays of supported types, and serializable types. This option is used under the covers by the Web Service Assembler utility (WSA) for publishing Java DB as Web service (see Chapter 15).

- The -dbjava option publishes static methods in Java DB to PL/SQL through the generation of Call Spec or PL/SQL wrappers on top of Java in the database. This option subsumes –java, since it generates a client-side stub as well, supports for more types, and works with pre-10*g* database versions. When coupled with -proxyopts, it also publishes instance methods at the expense of an additional server-side Java wrapper.

13.4   **Conclusion**

JPublisher is a versatile code generator, which offers many more possibilities than this chapter could cover. It shields the Java developer from the learning curve and many of the logistical details and inconveniences of manually creating Java database access programs. Furthermore, JPublisher simplifies the process of publishing database operations as Web services as well as the process of consuming external Web services from within the database, which is the topic of the next chapter.

Part V: Programming the Oracle Database with Web Services

Unless you have been living in a cave for the last four or five years, you have repeatedly heard about Web services and service-oriented architecture (SOA) as the new trend in IT, which allows resource consolidation, virtualization, and provisioning for optimized use, thereby reducing IT costs.

In Part I, we looked at Java within the database. In Part II, II, and IV, we looked at the APIs for persisting Java states or retrieving SQL data; the resulting code may run either within the database (i.e., manipulate the data in situ) or as a Java applet, Java EE framework/component, or stand-alone Java SE application/framework connected to the database.

In Part V, we'll switch our focus from programming the database with Java to programming the database with Web services. As we will see, the exact term would be "assembling database Web services" but the association of "database" and "Web services" immediately raises eyebrows and the following questions:

- What do Web services have to do with databases in general and the Oracle database in particular?

- What will Web services assemblers get from the integration of Web services with the database? Will they have to learn SQL and PL/SQL programming?

- What will database developers, DBAs, and data architects get from the integration of the database with Web services? Will they have to learn Java and/or Web services technologies or APIs?

Chapter 14 introduces the Web services technology and the service-oriented architecture for database developers, DBAs, and data architects (those familiar with these concepts and technologies may skip this chapter). Chapter 15 describes how you can turn your Oracle database into a Web services provider. Chapter 16 describes how you can configure your Oracle database to invoke external Web services from SQL, PL/SQL, and Java in the database. For starters, let's (re)visit the rationales for coupling Web services with the Oracle database.

Rationales for Database Web Services

Chances are you have already heard about Web services as additional means for accessing and manipulating data in the database and, conversely, as means for the database to reach external services. According to an Evans Data Corporation survey among database developers (Winter 2004), "More than two out of three respondents, 68%, say they are in the process of exposing or invoking their database operations through standard Web services mechanisms."

As another sign of the growing importance of database Web services, the leading RDBMS vendors, including Oracle, DB2, and SQL Server, furnish support with their database in a more or less integrated fashion. A summary of their implementations, the pros and cons, and how these compare is beyond the scope of this book. However, Chapter 15 contrasts the current implementation of Oracle database Web services with alternative implementation.

Motivations for exposing Oracle database functionality as Web services:

- Reuse existing database applications, such as PL/SQL packages and Java classes in the database, as Web services.

- Implement your own database-centric Web services, such as catalog services (i.e., Amazon Web services) and search services (i.e., Google Web services, Yahoo Web services) using database functionality[1] (i.e., SQL, PL/SQL, Streams/AQ, and Java).

- Furnish new database-centric Web services such as XML documents storage and retrieval e.g., client applications can insert new XML documents or retrieve existing ones from a central corporate database, edit locally, and finally store the updated document; and client applications can transmit audit and logging information to the database for archiving.

- Turn your database into a first-class member of your SOA.

---

1.   I am not implying that Yahoo, Google, and Amazon use database operations to implement their Web services.

Motivations for invoking external Web services from the database:

- Allow your Oracle database to consume data produced by external Web services.

- Federate legacy/heterogeneous data; build new applications that combine data from multiple sources, including Web services.

- Implement automated applications, such as parcel tracking, stock prices tracking and analysis, scientific data tracking and analysis, maintain/refresh policies and/or tax tables, and weather information tracking and analysis.

- Invoke business operations implemented as external Web services, such as placing new orders based on defined thresholds (i.e., number of products in inventory), batch processing of orders shipment, and batch processing of orders payment (using valid authorization numbers).

14

Web Services and SOA for DBA, Data Architects, and Others

Things should be made as simple as possible, but not any simpler.

—Albert Einstein

The promise of Web services is simplified interfaces for application-to-application interaction in heterogeneous and distributed environments. This chapter describes the key technologies that enable Web services (i.e., XML, WSDL, SOAP, UDDI) and then peeks at the bigger picture, the service-oriented architecture (SOA). After reading this chapter, you will be well armed to understand database Web services, our final destination.

14.1 Web Services 101

In traditional Web interactions, humans interact with applications through browsers, which interpret HTML to produce graphical displays and accept user inputs. As depicted by Figure 14.1, Web services, by contrast, allow *application-to-application interaction* through XML messages *irrespective of the implementations, the location, and the platforms* of the client and the server application modules. The World Wide Web Consortium (W3C) defines Web services as "software applications or components identified by a URL that describes their interfaces (i.e., services or operations they furnish) and their binding in XML, and that can be accessed by client-applications using XML messages and Internet protocols."

Figure 14.1
A Simplistic View of Web Services

The key benefits are interoperability (language/platform neutral); simpler, flexible, and dynamic integration (provision to support new protocols, dynamic service discovery and binding, defined interfaces foster composition); automation (application-to-application interaction, services orchestration/workflow); and time to market (reuse of existing applications). These benefits are made possible by the standards technologies (formats, protocols, and description) that compose the Web services stack. We can distinguish the core Web services technologies and then the infrastructure/deployment requirements, as well as higher-level technologies.

14.1.1 Core Web Services Technologies

The core technologies that make up Web services are XML, SOAP, WSDL, and UDDI. Figure 14.2 depicts how these technologies come into play. Let's look briefly into each of these.

Figure 14.2
Web Services Interaction

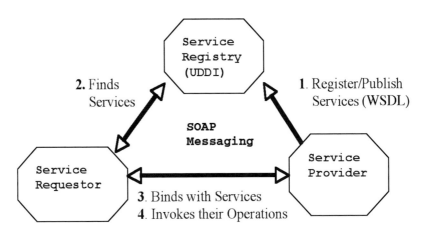

XML

The eXtended Markup Language (XML) is the *lingua franca* of Web services (and many other technologies); it serves as the base language for type definition, service description, data format, data transfer, messaging, discovery, security, and so on. Web services requesters and providers exchange information using XML documents, which are formatted according to either XML Document Type Definition (DTD) rules or XML schema rules (XSD).

As briefly described in Chapter 8, XML Schema Definition (XSD) is a W3C recommendation, an alternative to DTD, for describing *the structure, content, and semantics of XML documents*, thereby allowing all parties involved to have a common and exact understanding of the document in question. The XSD defines which elements the document may contain, their attributes, and their relationship. Because XML does not come with predefined tags, the role of XML namespaces and XML schemas is integral for a shared understanding of the document.

An XML document contains:

- A prolog or processing instruction, which starts and ends with "?" into brackets, and are the only "predefined" tags in XM; everything else is self-described, which is the "eXtensibility" in XML.

- XML namespace (`xmlns`), namespace instance (`xmlns:xsi`), and an association of the schema and the instance (`xsi:schemaLocation`). According to the W3C,[1] "XML namespaces provide a simple method for qualifying element and attribute names used in Extensible Markup Language documents by associating them with namespaces identified by URI references."

- A root element (address), which may have attributes and a cascade of subelements:

```
<element>
  <subelement>
    <field1>.....</field1>
  </subelement>
</element>
```

Here is a basic XML document representing an address:

```
<?xml version="1.0" encoding="ISO-8859-1" standalone="yes"?>
<! This is a comment -->
<Address
     xmlns=http://www.basicxml.org/AddressDoc
     xmlns:xsi=http://www.w3.org/2001/XMLSchema-instance
     xsi:schemaLocation=
        "http://www.basicxml.org/AddressDoc
         file:./AddressDoc.xsd">
     <Street> 24 Benin Drive</Street>
     <City> San Francisco </City>
```

---

1.   http://www.w3.org/TR/REC-xml-names/.

```
<State> California</State>
<Country>USA</Country>
</Address
```

XML defines simple types, such as `string`, `Base64Binary`, `hexBinary`, `integer`, `date`, `positiveInteger`, `genativeInteger`, `nonNegatveInteger`, `nonPositiveInteger`, `decimal`, `boolean`, `time`, `dateTime`, `duration`, `date`, `Name`, `QNane`, `anyURI`, `ID`, `IDREF`, and so on.

XML allows user-defined complex types such as the following:

```
<complexType name"myComplexType">
<sequence>
<element name="tname" type="string" minOccurs="0"/>
<element name="description" type="string"  minOccurs="0"/>
...
</sequence>
<attribute name="objid" type="ID"/>
<attribute name="objref" type="IDREF"/>
</complexType>
```

See Chapter 15 for more information.

XML documents can be processed and consumed directly by an application as a character stream or serialized and parsed by XML serializers and parsers (e.g., `DOM`, `SAX`, `StAX`).

XML documents can also be displayed using XSL and XSL transformers (XSLT) and style sheets. There is a whole range of XML standards, APIs, tools, editors, and utilities. However, their coverage is beyond the scope of this book. There are tons of online resources, tutorials, and FAQs about XML, such as the following:

- http://www.w3.org/XML/Schema
- http://www.w3.org/TR/xmlschema-0
- http://www.w3schools.com/xml/default.asp

WSDL

The Web Services Description Language (WSDL) is an XML language, based on a general-purpose XML schema, for describing how to access a service, including:

- Messages and their style (i.e., document versus RPC)
- Bindings of abstract operations and messages to a concrete network protocol
- Format of messages that a service can receive (see SOAP messages formats discussion)
- Supported operations, their parameters, and return types
- Location of the service

A WSDL structure is made up of two substructures: a service interface definition and a service implementation definition. The service interface definition contains initially an implementation neutral (abstract or reusable) of the service that will be instantiated by the service implementation and includes messages, types, port type, and binding.

- `Message`: Describes supported messages and parameters; may contain parts for RPC arguments.
- `PortType`: Describes the interface of a service (i.e., the set of supported operations with input message, output message, and fault message).
- `Operation`: A message signature, part of `PortType`; can be one-way of request-response.
- `Binding`: How to invoke the operations—that is, style (e.g., `RPC`), transport (e.g., `HTTP`, `SOAP`, `HTTP/MIME`, `SMTP/MIME`), encoding, and security. *Note:* WSDL does not require SOAP.
- `Types`: Describes XSD-related items and user-defined types.

The service implementation definition contains implementation details of the service, including a collection of WSDL ports service and a concrete endpoint or port.

- Service: Set of endpoints or port type ports (i.e., groups endpoints into service).

- Port: Concrete endpoint corresponding to a WSDL binding (i.e., network address of the Web service).

Do you have to learn how to write WSDL? Remember, "Things should be made as simple as possible." The WSDL is generated for each service by the Web services framework when you deploy or publish the service (see Chapter 15). As depicted in Figure 14.2, the requester retrieves the WSDL from a registry (see UDDI later) but could also find/receive it by other means; it then interacts with the service, either via a dynamic invocation (remember the old-time CORBA DII?) or more commonly via a static client or proxy. The other good news is that you don't have to code against the WSDL, because the Web services framework generates the Web service client (also called proxy) corresponding to your platform (e.g., Java client, .Net client), which shields you from SOAP/WSDL programming.

The following listing is a fragment of the WSDL generated for the Google Spell Check Web Service (see a complete demo in Chapter 16):

```
<definitions name="GoogleSearch"
targetNamespace="urn:GoogleSearch"
  ...
  <types>
    <xsd:schema
      xmlns="http://www.w3.org/2001/XMLSchema"
      targetNamespace="urn:GoogleSearch">
    <xsd:complexType name="GoogleSearchResult">
    <xsd:complexType name="ResultElement">
  ...
    </xsd:schema>
  </types>

  <message name="doSpellingSuggestion">
    <part name="key" type="xsd:string" />
    <part name="phrase" type="xsd:string" />
  </message>
  <message name="doSpellingSuggestionResponse">

  portType name="GoogleSearchPort">
    <operation name="doSpellingSuggestion">
```

```
            <input message="typens:doSpellingSuggestion" />
            <output message="typens:doSpellingSuggestionResponse" /
>
        </operation>
      </portType>

      <binding name="GoogleSearchBinding"
type="typens:GoogleSearchPort">
          <soap:binding style="rpc"
transport="http://schemas.xmlsoap.org/soap/http" />
          <operation name="doSpellingSuggestion"></operation>
      </binding>

      <service name="GoogleSearchService">
        <port name="GoogleSearchPort"
         binding="typens:GoogleSearchBinding">
           <soap:address location="http://api.google.com/search/
beta2" />
        </port>
      </service>

</definitions>
```

A Web service can be assembled from an existing WSDL, using a top-down approach. See Chapter 5 of the Oracle Application Server 10.1.3 Web Services Developer's Guide. Database Web services start from database functionality and correspond therefore to the bottom-up approach. Also, WSDL specifications versions (1.1, 1.2) are not covered but can be seen at the following Web sites:

- http://www.w3.org/TR/wsdl

- http://www.w3.org/2002/ws/desc/

SOAP

The Simple Object Access Protocol (SOAP) is a simple, lightweight, XML-based RPC protocol, which defines a common shape as well as the processing rules for messages exchanged between objects (remember old-time IIOP?). SOAP enables Web services interoperability by providing XML messaging, which is transport neutral (e.g., HTTP/HTTPS, FTP, SMTP, Messaging Protocols, RPC, BEEP); implementation language neutral (e.g., Java, C/

C++, C#, J#, JScript, Perl, VB, PL/SQL, SQL), and platform neutral (e.g., Java, .NET).

As depicted by Figure 14.3, a SOAP message is represented as a SOAP envelope, which contains an optional header (i.e., SOAP header) and a mandatory body (i.e., SOAP body).

- The `SOAP Envelope` must define a namespace for the envelope (i.e., `xmlns:SOAP-ENV`) and a namespace for the encoding style (covered later; i.e., `SOAP-ENV:encodingStyle`).

- The optional `SOAP Header"` is used for metadata, security/authentication, transaction management, routing/delivery, and other attributes. As an example, in SOAP 1.1, the `actor` attribute, when present, specifies the final destination of the header; if the recipient is not the final, it must forward/route the message to its final destination (this is replaced by the `role` attribute in SOAP 1.2).

- The mandatory `SOAP Body` carries the message content (i.e., payload) or instructions. The SOAP body may contain a SOAP fault message with the `Code`, the `Reason,` and optionally the `Details` of the fault. When large data such as LOB cannot fit within the SOAP body, the "SOAP with Attachment" specification (`SwA`) allows carrying a SOAP envelope within a `MIME` multipart structure and referencing `MIME` parts from the SOA envelope.

Figure 14.3
SOAP Envelope

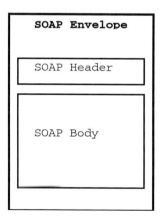

```
<SOAP-ENV:Envelope
  xmlns=:SOAP-ENV="SoapEnvelopURI"
  SOAP-ENV:encodingStyle="...">

  <SOAP-ENV:Header>
  ...
  </SOAP_ENV:Header


  <SOAP-ENV:Body>

    ...

  </SOAP-ENV:Body>

</SOAP-ENV:Envelope>
```

The following code is a fragment of a SOAP message sent to the Google Spell Check Web Service (see Chapter 16):

```
<?xml version="1.0" encoding="UTF-8" ?>
<SOAP-ENV:Envelope
  xmlns:SOAP-ENV="http://schemas.xmlsoap.org/soap/envelope/"
  xmlns:xsi="http://www.w3.org/1999/XMLSchema-instance"
  xmlns:xsd="http://www.w3.org/1999/XMLSchema">

  <SOAP-ENV:Body>
    <ns1:doSpellingSuggestion
      xmlns:ns1="urn:GoogleSearch"

      SOAP-ENV:encodingStyle=
          "http://schemas.xmlsoap.org/soap/encoding/">
      <key
xsi:type="xsd:string">00000000000000000000000000000000</key>
      <phrase xsi:type="xsd:string">Nelson Mandelo</phrase>
    </ns1:doSpellingSuggestion>
    </SOAP-ENV:Body>
  </SOAP-ENV:Envelope>
```

The SOAP messages can be transmitted either synchronously or asynchronously using either a Remote Procedure Call (RPC) or document messaging style:

- In the RPC messaging style, the structure of the SOAP body (i.e., the request) must conform to section 7 of the SOAP 1.1 specification and specify the method, the parameters, and the procedure (its URI). Upon execution, the service provider sends back a SOAP message (i.e., the response). The request/response messages are exchanged synchronously.

- In the document messaging style, the structure of the SOAP body is less constrained, because it does not contain direct method invocation, but rather an XML document, which may contain method invocation as well as other information (e.g., status, notification); the XML schema is defined by the type element in the WSDL (see WSDL previously). The messages can be exchanged synchronously or asynchronously.

The physical representation (i.e., the wire format) of the SOAP messages exchanged between the service requester and the service provider is controlled by settings in the WSDL, particularly the value of the use attribute of the WSDL binding, which specifies the encoding styles of the message:[2]

- *Literal use*: The encoding and interpretation of the SOAP body is dictated by the specified XML schema.

- *Encoded use*: The encodingStyle attribute of the SOAP body specifies the encoding and interpretation rules to use. The SOAP 1.1, section 5, defines a set of serialization rules for structures, object graphs, and so on.

The following classification—sometimes referred to as the WSDL style—combines the encoding style or wire format (literal versus encoded) and the message exchange style (RPC versus document) to determine how the SOAP message is interpreted/processed:

- *Document-literal format*: Specifies a document style message with "literal" format. The SOAP body maps only one parameter; other parameters are mapped by the SOAP header. This format conforms to the Web services interoperability.

- *Wrapped-document-literal:* A variant of document-literal used primarily in .NET environments. In this format, the parameters of the method are wrapped by a schema definition.

- *RPC-encoded format*: Specifies RPC message style, with "encoded" format. It is primarily used for object graphs.

- *RPC-literal format*: Specifies an RPC message style, with "literal" format.

REST

SOAP is by no contest *the* standard XML messaging technology for Web services. However, the Representational State Transfer (REST) is an alternative XML messaging technology being adopted by Web retailers such as Yahoo, Amazon, and Google for online shopping and search applications. REST Web services use XML documents directly as message payload, instead of SOAP envelopes and HTTP GET/POST and XML to share URIs

---

2.   See "SOAP Encoding." in section 5 of the SOAP 1.1 specification at http://www.w3.org/TR/2000/NOTE-SOAP-20000508/#_Toc478383512 and section 3 of the SOAP 1.2 specification at http://www.w3.org/TR/2003/REC-soap12-part2-20030624/#soapenc.

between distributed applications; the applications or end users perform state transitions (navigate following links), and the next state (next page) is transferred to the application or end user (and rendered). REST is not a standard, but rather an architectural style; however, it is based on standards such as HTTP, URL, XML/HTML/GIF/JPEG, and MIME types (e.g., text/xml, text/html, image/gif, image/jpeg). Products such as Oracle Application Server 10.1.3 support REST with the literal encoding style (use=literal).

UDDI

The Universal Description Discovery and Integration (UDDI) is an industry standard (supervised by OASIS) for publishing and locating Web services and their descriptions (dynamic discovery) in registries. UDDI also designates a collection of peer directories, known as UDDI Business Registries (UBR), which host information about businesses and their services.

The UDDI specification includes:

- An XML schema, which defines the documents that describe the key UDDI data structures relative to: (1) the business/organization/individual that offers services (i.e., businessEntity); (2) the set of services being offered (i.e., businessService); (3) binding information for invoking and using the services (i.e., bindingTemplate); more technical information for connecting to services (i.e., tModel); the relationship between entities (i.e., publisher Assertion)—new in UDDI version 2; and standing orders or requests (i.e., Subscriptions)—new in UDDI version 3.

- A set of UDDI APIs (Inquiry, Publication, Security, Subscription) for querying/browsing (also known as Inquiry API) the directories for details about a given Web service, such as supported security and transport protocols, and publishing/registering information in directories. The Information in UDDI registries is stored/classified in three parts: (1) white pages (general business information), (2) yellow pages (taxonomies industry/category/location), and (3) green pages (technical information). Vendors furnish Web-based interfaces as well.

- The Replication and Custody Transfer APIs for replicating directory entries between peer UDDI registries for failover and custody transfer.

Browse the following links for more UDDI resources:

`www.oasis-open.org`
`www.uddi.org`
`www.uddi4j.org`

Final Thoughts

Throughout this section, we have seen that Web services are standards-based, XML centric, platform independent, programming language neutral, self-contained, self-describing, and self-advertising software modules allowing application-to-application interaction over the Web.[3] Let's revisit Figure 14.2 to see how the core Web services technologies (i.e., SOAP, WSDL, UDDI) come into play:

Step 1: The provider sends the WSDL to the UDDI registry.

Step 2: The requester retrieves the WSDL from the registry.

Step 3: Based on information in the WSDL, the requester binds to the provider.

Step 4: The requester invokes operations on the provider.

All interactions are SOAP message based. This concludes a high-level "tour d'horizon" of the base technologies that enable Web services, and invokes operations on the services, but while you can publish and deploy Web services using the base technologies, you will rapidly be confronted with solving the usual enterprise deployment requirements of security, reliability, manageability, and so on—and this time with a new dimension: the Web! In order to address these requirements, a set of new Web services–related specifications, recommendations, de facto standards, APIs, and component models are being consolidated into the SOA, which is our next topic.

14.2 Service-Oriented Architecture (SOA): The Bigger Picture

Java brought portability across systems, but Web services go one step beyond and bring interoperability. It is no surprise then that all of the players in the IT industry are actively engaged in making Web services a reality.

---

3.   Take a deep breath first!

As already mentioned, however, it takes more than the core Web services technologies to interoperate across platforms, languages, corporations, and the Web. This section looks at the bigger picture of Web services: the service-oriented architecture (SOA), its specifications, recommendations, de facto standards, APIs, component models, and so on.

SOA 101

To get a feel for the pervasiveness of the concept of SOA, just Google "service-oriented architecture" and you get about 17 million hits. This is probably not the best definition, but SOA can be summarized as *the ability to implement a corporate architecture based on Web services standards, wherein client applications with proper authorization, simply register, discover, and use available services reliably and securely.*

The implications, requirements, and concerns for implementing SOA include advertising, business process, description, discovery, architecture, interoperability, management, messaging and reliable messaging, security, transport, policy, transaction, and user interface.

The following charts list some of the various specifications, standards, initiatives, recommendations, working drafts, and so on that address SOA infrastructure services requirements. Some of these services will be widely adopted and persist, while others will be subsumed by new ones and disappear.

Advertising

	Description	Status/Sponsor
UDDI	Web-based registry to publicize and locate services	OASIS standard

Architecture

	Description	Status/Sponsor
EbXML	Electronic Business XML	Superseded by various WS specs.
ebSOA TC	Electronic Business Service-Oriented Architecture	TC formed

Business Process

	Description	Status/Sponsor
BPEL4WS	Notation for specifying business process behavior	OASIS Standard
WS-Choreography	Ability to compose and describe the relationships between WS	W3C, WG formed
Web Services Choreography Description Language	Describes peer-to-peer collaborations	W3C, Working draft
Business Process Execution Language (BPEL)	Continue business process language work	OASIS, TC formed

Description

	Description	Status/Sponsor
XML	Extended Markup Language	W3C Recommendation
WSDL	Model and format for describing Web services	W3C
Web Services Architecture	Reference Architecture	W3C

Discovery

	Description	Status/Sponsor
Web Services Inspection Language (WS-Inspection)	Allow WS requester to drill down into WS	Proposal

Interoperability, Specification Profiles

	Description	Status/Sponsor
WS-I Basic Profile	Mandate support for SOAP 1.1, WSDL 1.1, HTTP 1.1, HTTP binding (or HTTPS), and XML Schema (1 and 2)	WS-I
Devices Profile	Interoperability between devices and Web services	

Implementation

	Description	Status/Sponsor
Framework for Web Services Implementation(FWSI TC)	Methods for broad, multiplatform, vendor-neutral implementation	OASIS, TC formed

Management, Auditing, Logging

	Description	Status/Sponsor
WS-Management	Interoperable and cross-platform management using Web services	Microsoft
WS-Management Catalog	Available endpoints or "resources," summary forms, compatible actions, schemas, and WSDL	Microsoft
WS-Manageability	Set of capabilities for discovering the existence, availability, health, performance, usage, and control of a Web service	OASIS, Spec Published

Messaging and Reliable Messaging

	Description	Status/Sponsor
WS-ReliableMessaging	Guaranteed delivery, guaranteed duplicate elimination	OASIS, Spec published
SOAP	Peer-to-peer RPC message exchange	W3C
WS-Addressing	Enables messaging systems to support message transmission in a transport-neutral manner	W3C, Spec published
MTOM (Attachments)	SOAP Message Transmission Optimization Mechanism (Supersedes WS-Attachments)	W3C, Working draft
WS-Enumeration	Enables an application to ask for items from a list of data that is held by a WS	Spec published
WS-Eventing	How to construct an event-oriented message exchange pattern using WS Addressing	Spec published

Messaging and Reliable Messaging (continued)

	Description	Status/Sponsor
WS-Transfer	Defines how to invoke a simple set of familiar verbs (Get, Post, Put, and Delete) using SOAP	Spec published
SOAP-over-UDP	Defines a binding of SOAP to use datagrams, including message patterns, addressing requirements, and security considerations	Spec published
Reliable HTTP (HTTPR)	Guarantees reliable delivery of HTTP packets	IBM

Metadata

	Description	Status/Sponsor
WS-Policy	Describes and communicates the policies of a WS (service requirements, preferences)	Spec published
WS-PolicyAssertions	Details messaging-related assertions for use with WS policy (encoding, language)	Spec published
WS-PolicyAttachment	Specifies three attachment mechanisms for using policy expressions with WS	Spec published
WS-Discovery	Multicast discovery protocol to locate services	Spec published
WS-MetadataExchange	Bootstrap communication with a WS, defines request-response message pairs to retrieve WS-Policy, WSDL, and XMl Schema	Spec published

Security

	Description	Status/Sponsor
WS-Security: SOAP Message Security	Message Integrity and confidentiality	OASIS proposal
WS-Security: Username-Token Profile	How a consumer will specify UsernameToken	OASIS proposal

Security

	Description	Status/Sponsor
WS-Security: X.509 Certificate Token Profile		
`WS-SecureConversation`, WS-Federation, and WS-Authorization	Authenticate message exchanges, security context exchange, and trust	Microsoft, Verisign & IBM proposal
WS-SecurityPolicy	Security policy assertions	Microsoft, Verisign, RSA, and IBM proposal
WS-Trust, WS-Policy, WS-Privacy	Trust, constraints of security policies, and privacy pactices	Microsoft, Verisign and IBM proposal
WS-Federation Active Requester Profile		
WS-Federation Passive Requester Profile		
WS-Security: Kerberos Binding		
Web Single Sign-On Interoperability Profile		
Web Single Sign-On Metadata Exchange Protocol		
XML-Signature	Integrity, message and user authentication	W3c recommendation
SAML	Security Assertion Markup Language	OASIS standard
XML Key Management Specifications (XKMS)	Public-key infrastructure integration	W3C Note
WS-Security Profile for XML-Based Tokens		

Transport

	Description	Status/Sponsor
WS-Coordination	Protocols to coordinate distributed applications	BEA, IBM, Arjuna, Microsoft, Hitachi, and IONA
WS-AtomicTransaction	Transaction completion, volatile two-phase commit, and durable two-phase commit	BEA, IBM, Arjuna, Microsoft, Hitachi, and IONA
WS-BusinessActivity	Protocols for the business activity coordination	BEA, IBM, Arjuna, Microsoft, Hitachi, and IONA

Policy and Binding

	Description	Status/Sponsor
WS-PolicyAttachment	Mechanisms for attaching policy expressions with one or more subjects or resources	BEA, IBM, Microsoft, and SAP
WS-PolicyAssertions	Messaging related assertions for WS-Policy	BEA, IBM, Microsoft, and SAP

Transaction

	Description	Status/Sponsor
WS Composite Application Framework (WS-CAF 3 parts: WS-CTX, WS-CF, WS-TXM)	Ability to compose an application out of multiple Web services	Oracle, Sun, Fujistu, Arjuna, IONA
WS-AtomicTransaction	See above	
WS-Coordination	See above	

User Interface

	Description	Status/Sponsor
Web Services for Remote Portlets (WSRP)	Set of interfaces and related semantics that standardize interactions with components providing user-facing markup	Oracle, SAP, IBM, Microsoft, Sun, BEA Novell, Tibco, Vignette

User Interface

Web Services for Interactive Applications (WSIA)	Standard based on XML and Web services for presenting interactive Web applications to users	IBM, Sun
Web Services Experience Language (WSXL)	Web services-centric component model for interactive Web applications	IBM

14.3 Conclusion

Web services frameworks vendors such as Oracle, Microsoft, IBM, BEA, Sun MicroSystems, and open source players/products are actively integrating these APIs/technologies while hiding their complexity from the developers/assemblers. Now that we have seen the core Web services technologies and the broader SOA landscape, let's look at how to turn your database into a first-class member of your SOA, including exposing database operations as a Web service and invoking external Web services from within the database.

15

Database as Web Services Provider Service

This chapter describes exposing database functionality as Web services, and the next chapter takes you through calling external Web services from within the database.

15.1 Rationales for Database as Web Services Provider

As database developers, DBAs, and data architects know, the Oracle database furnishes a rich set of functionality and APIs for building data-centric applications; if you visit the popular askTom[1] Web site, you will get a feel for the depth and breadth of the possibilities. It is no surprise then that, as already mentioned in Chapter 14, an Evans Data survey (Winter 2004) found that, "more than two out of three respondents, 68 percent, say they are in the process of exposing or invoking their database operations through standard Web services mechanisms." The question is no longer "Why?" but "How can I amortize my investment in the Oracle Database 10*g* and expose some of these application modules as Web services?"

15.2 How Does Database as Web Services Provider Work?

This section first discusses the implementation of Web services with RDBMSs in general, and then looks more specifically at the Oracle's implementation of database as Web service provider.

---

1.   http://asktom.oracle.com.

15.2.1   Implementation and Packaging

Simply put, Web services consist of a service client and service provider exchanging SOAP messages. As depicted in Figure 15.1,[2] the Web service provider is composed of a Web service layer and the service implementation. These two parts usually live within the same container (Figure 15.1). However, these parts may also sit in separate entities (Figure 15.2) such as a Java EE container for the Web service layer and an RDBMS for the service implementation. This is how the Oracle database as Web service provider is currently implemented (Figure 15.3).

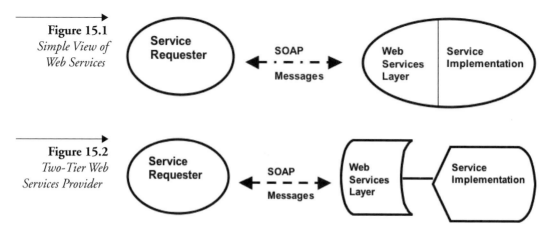

Figure 15.1
Simple View of Web Services

Figure 15.2
Two-Tier Web Services Provider

Some developers prefer a native support for Web services framework integrated within the RDBMS, while others are unwilling to directly expose their database to the Web and prefer the separation of the Web services framework from the RDBMS mostly for security reasons (i.e., peace of mind). Even though this book is not the place to discuss product packaging and strategy, here are some thoughts on the pros and cons of each implementation:

1.   It is technically possible to support the core Web services framework directly in most RDBMSs, including the Oracle database, and this can be useful for bare Web services.

2.   Web services and SOA players are actively beefing up existing technologies and adding new specifications, recommendations, and initiatives all the time. It is therefore desirable to use and

---

2.   Inspired by Figure 3.2 in Designing Web Services with the J2EE 1.4 Platform (Reading, MA: Addison Wesley).

maintain a single Web services, and SOA stack, so as to furnish consistent development, deployment, management, and quality of services, irrespective of where the module implementing the service is deployed (i.e., database or middle tier).

15.2.2   How Does Oracle Database as Web Services Provider Work?

Assume you have published selected database resources as Web services. The following software pieces come into play during the invocation of the service operations:

1. A SOAP request for a database Web service is received at the service endpoint in the Oracle AS OC4J Web Services layer.

2. A SOAP Servlet processes the message.

3. The Servlet transfers the request to the Java proxy within the OC4J container, which represents the service implementation (i.e., PL/SQL packages, Java in the database, SQL queries, SQL DML, AQ streams). The Java proxy is generated by the JPublisher utility invoked under the covers by the Web Services Assembler utility (WSA).

4. The Java proxy invokes the operations on the service implementation in the database through JDBC.

5. The database executes the requested operation and passes the response back to the Java proxy.

6. The Java proxy transfers the response to the SOAP Servlet.

7. The SOAP Servlet encodes the SOAP response in accordance with the WSDL and returns it to the client (service requester).

Because the Web services framework is constantly evolving, and independent of the Oracle Database release, I strongly suggest using the latest release of the Oracle Application Server (OC4J) Web Services stack whenever possible. For development purposes, you can just download the standalone OC4J.

15.2.3   Web Services and SOA Features in Oracle Application Server 10.1.3

What do you get when deploying database functionality as Web services through the Oracle AS Web services and SOA layer? As depicted in Figure 15.3, Release 10.1.3 brings the following new Web services features: interoperability, security, reliability, management, auditing, logging, BPEL integration, WSIF support, and other enhancements.

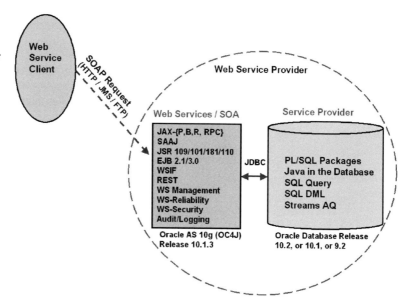

Figure 15.3
The Oracle Implementation of Database as Service Provider

Web Services Interoperability

Interoperability is the key to fulfillment of the Web services promises. In heterogeneous environments, incompatibility issues might be encountered at the protocol level (beyond basic HTTP), the message level (data type conversion across platforms), or the WSDL level (quality of services). The WS-I organization specifies what it means for a Web services framework to be interoperable via the WS-I Basic Profile. The WS-I Basic Profile 1.0[3] mandates support for SOAP 1.1, WSDL 1.1, HTTP 1.1, HTTP binding (or HTTPS), and XML Schema (Parts 1 and 2). The Oracle AS Web Service framework is compliant with WS-I Basic Profile 1.0, but also focuses pragmatically on interoperability with the specifics of other vendors and open source frameworks.

---

3.   http://www.ws-i.org/Profiles/BasicProfile-1.0-2004-04-16.html.

Web Services Security

Web Services security ensures transport-level security (TLS), as well as message-level security (MLS) and furnishes the following services: identification, authentication, authorization, data integrity, confidentiality, and nonrepudiation. The Oracle AS (OC4J) 10.1.3 Web services implements WS-Security and integrates it with the Oracle Web Services Manager (see later) and enterprise security frameworks, such as JAAS Security Provider (Oracle SSO integration), Oracle Identity Management (SAML token propagation, SSO support), third-party LDAP, COREid Access, and COREid Identity. The Oracle Web Services Manager tool lets you secure database Web services via WS-Security using agents and gateways and/or Oracle Enterprise Manager.

Web Services Management

The Oracle Web Services Manager (OWSM) furnishes Web services access control, single sign-on, centralized security policy management, enforcement of regulations (e.g., Sarbanes-Oxley, Gramm-Leach-Bliley, and HIPAA), monitoring of WS-Security, and Web Services Reliable Messaging. These features are exposed through a series of Java Management Extensions (JMX) Management beans (Mbeans). The Policy Manager allows configuring operational rules and propagating them to the enforcement components. The Monitoring Dashboard collects data from gateways and agents and displays results in a graphical format.

Web Services Reliable Messaging

Reliable messaging for SOAP-based Web services ensures that the message is sent at least once (guaranteed delivery), sent at most once (guaranteed duplicate elimination), sent exactly once (guaranteed delivery and duplicate elimination), and received in the same sequence (message ordering). The Oracle Application Server Web Services currently implements the OASIS standard WS-Reliability, and Oracle is working as part of the OASIS WS-ReliableExchange group to converge WS-Reliability with WS-ReliableMessaging to ensure an interoperable, industry-wide adopted reliable messaging standard (WS-RX). In the meantime, the Oracle database as Web services provider can benefit from WS-Reliability; however, the Web Services requester's framework must also support WS-Reliability.

SOAP Message Auditing and Logging

Auditing allows saving and accessing copies of SOAP requests, responses, and fault messages at both the client and server ends.

Logging allows administrators to log parts of the SOAP messages at the provider end. The configuration is accomplished as follows:

1.   Register the different namespaces at the port level.

2.   Create the XPath expression on request, response, or fault messages.

BPEL Integration

BPEL is the emerging standard for business process definition; think of it as the workflow for Web services. The Oracle BPEL Process Manager[4] (BPEL PM) supports RPC encoded and document literal message formats. A database Web service can be part of a complex Web service workflow process orchestrated by the BPEL PM.

Web Services Invocation Framework (WSIF) Support

WSIF provides a standard API allowing the Web service client to use native protocols such as RMI, IIOP, or JDBC, instead of SOAP, for interacting with the server (in connected environments). Adding WSIF binding to the WSDL enables supporting other protocols, in addition to HTTP, JMS, and UDP. Database Web services can be reached directly through WSIF. See Chapter 9 of the Oracle Application Server, Advanced Web Services Developer's Guide 10*g* Release 3 (10.1.3) for more details.

Other Web Services Features

The other new features and enhancements in 10.1.3 include the following:

- Support for REST Web services
- Enhanced Web service home page for testing with the addition of REST, security, and reliability testing
- Support for JSR-181 Web services annotation (requires J2SE 5.0)
- Ant tasks for configuration and scripting
- Custom type-mapping framework for serialization
- Enhanced database Web services support
- WS-I swaRef (in addition to SwA)
- MIME and DIME document support
- JMS transport as an alternative to HTTP

---

4.   http://www.oracle.com/technology/products/ias/bpel/index.html.

See the Oracle Application Server, Web Services Developer's Guide 10*g* Release 3 (10.1.3) for more details.

15.3 Turning Oracle Database Functionality into Web Services

The database functionality to be exposed as Web services (i.e., PL/SQL packages, Java classes in the database, queries, DML, and streams AQ queues) usually already exists in your database. Creating a database Web service from an existing resource is called a bottom-up approach as opposed to a top-down approach consisting of creating/generating the service implementation from the WSDL.

There are two approaches for assembling, deploying, testing database Web services, and generating their client proxy: using the JDeveloper Web Services Wizard and using the Web Services Assembler (`wsa`) command-line tool (which is used under the covers by JDeveloper). For each approach, we'll look at the installation and configuration of the required software pieces.

We'll start with an overview of type conversion between SQL types and XML types, then installing and configuring OC4J stand-alone, assembling PL/SQL Web services using JDeveloper, introducing the Web Service Assembler and the steps for assembling database Web services, deploying PL/SQL Web services, deploying Java DB Web services, deploying SQL queries Web services, deploying DML Web services, and deploying streams AQ Web services.

15.3.1 Type Conversions and Result Set Representation

Type Conversion between SQL Types and XML Types

The service implementation in the database manipulates SQL types while the Web services manipulate XML types. Table 15.1 summarizes SQL types mapping to XML types according to the message style (i.e., `Literal` or `Encoded`).

SQL Result Sets Representations

A PL/SQL stored procedure or a SQL statement can be mapped into one or several Web service operations. Typically, a SQL query or a PL/SQL function (i.e., <name>), which returns a REF CURSOR, will be mapped to the following methods: *<name>*Beans, *<name>*XMLRowSet, and *<name>*XMLSource:

Table 15.1   *SQL Type to XML Type Mapping*

SQL Type	XML Type (Literal)	XML Type (Encoded)
INT	int	int
INTEGER	int	int
FLOAT	double	double
NUMBER	decimal	decimal
VARCHAR2	string	string
DATE	dateTime	dateTime
TIMESTAMP	dateTime	dateTime
BLOB	byte[]	byte[]
CLOB	string	string
LONG	string	string
RAW	byte[]	byte[]
SQL object	complexType	complexType
PL/SQL RECORD	complexType	complexType
Index-by-Table of Scalar types	Array	Array
SQL table	complexType	complexType
Index-by-Table of Complex types	complexType	complexType
PL/SQL Boolean	boolean	boolean
REF CURSOR (<*name*>Beans)	Array	Array
REF CURSOR (<*name*>XMLSource)	any	text_xml
REF CURSOR (<*name*>XMLRowSet)	swaRef	text_xml
SYS.XMLTYPE	any	text_xml

- <name>Beans: Returns an array of instances of XSD complex types, each element representing one row in the cursor. Each subelement corresponds to a column in a row.

- <name>XMLRowSet: Returns a `swaRef` or `text_xml` response that contains an OracleWebRowSet instance in XML format. See "Working with MIME Attachments" in the *Oracle Application Server*

Advanced Web Services Developer's Guide for more details on the
`swaRef` MIME format.

■ `<name>XMLSource`: Returns XML `any` or `text_xml` response that
contains XMLType row set.

15.3.2 Setting up the Oracle AS OC4J for Database as Web Services Provider

As explained earlier, we utilize the Web services framework in the Oracle AS
for exposing database functionality as Web services. For development purposes, you can download a stand-alone OC4J from the Oracle Technology
Network (OTN).[5]

Once you've downloaded the oc4j_extended.zip:

■ Unzip into a location on your file system (i.e., a directory); let's call it
`OC4J_HOME`.

■ Set the `J2EE_HOME` environment variable to `$OC4J_HOME/j2ee/
home`.

■ Provide a JNDI location for the JDBC datasource by modifying the
`data-sources.xml` entry under `$J2EE_HOME/config/` with your
own hostname, port, and global database name as follows.

Note: The datasource `jdbc/OracleDS` must point to a running database.

```
data-sources.xml
================

<?xml version="1.0" standalone='yes'?>

<data-sources
  xmlns:xsi="http://www.w3.org/2001/XMLSchema-instance"
  xsi:noNamespaceSchemaLocation="http://xmlns.oracle.com/
oracleas/schema/data-sources-10_1.xsd"
  schema-major-version="10"
  schema-minor-version="1"
  >
```

5.   http://www.oracle.com/technology/software/products/ias/index.html.

```
<connection-pool name="Example Connection Pool">
  <connection-factory factory-
class="oracle.jdbc.pool.OracleDataSource"
    user="scott"
    password="tiger"
    url="jdbc:oracle:thin:@//<hostname>:<port>/<global
database name>">
  </connection-factory>
</connection-pool>


<managed-data-source name="OracleDS"
  connection-pool-name="Example Connection Pool"
  jndi-name="jdbc/OracleDS"/>


</data-sources>
```

1.   Go to the J2EE_HOME and start the OC4J instance as follows:

```
$ java -jar oc4j.jar

Oracle Containers for J2EE 10g (10.1.3.0.0) initialized
```

15.3.3   Assembling PL/SQL Web Services Using JDeveloper Wizard

PL/SQL packages are the typical service implementation, since Oracle database users have built or inherited PL/SQL packages over years and would like to reuse these. Even though we'll be using a Java/J2EE-based Web services framework, DBAs, database developers, and data architects will be shielded from the need to know Java or Web services; conversely, Java and Web services developers won't need to know PL/SQL; however, a functional knowledge of each package (i.e., what it does), its functions/procedures, and their signatures and parameters, is useful. Luckily, JDeveloper inspects the package to be published and furnishes such information.

Let's create a purchase order table (PO_TAB) storing XML documents representing purchase orders (XMLType column). Then let's create a PL/SQL package (PORDER), which has a function (GETPO), takes a PO number, and returns the XML document representing the purchase order.

Setup

```
po_tab.sql
==========

set echo on
drop table po_tab;
create table po_tab (po XMLType);
insert into po_tab values (XMLTYPE(' <PORDER PONUM="2004"> <CLIENT>
<CLNUM>2000</CLNUM> <CLNAME>Bobo Lafleur</CLNAME> <ADDRESS>
<STREET>24 Cartoon Drive </STREET> <CITY>San Francisco</CITY>
<STATE>CA</STATE> <ZIP>94313</ZIP> </ADDRESS> <PHONES> <VARCHAR2>415-
666-0000</VARCHAR2> </PHONES> </CLIENT> <ORDERDATE>10-FEB-06</
ORDERDATE> <SHIPDATE>12-FEB-06</SHIPDATE> <LITEMS> <LITEM_TYP
ItemNum="1"> <ITEM StockNo="1324"> <PRICE>199</PRICE> <TAXRATE>8</
TAXRATE> </ITEM> <QUANTITY>11</QUANTITY> <DISCOUNT>10</DISCOUNT> </
LITEM_TYP> <LITEM_TYP ItemNum="2"> <ITEM StockNo="2324"> <PRICE>299</
PRICE> <TAXRATE>8</TAXRATE> </ITEM> <QUANTITY>22</QUANTITY>
<DISCOUNT>20</DISCOUNT> </LITEM_TYP> </LITEMS> <SHIPTOADDRESS /> </
PORDER>'));
commit;
rem
set long  10000
set pagesize 80
select x.po.getCLOBVal() from po_tab x;
exit;



porder.sql
==========
create or replace package porder as
    function getpo (PONO number) return XMLTYPE;
end porder;
/
show errors
/

create or replace package body porder as
  function getpo (PONO number) return XMLTYPE is
   xmldoc XMLTYPE;
   begin
     select x.PO into xmldoc from po_tab x
        where x.po.EXTRACT('/PORDER/@PONUM').getNumberVal() = PONO;
```

```
        return xmldoc;
    end getpo;
end porder;
/
show errors
/
```

Generating the PL/SQL Web Service

First, download the latest release of JDeveloper (i.e., `jdevstudio1013.zip`) from the Oracle Technology Network (see OC4J download link). JDeveloper installation consists of unzipping the download object. Upon the installation, launch the IDE by clicking on its icon.

Assume you have a running JDeveloper, and now you need to:

- Create an application (`DBWS.jws`) and a new project (`PLSQLWS.jpr`).

- Create a connection to an Oracle database where the table and package have been created.

- Create a connection to the stand-alone OC4J (installed previously) or to an Oracle application. For development purposes, you can just use the embedded OC4J in JDeveloper.

The following screenshots illustrate the various steps for assembling the PL/SQL Web service from the package; alternatively, you may create the Web service from a project.

Step 0: This initial step consists of opening the database schema by right-clicking on the database connection in the navigator and locating the existing packages.

Step 1: Right-click on the desired package and select "Publish as Web Service" to launch the PL/SQL Web Services wizard. Accept or set the Web services name and the Java package.

Step 2: As Figure 15.4 depicts, the wizard lets you specify the Web service name, the Java package for the service wrapper, and the binding options: SOAP 1.1, SOAP 1.2, and WSIF. For this demo, accept or edit the default and go to the next step.

Step 3: As depicted by Figure 15.5, the wizard lets you choose the message format; accept the default SOAP message format (i.e., `Document Wrapped`).
Step 4: As depicted by Figure 15.6, the wizard lists all the functions in the

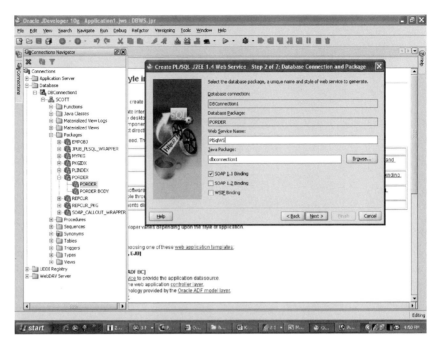

Figure 15.4
PL/SQL Web Services: Name, Package, and Binding

Figure 15.5
PL/SQL Web Services: Message Format

Figure 15.6
PL/SQL Web Services: Operations Selection

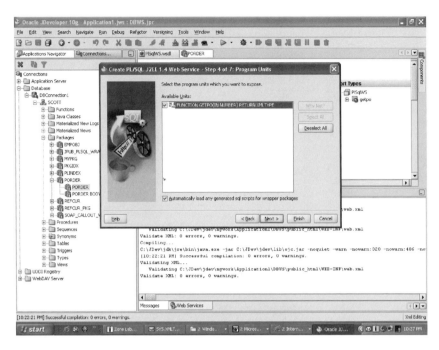

package. Select/check the ones you want to be accessible as service operations and go to the next step.

Step 5: As depicted by Figure 15.7, the wizard lets you specify the type mappings. Click on the Help button at the bottom of the screen for more details on the various choices. For this demo, we'll accept the default settings and go to the next step.

Step 6: Optionally, as depicted by Figure 15.8, you may specify the user-defined type mapping between SQL or PL/SQL types and Java wrapper classes, as discussed in Chapter 13 and summarized in Table 13.2. You may also specify the mapping of the PL/SQL types unsupported by JDBC or the Web services framework, using the in-database conversion approach covered in Chapter 13. This demo does not have such a requirement, so you can go to the next step.

Step 7: During this step, as depicted by Figure 15.9, you may specify user-defined SOAP message handlers. These classes are used to process request messages (client handlers) and response messages (server handlers) and implement logging, auditing, and encryption/decryption. There is no user-defined handler for this demo, so click on the `Next` or `Finish` button to trigger the generation of the Web service.

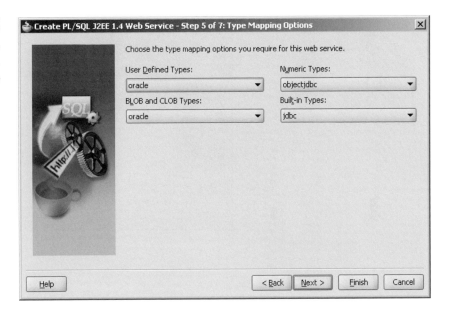

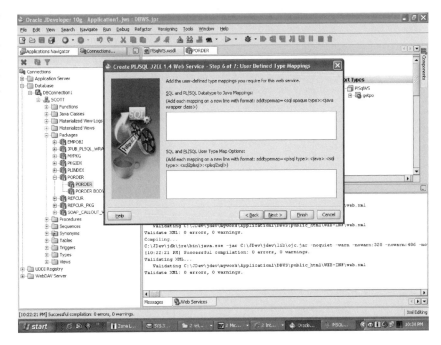

Figure 15.9
*PL/SQL Web
Services: SOAP
Message Handler*

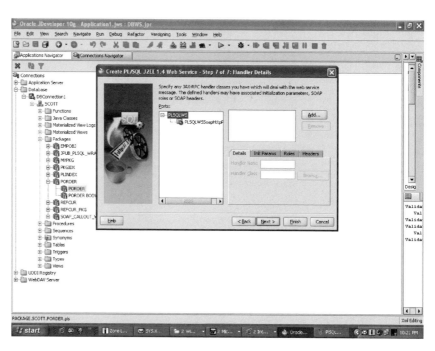

Figure 15.10
*PL/SQL Web
Services: WSDL
Structure*

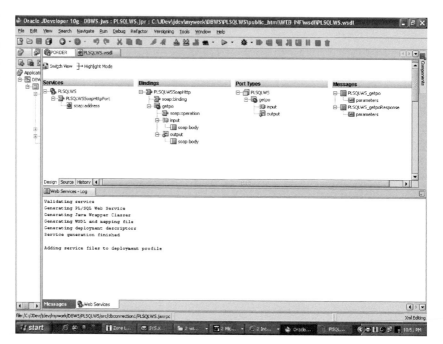

At this stage, the WSDL has been generated, as depicted by Figure 15.10, which shows a nice structure of the WSDL, including the services, bindings, port types, and messages. Chapter 14 explains the meaning of each component of the WSDL. See, in the following text, the actual values of the services, bindings, port types, and message components of the PL/SQL Web Services WSDL.

- Service:

```
<service name="PLSQLWS">
    <port name="PLSQLWSSoapHttpPort" binding="tns:PLSQLWSSoapHttp">
        <soap:address location="http://141.144.72.251:8888/DBWS-
        PLSQLWS-context-root/PLSQLWSSoapHttpPort"/>
    </port>
</service>
```

- Binding:

```
<binding name="PLSQLWSSoapHttp" type="tns:PLSQLWS">
    <soap:binding style="document"
        transport="http://schemas.xmlsoap.org/soap/http"/>
    <operation name="getpo">
        <soap:operation
            soapAction="http://dbconnection1/PLSQLWS.wsdl/getpo"/>
        <input>
            <soap:body use="literal" parts="parameters"/>
        </input>
        <output>
            <soap:body use="literal" parts="parameters"/>
        </output>
    </operation>
</binding>
```

- Port type:

```
<portType name="PLSQLWS">
    <operation name="getpo">
        <input message="tns:PLSQLWS_getpo"/>
        <output message="tns:PLSQLWS_getpoResponse"/>
    </operation>
</portType>
```

■ Message:

```
<message name="PLSQLWS_getpo">
        <part name="parameters" element="tns0:getpoElement"/>
</message>

<message name="PLSQLWS_getpoResponse">
        <part name="parameters"
element="tns0:getpoResponseElement"/>
</message>
```

■ Types: (see Table 15.1 for SQL type to XML type mapping).

The following XML fragment specifies the mapping of SQL NUMBER to XML decimal:

```
<element name="pono" type="decimal" nillable="true"/>
```

The following XML fragment specifies the mapping of SYS.XMLTYPE to XML any (literal style):

```
<element name="result" nillable="true">
      <complexType>
           <sequence> <any/> </sequence>
      </complexType>
  </element>
```

Step 8: Deploy the PL/SQL Web service; as depicted in Figure 15.11, right-clicking and selecting Run on the WSDL results in the deployment of the generated Java proxy representing the PL/SQL package at the returned endpoint. In this example, the Web service has been deployed against the embedded OC4J in JDeveloper, but, depending on the application server connection specified, you may deploy against a stand-alone OC4J or a full-fledged Oracle Application Server.

The wizard returns the endpoint at which the PL/SQL Web service is listening:

```
http://kmensah-lap1:8988/DBWS-PLSQLWS-context-root/
PLSQLWSSoapHttpPort
```

Figure 15.11
*PL/SQL Web
Services
Deployment*

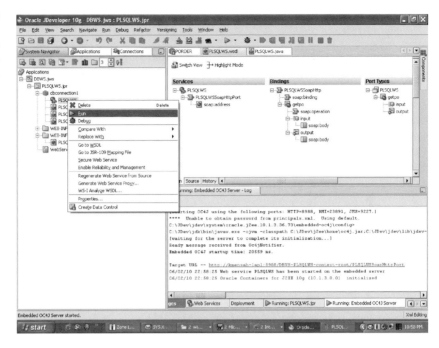

Figure 15.11
*PL/SQL Web
Services
Deployment*

Step 9 (Optional): At this stage, you may add quality of services, such as security, reliability, logging, auditing, and analyze the WSDL for WS-I interoperability, using the Web Services Editor, as depicted in Figures 15.12 and 15.13.

These quality of services can also be added using Oracle Enterprise Manager 10*g* Application Control.

As depicted in Figure 15.14, a browser-based test page (i.e., Web Service Home Page) has been generated at the following endpoint:

```
http://kmensah-lap1:8988/DBWS-PLSQLWS-context-root/
PLSQLWSSoapHttpPort
```

Step 10: Invoking the Web service through the test page. As illustrated by Figure 15.15, you can invoke the service using the purchase order number.

As illustrated by Figure 15.16, you can see the SOAP request and the SOAP response messages:

Figure 15.12
*Web Services
Editor: Reliability*

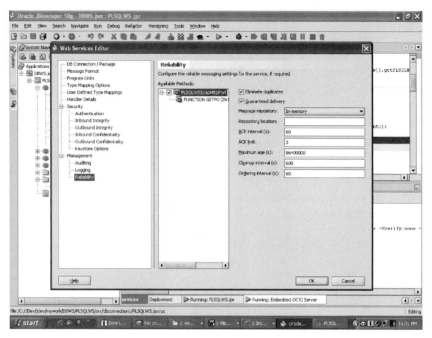

Figure 15.13
*Web Services
Editor: Security*

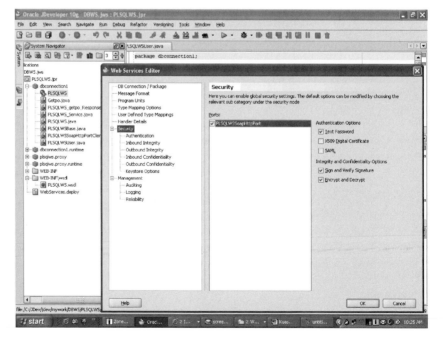

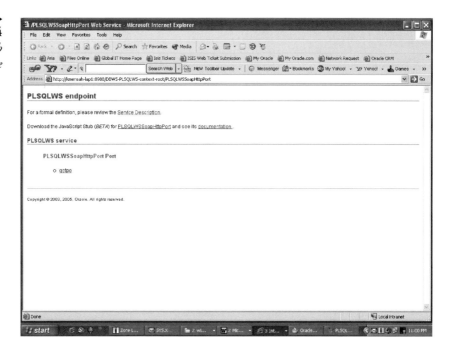

Figure 15.14
PL/SQL Web Service Test Page

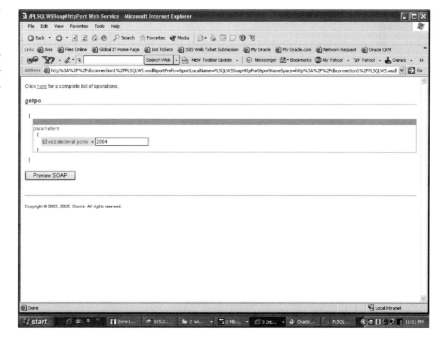

Figure 15.15
Invoking PL/SQL Web Service through the Test Page

SOAP Request

```
<soap:Envelope xmlns:soap="http://schemas.xmlsoap.org/soap/
envelope/">
    <soap:Body xmlns:ns1="http://dbconnection1/PLSQLWS.wsdl/
types/">
        <ns1:getpoElement>
            <ns1:pono>2004</ns1:pono>
        </ns1:getpoElement>
    </soap:Body>
</soap:Envelope>
```

SOAP response

```
<?xml version="1.0" encoding="UTF-8"?>
<env:Envelope xmlns:env="http://schemas.xmlsoap.org/soap/
envelope/" xmlns:xsd="http://www.w3.org/2001/XMLSchema"
xmlns:xsi="http://www.w3.org/2001/XMLSchema-instance"
xmlns:ns0="http://dbconnection1/PLSQLWS.wsdl/types/
"><env:Body><ns0:getpoResponseElement><ns0:result><PORDER
PONUM="2004"> <CLIENT> <CLNUM>2000</CLNUM> <CLNAME>Bobo
Lafleur</CLNAME> <ADDRESS> <STREET>24 Cartoon Drive </STREET>
<CITY>San Francisco</CITY> <STATE>CA</STATE> <ZIP>94313</ZIP>
</ADDRESS> <PHONES> <VARCHAR2>415-666-0000</VARCHAR2> </
PHONES> </CLIENT> <ORDERDATE>10-FEB-06</ORDERDATE>
<SHIPDATE>12-FEB-06</SHIPDATE> <LITEMS> <LITEM_TYP
ItemNum="1"> <ITEM StockNo="1324"> <PRICE>199</PRICE>
<TAXRATE>8</TAXRATE> </ITEM> <QUANTITY>11</QUANTITY>
<DISCOUNT>10</DISCOUNT> </LITEM_TYP> <LITEM_TYP ItemNum="2">
<ITEM StockNo="2324"> <PRICE>299</PRICE> <TAXRATE>8</TAXRATE>
</ITEM> <QUANTITY>22</QUANTITY> <DISCOUNT>20</DISCOUNT> </
LITEM_TYP> </LITEMS> <SHIPTOADDRESS/> </PORDER></
ns0:result></ns0:getpoResponseElement></env:Body></
env:Envelope>
```

At this stage, the PL/SQL Web service has been deployed and listening for incoming requests at its endpoint. But remember, Web services are about application-to-application interaction using XML messaging such as SOAP, and the client application can be implemented in any language and reside on any platform. As a Web service assembler ("developer" is not appropriate here), you certainly don't want to code to SOAP; fortunately, most Web services frameworks furnish tools/utilities that generate the client proxy specific to the Web service client framework from the WSDL (i.e., a Java proxy for a Java Web services framework, a .NET proxy code for .NET framework). So, for this demo to be complete, the next section takes you

Figure 15.16
*PL/SQL Web
Service Request
and Response
SOAP Messages*

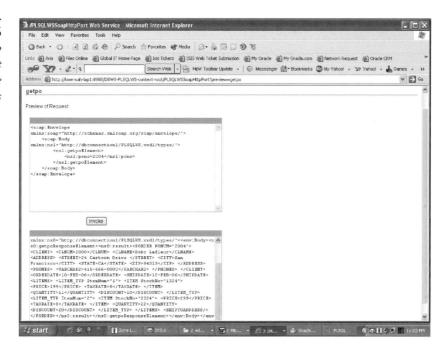

through the generation of a Java client proxy from the PL/SQL Web service WSDL.

Generating the PL/SQL Web Service Proxy

Step 1: Generate the proxy template.

JDeveloper lets you specify the target platform hosting the service, since the Web service may be hosted on the embedded OC4J, a stand-alone OC4J, or a full-fledged Oracle Application Server.

For this demo, we have deployed the service on the embedded OC4J in JDeveloper, so right-click on the PLSQLWS.wsdl, and select *Generate Web Service Proxy*; accept the default and proceed to the generation of the Java proxy. And here is the generated PLSQLWSSoapHttpPortClient.java.

```
PLSQLWSSoapHttpPortClient.java
==============================
package dbconnection1;


import oracle.webservices.transport.ClientTransport;
import oracle.webservices.OracleStub;
import javax.xml.rpc.ServiceFactory;
```

```
import javax.xml.rpc.Stub;

import oracle.xml.parser.v2.XMLElement;

...
public class PLSQLWSSoapHttpPortClient {

/**
 * @param args
 */
  public static void main(String[] args) {
  try
  {
    dbconnection1.PLSQLWSSoapHttpPortClient myPort =
      new dbconnection1.PLSQLWSSoapHttpPortClient();
    System.out.println("calling " + myPort.getEndpoint());
    // Add your own code here

  } catch (Exception ex) {
          ex.printStackTrace();
  }
 }
}
```

The code generator cannot guess which parameter to use from the client application, so this is the only place where you need a little Java expertise to come up with the following instruction to invoke the service with the appropriate parameter (as we did using the test page).

```
((XMLElement)myPort.getpo(new
java.math.BigDecimal("2004"))).print(System.out);
```

Update the proxy code as follows:

```
/**
 * @param args
 */
  public static void main(String[] args) {
  try
  {
```

```
dbconnection1.PLSQLWSSoapHttpPortClient myPort =
    new dbconnection1.PLSQLWSSoapHttpPortClient();
  System.out.println("calling " + myPort.getEndpoint());
  // Add your own code here
  ((XMLElement)myPort.getpo(new
      java.math.BigDecimal("2004"))).print(System.out);


  } catch (Exception ex) {
        ex.printStackTrace();
  }
}
```

Note: You also need to accept the following import statement that JDeveloper has inserted in the resulting `PLSQLWSSoapHttpPortClient.java`:

```
import oracle.xml.parser.v2.XMLElement;
```

Save and proceed to step 2.

Step 2: Compile and run the Web Services Proxy.

To see the HTTP traffic between the WS Proxy and the WS, select "HTTP Analyzer" in the View panel. Then, in the application navigation panel, right-click on `PLSQLWSSoapHttpPortClient.java` and select *Run*. As depicted in Figure 15.17, you will see the SOAP request (same as in the test page case) and the SOAP response (more nicely displayed than in the test page invocation).

That's it.

PL/SQL Web Services Limitations with JDeveloper

The following restrictions apply to PL/SQL Web services generation using JDeveloper (some of these limitations are specific to JDeveloper):

- Stored procedures of the same name that are accessible in multiple schema will fail the code generators.

- An overloaded program unit sharing the same name with another program unit in the same package. The WSDL processor cannot determine which program unit to execute; therefore, such PL/SQL program units cannot be deployed as Web services.

Figure 15.17
*PL/SQL Web
Services Invocation
from Proxy*

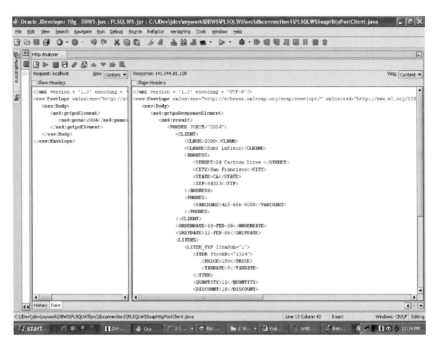

- The BFILE type can only be used as an OUT argument or as a function return value.

- PL/SQL pads CHAR type data into a string of length 4,001, which exceeds the 4,000 limit and results in a JDBC SQL exception.

- The PL/SQL BCLOB type is not supported.

- PL/SQL record type is not supported for creating directly, so you need to explicitly use JPublisher to produce a new package that uses supported types as parameters or specify the type map (see step 6).

- Ref cursors return types: A PL/SQL package that returns a ref cursor type, such as the following code fragment, is not exposable as Web services:

```
package refcur_pkg as  type refcur_t is ref cursor;
function RetRefCur  return refcur_pkg.refcur_t;end;
```

- SYS schema: It is generally a bad practice to allow user objects in the SYS schema; consequently, JDeveloper docs not allow creating a Web service from a package owned by SYS schema.

- Types declared within a package spec: PL/SQL packages that declare new types within the package specification cannot be published as Web services. The workaround is to create the types externally to the package.

- Nested Tables: JDeveloper does not allow creating Web services from PL/SQL packages that use PL/SQL Nested Tables.

This concludes the wizard-driven approach for assembling PL/SQL Web services. The next section introduces you to the command-line approach, which supports more database programming models than JDeveloper, including PL/SQL, Java in the database (see Part I), SQL query, SQL DML, and streams AQ.

15.4   Assembling Database Web Services Using the Command-Line Tool

Contrasted with the JDeveloper wizard-driven approach, the WSA approach may appear cumbersome but currently supports more models than JDeveloper. This section briefly describes the Web Service Assembler, then the generic steps for exposing database functionality with it, showing a complete example of publishing database functionality using WSA.

Introducing the Web Services Assembler

The Web Services Assembler utility furnishes options and APIs for assembling and deploying Web services on the Oracle AS Web Services layer.

It uses JPublisher under the covers and is delivered as a JAR file (wsa.jar) under $OC4J_HOME/webservices/lib. It is integrated with the Apache Ant and Oracle JDeveloper. It can be invoked:

- Using either the following command:

      -java -jar wsa.jar ...

- Or as Ant tasks, with the WSA option corresponding to the database functionality to be exposed:

      <oracle:plsqlAssemble .../>

```
<oracle:sqlAssemble .../>
<oracle:dbJavaAssemble .../>
<oracle:aqlAssemble .../>
```

Prerequisites:Make sure `JAVA_HOME/bin` and `JDK 1.4` or later are in the `PATH`.

The following `wsa` options are required for all database Web services types:

- `appName`: Web service application name
- `dbConnection`: Database connection URL used at code generation time (assume it will be different from the production database used at runtime)
- `dbUser`: Database user and password used at code generation time (assume same schema and objects at runtime)
- `dataSource`: JNDI location of the datasource used at runtime

As described in Chapter 13, JPublisher now generates code to retry database connection in case of loss of database connection.

The following `WSA` options may be used to specify additional details:

- `context`: Root context for the Web application
- `debug`: Displays detailed diagnostic messages
- `ear`: Name and location of the generated J2EE `EAR` file, which contains the Java wrapper for the database functionality exposed as Web service
- `jpubProp`: JPublisher options to fine-tune code generation
- `output`: Location for storing generated files
- `portName`: Name of the port in the generated WSDL
- `serviceName`: Local part of the service name in the generated WSDL
- `style`: Style part of the message format used in the generated WSDL
- `uri`: URI for the Web service to use in deployment descriptors
- `use`: Use part of the message format used in the generated WSDL

Generic Steps for Publishing Database Functionality Using Web Services Assembler

Assembling database Web services using the command line involves the following eight steps:

Step 1: Determine the functionality to be exposed.

Step 2: Run the Web Services Assembler tool to assemble the Web service, based on the specified database functionality.

Step 3: If PL/SQL wrappers are generated and the sysUser argument is not set, you will have to load the generated PL/SQL wrapper(s) into the database. The Web Services Assembler tool (WSA) will load the wrapper automatically otherwise.

- A PL/SQL wrapper is generated (under the covers by JPublisher) when the PL/SQL RECORD and INDEX BY TABLE types are used in the PL/SQL package.

- Similarly, a PL/SQL wrapper is also generated for exposing Java in the database; otherwise, you will have to load it manually using sqlplus.

Step 4: Configure the OC4J datasources to ensure that the JPublisher-generated Java proxy class can connect to the database and the functionality it represents.

Step 5: Deploy the Web service application into a running instance of OC4J.

Step 6: Optionally, check that the deployment is successful using the generated test page (i.e., Web service home page).

Step 7: Use the Web Services Assembler tool (WSA) to generate the Web services client proxy and incorporate it into your client application.

Step 8: Invoke the Web service using the client proxy.

The rest of this chapter describes the steps mentioned here for assembling and publishing PL/SQL packages, Java in the database, SQL Query/DML, and streams AQ using the Web Services Assembler.

15.4.1 Assembling PL/SQL Web Services Using Web Services Assembler

Prerequisite:

- Select the PL/SQL package that you want to expose as a Web service:
  REFCUR

```
package refcur as
   type curstype is ref cursor return emp%rowtype;
   FUNCTION getcurfunc RETURN curstype;
   PROCEDURE getcurproc(a curstype);
end;

package BODY refcur as

   FUNCTION getcurfunc RETURN curstype IS curs curstype;
    BEGIN
      open curs for select * from emp where ename='SCOTT';
      return curs;
    END;

   PROCEDURE getcurproc(a curstype) IS name emp%rowtype;
    BEGIN
       LOOP
         FETCH a INTO  name ;
         EXIT WHEN a%NOTFOUND;
         dbms_output.put_line(name.ENAME);
       END LOOP;
     close a;
    END;

END;
```

- The name for the Web service application. REFCURWS

- The JNDI location for the JDBC datasource to be used at runtime:
  jdbc/OracleManagedDS

- The JDBC URL for database connection and the username and password to be used at compile/generation time:

```
"jdbc:oracle:thin:@//localhost:5521/<global database name>
     scott/tiger
```

Step 1a

Provide the PL/SQL package and the information described in the Prerequisites section as input to the Web Services Assembler `plsqlAssemble` command described hereafter:

```
java -jar wsa.jar
-plsqlAssemble
-appName RefCurWS
-sql refcur
-dataSource jdbc/OracleManagedDS
-dbConnection jdbc:oracle:thin:@//<your global database name>
-dbUser scott/tiger
-style rpc
-use encoded
```

Here is the effective command (you need to replace `<your global database name>` with the actual global database name in your environment):

```
$ java -jar $ORACLE_HOME/webservices/lib/wsa.jar -
plsqlAssemble -appName PLSQLRefCurWS -sql refcur -dataSource
jdbc/OracleManagedDS —dbConnection jdbc:oracle:thin:@//
localhost:5521/<global database name> -dbUser scott/tiger -
style rpc -use encoded
```

This command generates the following files and directory structures:

- `PLSQLRefCurWS.ear`
- `ear`
  - `META-INF`
  - `PLSQLRefCurWS-web.war`
- `WarW`
  - `WEB-INF`
- `src/server/oracle/generated`
  - `GetcurfuncRowBase.java`
  - `GetcurfuncRowUser.java`
  - `refcur.java`
  - `refcurBase.java`
  - `refcurUser.java`

As mentioned in Table 15.1, WSA generates the following three interfaces to map REF CURSOR according to the encoding (literal/encoded) to: an Array of Beans (Array/Array), an XMLType (any/text_xml), and an OracleWebRowSet (swaRef/text_xml). See the getcurfuncXMLSource(), getcurfuncXMLRowSet(), and getcurfuncBeans() interfaces in refcur.java.

```
refcur.java
===========


package oracle.generated;

import java.sql.SQLException;
import java.sql.Connection;
import java.io.*;

public interface refcur extends java.rmi.Remote{



   public javax.xml.transform.Source  getcurfuncXMLSource()
   throws java.rmi.RemoteException;
   public javax.xml.transform.Source  getcurfuncXMLRowSet()
   throws java.rmi.RemoteException;
   public GetcurfuncRowUser[] getcurfuncBeans() throws
   java.rmi.RemoteException;
   }
```

For more details, see the "*Mapping PL/SQL IN and IN OUT Parameters to XML IN OUT Parameters*" section in the Oracle AS 10.1.3 Web Services Guide.

Step 1b

Alternatively, you can use an Ant task for generating PL/SQL Web services. The following code fragment is an Ant task for the Web Services Assembler to be inserted in the build.xml:

```
<oracle:plsqlAssemble
dbUser="scott/tiger"
sql="refcur"
dbConnection="jdbc:oracle:thin:@ :@//localhost:5521/
lab.regress.rdbms.dev.us.oracle.com "
```

```
dataSource="jdbc/OracleManagedDS"
appName="RefCurWS"
style="rpc"
use="encoded"
/>
```

Step 2 (Optional)

If WSA generates PL/SQL wrappers (RECORD and INDEX-BY-TABLE), these must be loaded into the user schema in the database either manually using SQL*Plus (just run the wrapper) or automatically by WSA using the following option of plsqlAssemble:

- -jpubProp plsqload for the command line
- jpubprop="plsqlload" for the Ant task

No wrapper has been generated for this demo.

Step 3 and 4

Not necessary (or already done).

Step 5

J2EE_HOME being the file system directory where the OC4J is installed, and 23791 the RMI port, you can deploy the service into a running instance of OC4J and bind the application, using the following command:

```
$ java -jar $J2EE_HOME/admin_client.jar
deployer:oc4j:localhost:23791 oc4jadmin welcome -deploy -file
PLSQLRefCurWS.ear -deploymentName PLSQLRefCurWS -
bindAllWebApps

06/02/12 20:48:49 Notification ==>Uploading file
PLSQLRefCurWS.ear ...
06/02/12 20:48:49 Notification ==>Application Deployer for
PLSQLRefCurWS STARTS.
06/02/12 20:48:49 Notification ==>Undeploy previous
deployment
06/02/12 20:48:49 Notification ==>Initialize /kmensah_oc4j/
j2ee/home/applications/PLSQLRefCurWS.ear begins...
06/02/12 20:48:49 Notification ==>Initialize /kmensah_oc4j/
j2ee/home/applications/PLSQLRefCurWS.ear ends...
```

```
06/02/12 20:48:49 Notification ==>Starting application :
PLSQLRefCurWS
06/02/12 20:48:49 Notification ==>Initializing ClassLoader(s)
06/02/12 20:48:49 Notification ==>Initializing EJB container
06/02/12 20:48:49 Notification ==>Loading connector(s)
06/02/12 20:48:49 Notification ==>Starting up resource
adapters
06/02/12 20:48:49 Notification ==>Initializing EJB sessions
06/02/12 20:48:49 Notification ==>Committing ClassLoader(s)
06/02/12 20:48:49 Notification ==>Initialize PLSQLRefCurWS-
web begins...
06/02/12 20:48:49 Notification ==>Initialize PLSQLRefCurWS-
web ends...
06/02/12 20:48:49 Notification ==>Started application :
PLSQLRefCurWS
06/02/12 20:48:49 Notification ==>Binding web application(s)
to site default-web-site begins...
06/02/12 20:49:03 Notification ==>Binding web application(s)
to site default-web-site ends...
06/02/12 20:49:03 Notification ==>Application Deployer for
PLSQLRefCurWS COMPLETES. Operation time: 14047 msecs


$
```

You can check that the Web service is indeed deployed, as depicted in Figure 15.18, by connecting to Oracle Enterprise Manager (oc4jadmin) at the following URL:

```
http://<hostname>:8888/em
```

See the *OC4J Deployment Guide* for more information on deploying EAR files.

Step 6 (Optional)

Test the service by clicking on Test Service on the OEM screen (top left), as depicted by Figure 15.19. The test page will give three functions: getcurfuncBeans, which retrieves an array of Beans; getcurfuncXMLSource(), which retrieves an XML (i.e., any/text_xml); and getcurfuncXML-RowSet(), which retrieves an XMLRowSet (i.e., swaRef/text_xml).

As you can see, getcurfuncBeans has been selected because the test page only support simple types such as primitive types and bean or array of such types; selecting the other functions will hang the browser.

Figure 15.18
Oracle Enterprise Manager (oc4jadmin)

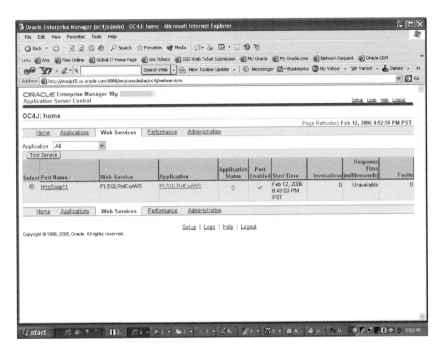

Figure 15.19
Web Services Test Page

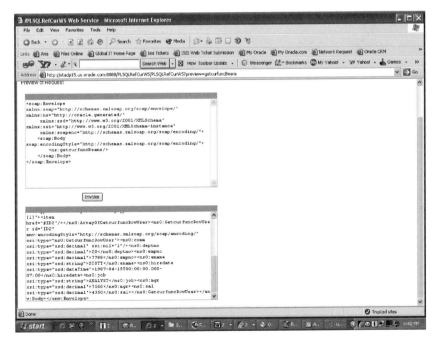

Step 7

Generate the Web Service Proxy using the -genProxy option of the Web Services Assembler:

```
$java -jar $OC4J_HOME/webservices/lib/wsa.jar -genProxy -wsdl
"http://<hostname>:8888/PLSQLRefCurWS/PLSQLRefCurWS?wsdl"   -
output ./wsclient
```

This command generates the following files and directories:

```
wsclient/oracle/generated/GetcurfuncRowUser.java
HttpSoap11Client.java
======================
...
/**
    * @param args
    */
    public static void main(String[] args) {
        try {
            oracle.generated.HttpSoap11Client myPort =
             new oracle.generated.HttpSoap11Client();
            System.out.println("calling " +
                myPort.getEndpoint());
            // Add your own code here

        } catch (Exception ex) {
            ex.printStackTrace();
        }
    }
PLSQLRefCurWS.java   Refcur.java
runtime/
```

Similar to the Web service proxy generated using JDeveloper, you need to edit HttpSoap11Client.java and insert the following fragment into the proxy class below the "//Add your own code":

```
GetcurfuncRowUser user;
GetcurfuncRowUser[] users = myPort.getcurfuncBeans();
int le = users.length;
for (int i=0; i<le; i++) {
```

```
user = users[i];
System.out.println("Employee " + user.getEname());
System.out.println("Emp# " + user.getEmpno());
System.out.println("Department# " + user.getDeptno());
System.out.println("Manager " + user.getMgr());
//System.out.println("Hiredate " + user.getHiredate());
System.out.println("Job " + user.getJob());
System.out.println("Salary " + user.getSal());
System.out.println("Commission " + user.getComm());}
```

Step 8

Compile and run the client using the following command (you may add
the additional JAR files to the CLASSPATH beforehand):

```
javac -classpath ${CLASSPATH}:${OC4J_HOME}/webservices/lib/
wsclient_extended.zip:${OC4J_HOME}/webservices/lib/jaxrpc-
api.jar oracle/generated/HttpSoap11Client.java
```

You may need to compile the Java classes in Oracle/generated/runtime:

```
javac oracle/generated/runtime/*.java
```

Then run the client application:

```
$ java -classpath ${CLASSPATH}: ${OC4J_HOME}/webservices/lib/
wsclient_extended.jar:
${OC4J_HOME}/webservices/lib/jaxrpc-api.jar:
${J2EE_HOME}/lib/jax-qname-namespace.jar:
${J2EE_HOME}/lib/activation.jar:${J2EE_HOME}/lib/mail.jar:
${J2EE_HOME}/lib/http_client.jar:
${OC4J_HOME}/lib/xmlparserv2.jar oracle/generated/HttpSoap11Client
$ java -classpath ${CLASSPATH}:${OC4J_HOME}/webservices/lib/
wsclient_extended.zip:${OC4J_HOME}/webservices/lib/jaxrpc-
api.jar:${J2EE_HOME}/lib/jax-gname-namespace.jar:${J2EE_HOME}/lib/
activation.jar:{J2EE_HOME}/lib/mail.jar:${J2EE_HOME}/lib/
http_client.jar:${ORACLE_HOME}/lib/xmlparserv2.jar oracle/generated/
HttpSoap11Client
calling http://<hostname>:8888/PLSQLRefCurWS/PLSQLRefCurWS
Employee SCOTT
Emp# 7788
Department# 20
```

```
Manager 7566
Job ANALYST
Salary 4350
Commission null
```

At this stage, you may add the quality of services using the Web Service Administration page of Oracle Enterprise Manager Application Control, as depicted in Figure 15.20.

Figure 15.20
OEM Application Control, Web Service Administration

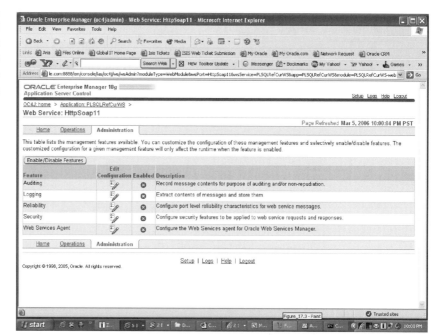

Voilà!

For retrieving XML documents instead of Array of Beans, try adding the following code fragment to `HttpSoap11Client.java` in Step 7:

```
System.out.println("*** XML Document ***");
 Element soapElem = eme.getcurfuncXMLSource();
 Source source = new DOMSource(soapElem);
 Transformer trans =
```

```
        TransformerFactory.newInstance().newTransformer();
            ByteArrayOutputStream buf = new ByteArrayOutputStream();
            StreamResult streamr = new StreamResult(buf);
            trans.transform(source, streamr);
            System.out.println(buf.toString());
```

For WebRowSet, try adding the following code in `HttpSoap11Client.java` in Step 7:

```
System.out.println("*** WebRowSet ***");
 soapElem = eme.getcurfuncXMLRowSet();
 source = new DOMSource(soapElem);
 trans = TransformerFactory.newInstance().newTransformer();
 buf = new ByteArrayOutputStream();
 streamr = new StreamResult(buf);
 trans.transform(source, streamr);
 InputStream istream =
        new ByteArrayInputStream(buf.toString().getBytes());
OracleWebRowSet rowset = new OracleWebRowSet();
System.setProperty("http.proxyHost", "www-proxy.us.oracle.com");
System.setProperty("http.proxyPort", "80");
//System.setProperty("javax.xml.parsers.DocumentBuilderFactory",
        "oracle.xml.jaxp.JXDocumentBuilderFactory");
System.setProperty("org.xml.sax.driver",
                "oracle.xml.parser.v2.SAXParser");
System.out.println("rowset read xml");
rowset.readXml(new InputStreamReader(istream));
System.out.println("rowset write xml");
rowset.writeXml(new PrintWriter(System.out));
System.out.flush();
```

15.4.2   Assembling Java in the Database as a Web Service

The idea here is to generate a client-side stub to be deployed in the Web Services layer.

Prerequisites:

The fully qualified name of the server-side Java class. It may contain any of the following types as parameters and return types:

- Primitive types (except `char`)

- Serializable types

- JavaBeans, whose attributes are supported types

- Standard JDBC types (i.e., `java.sql.*`) and Oracle JDBC types (i.e., `oracle.sql.*`)
- Arrays of supported types
- Select a Java class in the database
- The name for the Web service application: `JavaDbWS`
- The JNDI location for the JDBC datasource to be used at runtime: `jdbc/OracleManagedDS`
- The JDBC URL for database connection and the username and password to be used at compile/generation time:

```
"jdbc:oracle:thin:@//localhost:5521/<global database
name>
scott/tiger
```

Step 1a

```
java -jar wsa.jar
-dbJavaAssemble
-appName JavaDbWS
-dbJavaClassName REFCUR
-dataSource jdbc/OracleManagedDS
-dbConnection jdbc:oracle:thin:@//<hostname>:<port>/<global
database name>
-dbUser scott/tiger
-sysUser system/manager
```

Step 1b

Alternatively, you may use an Ant task with the Web Services Assembler `dbJavaAssemble` command:

```
<oracle:dbJavaAssemble
appName="javacallin"
dbJavaClassName="REFCUR"
dbConnection="jdbc:oracle:thin:@<hostname>:<port>/<service>"
dataSource="jdbc/OracleManagedDS"
dbUser="scott/tiger"
sysUser="system/manager"
/>
```

Steps 2 through 6 are similar to the PL/SQL equivalent.

15.4.3 Assembling SQL Queries or SQL DML Statements as Web Services

Prerequisites:

- Determine the SQL queries and DML to be published. Multiple `sqlstatement` arguments can be specified on the command line (or on the Ant task). *Note:* The DML statements (`INSERT`/`UPDATE`/`DELETE`) are auto-committed.

- The name for the Web service application.

- The JNDI location for the JDBC datasource to be used at runtime.

- The JDBC URL for database connection and the username and password to be used at compile/generation time.

Assembling a SQL Query Web Service from a SQL Statement

Step 1a

Provide the SQL statements or query, the name and password for the database that they are based on, and the other information described in the Prerequisites section as input to the Web Services Assembler `sqlAssemble` command, as in the following example:

```
java -jar wsa.jar
-sqlAssemble
-appName query
-dataSource jdbc/OracleManagedDS
-sqlstatement "getEmpCount=select ename, sal from emp where
sal>:{mysal NUMBER}"
-sqlstatement "getEmpBySal=select ename, sal from emp where
sal>:{mysal NUMBER}"
-sqlstatement "updateEmp=update emp SET sal=sal+500 where
ename=:{myname VARCHAR}"
-dbConnection jdbc:oracle:thin:@stacd15:1521:lsqlj
-dbUser scott/tiger
```

Step 1b

Use the Ant task for generating Query or DML Web Services: The current release provides Ant tasks for Web services development. The following example shows how the Web Services Assembler `sqlAssemble` command can be performed as an Ant task:

```
<oracle:sqlAssemble
appName="query"
dataSource="jdbc/OracleManagedDS"
dbConnection="jdbc:oracle:thin:@dsunrde22:1521:sqlj"
dbUser="scott/tiger">
<sqlstatement="getEmpCount=select ename, sal from emp where
sal>:{mysal
NUMBER}"/>
<sqlstatement="getEmpBySal=select ename, sal from emp where
sal>:{mysal
NUMBER}"/>
<sqlstatement="updateEmp=update emp SET sal=sal+500 where
ename=:{myname
VARCHAR}"/>
/>
```

15.4.4 Assembling Oracle Streams AQ as Web Services

The WebServicesAssembler tool can generate a Web service from an AQ existing in a database. Each stream AQ queue belongs to a queue table (persisted in the RDBMS), which defines the type of the payload. Stream AQ queues can have single or multiple consumers:

- A single consumer is often referred to as a queue.

- A multiple consumer AQ is often referred to as a topic.

The generated Java code employs the Oracle Streams AQ JMS APIs.
Prerequisites:

- The name of the queue or topic to be exposed (single queue or topic):

    The followng PL/SQL script defines a queue, `sample_queue`, and a topic, `sample_topic`. The payload of the queue is of type `queue_message` (SQL object type). The payload of the topic is of type `topic_message` (SQL object type).

- The name for the Web service application.

- The JNDI location for the JDBC datasource to be used at runtime.

- The JDBC URL for database connection and the username and password to be used at compile/generation time.

Assembling Streams AQ Web Services Using Web Services Assembler

Step 1a

Furnish the inputs to Web Services Assembler -aqAssemble command:

```
java -jar $ORACLE_HOME/webservices/lib/wsa.jar
-aqAssemble
-appName queue
-dataSource jdbc/OracleManagedDS
-portName assembleQueuePort
-sql sample_queue
-dbConnection jdbc:oracle:thin:@stacd15:1521:lsqlj
-dbUser scott/tiger
```

Queues and topics must be deployed in different services using different values for `sql` and `appName` options.

Step 1b

Alternatively, an Ant task may be used instead:

```
<aqAssemble
appName="queue"
dataSource="jdbc/OracleManagedDS"
sql="sample_queue"
portName="assembleQueuePort"
dbConnection="jdbc:oracle:thin:@localhost:1521:lsqlj"
dbUser="scott/tiger"
/>
```

Steps 2 to 4 are identical to previous models.

Step 5

Developing Client Code to Access a Stream AQ Queue Web Service

```
SampleQueuePortClient queue = new SampleQueuePortClient();
QueueMessageUser m;
queue.send(new QueueMessageUser( "star chopper", "sample
1"));
queue.send(new QueueMessageUser("easy blocks", "sample 2"));
```

```
queue.send(new QueueMessageUser("back to future", "sample
3"));
m = queue.receive();
while (m != null) {
System.out.println("Message received from SampleQueue: " +
m.getSubject()
+ ": " + m.getText());
m = queue.receiveNoWait();
}
```

This client returns the following responses.

```
Message received from SampleQueue: sample 1: star chopper
Message received from SampleQueue: sample 2: easy blocks
Message received from SampleQueue: sample 3: back to future
```

Accessing an Oracle AQ Queue with JMS

The Web Services Assembler `aqAssemble` option lets you access the Oracle Streams AQ queue via the JMS queue instance. By setting either of the following options instead of datasource, the Web service will use a JMS queue at runtime instead of a JDBC-based queue:

- `aqConnectionLocation`: JDNI location of the Oracle Streams AQ/JMS queue connection

- `aqConnectionFactoryLocation`: JNDI location of the Oracle Streams AQ/JMS queue connection factory

15.5   Data Type Restrictions

- Streams are not supported in Oracle Streams AQ Web services.

- SQL Type `SYS.ANYDATA` is not supported in PL/SQL Web services.

- `REF CURSOR` is not supported as a parameter in PL/SQL Web services.

- `REF CURSOR` returned as Oracle `WebRowSet` and `XDB RowSet` does not support complex types in the result.

- PL/SQL stored procedures do not currently support the char types, including `char`, `character`, and `nchar` as `OUT` or `INOUT` parameters, and `long` types, including `long` and `long raw` as `OUT` or `INOUT` parameters.

15.6 Conclusion

In summary, the Oracle AS Web Services framework lets you turn database Web services into first-class citizens of the service-oriented architecture, since they inherit all the quality of services (e.g., Web services security, Web services reliability, Web services logging, Web services auditing).

Let's move to the next chapter, which is about the Database as Web service consumer.

16

Database as Web Services Consumer

"Si tu ne vas pas a Lagardere, Lagardere ira a toi."[1]

—*Le Bossu*, Alexandre Dumas

This chapter takes you through the required steps for turning your database into a Web services consumer and explains how to invoke external Web services from within SQL, PL/SQL, or Java in the database. To begin, as already covered in Chapter 14, why should you consider calling external Web services from the database?

16.1   Rationales for Database as Web Services Consumer

In Chapter 17, I describe how the new corporate registry application of the British Columbia government in Canada exchanged data produced between the Oracle database and its legacy mainframe, which processes part of the application using a set of Web services initiated by database triggers. I must add that Web services call-out is not a response to massive data transfer or replication across systems; the Oracle database furnishes more appropriate mechanisms such as Streams for that function.

In summary, you might consider calling out external Web services from the Oracle database when you need to implement applications such as the following:

■ Federate legacy/heterogeneous data; build new applications that combine data from multiple sources, including Web services

---

1.   Lirrerally, "If you don't go to Lagardere, he'll come to you."

- Automate the tracking and analysis of external and dynamic data (e.g., stock price, scientific data, policy tables, tax tables, weather information)

- Invoke business operations implemented as external Web services, such as placing new orders, orders shipment, credit card payment transactions (and getting valid authorization numbers)

16.2   How Database as Web Services Consumer Works

In this section, we'll look at the software pieces and the steps for invoking external Web services from within the database.

16.2.1   The Software Pieces

As illustrated in Figure 16.1, the following software pieces come into play during the invocation of the external Web services:

- The Java Web Service Client stack.

- A Web Services proxy Java class generated by JPublisher for each external Web service. Static invocation refers to the generation of a Web service client proxy, which is loaded into the database for calling external Web services. Similar to CORBA Client Stubs (for old-timers), this proxy simplifies Web services programming. The client proxy handles the construction of the SOAP request and the marshaling and unmarshaling of parameters.

- A PL/SQL wrapper (Call Spec) to be used by SQL and PL/SQL for invoking operations in the static Web service proxy class. As discussed in Part I, Call Specs allow invoking Java methods from SQL and PL/SQL.

- A table function on top of the PL/SQL wrapper. A table function[2] treats the range of returned values from a single or multiple Web services invocations as a table. The rows of such table function are typically pipelined (i.e., streamed directly to the consumer without intermediate storing).

- The Java DII stack is an alternative to the static proxy part of the Java Web service client stack that dynamically inspects the Web services

---

2.   The combination of Table Function and Web Services is called Web Services Data Sources.

WSDL to determine the supported operations and their profiles, and then constructs the SOAP request without generating and using a static client proxy.

■ The UTL_DBWS is a PL/SQL package, which is a wrapper on top of the Java DII.

■ XML to SQL mapping: Web service sends data in XML format that can be used and stored as is using XDB; however, you probably and predominantly want to deal with SQL data. Table 16.1 gives a mapping of XML types (originating from Web services) to SQL types (consumed by the database).

Figure 16.1
*Software
Components for
Web Services Call-
Out*

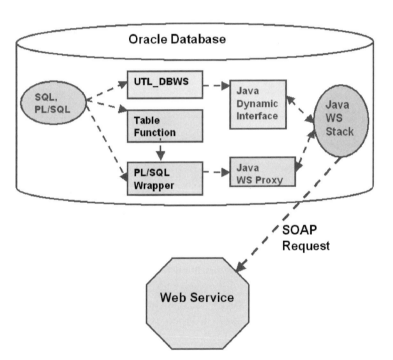

16.2.2 The Required Steps

The following simple steps let you invoke external Web services from the Oracle database.

Step 1: Load the Web services call-out utility in the database:

You need to configure your database to consume/invoke external Web services. See section 16.3 for more information hereafter.

Table 16.1 *Mapping XML Types to SQL Types*

XML Type	SQL Type
int	NUMBER
float	NUMBER
double	NUMBER
decimal	NUMBER
dateTime	DATE
string	VARCHAR2
byte[]	RAW
complexType	SQL OBJECT
Array	SQL TABLE
text_xml	XMLType

Step 2: Identify the target Web services and save the location of the WSDL and the endpoint where the Web services are listening to requests; in one of the following examples, the WSDL is located at:

```
http://services.xmethods.net/soap/urn:xmethods-delayed-
quotes.wsdl
```

In this example, the `Analyze WSDL` link takes you to the location of the endpoint, where the Web services are listening to incoming requests; in this example, the endpoint is located at `http://64.124.140.30:9090/soap`. The "`Operations`" link points to the description of supported operations.

Step 3a: Use static invocation:

Invoke JPublisher with the WSDL location and the endpoint as follows; it will generate the Java WS client proxy (which can be used directly by Java in the database), the PL/SQL wrappers, and a Table Function interface; it will then load everything in the database:

```
$ jpub -u scott/tiger -sysuser system/manager
-proxywsdl=http://services.xmethods.net/soap/urn:xmethods-
delayed-quotes.wsdl
-proxyopts=tabfun -httpproxy=www-proxy.us.oracle.com:80
-endpoint=http://64.124.140.30:9090/soap -dir=quotes
```

The following JPublisher options support Web service call-outs:

- `proxywsdl`: The URL of the WSDL file for the Web service to be. Note: You might need to enclose the WSDL URL with " " if it contains wild char such as "?".
- `user`: The database schema (and password) for which the PL/SQL wrapper is generated.
- `httpproxy`: The HTTP proxy host and port for accessing the WSDL file. *Note:* replace the Oracle HTTP proxy used below with yours.
- `sysuser`: The database user (and password) with SYSDBA privileges allows Oracle JPublisher to load the generated file into the database. Note: you may need to configure SYS account for remote access. If this option is not declared, you must manually load the generated file into the database to invoke the Web service from PL/SQL.
- `proxyopts`: A list of options specific to `proxywsdl`.
- `dir`: The directory storing all the generated files.

Following the JPublisher command, you can invoke the Web service operation either directly from Java in the database or from SQL and PL/SQL through the PL/SQL wrapper. The following SQL script invokes the Quote Web services through the Static proxy wrapper:

```
SQL> select jpub_plsql_wrapper.getQuote('ORCL') as Quote from
dual;

QUOTE
----------
12.6
```

That's it, because you don't have to know the Web services technologies; you just need to be able to locate the WSDL and the endpoint of the service, and then JPub takes care of the rest.

You may also use the table function. The JPublisher proxyopt option specifies the generation of a table function (`-proxyopts=tabfun`). Here's how you would use the table function resulting from the invocation of the getQuote Web services with a list of parameters (selected from a table of symbols):

1.   Create the table of symbols.

```
SQL> create table symbtab (quote varchar2(4));
SQL> insert into symbtab values('ORCL');
SQL> insert into symbtab values ('CSCO');
SQL> insert into symbtab values ('QCOM');
SQL> insert into symbtab values ('QQQQ');
SQL> insert into symbtab values ('GOOG');
SQL> insert into symbtab values ('EBAY');
SQL> insert into symbtab values ('YHOO');
SQL> commit
```

2.   Issue the following SQL command, which invokes the Web services iteratively on each symbol in the parameter list, and then pipeline the return values as a table (i.e., result set). Ideally, you'd want a Web service that takes several symbols as arguments and returns their values.

```
SQL> col ARG0 format a20
SQL> select * from
       table(jpub_plsql_wrapper.to_table_getQuote(cursor(select
       * from symbtab)));


ARG0                            RES
--------------------   ----------
ORCL                        12.64
CSCO                        17.12
QCOM                         43.4
QQQQ                      38.2799
GOOG                       353.58
EBAY                         38.2
YHOO                        35.42
7 rows selected.
```

The output shows the quotes of the given symbols (at the time of the execution of this command). You may apply SQL operators (e.g., MIN, MAX, AVG) on the table function. You may also store the values and schedule a batch job, which periodically collects these values, and then analyze the table using the power of SQL.

Step 3b: Use dynamic invocation (a bit more complex syntax):

Alternatively to the static proxy option, you may use the dynamic invocation interface (DII). The UTL_DBWS package is described in detail in the "Oracle Database 10*g* PL/SQL Packages and Type Reference." Table 16.2 summarizes the UTL_DBWS functions and procedures.

Table 16.2 *UTL_DBWS Functions and Procedures*

Subprogram	Description
CREATE_CALL Function	Creates a Call instance
CREATE_SERVICE Function	Creates a Service instance
GET_IN_PARAMETER_TYPES Function	Lists the XML type of the input parameters of the Call that is returned
GET_OUT_PARAMETER_TYPES Function	Lists the XML type of the output parameters of the Call that is returned
GET_OUTPUT_VALUES Function	Obtains the output arguments after a Call invocation
GET_PORTS Function	Lists the qualified names of all of the ports in a service
GET_PROPERTY Function	Returns the value of a particular property on a Call
GET_RETURN_TYPE Function	Lists the XML type that is returned by the given Call
GET_SERVICES Function	Lists the qualified names of the services defined in a WDSL document
INVOKE Function	Invokes a specific operation using a synchronous request-response interaction mode
RELEASE_ALL_SERVICES Procedure	Releases all Service instances
RELEASE_CALL Procedure	Releases a particular Call instance
RELEASE_SERVICE Procedure	Releases a particular Service instance
REMOVE_PROPERTY Procedure	Clears the value of a particular property on a Call
SET_PROPERTY Procedure	Sets the value of a particular property on a Call

The dynamic invocation using RPC-style messages works well with XML types that can be mapped into built-in SQL or PL/SQL types but may face serialization issues with complex XML types. DII with document-style messaging does not have these serialization issues.

- Here is an example of DII invocation using RPC message style. Note, this is not about the same Web service:

```
set serveroutput on size 999999
 drop table diioutput;
 create table diioutput (line varchar2(3000));
 declare
service_ sys.utl_dbws.SERVICE;
call_ sys.utl_dbws.CALL;
service_qname sys.utl_dbws.QNAME;
port_qname sys.utl_dbws.QNAME;
operation_qname sys.utl_dbws.QNAME;
string_type_qname sys.utl_dbws.QNAME;
retx ANYDATA;
retx_string VARCHAR2(100);
retx_len number;
params sys.utl_dbws.ANYDATA_LIST;
  begin
service_qname := sys.utl_dbws.to_qname(null, 'DBRpcEchoService');
service_ := sys.utl_dbws.create_service(service_qname);
port_qname := sys.utl_dbws.to_qname(null, 'EchoInterfacePort');
operation_qname := sys.utl_dbws.to_qname('http://echo.demo.oracle/',
        'echoString');
call_ := sys.utl_dbws.create_call(service_, port_qname,
        operation_qname);
sys.utl_dbws.set_target_endpoint_address(call_,
            'http://localhost:8888/echo/DBRpcEchoService');
  sys.utl_dbws.set_property(call_, 'ENCODINGSTYLE_URI',
            'http://schemas.xmlsoap.org/soap/encoding/');
string_type_qname :=
            sys.utl_dbws.to_qname('http://www.w3.org/2001/XMLSchema',
            'string');
  sys.utl_dbws.add_parameter(call_, 's', string_type_qname,
    'ParameterMode.IN');
      sys.utl_dbws.set_return_type(call_, string_type_qname);
params(0) := ANYDATA.convertvarchar('hello');
retx := sys.utl_dbws.invoke(call_, params);
```

```
    retx_string := retx.accessvarchar2;
    insert into diioutput values('echoString repsonse: ' ||
retx_string);
    end;
/
```

- Here is an example of DII invocation using document style:

```
set echo on
set serveroutput on size 999999
drop table diioutput;
create table diioutput (line varchar2(2000));
declare
    service_ sys.utl_dbws.SERVICE;
    call_ sys.utl_dbws.CALL;
    service_qname sys.utl_dbws.QNAME;
    port_qname sys.utl_dbws.QNAME;
    xoperation_qname sys.utl_dbws.QNAME;
    xstring_type_qname sys.utl_dbws.QNAME;
    response sys.XMLTYPE;
    request sys.XMLTYPE;
  begin
    service_qname :=
        sys.utl_dbws.to_qname('http://echo.demo.oracle/', 'tns');
    service_ := sys.utl_dbws.create_service(service_qname);
    call_ := sys.utl_dbws.create_call(service_);
    sys.utl_dbws.set_target_endpoint_address(call_,
            'http://localhost:8888/echo/DBDocEchoService');

    request := sys.XMLTYPE('<tns:echoStringElement
                    xmlns:tns="http://echo.demo.oracle/">
                        <tns:s>Bob</tns:s></tns:echoStringElement>');
    response := sys.utl_dbws.invoke(call_, request);
    insert into diioutput values('echoString:: response : ');
    insert into diioutput values(response.getstringval);

    request := sys.XMLTYPE('<tns:echoBeansElement
            xmlns:tns="http://echo.demo.oracle/"> <tns:b> <tns:age>13</
                tns:age>
            <tns:name>Bob</tns:name> </tns:b> <tns:b> <tns:age>33</tns:age>
            <tns:name>Smith</tns:name> </tns:b> </tns:echoBeansElement>');
```

```
     response := sys.utl_dbws.invoke(call_, request);
     insert into diioutput values('echoBean[]:: response : ');
     insert into diioutput values(response.getstringval);
   end;
  /
```

16.3   Turning Your Oracle Database into a Web Service Consumer

In order to turn an Oracle Database into a Web service consumer, you need to perform the following one-time configuration: ensure that Java is installed in the database; ensure that JPublisher is installed on the client machine; and install the call-out utility.

16.3.1   Ensure That Java Is Installed in the Database

If you have been running the examples in Part I, you can skip this section. The following basic test will tell your database whether Java is enabled or not:

```
$ sqlplus scott/tiger

SQL*Plus: Release 10.2.0.1.0 - Production on Sun Feb 5
16:54:21 2006
Copyright (c) 1982, 2005, Oracle.  All rights reserved.


Connected to:
Oracle Database 10g Enterprise Edition Release 10.2.0.1.0 -
Production
With the Partitioning and Data Mining options

SQL> select dbms_java.longname('coffee') from dual;

DBMS_JAVA.LONGNAME('COFFEE')
--------------------------------
coffee

SQL>
```

Otherwise, install Java from a download or the main Oracle Database CD. In order to get the natively compiled libraries of the system classes and also the ability to natively compile your own classes, you need to additionally install those libraries and the native compiler (NCOMP) from the Oracle Database companion CD.

16.3.2 Installing JPublisher on the Client Machine

The following command will tell you whether JPublisher is installed in your client environment:

```
$ jpub
JPub: Java Object Type Publisher, version 10.2.0.0.0
Production
Copyright (c) 1997, 2004, Oracle Corporation. All Rights
Reserved.

JPub generates Java or SQLJ source code for the following SQL
entities:
    object types, collection types, and packages.

Invocation:
    jpub <options>

The following option is required:
    -user=<username>/<password>
Other options are:
    -input=<input file>
        ...
```

Otherwise, install SQLJ (JPublisher is currentlly installed as part of SQLJ install) from an Oracle Database download or the client CD through the following steps:

- Launch the installer via **setup.exe**.
- Select Custom Install type.
- Select **Oracle SQL**.
- Then proceed with the installation.

16.3.3 Installing the Web Services Call-Out Utility in Your Database

The Oracle Database does not currently natively embed the required Web services libraries for call-out, even though the UTL_HTTP[3] package can be used to construct and unpack SOAP messages programmatically. By loading the Oracle-provided Web services call-out utility in the embedded Java VM, you can instantaneously extend the capabilities of your database.

Step 1: Select the appropriate Web service call-out stack:

This utility is a subset of the Oracle application server Web services stack (made available for free to database customers), you need to load the appropriate version of the libraries that suits your RDBMS release. Select the appropriate call-out utility for your database, using the compatibility matrix shown in Table 16.3:

Table 16.3   *Web services Callout Matrix*

Target Database Release	Java SE	Oracle AS (OC4J) Release	Call-Out Utility(*)
10.2	1.4.x	10.1.3	dbws-callout-utility-10R2.zip
10.1	1.4.x	10.1.3	dbws-callout-utility-10R2.zip
9.2	1.3.x	10.1.2	dbws-callout-utility.zip

* http://www.oracle.com/technology/sample_code/tech/java/jsp/dbwebservices.html

Notes:

- It is important that the JDK in your environment be in sync with the J2SE level of the Java runtime in the database; in other words, don't load code generated with JPublisher under JDK 1.5 in Oracle Database 10*g*; use JDK 1.4 for 10.2 and 10.1 and JDK 1.3 for 9.2.

- Web services call-out supports RPC encoded in Oracle Database 9.2 and any format in Oracle Database 10*g*.

---

3.   http://www.oracle.com/technology/tech/webservices/htdocs/samples/dbwebservice/DBWebServices_PLSQL.html.

Step 2: Extract the contents of the file into your `ORACLE_HOME` directory and set the `CLASSPATH` environment variable to include the following (replace Windows notation with UNIX equivalent):

```
%oracle_home%\jdbc\lib\ojdbc14.jar; // for JDK 1.4
%oracle_home%\jdbc\lib\orai18n.jar;
%oracle_home%\sqlj\lib\translator.jar;
%oracle_home%\sqlj\lib\runtime12.jar;
%oracle_home%\sqlj\lib\dbwsa.jar;
%oracle_home%\jdbc\lib\classes12.jar // for JDK 1.3
```

Step 3: Tune OracleJVM memory:

As explained in Chapter 2, the Java class loader in OracleJVM allocates memory from the Java pool during the resolution of new classes/JARS and for loading their metadata in SGA. You might need to increase the Java pool in order to accommodate the Web service client stack. Make sure that `shared_pool_size` and `java_pool_size` in the `pfile` (`.ora`) are set at minimum to the following values:

```
shared_pool_size=96M
java_pool_size=80M
```

You might need to recycle the database if you have altered the `pfile`; check with your DBA, if you don't know.

Step 4: Load the web service client stack:

Load the call-out utility library corresponding to your RDBMS (see Table 16.3).

- For 10*g* RDBMS:

    Use the following command if you are loading the JARS in `SYS` schema; note "`-s -grant public`" for creating synonyms to make the JARS publicly accessibles to other schemas:

    ```
    $loadjava -u sys/oracle -r -v -f -s -grant public
              -genmissing sqlj/lib/dbwsclient.jar
    ```

Use the following command if you are loading in a user schema such as SCOTT; note the absence of "-s -grant public" option; in this case, the libraries will only be accessible to SCOTT schema.

```
$loadjava -u scott/tiger -r -v -f -genmissing
dbwsclient.jar
```

- For 9.2 RDBMS:

  You might need to grab some of these jars from an expanded OC4J 10.1.2 (at the ORACLE_HOME location), if not present in the Call-Out utility. Use the following command to load the Web services client stack into the SYS schema; for Windows platforms, replace ${ORACLE_HOME} with %ORACLE_HOME%:

  ```
  % loadjava -u sys/change_on_install -r -v -s -f -grant
  public -genmissing ${ORACLE_HOME}/j2ee/home/lib/jssl-
  1_2.jar ${ORACLE_HOME}/soap/lib/soap.jar
  ${ORACLE_HOME}/dms/lib/dms.jar ${ORACLE_HOME}/j2ee/
  home/lib/servlet.jar ${ORACLE_HOME}/j2ee/home/lib/
  ejb.jar ${ORACLE_HOME}/j2ee/home/lib/mail.jar
  ```

  Use the following command to load the Web services client stack into the SCOTT schema:

  ```
  % loadjava -u scott/tiger -r -v -f -genmissing
  ${ORACLE_HOME}/j2ee/home/lib/jssl-1_2.jar
  ${ORACLE_HOME}/soap/lib/soap.jar ${ORACLE_HOME}/dms/
  lib/dms.jar ${ORACLE_HOME}/j2ee/home/lib/servlet.jar
  ${ORACLE_HOME}/j2ee/home/lib/ejb.jar ${ORACLE_HOME}/
  j2ee/home/lib/mail.jar
  ```

  If you used JDeveloper 10.1.2 to generate the web service client proxy, you also need to load $ORACLE_HOME/jdev/lib/jdev-rt.jar.

  At this stage, the RDBMS is ready for calling out external Web services.

Step 5: Enable DII:

The call-out utility loaded in the previous step already installs the Java DII stack; the downloaded ZIP file also contains the SQL scripts utl_dbws_decl.sql and utl_dbws_body.sql to create the wrappers on top of the Java DII stack. Execute utl_dbws_decl.sql and `utl_dbws_body.sql` as `SYS`. Your RDBMS is ready to use `SYS.UTL_DBWS` to call Web services.

16.4   Database Web Services Call-Out Samples

Before invoking JPublisher, set the `CLASSPATH` environment variable to include the following (replace Windows notation with UNIX equivalent):

Note: `oracle_home` here, refers to database home.

```
%oracle_home%\jdbc\lib\ojdbc14.jar; //for JDK 1.4
%oracle_home%\jdbc\lib\orai18n.jar;
%oracle_home%\sqlj\lib\translator.jar;
%oracle_home%\sqlj\lib\runtime12.jar;
%oracle_home%\sqlj\lib\dbwsa.jar;
%oracle_home%\jdbc\lib\classes12.jar //for JDK 1.3
```

16.4.1   Calling Out Google Search Web Service

In order to use Google Web services APIs, you need to register and get a valid license key at http://www.google.com/apis.

Step 1: Locate the Web service:

WSDL: `http://api.google.com/GoogleSearch.wsdl`

Endpoint: `http://api.google.com/search/beta2`

Connect to the endpoint from a browser to check that the Web service is up and listening at the endpoint in question; if so, you should receive the following message:

```
SOAP RPC Router
Sorry, I don't speak via HTTP GET- you have to use HTTP POST
to talk to me.
```

Step 2: Invoke JPublisher, as follows:

```
C:\>jpub -u scott/tiger -sysuser=scott/tiger
-proxywsdl=http://api.google.com/GoogleSearch.wsdl
-proxyopts=tabfun,soap
-httpproxy=www-proxy.us.oracle.com:80
-endpoint=http://api.google.com/search/beta2 -dir=tmp

tmp\GoogleSearchServiceProxyJPub.java
tmp\plsql_wrapper.sql
tmp\plsql_dropper.sql
tmp\plsql_grant.sql
tmp\plsql_revoke.sql
Executing tmp\plsql_dropper.sql
Executing tmp\plsql_wrapper.sql
Executing tmp\plsql_grant.sql
Loading tmp\plsql_proxy.jar
```

Note: When the –plsqlpackage option is not present, JPublisher uses
JPUB_PLSQL_WRAPPER as the default name of the wrapper.

Granting 'java.lang.RuntimePermission' permission to the invoking schema:

This permission is missing in early versions of plsql_grant.sql: (see Chapter 2 for an explanation of permissions with Java in the database):

```
SQL> connect / as sysdba
Connected.
SQL> exec dbms_java.grant_permission('SCOTT',
'SYS:java.lang.RuntimePermission','setFactory', '');

PL/SQL procedure successfully completed.
```

Step 3: Invoke Web services Spell Check operation through the PL/SQL wrapper:

```
SQL> select jpub_plsql_wrapper.dospellingsuggestion(
  2                '<enter your key here>',
  3                'licencing')
  4                as GOOGLE_Spell_Check_Web_Service
  5                from dual;
```

```
                GOOGLE_SPELL_CHECK_WEB_SERVICE

                ------------------------------------------------------
                licensing

                SQL> select jpub_plsql_wrapper.dospellingsuggestion(
                  2                      '<enter your key here>',
                  3                      'Nelson Mandelo')
                  4                   as GOOGLE_Spell_Check_Web_Service
                  5                   from dual;


                GOOGLE_SPELL_CHECK_WEB_SERVICE

                ------------------------------------------------------
                Nelson Mandela
```

Let's use the table function interface:

```
SQL> create table searchtab (key varchar2(32) default '<your key>', word
varchar2(30));

Table created.

SQL> insert into searchtab (word) values ('Ophrah Winfrid');

1 row created.

SQL> insert into searchtab (word) values ('Mariam Makebo');

1 row created.

SQL> insert into searchtab (word) values ('licenzing');

1 row created.

SQL> commit;

SQL> col arg0 format a32
SQL> col arg1 format a30
SQL> col arg1 format a23
SQL> col res format a20
```

```
SQL> select * from table(google.to_table_dospellingsuggestion(cursor(select *
from searchtab)));
```

ARG0	ARG1	RES
\<your key	> Ophrah Winfrid	Oprah Winfred
\<your key	> Mariam Makebo	Mariam Makeba
\<your key	> licenzing	licensing

16.4.2   Calling Out the Phone Verifier Web Service

This phone verification Web service (with a free testing at the time of this writing) lets you retrieve public details about a phone number. The following XML document is the SOAP response message template/profile.

```
HTTP/1.1 200 OK
Content-Type: text/xml; charset=utf-8
Content-Length: length

<?xml version="1.0" encoding="utf-8"?>
<soap:Envelope xmlns:xsi="http://www.w3.org/2001/XMLSchema-
instance" xmlns:xsd="http://www.w3.org/2001/XMLSchema"
xmlns:soap="http://schemas.xmlsoap.org/soap/envelope/">
  <soap:Body>
    <CheckPhoneNumberResponse xmlns="http://ws.cdyne.com/
PhoneVerify/query">
      <CheckPhoneNumberResult>
        <Company>string</Company>
        <Valid>boolean</Valid>
        <Use>string</Use>
        <State>string</State>
        <Switch>string</Switch>
        <RC>string</RC>
        <OCN>string</OCN>
        <OriginalNumber>string</OriginalNumber>
        <CleanNumber>string</CleanNumber>
      </CheckPhoneNumberResult>
    </CheckPhoneNumberResponse>
  </soap:Body>
</soap:Envelope>
```

Step 1: Locate the Web service:

Point your browser to:

> http://www.cdyne.com/developers/overview.aspx

Locate "Phone Verifier" and click on Get WSDL.

■ **Postal Address Corrector & Geocoder**	Get WSDL	Test	Example(s)	Price
■ **IP2Geo**	Get WSDL	Test	Example(s)	Price
■ **Phone Verifier**	Get WSDL	Test	Example(s)	Price
■ **Email Verifier**	Get WSDL	Test	Example(s)	Price
■ **NatTax**	Get WSDL	Test	Example(s)	Price
■ **Credit Card Verifier**	Get WSDL	Test	Example(s)	Free

Locate the endpoint (address location):

```
<wsdl:port
name="PhoneVerifyHttpGet"binding="tns:PhoneVerifyHttpGet">
<http:address location="http://ws.cdyne.com/phoneverify/
phoneverify.asmx" />
```

Step 2: Invoke JPublisher, as follows:

```
C:\My_Data\PM\Book>jpub -u scott/tiger -sysuser scott/tiger
   -proxywsdl=http://ws.cdyne.com/phoneverify/
phoneverify.asmx?wsdl
   -proxyopts=tabfun -httpproxy=www-proxy.us.oracle.com:80
   -endpoint=http://ws.cdyne.com/phoneverify/phoneverify.asmx
   -dir=phone

Multiple ports available. To publish a particular port,
use -proxyopts=port:PhoneVerifySoap,
or -proxyopts=port:PhoneVerifySoap12.
Use the default port PhoneVerifySoap.
phone\src\genproxy\PhoneVerifySoapClientJPub.java
phone\plsql_wrapper.sql
phone\plsql_dropper.sql
phone\plsql_grant.sql
phone\plsql_revoke.sql
Executing phone\plsql_dropper.sql
Executing phone\plsql_wrapper.sql
Executing phone\plsql_grant.sql
Loading phone\plsql_proxy.jar
```

Don't forget to grant the additional permission:

```
SQL> connect / as sysdba
Connected.
SQL> exec dbms_java.grant_permission('SCOTT',
'SYS:java.lang.RuntimePermission',
    'setFactory', '');

PL/SQL procedure successfully completed.
```

Step 3: Invoke the Web services from SQL:

```
SQL>select
jpub_plsql_wrapper.checkphonenumber('6505067000','0') from
dual;
```

This example is also fully highlighted in the Oracle By Example at

```
http://www.oracle.com/technology/obe/10gr2_db_single/develop/
java/java_otn.htm
```

These examples are just proof of the ability to invoke external Web services from within the database. Try your own examples, but more important, you need to determine if such an approach makes sense for your specific requirements.

16.5 Conclusion

This concludes Part V, which is dedicated to the emerging concept of Database Web services. This is just the beginning of a trend; I anticipate that Database Web services will mature and be an integral part of the larger Web services and service-oriented architecture.

The next part of the book "Putting Everything Together" will describe use cases that involve the pieces we have covered in Part I, II, III, IV, and V.

Part VI: Putting Everything Together

After climbing a great hill, one only finds that there are many more hills to climb.

—Nelson Mandela

In this book, I have tried to give you a good feel for the APIs and utilities available to Java and Web services developers for programming the Oracle database. Using those APIs and utilities, you can build tactical Java stored procedures, JDBC and or SQLJ based applications, and database Web services, but as you will see, you can also integrate these technologies with strategic applications or build custom frameworks and products. How far can you go? When you combine Java in the Oracle database, JDBC, SQLJ, JPublisher, and database Web services with the rich features set of the Oracle database (including PL/SQL, XMLDB, streams/AQ, JMS), the sky is the limit! Now, I'll describe real-world systems and products that exploit the technologies described in this book.

17

360-Degree Programming the Oracle Database

Step back, look at your Oracle database from all angles including: (1) the database functionality itself, (2) calling database functionality from within the database, (3) calling database functionality from outside (client, middle-tier, etc), and (4) calling external system/functionality from within the database. Far from being exhaustive, the case studies presented here will give you a broader, 360-degree view of how you can program the database using Java, JDBC, SQLJ, JPublisher, and Web services. Here are synopses of the case studies in question:

- **TECSIS Systems:** This case study describes how TECSIS Systems reduced its costs by integrating its platform using Java in the database, JDBC, PL/SQL, AQ, RMI Call-out, SAP Java Connector, JDBC Call-out, and Oracle XDK. The platform comprises SAP systems, custom applications, SQL Server, Natural Adabas, AS400 RPG-DB, and Tandem COBOL.

- **Oracle *inter*Media:** This is an Oracle database component that enables you to store, manage, and retrieve images, audio, video, or other heterogeneous media data in an integrated fashion with other enterprise information. This case study describes how Oracle *inter*Media built a server-side media parser and an in-database image processor using Java in the database.

- **British Columbia, Online Corporate Registration**: This case study describes how the British Columiba Corporate and Personal Registries have put legal filings online, as part of their Online e-Government Applications, using Java in the database, database Web services, XML DB, JMS/AQ, and Message-Driven Beans in OC4J.

- **Information Retrieval Using Oracle Text, XML DB Framework, and Java in the Database:** This case study describes the design and implementation of a search engine for a controlled environment, such as a text warehouse or a corporate intranet.

■ **Database-driven Content Management System (DBPrism CMS):** This is an open-source and database-oriented content management system (CMS), using Java in the database, XML DB framework, and the Apache Cocoon framework.

17.1 TECSIS Systems: Custom Enterprise Integration Framework

This case study has been presented and demonstrated at Oracle World in San Francisco, California, and is reproduced here with the authorization and courtesy of my good friend Esteban Capoccetti, System Architect at TECSIS and the mastermind behind this architecture.

17.1.1 About the Company

Tenaris, the world leader in tubular technologies, represents eight established manufacturers of steel tubes: AlgomaTubes, Confab, Dalmine, NKKTubes, Siat, Siderca, Tamsa, and Tavsa. Tenaris is a leading supplier of tubular goods and services to the global energy and mechanical industries, with a combined production capacity of 3 million tons of seamless and 850,000 tons of welded steel tubes, annual sales of $3 billion, and 13,000 employees on five continents. Our market share is about 30% of world trade in OCTG seamless products and 13% of total world seamless tube production. The main goal of TECSIS, the System Technology division of Tenaris, is to validate and disseminate technology throughout the companies within the Tenaris group. This case study describes their experience of using Java in the Oracle database and how it solved our integration requirements.

17.1.2 About the Application

For the last three years, our company has been using Oracle database, not just as a database, but also as an integration infrastructure. We started by implementing the business rules, using PL/SQL stored procedures, which gave us many advantages. With the Java virtual machine embedded in the database (OracleJVM), we extended the capabilities of our database and turned it into a data integration hub.

17.1.3   Our Business and Technical Requirements

Business Requirements

Our business requirements made it necessary to integrate online information from different platforms, including SAP, AS400, ADABAS/NATURAL, and COBOL Tandem. Our PL/SQL-based business rules needed to send and get data from these platforms. Existing legacy systems, as well as new intranet/Internet-based development, required cross-platform integration. Our main goal was cost savings through reuse of software, systems, and skills.

Technical Requirements

We needed to integrate the following platforms: Oracle PL/SQL Stored Procedures, SAP R3, Natural/Adabas, RPG/DB400, COBOL Tandem, COM Components, and non-Oracle databases (Adabas-D, MSSQL Server). We tried different RPC technologies to integrate legacy systems, but we were unhappy with their degree of integration. By that time, it became crucial for us to reach information available online on other platforms, from existing PL/SQL packages.

In summary, our most important requirements were to:

- Simplify cross-platform integration.
- Save costs: Instead of adding a new integration layer, we decided to leverage existing components and use each of these components to the best of its capacity.
- Avoid the explosion of communication that would be generated by point-to-point integration.

Design and Programming Choices

We choose to leverage OracleJVM and its ability to run Java libraries in the database, because all existing ERP systems, as well as non-Oracle databases, furnish either a Java-based Remote Procedure Call (RPC) software or a pure Java JDBC driver that can be loaded into the Oracle JVM. PL/SQL wrappers make these mechanisms available to the SQL world as Java stored procedures. Existing or new PL/SQL-based business rules can easily interact with other systems. By centralizing our business rules in the Oracle database, along with transformation rules and making the whole thing accessible by both Web clients and batch jobs, the Oracle database became our integration engine.

All of our new systems are based on Web pages that call stored procedures, which access the business rules. Existing batch jobs, as well as client applications, share the same business rules. We have also been able to standardize the way in which we call the procedures, using XML-based IN and OUT parameters. These XML parameters are parsed or generated using Oracle XDK.

The fact that the system became operational in a few days, without costly retraining of our PL/SQL programmers, is the best illustration of the simplicity of the solution. In addition, we accomplished the integration of batch jobs through three-line SQL* Plus scripts.

Using a traditional Enterprise Application Integration (EAI) product would have been more complex and expensive. Instead, employing Java in the database not only simplified our integration process, but it also saved us money.

17.1.4   The Architecture of the Integration Framework

This section describes our use cases and the two pillars of our architecture, which are Java stored procedures calling out external components from within the database and external systems calling in Java stored procedures.

Typical Use Cases

We had three use cases: (1) Code Validation, system A (COBOL Tandem) needs to check whether a specific code value exists in system B (Oracle Database); (2) Pop-Up Lists, system A (AS400 screen) needs to display a list of values using content from system B (Natural Adabas); and (3) Cross-Platform Modifications, a new product is added to system A (Oracle Database), and the same product must also be added to system B (Natural Adabas).

Java Stored Procedures Calling External Systems

We selected the Software AG EntireX Communicator (formerly EntireX broker) to make remote calls to Natural/Adabas programs (OS/390), RPG programs (AS400), and Tandem COBOL programs.

Although SAP Java connector (SAP JCO) is distributed as a JAR file, it is not 100% Java based because it uses several `.sl` (libraries). For security reasons, OracleJVM does not allow Java classes to use external `.sl` libraries (i.e., JNI calls). We worked around this restriction by running the SAP JCO as an external RMI server. Doing this allows us to issue RMI calls to the SAP JCO from within Java stored procedures (See SAP Call-Out in Part I).

We loaded third-party pure Java JDBC drivers into the database for interaction between Java stored procedures and non-Oracle databases (JDBC Call-out is described in Part I). If we needed to interact with a remote Oracle database, we would just use the pure Java server-side Oracle JDBC-Thin driver, from within the database. Then we created standard PL/SQL wrappers, called EAI_PKG, for each loaded module to allow uniform invocation from the PL/SQL-based business rules. Finally, we distributed an application integration guide internally to all PL/SQL programmers. In a few days, they were able to build procedures that interact with other platforms.

By centralizing the business rules, and adding integration and transformation rules, we created a complete data integration framework. These business, integration, and transformation rules all interact with external systems through Java stored procedures, using the EAI_PKG. Our new system comprises a Web-based presentation layer, as well as batch jobs (SQL*PLUS scripts). We use Oracle Object for OLE (OO4O) to execute Oracle procedures from our presentation layer (`.asp`). Both the presentation layer and the batch jobs use this same integration framework.

Figure 17.1 illustrates this architecture. Although the concept of the Oracle Advanced Queuing system does not appear in Figure 17.1, which illustrates how to call external systems from within the database, the EAI_PKG furnishes a queue corresponding to every remote system. If a remote system is down or unreachable, the EAI_PKG package automatically enqueues the message in the corresponding queue. An internal DBMS_JOB job is associated with every queue and is scheduled to run at a determined frequency. This job dequeues the pending messages and attempts to process them until the target system becomes available. Compared with Java stored procedures, traditional EAI products do not offer the same level of ease of use.

External Systems Calling Java Stored Procedures

After we were able to call all our external systems from Java stored procedures, the next step was enabling external systems to call Java stored procedures, as illustrated by Figure 17.2. To accomplish this second step, we reused both the EntireX Communication and the SAP Java connector. Natural Adabas, AS400, and COBOL Tandem place a call against EntireX, which, in turn, invokes a Java stored procedure. The response from the Java stored procedure is sent back to the legacy system.

Figure 17.1
Calling External
Systems

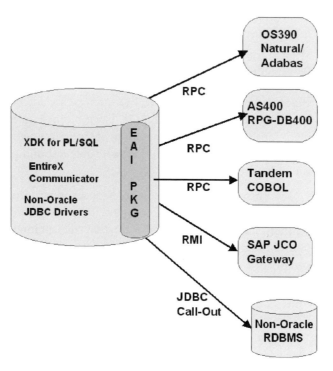

Similarly, SAP/ABAP applications call the SAP Java connector, which, in turn, calls the Oracle stored procedure. The response from the stored procedure is returned to the ABAP application.

17.1.5   The Complete Picture

As Figure 17.3 illustrates, by using the Oracle database as a central point of communication, we enabled any system to talk to any other system, while avoiding point-to-point communication.

The entire framework is monitored by an Oracle stored procedure, which, at a determined frequency, performs a call to each target system as well as the EntireX and SAP connector.

If one of the monitored systems returns an error, the procedure sends a notification email. Our next step will be to send SNMP traps to a central console. We are currently working on this.

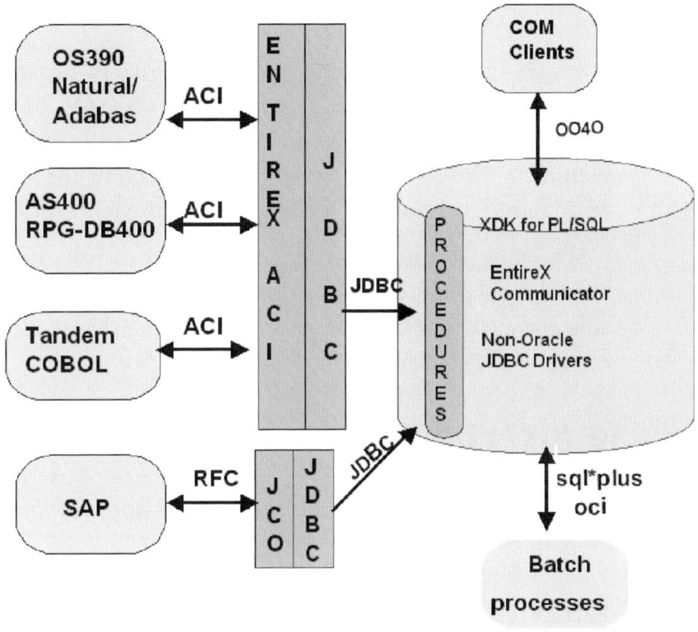

Figure 17.2
Calling In

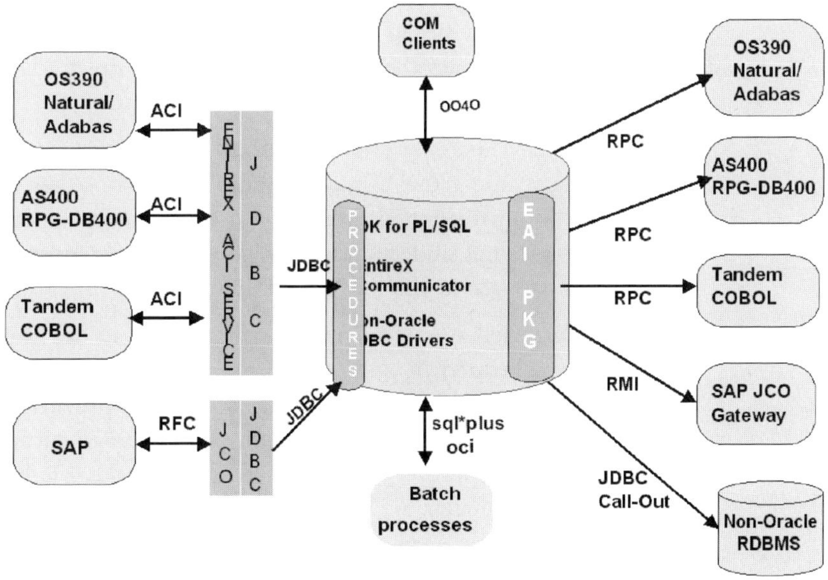

Figure 17.3
*TECSIS: The
Complete Picture*

17.1.6 Conclusion

We were able to implement a complete, easy-to-use integration framework employing Java and PL/SQL procedures. PL/SQL procedures were easy to create and maintain, and we were able to use the existing skills of our programmers. We do not see Java as a replacement for PL/SQL but, rather, as an enabling technology to extend and improve PL/SQL usage.

By using Java in the Oracle database to its full capacity, we were able to turn the database into an online integration broker. In addition, we were able to shield our developers from the underlying complexity of our platform, thereby simplifying the integration process.

17.2 Oracle *inter*Media

This use case has been kindly provided by the head of the interMedia development (she will recognize herself).

17.2.1 What Is Oracle *inter*Media?

As explained previously, Java in the database is more than just an alternative to proprietary stored procedure languages; the combination of the RDBMS and Java enables the implementation of complete database-resident products and component such as Oracle *inter*Media.

*inter*Media is an Oracle database component that enables you to store, manage, and retrieve images, audio, video, or other heterogeneous media data in an integrated fashion with other enterprise information. It makes native format understanding available for popular image, audio, and video formats, such as JPEG, TIFF, ASF, and MP3.

*inter*Media provides methods for metadata extraction, making the metadata embedded in popular image, audio, and video formats available for database searching and indexing. *inter*Media provides methods for embedding metadata into images, making it possible to encapsulate metadata and image data together into the same binary image. Methods are also provided for image processing, such as format conversion and thumbnail generation.

*inter*Media supports popular streaming technologies, allowing audio and video data stored in Oracle database to be streamed using Windows Media and Real Networks Streaming Servers. *inter*Media also integrates with JDeveloper ADF components (previously known as BC4J) and UIX (i.e., a framework for building Web applications) and Oracle Application

Server Portal, allowing for rapid development of media-rich applications using these tools.

17.2.2   How Does It Work?

interMedia Object Interface: New Database Types

To support multimedia data in the database, *inter*Media defines a set of new database media data types to handle image, audio, video, or other heterogeneous media data.

ORDAudio is the data type defined to hold digital audio. It includes a source attribute that points to the media data, defines audio-specific attributes such as `mimeType` and `duration`, and methods such as `setProperties` to extract embedded metadata.

ORDImage is the data type defined to hold digital images. It includes a source attribute that points to the media data, defines image-specific attributes such as `mimeType`, `height`, and `width`, and methods such as `setProperties` to extract metadata and `processCopy` to copy the image and generate an image thumbnail.

ORDVideo is the data type defined to hold digital video. It includes a source attribute, defines video-specific attributes such as `mimeType`, `duration`, `height`, and `width`, and methods such as `setProperties`.

ORDDoc is the data type defined to hold any type of media. If a column can hold mixed media (i.e., image, audio, or video data) in a single column, it should be defined to be of type ORDDoc. It includes a source attribute, defines attributes that are common to all types of media, such as `mimeType` and `format`, and methods such as `setProperties`.

BLOB/BFILE Support

For applications that already have large volumes of media data stored in database BLOBs or BFILEs, *inter*Media provides a relational interface that makes the services of *inter*Media available without requiring an *inter*Media object type to be instantiated. With the relational interface, the application manages the BLOB or BFILE and metadata columns, and calls object static methods for metadata extraction, image processing, and so on.

interMedia Object Interface

While the relational interface is a standard and supported part of Oracle *inter*Media, the recommended way of storing media in Oracle is the *inter*Media object interface. The *inter*Media object types are recommended because they are self-describing and easy for applications and other Oracle tools such as JDeveloper ADF Components and Oracle Application Server Portal to understand. If you use BLOBs in your application instead of *inter-Media* object types, the knowledge of what is in the BLOB must be hard-coded into the application.

17.2.3   Rationales for Storing Media Data in the Database

Many considerations drive *interMedia* adoption, including synchronization with related relational information, robustness, reliability, availability, security, scalability, integrated administration, search/query capabilities, integrated transactionality, simplicity, and cost reduction.

Synchronization with Related Database Information: Just Another Data Type

The media data stored in the database can be directly linked with corresponding relational data. Related information is kept in sync. If media are stored in a file system, it is possible for external processes to delete or modify the data, causing it to be orphaned or to lose synchronicity with its corresponding relational data.

Robustness, Reliability, Availability, Security, Scalability

Oracle *inter*Media extends Oracle database's robustness, reliability, availability, and scalability to multimedia content in traditional, Internet, electronic commerce, and media-rich applications.

Security

The database allows for fine-grained (row-level and column-level) security. The same security mechanisms are used for both media data and corresponding relational data. When using many file systems, directory services do not allow fine-grained levels of access control. It may not be possible to restrict access to individual users; in many systems, enabling a user to access any content in the directory gives access to all content in the directory. Oracle also makes it possible to attach timeouts to the content, to include check-in/check-out capabilities, to audit who accesses the content, and to enable exclusive access to the content.

Scalability

In many cases, the ability to index, partition, and perform operations through triggers, view processing, or table- and database-level parameters allows for dramatically larger data sets to be supported by applications that build on the database rather than on file systems.

Administration, Backup, Recovery/Disaster Recovery

Oracle provides a single administrative environment for managing, tuning, administering, backing up, and recovering the content. The media data is treated operationally in exactly the same manner as all other content. It can be partitioned, placed in transportable tablespaces, incrementally backed up, and recovered to the last committed transaction.

Because media data may have different characteristics than related relational data (e.g., multimedia content tends to be very large and not often updated), it can be treated differently using the same infrastructure. For example, older content can be placed on inexpensive disks with slower retrieval properties, storage areas can be excluded from nightly backups, and so on.

Zero data-loss configurations are also possible. Unlike configurations where attribute information is stored in the database with pointers to media data in files, only a single recovery procedure is required in the event of failure.

Search, Query, and Transactional Capabilities

*inter*Media extracts embedded metadata (information about the content) from the media data and makes it available for indexing and querying purposes. Using the specialized media object types enables the database to have knowledge of the data types, their behavior, and permitted operators (over and above BLOBs). In numerous domains, there is a rapidly increasing trend toward embedding much more searchable metadata within commonly used formats. For example, in medical imaging, patient data, modality (equipment) settings, physician data, and diagnostic information are being included as metadata in the DICOM format.

Unlike file system–based media products, storing media data in the database enables transaction-based, programmatic access through SQL and Java to this data, integrated with other database attributes, in a secure environment.

Simplicity and Reduced Development Cost

Oracle *inter*Media provides SQL language extensions, PL/SQL and Java APIs, and JSP Tag Libraries, which simplify the development of multimedia applications. The applications have much less code than applications that do not use these language extensions, resulting in substantial productivity. In addition, *inter*Media adds algorithms that perform common or valuable operations through built-in operators (see next item).

Code Reduction: Built-in Operators

Much of customers' motivation to use Oracle's support for media data comes from the power of the built-in functions and operators. By including operators that perform format conversion or thumbnail generation of images, the database reduces the need for application logic.

17.2.4 *inter*Media Powered by the Oracle Database Extensibility Framework

The foundation for *inter*Media is the extensibility framework of Oracle database, a set of unique services that enable application developers to model complex logic and extend the core database services (e.g., optimization, indexing, type system, SQL language) to meet the specific needs of an application. The Oracle database holds rich content in tables along with traditional data. Media data can be held in separate audio, image, or video columns or together in one column (ORDDoc). Oracle used these unique services to provide a consistent architecture for the rich data types supported by *inter*Media.

17.2.5 *inter*Media Powered by Java in the Database

Using Java in the database, Oracle *inter*Media built a server-side media parser and an in-database image processor. These features were implemented using more than 1,000 Java classes in the database, most of which are natively compiled for faster execution performance. As illustrated by Figure 17.4, the main Java enablers are the media parser and the Image Processor (JAI).

The Java Media Parser

The database-resident, Java-based media parser supports image, audio, and video data formats and application metadata extraction; it can be extended to support additional formats.

The Java Image Processor (based on JAI)

Using the embedded OracleJVM allowed *inter*Media to take advantage of the Sun Microsystem Java Advanced Imaging (JAI) package. The JAI API furnishes a set of object-oriented interfaces that enable developers to easily

Figure 17.4
interMedia Java
Components

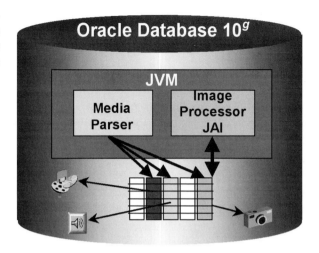

perform complex digital imaging operations. The image processor provides operations such as thumbnail generation and image format conversion.

Image Metadata Extraction

Embedded image metadata can be extracted and returned as a collection of schema valid XML documents that can be stored in Oracle database, indexed, searched, and made available to applications using XML DB and standard mechanisms of Oracle database.

Image Metadata Writing

Metadata, which has been formatted into XML format, can be stored into popular binary image formats, allowing metadata and image data to be encapsulated and shared and exchanged reliably as a unit.

Audio and Video Metadata Extraction

Embedded audio and video metadata is stored as XML in a CLOB column of the *inter*Media data types and is available for indexing and searching using standard mechanisms of Oracle database.

Image Processing and Image Format Conversion

Oracle *inter*Media provides a set of image processing operators for server-side image processing. Taken together, the scale and crop operators provide efficient and flexible thumbnail generation capability. Other image processing operations include arbitrary image rotate, flip, mirror, gamma correction, contrast enhancement, quantization methods, page selection, and alpha channel. Most applications only use a subset of the large set of different image formats. Oracle *inter*Media provides format-to-format conversion (transcoding) on demand.

Oracle interMedia Java Classes

*inter*Media Java Classes enable Java applications on any tier (client, application server, or database) to manipulate and modify audio, image, and video data, or heterogeneous media data stored in a database. Oracle *inter*Media Java Classes make it possible for Java database connectivity (JDBC) result sets to include both traditional relational data and *inter*Media media objects. This support enables applications to easily select and operate on a result set that contains sets of *inter*Media columns plus other relational data. These classes also enable access to object attributes and invocation of object methods.

Client-side JAI Applications

*inter*Media allows applications to take advantage of all the features of Java Advanced Imaging by allowing client-side JAI applications to access images stored in the database. The *inter*Media Java Classes provide APIs for three types of stream objects, which let you read data from BLOBs and BFILEs and write to BLOBs from your JAI applications. interMedia allows applications to take advantage of all the features of JAI by allowing client-side JAI applications to access images stored in the database. The *interMedia* Java Classes provide APIs for three types of stream objects, which let you read data from BLOBs and BFILEs and write to BLOBs from your JAI applications.

These methods include the following:

- *BfileInputStream*: A `SeekableStream` that reads data from an Oracle BFILE associated with the stream

- *BlobInputStream*: A `SeekableStream` that reads data from an Oracle BLOB associated with the stream

- *BlobOutputStream*: An `OutputStream` that writes buffered data to an Oracle BLOB associated with the stream

These stream objects are not meant to replace the input and output stream objects provided by Sun Microsystems; these objects are included to provide an interface to image data stored in BLOBs and BFILEs in `OrdImage` objects that can be used by JAI without loss in performance.

17.2.6 Developing Feature-Rich Multimedia Applications Using *inter*Media

We have seen the core *inter*Media framework, so how do you develop *inter*Media applications using the provided APIs? Figure 17.5 captures the big picture. This section describes the steps necessary to build PL/SQL and Java applications that exploit *inter*Media.

Figure 17.5
interMedia: The Big Picture

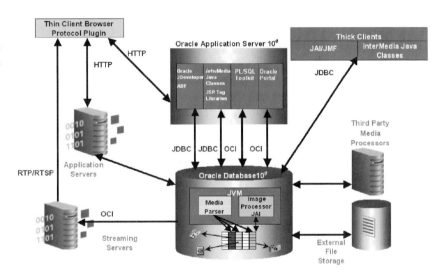

A PL/SQL Example

The following is a set of simple PL/SQL examples that upload, store, manipulate, and export image data inside a database using *inter*Media. We assume that only Oracle Database Release 10*g* with Oracle *inter*Media is installed (the default configuration provided by Oracle Universal Installer). Although this example uses the `ORDImage` object type, the `ORDAudio`, `ORDDoc`, and `ORDVideo` object types are similar, with the exception of processing, which is supported for `ORDImage` only.

Note: Access to an administrative account is required in order to grant necessary file system privileges. In the following examples, you should change the command `connect / as sysdba` to the appropriate `connect username/password as sysdba` for your site. The following examples also connect to the database using `connect scott/tiger`, which you should change to an actual username and password on your system. You should also modify the definition of IMAGEDIR to point to the directory where you have downloaded the sample image files goats.gif and flowers.jpg. The sample image files and these examples can be found here: www.oracle.com/technology/sample_code/products/intermedia/index.html.

Creating a Table with an ORDImage Column

First, we create a simple table with two columns: a numeric identifier (id) and an ORDSYS.ORDImage object (image). Note that all *inter*Media objects and procedures are defined in the ORDSYS schema.

```
connect scott/tiger
create table image_table (id number primary key, image
ordsys.ordimage);
```

Importing Images

This section shows how to bring images from the file system into the newly created table named image_table.

1. Create a *directory* object within the database that points to the file system directory that contains the sample image files. This is the directory where you saved the image files mentioned previously.

    ```
    connect / as sysdba
    create or replace directory imagedir as '/home/alamb/
    quickstart/';
    -- For windows: create or replace directory imagedir as
    'c:\quickstart';
    grant read on directory imagedir to scott;
    ```

2. Create a PL/SQL procedure image_import() that inserts a new row into image_table and then imports the image data in file name into the newly created ORDImage object.

    ```
    create or replace procedure image_import(dest_id
    number,
        filename varchar2) is img ordsys.ordimage;
      ctx raw(64) := null;
    begin
    ```

```
          delete from image_table where id = dest_id;
          insert into image_table (id, image)
            values (dest_id, ordsys.ordimage.init())
            returning image into img;

          img.importFrom(ctx, 'file', 'IMAGEDIR', filename);
          update image_table set image=img where id=dest_id;
       end;
       /
```

3.   Call the newly created procedure to import two sample image files.

```
      call image_import(1,'flowers.jpg');
      call image_import(2,'goats.gif');
```

Note: The directory object is named IMAGEDIR (in uppercase letters) even if it was created with upper or lowercase letters. Thus, the command img.importFrom(ctx, 'file', 'imagedir', filename); **will not work** and the following error is returned:

```
  ORA-22285: non-existent directory or file for FILEOPEN
  operation error.
```

Note: If the image you are importing is not one of *inter*Media's supported formats (e.g., JPEG2000), the following error is returned:

```
  ORA-29400: data cartridge error
  IMG-00705: unsupported or corrupted input format
```

Selecting and Viewing Image Properties

Once image_table has been populated, you can access image attributes using SQL queries. In the following example, we demonstrate how to select some information from the imported images:

1.   Height and width

2.   File format and compression format

3.   Content format (e.g., RGB, grayscale) and content length (number of bytes of image data)

Note: The ORDImage import() and importFrom() methods automatically invoke the ORDImage setProperties() method to extract image properties from the imported image. For the ORDAudio, ORDDoc, and ORDVideo data types, the setProperties() method is not implicitly called by import() and importFrom(). It must be explicitly called by your application to extract properties from the media after import.

```
connect scott/tiger
select id,
       t.image.getheight(),
       t.image.getwidth()
from image_table t;

select id,
       t.image.getfileformat(),
       t.image.getcompressionformat()
from image_table t;

select id,
       t.image.getcontentformat(),
       t.image.getcontentlength()
from image_table t;
```

The resulting output looks like the following:

```
id      height   width
------- -------- --------
  1      600       800
  2      375       500


id fileformat                     compression
------- --------------------------- -----------------------
  1 JFIF                            JPEG
  2 GIFF                            GIFLZW
```

```
     id contentformat                               length
---------- ------------------------------------   ----------
         1 24BITRGB                                    66580
         2 8BITLUTRGBT                                189337
```

Creating Thumbnails and Changing Formats

We next illustrate some image processing operations that can be invoked within the database. To generate a new ORDImage object from an existing one, the programmer describes the desired properties of the new image.

For example, the following description generates a JPEG thumbnail image of size 75 × 100 pixels: 'fileformat=jfif fixedscale=75 100'.

Note: Process operations are only available for the ORDImage object type.

The following example defines image_processCopy(), which adds a new row to image_table with identifier dest_id and generates an ORDImage in the new row by processCopying of the ORDImage in the source row.

```
connect scott/tiger
create or replace procedure image_processCopy(source_id number,
dest_id number, verb varchar2) is
     imgSrc      ordsys.ordimage;
     imgDst      ordsys.ordimage;
begin
  delete from image_table where id = dest_id;
  insert into image_table (id, image)
    values (dest_id, ordsys.ordimage.init());
  select image into imgSrc from image_table where id = source_id;
  select image into imgDst from image_table where id = dest_id for
  update;
  imgSrc.processCopy(verb, imgDst);
  update image_table set image = imgDst where id = dest_id;
end;
/


-- Scale flowers.jpg to 10% into row with id=3
call image_processcopy(1,3,'scale=.1');


-- convert goats.gif to grayscale jpeg thumbnail into row with id=4
call image_processcopy(2,4,'fileformat=jfif contentformat=8bitgray
    maxscale=100 100');
```

```
-- look at our handiwork
column t.image.getfileformat() format A20;
select id, t.image.getWidth(), t.image.getHeight(),
        t.image.getFileFormat() from image_table t;
```

The preceding example generates the following output:

```
ID     T.IMAGE.GETWIDTH()   T.IMAGE.GETHEIGHT() T.IMAGE.GETFILEFORMA
---------- ------------------- -------------------- --------------------
        1                 800                  600 JFIF
        2                 500                  375 GIFF
        3                  80                   60 JFIF
        4                 100                   75 JFIF
```

Exporting Images with ORDImage.export()

Exporting image data from the database with *inter*Media's export method requires that the database write to the file system. Writing to the file system requires granting Java permissions to your user (scott in the examples) *and* to the ORDSYS schema, as shown in the following example:

```
connect / as sysdba
create or replace directory imagedir as '/home/quickstart';
-- For windows:
--create or replace directory imagedir as 'c:\quickstart';
grant read on directory imagedir to scott;

call dbms_java.grant_permission('SCOTT','java.io.FilePermission',\
                        '/home/alamb/quickstart/*','WRITE');
call dbms_java.grant_permission('ORDSYS','java.io.FilePermission',\
                        '/home/alamb/quickstart/*','WRITE');
-For windows:
--call dbms_java.grant_permission('SCOTT','java.io.FilePermission',
--      'c:\quickstart\*','WRITE');
--call dbms_java.grant_permission('ORDSYS','java.io.FilePermission',
--      'c:\quickstart\*','WRITE');

connect scott/tiger
-- Writes the image data from ORDImage with id=<source_id>
```

```
-- in image_table
-- to the file named <filename> in the IMAGEDIR directory
create or replace procedure image_export (source_id number,\
 filename varchar2) as imgSrc ordsys.ordimage;
  ctx raw(64) := null;
begin
  select image into imgSrc from image_table where id = source_id;
  imgSrc.export(ctx, 'FILE', 'IMAGEDIR', filename);
end;
/


call image_export(3, 'flowers_thumbnail.jpg');
call image_export(4, 'goats_grayscale.jpg');
```

A Java Example

The following is a set of simple Java client examples that establish a connection, upload, set properties, get and display properties, manipulate, and download image data inside a database using *inter*Media. We assume that only Oracle Database Release 10*g* with Oracle *inter*Media is installed (the default configuration provided by Oracle Universal Installer). Although this example uses the ORDImage Java Class, the ORDAudio, ORDDoc, and Ord-Video Java Classes are similar, with the exception of processing, which is supported for ORDImage only.

Note: This example assumes the user account has access to the Sample Schema.

Establishing a Connection

First, we establish a connection to the database. Note when using inter*Media*, **auto-commit** must be set to **false** if updating LOBs, since they require selecting for update and then changing before a commit. Note that with a connection, the user can select either auto-commit after every transaction or manual commit.

```
    public OracleConnection connect(String user, String
  password)
      throws Exception
  {
    String connectString;
    DriverManager.registerDriver(new
  oracle.jdbc.OracleDriver());
```

```
      connectString = "jdbc:oracle:oci:@";

      OracleConnection conn = (OracleConnection)
         DriverManager.getConnection(connectString, user,
   password);

      conn.setAutoCommit(false);
      return conn;
   }
```

Uploading from a File

This section shows how to upload a media file from a local disk file into a media row in the database table. Oracle callable statements are used to make it easy to bind parameters to the SQL involved and to allow return of a client-side object. A new row is inserted into the PM.Online_Media table with an empty ORDImage object, and the newly inserted ORDImage object is returned on insert. Next, image data is loaded from a local disk file into the ORDImage object, and the online_media table is updated.

```
public void upload(OracleConnection conn, String fileName,
      int productId) throws Exception
{
  OracleCallableStatement cstmt = null;

  String queryInit = new String(
      "begin insert into pm.online_media " +
      "  (product_id, product_photo, product_thumbnail) " +
      "  values(?, ORDSYS.ORDImage.init(), ORDSYS.ORDImage.init())"
    + "  returning product_photo into ?; end; ");

  cstmt = (OracleCallableStatement) conn.prepareCall(queryInit);
  cstmt.setInt(1, productId);
  cstmt.registerOutParameter(2, OrdImage._SQL_TYPECODE,
                                   OrdImage._SQL_NAME);
  cstmt.execute();

  OrdImage img = (OrdImage)cstmt.getORAData(2,
                            OrdImage.getORADataFactory());
  cstmt.close();

  img.loadDataFromFile(fileName);
```

```
                String queryUpload = new String(
                  "update pm.online_media set product_photo = ? \
                              where product_id = ?");
                OraclePreparedStatement pstmt =
                    (OraclePreparedStatement)conn.prepareStatement(queryUpload);
                pstmt.setORAData(1, img);
                pstmt.setInt(2, productId);

                pstmt.execute();
                pstmt.close();

                conn.commit();
          }
```

Setting Properties

The *inter*Media setProperties method causes *inter*Media to examine the media object, determine its type (e.g., JPEG), and parse out both format and application metadata. In the following example, an image is queried for update, a proxy image is retrieved to the client, the setProperties() method is executed on the server, metadata attributes are parsed out of the media and then populated into the image object, and finally the image object is updated in the database.

```
public void setPhotoProperties(OracleConnection conn, int productId)
    throws Exception
  {
    String querySelect = new String(
        "select product_photo from pm.online_media where product_id = ? for
update");
    OraclePreparedStatement pstmt =
        (OraclePreparedStatement)conn.prepareStatement(querySelect);
    pstmt.setInt(1, productId);

    OracleResultSet rs = (OracleResultSet)pstmt.executeQuery();
    OrdImage img = null;
    if (rs.next() == true)
    {
      img = (OrdImage)rs.getORAData(1, OrdImage.getORADataFactory());
    }
    else
      throw new Exception("No row found for the product " + productId);

    rs.close();
```

```
    pstmt.close();

    img.setProperties();

    String queryUpdate = new String(
        "update pm.online_media set product_photo = ? \
                where product_id = ?");
    pstmt = (OraclePreparedStatement)conn.prepareStatement(queryUpdate);
    pstmt.setORAData(1, img);
    pstmt.setInt(2, productId);

    pstmt.execute();
    pstmt.close();

    conn.commit();
}
```

Getting and Displaying Properties

*inter*Media provides a set of getter methods for accessing the format meta-data from a client-side proxy object, which has had the `setProperties()` method performed on it. In the following example, an image is queried from a database table and then bound to a local image variable. Various image attributes are then accessed using getter methods and output to the command line.

```
    public void getPhotoProperties(OracleConnection conn, int
productId)
        throws Exception
    {
      String querySelect = new String(
          "select product_photo from pm.online_media \
where product_id = ? for update");
      OraclePreparedStatement pstmt =
          (OraclePreparedStatement)conn.prepareStatement(querySelect);
      pstmt.setInt(1, productId);

      OracleResultSet rs = (OracleResultSet)pstmt.executeQuery();
      OrdImage img = null;
      if (rs.next() == true)
      {
        img = (OrdImage)rs.getORAData(1, OrdImage.getORADataFactory());
      }
      else
```

```
      throw new Exception("No row found for the product "\
        + productId);

    rs.close();
    pstmt.close();

    System.out.println("MIME Type: " + img.getMimeType());
    System.out.println("Height: " + img.getHeight());
    System.out.println("Width: " + img.getWidth());
    System.out.println("Content Length: " + img.getContentLength());
  }
```

Processing an Image

In the following example, we illustrate some image processing operations that can be invoked within the database. This example copies an image and scales the copy, making a thumbnail and changing its format to GIFF.

Note: Process operations are only available for the ORDImage object type.

```
public void generateThumbnail(OracleConnection conn, int productId)
  throws Exception
{
  String queryGetThumb = new String(
      "select product_photo, product_thumbnail from pm.online_media
" +
      " where product_id = ? for update");
  OraclePreparedStatement pstmt =

(OraclePreparedStatement)conn.prepareStatement(queryGetThumb);
  pstmt.setInt(1, productId);

  OracleResultSet rs = (OracleResultSet)pstmt.executeQuery();
  OrdImage img = null;
  OrdImage imgThumb = null;
  if (rs.next() == true)
  {
    img = (OrdImage)rs.getORAData(1, OrdImage.getORADataFactory());
    imgThumb = (OrdImage)rs.getORAData(2,
OrdImage.getORADataFactory());
  }
  else
```

```
        throw new Exception("No row found for the product " +
productId);

    rs.close();
    pstmt.close();

    img.processCopy("maxScale=64 64, fileFormat=GIFF", imgThumb);

    String queryUpdate = new String(
        "update pm.online_media set product_thumbnail = ? \
                where product_id = ?");
    pstmt =
(OraclePreparedStatement)conn.prepareStatement(queryUpdate);
    pstmt.setORAData(1, imgThumb);
    pstmt.setInt(2, productId);

    pstmt.execute();
    pstmt.close();

    conn.commit();
  }
```

Downloading to a File

In the following example, we query an image from the online_media table, bind the image to a client-side image proxy object, download the image from the database, and then write the image to a local disk file.

```
  public void downloadThumbnail(OracleConnection conn, int productId,
String fileName)
    throws Exception
  {
    String queryGetThumb = new String(
        "select product_thumbnail from pm.online_media where
product_id = ?");
    OraclePreparedStatement pstmt =

(OraclePreparedStatement)conn.prepareStatement(queryGetThumb);
    pstmt.setInt(1, productId);
    OracleResultSet rs = (OracleResultSet)pstmt.executeQuery();
    OrdImage imgThumb = null;
    if (rs.next() == true)
    {
```

```
        imgThumb = (OrdImage)rs.getORAData(1,
OrdImage.getORADataFactory());
    }
    else
      throw new Exception("No row found for the product " +
productId);

    rs.close();
    pstmt.close();

    boolean isSuc = OrdMediaUtil.getDataInFile(fileName,\
                  imgThumb.getContent());
    if (isSuc)
      System.out.println("Download thumbnail for product \
        " + productId +
      " is successful");
    else
      System.out.println("Download thumbnail for product "
        + productId + " is unsuccessful");
  }
```

17.3 British Columbia: Online Corporate Registration

This case study has been presented and demonstrated at Oracle World; it is reproduced here with the authorization and courtesy of my longtime friend Thor Heinrichs-Wolpert, System Architect at Lunartek, and the mastermind behind this architecture. The first time I met Thor, he and his associate Jeff wanted to implement Jini/JavaSpace services in the database, using the OracleJVM. I thought he was crazy, but when you think about it, the JavaSpace object state information is currently captured in a file system, so, when it comes to capturing millions of performance metrics in large ISP/ASP environments, the Oracle Database, RAC, and OracleJVM are definitely more robust, reliable, and scalable than file systems. But I suspect the Jini/Javaspace thing is at rest—at least for now—as Thor has been recently working on the award-winning[1] Corporate Online project for the British Columbia Corporate and Personal Registries.

---

1.   International Association of Commercial Administrators in the category of "government to government."

17.3.1   Corporate Online: Background

The legal records of corporations are usually filed on paper. Lunartek and the British Columbia Corporate Registry have developed and deployed in production a new application that stores and maintains the legal records of corporations electronically in an Oracle Database 10*g*, using Java in the database, PL/SQL, database Web services, XMLDB, and Oracle JMS over Streams/AQ. Prior to Corporate Online, companies had to wait several weeks or more to get their business number. With this application, the Corporate Registry issues the business number and sends it to the company within a few days.

17.3.2   How It Works

The Corporate Registry database communicates incorporations or changes in a company to its partners and legacy systems via a set of Streams/AQ Queues, Java stored procedures, and Web service call-out, using XML documents stored in Oracle's XMLDB. Simple database triggers place small messages into the queues that only propagate upon commits. Callbacks within the database receive the messages and generate the XML documents, which are then passed to Java Stored Procedures for delivery by regular Web service mechanisms. The latest release of Corporate Online also uses XMLDB and stored procedures to generate XML summaries and client receipts, which are transformed into PDFs in the middle tier.

In all of these instances, the Oracle database does the real heavy lifting of ensuring that a legal transaction has completed, that any future dated filings have come to pass, and that the appropriate XML documents are then delivered.

17.3.3   Architecture: Requirements and Design

Figure 17.6 depicts the key database components that participate in the implementation of the application.

Requirement 1: How to Submit Only Committed Changes

The mainline business system *must* be able to complete its business transaction without delay. Partners *must* be notified of any business change they are registered for, once the mainline business transaction has fully completed. But how to submit changes to the hub only if these were committed?

Figure 17.6
Corporate Online,
Architecture

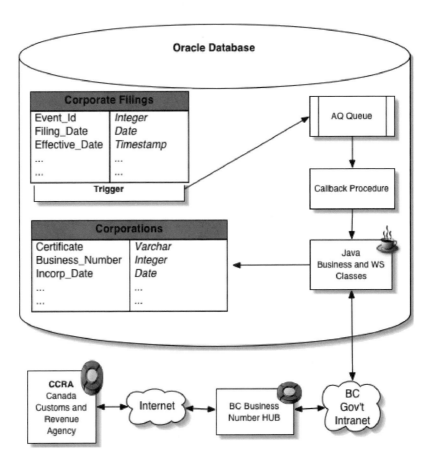

Ideally, the change or addition is monitored by a trigger on a table in the database, so that any application effecting a change has that change propagated. The problem with triggers is that they "fire" during a transaction and either execute a procedure as part of the transaction or out-of-band, but they do not fire *after* a commit has completed. Using Streams AQ, the messages are posted in queues that only propagate upon commits. To accomplish this task, we must use queues to propagate the event after completing a transaction in one system and then notifying the next.

First, create a type that will hold our message:

```
CREATE or REPLACE TYPE event_message_t AS OBJECT (
      event_id       NUMBER
     ,effective_dt DATE
);
/
```

We'll also create a log table to easily watch the status of our message:

```
Create table bn_message_log
       (event_id          NUMBER
       ,msg               event_message_t
       ,msg_q_handle      RAW(16)
       ,status            CHAR(1)
       ,transaction_id    VARCHAR2(4000)
       ,error_msg         VARCHAR2(4000)
     );
```

This will hold our event and the date on which it should be processed. Next, we create the queue, the procedure to add a message to the queue, and the trigger to "fire" off the event:

```
prompt creating CREATE_QUEUE_TABLE
begin
DBMS_AQADM.CREATE_QUEUE_TABLE
  ( queue_table         => 'event_qt'
   ,queue_payload_type => 'event_message_t'
   ,multiple_consumers => TRUE );
end;
/


prompt creating CREATE_QUEUE
begin
DBMS_AQADM.CREATE_QUEUE
     ( queue_name   => 'eventqueue'
   ,queue_table => 'event_qt' );
end;
/

prompt creating START_QUEUE
begin
DBMS_AQADM.START_QUEUE
     ( queue_name => 'eventqueue' );
end;
/

prompt creating enqueue_event_msg
```

```
create or replace procedure enqueue_event_msg( p_msg in
event_message_t
                    ,effective_dt in DATE )
  as
enqueue_options      dbms_aq.enqueue_options_t;
message_properties dbms_aq.message_properties_t;
message_handle       RAW(16);
message              event_message_t;
delay                integer;
  begin

-- we can delay the message so that the queue
   -- will deliver this message sometime in the future
   delay := (24*60*60)*(effective_dt - sysdate);

— no delay for dates in the past
   if ( delay > 1 ) then
   message_properties.delay := delay;
   end if;

-- only send our message if the transaction commits!!!
   enqueue_options.visibility := dbms_aq.ON_COMMIT;

dbms_aq.enqueue( queue_name            => 'eventqueue'
       ,enqueue_options     => enqueue_options
       ,message_properties => message_properties
       ,payload             => p_msg
       ,msgid               => message_handle );

insert into message_log
            ( event_id
             ,msg
             ,msg_q_handle
             ,status
             ,transaction_id
             ,error_msg)
     values ( p_msg.event_id
         ,p_msg
       ,message_handle
       ,'P'
       ,null
       ,null );
```

```
end;
/
```

Let's create our EVENT table, which we'll use to propagate a message from:

```
Create table EVENT ( event_id          NUMBER
                                        CONSTRAINT event_pk PRIMARY
KEY
                    ,event_type        VARCHAR2(25)
                    ,effective_dt      DATE
                    ,note              VARCHAR2(4000)
);
```

```
create or replace trigger event_propagate_trg after insert on
event
  for each row
  declare
    flag CHAR(1) := 'Y';
  begin
-- are we propagating?
-- This would be a bigger function in a real app
    if ( flag = 'Y' ) then
      enqueue_event_msg( event_message_t( :new.EVENT_ID
                                          ,:new.EFFECTIVE_DT
              )
              ,:new.EFFECTIVE_DT );
    end if;
  end;
/
```

We also use the ability of AQ to tag an effective time on a message, to allow filing to have future effective dates. We can make the determination if a filing is immediately active or if it is to take effect in the future.

Requirement 2: Processing the Received Message

This is pretty good so far, but what happens to the message in the queue? Callbacks within the database receive the Streams/AQ messages and generate the XML documents, which are then passed to Java stored procedures (as database trigger), which initiate the delivery using Web service mechanisms. In this sample, we'll create a callback that will execute once a message is ready to be processed from the queue.

```
prompt creating queueCallBack
create or replace procedure queueCallBack ( context  raw
    ,reginfo  sys.aq$_reg_info
    ,descr    sys.aq$_descriptor
    ,payload  raw
  ,payloadl number)
  as
  dequeue_options     dbms_aq.dequeue_options_t;
  message_properties dbms_aq.message_properties_t;
  message_handle      RAW(16);

    message              event_message_t;

  xml_view           VARCHAR2(30);   -- we'll use this later
  err_msg            VARCHAR2(4000) := null;
  withdrawn          NUMBER := null;
    my_code              NUMBER;
    my_errm              VARCHAR2(4000);

  begin

    dbms_output.put_line( 'about to process queue event' );

    dequeue_options.msgid := descr.msg_id;
      dequeue_options.consumer_name := descr.consumer_name;
      DBMS_AQ.DEQUEUE( queue_name         => descr.queue_name
                   ,dequeue_options    => dequeue_options
                  ,message_properties => message_properties
                   ,payload            => message
                   ,msgid              => message_handle);



      BEGIN
        update message_log
      set status  = 'R'
        where event_id = message.event_id;
```

```
    EXCEPTION
        when OTHERS then
        my_errm := substr( SQLERRM, 1, 4000 );

          ROLLBACK;
    END;

    if (my_errm is not null) then

    update message_log
       set status   = 'E'
           ,error_msg = my_errm
    where event_id = message.event_id;
    end if;

    commit;

  end;
/
```

Requirement 3: Database Web Services

Database Web services were covered earlier. We're doing Web services directly from the database to move critical program information to/from our Oracle database from/to our leagcy IMS/CICS/DB2 mainframe. We are exchanging information between these older systems directly from the database via a set of Web services that are initiated by database triggers. We went with Web services directly from the database rather than from the application server, because many processes interact with the data and create items of interest for the mainframe systems. (See Figure 17.7.)

The SOAP wrappers can be generated by the Web services client stack, but because we are running in the database, we choose to use XMLDB to create the content of the SOAP message, using the following steps:

1.   Create message types:

```
    CREATE or REPLACE TYPE header_message_t AS OBJECT (
        event_id     NUMBER
        ,priority     NUMBER(1)
        ,effective_dt DATE
    );
    /
```

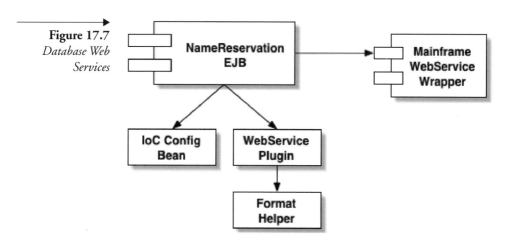

Figure 17.7
*Database Web
Services*

```
CREATE or REPLACE TYPE body_message_t AS OBJECT (
      message        VARCHAR2(400)
      ,note          VARCHAR2(50)
);
/


CREATE or REPLACE TYPE propagated_message_t AS OBJECT (
      header header_message_t
      ,body    body_message_t
);
/
```

2.   Create an object_view on propagated_message type:

```
CREATE OR REPLACE VIEW propagated_message_ov OF
propagated_message_t
      WITH OBJECT ID (header.event_id) AS
      SELECT
            header_message_t ( e.event_id
                                    ,1                    -- priority
                                    ,e.effective_dt --
effective_dt
                  )
            ,body_message_t ( 'the message body'     --
message
                              ,'note to the partner' — note
                  )
```

```
                        from event e
                /
```

3.   Generate a schema for the XML message:

```
        SELECT
        DBMS_XMLSCHEMA.generateschema('SCOTT','PROPAGATED_MESSA
        GE_T') FROM DUAL;
```

4.   Edit and load the view as appropriate.

Note: We can alter case of tags and even change them in the schema.

```
        BEGIN
         dbms_xmlschema.deleteSchema('http://www.lunartek.com/
        schema/v1/PartnerMessage.xsd', 4);
        END;
        /

        BEGIN
         dbms_xmlschema.registerSchema('http://
        www.lunartek.com/schema/v1/PartnerMessage.xsd',
                '<?xml version="1.0"?>
        <xsd:schema xmlns:xsd="http://www.w3.org/2001/
        XMLSchema" xmlns:xsi="http://www.w3.org/2001/XMLSchema-
        instance" xmlns:xdb="http://xmlns.oracle.com/xdb"
        xsi:schemaLocation="http://xmlns.oracle.com/xdb http://
        xmlns.oracle.com/xdb/XDBSchema.xsd">
         <xsd:element name="PartnerMessage"
        type="PROPAGATED_MESSAGE_TType"
        xdb:SQLType="PROPAGATED_MESSAGE_T"
        xdb:SQLSchema="SCOTT"/>
         <xsd:complexType name="PROPAGATED_MESSAGE_TType"
        xdb:SQLType="PROPAGATED_MESSAGE_T"
        xdb:SQLSchema="SCOTT" xdb:maintainDOM="false">
          <xsd:sequence>
           <xsd:element name="header"
        type="HEADER_MESSAGE_TType" xdb:SQLName="HEADER"
        xdb:SQLSchema="SCOTT" xdb:SQLType="HEADER_MESSAGE_T"/>
            <xsd:element name="body" type="BODY_MESSAGE_TType"
        xdb:SQLName="BODY" xdb:SQLSchema="SCOTT"
        xdb:SQLType="BODY_MESSAGE_T"/>
```

```
    </xsd:sequence>
  </xsd:complexType>
  <xsd:complexType name="HEADER_MESSAGE_TType"
xdb:SQLType="HEADER_MESSAGE_T" xdb:SQLSchema="SCOTT"
xdb:maintainDOM="false">
    <xsd:sequence>
    <xsd:element name="event" type="xsd:double"
xdb:SQLName="EVENT_ID" xdb:SQLType="NUMBER"/>
    <xsd:element name="priority" type="xsd:double"
xdb:SQLName="PRIORITY" xdb:SQLType="NUMBER"/>
    <xsd:element name="messageDate" type="xsd:date"
xdb:SQLName="EFFECTIVE_DT" xdb:SQLType="DATE"/>
    </xsd:sequence>
  </xsd:complexType>
  <xsd:complexType name="BODY_MESSAGE_TType"
xdb:SQLType="BODY_MESSAGE_T" xdb:SQLSchema="SBNDB"
xdb:maintainDOM="false">
    <xsd:sequence>
    <xsd:element name="message" xdb:SQLName="MESSAGE"
xdb:SQLType="VARCHAR2">
      <xsd:simpleType>
       <xsd:restriction base="xsd:string">
        <xsd:maxLength value="400"/>
       </xsd:restriction>
      </xsd:simpleType>
    </xsd:element>
    <xsd:element name="note" xdb:SQLName="NOTE"
xdb:SQLType="VARCHAR2">
      <xsd:simpleType>
       <xsd:restriction base="xsd:string">
        <xsd:maxLength value="50"/>
       </xsd:restriction>
      </xsd:simpleType>
    </xsd:element>
    </xsd:sequence>
  </xsd:complexType>
</xsd:schema>', TRUE, FALSE, FALSE);
END;
/
```

Test out the schema and see what we get!

```
SELECT SYS_XMLGEN (value(s),
 xmlformat.createformat( 'PartnerMessage',
'USE_GIVEN_SCHEMA', 'http://www.lunartek.com/schema/v1/
PartnerMessage.xsd')).getclobval()
 FROM propagated_message_ov s
 WHERE s.header.event_id = 2;
```

It should output something like this:

```
<PartnerMessage>
  <header>
    <event>2</event>
    <priority>1</priority>
    <messageDate>2005-09-27</messageDate>
  </header>
  <body>
    <message>the message body</message>
    <note>note to the partner</note>
  </body>
</PartnerMessage>
```

Notice the mixed case and altered tags ... very cool!

17.3.4 **Messaging across Tiers**

What if one of the partners was using some specific security toolkit—different from the standard JCE stack—that you couldn't use from within the database? The current implementation of JCE in OracleJVM does not yet allow any JCE provider other than the Sun-provided one (part of J2SE). The Streams/AQ system once again came to the rescue, because it can be used as a transport for JMS messages. As depicted by Figure 17.8, we can forward the message using JMS/AQ and have a J2EE message bean accept the message and process it using the specific partner requirements! You may also use messaging across tiers to partition the workload between the middle tier and the database.

First, set up the JMS Queue.

Note: This example uses the default JMS queue setup within OC4J as the J2EE container.

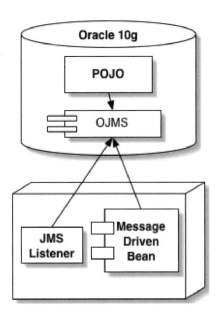

Figure 17.8
Messaging across
Tiers

1.   Build the JMS queue:

```
BEGIN
   DBMS_AQADM.CREATE_QUEUE_TABLE(
         Queue_table              => 'demoQTab',
         Queue_payload_type       => 'SYS.AQ$_JMS_MESSAGE',
         sort_list => 'PRIORITY,ENQ_TIME',
         multiple_consumers  => false,
         compatible               => '8.1.5');

   DBMS_AQADM.CREATE_QUEUE(
         Queue_name               => 'demoQueue',
         Queue_table              => 'demoQTab');

   DBMS_AQADM.START_QUEUE(
         queue_name               => 'demoQueue');
   END;
   /
```

2.   Load the Java source in the database (Listing 17.1):

Listing 17.1   *JMSSender.java*

==================================

```java
import oracle.jms.AQjmsQueueConnectionFactory;
import oracle.jms.AQjmsSession;

import oracle.jdbc.driver.OracleDriver;
import javax.jms.*;

public class JMSSender {

    public static void send( String msgBody )
    {

        OracleDriver oraDriver = null;
        java.sql.Connection dbConnection = null;

        // Variables for the sender
        QueueConnection senderQueueConn = null;
        QueueSession senderQueueSession = null;
        QueueSender sender = null;
        Queue senderQueue = null;
        TextMessage sendMsg = null;

        try
        {

            // get database connection
                oraDriver = new OracleDriver();
            dbConnection = oraDriver.defaultConnection();

            // setup sender
            senderQueueConn =
                AQjmsQueueConnectionFactory.createQueueConnection(
        dbConnection );
            senderQueueConn.start();
            senderQueueSession =
            senderQueueConn.createQueueSession( true,
        Session.CLIENT_ACKNOWLEDGE );
            senderQueue =
```

```
             ((AQjmsSession) senderQueueSession).getQueue( "scott",
"demoQueue" );
        sender = senderQueueSession.createSender( senderQueue );
        System.out.println( "sender created" );

        // create message
        sendMsg = senderQueueSession.createTextMessage( msgBody );
        sendMsg.setStringProperty ( "RECIPIENT", "MDB" );
        sendMsg.setJMSReplyTo( senderQueue );
        System.out.println( "message created" );

        // send message
        sender.send( sendMsg );
        senderQueueSession.commit();
        System.out.println( "message sent" );

        // cleanup
        senderQueueSession.close();
        senderQueueConn.close();
    } catch (java.sql.SQLException ex) {
            ex.printStackTrace();
    } catch (JMSException e) {
        e.printStackTrace();
    }
    finally
    {
            try{ dbConnection.close } catch (Exception x) ;
    }
  }
}
```

3.   Wrap it with a package.

Note: You don't have to wrap it, but it's nice to bundle all of the calls you need into a single package.

```
        create or replace package jmsPartner as

        procedure sendJMSMessage(msg VARCHAR2);
```

```
end jmsPartner;
/

create or replace package body jmsPartner as

  procedure sendJMSMessage(msg VARCHAR2)
  is language java
  name 'JMSSender.send (java.lang.String)';

end jmsPartner;
/
```

Now, in the QueueCallBack procedure we can change the code:

```
BEGIN
      update message_log
      set status  = 'R'
            where event_id = message.event_id;
EXCEPTION
```

to the following:

```
BEGIN
    SELECT jmsPartner.sendJMSMessage(
        SYS_XMLGEN (value(s), xmlformat.createformat(
'PartnerMessage'
        ,'USE_GIVEN_SCHEMA' ,'http://www.lunartek.com/schema/
v1/PartnerMessage.xsd')).getstringval()
    FROM propagated_message_ov s
    WHERE s.header.event_id = message.event_id;

  update message_log
    set status  = 'R'
  where event_id = message.event_id;
EXCEPTION
```

We're almost there. The last step consists of creating a message-driven Bean in OC4J that will listen on the JMS/AQ for the incoming message!

```
public void onMessage(Message msg)
```

```
    {
     System.out.println( "Entering the onMessage call" );
     try

     {
      String txnId = sendMessage( ((TextMessage)msg).getText() );
     } catch ( Exception e ) {
       e.printStackTrace();
       mdc.setRollbackOnly();
     }
    }
```

17.3.5   Future Work

Future developments may also improve the turnaround time and issue the business number at the end of the filing transaction. We will be adding in Web service interactions with partner systems via a WebMethods Broker, but our connection to the hub will again be initiated by the database, because it is the central point where things can converge and we can inescapably control the data management in one place.

17.3.6   Conclusion

Similar to the TECSIS use case, this real-life use case makes use of many components of the Oracle database, including SQL, PL/SQL, Java in the Database, XDB, Streams-AQ, and OJMS. Furthermore it straddles the Oracle database and Oracle application server (messaging across tiers), which is another example of cooperation between database applications and middle-tier applications.

17.4   Information Retrieval Using Oracle Text

This case study was demonstrated at the last Oracle World by my good friend Omar Alonso, who works in Oracle's Secure Enterprise Search group. Like many visitors, I was so impressed that I asked him to write this section for the book. Despite the tight schedule for submitting the manuscript, he busted his back, and here you are with a descriptrion of the design and implementation of a search engine for a controlled environment such as a text warehouse or corporate Intranet.

This section will briefly introduce the main technical features of Oracle Text, the rationale for using Java in the database, and the types of applications that you can build with the existing API. It then presents the built-in capabilities of the database for text searching, and finally you will learn how to build and experience Yapa, the nice demo, which prompted the writing of this case study.

17.4.1   What Is Oracle Text?

Oracle Text is an Oracle database component that lets you build general-purpose information retrieval applications.[2] Oracle Text provides specialized text indexes for textual content search or traditional full-text retrieval, such as:

- Intranet and extranet searches

- Web-based e-business catalogs

- Document archives and text warehouses

- CRM and other document-oriented applications

Oracle Text can filter and extract content from different document formats. It supports several document formats, including popular ones such as Microsoft Office file formats, Adobe PDF, HTML, and XML.

It offers a complete set of multilingual features, supporting search across documents in Western languages (e.g., English, French, Spanish, German), Japanese, Korean, and traditional and simplified Chinese. The technology also supports the combination of different lexical analyzers (lexers), as well as the ability to define your own lexer for particular languages.

As part of the Oracle database, Oracle Text transparently integrates with and benefits from a number of key enterprise features, such as data partitioning, RAC, query optimization, tools and development environments, administration and manageability, and integrated security. Oracle Text is included with both the Oracle 10*g* Database Standard and Enterprise Editions.

Let's take a quick look at how it works. First, we have to create a table and populate with some data—for example, a product table where we want to search product descriptions:

---

2.   The Oracle Text home page is http://www.oracle.com/technology/products/text/index.html.

```
create table products (
  id          numeric,
  name        varchar2(100),
  description varchar2(200));

insert into products values(1,'VT21','Monitor with high
resolution');
insert into products values(2,'VT100','Flat panel. Color
monitor');
commit;
```

Then create an index type called `context` that allows us to use the `contains` clause in SQL for text searching:

```
create index desc_idx on products(description)
indextype is ctxsys.context;
```

Finally, with SQL we retrieve the product's name where the description contains `monitor` and is `near` to the term `resolution`.

```
select name from products
where contains(description,'monitor near resolution') > 0
```

```
NAME
--------------------
VT21
```

17.4.2   Why Java in the Database?

The Oracle database furnishes an embedded Java run time, which can be used by database components such as XDB, *inter*Media, Spatial, Text, XQuery, and so on. Oracle Text leverages the XML DB framework, which includes a protocol server and a specialized Java Servlet runner, all running within the database. I need to clarify here that the J2EE stack has been discontinued from the database since Oracle 9*i* Release 2. This Servlet runner is by no means a reintroduction of J2EE in the database; it is not a full-fledged and general-purpose Servlet container; it's sole purpose is to support the XDB framework. The servlets are configured using the `/xdbconfig.xml` file in the XDB Repository. The protocol server supports FTP,

HTTP 1.1, and WebDAV. We describe the XDB repository and the configuration in the case study section later.

From development and deployment perspectives, there are some advantages of running Java in the database:

- Simplified all-in-one environment in which you only need a Java-enabled database, no external JDK, no external Web Listener.

- Easy to test and debug: no need to recycle a Web server or container.

- The database does the heavy lifting, including the processing of SQL, XML, PL/SQL, and Java operations. Moving data across tables and data-intensive computations are better handled directly within the database.[3]

17.4.3 Technical Features

In this section, we present a high-level technical overview of the main features. The YAPA demo complements this section with more details and source code.

Index Types

Oracle Text provides three types of indexes that cover all text search needs: standard, catalog, and classification.

- Standard index type: For traditional full-text retrieval over documents and Web pages. The `context` index type provides a rich set of text search capabilities for finding the content you need, without returning pages of spurious results. The first example showed this index type in action.

- Catalog index type: The first text index designed specifically for eBusiness catalogs. The `ctxcat` catalog index type provides flexible searching and sorting features. For example, a catalog index on a table that contains auction items:

```
create index auctionx on auction(item_desc)
indextype is ctxsys.ctxcat;
```

---

3.   In Part I, you have experienced that SQL-intensive JDBC applications run faster in the database.

Once the `ctxcat` index is created, you use the `catsearch` operator for queries:

```
select item_desc from auction
where catsearch(item_desc, 'oracle', null)>0;
```

- Classification index type: for building classification or routing applications. The `ctxrule` index type is created on a table of queries, where the queries define the classification or routing criteria. For example, a rule index for classifying incoming news:

```
create index newscats_idx on news(categories)
indextype is ctxsys.ctxrule;
```

Once the `ctxrule` index is created, you use the `matches` operator for queries:

```
select message from news
where matches(categories,'Soccer and football news')>0
```

Oracle Text also provides substring and prefix indexes. Substring indexing improves performance for left-truncated or double-truncated wildcard queries. Prefix indexing improves performance for right-truncated wildcard queries.

Query Operators

Oracle Text can intelligently process search queries using several strategies:

- *Keyword searching.* Searching for keywords in a document. User enters one or more keywords that best describe the query.
- *Context queries.* Searching for words in a given context. User searches for text that contains words near to each other.
- *Boolean operations.* Combining keywords with Boolean operations. User can express a query connecting Boolean operations to the keywords.
- *Linguistic features.* Using fuzzy and other natural language processing techniques. User searches for text that is about something.

- *Pattern matching*. Retrieval of text that contains a certain property. User searches for text that contains words that contain a string.

Document Services

A document service is any ad hoc operation on a particular document. Oracle Text provides the following document services: highlighting, markup, snippet, themes, and gist. These types of services can be very useful for browsing strategies and for document presentation. The PL/SQL CTX_DOC package exposes all document services.

Highlighting

The highlighting service takes a query string, fetches the document contents, and shows you which words in the document cause it to match the query.

Markup

Markup takes the highlighting service one step further and produces a text version of the document with the matching words marked up.

Snippet

This procedure returns text fragments containing keywords found in documents. This format enables you to see the keywords in their surrounding text, providing context for them.

Theme Extraction

A "theme" provides a snapshot that describes what the document is about. The procedure returns a list of themes for a document with their associated weight.

Gist

A generic gist is a summary consisting of the sentences or paragraphs that best represent the overall subject matter of the document. You can use the generic gist to skim the main content of the text or assess your interest in the text's subject matter.

Advanced Features

Classification

A document classification application is one that classifies an incoming stream of documents based on their content. These applications are also known as document routing or filtering applications. For example, an online news agency might need to classify its incoming stream of articles as they arrive into categories such as politics, economy, or sports.

Oracle Text enables you to build such applications with the `ctxrule` index type. This index type indexes the rules (queries) that define classifications or routing criteria. When documents arrive, the `matches` operator can be used to categorize each document. The `CTX_CLS` PL/SQL package enables you to perform classification and clustering.

Classification Training

We can summarize the following steps to set up a basic document classification application:

1.   Group related sample documents together.

2.   For each group, write rules that explain why the documents belong in the group.

3.   Using the rule set, classify incoming documents into appropriate groups.

The `ctxrule` index type automates step 3 of the process, but the user has to write the rules. The `CTX_CLS` package automates step 2 by generating `ctxrule` query rules for a set of documents. The user has to supply a training set consisting of categorized documents, and each document must belong to one or more categories. The package generates the queries that define the categories and then writes the results to a table.

Clustering

Contrary to classification, clustering is the unsupervised classification of patterns into groups. As part of `CTX_CLS`, the clustering procedure automatically clusters a set of documents according to their semantic meanings. The document in a cluster is believed to be more similar with each other inside the cluster than with outside documents.

Knowledge Base

Oracle Text's knowledge base contains more than 400,000 concepts from very broad domains classified into 2,000 major categories. These categories are organized hierarchically under six top terms: business and economics, science and technology, geography, government and military, social environment, and abstract ideas and concepts. Users can extend and customize this knowledge base by adding new terms or redefining existing ones.

XML Support

XML features include the operator `within`, nested section search, search within attribute values, mapping multiple tags to the same name, path searching using `inpath` and `haspath` operators. Also, you can use the Oracle XDB features for manipulating of XML content.

17.4.4 Benefits of an Integrated Search Capability

Oracle Database 10*g* provides an extensibility framework[4] that enables developers to extend the data types understood by the database kernel. Oracle Text uses this framework to fully integrate the text indexes with the standard Oracle query engine. This means the user has:

- A single repository for all data (text and structured). This is easy to maintain, back up, and so on.

- A single API for developing applications.

- Optimizer integration.

The advantages of integration:

- *Cost-effective solution.* Oracle Text is part of all editions of the Oracle Database 10*g* (Enterprise and Standard Editions). There are no separate products to buy or integrate.

- *Efficient.* The database will choose the fastest plan to execute queries that involve both text and structure content.

- *High integrity.* Because text is stored in the database, it inherits all of the integrity benefits (e.g., any update to the database can be reflected to the text search functionality), which means users can get an integrated, holistic view of all their data.

- *Low complexity.* Text is treated just like structured data, which makes it easy to develop and integrate search applications with existing systems.

- *Manageable.* Oracle Text can be managed by DBAs, using standard enterprise management tools.

---

4.   The interMedia case study, highlighted the importance of the extensibility framework.

17.4.5   Yapa

In this section, you will build and play with Yapa;[5] it demonstrates the main features of Oracle Text. Although it runs entirely in the database, it has two constituents: the back end and the user interface handler.

The back end consists of the following components: the search component, the browser, the clusterer, and the query logger. The search component consists of a text index for traditional information retrieval queries and a classification index for categorizing the documents. The text index type provides a rich set of text search capabilities for finding content, without returning pages of spurious results. The classification index type is the inverse of the usual text index. The index is created on a table of queries, where the queries define the classification or routing criteria.

The user interface is based on a two-view model, where the left side shows structure and the right side shows content. The left view presents the results in the following structures: list, categories, and clusters. The right view shows content and operations. The operations are documents with highlighted query terms, document themes, document summary, and document gist.

Architecture and Implementation

As we mentioned earlier, Yapa runs within an Oracle Database 10*g* with no extra components, such as external Web Listener or external Java VM. The architecture consists of SQL scripts (for the schema preparation) and a Java code (for the search application). The scripts perform the schema and index creation, along with the classification and clustering of the document collection. The Java code leverages a specialized and embedded XDB Servlet engine, which provides methods for searching, browsing, query logs manipulation, and document services. All that is available in the context of a two-view interface model. (See Figure 17.9)

Database schema and indexing

In this implementation, we decided to store the document in a regular database table using the LOB (Large Object) data type for the actual text. In case you don't want to store the documents in the database, you can store them in the file system or on the Web. The `context` index type creates the text index on that LOB column. There is a second table, which contains the categories for the collection. The `ctxrule` index type creates a classification

---

5.   Yapa is a South American Spanish word, which means "a little bit more for free."

Figure 17.9
*Main Architecture
of the Yapa Demo*

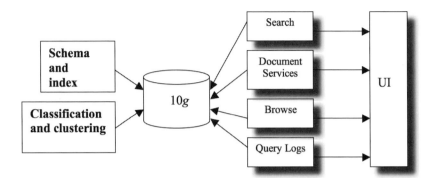

index on the categories column. This index type indexes the rules (queries) that define classifications or routing criteria. When documents arrive, the matches operator can be used to categorize each document. The following SQL script fragment shows the tables and indexes creation:

```
-- Enable theme indexing
exec ctx_ddl.create_preference('mylex','BASIC_LEXER');
exec ctx_ddl.set_attribute('mylex','MIXED_CASE','NO');
exec ctx_ddl.set_attribute('mylex','THEME_LANGUAGE','ENGLISH');
exec ctx_ddl.set_attribute('mylex','index_themes','YES');
exec ctx_ddl.set_attribute('mylex','index_text','YES');

-- Create HTML sections for searching within tags
exec ctx_ddl.create_section_group('htmlgroup','html_section_group');
exec ctx_ddl.add_zone_section('htmlgroup','title','TITLE');
exec ctx_ddl.add_zone_section('htmlgroup','heading','H2');
exec ctx_ddl.add_zone_section('htmlgroup','body','BODY');

-- Create index for documents
create index med_idx on med_table(text)
indextype is ctxsys.context
parameters('lexer mylex filter ctxsys.null_filter section group
htmlgroup');

-- Create index for categories
create index mesh_cat_idx on mesh_cats(query)
indextype is ctxsys.ctxrule;
```

Classifier Outline

In this particular example, we have created a simple batch classifier. This classifier is rudimentary and is intended to show how the basis works. For real production classifiers, you should look at the decision tree approach or Support Vector Machines (SVM). Both are supported in 10*g*.

```
for doc in (select tk, text from med_table)
   loop
     v_document := doc.text;
     v_doc := doc.tk;
     for c in (select queryid, category
               from mesh_cats
               where matches(query, v_document) > 0 )
       loop
          insert into med_doc_cat values (doc.tk, c.queryod);
       end loop;
     update med_table set category = v_categories where
tk=doc.tk;
   end loop;
```

Clustering

Once the index has been created, we just run a script that computes clustering on the entire collection. The CTX_CLS package has a number of parameters in case you want to tune the quality of the output.

```
exec
ctx_ddl.create_preference('ycluster','KMEAN_CLUSTERING');
exec ctx_ddl.set_attribute('ycluster','THEME_ON','YES');
exec ctx_ddl.set_attribute('ycluster','TOKEN_ON','YES');
exec ctx_ddl.set_attribute('ycluster','CLUSTER_NUM',12);
exec
ctx_cls.clustering('med_idx','tk','clu_restab','clu_clusters'
,'ycluster');
```

User Interface

The user interface is HTML-based, entirely generated and rendered from within the database. A Web page is divided into three parts: the search panel, the structure view, and the content view. The top frame consists of the search box for simple and advanced search. The left frame presents search results in three views: list, categories, and cluster. The traditional search results are presented in a list. For the categories view, the interface presents folders as categories. You can click on a category and present the documents. The cluster view presents a description of each cluster and its set of documents. The right frame presents the document content and its operations (e.g., the document with highlighted terms). The number of operations is implemented as tabs, allowing you to apply different services to the same document. Figure 17.10 shows the two-view interface.

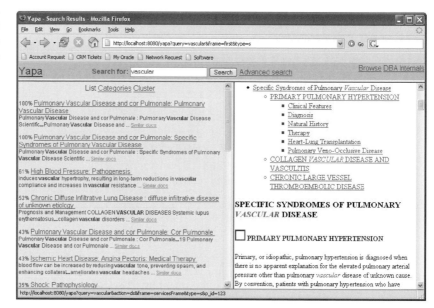

Figure 17.10
Two-View Search Interface

Search Panel

The panel presents two options for search: simple search and advanced search. The latter provides the ability to search within the structure of the document (e.g., within tags of HTML/XML documents). The following code snippet shows the main search block:

```
...
Connection conn = null;
try
    {
    String stateT =  "select /*+ FIRST_ROWS */ rowid, tk,
title, " + " category, score(1) scr," +
"ctx_doc.snippet('med_idx',tk,'"+query+"') snippet "     +
"from med_table " + "where contains(text,'" + query + "',1) >
0 " + "order by ctxsys.score(1) desc ";
```

```
      // text search is performed using the contains clause
      // score returns the relevance for a returned document in
      // a query
      // ctx_doc.snippet returns the keyword in context for a
      // query

      OracleDriver ora = new OracleDriver();
      conn = ora.defaultConnection();
      OracleCallableStatement state =
                  (OracleCallableStatement)
      conn.prepareCall(stateT);
      state.execute(stateT);
      ResultSet rs = state.executeQuery(stateT);

      int items = 0;
      while(rs.next() && items < 20) {
            items++;
            String tk = rs.getString(2);
            String title = rs.getString(3);
            String category = rs.getString(4);
            String score = rs.getString(5);
            out.println("<p class=OraCrumbs>");
            out.println(score+ "% ");
            out.println("<a class=OraLine href=\
"yapa?query="+query+"&action=ds&frame=servicesFrame&type=s&p_
id=" + tk +"\" target=\"servicesFrame\">");
            out.println(title);
            out.println("</a><br>");

            String kwic = rs.getString(6);
            out.println(kwic+ " ... ");
      }
      rs.close();
      conn.close();
      state.close();
   }
  catch(SQLException e) {
   out.println("SQLException: " + e.getMessage() + "<B>");

   }
```

Structure View

The list of views (list, categories, clusters) is presented as tabs. The default view for a search is the list view, which presents the results sorted by score. The categories view presents the results as a folder (category), where the user can expand the folder to see the list of documents. The cluster view presents a list of a cluster and its description (usually themes). The user can expand the cluster folder to see all the documents.

List

The traditional search results are presented as a list of documents sorted by score. For each document, the view displays the title and its metadata (e.g., URL, data, size). The metadata and the number of items per page can be set in the settings area. Figure 17.10 shows the result set for a search using the list view on the left and displays a highlighted version of the document on the right frame. The list view also presents the document snippet (also know as kwic) using the `ctx_doc.snippet` package, as presented in the previous code sample.

Categories

For the categories view, the interface presents search results arranged by folders (categories). The user can click on the category to show all the documents. Figure 17.11 shows an example using a collection of medical documents where the categories are based on the MeSH taxonomy.[6]

Cluster

The cluster package calculates the clusters plus other information and returns the data set in a couple of tables. The cluster view displays the description of the clusters with the option to display the documents that belong to that particular cluster. The cluster package is useful for implementing features such as "more similar documents." Figure 17.12 shows the search results by clusters.

Content View

At any point, and independently of a particular view that the user has selected, it is possible to operate on a document. The basic operation of a document is to click on it and display its content in HTML on the right frame. The number of operations is implemented as tabs, allowing the user

6.   http://www.nlm.nih.gov/mesh/meshhome.html.

Figure 17.11
*Categories View
Using MeSH*

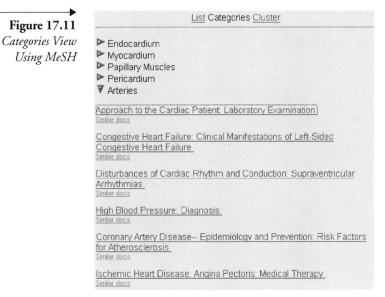

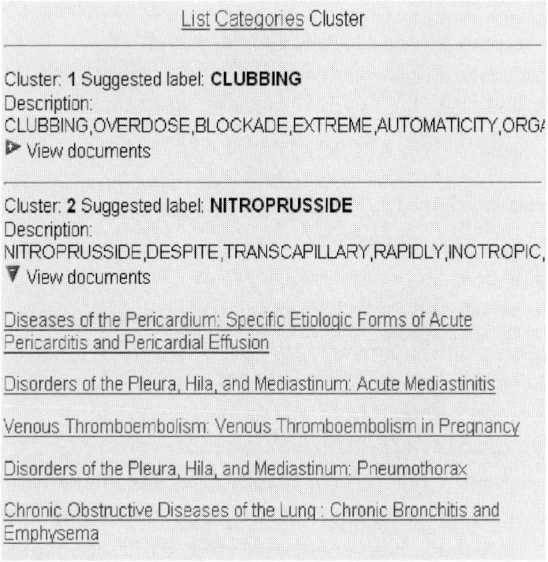

Figure 17.12
*Cluster View Text's
Clustering*

to apply different services to the same document in context. We will describe the implementation of the highlighting and theme services.

This operation displays the document with highlighted query terms in a particular format. The following Java snippet shows how the highlighting method is implemented. The service executes the `CTX_DOC.MARKUP` procedure that returns an in-memory LOB structure with the content. To display the document, we read by chunks from the data structure and print to the Web browser.

```
...
Connection conn = null;
String highlightQuery = "begin"
                    +" ctx_doc.markup(index_name=>'med_idx',"

                    +"   textkey=>?,"
                    +"   text_query=>?,"
                    +"   restab=>?,"
                    +"   starttag=> '<i><font color=red>',"
                    +"   endtag=> '</font></i>' "
                    +"   ); "
                    +"end; ";

try {
      OracleDriver ora = new OracleDriver();
      conn = ora.defaultConnection();
      conn.createStatement().execute("begin
ctx_doc.set_key_type('PRIMARY_KEY'); end;");
      OracleCallableStatement stmt =

(OracleCallableStatement)conn.prepareCall(highlightQuery);
      // get paramters

      stmt.setString(1,doc_id);
      stmt.setString(2,query);
      stmt.registerOutParameter(3, OracleTypes.CLOB);
      stmt.execute();
      oracle.sql.CLOB text_clob = null;
      text_clob = ((OracleCallableStatement)stmt).getCLOB(3);
      int chunk_size = text_clob.getChunkSize();
      Reader char_stream = text_clob.getCharacterStream();
      char[] char_array = new char[chunk_size];
      for (int n = char_stream.read(char_array); n >0;
               n = char_stream.read(char_array)) {
            out.print(char_array);
      }
} catch (SQLException e)
```

```
        {
            out.println("SQLException: " + e.getMessage() +
"<B>");
        }
    ...
```

Browse

Sometimes, searching for content is not enough, and users would like to browse or navigate the collection. In our example, you can browse by categories (based on MeSH) or by clusters.

We use an information visualization metaphor to present information in ways other than hit lists or folders. Visualization can show relationships across items in addition to satisfying query results. Figure 17.13 shows a stretch viewer visualization to browse the collection by categories. By issuing a double-click on the title of a document, you can view the content on the right frame.

Figure 17.13
Navigating Categories Using Visualization

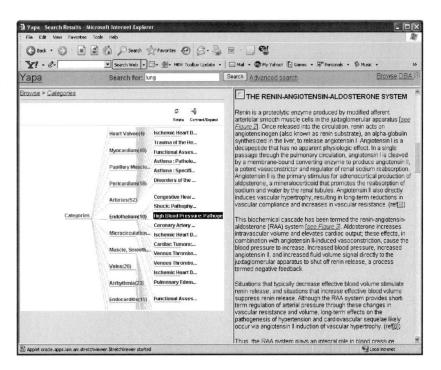

The visualization involves two steps. The first one is to generate the necessary HTML code on the fly that contains the following snippet. As we can see, apart from the usual code directory, we need to specify where the data comes from.

```
<object classid="clsid:8AD9C840-044E-11D1-B3E9-00805F499D93"
        width="100%" height="500" align="baseline"
        codebase="http://java.sun.com/products/plugin/1.3/
jinstall-13-win32.cab#Version=1,3,0,0">
    <param name="code"
value="oracle.apps.iam.am.stretchviewer.StretchViewer.class"/
>
    <param name="ImageDirectory" value="images/"/>
    <param name="codebase" value="http://localhost:8080/
classes_g/"/>
    <param name="DATA" value="http://localhost:8080/
yapacats?p_format=sv"/>
    <param name="DATALENGTH" value="66308"/>
    <param name="MODE" value="horizontal"/>
    <param name="BACKGROUND" value="white"/>
    <param name="STICKCOLOR" value="lightGray"/>
    <param name="AUTOEXPAND" value="true"/>
    <param name="CONTRACTABLE" value="true"/>
    <param name="TARGET" value="servicesFrame"/>
</object>
```

The generation of the categories involves a SQL query that returns all the necessary data.

```
select med_table.tk, title from med_table, med_doc_cat
       where med_doc_cat.category_id = v_category
       and med_table.tk=med_doc_cat.tk
```

Configuring, Compiling, and Testing the Demo

Here, we are going to configure the Servlet, compile it, and test it. First, we need to start the Web server and `ftp` server from the command line. Connected as sys, you have to run:

```
SQL> call dbms_xdb.setHttpPort(8080);

Call completed.

SQL> call dbms_xdb.setFtpPort(2100);
```

```
Call completed.
```

Now, via FTP or WebDAV, we need to edit the /xdbconfig.xml file by inserting the following XML element tree in the <servlet-list> element:

```
<servlet>
    <servlet-name>Yapa</servlet-name>
    <servlet-language>Java</servlet-language>
    <display-name>Yapa Servlet</display-name>
    <servlet-class>Yapa</servlet-class>
    <servlet-schema>med</servlet-schema>
</servlet>
```

We also have to add the following element tree in the <servlet-mappings> element:

```
<servlet-mapping>
      <servlet-pattern>/yapa</servlet-pattern>
      <servlet-name> com.oracle.demo.yapa.Yapa </servlet-name>
</servlet-mapping>
```

To install the Servlet, compile it, and load it into the Oracle database, you need to issue the following command:

```
>loadjava -grant public -u med/med -r Yapa.class
```

To launch the demo, open the search.html file or just edit a different one adding the following code that calls the servlet. As usual, replace the hostname and port number as appropriate:

```
<form action="http://localhost:8080/yapa" target="_top">
<center>Search for:
<input type="text"    name="query" size=20>
<input type="hidden" name="frame"  value="first">
<input type="hidden" name="type"   value="s">
<input type="submit" value="Search" >
</center>
</form>
```

The home page is shown in Figure 17.14.

Figure 17.14
Search Home Page

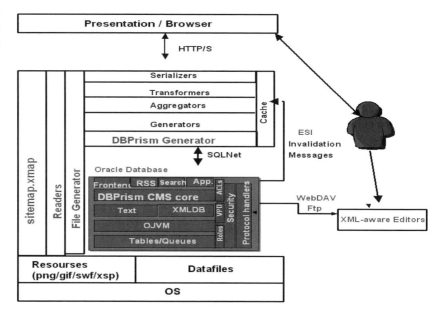

17.4.6   Conclusion

Oracle Text provides a complete API for building any type of information retrieval application. We also demonstrated that with Java in the database and XML in the database (XDB), the database becomes a content repository and also a full development and deployment platform. We presented Yapa, a demo system that combines search, classification, and clustering, as well as an integrated user interface based on a two-view model. We also demonstrated that it is possible to build and/or integrate visualization metaphors on top of the existing API. The complete source code is available from the book's Web site as well as from the Oracle Technology Network (OTN) Web site.

17.5   Database-Driven Content Management System (DBPrism CMS)

This innovative and open-source based case study has been provided by my new friend Marcelo Ochoa.

17.5.1   DBPRISM CMS: Key Features and Benefits

DBPrism CMS is the first open source database-oriented CMS using Java inside the database and XMLDB repository. It takes all the benefits from *Oracle XML Enable Database* and the Apache Cocoon Framework for CMS functionalities.

The following list describes the functionalities of DBPrism CMS:

- *Simple and Compact.* Unlike other CMS systems, the core functionality of DBPrism CMS is only 962 lines of Java code, which runs as Oracle Java Stored Procedure.

- *Powerful.* It is built on powerful capabilities such as XML, Oracle Text indexing and portal content aggregation functionality from Cocoon such as My Yahoo (TM).

- *Dynamic content.* It furnishes simple services written in Java or PL/SQL for producing dynamic content.

- *Multilanguage support.* It includes attributes inside its document schema definition to provide multilanguage support.

- *Secure.* It runs as a Java Stored Procedure, hence it inherits all the security mechanisms of Java in the database (described in Part I), as well as XMLDB repository ACLs.

- *Concurrency control.* All the assets are stored in database tables, which are controlled by the concurrency features of the database.

- *Performance.* It uses ESI invalidation protocol to provide a cache coherence between the Cocoon internal cache system and the database assets (i.e., the user can edit content into the database, and immediately after the page is updated an XML ESI invalidation message is sent by the database to the Cocoon to invalidate the cached pages).

- *Separation of layout and content.* Presentation concerns are responsibilities of Web designers; content authors don't deal with presentation concern, but they write a neutral XML document that will be rendered to HTML or PDF documents by Cocoon. In addition to this, a Web look and feel could be changed in seconds, and it will be applicable to all the Web pages of the Web site.

- *Scheduling system.* Using the database DBMS_SCHEDULER package, it is possible to invoke any CMS task at any specific time or periodically; pages can be programmed to be public at a specific date or time.

- *Enterprise support.* Oracle Java Stored Procedures are ready-to-use enterprise services such as Web services, so it is possible to easily integrate other applications into the CMS as a dynamic service.

- *Native XML support.* DBPrism CMS uses XML documents complying with Apache's `documentv20.dtd`, images in SVG format, and i18n support.

- *Editing tools.* It is possible to use any XML-aware editor with Web-DAV support, such as XMLSpy or Oracle JDeveloper. In addition, the CMS front-end application furnishes a simple WYSIWYG HTML editor, which supports basic CML functionalities such as creating, deleting, updating, and publishing pages and directories.

- *Workflow.* A simple workflow of two stages can be used to maintain private and public pages. It means that the user can edit private pages located under the XMLDB `/home` directory and publish them with the front-end application to the `/public` directory, which is used by Cocoon for the public Web site. An N-state workflow can be implemented using multiples CMS users, in which case pages move into a sequence of steps (schema) waiting for the approval of the owners.

- *Everything is a URL.* Cocoon provides a powerful rewrite engine to transform plain URLs to everything else, so you don't deal with cryptic URLs like `/portal//index.jsp?&pName=products2col&path=membership&file=coa.xml&xsl=generic.xsl`. These types of URLs will frustrate users who read them on a printed page. In addition to this, by using plain URLs, it is possible to store the Web site in a CD-ROM or other media using *wget,* for example.

- *Support for Creative Commons digital signatures.* The user can choose these licenses for every page, and CMS will put the RDF header for search engines and extensions such as *mozcc*.

17.5.2 The Architecture of DBPrism CMS

The DBPrism CMS has several components, as illustrated by Figure 17.15.

The main components are:

- *Browser*: Users can interact using regular Web browsers such as Explorer or Firefox.

Figure 17.15
CMS Architecture

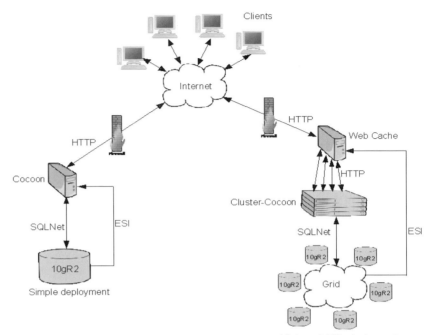

- *Cocoon*: Represented by the components in dark blue. This framework provides many architectural components to DBPrism CMS and is a proven technology used by CMS products such as Apache Lenya or Forrest. Cocoon separates the XML content, the style, the logic, and management functions of a Web site.

- *sitemap.xmap*: A configuration file, which controls all the behavior of the Cocoon framework.

- *Serializers*: Used to render an input XML structure into some other format (not necessarily XML, e.g., HML Serializer, Text Serializer, XML Serializer).

- *Transformers*: Used to map an input XML structure into another XML structure (e.g., XSLT Transformer, Log Transformer, SQL Transformer, I18N Transformer).

- *Aggregators*: Compound new documents by the aggregation of different parts or subdocuments; in DBPrism CMS every page consists of the content asset and the RSS of the site, but the site administrator can modify this configuration according to preferences.

- *Generators*: Used to create an XML structure from an input source (file, directory, stream, DBPrism). DBPrism Generator generates the dynamic XML inside the database by executing a Stored Procedure. It also provides parallel content generation, which means that during the setup stage of an aggregated document, multiple requests will be started to the database for execution, and the result will be collected in a serialized form.

- *Readers*: The starting and endpoints of an XML pipeline. They collapse the features of a generator, transformer, and serializer. Readers are useful for delivering binary content-like images; more general readers deliver content as is.

- *Cocoon cache system*: Responsible for caching every component through the execution pipeline. This cache system evaluates for changes in every part of the CMS document; parts are the content assets, RSS channels, style sheets, files, and so on. DBPrism adds a new cache component to Cocoon, which provides an external cache invalidation system, so the content is considered valid until an ESI invalidation message arrives to the system. This message is sent using HTTP, and in that case it is thrown by a database trigger.

- *DBPrism CMS core*: Basically a set of Java Stored Procedures and some PL/SQL utilities. This Java code will be explained in more detail in the following sections.

- *Front end/RSS/Search/App*: Components running using the CMS core components. They use some common functionalities, such as metadata of the documents, static resources, and so on.

- *XMLDB*: Another key component of DBPrism CMS, it provides all the repository metaphor for the CMS; up to release 2.0, DBPrism CMS uses regular Oracle tables with CLOB columns for storing the content assets. Now, with the addition of XMLDB DBPrism, CMS stores the content assets using native XMLType data types, obtaining good performance, security through ACLs, and support for external access to the repository using FTP or WebDAV.

- *Oracle Text*: Used to index the content assets to provide full searching facilities on the site using AltaVista syntax for writing queries.

- *OJVM*: The core code of DBPrism CMS is written in Java, and it runs inside the Oracle Database as a Java Stored Procedure. The availability of Java inside the database simplifies the code of DBPrism CMS, because working with XML is simple and all APIs working with XML are native.

- *Security*: DBPrism CMS inherits the security system of the database, including authentication, authorization, access control on database resources, and WebDAV ACLs on the content assets.

- *The XMLDB protocols server*: Furnishes an alternative access to the XMLDB repository with protocols other than SQLNet, including HTTP(s), FTP, and WebDAV. Users can access the repository, and insert, delete, and update CMS content assets using external and third-party editors and tools.

- *OS level resources*: These resources, handled by the operating system, are the static resources of the Web site, such as graphics files in `png`, `gif`, and `swf` formats and the database data files, log files, and so on.

DBPrism CMS typically is deployed in two servers, one for the application server (e.g., OC4J) and one for the database server.

A scalable architecture can be implemented using a cluster installation for the application servers. It means Cocoon replicated N times behind an Oracle Web Cache, in that case the ESI invalidation messages will be routed directly to it instead of to the cache of Cocoon. Also, an Oracle RAC installation can be used for scaling up the database counterpart. Figure 17.16 shows a simple deployment and a high availability deployment.

17.5.3   DBPrism CMS Internals

This section is a bit advanced and might be intimidating.

How DBPrism CMS Works

The simplified execution flow of a CMS is illustrated in Figure 17.17.

1.   A client browser sends an HTTP request asking for a CMS page (e.g., `/demo/doc/Documentation/Distribution/index.html`).

2.   The HTTP Listener will route this request to Cocoon, which will execute a stored procedure on the database using DBPrism Generator.

3.   The execution of the stored procedure will return an XML page using the client credentials and other HTTP information. This XML page has a `content` document root node with a `header`, `body`, and `footer` subnodes.

Figure 17.16
Deployment
Scenarios

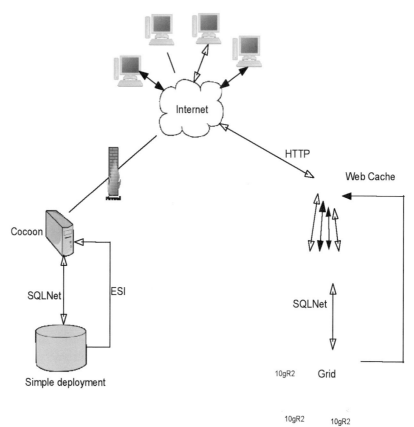

Figure 17.17
Simplified CMS
Execution Flow

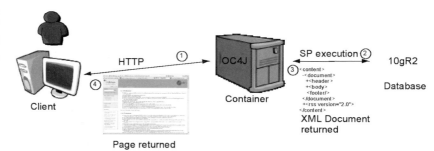

4.   With the XML document returned by the database, Cocoon will apply a set of preconfigured steps, such as extraction, transformation, and serialization, to generate the HTML page for the browser.

Complete Execution Flow

The complete execution steps involved for every page loaded from the CMS is depicted in Figure 17.18.

Figure 17.18
*Sitemap.Xmap
Matching Steps*

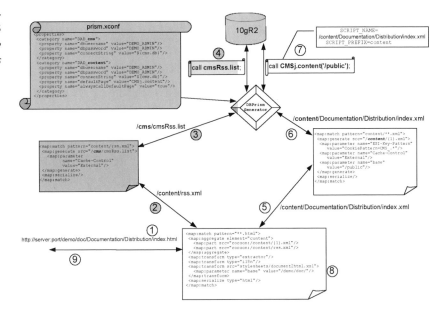

1. A CMS user asks for the page http://server:port/demo/doc/ Documentation/Distribution/index.html. This URL matchs with the sitemap.xmap pattern "**.html". The configuration values tell the Cocoon engine that the document will be generated by the aggregation of two new subdocuments, /content/ rss.xml and /content/Documentation/Distribution/ index.html, the path components *demo* and *doc* were extracted by the Servlet Container, and the mount point was defined on the Cocoon installation, respectively.

2. The component /content/rss.xml is generated by DBPrism-Generator, which is the default generator in this configuration.

3. The generation involves the URL /cms/cmsRss.list. DBPrism uses the same mechanism as Oracle mod_plsql, extracting the first part of URL as DAD key, so the Database Access Descriptor cms is used to find the username, password, and connect string for the target database into the prism.xconf configuration file.

4. DBPrism will execute at the database side the stored procedure `cmsRss.list` connected as DEMO_ADMIN user. This stored procedure will return the RSS XML shown in the next section, and the content will be cached by the Cocoon Cache system, because the Cache-Control parameter is given with the value External.

5. The component `/content/Documentation/Distribution/index.xml` is evaluated at this branch.

6. Unlike the previous branch, the used DAD is *content,* and due to the parameters `defaultPage` and `alwaysCallDefaultPage`, the stored procedure CMSj.content will be used irrespective of the URL evaluated. The parameter ESI-Key-Pattern is used to designate the cookies CMS_* as a discrimination pattern for storing pages. This configuration is required because the same URL for one page will be different if the CMS_LANG cookie is *es* or *en*.

7. The stored procedure `CMSj.content('/public')` is executed using the DEMO_ADMIN user to get the document content shown in the next section. This stored procedure will use the CGI environment variables `SCRIPT_NAME` and `SCRIPT_PREFIX` to know which CMS page is returned.

8. Once the two components are returned (document and rss), Cocoon will apply the extractor transformer to extract SVG images into the document. Then it will transform the document, analyzing the i18N tags, and finally the XML document is transformed into HTML using the XSL style sheet `document2html.xsl`.

9. The HTML page is returned to the browser.

Document Structure

The previous section shows that the aggregation configuration of the Cocoon sitemap will consist of an XML document with a root node `content` and two subnodes, `document` and `rss`.

Here is a simplified version of this document, which will help clarify the Java code used in the next sections:

```
<?xml version="1.0" encoding="UTF-8"?>
<content>
 <document xmlns:i18n="http://apache.org/cocoon/i18n/2.0">
```

```
<header xmlns:rdf="http://www.w3.org/1999/02/22-rdf-syntax-ns#">
 <!-- WebDAV Metadata tags here-->
 <!-- other metadata information about the page such as owner, last
modifier, etc.>
 <title>Distribution</title>
 <subtitle>Distribution Section</subtitle>
 <rdf:RDF xmlns="http://web.resource.org/cc/"
          xmlns:dc="http://purl.org/dc/elements/1.1/"
          xmlns:rdf="http://www.w3.org/1999/02/22-rdf-syntax-ns#">
    <!-- CreativeCommons license tags -->
 </rdf:RDF>
 <categories/>
 <map>
  <!-- Information about the two first level of the web site-->
 </map>
 <path>
  <!-- path information from the root directory to the current page -->
 </topics>
 </header>
 <body>
  <section>
   <title>Distribution Section</title>
  </section>
 </body>
 <footer/>
</document>
<rss version="2.0">
 <channel name="OTN News">
  <!-- RSS chanel 2.0 content -->
  .....
 </channel>
</rss>
<!-- Toolkit version 2.0.0.3 Author: Marcelo F. Ochoa "mochoa@ieee.org" -
->
</content>
```

- CMS contents are compounded by document and rss channels.

- Document is divided into header, body, and footer.

- Header includes WebDAV, CMS, and Apache document-v2.0.dtd header tags.

- Body is the content author's edited text.

- Footer includeds `Creative Commons` license links.

- Finally, a `RSS 2.0` channel is included.

Basically, the header information is used by Cocoon to render some contextual information of the Web site, such as the menu of the first and second depth of the hierarchy, title, license tags for the search engine, and so on.

Generation of the XML Document

As mentioned previously, the execution of a stored procedure leads to the generation of the XML structure shown in the previous paragraph. The code is located on the package com.prism.cms.core and is named wwwIndex.java; it has some static entry point for the PL/SQL wrapper defined on the package CMSj. The main entry point is the static method content(String user, String base).

```
public static void content(String user, String base)
throws SQLException {
  String source = Jowa.GETCGIVAR("SCRIPT_NAME");
  if (source==null) // provides a default page
    source = Jowa.GETCGIVAR("SCRIPT_PREFIX")+"/index.html";
  source = source.substring(source.indexOf('/',
    Jowa.GETCGIVAR("SCRIPT_PREFIX").length())); // removes
                                        // DAD info
  wwwIndex thisPage = new wwwIndex(user,source,base);
  Jxtp.tagOpen("document","xmlns:i18n='http://apache.org/
cocoon/i18n/2.0'");
    if (thisPage.showMetaData()) {
      Jxtp.tagOpen("body");
        thisPage.showContent();
      Jxtp.tagClose("body");
      Jxtp.tagOpen("footer");
        thisPage.showFooter();
      Jxtp.tagClose("footer");
    } else
      return;
  Jxtp.tagClose("document");
}
```

This code creates an instance of wwwIndex class using the source value extracted from the HTTP header attribute `SCRIPT_PREFIX` without the DAD information. Following the example of Figure 17.18, *user* is provided by the PL/SQL wrapper, `base` is hard-coded on the sitemap.xmap to '/public', and the `SCRIPT_NAME` is `/Documentation/Distribution/index.html`. This object, then, is used to get the metadata, content, body, and footer. The Stored Procedure `cmsRss.list`, which generates the RSS information, is not shown here. The class constructor is shown as follows:

```
public wwwIndex(String cmsUser, String p_info, String base)
throws SQLException {
    this();
    // Override cms user
    user = cmsUser;
    path = Util.getPath(p_info);
    name = Util.getName(p_info);
    ext = Util.getExt(p_info);
    OraclePreparedStatement stmt = null;
    ResultSet rset = null;
    try {
      baseUrl = base+"/"+user+"/cms/"+lang;
      stmt =
       (OraclePreparedStatement) conn.prepareStatement(
        "SELECT extract(res,'/Resource/Contents/*'),res   FROM
           resource_view "+ "WHERE equals_path(res, ? ) = 1");
      stmt.setString(1,baseUrl+path+name+".xml");
      rset = stmt.executeQuery();
      if (rset.next()) {
        doc = (XMLType)rset.getObject(1);
        xdbresource = (XMLType)((OracleResultSet)rset).getObject(2);
      } else if (directoryScan) {
        // default page not found try to generate a directory listing.
              directoryListing();
            } else { // Shows Page Not Found
              rset.close();
              rset = null;
              stmt.close();
              stmt =
                (OraclePreparedStatement) conn.prepareStatement(
          "SELECT extract(res,'/Resource/Contents/*'),res   FROM
```

```
        resource_view "+  "WHERE equals_path(res, ? ) = 1");
            stmt.setString(1,baseUrl+NotFoundUrl);
            rset = stmt.executeQuery();
            rset.next();
            doc = (XMLType)rset.getObject(1);
            xdbresource = (XMLType)rset.getObject(2);

        }
} catch (SQLException e) {
  throw new SQLException(".wwwIndex - SQLException on: "
      +e.getLocalizedMessage());
} catch (Exception e) {
  StringWriter sw = new StringWriter();
  e.printStackTrace(new PrintWriter(sw));
  throw new SQLException(".wwwIndex - Exception on: "
      +sw.getBuffer().toString());
} finally {
  ....
}
}
```

The code starts creating some auxiliary variables and then gets from the XMLDB repository, using the resource_view, the XML document requested by the user. That is, for the original request /Documentation/Distribution/index.html, it instantiates an XMLType object ***doc*** for the document stored at /public/DEMO_ADMIN/cms/en/Documentation/Distribution/index.xml and its WebDAV metadata in xdbresource. If the document is not on the repository, the content will be replaced by a directory listing, if it was enabled at installation time, or replaced by the content of the document notFound.xml.

Then, the method showMetaData() is called. The code of this method is shown as follows:

```
public void metaData() throws SQLException {
  // WebDAV Properties from resource_view

Jxtp.tag("DisplayName",Util.getResourceAttribute(xdbresource,"Display
Name"));
Jxtp.tag("Language",Util.getResourceAttribute(xdbresource,"Language")
);
Jxtp.tag("CharacterSet",Util.getResourceAttribute(xdbresource,"Charac
terSet"));
```

```
Jxtp.tag("VCRUID",""+Util.getResourceAttribute(xdbresource,"VCRUID"))
;
Jxtp.tag("ModificationDate",Util.getResourceAttribute(xdbresource,"Mo
dificationDate"));
Jxtp.tag("LastModifier",Util.getResourceAttribute(xdbresource,"LastMo
difier"));
    // page context properties
    Jxtp.tag("urlname",this.name);
    Jxtp.tag("urlpath",this.path);
    Jxtp.tag("urlext",this.ext);
    Jxtp.tag("lang",this.lang);
    Jxtp.tag("country",this.country);
    Jxtp.tag("user",this.user);
    Jxtp.tag("time",DateFormat.getDateTimeInstance(DateFormat.SHORT,
            DateFormat.SHORT, new Locale(Actions.getLang(),
Actions.getCountry())).format(newDate(System.currentTimeMillis())));
    // document-v20.xsd header information
    XMLType title = ((doc==null) ? null : doc.extract("/document/
header/title",""));
    Jxtp.p(""+((title==null) ? Jxtf.tag("title",
Util.getResourceAttribute(xdbresource,"DisplayName")) :
title.getStringVal()));
    XMLType subtitle = (doc==null) ? null : doc.extract("/document/
header/subtitle","");
    Jxtp.p(""+((subtitle==null) ? Jxtf.tag("subtitle","") :
subtitle.getStringVal()));
    XMLType license = (doc==null) ? null
: doc.extract("/document/footer/legal/a/@href","");
    String sLicense = (license==null) ? "http://creativecommons.org/
licenses/by/2.0/" : license.getStringVal() ;
    Jxtp.tagOpen("Work","rdf:about=''");
      Jxtp.tag("license","","rdf:resource='"+sLicense+"'");
    Jxtp.tagClose("Work");
    Jxtp.tagOpen("License","rdf:about='"+sLicense+"'");
    licenseTags(sLicense);
    Jxtp.tagClose("License");

Jxtp.tag("categories",Util.getResourceAttribute(xdbresource,"ResExtra
/Categories"));
  }
```

showMetadata() makes all the XML nodes of the header part (i.e., Web-DAV metadata) as other document-related information. Following this information, the CMS contextual information of the document is placed—that is, all the directories at levels 1 and 2 of depth into the Web site (showMapInfo) to make the menu information of the site, the path to the page in the hierarchy to make go back links (showPath), and finally related topics (relatedTopics), pages that are neighbors of the current page or linked using the CMS table cms_related, which provides many-to-many relations.

Here is the Java code:

```java
public void showMapInfo() throws SQLException {
  OraclePreparedStatement stmt = null;
  ResultSet rset = null;
  Jxtp.tagOpen("map");
  try {
    stmt =
      (OraclePreparedStatement) conn.prepareStatement(
         "select depth(1),path(1),res "+
              "from resource_view "+
              "where under_path(res,2,?,1)=1 and "+
            "extractValue(res,'/Resource/@Container')='true'");
    stmt.setString(1,baseUrl);
    rset = stmt.executeQuery();
    while(rset.next()) {
      int    depth = rset.getInt(1);
      String link = rset.getString(2);
      String name = Util.getName(link);
      XMLType res =  (XMLType)rset.getObject(3);
      Jxtp.tagOpen("linkmap","level='"+depth+"' name='"+name+"'
DisplayName='"+
              ((res==null) ? name :
Util.getResourceAttribute(res,"DisplayName") )+
              "' href='"+((link.endsWith(".xml")) ?
link.substring(0,link.length()-4)+".html" : link+"/" )+"'");
      Jxtp.tagClose("linkmap");
    }
  } catch (SQLException e) {
      throw new SQLException(".showMapInfo - SQLException: "
        +e.getLocalizedMessage());
  } finally {
    .....
    Jxtp.tagClose("map");
  }
}
```

```
    }

    public void showPath() throws SQLException {
      OraclePreparedStatement stmt = null;
      ResultSet rset = null;
      int level = 1;
      Jxtp.tagOpen("path");
      try {
        stmt =
          (OraclePreparedStatement) conn.prepareStatement(
              "SELECT path(1),res "+
                     "FROM resource_view "+
                     "where under_path(res,?,1)=1 and ? like
any_path||'/%'");
        stmt.setString(1,baseUrl);
        stmt.setString(2,baseUrl+path+name);
        rset = stmt.executeQuery();
        while(rset.next()) {
          String link = rset.getString(1);
          String name = Util.getName(link);
          XMLType res =  (XMLType)rset.getObject(2);
          Jxtp.tagOpen("linkmap","level='"+level+"' name='"+name+
                      "' DisplayName='"+((res==null) ? name :
Util.getResourceAttribute(res,"DisplayName"))+
                      "' href='/"+link+"/'");
          Jxtp.tagClose("linkmap");
          level++;
        }
      } catch (SQLException e) {
          throw new SQLException(".showPath - SQLException: "
            +e.getLocalizedMessage());
      } finally {
        .....
        Jxtp.tagClose("path");
      }
    }

    public void relatedTopics()
    throws SQLException {
      Jxtp.tagOpen("topics");
        OraclePreparedStatement stmt = null;
        ResultSet rset = null;
```

```
        try {
          stmt =
                (OraclePreparedStatement) conn.prepareStatement(
                   "SELECT  '/'||path(1) link, '1', "+
                           "r.res "+
                           "FROM cms_related,resource_view r "+
                           "WHERE owner = ? and page_from = ? and "+
                                 "under_path(r.res,?,1)=1 and "+
                                 "equals_path(r.res, ?||page_to ) = 1 "+
                           "UNION ALL "+
                           "SELECT  ?||path(2) link, '0', "+
                           "rv.res "+
                           "FROM resource_view rv "+
                           "WHERE under_path(rv.res,1,?,2)=1");
          stmt.setString(1,user);
          stmt.setString(2,path+name+".xml");
          stmt.setString(3,baseUrl);
          stmt.setString(4,baseUrl);
          stmt.setString(5,path);
          stmt.setString(6,baseUrl+path);
          rset = stmt.executeQuery();
          while(rset.next()) {
              String link = rset.getString(1);
              String name =  Util.getName(link);
              String level = rset.getString(2);
              XMLType res =  (XMLType)rset.getObject(3);
              link = (link.endsWith(".xml")) ?
link.substring(0,link.length()-3)+"html" : link+"/" ;
              Jxtp.tagOpen("linkmap","level='"+level+"' name='"+name+"'
DisplayName='"+
                       ((res==null) ? name :
Util.getResourceAttribute(res,"DisplayName") )+
                       "' href='"+link+"'");
              Jxtp.tagClose("linkmap");
          }
        } catch (SQLException e) {
          throw new SQLException(".relatedTopics - SQLException:
"+e.getLocalizedMessage());
        } finally {
          .....
          Jxtp.tagClose("topics");
        }
      }
```

Finally, the body and the footer are placed into the content nodes. These operations only copy the content as is, extracted from the ***XMLType doc*** variable using the native implementations of the operation extract.

```
public void showContent()
throws SQLException {
  try {
    if (doc==null) {
      Jxtp.p(defaultDoc);
      return;
    }
    XMLType podoc = doc.extract("/document/body/*","");
    if (podoc==null) {
      Jxtp.tag("s2","/document/body is null");
      return;
    }
    Jxtp.p(podoc.getStringVal());
  } catch (Exception e) {
    Jxtp.tag("s2","Exception type: "+e.getClass().toString());
    Jxtp.tagOpen("s3");
      Jxtp.tagOpen("source");
        Jxtp.p("<![CDATA[");
          e.printStackTrace(new PrintWriter(Jxtp.getWriter()));
        Jxtp.p("]]>");
      Jxtp.tagClose("source");
    Jxtp.tagClose("s3");
  }
}

public void showFooter()
throws SQLException {
  try {
    if (doc==null)
      return;
    XMLType legal = doc.extract("/document/footer/*","");
    if (legal!=null)
      Jxtp.p(legal.getStringVal());
  } catch (Exception e) {
    Jxtp.tagOpen("legal");
      Jxtp.tag("em","Exception type: "+e.getClass().toString());
      Jxtp.tagOpen("code");
```

```
        Jxtp.p("<![CDATA[");
           e.printStackTrace(new PrintWriter(Jxtp.getWriter()));
        Jxtp.p("]]>");
      Jxtp.tagClose("code");
    Jxtp.tagClose("legal");
   }
 }
```

17.5.4   Extended Capabilities

In addition to the plain core CMS capabilities, the following features are made possible by the power of the Oracle database and its embedded XML (also known as XML DB).

Searching for Nonpublic Pages

The following code shows how to compare nonpublic documents on the private area of the CMS. Remember that the CMS uses a workflow of two stages for publishing, meaning that only pages copied to the directory /public/ USER/cms/[en|es] will be visible at the Web site.

```
stmt =
      (OraclePreparedStatement) conn.prepareStatement(
        "select * from (select rownum as ntop_pos, q.* from ("+
            "select ?||path(1) p from resource_view e "+
                  "where under_path(e.res,HOME_PATH,1)=1 "+
                        "and instr(e.any_path,HOME_LIVE_DIR)=0 "+
                        "and extractValue(e.res,'/Resource/
@Container')='false' "+
                  "minus "+
                  "select ?||path(2) p from path_view f "+
                        "where under_path(f.res,PUBLIC_PATH,2)=1 "+
                              "and extractValue(f.res,'/Resource/
@Container')='false'"+
                  ") q) where ntop_pos>=? and ntop_pos<?");
```

This code fragment is part of the com.prism.cms.frontend.Reports source, and is part of the CMS front-end application. In order to get nonpublic pages, it's necessary to select all the resources under the home directory of the user (HOME_PATH), except the resources under the public area (PUBLIC_PATH), and that's all; the outside query is Top-N query for pagination purpose.

Updated Pages

Looking for updated pages is a task similar to the previous example. The goal is to locate pages under the public area that have a modification date older than the private area. The following JDBC statement and SQL query are used:

```
stmt =
      (OraclePreparedStatement) conn.prepareStatement(
          "select * from (select rownum as ntop_pos, q.* from ("+
              "select substr(e.any_path,?) p, e.res "+
                  "from resource_view e,resource_view f "+
                      "where under_path(e.res,HOME_PATH,1)=1 "+
                          "and instr(e.any_path,HOME_LIVE_DIR)=0 "+
                          "and extractValue(e.res,'/Resource/
@Container')='false' "+
                          "and equals_path(f.res,PUBLIC_PATH||'/
'||path(1))=1 "+
                          "and extractValue(e.res,'/Resource/
ModificationDate')> "+
                              "extractValue(f.res,'/Resource/
ModificationDate')"+
              ") q) where ntop_pos>=? and ntop_pos<?");
```

This code is also part of the `Reports.java` source of the CMS front-end application. It looks for pages under the private area that have their WebDAV modification date greater than the same document on the public side. It also excludes documents under the `/home/USER/cms/[en|es]/live` directory because these are part of the CMS front end.

Broken Links

This query is a bit complex and is used to search for broken links after renaming or moving operations on the CMS pages. It uses the Oracle Text index for checking link tags; these tags are `<a href="/path/page.html" title="title of the link"/>`, and the query will produce a report of the CMS pages with possible broken links.

```
stmt = (OraclePreparedStatement) conn.prepareStatement
  ( "select substr(any_path,?) path,r.res,"
  + "c.object_value.transform(XMLType(xdbURIType(
  '/home/USER/cms/en/live/stylesheets/
  brokenlinks.xsl').getClob()),"
```

```
    + "'base=\"'''..//..'||substr(any_path,?,instr(any_path,'/
',-1)-?)||
'''\" file=\"'''test.html''\"').getStringVal() "
    + "from cms_docs c,resource_view r "
    + "where contains(c.object_value,'test.html within
a@href')>1 and "
    + "sys_op_r2o(extractValue(r.res,'/Resource/
XMLRef'))=c.object_id and"
    + "under_path(r.res,?)=1");
```

This query will search for pages that have `test.html` within the attribute `href` of the tag **a,** using the Oracle Text operator CONTAINS on the table CMS_DOCS. The CMS_DOCS table is the object relational table that stores all the CMS documents associated with the schema "http://www.dbprism.com.ar/xsd/document-v20.xsd." XMLDB automatically detects XML documents with this signature and stores the content in the object relational storage of the CMS_DOCS table.

Once the document is located, this object is joined to the resource_view using the XMLRef value, which is a pointer to the content stored outside this view to get the path of the page. With this path, an XSLT transformation is made inside the database for making a report of the possible broken links, the style sheet that makes the report looks like this:

```
<xsl:stylesheet version="1.0" xmlns:xsl="http://www.w3.org/1999/XSL/
Transform">
  <xsl:output method="xml" indent="yes"/>
  <xsl:param name="base"/>
  <xsl:param name="file"/>
  <xsl:template match="a">
    <xsl:if test="contains(@href,$file)">
      <xsl:choose>
        <xsl:when test="starts-with(@href,'/')">
          <a href="{@href}" title="{@title}">
            <xsl:copy-of select="*|text()"/>
          </a>
        </xsl:when>
        <xsl:when test="starts-with(@href,'http://')">
          <a href="{@href}" title="{@title}">
            <xsl:copy-of select="*|text()"/>
          </a>
        </xsl:when>
        <xsl:when test="starts-with(@href,'ftp://')">
```

```
        <a href="{@href}" title="{@title}">
          <xsl:copy-of select="*|text()"/>
        </a>
      </xsl:when>
      <xsl:when test="starts-with(@href,'mailto://')">
        <a href="{@href}" title="{@title}">
          <xsl:copy-of select="*|text()"/>
        </a>
      </xsl:when>
      <xsl:otherwise>
        <a title="{@title}">
          <xsl:attribute name="href">
             <xsl:value-of select="concat($base,@href)"/>
          </xsl:attribute>
          <xsl:copy-of select="*|text()"/>
        </a>
      </xsl:otherwise>
    </xsl:choose>
    <br/>
  </xsl:if>
</xsl:template>
<xsl:template match="text()">
  <!-- ignore -->
</xsl:template>
</xsl:stylesheet>
```

The style sheet receives as parameters a base directory of the page that has broken links and a *file* name that was renamed or moved; *base* is used to produce a correct link to the target page on the report. Note that the style sheet is also stored on the CMS repository and is accessed using xdbUri-Type object.

Obviously, the previous query is executed in seconds within the Oracle-JVM, so this report is automatically displayed to the user with options for correcting the links. Management of broken links is usually a nightmare for CMS implementers, but when using the correct tools it's quite simple.

17.5.5   Text Searching

A key feature of CMS is the ability to search the content repository. Newspapers on the Web use public search engines such as Google or Yahoo, but these engines use a crawler tool for indexing the content. So for recent news, your query will return no hits because of the latency between index update (inherent to the batch nature of the crawler).

On DBPrism CMS, the content repository is indexed using the Oracle Text engine. The following Java code shows the query using this index:

```
stmt = (OraclePreparedStatement) conn.prepareStatement(
        "select * from (select rownum as ntop_pos, q.* from ("+
            "select score(1) rank,"+
                "extract(c.object_value,'/document/header/*'),"+
                "substr(r.any_path,?) "+
                "from cms_docs c,resource_view r "+
                "where under_path(r.res,PUBLIC_DIR,2)=1 and "+
                "sys_op_r2o(extractValue(r.res,'/Resource/
XMLRef'))=c.object_id "+
                "and contains(c.object_value,QUERY_STRING,1)>1 "+
                "order by rank desc "+
            ") q) where ntop_pos>=? and ntop_pos<?");
```

The outside query is the Top-N pagination. The inner query first limits the rows where the search is made to only the pages under the public directory of the user, and then the operator contains is used to query the content assets.

Reindex operations on Oracle Text indexes are not expensive in time consumption, so they can be executed after insert or update table actions or at a fixed time (e.g., 5 minutes). The collateral action of this task is that the user is always querying on the up-to-date content.

The code at com.prism.cms.ext.AvQuery class also includes a transform method, which takes the Alta Vista query syntax and transforms it into Oracle Text syntax; this code can be found in the OTN Samples section. Also, the Oracle Text index is configured to recognize documents in different languages, so the user can define the language of the content asset, providing the attribute lang on the root node. Here is an example for a Spanish document:

```
<?xml version="1.0" encoding="UTF-8"?>
<document lang="es"
    xmlns:xsi="http://www.w3.org/2001/XMLSchema-instance"
    xsi:noNamespaceSchemaLocation="http://www.dbprism.com.ar/xsd/
document-v20.xsd">
...
</document>
```

English documents are configured as the default language, so the attribute can be ignored.

17.5.6 Installing DBPRism CMS

This section covers the minimal steps to get DBPrism CMS up and running with a demo Web site. DBPrism CMS can be downloaded from the SourceForge Web site at the URL `http://prdownloads.source-forge.net/dbprism/cms-2.1.0-production.zip?download` and was tested against these dependencies:

- Apache Ant 1.6.2+ plus the extension for using FTP (jakarta-oro, commons-net)
- Oracle 10*g* R2 with Oracle Text installed
- OC4J 10*g*, Tomcat 4.1.12
- Red Hat Linux Advanced Server 4.0 on the database server, and Linux Mandrake 10.2 on the OC4J/Tomcat container

Note: The Apache Cocoon framework requires some related libraries to run; these libraries can be downloaded from the SourceForge Web site at the URL `http://prdownloads.sourceforge.net/dbprism/cms-2.1.0-applib-production.zip?download`; these JARS can be extracted in a common place of the Container (e.g., the `app-lib` directory of an OC4J 10*g*).

Configuration

As mentioned in the previous paragraph, all of the CMS components are installed using the Apache Ant utility, so you need to check the availability of this tool by executing the following command:

```
# ant -v
Apache Ant version 1.6.2 compiled on July 16 2004
```

Common deployment settings are placed into the *common.xml* file located under the root directory of the distribution. This file has parameters such as the following:

```
<property name="database" value="devel"/>
<property name="db.host"  value="reptil"/>
```

```
    <property name="db.port"  value="1521"/>
    <property name="db.sid"   value="devel"/>
    <property name="thin_string"
value="${db.host}:${db.port}:${db.sid}"/>
    <property name="jdbc_string"
value="jdbc:oracle:thin:@${thin_string}"/>
```

These parameters define the connect string of the SQLNet and JDBC for the target database. The user can check it using the *tnsping* utility:

```
# tnsping devel

TNS Ping Utility for Linux: Version 9.2.0.4.0 - Production on
18-JUL-2005 09:56:42

Copyright (c) 1997 Oracle Corporation. All rights reserved.

Used parameter files:
/u01/app/oracle/product/9.2.0/network/admin/sqlnet.ora



Used TNSNAMES adapter to resolve the alias
Attempting to contact (DESCRIPTION = (ADDRESS_LIST = (ADDRESS
= (PROTOCOL = TCP)(HOST = reptil)(PORT = 1521)))
(CONNECT_DATA = (SERVICE_NAME = devel.mochoa.dyndns.org)))
OK (0 msec)
```

A DBA database username and password of the target database:

```
    <property name="dba_user" value="sys"/>
    <property name="dba_pass" value="change_on_install"/>

    <!-- Database Schema used for storing CMS code -->
    <property name="cms.owner.user" value="CMS_CODE"/>
    <property name="cms.owner.pass" value="CMS_CODE"/>

    <!-- Database Schema used for CMS primary user (owner of
cms_docs table)-->
    <property name="cms.admin.user" value="CMS_DATA"/>
    <property name="cms.admin.pass" value="CMS_DATA"/>
```

dba_user will be used to create the CMS_CODE and the CMS_DATA on this example. Note that the installation scripts will first delete this schema.

Network-related settings:

```
<property name="proxy.host" value="null" />
<property name="proxy.port" value="null" />
```

If the database is behind a proxy firewall, change these values with the host and port values; if not, leave them with "null" string.

```
<property name="web.host" value="p1"/>
<property name="web.port" value="8888"/>
<property name="admin.port" value="23791"/>
<property name="admin.user" value="admin"/>
<property name="admin.pass" value="admin"/>
```

The hostname and the port of the container define where Cocoon will run. If you deploy the CMS behind an Apache server, leave these values to the container values, because they will be used by ESI invalidation triggers to send the messages.

The other three values are used for a remote deployment using the OC4J administrative interface, so you can easily deploy DBPrism CMS application using Ant.

Finally, check some environment variables used by an administrative tool:

```
<property name="env" environment="env" value="env"/>
<property name="ORACLE_HOME" value="${env.ORACLE_HOME}"/>
```

ORACLE_HOME needs to point to a valid Oracle Home installation; if you are installing DBPrism CMS remotely, this Oracle Home could be a minimum 9.2.0. If you are using Oracle JDeveloper, you can set ORACLE_HOME to the directory where JDeveloper was uncompressed, create a network/admin and bin directories on it, and move the SQLPlus utility under the bin directory. These parameters are common to all the sites that DBPrism will manage within a unique Oracle database instance. You can find a sample Web site on the directory `sites/www.mycompany.com/`; this directory could be used as a skeleton for any other custom installation.

The site environment settings of the `build.xml` file are described as follows:

```
<property name="cms.esi.user" value="dbprisminvalidator"/>
<property name="cms.esi.pass" value="dbprism259"/>

<property name="cms.rep.user" value="DEMO_ADMIN"/>
<property name="cms.rep.pass" value="DEMO_ADMIN"/>

<property name="project.web" value="demo" />
<property name="project.app" value="demo" />

<property name="project.base.web" value="/${project.web}/
doc/" />
<property name="project.base.live" value="/${project.web}/
ldoc/" />
```

ESI username and password are used by Cocoon to validate the access of incoming invalidation messages. These values are sent as part of the HTTP authorization header by the database triggers.

Repository username and password are the database schema used to validate site access to the content authors. The username will be the owner of the XML pages stored on the XMLDB repository. For the example shown previously, the private content assets will be stored on `/home/DEMO_ADMIN/cms/[en|es]` directories. Once the page becomes public, a copy of it will be in the XMLDB directory `/public/DEMO_ADMIN/cms/[en|es]`. `project.web` and `project.app` are values used to name the .war and .ear files during the application deployment. `project.base.web` and `project.base.live` are directories of the static resources on the container space; these resources are JPG and GIF images, css, Java Script files, and so on. During the deployment task, Ant will use these constants to rewrite some paths on the files located under the `sites/sitename/etc` directory.

Four-Step Installation

1. *Install the required JARS on the database.* This step is executed one time, because these JARS are uploaded to sys schema and granted to public access. These libraries are in binary format and are the

DBPrism Jxtp toolkit (a toolkit similar to Oracle mod_plsql HTP toolkit but written in Java) and the HTML parsing utility Jtidy, used to process documents edited with the WYSIWYG HTML editor of the front-end application.

```
# cd sites/www.mycompany.com
# ant pre-install
Buildfile: build.xml

Ant output goes here......

BUILD SUCCESSFUL
Total time: 35 seconds
```

2.   *Install the CMS code and data.* This step is executed one time; the task will delete and create the database schema, which holds the code and the data of the CMS. These code and data are shared by all the CMS sites and users.

```
# ant install-cms
Buildfile: build.xml
Ant output goes here......
```

3.   *Add the CMS user and upload the initial content.* This step is run for each CMS user on the system. Unlike the previous task, the add-cms-user task does not drop an existing database user; if you need to do this, execute first ***ant del-cms-user*** to drop the schema and XMLDB folders associated with it.

```
# ant add-cms-user
Buildfile: build.xml

Ant output goes here......

# and demo-web-install
Buildfile: build.xml

demo-web-install:

upload-demo-docs:
```

```
    [ftp] sending files
    [ftp] transferring /home/oracle8i/jdevhome/mywork/
cms-2.1/sites/www.mycomp
any.com/cms/en/About/Credits.xml
.....
    [exec] Trigger altered.
    [exec] Disconnected from Oracle Database 10g
Enterprise Edition Release 10.
2.0.1.0 - Production
    [exec] With the Partitioning, OLAP and Data Mining
options


BUILD SUCCESSFUL
Total time: 1 minute 47 seconds
```

4. *Deploy static resources to the container.* This task will create a war/ ear file and deploy them to an OC4J, which is up and running. If you are using Tomcat, execute the ant cms-war task, and it makes a {project.web}.war file for manual deployment.

```
# ant deploy-app
Buildfile: build.xml

Ant output goes here......

# ant deploy-web
Ant output goes here......

# ant demo-doc-ldoc-app
Ant output goes here......

# cd /usr/local/JDev10g/j2ee/home/applications/demo/
demo
# unzip /home/oracle8i/jdevhome/mywork/cms-2.1/deploy/
demo-doc-app.zip
# unzip /home/oracle8i/jdevhome/mywork/cms-2.1/deploy/
demo-ldoc-app.zip
```

Once these steps are completed, you can test the CMS at URL http:// localhost:8888/demo/ldoc/. The CMS will prompt for a valid CMS

Figure 17.19
CMS Test Screen

user; log in using demo_admin/demo_admin as user name and password, and you will get the screen pictured in Figure 17.19.

17.5.7 Future Work

From its Release 1.0, which was based on Cocoon 1.x architecture to the latest release, which uptakes Oracle Database 10*g* Release 2, DBPrism CMS is continually enhanced with new capabilities. It currently provides a linear versioning system based on the `archived_cms_docs` table, which backs up every page modified by users. XMLDB provides a Versioning API, but only for resources stored inside the resource_view (i.e., documents based on registered schema cannot be versioned). The challenge for the next release of DBPrism CMS will be to unify XMLDB versioning with the linear versioning. An object-oriented API for XML resource access such as JSR 170[7] or JNDI will be implemented, instead of using queries on the resource_view. A simpler import and export mechanism of the XML content and metadata using ZIP files will be added to the front-end application; these operations are currently manual using FTP clients and SQLPlus. Last, but not least, a shopping cart application will demo how to use `XForms` with CMS.

---

7. Content Repository for JavaTM Technology API.

17.6 Conclusion

This case study shows how a complete database-oriented CMS can be implemented with a few lines of Java code. I also walked you through the architecture and the motivations behind our design choices. Java is a natural language for processing XML; a corresponding PL/SQL code implementing the same functionality would be too complex and incomplete, because some operations would not be possible. Using Java, we could perform all the data-intensive processing in the database and only return the XML to Cocoon. By doing so, we eliminate unnecessary information transfer between the database and the middle-tier container and avoid unnecessary JDBC roundtrips. The XML DB abstraction layer and its protocol server greatly simplify the development of DBPrism CMS. The Cocoon presentation framework is a crucial component of the CMS, which provides caching, transformation, and many other features.

Index

Team For Counter

President Heuss
Greg ~~Hike~~

CTO

Amad Zoghlami

eyelike.com

Siemens

↕ sigl.

① image similarity,

2 products

② facial recognition

③ Target driven
logical.

① Flickr

②

VC

competitor